THE SADDEST STORY

A Biography of Ford Madox Ford

Arthur Mizener

THE SADDEST STORY

A

Biography

of

FORD MADOX FORD

THE WORLD PUBLISHING COMPANY
New York and Cleveland

*Published by The World Publishing Company
Published simultaneously in Canada
by Nelson, Foster & Scott Ltd.
First printing—1971
Copyright © 1971 by Arthur Mizener
All rights reserved
Library of Congress catalog card number: 73–124285
Printed in the United States of America*

WORLD PUBLISHING
TIMES MIRROR

For Rosemary
*Who did much of the work
and more of the worrying*

Contents

Foreword

Ford Madox Ford wrote eighty-one books during his life, thirty-two of them novels. These books were the purpose of his existence, the one commitment of his life that nothing—disaster, illness, despair—was allowed to interfere with. They are the meaning of his life, and its most valuable product. Some of them are important books; some are imperfect—interesting but tentative; some are failures. But every one of them shows something about a human imagination perhaps not radically different from other men's but made to seem so by being revealed to us in unusual detail by these books, and everyone of them helps us to understand the process by which Ford slowly learned to reveal his imagination.

Most readers, however, will know only a few of Ford's books—*The Good Soldier*, perhaps one or two of the four novels of *Parade's End*, perhaps some of the *Fifth Queen* trilogy. Even the reader with the energy to learn more will find it impossible to get hold of most of Ford's novels; I hope this will not always be the case, but it is now. Critical discussion of books a reader does not know are not very meaningful. For the reader who is familiar with Ford's work, his novels are the most important thing about him and demand careful attention; for the reader who is interested in Ford but unfamiliar with most of his books, discussions of them are a bore.

I have tried to meet the needs of both these readers. Where one of Ford's books is of major importance and likely to be known to readers, as is *The Good Soldier*, or is particularly revealing of Ford, as is *The New Humpty-Dumpty*, I have discussed it fully in the text. Where neither of these things is true, I have put the critical discussion of the novel at the back of the book. Each of these discussions was originally written as part of the narrative and can, I hope, be read without difficulty as a part of it by readers who are interested in doing so.

The reader of Ford's novels will be aware that Ford frequently used the ellipsis to indicate pauses. These ellipses are easily distinguishable from those which indicate the omission of quoted material.

Acknowledgments

This book would not have been possible without the help of Janice Biala, who is both Ford's literary executor and the owner of a major collection of Ford papers. She put her collection on deposit at Cornell for my convenience and has in many other ways been extraordinarily generous to me. I also owe much to Mrs. Charles Lamb, who put up with me and my wife for a long visit at Carraroe while we studied her mother's papers and was endlessly patient in answering questions about them. Mrs. Roland Loewe let me use the Ford papers in her possession, including the crucial correspondence between Stella Bowen and Ford. The Violet Hunt papers, the fourth major source of information about Ford, were bought by the Cornell Library when they suddenly reappeared after being lost for over thirty years; together with the bulk of Stella Bowen's papers, which are also in the Cornell Library, they constitute the largest single source of information about Ford. The best private collection of Ford material is in the possession of Mr. Edward Naumburg, Jr., a fellow Princetonian who made his papers available to me and even fed me while I worked on them. Great as is my debt to these friends, they are not in any way responsible for the conceptions of the people described in this book. It is, in fact, a part of the unusual generosity of Janice Biala and Mrs. Lamb that they have let me use the unpublished material in their possession despite the fact that Janice Biala believes my portrait of Ford does him an injustice and that Mrs. Lamb believes my portrait of her mother is unfair.

Ford's friends have also given me a great deal of help. Allen Tate has answered endless questions; he also read my manuscript and caught many mistakes. Edward and Clare Crankshaw have been equally generous; they too read this book in manuscript, and it was Mrs. Crankshaw who put me on the trail of Violet Hunt's papers. Many others have helped me too, especially Iris Barry, Kathleen Cannell, Margaret Cole, Edward Davison, David Garnett, Mrs. Oliver Hueffer, Professor Frederick Karl, Lady Rosalie Mander, Mrs. Charles Masterman, Mrs. Brigit Patmore, James Randall, Sir Herbert Read, Jean Rhys, and Dame Rebecca West. My old friend, the late W. K. Rose of Vassar, who was working on a book about The Men of 1914, gave me many leads. I am also indebted to many libraries, especially those of the University of Chicago, Harvard University, the University of Illinois, the University of Indiana, the University of Kansas, Northwestern University, Princeton University, the University of Texas, Yale University, the Huntington Library, and the New York Public Library. The Cornell University Library, and especially its remarkable Curator of Rare Books, Professor George Healey, have given me invaluable help.

A great deal of the primary research on Ford's life was done by David Harvey during the preparation of his magnificent bibliography of Ford, and again and again I have simply followed the path he laid out in his bibliography and in the notes he collected for it, which he generously turned over to me.

Grants from the National Endowment for the Humanities, the Guggenheim Foundation, and the American Council of Learned Societies, the research fund attached to the Mellon Foundation Professorship at Cornell, and the patience of the Cornell English Department gave me the time for research and writing.

I would not have started this book without the encouragement of my editor, Robert Gutwillig, who worked with me patiently throughout the six years it took me to finish it.

Introduction

The *Saddest Story* was the title Ford Madox Ford himself chose for his most brilliant novel; it was only when his publisher protested that it was an unfortunate choice for a novel issued during a war that, half ironically, he suggested *The Good Soldier*. *The Good Soldier* is not a bad title, either for Edward Ashburnham's life or for Ford's. Edward was a fine officer and an honorable man: the Asburnhams were "good people." He was also a simple man with the simple man's sense of duties and responsibilities. He was a good soldier, both literally and figuratively. There was a part of Ford that was like that too; much of the time he acted the role of the good soldier, fulfilling his responsibilities, sacrificing himself for literature as the editor of *The English Review* or for his country as a soldier in the First World War.

But *The Good Soldier* contains more than Edward Ashburnham; it in-cludes a judgment of the world in which Edward Ashburnham has to exist and an ironic awareness of the impossibility of Edward's conduct in that world. John Dowell, the novel's narrator, would not have had Edward differ-ent; he loved and admired what Edward was. But he could see—if Edward could not—that Edward's conception of how he ought to live, however admirable, was impossible to realize; neither the world nor strong elements in Edward's own very human nature would permit it. Dowell's judgment of Edward's defeat is not that Edward was a tragic hero; you do not have tragedy in a comedy-of-manners world or with a nature like Edward's that is fulfilled by the good soldier's wholehearted performance of his role. The lives of such simple souls are only sad. But they can be very sad, as Edward was. There are no cheerful resolutions for dilemmas like this. Edward's innocent conception of his life as a Tory landlord redeemed by the love of a good woman so that he could devote himself to the care of his tenants, especially the women and children, was—perhaps always has been and always will be—impossible; it was, in a key word of John Dowell's, "sentimental." It was nonetheless the finest idea of a life Ford could conceive, sentimental not simply in the sense that it was impossibly idealistic but also in the sense that it was based on the finest sentiments.

Ford saw the sad impracticality of the life Edward innocently imagined he could live; he was as much John Dowell as he was Edward Ashburnham. His own dream of a life was the life of Edward Ashburnham, and he dreamed—both his good dreams and his bad dreams—with an intensity that it is difficult for ordinary people to comprehend. "That Ford was almost an *halluciné*," Ezra Pound said, "few of his intimates can doubt. He felt until it paralysed his efficient action, he saw quite distinctly the Venus immortal crossing the tram tracks." Perhaps Pound's image makes Ford's imagination too like that of the Cantos, where we constantly see the "daughter of Lir" in the "spray-whited circles of cliff-wash" and "fair Dafne of sea-boards" "pale in the wine-red algae." But Pound was altogether right about the sheer intensity with which Ford's fancy committed itself to possibilities of experience that were beyond realization. "He was the helpless victim of his own imagination. . . . He could not extricate himself from what he imagined and what actually happened. . . . He told stories about himself constantly and as the stories were retold he embroidered them. . . . He fabricated and elaborated his life as assiduously as he fabricated and elaborated his books." "It was," Stella Bowen said of Ford's dream of living in the country as Small Producer, poet, and philosopher (the image of himself he presented as Gringoire in *No Enemy*), "what he wanted, and when Ford wanted anything, he filled the sky with an immense ache that had the awful simplicity of a child's grief. . . . "[1]

Just as *The Good Soldier* has its Dowell to look at Edward Ashburnham with irony for his simplicity as well as with admiration for his idealism, so *No Enemy* has its Compiler, with his limited patience for Gringoire's easy assumption that he can live the life his romantic poet's imagination has conceived. When Ford talked directly about the Gringoire in himself, he usually did so half jokingly, as when he said toward the end of his life,

> I have written at least fifty-two books, of which a couple might stand;
> I have dug, hoed, pruned, and sometimes even harvested twenty-six
> kitchen gardens that I can remember . . . and thirteen times I have
> travelled the round that goes from London to New York, New
> Orleans, the Azores, Gibraltar, Marseilles, Paris, London. . . . If I had
> not so constantly travelled, I should have reaped better harvests and

written more and better books; if I weren't, when travelling, constantly impeded by the desire to settle down somewhere and start something growing and write something, I should have travelled more happily and farther. And if suddenly, when dunging or irrigating in . . . Provence . . . I hadn't been filled with the itch to be walking across Sheridan Square . . . and if I hadn't incontinently gone and done it all—I should have eaten many more cabbages, oranges, and ears of corn of my own growing.

Attractive as this is in its frank recognition of a tendency to go in too many directions at once, it still leaves the impression that this fault has hardly been serious: the fifty-two books and the twenty-six kitchen gardens were still achieved. This was the best Ford could do when he spoke in his own character about this aspect of himself (most of the time he did much worse), and it seems scarcely to recognize how serious the consequences of his own divided nature were.[2]

But his best fiction does recognize those consequences. As early as the *Fifth Queen* trilogy he produced what is in some ways his subtlest dramatization of this fundamental division in his nature. Here he not only doubled his hero, as he did in *The Good Soldier, No Enemy,* and a number of other novels, but, in Henry VIII, produced a believable character who is almost as radically mixed in his impulses as Ford himself was. He faced the complexity of his own nature this way in all his best novels; it is what gives them the insight and the passion that raises them above his other work, however skillful.

When Ford fell in love with Elsie Martindale, his deepest feeling was that she would give him rest; "Du bist die Ruhe," he told her again and again, as he told every woman he fell in love with for the rest of his life. "I must," Edward Ashburnham says as he kills himself believing he has lost Nancy Rufford, "have a bit of rest, you know." The pain of living with his own divided nature was unendurable to Ford, and he spent much of his life and his imaginative energy inventing an alternative and more flattering image of himself that he could endure; the major source of the romancing Ford did all his life lies here.

There is thus a sense in which Ford's life was the saddest of stories in the way the paired lives of Edward Ashburnham and John Dowell were. Part of him believed in the honorable and simple life of the Tory gentleman and gifted poet of his dream and believed in it so intensely that he could not imagine it was unachievable, and part of him was the skeptical observer who was reduced to hopeless inaction by his common-sense recognition that it was. It was only in the best and most creative moments of his life that he could endure to face steadily the conflict between these two sides of his nature and to admit that for such natures life is, as Dowell says, "all a darkness." It is impossible not to believe that, most of the time, the vision of the Ashburnham in him dominated his consciousness and made him, as Ezra Pound said, a *halluciné*. But it is not easy to suppose either that he could permanently suppress the voice of Dowell; in some hidden and mostly neglected corner of his mind he must always have heard Dowell commenting on his conduct, pointing out how much of a fool, practically speaking, he was making of himself.

The effect of this division in his nature on his work is even sadder. Pound was always irritated by what seemed to him Ford's refusal to write the book Pound was sure he had it in him to write, and everyone who studies Ford's career has to face the problem of why Ford's achievement was not what his gifts would lead us to expect. Taken in one way—at the level of judgment that looks for talent and skill—Ford's career was brilliant. But when, like Pound, one applies to this career the standard that is set by Ford's own best work and asks why he wrote so many merely promising or clever books—not to mention that formidable mass of journalism—one is confronted by a further consequence of his divided nature. He had a romantic need, far more developed—or at least far more indulged—than in most men, to see himself as admirable and his defeats as undeserved, to revise in his imagination his actual conduct in such a way as to make himself the virtuous victim of a malicious world. Stella Bowen, who loved him, called this "weakness of character" quite simply "vanity."

This irrepressible need to invent and to impose on others an improved account of his own life and character did him very great harm. Even those who admired him found it impossible not to be irritated by it. Thus Robert Lowell, who respected Ford and was indebted to him, could not resist exposing him.

> The lobbed ball plops, then dribbles to the cup . . .
> (a birdie Fordie!) But it nearly killed
> the ministers. Lloyd George was holding up
> the flag. He gabbled, 'Hop-toad, hop-toad, hop-toad!
> Hueffer has used a niblick on the green;
> it's filthy art, Sir, filthy art!'
> You answered, 'What is art to me and thee?
> Will a blacksmith teach a midwife how to bear?'
> That cut the puffing statesman down to size,

Ford. You said, 'Otherwise
I would have been general of a division.' Ah Ford!

It is just possible Ford played golf with Lloyd George. But it is not easy to
believe Ford's shot was so brilliant, Lloyd George so silly, and Ford's retort
so apt; and it is inconceivable that a busy wartime minister devoted his time
to seeing that Second Lieutenant Hueffer was deprived of the command of
a division. On the other hand, it is all too easy to imagine Ford—sharing the
combat soldier's hatred of Whitehall, deeply humiliated by his colonel's
scorn of him as a soldier, and disappointed by the failure of his efforts to get
a staff appointment—inventing this daydream.*³

Such ill-calculated self-flattery was particularly damaging when Ford got
on the delicate subject of gentility.

> The merit of the Englishman—my own merits as far as they went
> —consisted in concealing as far as possible one's qualities. I might be
> an authority on Aryan dialects, or I might be plus one at golf; but at
> dinner I should never mention the one fact to the aspiring lady seated
> next to me, or, when challenged to take a turn over the links, I should
> say that I was pretty rotten and hadn't had a club in my hands for
> six months.

This offers us a dubious cliché about the upper-class Englishman's habit of
understatement as a piece of inside information; it makes claims of accomplishments that are hard to swallow and in fact not true, and it boasts of these
accomplishments by claiming that, as an English gentleman, Ford never
boasts.⁴

Ford was least able to control these consoling descriptions of himself
when he was emotionally disturbed. It was in this state that he told Herbert
Read that Conrad

> has done an immense deal for the Nuvvle in England—not as much

---

*In *Return to Yesterday* (p. 250) Ford has another version of this triumph over Lloyd George;
there Lloyd George is slightly disguised as "a future Prime Minister," the debated shot consists
of Ford's "using a wooden putter when [Lloyd George] said an artist would have used a
niblick," and Ford's retort was "that for him to talk to me about Art was like a blacksmith
telling a lace-maker how to make lace." Ford was particularly fond of representing himself as
a gifted golfer, perhaps because it was an accomplishment of a gentleman. "You know," he told
Curtis Brown, "what the third hole [at Littlestone-on-Sea] is like . . . a good player such as I was
would carry the ridge and find the green below. I recently did so, but my ball was lost. After
a prolonged search for it by all concerned, I was on the point of giving it up when I happened
to look in the hole, and there it was. I said to myself: When one can play as well as that, golf
ceases to be a sport and becomes a mere matter of mechanics. With play of such excellence and
accuracy one might as well pick up the ball and walk over to the hole and drop it in. I felt that
golf had no further charm for me, and I have now abandoned it" (Curtis Brown, *Contacts*
[London, 1935], pp. 10-11).

as I, no doubt . . . I learned all I know of Literature from Conrad—and England has learned all it knows of Literature from me. . . . I do not mean to say that Conrad did not learn a great deal from me when we got going; I daresay he learned more actual stuff of me than I of him. . . .

"This," as Read remarks, "might be read as humorous bluffing, but not by anyone who knew Ford."[5]

Uncontrollable vanity of this kind begins to creep into Ford's work about the time of the First World War and is never again absent. Even when he was writing about men he admired very much, he could not keep it out. In *Portraits from Life*, for example, he tells an amusing anecdote about Henry James's struggles with the servant problem.

He would pass his time, he said, interviewing ladies all of a certain age, all of haughty—the French would say *renfrognée*—expressions, all of whom would unanimously assure him that, if they demeaned themselves merely by for an instant considering the idea of entering the household of an untitled person like himself . . . if they for a fleeting moment toyed with the idea, it was merely, they begged to assure him . . . "forthegoodoftheirhealths."

But he cannot resist beginning this anecdote by describing how he was at work in his study at Winchelsea one day when he was disturbed by a conversation at his front door. Going out to quell this disturbance, he found James deep in conversation with their housemaid. "Would you then advise me . . . for I know that such an ornament decorates your master's establishment and you will therefore from your particular level be able to illuminate me . . . " James is saying. This is calculated to suggest that Ford lived a quietly elegant, dedicated writer's life at Winchelsea—something like the life Galsworthy, for example, actually lived—and did so with sufficient success to make Henry James, with whom he is on intimate terms, anxious to emulate it. These things were not true; even if they had been, Ford was not the man to tell them.[6]

Even Ford's book about Conrad does not escape damage. Ford loved and admired Conrad. "His native arrogance," Violet Hunt said truly, "appeared to be completely obliterated when Conrad was in the room." There is an aspect of Conrad's nature, and an important one, that no one has ever represented so convincingly as Ford does. Yet there is far too much irrelevant information about "the writer" (as Ford always calls himself) in *Joseph Conrad* and a great deal of it is grossly flattering. Possibly Ford saw these passages as gracefully casual asides, but the effect of silly vanity they produce damaged him badly even in the eyes of sympathetic critics. When Granville Hicks was trying to help Ford get recognized, he was forced to say that *Thus to Revisit*

> is, of Ford's many books, the most amusing and the most irritating. Ostensibly a treatise on contemporary writers, it concerns itself primarily with one Ford Madox Ford. This Ford, we learn, has "the faculty of absolute indifference to my personal fate or the fate of my work." He is often hailed as the greatest living critic, novelist, and poet. When he is attacked or slandered he merely shrugs his shoulders.
>   . . . it is difficult to take seriously a man who so recklessly exposes himself to the charge of asininity.

The feelings these little asides about himself roused in people who did not like Ford were violent. When Ford fell on evil days in the thirties, people made an effort to get Jessie Conrad to stop attacking him. She couldn't see it. When Hugh Walpole tried to say a word for Ford after Jessie's attack on him in *Joseph Conrad and His Circle*, she wrote:

> F. M. H. cannot complain. I have before me his preposterous claims to the plots of . . . Conrad's books. . . . The Trustees and Pinker have tried to pacify me by saying that both here and in America he is utterly discredited and that the total sale of Return to Yesterday and the Nightingale together was under 3,000 copies. All the more reason for him to be kept off the fringes of Conrad's reputation.[7]

Ford was a gifted man unqualifiedly devoted to literature—an old man, as he liked to say, mad about writing. He never questioned that "a writer committed himself at the beginning and had to remain committed through all the mischances of life. . . . He thought of it as something like a priest's vocation. . . . To write honestly and well was the most important thing in the world"; and throughout his life this dedicated man was frustrated by what Stella Bowen called an uncontrollable "weakness of character." It is not easy to imagine a sadder story than that.[8]

Ford had considerable charm. He was a sympathetic, even a sentimental man, and his sensitivity to the feelings of others often seemed to them almost uncanny; it made him especially attractive to women.

> I have known this heavy man [Violet Hunt said] repeat to me, word for word, parts of a conversation held between myself and a soldier friend of his in a cottage parlour in England while he himself was in France. . . . The author in the seër knew precisely what this so ordinary soldier-man was likely to say to this so ordinary, jealous woman.

When he gave his attention to someone he gave it all, and when he was not distracted by his anxiety to be admired, he could be wonderfully gentle and understanding so that, as D. H. Lawrence's Jessie Chambers said of him, "I suppose never before or since has anyone talked to me with quite such charm, making me feel in the most delicate way that what I said was of interest."[9]

He was also a brilliant talker. He was widely read; he had a tenacious if impressionistic memory and quick intelligence. He also had a talent for making his conversation dramatic; the emphasis on verisimilitude in his theory of fiction is a reflection of his interest in producing these effects in conversation. His fiction is always at its best when he uses a narrator's voice or is representing the interior dialogue of a character. "Ford," said Robert Lowell, "was large, unwieldy, wheezy, unwell, and looked somehow like a British version of the Republican elephant. His conversation, at least as finished and fluent as his written reminiscences, came out in ordered, subtly circuitous paragraphs. His marvelous, altering stories about the famous and colorful were often truer than fact.... His humility was edged with a mumbling insolence. His fanatical life-and-death dedication to the arts was messy, British, and amused. As if his heart were physically too large for his body, his stamina, imperfection, and generosity were extreme."[10]

He also had a kind of wisdom. It was his misfortune that he could seldom apply it to his own affairs, but he could use it for others in fact and in fiction, and often did. Nearly all of the women—and some of the men— who knew him well, however unjustly he sometimes treated them, felt gratitude to him for the sympathy he had shown them, his delicate insight, and the attractiveness of his mind. This is equally true of women so different as his wife, Elsie Martindale, who was unworldly, earnest, even rigid in character; of the woman he left her for, Violet Hunt, who was romantic, impulsive, and unconventional; and of the woman he left Violet for, Stella Bowen, a conventional, generous, and humorous woman.

No one could have been more aware than Ford himself of the discrepancy between the image these women who had loved him had of him and the image any biographer would present. He spent his life as a professional novelist, a man whose business it was to use the biographer's kind of curiosity about people to collect material for his fiction, and in *The March of Literature* his handling of the biographical details about the writers he admires, such as Horace, Villon, and Shakespeare, brings them vividly to life. But, like the doctor who knows far too much about disease ever to accept a colleague's encouraging lies about his incurable illness, Ford knew far too much about the indignity to the ego of such curiosity ever to contemplate without uneasiness its application to himself. His gloomiest expectations were confirmed by the publication in 1926 and 1927 of Violet Hunt's *The Flurried Years* with its indiscreet description of their love affair, and of Jean-Aubry's *Joseph Conrad* with its carefully touched-up and, as it seemed to him, corpselike image of Conrad. As a result he committed himself to the view that the biographical part of literature is a menace to art. This made his skillful biographical "digressions" in *The March of Literature* a little embarrassing, especially as he observes, quite rightly, that they are "valuable because they [permit] us to realize to what a great extent the life that a writer [leads] influence[s] his product." It is difficult to think of a writer of whom that is truer than it is of Ford.[11]

But however understandable Ford's reluctance to let others describe him was, the image he himself invented was a disaster; it creates an impression of his personality less sympathetic than he deserves and has led to a judgment of his work that undervalues it. He was not the greatest writer of his time, and despite the unfortunate things he occasionally said about himself, he never believed he was. He looked up to Conrad with selfless admiration and affection; he worshiped Henry James as a writer and would have devoted himself to James personally, too, if James would have allowed him to; he admired H. G. Wells only a little less; he deeply respected the work of W. H. Hudson, Stephen Crane, and R. B. Cunninghame Graham. He always recognized and paid generous tribute to good writers, even when they were unsympathetic to him, as was D. H. Lawrence.

But if he neither was nor thought himself the greatest writer of his time, he was nonetheless a superbly talented man. It is almost literally true that he could, in the words Conrad ascribed to their agent, J. B. Pinker, write anything and write it well. He wrote poetry that anticipates—in style if not feeling—some of the essential qualities of twentieth-century poetry. He was, at moments, a fine novelist and produced at least five distinguished novels; even more frequently he was a very good novelist who wrote half-a-dozen period books that will stand comparison with the work of contemporaries such as Galsworthy and Bennett and Wells and several clever experimental novels. He practically invented a form of fictional reminiscence; it may be a dubious genre, but in it he wrote two fascinating books. He wrote half-a-dozen books of intelligent literary criticism, at least one of which, his much-abused book about Conrad, is a remarkable achievement. Despite his scorn for facts, he wrote half-a-dozen books of a scholarly nature on literature and painting, one of which—his life of Ford Madox Brown—is still, after more than sixty years, the standard work on the subject.*

Ford also had a remarkable eye for talent in other men and he loved good writing with a devotion that made him able to bear almost anything for it, so that he was a great editor, especially during the period of *The English Review*. He was also for more than thirty years one of the most effective literary journalists in the English-speaking world, able to write interestingly on anything from Amenemhet I's advice to his son to Joyce's *Ulysses*. We ought to remind ourselves that this last achievement is not so insignificant as we are sometimes asked to believe. It was to a considerable extent motivated by a desire not to allow the growing gap between literature and the general audience to become unbridgeable. The writers of the period who made a virtue of "alienation" believed that their integrity as writers depended on their ignoring the general audience, and they were inclined to assure themselves of their virtue by offending it. When their work was, as a consequence, not immediately accepted, they were convinced that they had proved their thesis, that the general audience was stupid beyond contempt, and that anyone it would listen to must be pandering to it out of the worst kind of desire for money and popularity. Such was Pound's idea of Arnold Bennett:

> "Follow me, and take a column,
> Even if you have to work free,
>
> Butter reviewers. . . .
>
> Accept opinion. The 'Nineties' tried your game
> And died, there's nothing in it."[12]

It is typical of Ford's range that he was, on the one hand, intimate with Wells and often allied with Bennett, and on the other, close to Pound and Wyndham Lewis. *The English Review* published *Tono-Bungay* and "The Matador of the Five Towns"; it also published Pound's "Sestina Alteforte" and Lewis' "Saltambiques."

Most of Ford's astonishing quantity of work was produced by the writer of talent in him, the skillful craftsman with his irrepressible delight in his

---

*Since judgments of this kind are necessarily to some extent subjective, these books ought to be specified. The five distinguished novels are *The Good Soldier* (1915), *Some Do Not...* (1924), *No More Parades* (1925), *A Man Could Stand Up—* (1926), and *Last Post* (1928). The good period novels are *The Fifth Queen* (1906), *Privy Seal* (1907), *The Fifth Queen Crowned* (1908), *A Call* (1910), *Ladies Whose Bright Eyes* (1911), and *The Young Lovell* (1913). The experimental novels are *The Inheritors* (1901), *Romance* (1903), *Mr. Apollo* (1908), *The Simple Life Limited* (1911), *The New Humpty-Dumpty* (1912), *Mr. Fleight* (1913), *The Marsden Case* (1923), and *No Enemy* (1929). The fictional reminiscences are *Return to Yesterday* (1931) and *It Was the Nightingale* (1933).

métier. But somewhere inside him, apparently beyond the control of his conscious will, there was another self in Ford, what he called in his novels "the under self." This under self is the source of his best work. Its voice can be heard from time to time in his early books, but it is clearest in *The Good Soldier* and *Parade's End*. It fades out in his later work, for much as he longed to be a part of the new literary world that he, as an Edwardian rebel, had helped to make possible, his under self remained an old Bolshevik. It is a false ascription of motive but a fair judgment of the fiction Ford wrote in his last years to say, as Ambrose Gordon, Jr., does, that "for his last ten years [Ford] subsided into the novelistic equivalent of anagrams or acrostics, the elaborate amusements of 'an old man mad about writing.' " These late novels are skillful exercises in the special form Ford had gradually developed over the great years of his career, but they have no significant subject. Only the final poems, the expression of his feelings for Janice Biala, speak with the voice of his under self.[13]

Ford saw before any other writer of his age the peculiar conflict be-tween the possible and the actual that has been the subject of twentieth-century literature, and at his best, he made images of it that are very moving. But they are all more or less limited by his inclination to make his heroes —like himself—"too like thee, tameless and swift and proud," so that they are subject only to romantic irony; and romantic irony, even when it is carried to the point where it actually deceives some readers—as the irony about Edward Ashburnham of *The Good Soldier* does—is never a measure of the hero's complicating defects: he has no defects. The irony is only a measure of the world's inadequacy to his fineness. "[Ford's limitations] de-prive him of co-status with Pound, Eliot, and Joyce," Hugh Kenner has said. "[He is] a little anachronistic, writing from a basis a little closer to the time in which the novels are set than to that in which they were conceived."[14]

Nevertheless, young and old, over a span of nearly fifty years, from the publication of *The Brown Owl* in 1891 to the publication of *The March of Literature* in 1938, Ford's love of literature and his productive energy were unflagging. David Harvey's fine bibliography of his work lists eighty-one books, 419 contributions to periodicals, and fifty-seven miscellaneous contri-butions to other men's books. This formidable achievement has never really been given its due, partly because the enemies Ford so effectively created and provided with such powerful ammunition have made good use of their opportunities and partly because the very quantity of Ford's work has tended to obscure the best of it.

Yes.   Yes.   F. a prubblum—knew more than any
—see how good———is, when obeyin F's formula—'n'
then F. don't & cobwebs, etc etc
        —*Ezra Pound to Stella Bowen, September 16, 1947*

. . . Ford's weakness of character, unfairness, disregard
of truth, and vanity *must* be accepted. . . . On the other
hand, his tenderness, understanding, wisdom (about
anything that didn't apply to himself!) and the tremen-
dous attraction of his gorgeous mind, must make him
always regretted. . . .
        —*Stella Bowen to Katharine Lamb, June 22, 1947*

Chapter I

Ford Madox Ford—as he eventually chose to call himself—was born December 17, 1873, at 5 Fair Lawn Villas, Merton, Surrey (now 245 Kingston Road), the first of three children born to Franz Carl Christoph Johannes Hüffer and Catherine Emma Brown. His brother, Oliver, was born four years after him and his sister, Juliet, eight. He was christened Ford Hermann Hueffer, his father having anglicized his name to Francis Hueffer, which he pronounced to rhyme with "hoof," so that much later in Ford's life Jessie Conrad could express her dislike of him with her customary vigorous vulgarity by asserting that one of her main objects in life was to "hoof out Hueffer."[1]

The Hüffers were an old family of Münster, where they owned a prosperous printing establishment called the Aschendorff Press. They also owned the *Westphalische Zeitung*. Two of Franz Hüffer's half-brothers became wealthy men, Wilhelm in Rome, where he was known as Barone Hueffer, and Leopold in New York and, later, in Paris. A third brother, Hermann, whose name Franz chose for his eldest son, was a professor of history at Bonn. The Hüffers were a devout Catholic family, a fact that was to have some influence on Ford's career, and it was perhaps Franz Hüffer's atheism and his devotion to Schopenhauer that led to his emigration to England in 1869.[2]

According to William Michael Rossetti, Franz Hueffer was "a rather bulky but not a tall man, of very Teutonic physiognomy: brilliant, ruddy complexion, brilliant yellow hair, blue eyes radiant with quickness and penetration ... though not a melancholy person in his ordinary demeanour, [he] had a certain tinge of hypochondria in his outlook on life." Ford's childhood memory was of a man "enormous in stature, [with] a great red beard and rather a high voice." Like his brothers, Franz was a man of considerable gifts. In addition to his philosophical interests, he was a distinguished

3

musicologist and the author of librettos for operas written by Sir Alexander Mackenzie (*Colomba*, 1883; *The Troubadour*, 1886), of one of the earliest serious books on Wagner, and of *The Troubadours, A History of Provençal Life and Literature in the Middle Ages* (1878). Like Ford, he was a great hand at starting intellectually serious, financially disastrous magazines, two of which (*The New Quarterly*, which boosted Schopenhauer, and *The Musical World*, which was Wagnerian) were creations of his English years. In 1879 he became music critic of *The Times*. By 1871 he was courting Catherine Madox Brown, the daughter of Ford Madox Brown by that second, oddly Pre-Raphaelite marriage of Brown's to a fifteen-year-old farmer's daughter, Emma Hill. In July, 1872, Franz and Catherine were engaged.*[3]

Ford Madox Brown's grandfather had been a famous eighteenth-century doctor, lucky enough to have Blake make an etching of him, and unlucky enough to be driven from England for stubbornly holding to medical views far in advance of his time. He settled in Calais, where Ford Madox Brown was born. The child was named Ford after his father (who had, in turn, been given the name Ford in honor of one of his father's favorite pupils) and Madox for his mother, Caroline Madox. Thus the two names that Ford Madox Ford would eventually take in memory of his grandfather came into the family. According to his grandson, Ford Madox Brown always had "a strong French tinge to his English"; his love of France unquestionably contributed to his grandson's lifelong devotion to it.[4]

Cathy Brown was, like everyone in the Browns' set, encouraged to become an artist. She painted well enough for her father occasionally to get a picture of hers into an exhibition. If one can fairly judge by the drawing of her made by her father as a study for "Stages of Cruelty," she was a pretty child. She was also an attractive woman. "My mother was very pretty," her daughter said. "She had fair hair and an absolutely straight nose, and a nicely shaped mouth with beautiful even white teeth, and her eyes were a bright clear blue." Though she seems to have inherited some of her father's notorious thorniness ("She didn't much like being contradicted because, she said, 'I never insist upon anything unless I'm *positively certain*' "), she was endlessly self-sacrificing and devoted to her husband and children, continuing to struggle with the problems of her son Oliver long after everyone else had given him up.[5]

*In addition to the famous cases of Watts and Ruskin, and of Brown himself, Pre-Raphaelite marriages to young or uneducated girls included Stephens and his Clara, and Shields and his Matilda. Something like the same impulse must have motivated Rossetti's enthusiasms for the fundamentally conventional Lizzie Siddal and the fundamentally unconventional Fanny Cornford.

She and Francis Hueffer were married in August, 1872; Sir Lawrence Alma-Tadema painted their wedding portraits. Shortly after the birth of their first son they moved to 90 Brook Green, Hammersmith, where they remained for the rest of their life together. " . . . there were pretty carpets . . . gay papers on the walls and flowers on the tables. . . . [Mrs. Hueffer] always chose books with the brightest and prettiest covers to put in front of the shelves in the bookcases and put the ugly ones behind, even if they were learned." The "Assyrian" curtains of her drawing room were much admired.[6]

In middle age Ford remembered his childhood as oppressive. " . . . by sheer reaction of inheritance," he wrote in 1920, "I had even then [1900], an absolute hatred for the 'toll-loll' Great Figure, the Quarterly Reviewer, the Bibliographer, and the ceaselessly mouthing Great Poet, who had overshadowed my childhood." He had greatly disliked the outlandish style imposed on him by the principles of his elders (a memory that did not prevent his making a strenuous effort to impose equally unconventional opinions on his daughter, Julia, when the time came). He was dressed in a "a suit of greenish-yellow corduroy velveteen with gold buttons, and two stockings, of which the one was red and the other green," and his yellow hair was kept in a pageboy bob that hung below his shoulders "as a token of my Pre-Raphaelite origin." He also felt, apparently with some justice, that his younger brother, Oliver, was his parents' darling.[7]

Francis Hueffer was, according to Ford, not an overly severe parent, but he was an earnest one. It was characteristic of him to write his wife, when she was away, a daily communiqué about the children's behavior ("[Ford] had his early dinner with me yesterday and behaved *exemplarily* which I promised him I would write to tell you"). The one thing about him Ford never forgot was his oft-repeated observation that Fordie was "the patient but extremely stupid donkey." Ford remembered this childhood as a time of "moral torture."[8]

Possibly it was Francis Hueffer's deep respect for the Victorian and Pre-Raphaelite Great that made Ford think he remembered them as so very unpleasant. " . . . the Middle Victorian, tumultuously bearded Great . . . were a childish nightmare to me. They ringed in my young horizon, miching and mowing and telling each other disagreeable stories, each one about all the others who were out of earshot." He could see that they had been quite funny:

Thus one great painter would write:
"Dear Brown—Tell Gabriel that if he takes my model Fanny

[Cornford] up the river on Sunday I will never speak to him again."
    Gabriel would take the model Fanny up the river on Sunday,
and a triangular duel of portentous letters would ensue.
    Or again, Swinburne would write:
    "Dear Brown—If P. says that I said that Gabriel was in the
habit of——, P. lies."
    The accusation against Rosetti being a Gargantuan impossibil-
ity which Swinburne . . . could impossibly have made, there ensued
a Gargantuan correspondence.

Nevertheless, the young Ford hated the kind of intimacy these quarrels
represented in a way that affected his whole life.[9]

The world in which Ford grew up thus produced in him an odd combination of feelings about artists. On the one hand, he was convinced that to
be an artist was the only serious occupation for a man and that there was
something very wrong with a society that did not allow artists to do as they
pleased and support them comfortably. "For myself," he said later with
amusement at an attitude that was nonetheless quite serious, "from my
childhood I was brought up to believe that humanity divided itself into two
classes—those who were creative artists and those who were merely the stuff
to fill graveyards. In that belief I tranquilly abide." On the other hand, he
suffered greatly from the backbiting competitiveness of the intellectual community—all his life Ford was extraordinarily thin-skinned and easily hurt—
and had a strong feeling that practical skills and executive powers were very
important. His ideal man had the intelligence, the innocent sincerity, and
the practical gifts that he divided between Christopher Tietjens and his
brother, Mark, in the greatest of his fictions, the tetralogy now called *Parade's End*. He began to conceive this man quite early in his career; he first
appears as Colonel Blood, the leading figure of *Mr. Fleight* (1913). This was
the man the adult Ford often strove—and even oftener pretended—to be.[10]

    Meanwhile there were those oppressive Victorian geniuses of his child-
hood to endure.

    If Mr. Swinburne was in the house we children knew of it up in the
    nursery. A hush communicated itself to the entire establishment.
    . . . We all of us, all the inhabitants of the back nooks and crannies of
    a large stucco house, fell to talking in whispers. I used to be perfectly
    convinced that the ceiling would fall in if I raised my voice in the very
    slightest.

Nevertheless, "brought up in the back rooms and nurseries of Pre-Raphael-
ism, which, for better or for worse, held that to be an artist was to be the

most august thing in life," he learned to believe "that the profession of the arts or the humaner letters was a priestcraft and of itself consecrated its earnest votary." As an adult he shared the Pre-Raphaelite conviction that "to speak to any one who made money by commercial pursuits was almost not to speak to a man at all. It was as if one were communicating with one of the lower animals endowed with power of speech." This feeling was, of course, a special variation on the Victorian feeling that people in trade were beneath notice. Artists were not prevented from sharing this feeling by the insignificant fact that they were not landed gentry either. As late as 1913, during a discussion of censorship at the Society of Authors, Maurice Hewlett told his fellow writers that "he thought it not only undignified but almost indecent that representative writers should discuss these matters with trades-men; that it was not for the tradesmen to dictate their terms to the Authors ... but that the Authors should, if possible, dictate terms to the tradesmen." All his life Ford, like his grandfather Brown, contributed to his own lack of success by assuming that it was not only possible for him to dictate to editors and publishers but necessary to his dignity as a gentleman and author that he do so.[11]

At the same time, the overwhelming presences of the Victorian Great filled the small boy with a nightmarish doubt of his own ability to become a great artist. This doubt could hardly have been allayed by the well-meant efforts of his aunt Lucy, the wife of William Rossetti and the mother of those pesky cousins Olive and Arthur, to turn all the children of the family into geniuses—"That terrible word 'genius,' " as Ford said. During the summers which the children of the Hueffer and Rossetti families spent together at the seashore, at Bournemouth or Hythe, he found himself "delivered over to the full educational fury of our aunt." This experience was all the more painful because the Rossetti children took to it with enthusiasm. Awesomely early Olive Rossetti wrote a Greek play in which Ford was required to take a minor role before a large audience of the Victorian Great. It did nothing to ease his embarrassment that his cousin Arthur Rossetti, who was much smaller than he, strode boldly about the stage in the heroic role of Theseus, or that, when it came time for him to speak his one or two words, the voice of Francis Hueffer could be heard from the audience firmly advising him to "speak up, Fordie!"[12]

The discomfort of experiences like this was intensified for him by the fact that he was an imaginative child. His nurse, Atterbury, had a powerful relish for the gruesome that she delighted to share with him.

When I lived with meyuncle Power in the Minories [she would say]

time of the Crimea Wower, meyuncle let 'is top front to a master
saddler. N wen wower broke out the master saddler worked niteand-
day, niteanaday for sevin weeks without stop er stay. N e took is
saddles to the Wower Orfis n drawed his pay. All in gowlden sovrins
in a Gledstun beg. N wen e got ome e cut his froat on the top front
landin n the blood n the gowld run down the staircase together like
the awtificial cascades in Battersea Pawk.

This did a good deal to fill his childhood with imaginary horrors and he once
said that "I can still see the shadows of wolves if I lie in bed with a fire in
the room." The dread thus fixed in his childhood endured all his life. "Ever
since he had been a tiny child," he once wrote of himself,

> He had . . . been so much a creature of dreads that [the war]was, in
> a sense, much less than dreads to which he had been well accustomed.
> The dreads of original sin, of poverty, of bankruptcy, of incredible
> shyness, of insults, misunderstandings, of disease, of death, of suc-
> cumbing to blackmailers, forgers, brain-troubles, punishments, un-
> deserved ingratitudes, betrayals.

He suffered all the more from these dreads because his pride required him
to maintain an offhand air and never admit he felt them.[13]

The Hueffer boys were not wholly defenseless against their brilliant
Rossetti cousins. They soon discovered that, if these cousins could outshine
them as Theseus, they were more skillful as Turpin the Highwayman and
Dick Harkaway, "who had a repeating rifle and a tame black jaguar, and
who bathed in gore almost nightly." Games of this order put the smaller
Rossetti children at a disadvantage, and Ford distinctly remembered "that I
bagged my cousin Arthur with one collar-bone, broken on a boat slide in my
company, while . . . Olive Rossetti, I also remember with gratification, cut
her head open . . . because she wanted to follow me down some dangerous
steps and fell onto a flower-pot." "My cousins, in the full glory of their
genius," he could console himself, "were never really all of them together
quite out of the bonesetter's hands."[14]

Broken Rossetti bones were doubtless some consolation, but Dick Harkaway was bound to be a losing game in a world where the only life any
adult could seriously imagine living was the life of the artist and even his
grandfather Brown could say, when Ford considered going into civil service,
"God damn and blast my soul! . . . I will turn you straight out of my house
if you go in for any kind of commercial life."[15]

Nevertheless, his grandfather's homes were the delight of his childhood.
His memories of the first of them, in Fitzroy Square, may well include much

that he learned later rather than remembered, for Ford Madox Brown left Fitzroy Square when he moved to Manchester in 1881 and was not much there after 1879, when he began on his painting for the Town Hall in Manchester; and Ford was only five in 1879.[16]

But it hardly matters if Ford's vague memories of having seen Bret Harte and Mark Twain and Joaquin Miller at Fitzroy Square and of having sat on the Queen's lap at a Liszt concert are rather stories he was told and improved than events remembered from his early childhood. They were images of the atmosphere of Fitzroy Square, just as were his memories of the Charlotte Kirby he trusted so confidently. Quite possibly he enlarged in his memory the account Charlotte gave him, as she put him to bed, of the cabdriver who knocked on the door to announce that "I've got your master in my cab. He's very drunk," only to be told by Charlotte—" and an immense intonation of pride would come into Charlotte's voice" as she reported to her small charge this grand retort—"My master's a-sitting at the head of his table entertaining his guests. That's Mr. [Swinburne]. Carry him up-stairs and lay him in the bath." The story that Ford Madox Brown pinned labels to the clothes of friends of this kind so that if they got in trouble they would be brought to his house to be cared for may also be exaggerated, but it is wholly in character, an example of Brown's "singular and quaint ingenuity" in serving his friends.[17]

Ford never forgot the house in Fitzroy Square with its "great stone urn, lichened, soot-stained, and decorated with a great ram's head by way of handle, elevated only by what looked like a square piece of stone of about the size and shape of a folio-book" which he always imagined, as he stood on the doorstep, might fall and crush him quite out of existence. He remembered the large rooms at Fitzroy Square as filled with "articles of furniture mostly after the 'Firm' taste," and "women more or less aesthetically garbed," and distinguished poets reading their own works aloud for two or three hours on end, and the bathroom that was, for the small Ford, "full of warmth and lightness" and safety. Even more vivid in his memory was the house at 1 St. Edmund's Terrace in which Ford Madox Brown lived when he returned in 1887 from his labors in Manchester to settle once more in London.[18]

Meanwhile, however, in 1881 Ford had been sent to boarding school. In later years he liked to hint that he had been sent to one of the famous public schools: he usually favored Winchester, though sometimes he chose Eton. In fact he was sent to just the kind of school Francis Hueffer and his friends the Garnetts and the Martindales would have admired. This seems to have been chosen because Dr. Alfred Praetorius and Mrs. Praetorius were friends of both Ford Madox Brown and the Martindales. The Martindale daughters, Elsie and Mary, attended the kindergarten run by the Praetoriuses in Weymouth Street and followed them to Folkestone when they set up a school there. Dr. Praetorius came from Bad Soden, near Frankfurt am Main; he had been a favorite pupil of the distinguished educator, Froebel, and had pleasingly modern ideas of education. At the same time he had a good deal of German admiration for English social customs and wanted his students to play cricket and become gentlemen of the public-school type.[19]

Most of the students at Praetorius were the children of professional people like the Martindales, and the Hueffer boys had a certain advantage over them with respect to languages and culture in general, matters much stressed at Praetorius, where life was conducted, on alternate days, in French and in German. But they suffered balancing disadvantages with respect to the more conventional activities encouraged by the school. These activities Ford entered into with equal energy and enthusiasm, and he eventually became the captain of the school's cricket team and one of its best tennis players. It was at Praetorius that he and Elsie Martindale got to know each other well. Ford was ten and Elsie seven when Elsie was first sent there; she and Ford saw so much of one another that their schoolmates began calling Elsie "the Captain's wife."[20]

Ford remembered Elizabeth Praetorius as "a very great educationalist ... from whom I suppose I learned everything that I ever learned in school, except the writing of Latin verse.... " To the end of his life he remembered a Scottish usher named David Watson who "used to spend every spare moment of his day and whole Sundays on end" with Ford "beside him at his pulpit and construing for him every imaginable kind of book from the *Artaxerxes* of Madame de Scudéry ... to ... *Don Quixote* in the original," and who also drilled him fiercely in English composition. Ford was child enough to notice that Mr. Watson "had the largest and reddest ears that can ever have been affixed to a human head"; but he never forgot what Mr. Watson had done for him: "May his soul be being read to by whole choirs of little Anglican angels!" he said.[21]

He was very happy at Praetorius. "There can scarcely have been at any stage of the world's history," he recalled, "a happiness greater than that, say, of an English schoolboy during the decades of the eighties and the nineties. There you were, vicariously ruling the waves of the world, building up the empire on which the sun never sets.... You were furnished without effort on your part, with traditions of valour and of physical perfection." His uncle

William Rossetti passed on to him a volume called *The Novelists and Roman-cers Library* that included *Captain Singleton*, *The Mysteries of Udolpho*, and Sue's *Mystères de Paris* and had been the delight of Christina and Gabriel and William Rossetti when they were young. Mathilde Blind, the formidable poetess whom Ford Madox Brown so much admired and Gabriel Rossetti could never be persuaded to meet, even presented him with a complete set of *The Great Writers*. Such was his reputation as a reader that his schoolmates sought him out to discover the indecent passages in *Tom Jones*. By the age of fourteen he had read a wonderful mixture of books ranging from Gibbon and Plutarch through Marryat, Scott, and Defoe, to *Westward, Ho!* and *Sweeny Todd, the Demon Barber.*[22]

Ford was also in Germany during these years on a visit that "repre-sented my first absolute freedom from parental control," during which he fell in love with a blond Flemish madonna, who sold him cigarettes.[23]

Chapter 2

This carefree life came to an end when Francis Hueffer died of a heart attack in January, 1889; he left almost nothing. Juliet went to live with the William Rossettis; Ford and Oliver left Praetorius and went with their mother to live with Ford Madox Brown at 1 St. Edmund's Terrace, two doors away from the Rossettis. These changes made the Hueffers cling together for support, and there developed a camaraderie between Mrs. Hueffer and the children that, despite the nominal authority of her position as a Victorian mother, made them allies and confidants. They saw themselves as an isolated detachment conducting a guerrilla war against the rest of society and always presented a united front to the enemy. Mrs. Hueffer was fiercely loyal to Ford throughout the difficulties he had with the Martindales during his courtship of Elsie; she was always ready to go to Germany to care for him when he was ill or to move to South Lodge to lend her countenance to him and Violet Hunt when they were living there notoriously unmarried.[1]

The "spirited and precocious" Rossetti children did not make the Hueffer children's lives easier. They had a printing press in the basement on which they turned out an anarchist journal called *The Torch*, which they sold in Hyde Park. Ford's aunt Lucy did not like the printing press. The children got very dirty and the press made a loud groaning noise that had to be explained to Uncle William's respectable visitors (William Rossetti was Secretary of the Inland Revenue). "But Uncle William stood up for us and protected [us]." On one occasion they marched down Primrose Hill to the corner of Avenue Road and St. John's Wood Road, their banner flying before them ("We took our banner . . . with us to give us confidence"), to convert the local policeman. They stood about him in a circle and he bent down with his hands on his knees to listen while Helen Rossetti explained to him the natural equality of all men. The policeman said to Juliet Hueffer, "I got a little lass your size, with hair that colour, and she makes a rare fuss when her mother puts it into papers of an evenin'."[2]

The Garnett boys, with whom the Hueffer boys were much thrown, were not easy for them either. "The young Garnetts ... were sceptical, unworldly and over-critical, and the Hueffer boys ... were credulous, worldly (without being worldly-wise) and over-confident. The young Garnetts were inclined to regard the Hueffer boys as half egregious asses and half charlatans. The Hueffers, who originally respected the Garnetts, became more and more exasperated by their sceptical attitude and their strait-laced almost puritanical contempt for success and notoriety, which constituted the breath of romance for Ford and Oliver." Yet as Ford later said, "The public opinion, as it were, of the younger Garnetts must have had a great effect in shaping my young mind," and his recollection of growing up between these two groups of children was that "such consciousness of the Higher Things as has been vouchsafed me awakened in the contemptuous companionship of the children of Doctor Garnett of the British Museum and the still more contemptuous society of the still younger Rossettis. ... The one ... represented orthodox Anglicanism and Virtue; the other stood militantly for Established Rationalism, which at the time was a menacing affair."[3]

The Hueffer boys were sent to the University College School in Gower Street, where "all education except the teaching of Latin verse and the reading of Plutarch was treated as a joke." David Garnett, who attended the school a decade and a half later, found it "a disagreeable institution." "We were unattractive, smelly, inkstained boys, wearing frayed Eton collars and Nórfolk jackets. ... And with two or three exceptions the masters were of much the same quality as the boys." But Ford was at the University College School less than a year and it had little effect on him. He was not very consistent in his attendance even then, partly because he was seriously considering becoming a composer and "most afternoons, in furtherance of my musical education I used to go to concerts." Moreover, he and Oliver were beginning to discover the life of London, particularly the argumentative café life of the young intellectuals, and were eagerly exploring the great city that appealed to the romantic side of their natures the Garnetts found so annoying.[4]

It was at this time that Ford became acquainted with some of the anarchists who were just then much in evidence around London. His acquaintance with Prince Kropotkin was close enough to allow him to take his young sister to Kropotkin's for tea, to her awed delight. Ford also had some acquaintance with Vaillant, who achieved a certain notoriety in 1893 by exploding a bomb in the French Chamber of Deputies, and occasionally during these years he walked the streets of London with Stepniak and Volkhofsky, both well-known Nihilists, and Prince Kropotkin, "dodged [by] the Russian spy allotted to each of these distinguished lecturers." He learned enough about such men to supply Conrad with much useful information about anarchist activities when Conrad was writing *The Secret Agent.*[5]

But much the most formative influence on him at this time was his grandfather. Ford Madox Brown was a rash, quick-tempered, belligerently independent man. When the Mayor of Manchester wished to show Lord Derby one of the Town Hall paintings Brown was working on, he took offense. "... that was too much," he wrote Mrs. Hueffer. "I could not be shown as one of the sights, so his lordship had to go through [Manchester] unenlightened as to my noble self. One must draw the line *somewhere.*" When young Gabriel Rossetti wrote him enthusiastically about his painting, *Wickliffe Reading his Translation of the Bible to John of Gaunt,* he suspected some impertinent whippersnapper was making fun of him and arrived on the Rossettis' doorstep, stick in hand, in a towering rage. Rossetti's charm and enthusiasm soon disarmed him, for he was as quick to forget his anger as to feel it, and he became the one really close friend Rossetti ever had.[6]

For all this thorniness Brown was a very lovable man. "My grandfather," Juliet remembered, "was one of the kindest, gentlest, handsomest old gentlemen that ever lived. Everybody loved him.... His cheeks were pink, and he had blue eyes, and his hair fell straight down on both sides of his face nearly to the bottom of his ears, and my grandmother cut it straight and even all the way round.... He wasn't very tall, but his shoulders were broad, and he looked somehow grand and important."

> ... Madox Brown [his grandson said] was the finest man I ever knew. He had his irascibilities, his fits of passion when, tossing his white head, his mane of hair would fly all over his face, and when he would blaspheme impressively after the manner of our great grandfathers.... But ... he was never either unjust or ungenerous in cold blood, and I am quite sure that envy had no part at all in his nature. ... I would give very much of what I possess to be able ... to live once more some of those old evenings in [his] studio.[7]

Brown's enthusiasm was as violent as his scorn, and he threw himself into life with great energy: he painted ten hours a day for days at a time and was capable, in his enthusiasm for young artists, of declaring Mathilde Blind's sonnets as fine as Shakespeare's or a young painter's works "equal to those of Raphael." "Ah," he would say, "how cleverly these young men sketch. I never remember to have seen such work. If only *I* could do anything so good."[8]

He was hopelessly unbusinesslike and frequently in financial difficulties. "As to the conduct of life," Ford said, he was "a little sketchy, a little romantic, perhaps a little careless," partly because he was unreasonably generous. Ford might have been describing himself. Brown's studio was a sort of junkshop of objects he had painted, including "a weak lay-figure with false yellow hair" so broken down that it would change its posture at the slightest movement in the room, in a way that terrified his young granddaughter. Here he sat, in his blue tam-o'-shanter and—in winter—with his legs encased in a fur-lined bag, in a chair that could be raised and lowered on a screw that came up out of "a kind of square barrel." He considered it all eminently comfortable and once assured Miss Blind that his establishment was "grandly picturesque." When the art critic Harry Quilter described his studio as "a place half-way between the Old Curiosity Shop of Dickens and a marine store in the suburb of Portsmouth," Brown exclaimed, "God damn and blast my soul! What does the fellow want?"

> The walls were covered with gilded leather; all the doors were painted dark green; the room was very long, and partly filled by the great picture that was never to be finished, and, all in shadow, in the distant corner was the table covered with bits of string, curtain-knobs, horseshoes, and odds and ends of iron and wood.

> ... I would sit there on the other side of the rustling fire [Ford remembered], listening, and he would revive the splendid ghosts of Pre-Raphaelites, going back to Cornelius and Overbeck and to Baron Leys and Baron Wappers, who taught him first to paint in the romantic, grand manner. He would talk on. Then Mr. William Rossetti would come in from next door but one, and they would begin to talk of Shelley and Browning and Mazzini and Napoleon III.... [9]

"Fordy," Brown would say, "never refuse to help a lame dog over a stile. ... Beggar yourself rather than refuse assistance to any one whose genius you think shows promise of being greater than your own." "I wish," Ford said, "I could have lived up to ["this rule of life"]." He often did.[10]

Like his grandson, Brown suffered from periods of melancholia when his eager independence would be exaggerated into insulting brusqueness and he would discover that plots were being hatched around him. Most of the time, however, "he was well enough aware [that "his quite preposterous prejudices were"] the mere emanations of persistent wrong-headedness."[11]

By the end of 1890 Ford had left school for good. For a while he drifted around London often ending up for tea at the British Museum, where the Garnetts had moved when Dr. Garnett became the Keeper of Printed Books. There he would listen to "Mr Gosse . . . trumpet the latest news from literary Scandinavia; and Mr Sidney Colvin . . . tell us how, in the latest letter from poor dear Robert Louis [Stevenson], that exiled invalid would talk minutely about his health in Samoa; and Samuel Butler . . . relate the latest fluctuations in the four per cents. And I would be kept in a corner by Mr Robert Garnett who would tell me the latest eccentricities of his extraordinarily eccentric clients; or by Miss Olive Garnett who . . . would tell me that I ought to become a Nihilist. And at last Dr Garnett would come in from behind his book-wall in the Museum, and Mrs Constance Garnett . . . would look in for a minute and beam absently with her blue eyes through her spectacles. . . . " "I was," he remembered later, "in and out of the Garnetts' house in the Museum courtyard every day and all day long. Their hospitality was as boundless as it was beneficent."[12]

He also remembered leaning idly against the railings of the Museum in Great Russell Street and having Edward Garnett come along "with his peculiar lounging stride" to lead him "to the Vienna Café where, in those days met all the youthful intelligentsia, and . . . lecture [him] on the Social Revolution." "[Ford] wore a black coat with a cape over the shoulders, and when [he] walked along it floated out a little way behind." This cape had been Gabriel Rossetti's and had come down to him through his grandfather; it was over thirty years old. The jacket he wore under it was "a water-tight German forester's pilot jacket," also secondhand, and under that was a fifteen-year-old blue-linen shirt of his grandfather's and a red-satin tie. This costume, he felt, was the proper wear for a young man of Pre-Raphaelite descent who sympathized with Morris' socialism; Morris' disciples, he noted, had much imitated Rossetti's cape.[13]

His life during these years appears idle enough, and in a way it was. But he was not yet eighteen and his pride made him try to appear indolent until some sort of success would allow him to admit he had been working hard to become a writer. He was also learning a great deal about London, and he always remembered with nostalgia the London of this period when "the streets were still gaslit—the electric arc-lamps, wavering from white to lurid purple, were only to be seen on the Thames Embankment or outside a few big buildings . . . the buses, hansoms and 'growlers,' or four-wheelers, were still horse-drawn . . . [and] the big railway station at King's Cross smelt strongly of horses and engine smoke." To Ford even the old Underground was glamorous. "It smelled of sulphur as hell is supposed to smell; its passages were as gloomy as Tartarus' was supposed to be, and smokes and fumes poured from all its tunnels, while its carriages were lit by oil lamps, so that little pools of oil swayed and trembled in the bottoms of the globe-like lamp-glasses."[14]

His mother preserved a poem dated September 12, 1890, called "In Memoriam"; it begins:

> Since you are gone and we are left—
> Since for you the veil is reft
> From dark Eternity....

But he did not always take himself so seriously. He enjoyed telling his younger sister, Juliet, fairy stories, and when he wrote one of these down, his grandfather was so delighted that he immediately made two illustrations for it, bullied Edward Garnett into seeing that Fisher Unwin published it, and rushed copies to all his friends. "Dear Watts," he wrote Watts-Dunton. "By the same post I send you, & I think you will like to see & have my grandson Ford's first book, *The Brown Owl*. Fisher Unwin and young Garnett have, between them, thought it worth publication.... "[15]

The success of *The Brown Owl* made Ford an author, and he quickly produced two more fairy stories, *The Feather* (1892) and *The Queen Who Flew* (1894), and a dozen short fairy tales. These stories deserved their success. Ford loved children and understood the queer combination of realism and simplicity that appeals to their imaginations. "The stories are about Princes and Princesses and magicians and such twaddle," as he put it.[16]

The Feather, for example, is the story of a princess who lives in a kingdom cut off by high mountains from the rest of the world. She is carried across the mountains by a great eagle.

> She expected that the eagle would set to and make a meal off her at
> once. But somehow or other, either it had had enough to eat during
> the day, or else did not like to begin to have supper so late for fear
> of nightmare; at any rate, it abstained....

Her later adventures include a journey to the moon to see the Parcae, who are known as the Misses Parker, and a return trip in Diana's chariot. Ford said he "had written [*The Brown Owl*] to amuse my sister Juliet" (*The Feather* is in fact dedicated to her); "the publisher ... " he added, "paid me ten pounds for it and ... it sold many thousands more copies than any other book I ever wrote."[17]

Though he was not yet twenty, he also attempted to write a sophisticated novel, *The Shifting of the Fire*, about an elegant young chemist named Clement Hollebrone. The girl he loves marries a rich old man in order to get his money. When the old man dies, Clem is torn between his love for her and his dedication to Berlioz' "Absolute Indifferentism in Universal Matters." " . . . he had no wish to enter another phase of philosophic psychology, to have his 'Indifferentism' overcome by passion." Needless to say, however, he does.[18]

The characters in *The Shifting of the Fire* are implausible and the plot absurd; Ford has the chemist-hero give his love a phial of a newly invented poison as a birthday present, in order that, later on, he may falsely suspect her of having poisoned her elderly husband. The novel is written in a ludicrously elegant style; the author puts his hero and a friend to bed after a hard day's travel this way:

> [Their host] was fain to let them go to their rooms above. Here the air struck cold on entry, despite the fires which burned bravely, with crackling red embers, yet were they glad without more ado to doff their clothes in cold and shivering haste, thrusting themselves between the sheets. . . .

Only the hero, who has a considerable resemblance to Ford's dream-vision of himself (he too quoted Berlioz when he was in love), has any complexity of character, however implausible.[19]

Conrad read *The Shifting of the Fire* shortly after he and Ford met.

> The book is delightfully young [he said]. Mind I say *delightfully* instead of drearily, or morally, or sadly, or frightfully or any of those things which politeness would have induced me to paraphrase. . . . Felicitous phrasing is plentiful and with that the writing is wonderfully level. There is certainly crudeness in the presentation of the idea. The facts, the emotions [,] the sensations are painted somewhat as the scenery for the stage is painted but youth does not make for fineness—except in inexpressible ideals, in acted dreams, in the spoiling or making of a life. Never in writing about it. More could have been made of the situations by a more spiritual method. . . . No doubt the general cause is (O happy man) youth—inexperience.[20]

During the summer of 1892 Ford began to court Elsie Martindale seriously: he was eighteen and Elsie was fifteen. The Martindales spent their summers in Winchelsea, and Ford went down there regularly to call; by August he had progressed far enough to get himself invited for a weekend.

Then there was an interruption: Mrs. Hueffer was worried about the future of both boys. Thinking it possible Ford might gain the interest of Francis Hueffer's wealthy German relatives, she decided to take him to visit them and have him become a Catholic. He went to Bonn to stay with his uncle Hermann, the professor, and to receive instruction. His strongest memories of this period, however, were of a tutor who was an atheistic Lutheran clergyman and of "a crowd of students with literary aspirations and Marxian views ... [and] a female cousin who, in sign of emancipation, wore a Russian, almost Nihilist, fur toque, smoked cigarettes and when bicycling appeared in knickerbockers."[21]

He went from Germany to the Riviera to stay with his uncle Leopold in a luxurious hotel, where he was sent "to bed early and read Eugène Sue to the music of the orchestra of the Café de Paris. They played over and over again in alternation 'Tararaboomde-ay' and 'The Man Who Broke the Bank at Monte Carlo.' " But the family's plan to have him become a Catholic and enter into the good graces of his rich German relatives now struck a snag. Whether owing to the influence of the atheistic Lutheran clergyman or the female cousin with the almost Nihilist toque or his own socialism, he rebelled against entering the Church and returned to England.[22]

There he resumed his courtship of Elsie Martindale, writing her solemn letters about practicing her violin and doing the household chores and being polite to her mother. On October 3, 1892 (Elsie's sixteenth birthday), he sent her a ring, at the same time writing Mrs. Martindale.

> Of course [he said] I am well aware that we are both of us too young for you to sanction anything like a definite engagement between us, & indeed, unreasonable as I am, I can see for myself that it would be wrong for me to wish to fetter her in any way.... If, however you should consider the matter entirely out of the question I beseech you to say as much & I will resign myself never to trouble you or her again.... Hoping that you will not think me impertinent or over troublesome in asking you to give the matter a few moments' consideration,
>
> I am—
Most sincerely yours'
Ford H. M. Hueffer.

That grand offer of renunciation would come back to haunt him.

Meanwhile he had been persuaded to go back to the Continent, now to Paris, to which his uncle Leopold had moved on. He remained there for the rest of the year, and on November 7, he was received into the Church, "absolutely baptized" at St. Joseph's in the Avenue Hoche. For the rest of his life, Ford would remain nominally a Catholic and, when it suited the image of himself that for the moment dominated his mind, an active one. The kind of Catholicism that appealed most strongly to his imagination was the Albigensian variety that had flourished in Provence in the Middle Ages, and from the time of his poem, "On Heaven," written in 1913, to his final books about the Great Trade Route, he wrote enthusiastically about the Albigenses. But Ford's Catholicism was essentially a by-product of his social and political views rather than a religious attitude. When, just before the war, he worked out his Tory radical attitude with its devotion to feudal values or when he was imagining himself as a good south German during the time he was trying to divorce Elsie, he would become enthusiastically Catholic, energetic in religious observations and full of scorn for "Prots." At such times he would assure people that only tempestuously religious natures were capable of clear thought. The rest of the time he was scarcely Catholic in either feeling or conduct.

In his memory this winter of living the opulent life with his uncle Leopold in Paris expanded into "winter after winter spent in an immensely luxurious, gilded and absolutely tranquil *appartement* of a millionaire's house ... " in " the rich Anglo-American Catholic circle that solidly ornamented in those days the French capital." As usual, he eventually carried this fanciful elaboration too far, imagining what was evidently impossible, that "my boyhood... was passed very largely in Paris, and very largely in exactly the same society as that in which Newman [the hero of Henry James's *The American*] himself moved."*[23]

By the beginning of the next year Ford was back home with his mother at 90 Brook Green, busy cultivating his socialism and courting Elsie Martindale. He remembered the self he presented to the world at this time as bumptious. Once he even corrected his beloved grandfather about the subject of his ponderously moral painting, *Cromwell, Protector of the Vaudois*, quite overwhelming the old gentleman with his superior learning on the subject; it was a piece of swagger he was always ashamed of.[24]

This youthful exuberance was concealed by Ford's air of indifference.

---

*"The great house of Bellegarde ... would, I now feel," James said in his Preface to *The American*, "given the circumstances, given the *whole* of the ground, have comported itself in a manner as different as possible from the manner to which my narrative commits it.... I doubtless at the time... believed I had taken my precautions; but truly they should have been greater, to impart the air of truth to the attitude—that is first to the pomp and circumstance, and second to the queer falsity—of the Bellegardes." The representation of Paris society in *The American* is, in short, pure romancing.

"It is recorded [in] some book or other against me as a defect that I never would argue with anyone thus giving the impression that I was too coldly conceited to care to listen to the counter-opinions of my fellow men." This was a gross injustice: "... having ... no opinions at all of my own, I find myself regarding the opinions of others as usually unanswerable." This is a revealing illustration of the way Ford's self-esteem led him to make foolish distortions of genuine perceptions. Nothing is more obvious than that he had a great many opinions. But he also had the novelist's habit of entering, with complete imaginative sympathy, into a large variety of moral attitudes. This habit made it impossible for him to believe, as other men seemed to, in a fixed moral attitude.

I can't believe [he said later to Stella Bowen] that I have any settled —or even unsettled—scheme of ethics, like you. I don't believe I *could* have—because I never had any 'views'—I have only had sympathies in this life. I don't think I ever 'presumed' to form, much less to formulate, any general scheme of life.

At a given moment, particularly when he was seeking to make his own conduct look admirable, he would commit himself with great energy and a wealth of opinions to a particular attitude, but this commitment seldom survived its occasion. But it was not simply his want of a fixed "scheme of ethics" that made him refuse to argue. At any given moment his view of things involved so many nicely shaded improvements and his self-esteem was so heavily dependent on it that he simply could not afford to contemplate any other view of it than his own.[25]

The book in which this defect is recorded against him and that he is pretending he cannot remember is his sister Juliet's *Chapters from Childhood*, in which it is also recorded that he was a very kind young man.

He was a fair, clever young man, rather scornful, with smooth pink cheeks and a medium-sized hooked nose like my grandfather's, a high, intellectual forehead, and quiet, absent-looking blue eyes that seemed as if they were always pondering over something. I was nervous with him, because he was very critical and thought that nearly every one was stupid and not worth disagreeing with. But he was very kind and liked to take me out to tea.[26]

Chapter 3

Ford was a romantic man; what counted for him in any serious love affair was intimacy, close sympathy, and understanding. He was like Edward Ashburnham of *The Good Soldier*, who, when he loved Nancy Rufford, felt it was "her effect on the moral side of his life [that mattered]. . . . I do not think that ["the sex instinct"] counts for very much in a really great passion." Or, as Christopher Tietjens puts it in his blunt eighteenth-century way:

> You seduced a young woman in order to be able to finish your talks with her. You could not do that without living with her. You could not live with her without seducing her; but that was the by-product. The point is that you can't otherwise talk. You can't finish talks at street-corners; in museums; even in drawing-rooms. You mayn't be in the mood when she is in the mood—for the intimate conversation that means the final communion of your souls.

"You," Ford wrote Elsie, "are my friend because to you alone I can talk with a feeling of perfect ease and your ideas alone fit mine." He was even less able than most young men in this condition to endure delays. "If we could only take our fate into our hands and drag it round," he said. "But there is the stupid creature God Almighty who sits grinning and says in dreary platitudes—'Wait, wait all things in the fitness of time.' How can one reconcile oneself to it when talent is wasting and death stalking over the land?"[*][1]

*This view of God as a "a plag[u]ing beast" and of religion as "humbuggery" is frequently asserted, with delighted daring, in Ford's letters. Sometimes, however, God was on their side: "It always seems to me when I hear the voice of the wind in London as if God had wandered out of the free country where one may hear him and see him and having got [to London] by mistake is saying 'Damn my eyes but this is a queer place. I wonder if I have got any influence here.' But a creature called Mrs. G[rundy] kicked him out long ago and reigns in his stead— so he howls out a bit and bangs himself against everything." A more sophisticated version of

As a consequence Ford's letters to Elsie during these months, when the Martindales began seriously to oppose them, are full of threats of suicide that were perfectly sincere despite their rather self-conscious literary air. "It does not very much matter either way what these folks [the Martindales] say or do because as I get to feel more and more we can always cut our throats and have it over"; "you see we are poor brave things or else we shouldn't go on living knowing as much as we do"; " . . . at worst there's a garter—or a second storey window—or your hair—your soft hair, that too would be like kisses. . . . You know as well as I do how much I am against self-slaying, but better that than let your mind fail beneath hopeless tyranny. And then we shall at least be forever together." The increasing lack of enthusiasm of Elsie's parents thus served mainly to accelerate their intimacy; by May they were writing each other daily, sometimes twice a day.[2]

There were good reasons for the Martindales' opposition, but they made the mistake—perhaps inevitable with somewhat old-fashioned parents—of not confiding these reasons to Elsie and Ford. By the middle of May the situation reached the point where Ford Madox Brown called formally on the Martindales to discuss it. But again the Martindales avoided the real issue. They said they were not trying separate Elsie and Ford but were worried about the health of their older daughter, Mary, and wished to send her in Elsie's care to Soden for the cure. From childhood Mary had been of such an excitable temper that her parents feared for her sanity. Now they had discovered that she cherished a passion for Ford and they were terrified of the effect on her of any special intimacy between Ford and her younger sister. Things might have gone very differently had the Martindales told the truth. Late in her life Elsie said that, had she known her parents' real reason for objecting to her relation with Ford, she probably would have obeyed them.[3]

This was the fundamental difficulty, but it was reinforced by the Martindales' conventional doubts about Ford as a suitor. They were substantial, conservative people. Dr. Martindale had come to London in 1862 from Carlisle, where he had been apprenticed to a chemist, to become a pharmacist and lecturer on Materia Medica at University College Hospital. In 1873, he bought a pharmaceutical business in New Cavendish Street and prospered rapidly, greatly aided by his authorship (with Dr. Wynn Westcott) of the *Extra Pharmacopeia*, the official handbook for all druggists. The Martindales were a handsome couple with handsome children, and in their newfound

---

this whimsical attitude governs Ford's novel, *Mr. Apollo.*

prosperity they were as little likely as most such people to look with enthusiasm on their daughter's interest in someone like Ford.[4]

To them he appeared an irresponsible young man unlikely ever to earn a decent living, a prospect that seemed especially dangerous for a delicate girl like Elsie. When she had been three or four she had been bedridden for nearly two years with tuberculosis of a vertebra of her neck. When she was ten she injured her knee. It too became tubercular and had to be operated on. She was left with only a slight limp but the knee remained weak and caused her frequent falls for the rest of her life.

Moreover, the Martindales had the darkest suspicions (some quite justified) of Ford's advanced ideas, especially about sex; they also suspected him of wanting to marry Elsie for her money. Ford certainly was not unaware of the Martindales' wealth, but their suspicion was unjustified: Ford was deeply in love with Elsie. In the sequel, as so often happens, Elsie turned out not to be the heiress everyone took her for. Dr. Martindale's money was badly invested and he left far less than had been anticipated.[5]

The Martindales' anxiety about Ford's reliability must have been greatly increased by the spectacular career of Oliver Hueffer, who, at the ripe age of seventeen, had involved himself in debt.

> One morning a week the early hours [at Ford Madox Brown's] would be pierced by [Brown's] imprecations. He would send for my brother who would look more than usually cherubic. He would fling his nightcap across the room and shout:
>
> "God damn and blast you, Oliver, what have you done with my watch and chain and spectacles?"
>
> Oliver would say, with an air of ingenuousness:
>
> "Well, you see, Granpa, I had to have a couple of quid for debts of honour and I knew you would not want me not to have them whilst I did not want to wake you. So I took them down to Attenborough's. But here are the pawn tickets."
>
> I think my grandfather was, in secret, rather proud of these exploits. At any rate he never locked his bedroom door. . . . [6]

Ford did not find them especially amusing. He told Elsie that "Oliver is ruining FMB" and "Oliver is gradually ruining the V[enerable] P[arent]." Early in 1893 Brown paid debts of £200 for Oliver "for use of horses Dog Carts &c." It was not enough. During that summer another financial crisis arose about which Brown wrote Cathy Hueffer in despair, "I can get nothing reasonable out of Oliver." Oliver, of course, had an elaborate and wholly implausible plan for dealing with his difficulties. He proposed that Brown lend him money to carry out some unexplained scheme with his uncle William Rossetti, the most practical man imaginable and the last one any-body would expect to involve himself in a scheme of Oliver's. When the family tried to persuade Oliver to go to Africa, he scornfully pointed out that "it would cost 200£ for the outfit alone"—at least of the kind he required.

This crisis was surmounted by various promises to Oliver's creditors, but immediately after Brown's death that fall they returned to haunt poor Mrs. Hueffer, who was driven to write her lawyers:

> My son Oliver was not living with me at the time he incurred the debt of 23£ to Mr. Clement Paul and was only 17 years old at the time, therefore I don't consider he [Paul] could claim it from me as I only saw him [Paul] the once when he came to my house to tell me about it after my fathers debt [*sic*: death].
>
> On that occasion I said I would pay my son Olivers debt from a point of honour—when my Fathers affairs were settled. I repeat that statement—indeed if you could let me have the 120£ remaining from the 500 coming from my Fathers will [Brown had left each of his daughters £500 outright]—I would send him the money & then I could pay another debt [of Oliver's] of 50£ quite as necessary to pay as Mr. Pauls. . . .

Presumably all this was done, but by the next year Oliver was back living with —and off—his mother, his consumption of the purse as incurable as ever. Throughout the rest of his life Oliver, "with the swiftness of the succession of the seasons at St. Agrève, ran through the careers of Man About Town, Army Officer, Actor, Stockbroker, Painter, Author and under the auspices of the father of one of his fiancées, that of valise manufacturer!" As Ford once observed, Oliver was, in temperament and character, a more extravagant version of Ford himself; the Martindales were not, perhaps, so wrong as Ford supposed them to consider Oliver's early career as a warning to them.[7]

In any event, they set themeselves to prevent the development of any serious relation between Ford and Elsie. For a time Dr. Martindale fancied he had the situation under control, but he was wrong. From the start Ford had felt —as he had carefully explained to Mrs. Martindale when he had sent Elsie her ring the previous October—that they "would not deem him over-boastful were I to say that I have been more successful than many boys of my age—and there seems to be no particular reason why I should not continue to succeed." Had he not already published a novel and two successful fairy stories? Was he not about to publish a volume of poems? Opposition to such a suitor was, he thought, hardly rational.

By the summer of 1893 this opposition had, in his judgment, become even more unaccountable. He was now beginning to make himself heard at what H. G. Wells called the "little conventical in the outhouse beside [William Morris'] Kelmscott House," where a good many young men who were soon to be famous were busy with denunciations of the bourgeois and a combined operation to save the Chicago anarchists and restore the thirteenth century. It was a colorful assembly.

> a blue serge jacket . . . a flannel collar, an inordinate orange tie, and a lank neck with a vast Adam's apple passing upward into mist. . . . Another faceless figure of black and gold, like a banker. And a wonderful girl, designed, it seems, by Mr. Walter Crane . . . [and] Mr. Bernard Shaw, physically individualized with extraordinary decision, a frequent speaker, and always explicit and careful to make himself misunderstood.[8]

Ford found this a highly stimulating forum; his sense of powers newly realized is evident in his description of an evening he spent there.

> I thought I would look in at Kelmscott House to get a breath of fresh air. But alas . . . for there I heard out a lecture on [the] "Foolishness of Anarchism" and there was an audience as unfair as any Tory pot-house meeting . . . all Socialists about 200 strong pitching into . . . just four Anarchists and they the A's took the wrong side or boggled about the dynamitards.
>
> I did my best and decried any kind of force physical or moral but it weren't no good. I got howled down by the entire audience inclusive of the four Anarchists.

Tory-Papist Anarchism was clearly not for Kelmscott House, but that hardly made a boldly dramatic assertion of it any less satisfying.[9]

Even Ford must have suspected that appearances at Kelmscott House were not the best means of impressing the Martindales. He had better hopes of his growing acquaintance among the artists and writers who gathered in St. Edmund's Terrace. "I want," he wrote Elsie, "to meet the great Le Gallienne. You see he is a great, great man and it is well to conciliate him." There is a more comfortingly youthful irreverence in his report of his actual meeting with Le Gallienne; "those wonderful great men . . . contrive to make a wonderful deal of small talk among them," he thought. By that fall he was publishing poems in the magazines, and he therefore no longer felt —if he ever really had—that it was entirely up to the Martindales to determine whether he and Elsie could be engaged. Such humbleness had looked well and cost little when he had been confident that the Martindales would eventually say yes. But now he was beginning to understand that, despite his impressive credentials, the Martindales were not going to come around.[10]

He therefore ceased advising Elsie to conciliate her mother and began to say that "Your Mama and her relatives are ignorant arrogant spiteful and unscrupulous," and to assure Elsie that she was "being tortured by an ignorant woman." When Elsie reported that her mother had injudiciously asserted she would rather see Elsie dead than married to Ford, he said that this "is a fairly good confrontation of all she said [to Ford Madox Brown] about not wanting to separate us and that sort of nonsense." Mrs. Martindale certainly talked indiscreetly to Elsie, for reasons that were well enough understood in the family. Before she married Dr. Martindale, she had been an overworked country nurse in Ireland; to get herself through she had begun to drink, a habit she had not conquered at this time, though she did so later. What Elsie delicately called her mother's "intemperance" certainly encouraged the young people's belief in their own superior good sense.[11]

The tension was momentarily relieved in August when Ford made a second trip to Germany with his mother; when they returned Ford Madox Brown's death made another truce. Ford and Elsie were allowed to go together to Birchington-on-Sea to look at the monument Brown had designed for the grave of Rossetti. Ford then went traveling again, this time about England, "to have a change." He was back in London by January, "feeling rather cowardly," as he wrote Elsie, "since I have left you in the jaws of death"—by which he meant "surrounded by the sounds of hymns or something almost as dismal if possible."[12]

The situation was bound to come to a head.

> On the evening of the 24th day of February 1894 [Dr. Martindale later reported] my eldest son [Harri] agreed to take his sister and some friends and also the said Ford Herman Madox Hueffer to the theatre. When my daughter Elsie came downstairs ready to start for the theatre she had on an old cloak to which my wife objected and asked her to change it for a new cloak which . . . my daughter had herself selected. This she refused to do and was supported by the said Ford Herman Madox Hueffer who said he had quite as much to do with my daughter's dressing as my wife had. I resented this interference with my household and angry words passed between the said Ford Herman Madox Hueffer myself and my wife on the subject.

The full significance of this defiance was not, however, immediately clear to Dr. Martindale. A hint of what was to come did reach him a week later when he undertook to remonstrate with Elsie for her disobedience.

I asked her how she could ask for the blessing of God if she behaved this way. Her answer was that she did not want the blessing of God. She further said that there was no need to obey her father and mother when she could think for herself and in reply to further questions from me said that it might be right to steal as all property ought to be in common.

The poor doctor was so shaken by this revelation of his daughter's views that he swallowed his pride and went around to discuss the matter with Mrs. Hueffer. "He does not," Ford was able to report, "seem to have effected anything or to have made up his [own] mind to do anything. . . . "*13

Dr. Martindale had, however, made up his mind. "On the 4th day of March," as he said later, "believing that the mind of my daughter had been corrupted by the said Ford Herman Madox Hueffer, I forbad him to come to my house again." When Ford learned of this edict he turned up on the Martindales' doorstep demanding to see Elsie. When he was refused he waited a short distance from the house until Elsie could slip out, and off they went. "We were," says Dr. Martindale, "unable to overtake them"—as usual. Ford hurried Elsie across Regent's Park to Ford Madox Brown's house, left her there, and returned to Devonshire Street with a letter from Elsie that he had doubtless helped to compose. It said: "Dear Daddy, As you have chosen to use force against me to-day and to lock me up I shall take effectual steps to prevent such a thing occurring again. Unless you give Ford an absolute promise that I shall be unmolested—I shall not return to the house of my own will. Your affectionate daughter, Elsie." At first Dr. Martindale was so enraged by this defiance that he seized Ford and shook him, but "I was most anxious that my daughter be restored to my house and I temporised," with the result that Ford brought Elsie home.[14]

The situation was now, however—in the eyes of Ford and Elsie, at least—impossible. The next day Ford was saying, "You may be certain that I shall leave no stone unturned and flinch before no threats in the giving you of your liberty. Of course the mayoress is capable of legal

*"I can only say," Mrs. Hueffer wrote Dr. Martindale, "that I do not consider you can or have any right to break the promise you made Fords grandfather to whom you gave your solemn word that you had no thought of breaking the engagement between Ford and Elsie" (March 5, 1894). This letter appears to have been composed by Ford. It is in his style rather than in Mrs. Hueffer's faintly illiterate one; and the exaggeration is characteristic of Ford's impressionistic way of handling such arguments: Dr. Martindale had promised Brown not to try to keep Ford and Elsie from meeting; he had not sworn he had no thought of breaking their engagement: there was no engagement when he talked to Brown.

proceedings (she is capable of many things) but I am by no means afraid of that." (Dr. Martindale had been the mayor of Winchelsea in 1893 and Ford delighted to refer to him and Mrs. Martindale as the mayor and mayoress.)

Even Dr. Martindale recognized that things could not go on as they had, and he decided to consult William Michael Rossetti. He could not have chosen better. Rossetti pointed out that by October of 1897 both children would be of age and free to make their own decision; would it not, he asked, be best to allow them in the meantime to see one another in a decorous way? But this sensible plan was more than Dr. Martindale could stomach. He began negotiations with Ford by asking Ford to agree not to see Elsie for a specific period. This Ford refused to do, in effect countering by suggesting to Elsie that, if worse came to worse, Mrs. Hueffer would be glad to have Elsie come to live in Brook Green.*[15]

In this crisis Robert Garnett turned out to be a tower of strength—even, perhaps, too helpful. Elsie's idea had been to run away to a sympathetic Martindale aunt in Carlisle, where she was confident she would be allowed the freedom she felt was her right. But Robert Garnett took them firmly in hand. He arranged with relatives of his in Bath to take Elsie in and helped her to plot her escape. His plan was much facilitated by Dr. Martindale's decision to send Elsie and her sister to Winchelsea, where he fondly imagined Elsie would be beyond the reach of the said Ford Hermann Madox Hueffer.

Once again he had seriously underrated his opponents, who at once recalled that to get from London to Winchelsea it was necessary to change at Ashford and that an up train from Dover passed through Ashford at the same time. When Elsie and Mary arrived in Ashford near noon on March 16, Elsie slipped across to the opposite platform and boarded the train for London, whence she made her way to Bath. The ensuing uproar is dramatically reflected in the series of telegrams that followed.

> Ashford SRR 1. 9p. Martindale Chemist London. Elsie has gone from Ashford Beware Dover Train Mary.

> Ashford SRR 2. 46p. Martindale Chemist London. Elsie not turned up look out at London stations Mary.

But Dr. Martindale did not entirely trust Mary's judgment in a matter of this importance.

---

*William Rossetti's diplomacy was not made easier for him by the fact that there was a long-standing feud between the half sisters, Lucy Rossetti and Cathy Hueffer.

Ashford SRR 3. 14p. Martindale Chemist London. One daughter here other not here [Sir Edward] Elgar.

That did frighten Dr. Martindale. At 7:45 he wired Mary from Euston: "Not found Elsie been Brookgreen and St. Edmund's Terrace." He even wired the Praetoriuses in Folkestone. The next morning he was inquiring of friends in Winchelsea with equal lack of success. He then went to Ashford himself to consult the stationmaster and the superintendent of police. But, as had so often happened before, Dr. Martindale had "been unable to overtake them"; Elsie had completely disappeared. He then hired detectives to search for her and arranged to have a policeman watch 1 St. Edmund's Terrace, remembering that Ford had taken Elsie there the first time she ran away.

Eventually his solicitors learned from Shaen Roscoe (Robert Garnett's firm) that Ford knew—but would not reveal—where Elsie was and that Elsie was quite safe with "a respectable lady . . . a client of their firm." Finally, on March 20, Elsie wrote her father to assert once more her claim to freedom. "I do not mean," she said firmly, "to return to you until you arrange something definite regarding the continuance of my old acquaintance with Ford. I had written you a note to let you know of my disappearance on Friday [March 16] but found no convenient opportunity to leave it for you." Evidently she was still hoping to persuade her father to give in and not force her to leave home permanently.

But by this time Dr. Martindale was so angry at Ford that he would not consider such a solution. After Elsie's disappearance he had broken open a box in which she kept Ford's letters and read them. What he got was perhaps no more than he deserved; he could not have been much pleased by Ford's references to the mayor, or by his quoting Berlioz' last words— "When I see the way in which certain people look on love and what they seek in artistic creation I am involuntarily reminded of hogs rooting and grunting under the grandest trees"—and then adding, "which is singularly appropriate." He was horrified by the revelation of Ford's ideas. "I am intensely shocked," he said, "to discover from the said letters that the said Ford Herman Madox Hueffer is an Anarchist frequenting places to which Anarchists resort a scoffer at all religion and that he has systematically incited my daughter Elsie to disobey her parents and has several times suggested suicide to her." He was now more determined than ever to separate Elsie from Ford and to this end he began the slow legal process of getting her made a ward in Chancery. He had his lawyers at once inform Ford that Elsie was a ward of the court, though in fact she did not become one until

April 11; Ford was unwise enough to acknowledge the receipt of this letter. These maneuvers gained Dr. Martindale only the dubious advantage of confronting Ford and Elsie with an unanticipated delay with Elsie alone in Gloucester (to which she had moved from Bath) and Ford in London.[16]

This unexpected delay made them anxious lest a scandal develop, and Robert Garnett began to press Elsie and Ford to marry at once. They were still not prepared for that, but they were ready to use it as a threat, as Elsie did when she wrote her father:

> I imagine you have not yet realized my firm determination not to return to you, a determination which increases daily.
>
> ... if it were possible for you to view the matter slightly from my point of view—I do not doubt but that it would lead you to seeing that I was perfectly justified in leaving your house.
>
> Perhaps you still do not understand my reasons for so doing.
>
> They are—Mother's continual intemperance & the weak, unhealthy condition of Mary's mind. ...
>
> No doubt you will still persist in thinking it is my duty to remain with such companions—but I, as you know, think differently. ...
>
> If you can propose any arrangement which will be at all bearable to me—I am quite ready to consider it—as I have no wish to utterly estrange myself from you. ... But I think it only right to say that unless you send me word that you intend to make some such arrangement, as you can understand [, that] we consider satisfactory, there remains no alternative but an early marriage.[17]

To this proposal Dr. Martindale made no reply except to go ahead with his plan to get the Court of Chancery to force Elsie to return, leaving Elsie and Ford no alternatives except surrender or marriage. They chose marriage, and on May 17, 1894, after falsely alleging to the Registrar that Elsie was over twenty-one, they were married at Gloucester. They went to the Doone Valley, on Exmoor, for their honeymoon, but it was cut short by Dr. Martindale, still busy locking the door after the horse had been stolen; he got a court order restraining "all communication" between Ford and Elsie and ordering Ford to appear in court. Ford did so on June 6, and foolishly swore that he had never heard of Elsie's being a ward. When this allegation was shown, by the production of his letter to Dr. Martindale, to be false, he played his trump card and informed the court that "there was no longer any Miss Martindale for the court to protect. That lady became Mrs Madox Hueffer some three weeks ago." Mr. Justice North, in some irritation, pointed out that Ford "had laid himself open to criminal proceedings under more than one head," but recognized that the marriage was nonetheless legal and stayed the operation of his restraining order.*18

*Justice North finally closed the case by rejecting several motions to find Ford guilty of contempt of court. Since Elsie was now Ford's wife, no parent or trustee could, in her name, move to have Ford committed for contempt, so that Dr. Martindale was deprived of even this consolation.

Chapter 4

The honeymoon had to be cut short anyhow; Ford wanted to be back in London for the sale of Ford Madox Brown's effects, which took place in St. Edmund's Terrace May 29–31. He also wanted to make the most of the romantic circumstances of his marriage, which struck him as a fine opportunity for advertising that rising young writer, Ford H. Madox Hueffer. Immediately after his appearance in court on June 6 he sought out at his club a journalist friend named Perris and together they concocted a story that appeared that afternoon in *The Star* under the alluring head, "A Poet's Love Affair. A Chancery Court Chapter of 'The Queen Who Flew.'" (*The Queen Who Flew* was the title of Ford's current book, a fairy story published a few weeks earlier.) *The Star*'s story begins: "In Chancery Court No. 2 to-day a rarely romantic story was unrolled before Mr. Justice North, who sat in private to hear the action. . . . " It then goes on to give a detailed account of Ford's career, describing him as "a young poet and novelist who has already achieved a certain measure of distinction." This story was promptly copied the next day by the *Morning* and the *Pall Mall Gazette* and, the following day, by the *People*.*[1]

After a period of such tension, a change was again in order, and Ford and Elsie took a quick trip to Germany. When they got home, they had to find a place to live. Both of them wanted to be in the neighborhood of the Romney Marsh where they had spent their childhood summers. They went down to Hythe and walked across through Aldington to Bonnington; there

*Ford and Perris risked contempt by publishing the proceedings after the judge had heard the case in his private room, especially as the judge believed they had deliberately referred to the privacy of the hearing in order to enhance what he called the "vulgarity and bad taste" of their article. They were probably lucky to get off with costs.

they found a house called Bloomfield Villa. It was a tall, rather bare house set in a hollow, and "the damp cold," Elsie complained, hung constantly about it. Ford made the most of its somewhat dubious attractions, asserting that from it one could see across the marsh to the sea seven miles away and that Bonnington had its saint (St. Rumwold) and was known locally by the colorful name of Hog Turd Green.[2]

Afterwards Ford thought that during the year and a half they lived at Bonnington he lost "almost all touch with intellectual life," but they entertained steadily and Ford was frequently in London, where he kept a small flat with Harrison Cowleshaw, Edward Garnett's brother-in-law. He also spent a great deal of time getting to know the local people like Meary Walker and Meary Spratt and Ragged Ass Wilson and "Shaking Ben who had been ruined by the bad gels of Rye," about whom he wrote eloquently in *Women & Men*. But their life at Bonnington was not easy. They were very poor. Before their marriage Mrs. Hueffer had promised them an allowance of £ 4 a week, but when the time came Oliver had got through so much of her money that the best she could do was £ 1, not a princely income even for that time.*[3]

Ford would not have been an easy domestic companion in the most comfortable circumstances for a wife like Elsie, who was extremely orderly. Ford once remarked that she would have made an excellent hospital matron. Ford, on the other hand, was uninterested in domestic comforts ("I love luxury but I hate comfort," he once observed). Like his grandfather, he was a dedicated worker, and once he began writing he forgot everything else. The idea that he should stop work at some predetermined time to eat seemed to him absurd. But he expected to be well fed when he was ready; he loved food and drink, and he was a big man, better than six feet in height, who could eat and drink astonishing amounts. In his later years, when he became a notable gourmet, he developed a monumental paunch and weighed close to 250 pounds.

As people without much income but with expectations, Ford and Elsie tended to live beyond their means. Elsie's upbringing had left her with no idea of what it is to manage on a small income, and money ran through Ford's fingers like water. Elsie never forgot her first experience of hiding behind the door when the butcher came because there was no money to pay

---

*The Grevilles of Ford's *An English Girl* (1907), living a life of some social pretensions, figure "you might live comfortably and decently upon twelve hundred a year." The magic figure for the working classes was £ 160: "A man who enjoys an income over £ 3 a week need not stint himself and his family of reasonable food or clothing or shelter," said Lloyd George in the House of Commons in 1909. The Hueffers' income was about £ 100 a year.

him. Whatever their ultimate expectations from Dr. Martindale, they were scant at this time; he would not even recognize their existence, and they had to make the first advance. On Christmas Day, 1894, Elsie wrote him, "Dear Daddy, My affection for you is sincere and in spite of everything, will be lasting and it will be to me a real cause of grief if the gulf between us cannot be bridged over." Dr. Martindale's answer was anything but conciliatory. He suggested that Elsie was writing at Ford's instigation and that Ford had probably composed her letter. Dr. Martindale should have known better. Elsie replied with true Martindale firmness: "As you seem to think it is Ford and not I who write," she remarked, "he shall [not] even see this letter."

Financial help came from an unexpected source a short time after this when Ford's uncle Leopold Hüffer died childless in Paris on February 18, 1897, leaving his money to his nephews and nieces; there were more of these than was desirable, but Oliver and Ford each got something over £ 3,000. Like any sum greater than the pound or two one might borrow from a friend, this seemed to Ford a limitless amount of money that would comfortably support the life of modest gentility he had begun to live—he had taken up golf at Hythe, where "my cousin, George Wilkes," had just started a links, and made friends with Dr. Macnamara, the Liberal Minister for Education, and Charles Masterman, with whom he was to be closely associated for a time during the war.[4]

These activities did not interrupt his work; nothing ever did. Sometime during 1895 he completed a novel that was never published. He also completed his biography of his grandfather. This project had been suggested by Longman to William Morris and, when he refused it, to William Rossetti, who suggested his wife, Brown's daughter Lucy. Lucy accepted, but she died before getting much work done on it and Rossetti then proposed Ford. It was a large undertaking, and Ford was just twenty. It was also a solemn obligation; Ford loved his grandfather. He took great pains over it; he and Elsie went to Manchester and Liverpool to see private collections and the Town Hall frescoes, and Elsie made careful lists of the dates, prices, and owners of all the paintings. Ford persuaded William Rossetti to revise his manuscript and got Edward Garnett to advise him: "—In point of style your suggestions would be gratefully received, the work being new to me is perhaps not up to much and I am not able to judge, so let me have your advice."[5]

The style of *Ford Madox Brown* and, indeed, of much of Ford's work up to the time of his collaboration with Conrad, has a wooden solemnity it is hard to believe Ford was ever capable of: "1876, a year again cut up by serious illnesses," he would write, "saw the completion of a number of the small works that go to fill up the interstices of the edifice of an artistic career." He was evidently determined to achieve the pompous tone of the official Victorian biography. He omitted any hint of a joke and—even more remarkable —any reference to himself. He calls his grandfather's portrait of him, *Tell's Son,* "a portrait of the artist's grandson," and Brown's illustrations for *The Brown Owl* "a couple of illustrations for a book of one of his grandsons." This is in striking contrast with Ford's later accounts of this period, in which he figures prominently as an influential man "attempting to promote the growing of corn, tobacco and wine on my own land in England," and as an acute observer of the political scene, watching ironically as Gladstone addresses the house in 1895 and as Oscar Wilde struggles to defend himself against the cross-examination of Sir Frank Lockwood.[6]

Ford Madox Brown was finished early in 1896 and published October 28, "very handsomely got up and illustrated," as William Rossetti said. By this time the Martindales had forgiven Ford and Elsie; in the last week of August they came to Bloomfield Villa for a visit and, in September, had Elsie and Ford come to Winchelsea to stay with them. Ford at once wrote Henry James to ask if he could call. "I shall be very glad to see you & talk with you," James replied, "—& am not insensible to the compliment of your wish." James, Ford says, was "bearded, composed, and magisterial. . . . After [luncheon] he let himself go in a singularly vivid display of dislike for the persons rather than the works of my family's circle." Ford did not see James again until they moved to Winchelsea in 1901.[7]

Dr. Martindale had been distressed when he was at Bloomfield Villa by its unhealthy dampness. He very much wanted them to move, so that when, during a bicycle tour, they saw a house they liked near Postling they hastened to rent it. This was Pent Farm; they moved into it October 15, 1896. The Pent was—and is—a small, square, red-brick farmhouse, but it seemed large to Elsie ("a room on each side of the door . . . both good-sized . . . [and] a huge kitchen . . . and . . . five good-sized bedrooms"); Ford restored the Pent "on the most approved lines to its original antique condition of great rafters and huge ingles with rackets and crocks." "We are," he said, "just under the most magnificent sheep-downs near Canterbury"—"at the foot of those bleak downs that we used to see from Aldington Corner," Elsie said. E. V. Lucas called the Pent "a damp and dark little farmhouse." It was to be the Hueffers' home until late 1898, when the Conrads took it over so that it remained almost a second home to Ford and Elsie until the Conrads left it in September, 1907.[8]

As soon as they were settled at the Pent Elsie, who was pregnant, took to her bed, to be followed at once by their small servant, Annie. Elsie's sister Mary came down to help a grumbling Ford care for them (having "the whole house on our hands ... is no kind of a joke"). He was himself just recovering from a spell of depression of the kind he frequently had after finishing a piece of work. The situation righted itself in time for him to go to Liverpool and Manchester to prepare the Brown exhibition at the Grafton Gallery in January, 1897. There were, as always, many weekend guests, including Jayme Batalha-Reis, the Portuguese Consul-General, on whom Ford would later model Tomas Castro of *Romance*. On July 3, 1897, "at half past four in the afternoon," their first child, Christina Margaret Madox Hueffer, was born. To rest from the strain, Ford bicycled to Guildford to see Cowleshaw and Henry Hyde, the cranky artist who would later illustrate *The Cinque Ports* and McClure's edition of *England and the English*.[9]

Ford was at this time "a long blonde with a drawling manner," "tall and Germanic in appearance, with a pink and white complexion, pale, rather prominent, blue eyes and a beard." He was still committed to the Tory conservatism, the Pre-Raphaelite medievalism, and "the simple life" so fashionable among advanced intellectuals of the kind he would later satirize in *The Simple Life Limited.*

> I carry my love for the enduring and old into every department of life [he asserted] preferring old clothes built after my own design, and suiting my own habits, to the most seemly showy garment designed with a view to the uniformity of the human species and destined to change with the waning of the moon.

"Fate," he liked to say, " ... a thought mercilessly ... leaves us with few of the old familiar faces, the old and trusted landmarks." He was devoted to the idea of the Small Producer, which had an unusually strong grip on his imagination just at this time ("I was at the time in a severely Small-Producer frame of mind"). In all these feelings Elsie was his devoted supporter, a "tall, high-breasted and dark [girl] with a bold eye and a rich, high colour, like a ripe nectarine," she "dressed in richly coloured garments of the William Morris style and wore earrings and a great amber necklace...."[10]

Their interest in advanced ideas made them eager to be at the center of things, and the center of things was what Edward Garnett, thinking of his wife's interest in all things Russian, called Dostoevsky Corner. This was the pair of houses known as the Cearne (because it was "encearned" or encircled by woods) and Gracie's Cottage on the High Chart near Limpsfield, where Edward and Constance Garnett had settled in 1896. Though Frederick Wishaw had made some translations of Dostoevsky in the eighties and in 1899 Constance Garnett completed her translation of Turgenev, there were at this time no English translations of Tolstoy and Gogol. Constance Garnett, however, knew all about the Russian novel and was acquainted with many of Russia's leading revolutionaries. Ford's sister, Juliet, learned Russian in order to help Mrs. Garnett with her translating, and Ford learned about Russian novelists and Russian politics from her. Edward Garnett was not only an advanced thinker but a man of considerable literary influence. Ford respected him, though they never got on. "A friend to me my enemy is," he said of Garnett, and when Garnett died, Ford wrote Stanley Unwin, "He was a pretty vindictive foe of me—or rather of what I stand for, but I had a certain affection for him."[11]

The Hueffers rented the Pent to Walter Crane and, on March 20, went to live in Gracie's Cottage. It was immediately filled with local guests—Garnetts and Stepniaks and Kropotkins, and David Soskice, who had only recently escaped from Siberia. Ford undertook to educate the innocent and literal-minded Soskice in English ways. Soskice would sit on the doorstep scribbling information into his notebook while Ford walked to and fro imparting it: most of it was improved information. D. H. Lawrence, who did not actually meet Ford until 1909 and must have heard about all this from David Garnett, was much amused by Ford's method of educating Soskice and loved to give imitations of it— "Yaws, yaws . . . rye . . . rye is one of our—ah—lawgest crops." Ford the Small Producer went about in smock and gaiters. He kept ducks, and because there was no pond for them, he sank a hip bath in the ground. He named the ducks after the ladies of Dostoevsky Corner and as they stood about him waiting to gobble up earthworms when he was digging in the garden, he would observe that "Lucy is so very greedy . . . she always manages to eat some of Connie's share"; or "Katie [is] such a clumsy thing, she broke one of my tomato frames. Really I could *not* feel fond of her, so we had her roast on Sunday. Rather tough." The namesakes of these ducks were not much amused.[12]

Ford was also busy being reformed by the local Fabians. The permanent secretary of the Fabian Society, Edward Pease, lived in the neighborhood and there were frequent meetings at his house, where one could improve oneself. It was there that Ford first saw Stephen Crane, fresh from Cuba. Later Edward Garnett brought Crane to see him, and Crane asserted that Gracie's Cottage was "a bully old baronial ruin"—a mistake to which the cottage's unfinished condition may have contributed. It was during this summer and fall that Ford wrote *Seraphina*, on which he and Conrad would base *Romance*.[13]

Ford says that he had been working for months on a life of Henry VIII

when he learned that the distinguished historian, A. F. Pollard, was writing a
biography of Henry. Convinced he could not compete with Pollard, he gave up
his book. Dr. Richard Garnett then suggested that he write a book about pirates. "I ejaculated: 'Good God: Pirates! Why not Palmistry?' Palmistry . . .
was . . . one of that great scholar's infatuations." But he laid aside his materials
on Henry VIII until he was ready to write his *Fifth Queen* trilogy and looked
into Dr. Garnett's pirates.

Dr. Garnett may well have suggested Ford look up the case of Aaron
Smith, the last man ever tried for piracy at the Old Bailey; this was just the
sort of thing Dr. Garnett would have known about, though in *Joseph Conrad*
Ford says, possibly correctly, that he came on the Aaron Smith story accidentally while he was doing research for *Ford Madox Brown*. But Ford did
not turn to the story of Aaron Smith because he had given up the idea of
a book on Henry VIII; he did not give up that idea until at least three years
later. Moreover, the idea for a book like *Seraphina* had been in his mind ever
since he had discovered the colorful history of the country around Bonnington and the Pent. "I am thinking of writing a novel all about smugglers,"
he wrote Edward Garnett in 1895. "—It seems this was the centre of one of
the famous gangs of smugglers & the people can tell some famously realistic
stories about those gentry." Stevenson's *Treasure Island* was in everybody's
mind at the time to make him think such a book might be successful and he
seems to have started *Seraphina* as early as 1896.[14]

In any event, what Dr. Garnett did (if he did) was to put Ford onto
Aaron Smith. Smith's trial in 1823 had been reported in the papers and there
was a sensational little book about it, the character of which is clear from its
title:

> The Atrocities/ of the/ Pirates;/ Being/ A Faithful Narrative/ of
> the/ Unparalleled Sufferings/ Endured by the Author during his
> Captivity/ Among the Pirates of/ The Island of Cuba;/ With an
> Account of the/ Excesses and Barbarities/ of Those/ Inhuman Free-
> booters./ By Aaron Smith,/ (Who was himself afterwards tried at the
> Old Bailey as a/ Pirate, and acquitted.)/ London: Printed for G. and
> W. B. Whittaker,/ Ave-Maria Lane./ 1824

The text of *Seraphina* makes it clear that Ford never saw this little book;
what he read was a fairly detailed summary of it called "Cuban Pirates: A
True Narrative" that was printed in *All the Year Round,* the popular magazine edited by Dickens, for January 22, 1870.[15]

Ford's alternative explanation, that he had come across this article in the
course of doing research for *Ford Madox Brown,* gets its plausibility from the

fact that Dickens made a notorious attack on Millais' *Christ in the House of His Parents* when it was exhibited at the Academy in 1850 and no Pre-Raphaelite or any of his heirs or assigns had ever forgiven Dickens. "The writer in his youth," Ford said, "lived amongst a set of artists and writers to whom the name of Dickens was almost anathema, most of them, indeed, having known him personally.... They would descant without end on his 'vulgarity.' " When H. G. Wells wanted to tease Ford in *Boon* he had Ford "contribute ... an exhortation not to forget that Henry James knew Turgenev and that he had known them both, and a flat denial that Dickens was a novelist. This last was the tail of the Pre-Raphaelite feud begun in *Household Words*, oh! generations ago.... " Perhaps, then, Ford did come on "Cuban Pirates: A True Narrative" on his own. In any event it was this "True Narrative" that he turned into "The Privateer./ A Romance of Cuban Waters./ Wherein are recorded the wanderings, perils/ & endurings of John Kemp, Duke & Grandee of Spain,/ & of Seraphina his wife./ By./ Ford Hueffer./ Author of 'The Brown Owl,' etc."[16]

From the "True Narrative" Ford copied all he could, almost word for word. He added a new beginning that describes Kemp's unhappy childhood at Pont Farm and the local smugglers who help him escape to Cuba. He turned the brief meetings between the hero and Seraphina of the "True Narrative" into a series of clumsy scenes of courtship that lead John Kemp to take Seraphina with him when he escapes to Havana. There he marries her, in another laboriously comic scene. Aaron Smith had dropped Seraphina unceremoniously when he escaped; he had a fiancée in London named Sophia Knight whom *The Atrocities* calls "a female of considerable personal attractions." Sophia testified for Smith when he was tried at the Old Bailey, and that suggested to Ford the idea of bringing Seraphina into Kemp's trial as a surprise witness. Finally he added a long "Envoi" in which our hero, now a "Duke and Grandee of Spain" by virtue of his marriage to Seraphina, returns in triumph to Pont Farm and his astonished family. These additions are awkward in construction and inflated in style. Edward Garnett told Ford *Seraphina* was unpublishable, and he was right. This was the mediocre narrative Ford and Conrad would turn into *Romance*.[17]

Chapter 5

Conrad and Ford met during the first week of September, 1898, when the Conrads were staying with Edward Garnett at Limpsfield and Garnett brought Conrad over to Gracie's Cottage.

> Conrad came round the corner of the house. I was doing something at the open fireplace in the house-end. He was in advance of Mr. Garnett who had gone inside, I suppose, to find me. Conrad stood looking at the view. His hands were in the pockets of his reefer-coat, the thumbs sticking out. His black, torpedo beard pointed at the horizon. He placed a monocle in his eye. Then he caught sight of me.
>
> I was very untidy, in my working clothes. He started back a little. I said: "I'm Hueffer." He had taken me for the gardener.
>
> His whole being melted together in enormous politeness. His spine inclined forward; he extended both hands to take mine. He said:
>
> "My dear faller ... Delighted ... Ench ... anté!"

With his admiration for all things English, Conrad very much wanted to appear an English gentleman, but nature, unbeknownst to him, kept breaking through. He was, as H.G. Wells said, "The strangest of creatures."

He was rather short and round-shouldered with his head as it were sunken into his body. He had a dark retreating face with a very carefully trimmed and pointed beard, a trouble-wrinkled forehead and very troubled dark eyes, and the gestures of his hands and arms were from the shoulders and very Oriental indeed.[*][1]

*Coming unexpectedly on Conrad in London one day and seeing him for a moment as a stranger, Ford saw "an old, shrunken, wizened man, in an unbrushed bowler, and ancient burst-seamed overcoat, one wrist wrapped in flannel, the other hand helping him to lean on a

Very soon after this first meeting Conrad wrote Ford to suggest that they collaborate on a revision of *Seraphina*.

In the Pent Farm, beneath the South Downs, there was a great kitchen with a wavy brick floor. On this floor sat a great many cats: they were needed to keep down the rats and they got some milk of a morning. Every morning a wild robin with a red breast and green-ish-khaki body would hop, not fly, across the floor of the kitchen between the waiting cats. The cats would avert their glances, pulsing their sheathed claws in and out. The robin would hop through the inner doorway of the kitchen, across an angle of the low dining-room and so up the bed-room stairs. When the maid with the morning letters and the tea-tray opened the bed-room door the robin would fly through the low, dark room and perch on a comb, stuck into a brush on the dressing-table, against the long, low leaded windows. It awaited crumbs of bread and tiny morsels of lump sugar from the tea-tray. It had never been taught to go on these adventures. This robin attended at the opening of the first letter that ... the writer received from Joseph Conrad. The robin watched with its beady eyes the sheet of blue-grey paper with the large rather ornamental hand-writing. ... It was afterwards drowned in a cream-jug which took away from its aspect of a supernatural visitant.[2]

In this letter Conrad "said that he had consulted his friends and that they had strongly recommended the experiment because he wrote so slowly and with such difficulty." Ford always supposed he must have told Conrad about *Seraphina* at their first meeting, but he could never actually remember doing so, and it seems a good deal more likely that it was Edward Garnett (one of the friends Conrad consulted about his situation) who told him about it. Garnett wanted to help Conrad and here was Ford with an unpublishable version of a promising story on his hands and Conrad haunted by "the particular devil that spoils my work for me" to the point where he could not write at all. We are probably hearing almost the exact words Garnett used to Conrad in Conrad's report to Henley of his motives: "I thought that ... the material [*Seraphina*] being of the kind that appeals to my imagination and the man being an honest workman we could turn out something tolerable—perhaps. ... " Conrad did not read *Seraphina* (and could not even spell its name) until after he had moved to the Pent; his assertion about "the material" is secondhand

---

hazel walking-stick, cut from a hedge and prepared at home. [He] had in one tortured eye a round piece of dirty window-glass."

and can only be Garnett's description of it, or Ford's own. Conrad also consulted Henley, as this letter shows.

Ford's recollection of Conrad's letter suggesting the collaboration is probably substantially correct; its "Oriental politeness" and elaborate flattery sound too like Conrad to have been invented.

> ... Conrad confessed to the writer that previous to suggesting a collaboration he had consulted a number of men of letters as to its advisability. He said that he had put before them his difficulties with the language, the slowness with which he wrote and the increased fluency that he might acquire in the process [of collaborating]. ... He stated ... that he had said to Henley ... "Look here. I write with such difficulty...." And Henley, according to Conrad ... had said: "Why don't you ask H. to collaborate with you. He is the finest stylist in the English language of to-day...."

Ford knew very well that Henley had never said any such thing, remembering that much later on Henley had once turned on him with "Who the Hell are you? I never even heard your name!" He realized that this flattering view of him as the finest stylist in English was Conrad's ("Conrad," as he put it, "liked to please as much as Henley liked to knock the nonsense out of you") and suspected that Conrad—no doubt at Garnett's suggestion—had proposed him as a possible collaborator during some discussion with Henley, and Henley had said something like "I daresay he'll do as well as anyone else."[3]

Ford got away from Limpsfield almost immediately after meeting Conrad. Limpsfield had not turned out the way he had hoped; he found the ideas that prevailed there unsympathetic. "I ... went to Limpsfield," he said later, "to be reformed by Mr. Edward Garnett and his friends. Limpsfield however disgusted me with the life of the Intelligentzia as lived in the London suburbs.... [The Fabian Society's] permanent secretary dwelt there and there meetings sanctioning the marriages of members—in the case of the Committee usually with wealthy American women—were held. Mr. Shaw's marriage was there sanctioned."[4]

By the middle of September, then, Ford and Elsie were back at the Pent, and it was there Ford received Conrad's letter suggesting that they collaborate. He must have replied immediately, for it was not more than a fortnight after their meeting at Limpsfield that they had completed their arrangements to work together and Ford had generously proposed to move out of the Pent and sublet it to the Conrads so that they could move out of their uncomfortable quarters at Stanford-le-Hope. The arrangement was completed by early October, but then Ford developed an eye infection and the Conrads' arrival was postponed. Conrad came down to have his first look at the Pent on October 7 and arrived to take possession on the 26th. He took to the house at once, in defiance of the disapproval of Garnett and others. "We are here . . . and the place is a success. I reckon Ford told you. I reckon you disapprove. . . . I feel hopeful about my work. Completely changed." Five days later he was eagerly writing Ford, "Have you written for *Serafina* (Seraphina?)," and as soon as Ford had, Conrad urged him to bring it to the Pent for discussion. This was an altogether different mood from the despair he had felt when he came to the Garnetts two months earlier, and it lasted: over a year later he was to write proudly to Cunninghame Graham, "in the fourteen months I've been at the Pent I've written upwards of 100,000 words."[5]

It is not easy to determine either writer's true motives for joining in this collaboration. In his letters Conrad had a misleading habit of taking the attitude he thought his correspondent would like; he seldom revealed his real feelings. "Behind that eyeglass," as E. V. Lucas said, "what was going on? . . . He was smiling, inscrutable, and, no matter in what company, living behind his mask, and always so polite as almost to terrify." This elaborate politeness makes Conrad's expressed opinions contradictory and unreliable, and nearly everything Ford wrote about their relations was written long after, when Ford's tendency to improve his stories was well developed.[6]

Conrad's motives almost certainly did not include personal affection. He had a curious incapacity for any of the feelings that ordinarily accompany friendship or love. His masterful courtship of Jessie is comically impressive. Yet from the very first days of their marriage, he showed none of the special consideration that ordinarily accompanies a happy marriage; he created the impression that "he found his family an oppression that kept him irritable." He seems to have suspected that he was in some way unusual and to have made an effort to compensate for it by his elaborate, artificial politeness. He was convinced that Ford could be useful to him and that he could help Ford; he seems to have thought nothing further—except a decorous pretense of friendship—was needed.[7]

But Conrad did need Ford. As his sporadic attempts to return to the sea and his anxious consultations with friends show, he was discouraged and floundering. He doubted his understanding of the English audience; "One could," as H. G. Wells said, "always baffle Conrad by saying 'humour.' It was one of our damned English tricks he had never learned to tackle." He also doubted his command of English. Ford has frequently been criticized for claiming Conrad said that "my intimate, automatic, less expressed thoughts are in Polish; when I express myself with care I do it in French. When I write I think in French and then translate the words of my thoughts into English." This description may be exaggerated, but to some extent Conrad certainly still thought in French: as late as the final version of *Romance*, nearly four years after this, he was writing such literally translated French sentences as "I understood, then, what meant this illusion of ghostly murmurs. . . . " To the end of his life his speech was unreliable: in a moment of anger Pinker suggested as late as 1910 that he try speaking English ("I have," Conrad wrote him with injured dignity, "asked Robert Garnett to be my mouthpiece—at any rate until my speech improves sufficiently to be acceptable"). As Ford once pointed out, the eloquence of Conrad's prose is partly the result of his using the Latin words of English as the French use theirs. Lewis Hind once said,

> It was a marvel to me then, and always has been how so un-
> English a man in temperament, looks, and utterance as Conrad
> should be able to write such perfect English. . . . That afternoon [in
> 1898] he dug his fists into the sand, I remember, and said, "Ah, if only
> I could write zee English, good, well! But you see, you will see."*[8]

These discouragements were piled onto a temperament at all times uncertain.

> I remember once we had been struggling with *Romance* for hours
> and hours, and [Conrad] had been in complete despair, and every-
> thing that I had suggested had called forth his bitterest jibes, and
> he was sick, and over ears in debt, and penniless. . . . And Mrs.
> Conrad came in and said that the mare had trotted from Postling
> Vents to Sandling in five minutes—say, twelve miles an hour! At
> once, there in the room was Conrad-Jack-ashore! The world was
> splendid; hope nodded from every rosebud that looked over the
> windowsill of the low room. We were going to get a car and go to
> Canterbury; the mare should have a brand new breeching strap.[9]

Conrad needed the moral support he found in Ford, perhaps in that very "characteristically casual and omniscient [and, as Conrad would have thought, very British] manner" that was otherwise so harmful to Ford's

---

*Conrad, said H. G. Wells, "spoke English strangely . . . with certain oddities. . . . He had for example acquired an incurable tendency to pronounce the last *e* in these and those. He would say, 'Wat shall we do with *thesa* things?' . . . When he turned to less familiar topics [than seafaring] he was often at a loss for phrases." "He spoke with a very strong foreign accent and in sentences not too well constructed," E. V. Lucas said. "To the end his accent remained exotic";" . . . on one occasion he . . . describe[d] a certain publisher as a man of a norrible per-son-al-i-ty.' "

personal relations. Throughout the decade of their intimacy, there was, beneath Conrad's fierce pride, a real dependence on Ford. It was never a dependence for a knowledge of his craft or for imaginative insight; despite the false impression Ford sometimes created, neither of them questioned that Conrad was the more gifted writer. It was psychological support— assurance that these gifts were really his—that Conrad needed, and for it he expressed extravagant gratitude. The characteristic note of his attitude throughout his intimacy with Ford is that of a letter of November, 1899:

> Whether I am worth anything to you or not, it is for you to determine. The proposal [that they work together] certainly came from me under a false impression of my power for work. I am much weaker than I thought I was....
> ... Don't you good people [Ford and Elsie] think hardly of me. I've been—I am!—animated by the best intentions. I shall always be![10]

Ford provided moral support for Conrad in two ways. He kept Conrad's spirits up by constantly assuring him of what he quite sincerely believed, that Conrad was a great writer. He also took over, in a way that appeared at least to Conrad very effective, many of the practical operations of Conrad's life, which Conrad's own considerable ingenuity in negotiation always tended to reduce to a hopeless muddle.

> I was useful to Conrad as writer and as man [as Ford put it] in a great many subordinate ways during his early days of struggle and deep poverty.... I did, at such times as he was not himself equal to them, absolutely all of his literary dustings and sweepings, correcting his proofs, writing from his dictation, suggesting words when he was at a loss, or bringing to his memory incidents that he had forgotten. It was still more, perhaps that I was large, blond, phlegmatic on the surface.... Conrad passionately needed some moral support of the type that such an individual could afford him."[11]

Ford's description of the ways he served Conrad is, if anything, an understatement because he was, as he wrote it, thinking mostly of how he nursed Conrad in his moods of black despair. This he indeed did. He once described in some detail the way he could keep Conrad going.

> I would ... walk up and down [the terrace at the Pent] in front of Conrad who would groan, extended in a steamer chair. I would say: "Well now, what about the *Tremolino*" or "What about the diamond mine you owned in the Transvaal?" and, after exclaiming a dozen times: "Nonsense, no one will want to hear about that," he would

begin to talk about the Ukraine of his uncle's day and Palmerston's Emissary with a sledgefull of gold or about Venice when he was a boy or about his exile in Siberia or, of course, if I suggested that he should talk about the Ukraine or Venice or Siberia, he would insist on telling anecdotes about the *Tremolino* or his Transvaal mine. In any case, once he was started, he would go on for a long time and as I wrote shorthand very fast, I could take him down without much trouble.

"The fact is," as Ford said elsewhere, "I could make Conrad write at periods when his despair and fatigue were such that in no other way would it have been possible to him"; and here even Jessie Conrad, much as she hated Ford, bears him out: "*The Mirror of the Sea* owes a great deal to [Ford's] ready and patient assistance. . . . That book would never have come into being if Joseph Conrad had had no intelligent person with whom to talk over these intimate reminiscences."[12]

But Ford did a good deal more than this for Conrad. He acted as Conrad's agent in dealing with Pinker when Conrad was not in a mood to do so. He struggled to control what Jessie called Conrad's "inherent extravagance" (of which she had a good deal too), and believed, perhaps rightly, that neither Jessie nor Conrad had ever quite forgiven him for preventing them from buying "a pair of trotting ponies and a phaeton of sorts with scarlet wheels" while they were at the Pent. He worked to make Conrad's reputation, writing an anonymous piece for *T. P.'s Weekly* about how "all through 'Romance' one catches what, for want of a more precise word, one may call the glamour of Mr. Conrad" or dropping in on Rothenstein to persuade him to do a drawing of Conrad. No wonder that Ford became for Conrad, as Conrad said to Wells, "a sort of lifelong habit."[13]

Ford's reasons for entering into collaboration are even less easy to feel sure of than Conrad's. It must have counted for something with Ford that Conrad was the older and more widely experienced man, forty to his twenty-four when they met, with an exotic life behind him; it was he who pushed Conrad into writing *The Mirror of the Sea* in the face of Conrad's firm conviction that "no one will want to hear about that." At bottom, however, it was perhaps quite simply Ford's "unchanging affection and admiration for [Conrad's] almost miraculous gifts." Ford was a very generous man; all his life he would give his time and energy to helping gifted writers. No doubt, too, he enjoyed the feeling of superior worldliness that managing Conrad's affairs gave him ("[I] had a good deal of knowledge of the practical sides of English life that Conrad naturally ignored"). Most important of all, his association with Conrad gave him a settled purpose in life. "When [Ford] first came along," H. G. Wells said, " . . . [he] had cast himself for the rôle of a very gifted scion of the Pre-Raphaelite stem, given over to artistic purposes and a little undecided between music, poetry, criticism, The Novel, Thoreau-istic horticulture and the simple appreciation of life." Conrad decided him.[14]

At one time or another in his life Ford said some very foolish things about his relation with Conrad that tend to obscure its real nature; for example: " . . . during a considerable part of the period of our collaboration I was not only much the more prosperous individual but greatly the more popular author; indeed at one period I must have been one of the most boomed writers in England." This is not only annoyingly vain; it is largely false. Ford and Conrad were both wildly improvident and neither of them was ever, during their years of collaboration, prosperous. But Ford could not resist this note of superiority: "The writer, it should be remembered, though by ten or fifteen years the junior of Conrad, was by some years his senior at any rate as a published author, and was rather the more successful of the two as far as sales went." But in sober fact, almost until the end of their relation, when Ford did acquire a certain amount of influence with publishers and journalists, their situation remained what it was at the start. "When talking with Hueffer," as Conrad told Henley, "my first thought was that the man there who couldn't find a publisher had some good stuff to use and that if we worked it up together my name, probably, would get a publisher for it."[15]

Yet despite the foolish remarks Ford made about Conrad, there was always the hard core of his abiding admiration for Conrad and his largely unreciprocated affection. The very passage about his prosperity and fame quoted above begins, "My own books of that period are entirely negligible"; and sometimes he put his real feeling quite simply, as when he said, "That [my relation with Conrad] was fortunate for me I am sure, for if I know anything of how to write almost the whole of that knowledge was acquired then."[16]

So, for nearly a decade, Ford and Conrad worked in happy intimacy, with what Ford quite rightly called "absolute one-ness of purpose and with absolute absence of rivalry." They were both acutely aware of how isolated they were by their belief that the novel should be a serious work of art. "Among [successful novelists of the late nineties]," as Ford later said, "the conception of the novel as a work of Art was unthinkable. . . . It was difficult in the England of those days to strike out on that path alone. I owe a great deal to Conrad. But most of all I owe to him that strong faith—that . . . the writing of novels is the only pursuit worth while for a proper man." To their endless discussions of the novel as a work of art Ford brought his lifelong concern for the exact implications of every word and every cadence of their prose, and this aspect of the novel was what Conrad felt most anxious about. To these discussions Conrad brought his "infinitely greater hold over the architectonics of the novel, over the way a story should be built up so that its interest progresses and grows up to the last word," which was the aspect of novel writing Ford had shown himself woefully clumsy with in *Seraphina.* "Conrad," as Ford later put it, "[sought] most of all a new form for the novel and I a limpidity of expression that should make prose seem like the sound of some one talking in rather a low voice into the ear of a person that he liked."[17]

The discovery of their common concern for the novel as a work of art and of their interests in complementary aspects of it made their collaboration an exciting release from isolation for them both. "They were," as Elsie said, "so happy talking and talking in that room [at the Pent] and up and down that path in front." Jessie also remembered how

> the two would elect to start work as we, Mrs. Hueffer and I, were retiring for the night. For hours after I had gone to bed the voices would reach me through the floor. Sometimes the tones would appear to mingle in pleasant accord, their ideas flowing easily, amused laughs and chuckles. At others sounds of wordy strife and disagreement penetrated to my ears, and raised voices came distinctly into my room. Then F. M. H., who was a very tall man, would relieve his feelings by thumping the oaken beam that crossed the ceiling below and my small son would stir in his sleep and mutter sleepily: "Mama, dear, moo-cows down there."

Jessie certainly never suspected the extent to which this life of the mind must have been to Conrad a relief from her, for, necessary to Conrad as Jessie was, the illiberality of her mind must often have been oppressive. It could not always have been easy to play up to Jessie's constant attention-getting self-dramatization.[18]

As soon as the Conrads were settled at the Pent, Ford and Elsie went off on a bicycling trip in the south of France, but by November they were back in England. It was a happy time. "Xtina Margaret," as Ford called her, was an enormous source of pleasure to them. She learned to open the gate in order to meet Ford when he returned from his golf at Hythe, and became a comically small tyrant about the house. The rooster had to go into the pot because he flew at her and she was determined that Cromwell, the dog, needed shaving as much as Ford and appeared one day with Ford's razor in hand to see that it was done. Ford and Conrad went over to Sandgate to pay a call on Wells, whose favorable reviews of Conrad's books made him a patron, to announce their collaboration.

> As we stood on the doorstep of Mr. Wells's villa . . . behold, the electric bell-push, all of itself went in and the bell sounded. . . . Conrad exclaimed: "Tiens! . . . The Invisible Man!" and burst into incredible and incredulous laughter. In the midst of it the door opened before grave faces. . . .
>
> For years after, a translation of Mr. Wells's book having appeared in Italian, you could never mention that author's name without Conrad's saying: "Tiens! . . . L'Uomo Invisib[i]le!"

Wells did not, however, approve of the collaboration. If Henley had thought that Conrad might "eat up" Ford, Wells was worried that Ford would "ruin Conrad's 'delicate Oriental style.'" He bicycled all the way over to Aldington later that spring of 1899 to lay this view of the matter before Ford. Henry James was equally discouraging. "To me this is like a bad dream which one relates at breakfast!" he said to Elsie. "Their traditions and their gifts are so dissimilar. Collaboration between them is to me inconceivable." Ford put up a bold front about these criticisms, but they hurt and depressed him.[19]

The Fords' lease on Gracie's Cottage at Limpsfield came to an end at quarter day (March 25), and by March 30 they were settled in a house they had found at Aldington, a farm laborer's cottage called Stocks Hill in the middle of a field. It was a primitive place, but its location under Aldington Knoll meant much to Ford.

> For that ol' Knoll is watched so well
> By drownded men let outen Hell,
> They watches well and keeps it whole
> For a sailor's mark—the goodly Knoll.

Among their first visitors were the Conrads. Pacing up and down and discussing continued unabated, but Ford and Conrad did not make much progress with *Romance*. "We each at intervals carried on work of our own," as Ford put it, "then we would drop it, and have another month's try at *Romance*. Then drop that again. . . ." Conrad was hard at work on *Lord Jim*, and Ford had—thanks to Edward Garnett—now found a publisher to commission "my colossal book on the Cinque Ports" and had carried a plan for a novel about Oliver Cromwell far enough to sell the idea to a publisher. All that ever came of that plan was the imaginary *Life of Cromwell* written by Churchill and Granger in Ford's later novel, *The Inheritors*, but, like Granger, Ford had momentarily "set about one of those glorious novels that one plans—a splendid thing with Old Noll as the hero or the heavy father."[20]

During the summer Ford gave up the Cromwell story and began the novel that would become *The Inheritors*. Elsie's diary shows that he was well into it by October, and on October 6 he drove "over to the Pent with the manuscript of the opening chapters of the novel rather shyly in his pocket." "Conrad [was] upset with novel," Elsie noted, but he was nevertheless ready to enter into the project, and the Fords came to the Pent for a fortnight's visit and "long heated discussion[s], lasting well into many nights" that were a great trial to Jessie. "The old farmhouse was not," she felt, "adapted for the shelter of two families, or capable of providing seclusion for the two authors engaged upon even such a book as 'The Inheritors.' " "No doubt our guests," she added, clearly not believing it, "suffered quite as much as I did." There was no question in the mind of either writer that the book was Ford's work; Conrad put his name to it in order to sell it. "If," he said, "I had influence enough with the publishers I would make them publish the book in your name alone—because the *work* is all yours—I've shared only a little of your worry." Ford once asserted that Conrad had written the last twenty pages of *The Inheritors*, but Conrad was ill for nearly a month during the final stretch of work, and it seems more likely his contribution was a scattering of revisions of the kind Ford illustrates in his discussion of *The Inheritors* in *Joseph Conrad*. On November 23, when Ford was back home plugging away, Conrad sent him a letter from McClure urging Conrad to send him "the 'Extravagant' novel when it is finished" and suggesting he might want to serialize it in the United States. "Let this cheer you up in your arduous labour" Conrad scribbled on the bottom of this letter when he sent it to Ford. But it was March 17 before Ford, once more at the Pent, was able to tell Walter Jerrold that the manuscript had gone off to Heinemann the day before.[21]

Chapter 6

ૐ

The Inheritors: An Extravagant Story was intended to be "a political work, rather allegorically backing Mr. Balfour in the then Government; the villain was to be Joseph Chamberlain who had made the [Boer] war. The sub-villain was to be Leopold II, King of the Belgians, the foul—and incidentally lecherous—beast who had created the Congo Free State in order to grease the wheels of his harems with the blood of murdered negroes.... " Ford had begun the book with the idea of writing "an allegorico-realist romance" showing "the superseding of previous generations and codes by the merciless young who are always alien and without remorse.... But... Conrad ... was avid of political subjects to treat.... "[1]

Ford was emotionally committed to the world of his young manhood with its ruling-class tradition of responsibility for the lower orders and its concern for the arts. Romantic idealist that he was, he early began to feel that this world had gone to the dogs since his youth; the scandals of Leopold II's Congo, with their commercialism, their corruption, their lack of chivalry, convinced him that this tradition had not survived. "And then," he said, "came the Boer War, which appears to me like a chasm separating the new world from the old. Since that period the whole tone of England appears to me to have entirely changed. Principles have died out of politics, even as the spirit of artistry has died out among the practitioners of the arts." It was not just Conrad who cared about the political aspects of The Inheritors.[2]

The Inheritors' political satire is often effective, though the decision to call the book's equivalent of the Congo "Greenland" is a little unfortunate, especially as Ford failed to make up his mind whether Greenland was inhabited by Eskimos or blacks. Even now it is possible for readers with a modest knowledge of the period to be entertained by the book's contemporary portraits—Balfour (Churchill), Chamberlain (Gurnard), Leopold II (the Duc de Mersch), Northcliffe (Fox). Some of them, however, are more nearly private jokes, like Callan, who, as Conrad playfully wrote Garnett, "Pawling says, must be Crockett"—that is, R. S. Crockett, the Scottish kailyard novelist (but Callan seems also to have a touch or two of Henry James about him). There is also a satiric sketch of Fisher Unwin as Polehampton, a natural victim for two authors he had been the first man to publish; and there are flattering portraits of Edward Garnett, as the critic Lee, and of Ford Madox Brown, as the great, unrecognized painter, Jenkins. *The Inheritors* shows how much Ford had already learned from Conrad about how to give his fiction vivid particularity, an effect no doubt increased by Conrad's revisions. One can almost hear Conrad's voice in certain passages.

> He proposed that we should stroll as far as the paper kiosque that he patronised habitually—it was kept by a fellow-Israelite—a snuffy little old woman.
> I understood that in the joy of his heart he was for expanding, for wasting a few minutes on a stroll.
> "Haven't stretched my legs for months," he explained.[3]

The allegory of this "allegorico-realist romance" is ingenious, and because Ford himself was torn between a conservative love of the past and sympathy with "the merciless young," it deals with a psychological conflict that was significant to him. He must have seen the objections of the reviewer that "the book never lives" and that "its realization seems to leave a good deal to be desired" as one more illustration of the popular audience's incapacity for serious literature. Twenty-five years later, though ostensibly belittling it, he was still half defending the book as "a monument as it were of silverpoint, delicacies and allusiveness."[*4]

The book's failure was all the more painful because it looked at first as if it were going to be a great success. Both Pawling (of Heinemann) and Stephen Gwynn (of McClure) were enthusiastic and favored not only publication but serialization. Gwynn's report called it "a work no publisher anxious to produce literature should think of refusing"; Pawling asserted that the last three chapters (in which the hero, inexplicably confident that it will win him the girl, decides to print the article that destroys his patron and friend) were "completely convincing." This could hardly have prepared Ford for reviews that said the book left the "bewildered student" feeling

that it is very clever book, and that he is a very stupid person for not

*For a discussion of *The Inheritors*, see pp. 464–66.

seeing what it is all about.... [Most] of the novel seems a kind of moral nightmare.... Obviously the book is a satire on the sham philanthropy.... Journalism of the venal kind and quack novelists are also fair game. But the lady of four dimensions is quite superfluous and remarkably destitute of interest. The story on the title-page calls itself "extravagant." It is not extravagant enough, or not in the right way.[5]

Conrad had taken a more realistic view of the book. He wrote Meldrum that he was a little surprised by the readers' reports. "There is something in [the book] no doubt. *What*, exactly, I can't say myself." To Edward Garnett, who enjoyed a more sardonic tone, he wrote:

What a lark! I set myself to look upon the thing as a sort of skit upon the sort of political (?!) novel, fools of the Morley Roberts sort do write. This in my heart of hearts. And poor *H* was dead in earnest! O Lord. How he worked! There is not a chapter I haven't made him write twice—most of them three times over.... And in the course of that agony I have been ready to weep more than once. Yet not for him. Not for him.

When Ford read this letter more than twenty-five years later he was deeply hurt, as he shows in the letter he wrote Edward Garnett.[6]

He begins with his usual assertion of indifference.

... if I resent, as I do with a good deal of sadness, your printing this letter it is entirely for the sake of Conrad and not in the least for my own sake. I am absolutely indifferent to anything that has been said about my relations with Conrad—except in so far as they do anything to injure his memory—and that Conrad himself was ashamed of the letter you can see from the fact that he asked you to burn it.

He then launches into an account of how he had written *Joseph Conrad* because Conrad had asked him "to amplify what I had written in 'Thus to Re-Visit...' "; of how Conrad had "*begged* [him] to write the joint preface to the Nature of a Crime ... although I was averse from doing so"; of how he feels no impulse whatsoever to question Garnett's sale of Conrad's letter, though "for myself I have never sold and never will sell anything of Conrad's, though I have had a great many things stolen." All of this has a certain plausibility but it is essentially false, however little Ford could endure knowing it was.

He concludes with a statement of the feeling for Conrad that made Conrad's brutality hurt him so deeply even after all this time.

Anyhow, I beg you not to take in bad part anything that I have writ[t]en. It is written with a great deal of emotion. My affection for Conrad was so great and remains so unchanged that I have never been able really to believe in his death, and at this moment it is as if he he were sitting behind me waiting to read what I have tapped out. You see, we did live together, day in day out, for many years— ten, I daresay and even towards the end he could not really get on without me any more than I could or can get ob [sic] without him, and I do not shrink from saying that at this moment I cannot see for tears.

Those tears are no mere rhetorical flourish. David Garnett has recalled an occasion when he walked with Ford from the Cearne to Westerham to catch the train.

He had been cheerful at tea, but in Squerries Park a mood of melan-choly stole over him, and he sang me one melancholy song after another, some French, some German, ending with the Westmorland folksong *Poor Old Horse.* Ford's voice was not bad, his ear was good, and the expression he put into the words of the horse's cruel master was pathetic in the extreme.... [Then]in the most unhappy voice Ford broke in to say something like this: "I am that poor old horse, David.... The world is cruel to the old, David. It is very cruel to me ... once I was a brilliant young poet, a famous writer ... now I am no more use to anyone and they kick me, now they have got me down.... Poor old horse.... ". I was in tears and, seeing this, Ford wept also; then brushed his tears aside for a moment to look at his watch and make sure that he was not late for his train.

The rapidity with which Ford moves from cheerfulness to melancholy and back to the practical problem of catching his train is typical.[7]

Even three years after he had first seen Conrad's letter, Ford could not keep the hurt out of his voice. "In [this] letter Conrad alludes to our strug-gles over *The Inheritors*... with a burst of mordant humour at my expense. ... That was all right between ourselves.... However, in this particular letter, he must have thought that he had gone a little too far, for he asked Mr. Garnett ... to burn it. Mr. Garnett preferred to publish it." Ultimately he was able to exorcise this terrible ghost of a Conrad who had scorned him just at the time he felt closest to him by thinking that "the faculty that made [Conrad] be able to prostrate himself in unbelievable politenesses before Messrs. Gosse, Garnett, and Galsworthy, not to mention such relatively humble persons as his child's nurse and myself, let him, at other times, perceive and express the bitterest, the almost most sadistic, contempt for those three gentlemen—and, of course, myself.... "[8]

As if to illustrate how completely he could change his feelings to suit the occasion, Conrad wrote Ford only four days after his letter to Garnett in an entirely different tone to invite him to luncheon with his beloved "aunt" (she was not actually related to Conrad), Marguerite Poradowska:

> My aunt is coming on Monday to stay a week, I would be awfully glad if your wife and yourself could come on Wednesday to lunch. Jessie thinks that if you started early to arrive here about 10 so as to give your wife some time to rest on a couch before lunch . . . there would be no imprudence in the proceeding. I am of course anxious very anxious to introduce my "collaborateur" to the good woman who represents to me so much of my family—she had known so many of them on whom no eye of man'll rest again. And the pleasure would be more than doubled if Auntie Elsie could come too.[9]

Conrad's concern for Elsie was due to her being a scant month and a half away from the birth of a second child, who was born at the hospital in Hythe at 9:50 P.M. on April 16, 1900, and named Katharine Mary Madox Hueffer. "Mrs. Hueffer has another daughter," Jessie wrote Marguerite Poradowska. " . . . I am afraid they are both awfully disappointed it is not a son."[10]

Meanwhile Ford had finished *The Cinque Ports*, though it was not published until fall. *The Cinque Ports* is a delightful book for anyone interested in the south coast of England. Ford knew well the Five Ports—Hastings, Romney, Hythe, Dover, and Sandwich—and the Antient Towns such as Winchelsea and Rye. Much of his boyhood had been spent on the south coast and since his marriage he had lived there, talking away long hours with the local people. He knew the back country intimately and had walked its remote roads and footpaths and worked his way to its lost villages such as the little settlement— "Lambarde calls it Nesh—[that] is perhaps as difficult of attainment as any in the kingdom." Most of all he loved Romney Marsh, which he delighted to explore. "On a dark night—and the nights here are sometimes incredibly dark —" he says with relish, "the finding of one's way is a perilous matter."

To this personal knowledge of the country he added all he could learn. He was "determined that I would print assertively no single statement for which I had not found chapter and verse . . . in the work of a chronicler as nearly as possible contemporaneous with the event asserted," a concern for accuracy the later, impressionistic Ford would have greatly scorned. Of the mayoring ceremony at Folkestone, for instance, he tells us that it

> did not always proceed without a hitch. Thus in 1650, at the very outset of the proceedings, one of the newly elected jurats became

contumacious. The good man's name was Medgett.... He flatly
refused to be made a jurat, and exhibited the utmost disrespect for
the mayor and his henchmen. "Before I come to be jurate in this
towne you shall first put my head in the stockes," he said.... The
mayor threatened him with imprisonment. "Over shoes, over boots,"
he answered.... It is pleasant to think of the consternation in the
churchyard. The wise mayor and the rather hot-headed jurats were
nonplussed. Their grey beards wagged together. In the end better
counsels prevailed, and Medgett consented to serve: his fine was
remitted.... But... in Rendavowe Street—we spell it "Rendez-
vous" to-day—a prototype of Mr. Bumble became suddenly contumacious—abusive indeed.... The mayor sorrowfully told him that
his language was incompatible with his high office and asked him to
resign. He replied by snapping his fingers in his worship's face, and,
becoming physically violent, was removed.

In this way Ford traces the history of each of the Ports and Antient Towns
from its origins in Roman and Saxon times, and describes its antiquities and
its present character—that is, as of 1900. *The Cinque Ports* is a modest, infor-
mative, and entertaining book, a remarkable achievement for a young man
of twenty-six.[11]

With these matters attended to and Conrad uncharacteristically confident that *Lord Jim* would be finished any minute, both authors began to
think it time they returned to *Seraphina*. They decided to get away from all
distractions by going to Bruges, where they fancied they would lead a restful, uncomplicated life: "... the writer would work in the mornings on
Romance whilst Conrad wrote—probably *Typhoon*—at the same time. We
would play dominoes in agreeable cafés during the afternoons and after
dinner collaborate gaily." This idea was almost certainly Ford's. He was
finding the violent jingoism of the Boer War intolerable and he wanted to
be anywhere but in England, though he did not find the mindless anti-British
feelings of the Belgians any more attractive: "... abroad, where I passed for
an Englishman, I witnessed and suffered from more ferocity... than I did
in England, where I passed for a pro-Boer." But it was nearly two years since
he had had a change, and he felt he had earned one. "My colossal book on
the Cinque Ports is hung up waiting for the war," he wrote Jerrold, "—the
Conrad-Hueffer novel went off to the printers on Friday [March 16]; that too
will appear in the autumn if serial arrangements permit. I've got a volume
of poems [*Poems for Pictures*], too, coming out next month, Macqueen being
the happy publisher, the others being Blackwood & Heinemann."[12]

The Hueffers got to Bruges in early July; the Conrads were to follow as soon as *Lord Jim* was finished. *Lord Jim*, however, refused to get itself finished. "Telegrams went backwards and forwards. . . . Book just being finished. . . . Pinker would come down with large sum . . . "; and time passed. "The disconsolate and much enduring Hueffers," as Conrad called them, were cooped up in the English Pension, in the rue Anglais, which "seemed to be distinguished chiefly by brown linoleum, bentwood chairs in long perspectives, long teeth in withered faces, dimness and placards forbidding you to take water between certain hours from certain taps." Finally, by writing practically the whole night of July 13–14, Conrad finished *Lord Jim* and they were able to set off for Bruges.[13]

Conrad landed at Ostend in an overworked and exasperated state, carrying Borys, who was feeling ill. As Ford put it long after, "Bearers staggering after that Congo caravan. . . . The scared face of Amy Foster, maid, who had never been abroad. . . . A swarm of frightened ticket-collectors running alongside. Conrad infuriated. . . . " Finally they got into the train for Bruges with Conrad "exhausted but volcanic" so that when the ticket collector arrived Conrad blew him out of the doorway. "Whether Conrad had any tickets," Ford says, "the writer never knew. He certainly never showed them." Conrad's "comminative gloom" was not relieved by the sight of the English Pension. Then, however, he went out for a walk and came back transformed. "He had met an admirable Abbé in the Place du Beffroi. . . . He had been directed to [Knocke-sur-Mer]. Admirable hotel. . . . Wonderful domino players. . . . Charming Dutch, French, Spanish, German, fellow guests. . . . Belgians not so bad. . . . Best class. . . . " The Grand Hôtel de la Plage at Knocke turned out to be very pleasant, an airy seashore resort with *écarté* tournaments and sand tennis and sand yachts in which one sailed up the beach to Sluis. Nevertheless the great life of work and dominoes was not to be; Borys had dysentry. "It was," as Jessie said, "a nightmarish time, that terrible August we spent in Knocke."[14]

This kind of crisis brought out the very best in Ford. Though he never afterwards mentioned his devotion during Borys' illness, it drew from Jessie the only kind words she ever spoke of him: "I have nothing but praise for F.M.H. He earned my gratitude and appreciation by the manner he showed his practical sympathy. He was always at hand to shift my small invalid, fetch the doctor or help with the nursing." But "poor H. did not get much collaboration out of me this time," Conrad remarked. As Ford said:

> The book [*Typhoon*] would not go in the mornings in the top room [where Conrad tried to work beneath "a portrait of Leopold, King of the Belgians . . . as he simpered down over his preposterous

beard" taking his revenge, as it were, for *The Inheritors*]: *Romance* in the mornings would not go, either, on the corner of the café table [where Ford tried to work]: doctors had to be fetched at midnights in the teeth of westerly gales. . . . Owing to the illness of the child it was impossible for Conrad to invent the escape of John Kemp from the Casa Riego in Rio Medio. The writer was set to invent. . . .

Conrad had an attack of gout, as he so frequently did in a crisis.[15]

Eventually Borys grew better and Conrad's gout subsided and he could concentrate enough to look over what Ford had written about John Kemp's escape from Rio Medio and "the villainous O'Brien's" cry of "Foiled! And by a stripling!" Not that Ford had really written anything quite so bad as that, "but that was how it felt as the writer sat by with Conrad reading the manuscript." Ford knew nothing about ships and sailing and never was able to take nautical matters seriously, so that when the villain of *The Feather* has to sail a ship, he observes that "He then went through various nautical exercises—such as boxing the compass, and shivering his timbers, and dangling his lee-deadlights, and other things which it takes a sailor, or a nautical novel-writer, to understand." In the end Conrad, the "nautical novel writer," had to do the whole episode over. So, about the middle of August, both families returned home with *Romance* no further along than when they had left.[16]

What they had at this time, in at least some form, was Parts I, II, and III and most of the conclusion. On their return to England, Ford came over to the Pent, where he remained until the middle of September, and in an excess of anxiety over the time lost at Knocke, they worked hard over *Romance*. "I am dropping still [from gout]," Conrad wrote Galsworthy on September 19. "Working at Seraphina. Bosh! Horrors!" And to Meldrum he said, "I ought to have written to you before but on my return I was distracted with Hueffer. When he went away I was half dead and crawled into bed for two days." When Hueffer went away, Conrad also stopped working on *Romance* and went back to his own stories.[17]

Chapter 7

ॐ

After their return from Belgium, the Hueffers began to see a good deal of the H. G. Wellses. There is a glimpse of Ford playing a part in one of Jane Wells's charades at Spade House "as the sole croupier at a green table in a marvellous Monte Carlo scene [in which] Jane was a gambling duchess of entirely reckless habits." One of Wells's visits ended in high comedy that he made the most of in his letter of thanks.

> I should further then have apologized to Mrs Hueffer for whirling past her upon my bicycle with an almost inconceivable lack of elegance & civility. It was my design in the event of meeting her to stop & express my respect for her & my gratitude for your hospitality in a few graceful & becoming sentences. But when at last Mrs Hueffer did appear in sight my mind was suddenly and disastrously disordered by the presence of a third person whom I did not until subsequent reflection understand must be your Swiss governess and a member of your family but whom [sic] at the time seen through the refractory mist of my shyness I imagined was some social personage of the class that fills my soul with terror and abasement. . . . [1]

The Hueffers were planning to move. Dr. Martindale had been appalled by the primitive conditions of Stocks Hill, and he had been urging them to move, preferably to Winchelsea, where they would be near the family. The Mayor had now found a house called "The Bungalow" not far from his own creeper-covered brick house, Glebe Cottage. The Bungalow was a frame cottage that—according to Ford—had been built in 1782 for his retirement by General Prescott, the first Governor-General of Canada. "The General," Ford thought, "had been homesick for Canada" and had built his house "in exact imitation of a Canadian [clapboard] frame-house." It was—and is—a charming place. There were hops growing over the shallow veranda that ran across the front, where Ford and Conrad would sit talking far into the warm summer nights. Across the road stood the ruins of the beautiful old parish church of St. Thomas of Canterbury. " . . . there is a certain pillar (visible from the southern outside), with a pair of arches soaring upwards from it, that looks like a radiant fountain, caught and rendered for all time. Ruined arches and buttresses, without, stand out against the evening sky; in the centre the dark mass of the church itself; and then the radiant pillar itself, shining through the tracery of the illuminated windows." The Mayor bought the Bungalow and they moved into it on April 10, 1901.[2]

The clan of Martindales and Hueffers standing before Glebe Cottage and the Bungalow in the old photographs made an impressive showing. Dr. and Mrs. Martindale were dignified and visibly substantial people, and the young people from the Bungalow, with their two blond little girls, were a handsome family. Elsie was still, at twenty-five, the slim-waisted, high-breasted girl the five-year-old David Garnett had been so eager to marry. She had discarded the "richly coloured garments of the William Morris style" that she had worn at Limpsfield, and now wore the long-sleeved blouse and dark skirt of the period or, for evenings, white chiffon and flowing sleeves (the little girls called that her "angel dress").

Ford was a tall, slender young man, conservatively but elegantly dressed, with his blond hair parted in the middle and combed flat to either side of his head. He was not conventionally handsome, but his air of the young man of talent was impressive. "He was," as Henry James said of Merton Densher, whom he is supposed to have modeled on Ford, "a longish, leanish, fairish young Englishman, not unamenable, on certain sides, to classification—as for instance by being a gentleman, by being rather specifically one of the educated, one of the generally sound and generally pleasant . . . " " . . . yet," James added, "though to that degree neither extraordinary nor abnormal, he would have failed to play straight into an observer's hands" —anyhow, the hands of an observer as shrewd as James, for there were problems among these people not visible on the surface of their lives; one of them, Elsie's sister, Mary, was still unmarried and living with her parents at Glebe Cottage.[3]

Mary Martindale was a tall girl with red-gold hair. After Ford and Elsie's marriage, she had become engaged to a young Frenchman, but she soon broke with him. Her feelings about Ford seemed to have been intensified by jealousy of the position marriage to him had given her younger sister; like so many women of her time who were theoretically believers in what they called, with unintentional irony, Free Love—Violet Hunt was another such woman—Mary Martindale longed for that position, or was at least jealous of Elsie's possession of it. Perhaps this feeling was, however inconsistent, unavoidable at that time when the social and economic security of women was almost completely dependent on marriage. Mary's feelings were certainly intensified by the move to Winchelsea that placed Ford so close to her.

Mary had a vivacity that was in marked contrast to Elsie's seriousness. How well Ford understood that this vivacity was the comparatively controlled expression of an hysterical nature it is not easy to say, but it appealed to him strongly at this moment, when marriage was beginning to be more a routine than a romance and the middle-class respectability of Winchelsea was closing in about him. Sometime after the Hueffers' arrival in Winchelsea, he and Mary became lovers.

It was inevitably an affair of snatched moments and clandestine encounters, of the cryptic telegram, the hansom cab, and the hotel. In their different ways, they must both have found these conditions romantically exciting— Ford as the uninhibited artist who had scornfully cast aside the small-minded prudence of the middle class in order to "live" and to gather experience; Mary as a budding Ann Veronica, the girl who would soon plunge into the bohemian life of intellectual London. Mary Martindale was certainly not the wisest choice a man ever made for a love affair which, when it was exposed, was sure to have unusually awkward consequences; but even the most prudent man is not likely to be prudent in matters of this sort, and Mary Martindale appealed to the romantic adventurer in Ford—the Bulldog Drummond of the new life of frankness and sensitivity in sexual affairs—as much as women like Stella Bowen would later appeal to the Ford who, exhausted by the formidable logistic problems of the free life, longed for rest and peace.

Elsie eventually found out about this affair, through one of those accidents that sounds as if it had been invented by Pinero, the mistaken delivery to her of a revealing telegram from Ford to Mary. But they managed to keep their relation secret for some time and continued to see each other—no doubt almost as a matter of principle—even after Elsie found out about them. It was not until Ford began to court Violet Hunt that this affair with Mary drifted out of existence, though it was of course never possible for them to be alone for any length of time; toward the end, after Ford's trip to America in 1906, when he became very busy with his London literary life, they could have seen relatively little of one another.

When Ford told Elsie at the time of their marriage that she was not to expect him to be faithful to her, he was probably only making the advanced young thinker's confident assertion of an abstract principle. But this warning turned out to be a disconcertingly accurate prophecy of his conduct, most strikingly—though not exclusively—with Mary Martindale. By the time he came to write *An English Girl* (1907) he had convinced himself that this was an obvious truth about all marriages; even the idealistic and naïve young American hero of *An English Girl* knows it. " . . . my mother," he says casually, "had too much knowledge of life to expect my father to be faithful to her."[4]

Ford was also extending his activities in a number of other directions at this time. He made the acquaintance of upper-middle-class people like Arthur Marwood, that "powerfully built, leisurely man" with his acute intelligence, "the heavy Yorkshire squire with his dark hair startlingly silver in places, his keen blue eyes, his florid complexion, his immense, expressive hands and his great shapelessness"; he discovered a value in people of this sort he had never before imagined they possessed, and it greatly strengthened his romantic attachment to the idea of the English gentleman. He became especially fond of Dr. Martindale, watching with fascination the minute reenactment of *The Enemy of the People* that occurred when the Mayor sought to modernize the drains in Winchelsea. These experiences— transformed beyond recognition by large infusions of Ford's daydreams about himself—he was to make into his novel *The Benefactor* a few years later.[5]

He also set about renewing his acquaintance with Henry James, paying a call on him during which James made a joke about *The Cinque Ports* that gave Ford the opportunity of sending him a copy.

I am [James wrote him] overwhelmed by your letter, touched by your sympathy, & almost appalled by your munificence:—in the light, that is, of my fear that my crude pleasantries, my reckless and accidental levity on the subject of your brave Book may have seemed (while you evidently sought, or awaited, but a pretext for kindness) to put a kind of pressure on you in respect to my deprived state. I thank you none the less cordially, but I feel embarrassed & confused; as if I were really inhuman to consent to receive from you an offering of such value. . . . For the rest I respond very gratefully to the charming things you tell me in relation to your friendly acquaintance with things of mine. . . . I shall read the Ports—I can't possibly not; & I shan't promise not to write you again. But I shall see you again before I do so. . . .

For the next few years there was a certain amount of calling back and forth between Winchelsea and Rye, but James and Ford were never so intimate as Ford liked to suggest ("In the writer's almost daily colloquies with Mr. James, which extended over a number of years . . . "). Ford knew very well "that Mr. James had [not] the least idea what I was, and I do not think that, till the end of his days, he regarded me as a serious writer." But Ford immensely admired James and did his best to cultivate the acquaintance. No doubt, in his eagerness, he sometimes pressed himself on James more than James found convenient; such at least was the impression David Garnett got when Ford proudly took David and his parents to call at Lamb House. But James was not unreceptive. He clearly enjoyed Ford's company and often during the next few years sought him out. Ford's motive for pursuing James was simple admiration, as is evident from a letter he wrote Elsie from Lamb House some years later.

> Dearest E:
> From the superscription you'll observe where I am. The Great Man came over to tea and as I lost in consequence the Winchelsea post I came on over here to write as I'd promised to you. . . . James brought with him a Mr. Owen Wister—a mild U.S.A. author. . . . It's curious to sit at this [James's] desk . . . near the window in the little room on the left of the hall door. . . . James himself has gone to see someone to the station. So I am the sole lord of the demesne.

It sounds a little like James's own Hyacinth Robinson writing Millicent from the princess' country house for the pleasure of seeing "Medley Hall" stamped at the top of the paper.[6]

During most of this time Conrad was busy with work of his own. When Ford had left the Pent in September, 1900, Conrad had completed *Typhoon* (January, 1901); he then wrote "Falk" and "Amy Foster." These two stories occupied him until early June, but they did not stave off a financial crisis and he resorted to his favorite device, borrowing. This time Ford was the willing victim. The two of them tried, like naughty boys, to hide what they were up to from Robert Garnett, who managed Ford's affairs. Their first idea was to persuade Robert that Conrad was turning over to Ford, as security, a life insurance policy with a surrender value of about £ 400. To their pained surprise, however, Robert agreed to produce the money only on actual receipt of the policy. "Ford Hueffer writes me to-day," he wrote Conrad, "about an advance which he contemplates making you—£ 80 cash and £ 20 which apparently is due for rent. . . . If you will send me the [life insurance] Policy . . . I will arrange to supply the £80 by sale of an investment of Ford's."[7]

Thus temporarily foiled, the conspirators next tried on Robert a cock-and-bull story about how Conrad had to leave the insurance policy at his bank as security against "any small drawing in excess of [his] balance there," an argument Robert quickly demolished by pointing out that a policy worth £400 was hardly necessary to secure a small overdraft. "Whatever [Ford] does lend," he concluded severely, "should be *secured.*" Ford had meanwhile been trying to circumvent Robert by getting the money from the sale of some first editions and autographs of Browning and Morris—presumably heirlooms. When this maneuver failed to produce enough money, they gave up and Ford confessed to Robert that he intended to lend Conrad the money on no better security than Conrad's I.O.U.[8]

Robert reluctantly agreed to this plan, only to have Conrad turn about and produce the insurance policy, on the understanding that Ford would let him have the whole £100 in cash. To Ford he then observed complacently, "Briefly, for the policy, I ask you to advance me £100 in actual cash. You are safe and I am pleased." When the check arrived, Conrad wrote to thank Ford:

> Dearest Ford,
>   I have today received the cheque from Robert—and many thanks to you for staving off the impending annihilation. . . .
>   Yes. D[aily] T[elegraph's] review of *The Inheritors,* published Friday, July 14, 1901] all right. And so in a measure D[aily] N[ews] and I feel more like a thief of your cleverness.
>   Upon the whole (apart from cash) this thing must do us good —at any rate as far as our next book is concerned. . . . [9]

Typhoon, which had its serial publication in *The Pall Mall Magazine* from January to March of 1902, was the first work of Conrad's to be handled by J. B. Pinker, who was to play such a significant part in the life of both Ford and Conrad. Literary agents were a novelty at this time; authors got what help they could from lawyers. But in the seventies, A. P. Watt began representing writers; he was followed shortly by Curtis Brown, and the literary agent came into existence. Watt, according to Ford, invented the practice of syndicating articles to widely separated newspapers, but he had the defect of an awe-inspiring manner—"something between [that of] a bishop and a butler"—which did not help him with editors. Pinker was a Scotsman, a small, lively man with "a grim gleam in [his] hard eyes, behind his benevolent spectacles" and "a singular accent." His authors liked to call him "Jy B," and D. H. Lawrence, enraged by the social humiliation of having Pinker dole out to him only what his books earned ("a pittance," he called it,

" . . . it is too insulting"), called Pinker "that little parvenu snob of a procu-
reur of books."[10]

There is no doubt that Pinker was the greatest agent of his time, "the
Pinker of Literary Agents," as Conrad once called him. He was a skillful
judge of the market and had wide connections among publishers in both
England and the United States and he dealt with them in an understanding
but firm way.

> He said candidly to one publisher, over a contract made directly with
> the author: 'But this is swindling!' 'Oh!' protested the publisher,
> 'that's a very strong word!' Pinker fixed those immovable eyes upon
> his victim. 'What other do you suggest?' 'Well', said the publisher, 'I
> admit it was sharp practice.' And so the contract was destroyed.[11]

He was a shrewd and patient judge of writers. All the great agents have been
men who gambled on their ability to judge the characters of writers. Pinker
did a great deal for his authors, but one would hardly guess it from the
writers themselves. The letters of Ford and Conrad are a gold mine of
eloquent complaints against Pinker. They also devoted considerable energy
to inventing witticisms at his expense: "Every time Pinker gets a new author
he gets a new pair of horses," they told each other. This was shrewd if
unjust: Pinker liked driving pairs in tandem and was a great fox hunter.

In other moods, however, Conrad at least knew how much he owed to
Pinker. "He has stepped gallantly into the breach left open by the collapse
of my bank," he said of Pinker in 1904, when his bankers, Watson & Co.,
failed. "He has treated not only my moods but even my fancies with the
greatest consideration." This was no more than justice. Pinker invested
heavily in Conrad: in 1908–09 he paid Conrad an allowance against future
work that Conrad was always busy figuring ways to cheat him over, even
though by this time Conrad owed Pinker something like £ 1,600.

Not nearly enough is known about Pinker's life. His first literary connection—if it can be called that—was a job on the *Levant Herald* in Constan-
tinople. At the beginning of the nineties, he became assistant editor of a
London magazine called *Black & White* that Violet Hunt wrote for and that
was edited by Oswald Crawfurd, of whom we shall hear more later; Pinker
also worked as a publisher's reader. From *Black & White* he went for a brief
spell to the newly organized *Pearson's Magazine* and then, in January, 1896,
he set up as an agent. One of his first clients was an old friend, H. G. Wells;
he quickly acquired others, the most important of whom was Henry James,
who left A. P. Watt to come to him. His most profitable client, Arnold
Bennett, followed quickly. It is some indication of Pinker's success that as

early as 1898 a writer of Stephen Crane's reputation should have sought him out in London and—if one can believe Ford—found what Pinker was able to do for him almost miraculous.[12]

Well aware of Conrad's extravagance and of the machiavellian ingenuity with which he could mismanage his affairs when he negotiated with publishers, Edward Garnett had, as early as 1896, brought Conrad and Watt together. Nothing came of it, but when Pinker wrote Conrad in August, 1899, Conrad responded immediately. "My method of writing is so unbusinesslike," he wrote, "that I don't think you could have any use for such an unsatisfactory person. I generally sell a work before it is begun, get paid when it is half done and don't do the other half till the spirit moves me. I must add that I have no control whatever over the spirit—neither has the man who has paid the money." Pinker was undaunted by this quite accurate account of Conrad's habits, and they came to an agreement at once.[13]

It was almost certainly through Conrad that Ford became one of Pinker's clients. This was the beginning of a relation that lasted until Pinker's sudden death in New York in 1922. Ill with influenza, Pinker had sailed on the *Aquitania* for New York in February; one of his objects had been to arrange a contract with Macmillan that was to have "kept [Ford] in clover for the rest of [his] life." By the time Pinker reached New York he had pneumonia; he died at the Biltmore the night of February 8.[14]

In April, 1901, just after Pinker had shown his metal by placing *Typhoon*, he wrote Ford. "I haven't had the grace to answer y^r letter," Ford wrote, "because I've been at the Pent until just this morning." He then comments on the material he is sending Pinker and describes his own efforts to sell it. He concludes by asserting a principle he was to stick to throughout his life.

> —I've been slaving—for years—at a novel that I've just upon finished rewriting for the fourth time.—I'd offer it to you instead of these things, only at various stages of its career I tried it on several publishers who just stopped short of taking it & to another who wanted to publish it without making an advance—wh. I refused.[15]

Ford's refusal to publish without an advance was made necessary by his habit of living on the future earnings of a book from the moment he signed a contract for it. He was never, for the rest of his life, able to put his affairs on a current basis. This improvidence was a product of his optimism working on his conviction that artists are a society's most valuable members and deserve a comfortable living from it. However right Ford may have been to think so, his society did not. But Ford never ceased to believe that any windfall was the precursor of an endless flow of checks with which society would at last show that it had seen the light. The mere possibility that Pinker might succeed in his negotiations with Macmillan in 1922 made him rich. "I have got an immense contract from New York which shd. last me all my life," he wrote Herbert Read. "*Thus to Revisit* is going into editions & I get cheques in excess of advance of royalty which never happened to me before ... and we pass our time speculating on whether it is to be a Rolls Royce or an Overland. . . . "[16]

Thus it was that he began to live on advances and to spend whatever money he laid his hands on as fast as he got it. He always fulfilled his contractual obligations to produce work, and he found it incomprehensible that the comfortable income he believed his due was not immediately forthcoming. This was the source of his lifelong suspicion of publishers, editors, and agents: he was sure they must be cheating; how else explain the failure of his work to bring in large sums of money? It was also the source of the constant financial crises that forced him to write too much journalism and popular fiction. It is one of the sad ironies of Ford's life that, with all his scorn of businessmen and his belief that as an artist he had risen above the vulgar pressures of money, he was constantly at the mercy of his need for money.

Ford never fairly recognized what Pinker had done for him. Conrad, who quarreled with Pinker as violently as Ford, knew that his "books owe their existence to Mr. Pinker as much as to me. For fifteen years of my writing life he has seen me through periods of unproductiveness, through illness, through all sorts of troubles." Ford took the attitude espoused by the Society of Authors and ingeniously set forth by Shaw. Shaw argued that if an agent takes what the publisher considers a reasonable attitude, he can probably place books regularly with the publisher at a royalty of ten or fifteen percent, whereas he may well kill the goose if he insists on a royalty of twenty percent for a particular book. It is not, therefore, to an agent's advantage to fight for the very best terms for a particular book or author. This was Ford's view of Pinker.

> I should say [he wrote] that on the whole an agent is of little use to the author who has any business faculties at all. . . . He will place a highly paid author in preference to another on his list; he gets more commission. He will place an author who is indebted to him rather than one who isn't. . . . It is not always to his interests to press dishonest or defaulting publishers. . . . I never could quite know how I felt towards [Pinker]. He was so good and helpful and patient with Conrad and Crane and James and so quarrelsome to myself. But on

the whole ... I very much regretted his death. ... I remember thinking that New York was no place to go if it could kill anyone as hard
as Pinker.[17]

The fact that Ford and Conrad made no great progress with *Romance*
during the ten or twelve months after their return from Belgium in August,
1900, does not mean that they were not still actively worrying about getting
it finished. They worked over it when they were together at Christmas, 1900,
and when the Conrads spent a "holiday" at Stocks Hill in March. As soon
as the Hueffers were settled at the Bungalow, Ford hurried over to the Pent
for another stint of work and then urged the Conrads to come to Winchelsea
for a long visit. Conrad wrote them:

> I think I shall run down in two-three days to you [to] make
> arrangements and then fetch wife and boy for 3 weeks. Something
> must be done [about *Romance*].
> I am finishing the Falk story but with me such a statement
> may mean anything.
> You two are excellent, worthy people deserving of testimonials
> in jeweled caskets and your own portraits in gold frames.

In the event, the Conrads did not come to Winchelsea until the middle of
May and Conrad did not finish "Falk" until after their arrival. Unfortunately
—at least for *Romance*—it was during this visit that Ford drew Conrad's
attention to the story that was to become "Amy Foster."[18]

Ford's involvement with "Amy Foster" has become notorious, because
in *Joseph Conrad* he said that "Amy Foster" was "a short story originally by
the writer which Conrad took over and entirely re-wrote." This claim caused
Jessie Conrad to make her infuriated public statement that "I deny most
emphatically that Joseph Conrad ever *poached* on Mr. Hueffer's vast stock of
plots and material. ... " She repeated her argument in more detail two years
later in *Joseph Conrad As I Knew Him.* "The only foundation for this claim
[Ford's claim to "Amy Foster"] is that there is in Winchelsea churchyard a
grave which bears on the head-stone no name, but recording the fact that the
bodies of one or two foreign seamen are buried there, after being washed
ashore. I very well remember F.M.H. pointing this grave out to us one day."
No doubt he did, thus fixing Conrad's imagination on the subject Ford had
—unbeknownst to Jessie—already been urging on his attention; that was an
anecdote about a shipwrecked sailor who, unable to speak English, wandered
the Romney Marsh knocking on doors and being driven away as a lunatic
or a ghost. Ford had come on this story when he was gathering material for
his *Cinque Ports.* The inclusion of this anecdote in *The Cinque Ports* is a far

cry from "a short story originally by the writer," but it did contribute the idea for Conrad's story.[19]

Conrad settled down to write "Amy Foster" when he got back to the Pent and did not return to Winchelsea and *Romance* until it was finished. But by June 20 he was writing Galsworthy from the Bungalow:

> I have finished Falk and I've written another story ["Amy Foster"] since. Now I am here working at Seraphina. There are 10,000 words that I am going to write in manu propria [presumably Part Fourth of *Romance*]. I reckon to be done on Sunday [June 23] sometime. On Monday we go to the Pent.

No sooner had Conrad returned to the Pent than Ford began urging him to come back to Winchelsea for more work on *Romance;* Conrad's reply, to Elsie, somehow offended Ford, and he wrote Conrad one of the haughty letters that were his customary expression of hurt feelings. Conrad replied:

> You can not really suppose that there is anything between us except our mutual regard and our partnership—in crime. "Voyons, señorita, quelle folie!" Upon my word I am quite confounded by your letter which my speaking a coeur ouvert to Auntie Elsie did not deserve. I was afraid of taking a course that would seem heartless or offensive to you—especially in your low state of health. . . . But of irritation or of any thought about you but of the most affectionate nature I have been utterly unconscious then or now. . . . Report: O'Brien just out of Kemp's room.—another 2 hours work'll push the story along.

O'Brien's departure from Kemp's room concludes Chapter IV of Part Third of *Romance.* There therefore remained a great deal of writing for both of them to do, and Conrad decided to send what they had finished to Pinker with instructions to dispatch it to *Blackwood's* as soon as it was typed, in the hope that it would be enough to persuade Blackwood to buy the serial rights immediately.[20]

Chapter 8

W̲hen the incomplete typescript of *Romance* went off to Blackwood, Conrad wrote them to make sure—if he could—that they took the proper view of the book. "I have," he said, "given rein to my unholy passion for revising, reconsidering, re-writting [*sic*] ... my concern being not the matter—which is all right—but the expression.... This tale ... has been grubbed out of the British Museum by Hueffer.... You'll see we do not go in for analysis of character seeking rather to present a succession of picturesque scenes and personalities."[1]

Romance, that is to say, was intended to be an adventure story, a "romance of Cuban waters," with all the exotic circumstances, the sophisticated stylization of character, and the ingeniously plotted melodrama that Robert Louis Stevenson had used so successfully. "It was easy," Conrad said, "to relate a few events without being otherwise involved in the subject. The idea we had was purely aesthetic: to depict in an appropriate way certain scenes and certain situations. Also it did not displease us to be able to show that we could do something which was very much in vogue with the public at the moment."[2]

They hoped to show just how vivid real craftsmen could make even a simple adventure story. They believed deeply in the "purely aesthetic" aspect of the novel, though they did not believe—as they thought many of their contemporaries did—that if you "treated" a subject thoroughly, you gave it profundity. The last man to share an idea of that sort was Conrad, with his conviction that moral significance depends, not on words, but on what men do when the universe opens up around them in all its awesome inhumanity, as it opens up around the *Nan-Shan*, when the typhoon strikes her, "like another night seen through the starry night of the earth—the starless night of the immensities beyond the created universe, revealed in its appalling stillness through a low fissure in the glittering sphere of which the earth is the kernel." These very words may have been in Conrad's mind as he considered the problem of *Romance*, much of which was written at the same time he was writing *Typhoon*.³

"The heroic gospel of St. Henry, dear sir," as he put it about *Romance*, "rules the entire world and, as you know, there is more than one way of laughing at it. There were moments when both Hueffer and I were very gay while working on this construction. Nevertheless we took pains with the technical side of the work." As he wrote Ford:

> One would not be far wrong if one wrote—"Ne voyez-vous pas que c'est une bonne farce!" But that would not do perhaps. Also one could write: "Le besoin de manger, de fumer, de boire, de porter une culotte comme tout le monde." . . . I suppose the estetic [sic] racket is the practicable answer, satisfying if incomplete. I should think that with the other two we cover the whole ground of our motives.

Conrad makes this double game of staying uninvolved with the subject and deeply involved with the composition of the work sound easier than it was; there came a point in their labors when he cried out that "*Seraphina* seems to hang about me like a curse." Still, this was what they were attempting to do in *Romance* and Conrad believed they had succeeded. "It has," he said confidently, "a certain originality—of *exposition*, I may say."⁴

It was a serious blow to their belief in the power of cleverness when Blackwood turned down *Romance*. "The fault of the thing," David Meldrum said, "stated in a word, is that it is Hueffer's story and Conrad's [story-] telling; and that the dramatic intensity, while there, appears a little forced" —which is to say that involvement with the composition without involvement with the subject had not worked. "I will admit," Conrad wrote Blackwood three months later, "the rejection of *Seraphina* had shaken the confidence with which I looked upon that work. So, as one can not turn back till the furrow is ploughed to the end, I took it in hand [again]. . . . "⁵

During the next six months Conrad rewrote the whole of Part Fourth —the best thing in the book—and Ford worked equally hard on his parts. The big push came in December, but before that there were plenty of sessions at the Pent, duly reported in Ford's letters to Elsie along with the latest news of their competition in ill health.

> We're getting ahead. . . . Conrad has actually killed Don Roderigo and I am just surrendering Kemp to the Admiral. C. was so obviously depressed at the idea of my departing or rather so elated at that

of my remaining that I thought that [since] I hadn't to go up to London that I'd stay. . . . Conrad once again sleeps. We're getting ahead now. About half the work done. I've been doing it so I'm both excited and exhausted. But another coup de collier tonight. I was writing till past one last night. Ought to see the end of it.

Then Conrad came to Winchelsea to stay over Christmas so that they could finish. He had to do more work than he had bargained for: at Ford's birthday party, December 17, Ford swallowed—"or rather didn't swallow," as he put it—a chicken bone and was prostrate for some days. This was a signal victory in the competition over which of them suffered more from illness and nerves. "I intended," Conrad wrote Meldrum, "to write you for the N[ew] Y[ear]'s day but being in Winchelsea, with Hueffer very unwell, and the wretched work on my hands I absolutely had no knowledge of the day incredible as it may appear." In his abstraction, he set fire to the tail of the Hueffers' blue angora cat, Hall Caine (Conrad was prone to starting accidental fires when he was overwrought; he once burned the manuscript of "The End of the Tether"). He was back at the Pent by New Year's Day "with piles of MS," and a week later he summed up for Meldrum.

> There is always something wrong . . . about [*Romance*]. After M^r B'wood's refusal of the same I first dropped it in disgust; Then took it up again and have been working very hard at it. It is now a satisfactory piece of work but not quite rearranged and adjusted all through to the changes in action and in the reading of characters which I have introduced. Hueffer was to do all that—instead of which he goes and tries to swallow a chicken bone, gets nearly choked, awfully shaken up, unable to work and so on. I could have wept. Still there was no remedy so I buckled-to again and am still at it driving hard. I had just one days respite—Xmas—that's all—but the book is a new book and really not bad at all this time.[6]

But in fact the job was still far from done. Ford was at the Pent in January, 1902, for more work, this time with his nose a little out of joint about the subordinate role assigned him. "Conrad apparently wants me to sit around and look pleasant," he wrote Elsie, "so that Heaven knows when I shall get back; I haven't cared to ask for fear of precipitating explanations. . . . I don't know when Seraphina will get finished. But it does make a slow way along." He returned to the Pent again in March, when they finally finished the book and Conrad was able to write Galsworthy with a sigh of relief, "Seraphina is finished and gone from the house she has haunted for this year past. I do really hope it will hit the taste of the street—unless the devil's in it."[7]

The result of all this writing and rewriting is a novel that is almost equally Conrad's work and Ford's; much of it, as Ford said, is a "mosaic of passages written alternately." He gives a sample of this mosaic work in the Appendix to *The Nature of a Crime* that is remarkably revealing of both writers. Thus, when Ford wrote, "For suffering is the lot of man," Conrad added, "but not inevitable failure or worthless despair which is without end—suffering, the mark of manhood, which bears within its pain a hope of felicity like a jewel set in iron. . . ."

But though each of them frequently revised the other's work, they agreed that, generally speaking, Ford had written the first two parts of the book (up to Kemp's arrival at Rio Medio), Ford about one-third and Conrad two-thirds of the third part, Conrad all of the fourth (up to the moment when Kemp is imprisoned in Havana), and Ford all of the fifth. Thus Ford provided the skeleton of the story, the historical detail, and most of the characters. But "the matchless Fourth Part," as he said, "is both in conception and writing entirely the work of Mr. Conrad."

Who but Conrad would ever have thought of that romantic Methodist spinster, Mrs. Williams, who, "with a sort of sweet absurdity . . . talked [to Kemp] in great agitation of the depravity of hearts, of the sin of light-mindedness, of the self-deception which leads men astray—a confused but purposeful jumble, in which occasional allusions to the errors of Rome, and to the want of seriousness in the upper classes, put in a last touch of extravagance"—all in the romantic excitement of assuring herself that Kemp would not betray Seraphina after having carried her off from Rio Medio. Who but Conrad would have married this woman to Captain Williams, whose legs moved in his "loose silk trousers" "like a contrivance made out of two gate-posts," the upward cast of whose eyes "invested his red face with an air of singularly imbecile ecstacy," and who was, for all his sailor's past, devoted to this romantic scarecrow. Even the ordinary seamen aboard the *Lion* have the imaginative energy of Conrad's best work, as does the carpenter, "a Shetlander—a sort of shaggy hyperborean giant with a forbidding face, an appraising, contemplative manner, and many nails in his mouth."

How far Ford had developed can be seen in the book too. When, in the third part, the pirates of Rio Medio attack the *Breeze*, Kemp saves the hysterical Mrs. Cowper by making her understand she must give her rings to them and by carrying her to safety.

> She could hardly walk at all. The child and the nurse ran in front of us, and, practically, I carried her there in my arms. Once [at] the

stateroom she struggled loose from me, and, rushing in, slammed the door violently in my face. She seemed to hate me.

And did, so that when Kemp is brought to trial for his life at the Old Bailey, Mrs. Cowper refuses to testify for him on the grounds that he filched her rings. Here is Ford's typical situation, in which the hero's admirable conduct is rewarded with hatred and malice.[8]

But the story, despite its nominally lively action, moves in slow motion; both Ford and Conrad were too interested in an impression—a static picture rich in atmosphere—to keep events moving as they must in an adventure story. In *The March of Literature* Ford imagines the author of *Beowulf* saying to himself, "If . . . I repeat the story very succinctly with atmospheric touches and little passages of corroboration, my whole work ought to leave an impression of great truth and greater unity." He then adds, "Conrad and the present author must have uttered similar sentences fifty or sixty times, whilst elaborating their plots during their decade of collaboration," with fatal results so far as the narrative drive of their novels was concerned.[9]

What is memorable in *Romance* is a series of images—Don Balthaser walking with senile dignity up and down the courtyard of the Casa Riego on the arm of the villainous O'Brien, Manuel surrounded by the boats of the other pirates adrift in the fog, holding them enthralled with the "inspired and grandiose strain" of his love song, like "a mournful parody, the odious grimacing of an ape to the true sorrow of the human face." This was not, alas, enough to "hit the taste of the street." The reviewers received *Romance* in a friendly but not very encouraging way; they thought that it was "not convincing, though admirably clever," and—most unkindest cut of all—that it almost justified comparison with Stevenson himself. Nor were the financial rewards what they had hoped for. In an injudicious effort to build up Conrad's morale, Pinker had suggested they might get an advance of as much as £ 400; now he was estimating it would be only £ 230, and they were outraged by what they assured one another was his betrayal of a firm promise. This outbreak of righteous indignation was to have further unhappy consequences.[10]

Conrad's need of Ford's moral support was still as great as ever and he clearly feared that, with the completion of *Romance*, he might lose it. He was at some pains to advertise his satisfaction with their work. "Strangely enough," he wrote Garnett, "it is yet my share of *Romance* (collab^on stuff with Ford) that fills me with the least dismay"; and he wrote Ford anxiously:

Dearest Ford,
    What becomes of you two and your work? And what of your young women?

These interrupted relations must be taken up again[.] The cause of my silence is as usual the worry about stuff that won't get itself written. Vous connaissez cela.

I miss collaboration in a most ridiculous manner. I hope you don't intend dropping me altogether....

In haste to catch post I ask: are you thinking of coming this way and of staying here? ... How rotten everything is! ...

Ever yours
Conrad

Conrad begins with that tactful reference to the work of both Ford and Elsie because Elsie had been hard at work during this spring on a novel and both Ford and Conrad had been careful to write her enthusiastic comments about it, partly perhaps with a view to keeping her content while Ford was at the Pent helping Conrad instead of at the Bungalow helping her.[11]

Ford did have work of his own to worry about. He had been writing a little book on Rossetti for Duckworth's Popular Library of Art. However unsympathetic he found Edward Garnett, he still trusted Garnett's judgment and sent him the manuscript of the Rossetti for his opinion. As usual, he found Edward's suggestions almost shocking. "Please," he said, "I cannot enter into the pathological details; I sh^d have to consider the matter for a long time, consult toxologists for symptoms and ponder for ever so long on a matter very repellent. Because how can I distinguish between the symptoms, on canvas, of chloral, uraemia, gout in the wrist and incipient blindness, all of wh. (not to mention chronic delusions) had a share." Ford liked to think about the psychological complications of other men's lives as little as he liked to think about his own; there was something almost indecent about the subject, something that derogated from the dignity of man.[12]

There were also family problems to confront. On February 2 Dr. Martindale was found dead in his laboratory, possibly from an overdose of drugs. Ford and Elsie rushed up to London to deal with the situation and that night Ford wrote Conrad all about it; "to think of you hung up in that hotel, waiting under the burden of that God-forsaken errand," Conrad replied, "was too awful." If Dr. Martindale did commit suicide, they managed to hush it up, and Ford produced a large wreath "From his daughter and grandchildren" and a set of verses for the funeral.

> He hath outsoared the darkness of our night
> Envy and heartache and all grief and pain
> And that unrest which men miscall delight
> Can touch him not and torture not again.[13]

After the funeral, Ford and Elsie took a quick trip to Germany to recruit their spirits; when they returned there were more troubles. Oliver Hueffer, who had married Miss Zoë Pyne, had been "doing business on a large scale and running heavy risks," with results so disastrous that Robert Garnett urged Mrs. Hueffer not to throw good money after bad by trying to help him, and Ford wrote her, "We expect Oliver down to-day.... It's been a fearful nuisance to me. And there have been other nuisances," including Ford's refusal to speak to Zoë, who "got ... perfectly outrageous in abuse of me.... I certainly hadn't done anything to deserve it," he said.[14]

Ford let himself go to his mother about these problems.

> Elsie is still writing. She's not at all well; indeed I despair of her ever getting well again. But the children continue to flourish & make unbearable noises....
>
> We've had plenty of trouble with servants.... Daisy remains nurse. Bessy [the cook] turned out not only no better, but very much worse, than she ought to have been. Then we had an interregnum of an Early Victorian Treasure, owning to 57.—But she could remember the birth of George III. She was a good cook but was too weak to cook more than one chop per day.... However, she was strictly virtuous.
>
> Now we have Mrs. Mitchell at a large salary & *she's* fallen ill to-day. Such are the agréments of a little house in the country.

He was beginning to tire of the life of a country gentlemen and to think of the challenge and romance of the city.[15]

It is typical that, at a time when he was finding domesticity in Winchelsea less enchanting, he should have written the most successful of all his "family" poems, "To Christina at Nightfall":

> Little thing, ah, little mouse,
> Creeping through the twilit house,
> To watch within the shadow of my chair
> With large blue eyes; the firelight on your hair
> Doth glimmer gold and faint....

Ford never wholly lost this feeling for domesticity, but he believed—as the next few years were to show—that most of its joys could be had without the annoyances of noisy children, servant problems, and sick wives. This delusion that one could have his cake and eat it too if only the "Victorian" notions clung to by older people could be cast aside was at the bottom of many of Ford's future troubles. By professing his old-fashioned love of domesticity he offended advanced thinkers, and by acting on the idea of free love he offended conservative people.

He sought consolation for his troubles in contemplating work accomplished and in dreaming of success.

> ... on Thursday, I finished [*The Benefactor*] & I am now recovering from my exhaustion & am taking a rest.... My novel with Conrad won't be out till next year I expect. It will have first to run as a serial [alas, it never did].—My Rossetti will be out in a day or two.

As this letter shows, Ford and Conrad were still hopeful of profitable serializations of *Romance* in England and America. S. S. McClure had been in London and they had worked hard to sell him *Romance;* when he returned to America, Pinker went to New York too in the hope of clinching the deal. When he returned it appeared he had, and Conrad wrote Ford hopefully:

> I ... look[ed] in upon the Pinker of Literary Agents. I reckon he had been very sea-sick and the Yanks must have been bullying him brutally between the two spells.
> He placed "Romance" for serial rights and book form with McClure. The Royalty arrangement is fairly good.... [16]

But Ford was in one of his frequent financial crises and began to make trouble over McClure. He first wrote Conrad and Conrad replied:

> I suggest that you should write Pinker saying that as co-author of *R* you object to its being disposed of to McClure till a statement and remittance of Inheritors is sent us.... I [may] be able to chime in with a small cheque.... In your letter to P say that you cannot enter into Conrad's position vis-a-vis of McClure and that you insist on payment of your half.... I am dropping a note to P saying: Hueffer's angry and my position most unpleasant.
> This is all I can do just now.

Ford followed this advice to the letter and, when Pinker attempted to placate him, insisted even more strongly:

> Robert McClure promised to deliver an acc^t by February last & to pay the Royalty then. He said this was a trade custom & I didn't offer any objection.... What I feel is that as an American firm they haven't any assets here—or indeed I sh^d have sued them before.... They haven't even answered letters addressed to them. That I resent as being both insolent and incomprehensible.

No doubt Robert McClure did say there would be an accounting in February (six months after publication), but he can hardly have promised that the royalty would be paid then, since that was (and is now) far from the custom of the trade. Ford's threat of a lawsuit and his outrage at the insolence of these tradesmen are characteristic of him in this mood. McClure's check arrived early in June, when it was due, accompanied by the belated accounting.[17]

Then Conrad had a disaster. In March he had told Elsie that "I am ... going to begin writing my B'wood stuff 'The End of the Song' ["The End of the Tether"]—as Ford has suggested and advised"; as usual he worked dangerously close to *Blackwood's* deadline. Then, on the night of June 23, an old-fashioned oil lamp with a glass reservoir exploded; it scorched the rug and burned a table Ford treasured because it had been designed for his grandfather by William Morris. Far worse, however, it destroyed the whole of the second installment of "The End of the Tether," which had been due in Edinburgh on June 24.

> The fire ran in streams and Jess and I threw blankets and danced around on them; the blaze in the window was remarked in Postling[.] Then all was over but the horrid stink. . . . This morning looking at the pile of charred paper—MS and typed copy—my head swam; it seemed to me the earth was turning backwards.[18]

Elsie had been ill in bed but fortunately was now better and the Fords rushed into the breach. They rented a cottage for the Conrads and there Conrad settled down to rewrite the lost installment.

> It became a matter of days: then of hours. Conrad wrote: the writer corrected the manuscript behind him or wrote in a sentence; the writer in his study on the street, Conrad in a two-room cottage that we had hired immediately opposite. The household sat up all night keeping soups warm.

Despite these heroic measures, Conrad did not finish the installment until the early hours of July 16.[19]

As soon as the Conrads had left Winchelsea, Ford set off on a walking trip through the New Forest. His complaints about his health had recently expanded into complaints about life in general, always a bad sign with him: "[Writing]'s an endless business, of course," he was saying to Elsie, "but then, so is life—and if occupation fills up life, passes it away, that's always so much to the good." This state of mind was not improved by the domestic difficulties he described to his mother or by the disappointment of McClure's not paying the royalty on *The Inheritors* when Ford needed it instead of when it was due. It was not much improved by the New Forest either: "I've seen 30 million bluejackets, Southampton Water and the King's train as that personage went up to town and I'm exceedingly lonely"—as he always was without plenty of companionship. "Congratulations," he wrote Elsie gloomily when he heard she had finished her novel. "Just as I'm never going to try to write again," and then added, "I expect you're tired of my letters as of me."[20]

Pinker had seen from the start that if *Romance* was to be serialized it would have to be cut, but he did not succeed in conveying this idea to Conrad until September.

> I happened to be at the Pent [Ford wrote] when yr. letter of the 26th arrived & Conrad asks me to answer it for my own part. I can't myself feel—& I don't think Conrad feels—inclined to let Romance go at the present terms [this was the suggested advance of £ 230].... If you think that cutting the story wd. help its chance as a serial I expect to have some leisure shortly & might see to it. The point is: supposing it cut down, say, to 70,000 words or less, what price could we expect to get for the serial? ...

Pinker then suggested they cut it and he would see what he could do, but Ford was reluctant. "I'll however see Conrad about it as soon as he has finished *The End of the Tether*. It would stop his work to introduce a new subject," he wrote Pinker. "Could you in the meantime make me an advance on what has been secured on the m.s.?—I ask you because you must be better aware than any one else of the value of the security & I haven't at the moment any investments I want to disturb & I have at the moment a need for about £ 75."[21]

While they were conducting this futile last stand, Elsie Hueffer was starting on a volume of de Maupassant translations, a task that drew from Conrad a number of letters of help and criticism. In return Elsie sent Conrad a shrewd comment on "Heart of Darkness," to the effect that Kurtz was too symbolic. Conrad answered good-naturedly,

> What I distinctly admit is the fault of having made Kurtz too symbolic or rather symbolic at all. But the story being mainly a vehicle for conveying a batch of personal impressions I gave rein to my mental laziness.... This is then the whole Apologia pro Vita Kurtzii —or rather for the tardiness of his vitality.

Elsie hoped to persuade Conrad to write the preface to her translations, but in the end she had to settle for one by Ford.[22]

Ford and Conrad had now to recognize that their attempt to produce in *Romance* an adventure story that would outsell Stevenson had failed. It made them both feel their health unequal to the demands of Christmas festivities. "We've got the Conrads coming for Xmas & several other people in the neighbourhood, so, much as we want to be quiet we've had to make

considerable preparations," Ford wrote his mother; and Conrad said to Galsworthy, "We are leaving in half an hour for W'sea to spend three weeks or
so. I don't know whether that sort of thing does me any good or not, but
as I can't work at home it doesn't matter where I am."[23]

Presently, however, Ford's spirits revived and Conrad was persuaded to
go back to work. Ford got him to start on *Nostromo,* since it would be,
Conrad thought, "something silly and saleable," like "Youth," and talked
him into "dispatch[ing] [*The Rescue*] into [Ford's] friendly hands for the
only real work of Rescue that will ever be found in its text."*[24]

It was probably in January, 1903, that Conrad arranged the elaborate
joint birthday party for Borys and Christina, the plans for which he described in a "Protocol of the Celebration (official)." It was in his best mock-
heroic style: "At 3.40 the Young Lady [Christina] having had barely time to
smoothe her plumes shall proceed (attended by the Lady Regent [Elsie]—
the Lord Regent [Ford] is at liberty to swoon for fifty minutes) shall proceed
—I say—to the Baronial Kitchen (where the feast is to be engulphed) to
receive the guests with the young Cavalier [Borys]." Conrad also wrote
Elsie in a somewhat less facetious vein.

> *Sixteenth* is the day, by the force of circumstances.
> My suggestion is that you should come on that very day
> by the 1.6 pm train from W'sea; arriving here in time for the festivi-
> ties which will begin (with the feed in the kitchen) at 3.45. This will
> enable the staff (Jess—Mrs. Graham—Mrs. Gates and Nellie [their
> maid]) to devote all their energies (from 10 in the morning) to the
> preparations. . . .
> Xna to take the head, Borys the foot of the table each before
> a birthday cake bearing their joined names (But we won't look
> upon this as a definite engagement if you doubt the wisdom of the
> step owing to the youthfulness of the parties)[.]
> Meantime Ford and I shall light up the tree in the empty
> dining room.
> On the stroke of 5 the portal is to be thrown open and the
> glory revealed.
> Carriages at 5.30. . . . [25]

Conrad was more interested in teasing Ford about his grand manner

---

*Ford's recollection was that he then suggested a rearrangement of the opening of *The
Rescue* that Conrad, when he finally completed the novel in 1916, adopted. So far as the evidence
of the manuscript goes, it supports this recollection, though Ford's suggestion did not help
Conrad at the time.

and his romantic medievalism than he was in amusing the children, but Ford always thought of the children on such occasions.

> There was an old Pumpums [Ford] who said
> "It is time little kids were in bed,"
>> So they took up Christina
>> And washed her much cleaner
> And carried her quickly to bed.

> There was an old Mummums [Elsie] who said,
> "It is time little girls were in bed,"
>> So they caught up Miss Katharine
>> And made a great lather in
> Her bath and then popped her in bed.

> There was an old Blank-dash [Conrad] who said,
> "It is time little scamps were in bed,"
>> So they bore Master Borys
>> Upstairs where the door is,
> And bathed him and put him to bed,
>> And they said
> "Oh it's peaceful now they are in bed!"

That winter Ford had got the idea of doing a book with Hyde about London, somewhat on the line of *The Cinque Ports*, and he now busied himself running about London with Hyde, who was to illustrate the book, and entangling himself in negotiations with editors and publishers; as always he greatly enjoyed the miseries of this kind of work.

> Here I am at Gatti's awaiting Joseph.
> I saw Dell [of the *Burlington Magazine*] who is literally no use: a sort of imbecile strikingly like Oliver in appearance, only thin. ... I have (five minutes ago) seen Pawling [of Heinemann's] and have decided not to bother about the Burlington.
> Pawling's ... asked me to do two more London draftings on more "popular" lines and says that if I achieve them he's practically certain to publish and to pay the £ 100. ...
> Trotting about London all day yesterday with Hyde was awful. ...
> Here's C.—more tonight. ...
> I've had a frightful rush for it: as my interrupted letter was beginning to tell you but I'm on the whole in good spirits. ... — Hyde rushed in to Gatti's to tell me that Constables had been sounding him & wanted me to do a book with him!!! on the Pilgrim's Way. ...

Tomorrow I *breakfast* with Galsworthy (fancy my early rising) in order to be able to get down to you if you want me....

You can see from this thing how tired I am: no sleep last night after a slanging match with Edward [Garnett]....

After I wrote you C. and I went to Pinker who was literally beaming....

After Pinker I went with C. to Heinemann's.... I then went with C. to the Monico & afterwards saw him off from Char[ing] X.

... It was quite restful and homelike to have him in the midst of all this racket.

After months of negotiations of this kind, with Hyde's uncertain temper adding appreciably to the complications, he gave up trying to place *The Soul of London* and settled down to writing it without a commission.[26]

In April the proofs of *Romance* brought Ford back to the Pent for a last session over it. "Joseph is very kick-uppy about Typhoon," he wrote Elsie.

It came out yesterday with a great flourish of trumpets. Three re- views on day of pub¹ which has driven Pawling into fits of triumph (there was one in the Chronicle, did you see it?).

I have just drafted my letter to Courtney [of the *Daily Tele- graph*, presumably written in the hope that Courtney would serial- ize *The Soul of London*] & we are getting through [the proofs of] Romance. I keep pretty well though last night I didn't sleep so I suppose that is going to begin all over again.

At last those terrible proofs—Ford always hated proofreading—were finished and they went triumphantly up to London to deliver them. Conrad kept working on the train, getting down on the floor on his stomach to do so because the train was jolting badly. He became so deeply absorbed that— according to Ford—when Ford tapped him on the shoulder to tell him they were at Charing Cross, "he sprang to his feet and straight at [my] throat."[27]

Chapter 9

Underneath his apparently phlegmatic suface, Ford took disappointments less well than did Conrad, for all Conrad's dramatic gestures of despair. His disappointment over the comparative failure of *Romance* was intensified by the financial difficulties it caused. He had been living on the anticipated profits of *Romance.* "I've had a most distressing year," he wrote his mother at the end of 1902. "I've hardly made £ 100 in all." By the autumn of 1903 he was really hard pressed. "Does 'Romance' burst on the world to-morrow?" he wrote Pinker on October 15 with a transparent show of casualness.[1]

When Pinker reported to him the actual sales of *Romance* he tried to appear philosophical. "I suppose," he said, "it's merely a matter of advertising—the sales stopped the moment they did.—It can't be helped, I suppose." There was nothing left except to borrow, and in December he had Robert Garnett arrange a loan of £ 150 for him.

> I've not settled anything with C. [he wrote Elsie] but I don't suppose the Rescue will be finished this year. Robert has settled that loan at 5% so if you like to send the bills down to me I'll settle them off and get rid of them.

Apparently most of the £ 150 went into these bills, since Robert borrowed another £ 100 for them in March, 1904. Elsie's stiff knee caused her to fall down some stone steps and break her arm and there were more expenses.[2]

Ford spent the fall looking for a way to start over again, revising *The Benefactor* for the second or third time and going back once more to his collection of notes on the reign of Henry VIII. Edward Garnett suggested he write a little book on Holbein for the Library of Popular Art, for which he had already written his *Rossetti*; this project was not likely to bring him immediate fame, but it had the merit of requiring a trip to Berlin and Basel to look at Holbeins: travel was always a consolation to him. He also began to think of doing a novel about Katharine Howard. Uncle William thought it a somewhat questionable idea. "You seem," he wrote, "to have got hold of a very good and unused subject: only I am afraid that she was a slightly scabreuse female, and that your romance, to be true, must partake of the scabreux." This little awkwardness seemed not to have discouraged Ford; perhaps he had already conceived the heroic view of Katharine that was to govern his trilogy about her. In any event, the combination of Holbein and Katharine was an admirably economical one: he was frequently able to use the same material in both books.[3]

Then suddenly Ford decided to move to London. In a way it is easy to understand why he wanted to, once the idea was put in his mind. He was disenchanted with life in the country, and he undoubtedly thought he would have a better chance of literary success if he were in London; that this was at least one of his motives is evident from the energy with which they began to entertain when they got to London. But going to London would have been a financially risky move for him under the best of circumstances.*

The move was suggested to him by Oliver. Oliver and his wife had been living for three years on Campden Hill, at 10 Airlie Gardens, a house owned by Zoë's family. They now decided (no doubt as a result of one of Oliver's many schemes for making a fortune) to move to Manchester and proposed that Ford take over their rather depressing liver-colored brick house. Ford rented it for the first quarter of 1904 and they moved to town early in January. The Conrads came to London too, taking "a couple of rooms [in a house at 17 Gordon Place] nearby, round the corner, as we used to do at Winchelsea."[4]

" . . . in 1903 . . . " Ford later wrote, "Campden Hill, in the royal borough of Kensington, was like a high class Greenwich Village in which all the artists should be wealthy, refined, delicate and well-born. It was high in the air. In its almost country roads you met ladies all of whom wore sable coats—or at least sable stoles; and admirable children all bursting with health; and Whistler and Abbey and Henry James. . . . " Despite his ironic tone, these features of Campden Hill may have had something to do with Ford's desire to go there; the ironic tone is a result of what happened after they arrived. They had anticipated a lively and interesting life among prominent and influential people; what they got was a nightmare.[5]

*Late in her life, Elsie said it was the success of *The Soul of London* that made them think they could afford to go to London, but that cannot have been true, since *The Soul of London* was not published until a year and a half later. Perhaps Elsie, taking the word for the deed as Ford so often did, was remembering some idea for serializing the book that Ford had counted on.

Ford knew he was going to have to make a good deal more money to maintain this "very large, absurd house," and he began at once to bombard Pinker with "a dozen fairy stories" (no doubt the stories eventually used in *Christina's Fairy Book* in 1906) and proposals for articles "on Jap.; French Literature & German subjects." This anxiety about money made it maddening that he could find almost no time to write. "We go on Tuesday to 10 Airlie Gardens," he had written Pinker just before they moved. "Whilst I was at the Pent Conrad did a good deal—I'm going to have him in Town & run him thro' *Nostromo* energetically."[6]

Conrad was even more depressed than usual during these months, and the job of keeping him running through *Nostromo* energetically was far from easy. In addition there were deadlines; *Nostromo* had already begun to run in *T.P.'s Weekly.* "[Conrad] used to come in [to Airlie Gardens] in the mornings and, having climbed the many stairs to my small, dreadful study, would sit for hours motionless and numb with a completely expressionless face. Every now and then he would say: 'I can't do it. It can't be done. *Je suis foûtu* [*sic*]!' " In addition to the burden of *Nostromo* there was the task of persuading Conrad to dictate the essays for *The Mirror of the Sea* while Ford took them down in his laborious amateur shorthand. "So in the day," as Conrad said, "*Nostromo*, and, from 11 to 1 A.M., dictation." As if this were not enough, Ford had persuaded the Conrads to take their meals at Airlie Gardens; he was certainly making an effort to live up to Ford Madox Brown's admonition to "beggar yourself rather than refuse assistance to anyone whose genius you think shows promise of being greater than your own."[7]

Things quickly became worse. Christina's hair caught fire as she was drying it before an open fire and she raced downstairs with it ablaze, setting her clothes afire in the process; only the prompt action of Johanna, the faithful German cook they had brought with them from Winchelsea, saved Christina from serious injury; Johanna threw a blanket about Christina, burning her own hands badly. Then, one by one, both the Hueffers and Conrads came down with influenza. Just as Ford was beginning to be convalescent and while Elsie was still in bed, "one day no voice from the kitchen answered mine in the speaking-tube. Johanna was lying face-downwards on the kitchen table with her varnished scarlet cheeks in a great sieve of flour. She had been cooking against influenza for a fortnight." Johanna was sent off to the hospital and Ford took on the cooking in addition to the nursing and the household chores. " . . . Conrad," he said, "noticed no difference as long as I imitated Johanna. But once I cooked a *civet de lièvre à la Parisienne.*"

Conrad inspected it as he always did, carefully and with his monocle screwed into his eye. He rubbed his hands and with enthusiasm unfolded his napkin. When, with head on one side and a look of pleased anticipation, he had tasted it, he started slightly. He said:

"My dear faller.... The admirable Johanna has of course surpassed herself.... But... eh... my gout!... *Une telle succulence, mon cher*... Tebb says the greatest abstinence...." He added that ... if there remained a little of the admirable saddle of lamb of the night before ... a small slice, cold, with a leaf of salad....

... I imitated Johanna from then on.[8]

None of this was allowed to interfere with their social life. Henry James was invited to dinner and to tea, Pinker was invited to drop in to supper even though Elsie was "absent ill," and Ford walked across the reservoirs to Aubrey Walk to breakfast with Galsworthy.

... the doors and windows [were] always open, the sunlight streaming in on the hissing silver teakettle, the bubbling silver entrée dishes, the red tiles of the floor, the bright rugs, the bright screens. And we would talk until it was time for me to go back along the waterworks wall and take up the interminable job of writing ... when Conrad was not writing *Nostromo* up in my study.

He and Galsworthy became good enough friends so that when Ford later left London, he wrote Galsworthy explaining his departure and replying to Galsworthy's comments on the fourth chapter of *The Soul of London*, which he had asked Galsworthy to read. His reply was evidently violent (he was starting into a serious nervous breakdown) and, on April 14, Galsworthy answered:

I feel like a pig and an imposter for having by a slipshod annotation opened the flood gates of your wrath.... My note was meant to say (I can't remember what it did say) that: *talking of the third state which you mention* (man looking out of club window all of which I took to mean an important quiescent enjoyment of things going on round you) non-artists would feel IT....

I'm so glad you're settled in comfortably, but I shall miss you very much—it was nice to feel one could "drop-in".... why not send me Chap V and risk some more slipshod annotations?

Meanwhile the at homes continued, too, not always with happy results. At one of them Lewis Hind ("a thin, slightly stuttering nervous, dark fellow who was noted as a critic, mostly of paintings") innocently congratulated Conrad on the fact that *T.P.'s Weekly* was splashing his name on all the hoardings of London. Conrad, who despised *T.P.'s Weekly* and thought its publicity almost an outrage on his honor, was convinced Hind meant to be sarcastic and was visibly insulted.[9]

Nor did these difficulties slow down Ford's work. By April 14 he had written all but the last chapter of *The Soul of London.* By the middle of May the book had been finished long enough for him to be fretting over Pinker's failure to arrange for its serialization. "I spoke to P of the *London,*" Conrad wrote. "He protested that he has not in the least slackened his efforts. He believes that the time will come for it. . . . You know how he failed with Falk and yet managed to do a stroke of business afterwards. . . . I tell you this for what it is worth." Then Ford heard that Henry James had agreed to write a similar book. James reassured him: "Lord bless you, it is all right about your book, of which I am delighted to hear. Go on with it to felicity and fortune and let it take my hearty benediction with it. Mine is a thing of the *far,* though not of the contingent future."[10]

Meanwhile there was the continual struggle to keep Conrad going; even Jessie Conrad recognized the help Ford gave Conrad at this time.

> F.M.H. has made the most fantastic claims with regard to my husband's various plots, yet *The Mirror of the Sea* owes a great deal to his ready and patient assistance—not perhaps to the actual writing, but that book would never have come into being if Joseph Conrad had had no intelligent person with whom to talk over these intimate reminiscences.

Mrs. Conrad's "perhaps" may need more emphasis than she knew; there is a real possibility that Ford wrote some of *The Mirror of the Sea.* Ford told Elsie at this time that "I've finished the chapter for B'w'd and it has gone off." Ford published nothing in *Blackwood's Magazine* at this time—or ever. But two of the essays in *The Mirror of the Sea* appeared there not long after this. A month or so later, when Pinker was struggling to sell these essays, Conrad wrote Ford, "Harpers are inclined to take the papers[.] Expect to hear from them next week. Of course I've done nothing more. 40,000 w would be required[.]" In his next letter he returned to this subject. "I saw Pinker the other day. No word yet from [Colonel] Harvey [of *Harper's*] as to the sketches. . . . As to the book form (which Harvey already is ready to take) a small calculation will fix our proportions; for I suppose we cannot now finish the whole together. Can we? Anyhow so far nothing is fixed." When Conrad sold the first two chapters of *The Mirror of the Sea* for serial publication, he sent Elsie a check, saying, "Cheque (endorsed) enclosed here is for Ford's proportion of Sketches. . . . Perhaps you will just note it in some small book. . . . Mark: on act/of two sketches disposed of up to now. (serial)." Possibly Conrad was sharing the payments for *The Mirror of the Sea* with Ford because Ford had taken it down from Conrad's dictation, but there are no other cases of Conrad's paying Ford when Ford helped him in that way. The first five papers of *The Mirror of the Sea* were finished before Ford left Airlie Gardens. At least two of the remaining seventeen sketches were written at the Bungalow with Ford after the Conrads' return from Capri in May, 1905. In any event, Ford did more to help Conrad during these months in London than at any other time during their long intimacy —and more that has aroused controversy.[11]

The main cause of controversy has been *Nostromo*. "Conrad," Ford said, "was very ill with mortification [after the Lewis Hind episode] and I had to write the part of the serial that remained to make up the weekly instalment [of *Nostromo*]. Our life was like that." Conrad was in fact suffering from a good deal more than Hind's gaffe. Shortly after their arrival in London Jessie had fallen in the street "putting out both her knee caps"; then she was discovered to have a "valvular defect of the heart"; and then Conrad's bankers, Watson & Co., failed. No wonder he was "taken with so violent an attack of gout and nervous depression that he was quite unable to continue his installments of NOSTROMO. . . . "[12]

It is the simple truth that Ford and Conrad's life then was, as Ford says, "like that." A couple of months later Conrad sent Ford a letter from the Northern Newspaper Syndicate asking for a story, and said, "I was going to fling [this letter] into the paper basket. Still—if you have something written that you do *not* care for *in the least* send it on. I'll put in a few of my jargon phrases and send it on. As I remarked—nothing matters—and we are intimate enough to say anything to each other. You may as well have this modest cheque."[13]

Of Ford's claim to have written an installment of *Nostromo* even so mildly anti-Fordian a scholar as Jocelyn Baines says: "Hueffer would have had to have known the story very well indeed to have written the passage [of the *Nostromo* manuscript that is in Ford's hand] himself; he may have done so, but it is more likely that he took it down from Conrad's dictation." The portion of the *Nostromo* manuscript Mr. Baines is here discussing consists of sixteen pages, a part of Chapter V of Part Two, entirely in Ford's hand. It constituted most of the installment of *Nostromo* that appeared in *T.P.'s Weekly* for April 9, 1904, and must therefore have been written about the middle of February, 1904. It is unlikely that Ford took this passage down at Conrad's dictation since, as we know, he wrote a kind of shorthand that he was using at this very time to take down *The Mirror of the Sea;* he would surely have used it to take down *Nostromo,* too, if he had done so.*[14]

Besides, the manuscript shows every sign of having been composed as it was written. For example (the words in square brackets have been written and then crossed out):

the silver [tea] and porcelain of the tea service

like a bit of a [boud] lady's boudoir [dropped] putting in a note of feminine and intimate delicacy.

The lights of the Casa Gould flung their [paralle] shining parallelograms upon the house of the Avellanos.

This is not a man taking down dictation; it is a man composing, and sometimes changing his mind, as he puts the words on the page. Moreover, the manuscript shows a good many small errors in the handling of the characters' names, errors it is hardly conceivable that Conrad could have made.[15]

The view that Ford's claim to have written these pages of *Nostromo* was a fiction invented to satisfy Ford's vanity was at least arguable before Professor Morey uncovered this evidence, which remained so long concealed because Mr. Keating feared that this manuscript "might be misunderstood . . . and some doubt thrown on the great Pole's novel." After consulting Ford, who agreed, he omitted all reference to this manuscript from the Conrad Memorial Library, and the Yale Library made no cross-reference to Conrad when it catalogued it. Mr. Keating also decided not to print a letter he had asked Ford to write for the Conrad Memorial Library to explain the whole matter. In that letter Ford said:

The circumstances in which I wrote that small portion of NOS-TROMO were as follows. . . . Whilst I was living in London with Conrad almost next door and coming in practically every day for meals, he was taken with so violent an attack of gout and nervous depression that he was quite unable to continue his installments of NOSTROMO that was then running as a serial in T. P.'s weekly. I therefore simply wrote enough from time to time to keep the

---

*When this fragment of manuscript became a part of the Keating collection (now in the Yale Library) it consisted of fifteen pages, numbered 588–89 and 591–603. Janice Biala later found page 590 among her Ford papers and presented it to Yale. The fragment begins with the words "The *Porvenir* must have a long and confident article . . . " (on p. 175 of the Concord Edition of *Nostromo*) and ends with the words, "She did not answer. She seemed tired and they . . . " (on p. 185 of the Concord Edition of *Nostromo*), breaking off in the middle of a sentence. The full installment in *T. P.'s Weekly* consisted of the first fourteen pages of Chapter Five of Part Two in the Concord Edition of *Nostromo.*

presses going—a job that presented no great difficulties to me. ... But to argue from that that I had any large share in Conrad's writing would be absurd. ... I was practically under oath to Conrad not to reveal these facts owing to the misconceptions that might arise and nothing in the world would have induced me to reveal it now but for the extremely unfortunate sale of these pages.[16]

What Ford did was to write a brief passage in which he made sure nothing significant happened, a set of variations on matter already invented by Conrad in a plausible imitation of Conrad's style. That certainly called for considerable intimacy with the story and considerable ingenuity, but it did not require Ford to create anything in the style of Conrad's imagination. That Ford could do the job he set himself with comparatively little difficulty is evident from the modest amount of revision in the manuscript. It is a pity he did not resist the temptation to point out that this task "presented no great difficulties to me," but it is true.

These three or four months at the beginning of 1904 were, as Ford said long afterwards, "the most terrible period of Conrad's life and of the writer's" and he sank into a depression that was to become much worse before he recovered; his only thought was to run away. He seems to have briefly considered joining George Gissing, the novelist, in Spain but eventually settled on his old haunt, the New Forest, to which he set off by himself late in March, as soon as he had finished *The Soul of London,* leaving Elsie to pack up and close Airlie Gardens.[17]

He found a place called Bridge House at Winterbourne Stoke and there Elsie and the children joined him in May. "This is rather a nice place," he wrote his mother, "very hidden among the downs & extremely remote from civilisation. We have two cottages—in one of which I'm writing & in the other the daily life of the house proceeds. The children are in rude health: Elsie is well and I'm—umberufen—picking up slowly. I trust it's surely, but in this vale of tears one never knows." His letters to Pinker do not pretend to even that much contentment.[18]

In April, 1904, his third volume of poems, *The Face of the Night,* was published; it was much the strongest collection he had yet put together. These are the poems Wells had in mind when he described Ford in *Boon* as "wandering to and fro up and down the corridor, with distraught blue eyes, laying his hands on heads and shoulders, the Only Uncle of the Gifted Young, talking in a languid, plangent tenor, now boasting about trivialities, and now making familiar criticisms (which are invariably ill-received), and occasionally quite absent-mindedly producing splendid poetry. . . . " It was these poems too that impressed Ezra Pound when they were reprinted in *From Inland* (1907). Ford had always had a fine ear for the rhythm of verse and he had had considerable musical training. The poems of *The Questions at the Well* (1893) and *Poems for Pictures* (1900) had been almost verse exercises, mechanically skillful but vague in intention and colorless in phrasing. The poems in *The Face of the Night* are in the post-Tennysonian manner that dominated the time, poems like "Grey Matter," on the baleful effects of science's discoveries (there is even a poem on the death of Queen Victoria to remind us of Tennyson himself); dialect poems spoken by shrewd country folk such as "Old Man's Evensong" and "From the Soil"; and Tennysonian lyrics, touched sometimes with an almost Swinburnian lilt, sometimes with an echo of Herrick. But they are written with considerable distinction.

When Ford echoes Tennyson's "Now sleeps the crimson petal, now the white," he does so with rhythmic subtlety:

> Come in the delicate stillness of dawn,
> Your eyelids heavy with sleep;
> When the faint moon slips to its line—dim-drawn,
> Grey and a shadow, the sea. And deep, very deep,
> The tremulous stillness ere day in the dawn.

If he echoes seventeenth-century songs, it is with real grace:

> You make me think of lavendar,
> And that is why I love you so:
> Your sloping shoulders, heavy hair,
> And long swan's neck like snow,
> Befit those gracious girls of long ago,
> Who in closed gardens took the quiet air. . . .

And just occasionally there is the faint sound of the voice that will dominate the finest of his poems in *On Heaven* and *Buckshee*,

> Up here, where the air's very clear
> And the hills slope away nigh down to the bay,
> It is very like Heaven. . . .

Skillful though they were, the poems in *The Face of the Night* were scarcely noticed. "They won't I fear, set the Thames on fire," he had written his mother, "but such as they are, they are." He was right; when Wells wrote him to express his admiration, Ford replied "that after 3 months of pub^{n} I have had FIVE reviews (of wh. three are provincial & four contemptuous.)."[19]

The worst thing about his breakdown was that he could not write.

Instead, he scribbled long letters to people that were more admonitions to himself than serious inquiries. "I am always," he wrote Dr. Garnett,

> digging into the times of Henry VIII F[ides] D[efensor] &c.
> ... What I particularly want to discover is: to what extent the theological struggles of the Reformation were affected—in the case, say of the upholders of the Six articles—by the Homoousian &c struggles of Athanasius—and to what extent the (Latin) Classicism of the Renaissance reacted upon, say, the same six articles.

He was not making these interests up, but he could not make himself write about them; he could only pretend he could. "How gladly," he wrote H. G. Wells, "I wd. change with you & sympathise, if only I cd. be 1/10th of a live man once more!"[20]

He began to brood in a damaging way about his inability to find a publisher for *The Benefactor* and *The Soul of London*, and developed a persecuted feeling that he had been talked into sacrificing *Seraphina* against his own best interests. As a result he asked Conrad to repay him the £ 100 Conrad owed him. Because Conrad understood Ford's condition, he took no offense at this request, though he could not resist a suggestion that he was more ill than Ford.

> I am awfully grieved to hear of your state. Mine though not identical is just as bad in its way and surely less excusable....
> I am making strenuous efforts and shall persevere therein till I am able to send you ... not the whole hundred as yet but some appreciable part at least.[21]

During that May at Winterbourne Stoke Ford thus got steadily worse, and it was decided he should go to Germany, the usual recourse at this time for anyone with nervous troubles. His condition was such that, though he could not endure family life, neither could he bear solitude. He found being shut up in the country with Elsie and the children intolerable. "Winterbourne Stoke," he wrote Elsie after he reached Germany, "was a fiasco." He left for Germany early in June, under some difficulties: his agoraphobia was so bad that he could not get up the ship's gangplank without support, a trouble that was to be with him in milder forms for the rest of his life; "And I suffer, anyhow, badly from the *maladie des hauteurs*," he remarked as late as *Great Trade Route*.[22]

> [Ford] has really in the last year had more worries & anxieties than any mortal can bear [Elsie wrote Mrs. Hueffer].
> He cannot get about at all or else he would come to see you.

I wonder if you could go to see him off. He will start on Saturday. . . . He thinks it better for me not to go up [to London] again
for many reasons. This letter I'm afraid is very incoherent but I am
tired & worn out to distraction with all this misery.

Yours affec^{ly}

Elsie M. Hueffer

Tunnycliffe [their doctor] thinks it better that he should go without
me—but it is hard to bear as we have never once been separated for
so long since our marriage.[23]

Ford went straight to Boppard, a town of approximately 5,500 people on
the Rhine some fifteen kilometers above Coblenz, where his two Hueffer
aunts lived. They were very good to him. "I get on remarkably well with
the Goesens," he wrote Elsie. "Here I am treated as a sort of demi-god.
. . . I can now walk anywhere, particularly when I've someone with me." As
some return for this kindness, he dedicated a book to each of his aunts, "To
Frau Laura Schmedding who has so often combated my prejudices and
corrected my assertions" he dedicated Privy Seal, and "To Frau Regierung-
srat Emma Goesen who returned from New York more than a generation
ago and has since beaten the author thirty-one times out of thirty-two games
of chess," An English Girl. But Ford needed something more than kindness.
It depressed him to think that all his troubles were probably imaginary. "For
supposing it to be nothing but hypochondria," he wrote Elsie after his arrival
in Germany, "I'm a pretty miserable skunk." What was worse, he became
unendurably homesick the moment he got to Germany:

> God, to be in Romney Marsh
> And see the ships above the wall—
> I'd give these lakes and alps and all
> For just an hour of storm and shower,
> And just a glimpse of Lydd church tower,
> And just to hear the wind in the thorns—
> Just not to hear the cowbells' din,
> Just not to hear the cowmen's horns—
> But just to mark the tide come in,
> Dear God by Romney Wall[.]

"I live," he said, "in a state of hourly apprehension of going mad. I fancy
homesickness does as much to pull me down as anything else." When he was
not convinced he was going mad, he was convinced that he was dying, and for
the rest of his life he thought he had been; at the very end of it he still saying,

. . . years ago . . . I was seized upon by one German nerve-specialist after another and sent further and further towards Central Europe in one hydropathic establishment after another. . . . I all but died.[24]

As soon as he reached Boppard he began struggling to write his book on Holbein; he knew how desperate Elsie was to find money for his trip. His efforts to write greatly distressed his aunts. Tante Emma attempted to combat them by depriving him of candles. When this did not work, Tante Laura offered to give him the amount of money he estimated he would make on the Holbein book if he would promise to stop working on it. He accepted this proposal and immediately made plans to visit Münster, the original home of the Hueffer family.

At first the visit was a great success; Ford was, as usual, happy when he was traveling. At Münster he found, as he said, "half a hundred Hueffers" who took him shooting at Markfurt and kept him busy in dozens of other ways. Even better, he met at Telgte—that "queer, Dutch-looking little town with its pleached alleys and its hidden ways amongst thorn-bushes and Wand-haecke" —the Schückings, with whom he could be literary in the most satisfactory way.

The feeling of age in the [Schücking] place was somehow tremen-dous [he wrote Elsie]: Mrs. L[evin] S[chücking] is still alive—and two grandsons, one Lothar and one Levin. Lothar is not interesting: but as for Levin I'm sure you'd have fallen in love with him. He's in face *exactly* like Stephen Crane, only quite dark, six foot six high and dressed in brown corduroy. He's naturally a poet. And to sit before the great grate, with big logs on the dogs, burning in the great Geor-gian drawing room with all the portraits of Schückings from centuries back, on the walls and an ancient garden, all alleys, clipped hedges, old trees and moonlight and mist—and to listen to Levin reading his own poems with tremendous force and verve in a sort of suppressed baying voice—all that was most memorable really.

I don't know that it was any less memorable to read my own verses—and to feel that one's own work—good as theirs was—was better. And to feel that they felt it was better—that too was an emo-tion!—You've no idea how d——d intelligent these people are (I mean the Schückings and the Droste-Hülshess who live next door in an old castle). . . .

This recovered confidence in the superiority of his own work sounds promis-ing, but the excitement of the Münster visit was too much for him and he had a bad relapse. When he was well enough to move, he went back to Boppard.[25]

Meanwhile Elsie's difficulties were multiplying. She had returned to Win-chelsea as soon as the Bungalow was free, but without the rent for it she was short of money. Ford urged her to press Robert Garnett for the income on his investments he believed had accumulated and urged her not to spend any of her own money, above all not to mortgage Hurst Cottage in Aldington, "which is after all a sort of final asylum." Ford's investments consisted of two properties in London that had been purchased in 1896 for £ 779.17.6, the Hurst Cottage, which had been purchased in 1901 for £ 150, and £ 500 invested at 5 percent. The income from these assets was £ 75.17.0 a year, but this income was offset by the interest owed on debts of £ 425 to Mrs. Hueffer, Martha Garnett, and Miss Wanostrom; this interest amounted to £ 27 a year and reduced the income from their investments to under £ 50, none of which was, for the moment, available, despite Ford's hopes. In addition to these assets, there was what Ford had lent Conrad, which, together with the arrears of rent on the Pent, came to nearly £ 200.

"As for Conrad," Ford said at the conclusion of this financial discussion, "of course I don't mind you writing him." The idea of asking Conrad for the money he owed had been suggested to Elsie by Robert Garnett, who had written her, "*Entre nous* I think F. wd. be very glad if Conrad paid up. . . . If he paid £ 3 a week thro Pinker it would be a very considerable help. I feel sure that if you do not yourself get the money or induce F. to do so it will eventually be *lost*." With Ford's permission, then, Elsie wrote Conrad, who answered,

> N[ostromo] is finished and in some fifteen days or so the money (what there's left of it) shall be coming in and I shall forward you £ *20*. . . .
> I would send at once but on delivery of MS (on the 31stAug) Pinker had to pay off my overdraft at Watson's. . . . Nearly £ 200! in one fell swoop.

But if, as usual, ready cash was beyond Conrad's powers, he was eager to give all the help he could.

> Yesterday I saw Pinker . . . [who] says that should F. feel able to write anything on Germany special efforts shall be made to place it to advantage. I could not see Dunn (of the Mg Pst) yesterday but shall write him a careful and cautious letter as to corrce from Gny—(so, you understand, as not to engage Ford who may be as yet unable to write) but to prepare the way.

Nothing came of these efforts; Ford published no journalism at all between March, 1904, and February, 1906. In spite of Ford's admonitions about mortgaging Hurst Cottage Elsie now decided to add a studio for Ford to the Bungalow at Winchelsea. It cost £ 250, which she obtained from a mortgage.[26]

In Boppard Ford went back to work on his Holbein book, despite his agreement with Tante Laura not to.

> I'm making good progress with the Holbein [he wrote Elsie]. I shall have to, though I rather dread it, make the rundreiser Bâle, Damstadt, Leipzig and Berlin. It seems to tax my eyes a good deal to write. Probably I shall go to Wiesbaden to Pagensticker about them. . . . I hope Conrad has forked up. If he hasn't I'd better send you some of my money. They've a regular name here for lack of walking power —platz angst.

He was, for the first time since his trouble had begun, able to sleep without bromides, but, as this letter shows, he was still suffering from agoraphobia. He had stopped smoking, which may have helped, for he was a chain smoker. Toward the end of the month he got over to Wiesbaden to see Dr. Pagensticker, who told him there was nothing the matter with his eyes: he had "gout in the brows"—whatever that may have been.[27]

But, like Christopher Tietjens in the trenches of the First World War, he found that his anxiety attached itself most to things back home. He worried about Christina, who was now seven. Ford had insisted on the girls' being brought up Catholics so that they might, as he put it, have something to hold on to when trouble came. Now an opportunity arose for Christina to go as a boarding student to La Sagesse Convent school in Rye and Elsie was eager to take advantage of it. The idea frightened Ford: "You never know what nuns get up to," he wrote Elsie, " . . . she's such a loyal little thing." Eventually he gave in—the opportunity was too good to miss—but he remained anxious. "I daresay," he said, "you're wise about Christina but I rather regret it." The wisdom—at least from his point of view—of that regret was to be proved by the event.

He also felt anxious about more pressing matters—his career as a serious writer, success, money. But much of his worry was neurotic, a product of the destructive clash between his dreams of glory and the actualities of his existence. In his concern for these things, there was the angry despair of a man confronted by difficulties he felt were wholly underserved. Before leaving England he had borrowed £ 50 from William Rossetti; he now insisted on paying it back at once, though where he proposed to get enough to do so it is not easy to imagine and perhaps he had not tried to. In his generous way, Rossetti wrote him, "Pray think no more about that tin. This stroke of the pen wipes it out, and it is a free gift. Were I otherwise minded, I might leave off signing W.M. Rossetti, and ought in conscience to sign henceforth Shylock—who was himself a most conscientious man." But since much of

Ford's anxiety was free-floating, the removal of any object to which it had momentarily attached itself only sent it in search of another. He immediately began to fret over *The Soul of London*'s failure to find a publisher.[28]

Like William Rossetti, Conrad was trying hard to think of ways to help Ford; when Ford wrote him a letter full of observations about Germany, he at once suggested that Ford go on writing him such letters, which he would arrange and, with Pinker's help, get published. "Directly I get something," he asserted with quite uncharacteristic confidence, "I shall make a sort of expedition [to London to sell it]—a crusade." He was eager to convince Ford of Pinker's desire to help.

> In the state of nerves from which you suffer any mention of Pinker may be exasperating. But it is unavoidable. . . . The fact is my dear boy that without understanding you in the least the man likes you personally. He also nurses in his mind a by no means irrational idea of your usefulness. You are for him the man who can write anything at any time—and write it well—he means in a not ordinary way.

This was not only a practical letter aimed at Ford's anxiety about his career and money; it was a letter calculated to encourage him to believe in himself once again. Ford always suspected that the businessmen of the writing world were, in some mysteriously wicked way, responsible for the failure of his career to satisfy his expectations. This suspicion was essentially defensive, the result of a fear that such people were better judges of his work than he was, that if they did not believe in it it did not deserve admiration. To be told by Conrad that Pinker was incapable of understanding him but nonetheless admired him and—what was perhaps even more important—liked him was the best medicine that could be given him.[29]

With the disconcerting insight that Ford showed even in his most disturbed times, he recognized Conrad's motives. "I had a long and particularly loving letter from C. this morning," he wrote Elsie. "He really seems to be doing his best for me." That best was not, unhappily, enough. In the very next paragraph of his letter to Elsie, Ford suggests that she and the girls come out to Germany and settle there permanently. Elsie replied by listing the difficulties in the way of such a plan. Then she was told by Ford that such suggestions were "mostly part of the disease." That was no doubt true enough, but it must have been disturbing to Elsie to realize that it was quite impossible to distinguish between Ford's responsible assertions and the assertions that were part of the disease. This was a kind of difficulty he was to create at other times for other people; he was a man capable at any moment of being wholly irresponsible in the most convincing way.[30]

When Ford showed no signs of improvement during September, the doctors hopefully pulled a number of his teeth. No benefits ensued from this measure either and Ford's despair grew deeper. "I have the feeling," he wrote Elsie, "that if I could be back with you my troubles would vanish, but alas they probably would not being deep within my nature." He was determined, whatever the doctors or his aunts might say, to get at least to Basel for work on his Holbein book; Berlin, he had decided, would be too expensive. He set off for Basel on October 3. As always, a new place cheered him up momentarily and he wrote Elsie at length about the "mountains of [Holbein] material" at Basel, about the Kaufmanns, cousins of his father in Basel who were very kind to him, and about the professor in whose house he lodged.

> He had lost his only daughter and could not bear the silence of his immensely tall, gloomy, ancient and crowstepped house. He had filled it with clocks—every imaginable type of Swiss clock. There was thus a continual ticking, striking, chiming and cuckooing whilst the poor man continually wept. The noise of the clocks was not disagreeable but the gloom of the house was profound.

Here he got a considerable amount of the Holbein written. But the gloom, the work, and his longing for home were soon troubling him again. He did not like Uhlemann, the doctor at Basel; he hated the baths; and "poor Uncle Hermann [in Bonn] was dying." In the middle of October Ford broke down again. He described himself as even worse than at Winterbourne Stoke. Elsie was so disturbed that she wired him twice asking if she could not come out to him, but Ford asked her not to.[31]

It was then decided that he should try the Kurabstalt at Mammern, on the Boden See, and the Kaufmann cousins took on the considerable task of transferring him there from Basel. He liked it no better than any place else he had been. "I [took]," he said later, "ninety cold baths and thirty tepid soda water douches in thirty days. I was so weak that, even if the so-called agoraphobia had not interfered with my walking I should hardly have been able to get about." "Dearest Kid," he wrote his daughter Katharine,

> Here is where pumpums is now: he has got to get up at 6 o'clock & sit in a bath for an hour: at 11 o'clock he has an electric bath & at 3 a cold footbath. . . .

Nonetheless he stuck it out at Mammern. His condition fluctuated throughout the month. Sometimes he was well enough to walk over to Stein for tea; then he would fall back into depression and agoraphobia. Finally the family

decided he would have to have someone with him, and since both the
English doctors and Ford himself objected to Elsie, Mrs. Hueffer decided to
go out: she got to Mammern late in October.[32]

On her arrival Ford wrote that he was feeling more cheerful and he
immediately decided to leave Mammern. He had another relapse at Basel,
but by the beginning of November he was back at Boppard, despite bad
feelings between Mrs. Hueffer and Tante Emma that made the situation
awkward there, and was being treated at the Marienberg Kaltwasser-Heilanstalt; one of the relatives there reported to Elsie that he looked twice as ill
as when he left Boppard a month earlier.

Marienberg seemed to him "the most horrible of all the monstrous
institutions that had tortured" him yet. "I was fed on pork and ice-cream and
salad made with lemon juice and white of egg," he said; there was nothing
he so much resented as a bad salad. "In the effort to prove that my troubles
had an obscure sexual origin ["the director of the Kaltwasser-Heilanstalt"]
would suddenly produce from his desk and flash before my eyes indecent
photographs of a singular banality." Given Ford's deeply romantic attitude
toward sex and his Victorian distaste for the clinical view of it, there is
something grimly comic about the persistence with which these German
doctors dwelt on the subject; it seemed to him to follow him everywhere.
Once, when he had been thinking about a gold christening cup he had seen
on the way to the doctor's office, the doctor "put his head suddenly around
the door" as he sat in the outer office "and asked menacingly":

> "*Uber was speculieren Sie?*"
> I said innocently and without premeditation:
> "*Eine goldene Tasse, Herr Wirklicher Geheimrath!*"
> His face lit up with the pleasure of cross-examining coun-
> sel who had caught out a hostile witness.
> "*Kurz und gut,*" he said, "you are suffering from ... " some
> sexual disorder or other.

Ford had now tried nearly six months of the most modern cures German nerve specialists could invent—soda-water douches, pork-and-ice-cream
diets, and indecent photographs—without any visible improvement. He decided to go home, a change that was made easier for him by William Rossetti's offering to lend him his house for the winter so that he did not have to
return to Winchelsea and the unavoidable strains of family life. By Christmas
he was back in London, at 3 St. Edmund's Terrace.[33]

Chapter 10

At first Ford isolated himself at 3 St. Edmund's Terrace, staying in bed a great deal and reading endlessly. He filled his bedroom with birds—"African wax-billed finches and parakeets"; he found watching them soothing. Conrad urged him to try the doctor who had helped with Jessie's knee during the previous fall; this was Albert E. Tebb, a friend of William Rossetti and a great admirer of Ford Madox Brown, at whose sale in 1894 Ford had first encountered him. Tebb eventually became the doctor for everyone in the group—Conrad and Jessie, Ford and Elsie, even Violet Hunt. He was a

> queer, clever, weedy man who stooped so for despair, not laziness. Himself he could not save. But you called him and he came, hasting, his baggy umbrella in front of him, the flaps of his greatcoat nearly touching the ground, looking like Santa Claus or the Old Clo' Man bringing the babies. . . . He was a magician, a wonder-doctor, as one would have expected from his quack-like appearance, white-complexioned, blue-eyed, bewildered. . . . He was always poor—and likely to remain so.

Poor, in fact, he did remain: in the thirties he wrote Ford from the Royal Hospital for the Incurables, an impoverished old man who had had to sell everything he owned, even his precious autographed Conrad first editions. Ford ascribed his recovery from his long breakdown to Tebb, and in *Return to Yesterday* he tells an unlikely story of the melodramatic method Tebb used to cure him.*[1]

*According to Ford, Tebb said to him "with a hollow and mournful vindictiveness" that he would be dead in a month. This immediately cured his agoraphobia. "As soon as he was gone I jumped up, dressed myself and . . . took a hansom to Piccadilly Circus. . . . I walked backwards and forwards across the circus for an hour and a half. I kept on saying: 'Damn that brute. I will not be dead in a month.'" At the end of the month he confronted Tebb and "said trium-

But Ford could not long endure to be alone. In January he went down to Sandgate for a week and by the first of February he had moved back to Winchelsea. Then Elsie fell ill and the whole family had to be moved to Mrs. Martindale's house at 93 Broadhurst Gardens so that she could be properly cared for. This was the first sign of Elsie's tubercular kidney. Unfortunately, it was not properly diagnosed until 1908.

At first, with the recollection of his own suffering vivid in his mind, Ford was very kind to Elsie, spending long hours reading to her and doing everything he could to make her happy, but as he himself recovered and—after 1905—became involved in the literary life of London, he grew less patient with her; he became convinced that her illness was imaginary. Elsie's unhappiness over this refusal to believe in her suffering led to scenes of the kind that upset Ford badly.[2]

Even when his sympathy with Elsie's illness was greatest, Ford could not stand the atmosphere of Broadhurst Gardens for long, and he was soon begging Jerrold to come with him to Winchelsea: "Supposing you could manage it, if you c^d turn up at B^{dhst} G^{dns} (Finchley Road) about lunch tomorrow we c^d start at once—for anywhere you like; even to the Isles of the Blest!" He was evidently feeling a good deal better. When Conrad, who had committed himself to an extravagant plan for taking Jessie to Capri to recuperate from her knee operation, sailed from Dover, Ford managed to get there to see them off. Then his books began to sell. Pinker finally placed *The Benefactor* with Brown, Langham, though without an advance. With unaccustomed good humor Ford told him, "As far as I am concerned, B.L. & C. can have the *Altruist* without advance. . . . I admire your patience [in persisting with the book]: I should certainly have despaired years ago!" Pinker also placed *The Soul of London*, with a new firm of publishers called Alston Rivers.[3]

By March Elsie was well enough to be up and about again, and she went on a trip to France to recuperate; she stayed abroad until May. During these months Ford wandered back and forth between Winchelsea and London, a pattern he continued to follow after Elsie's return, on the theory that his illness required it. He was certainly not entirely well that spring and lived much of the time at Dr. Tebb's house in Finchley Road. In April he remarked sardonically to Walter Jerrold that he was "writing, at the rate of 20 words a day, a life of Holbein for Duckworth." Still, he was writing, and

---

phantly: 'You see, I am not dead.' " Tebb said, "If I hadn't told you you would be dead you would have been dead."

when Pinker placed his books, Ford began to recover rapidly from the depression he had lived with so long—for years, it seemed to him. "The illness," he said afterwards, "was purely imaginary; that made it none the better. . . . I had nothing specific to be depressed about. But the memory of those years is one of uninterrupted mental agony. Nothing marks them off one from the other. They were lost years."[4]

Then he had another piece of luck. René Byles, the managing director of Alston Rivers, the publishers of *The Soul of London*, made the book a success. According to Ford, Byles "succeeded in buttonholing Lord North-cliffe actually in the composing room of [the *Daily Mail*] and then and there read him some extracts from [Ford's] book," and Northcliffe promised to review the book himself and give it at least a column in "the precious middle page" of the paper. Only Ford was likely to believe the magic of his prose so powerful that a few extracts could produce these results; and in fact they did not: *The Soul of London* was reviewed in the *Daily Mail* by Edmund Candler. Still, it was given special treatment; Candler gave it a full column of praise on the day of publication, a Tuesday (the *Daily Mail* usually printed reviews only on Thursdays).

Ford also said that Byles, having extracted the promise of a personal review from Northcliffe, then used this promise to persuade the other papers to give equal prominence to *The Soul of London*, so that on publication day Ford felt "like a cat in a coruscation of fireworks. I could not open a paper, morning or evening, without seeing my name in 'leaded caps.' " This is exaggerated, but in addition to the *Daily Mail*, the *Daily News* and the *Morning Post* carried enthusiastic reviews on publication day. In reporting the news of Ford's success to Galsworthy, Edward Garnett says Byles "happened to strike on Harmsworth accidentally—and H. read the book for 10 minutes, and said 'We'll give it a column.' " He then adds that Byles used this promise to get space in the *Chronicle* and the *Daily News;* this sounds possible, but Garnett may be repeating an early version of Ford's story rather than anything he got directly from Byles.[5]

In any event, Ford's account of this episode shows the effect it had on his morale. This effect grew with the appearance of enthusiastic reviews in the weeklies and monthlies. Ford often claimed that he found reviews of his own books painful and never read them. His account of seeing his name in every paper the day *The Soul of London* appeared hardly supports this claim, though he certainly found reviews painful, as do most authors—who nevertheless do read their reviews. As Ford disarmingly said of reviews: "If they praised me I used to think that I could do it better myself; if they blamed me it upset me." When *The Heart of the Country* appeared in May, 1906, he fled to Oxford in the hope of escaping the temptation to read its reviews. On the other hand, in a canceled passage of "Working with Joseph Conrad," Ford defended himself against the charge that he "was a seedy sort of fellow, parasitic on a popular author" in his relations with Conrad by asserting that "three times did books of mine receive seventeen reviews in the papers on the days [of] their issue and Lord Northcliffe himself wrote a review of one of them which the publisher told me—for I did not see it—took up the greater part of a page in the *Daily Mail.*" However vague Ford's memory of the reviews of *The Soul of London* may have become later, it seems unlikely that he did not read them or that they were not a major cause of his dramatic recovery. "But for [Byles]," he said later, "it is almost certain that I should have given up writing. But his enthusiasm for my work was extraordinary and infectious. He almost made me believe in myself. He certainly made the newspapers believe in me. . . . " This at least was the opinion of his friends. " . . . you will be interested to hear that Hueffer has at last been boomed, boomed furiously!" Edward Garnett wrote Galsworthy, "and has come into his own. I am so very, very glad. I think that this success may go a long way to putting him definitely on his feet . . . for if ever a man wanted recognition, poor Ford does." "May it," Galsworthy answered, "be more than a passing boom, and cheer him into perfect health again."[6]

This was a shrewd qualification; all those leaded caps, "the rather overpowering reception of the work," as Ford called it, overstimulated him; he swung from depression to hysterical cheerfulness and an exaggerated opinion of his own fame and influence. *The Soul of London* did not make him a fortune. Still, its acclaim put him on his feet again. "I had neither aims nor strong motives before [his breakdown]," he said. "I have had some since."[7]

Ford's conduct throughout the rest of his life was not so reasonable as that suggests, but it is true that those agonizing years of depression followed by this success gave him a new view of himself. He now saw himself as an important writer with considerable influence, and except during his second breakdown a decade later, he was never again quite so uncertain about what he was as he had been up to this time. This new view of himself often led him to make claims that did him a good deal of harm; it encouraged him to show much too openly his feeling of superiority to everyone not his particular kind of artist.

It also created a psychological problem for him. He had become convinced that he was an important writer before he had anything serious to say, or at least before he could consciously command what he had to say. For all his devotion to great literature, Ford never could consistently distinguish between his real insights and the merely clever ideas of his surface self. His best work depended, not so much on an act of the will, as on moments when a combination of accidental circumstances made it possible for him to express his deepest understanding of his experience. This situation made it extraordinarily difficult for him to recognize his own best insights. He was not in fact to do so fully until he had begun to suffer his second major breakdown just before the war. But this first breakdown did make it possible for him to define, if not very clearly, something that was new to his work, and the best novels he was to write between 1905 and 1915 are different from the work he had done up to this time, none of which, with the exception of a few poems, was more than charming.

This was certainly true of *The Soul of London* and its two sequels, *The Heart of the Country* (1906), and *The Spirit of the People* (1907). They are the best of his early nonfiction; "it *is* very good, you know," Edward Garnett said of *The Soul of London;* "the best thing he's done." These books have an easiness and an insight Ford had not before shown. When he comes, for example, to consider the poor of London, he has what is for his time the rare insight that the poor have their own values and their own pride that make the ideas of reformers irrelevant. Watching a woman who makes matchboxes at 2 3/4d. the 144, he thinks,

> You could not pity her because she was so obviously and wonderfully equipped for her particular struggle: you could not wish to "raise" her, for what could she do in any other light, in any other air? Here at least she was strong, heroic, settled and beyond any condemnation.
>
> As for ideals . . . she would utter long bursts of language that was a mixture of meaningless obscenities and of an old fashioned and formal English. She did not see why the Irish were allowed in Southwark, and . . . she had stuck the carving knife through the arm of a drunken man because he had tried to come into her room one night when her man was in hospital. She laughed hoarsely at the idea and made feints with her hands.

A passage like this shows a remarkable imaginative grasp of the life of the urban poor. Rowntree and the Edwardian sociologists were studying these people, but as Samuel Hynes has pointed out, "for nearly twenty years, from Maugham's *Liza of Lambeth* to Frank Swinnerton's *Nocturne,* there was no important realistic novel published" about the urban poor, no work, that is, with Ford's kind of understanding of their lives.[8]

But all three of these books are limited by Ford's commitment to impressionism; they are, as he says, "not a statement of facts [but] precisely a set of analyses of feelings" about a random selection of subjects such as "Roads into London" or "Work in London." They are collections of personal essays within each of which Ford allows his thoughts to drift from vignettes of London life to random personal feelings ("For myself, when on a train into London, I feel almost invariably a sense of some pathos and some poetry," etc.). He plays with contrasts of "the psychological London," "the Administrative County," and "the London of natural causes"; he muses over why the greater talkers of an earlier London have disappeared; he allows "It would be fanciful to make Buonaparte too responsible for the Modern Type [of London adventurer]" and then develops that fancy at length. The only persistent attitude in these books is their unanalyzed mixture of Ford's love of things as they are, especially if they have been that way for a long time, and his almost Wellsian feeling for the romance of technology and social change.

It is typical of him that he notes—"alas perhaps"—that the old steam-driven, smoke-choked underground "has been 'electrified,' at American hands and there is one of our glamours [of London] gone." At the same time he draws a horrifying picture of the London this sentimental conservative would in fact create, "a vast stretch of mounds, a gigantic quagmire with here and there a pillar of a mediaeval church serving as a perch for a hawk's nest . . . an immense Town, shut off from the rest of the world, black, walled in, peopled by gibbering neurasthenics, a prey to hysterias, useless for work, getting no pleasures from horrible self-indulgences . . . a City of dreadful Night. . . . "

What gives these books the superiority to Ford's earlier work that Edward Garnett noted is not a change in his ideas or even in his capacity to organize them; in them he does what he has always done, give us his personal impression; but here he does so with much greater skill.

> And in the hearts of [London's] children [London] will still be
> something like a cloud—a cloud of little experiences, of little personal
> impressions, of small, futile things that, seen in moments of stress and
> anguish, have significances so tremendous and meanings so poignant.
> A cloud—as it were of the dust of men's lives.[9]

The critical success of *The Soul of London* made the summer of 1905 hectically exciting for Ford. "This is SUCCESS at last," he wrote his mother when he sent her half-a-dozen newspaper clippings of reviews. At the same time he was sending his usual letter to Pinker: "I'd be glad if you'd make [Alston] Rivers fork up for the *London*, the money being due & I mildly hard up." He had joined the National Liberal Club, where he saw Masterman and Wells and several friends of more recent times, such as Jerrold and Byles. He began turning up regularly at Edward Garnett's Tuesday luncheons at the Mont Blanc restaurant in Gerrard Street, where he met Thomas Seccombe, Hilaire Belloc, Chesterton, W. H. Hudson, J. D. Beresford and H. M. Tomlinson, Conrad and Arthur Marwood. At these meetings, Ford said, "the elect of the city's intelligentsia lunched and discussed with grave sobriety the social problems of the day . . . under the presidency of Mr. Edward Garnett, who has for so long been London's literary—if Nonconformist—Pope. . . . " One of them remembered how Ford's "light blue [eyes] . . . twinkled gaily when he was amused . . . [and] his too mobile lips were sensitive and in some of his moods would open into an engaging smile. He was tall and, at that time . . . still comparatively slender; the paunch which a little later was to become too pronounced had not yet developed—or not much; and the flabbiness under the chin which in middle life overemphasized his Teutonic origin was not yet conspicuous." "In my day in London," Ford said later, remembering his mood of this time, "one —if you will pardon the expression—bloody well knew that London was the bloody world and if anything went wrong anywhere one said that something must be done about it . . . and something was done about it. That at least was the frame of mind."[10]

Ford and Conrad had seen little of each other for the last year and a half. Ford had been abroad for most of 1904 and during the spring of 1905 Conrad was in Capri and Ford preoccupied with his new career. They would never again be as close as they had been at Airlie Gardens, but this summer they saw more of each other. Conrad wanted to turn his short story, "To-morrow," into the play that was eventually produced at the Royal Theatre under the title *One Day More* on June 25, 26, and 27, a production that, according to Conrad, "the very smart audience did not catch on" to but Shaw admired. Conrad first mentioned this play in a letter to Wells of February 7, 1904, in which he also discussed the way he was dictating *The Mirror of the Sea* to Ford. Nothing more is heard of it until sometime early in 1905, when Ford wrote Pinker:

I am sending you herewith
I m.s. of the Fifth Queen—the 2/3ds finished novel
    I spoke of—which you might offer Methuen.
II The second chapter of The Heart of the Country, which

pray have typed.
III The m.s. of the play.

Shortly after this he wrote Pinker:

> Granville Barker—of the Court Theatre—is "anxiousish" to see
> a play of mine.
> Would you in a day or two—since I don't want to impress him
> with a sense of my anxiety—forward him that one I sent you—&
> would you impress him with the idea that it's merely in a sketchy
> stage? & that C. & I would work it up any amount if there were a
> definite chance of production—but not otherwise?

In his next letter to Pinker, he says, "Certainly you can say the play is by
self & Conrad—C., that is, will do more to it if there is a reasonable certainty
of its being accepted—&, for all I sh^d care, he c'^{d} call it quite his own." The
suggestion of these letters that Ford had done the actual dramatization of
One Day More is borne out by the existence of forty-three pages of manuscript of the play in Ford's hand.

Conrad had told Wells that he was doing the dramatization of "To-
morrow" at the suggestion of Sidney Colvin, and in April Colvin asked him
whether the play was actually his. Conrad's answer is curiously defensive.

> The facts are that Hueffer ... helped me by ... taking out the dia-
> logue of the story in a typewritten extract. ... The play ... has been
> written entirely in my own hand. ... Five minutes' perusal will show
> you the genuineness of [Ford's] disclaimer.

When all the arrangements for the play's production had been completed,
Conrad wrote Ford that "I hadn't the pluck to write you—not even after the
telegram about the Play.—not after your good letter which saddened me a
little and augmented my desire to see you very much." This makes it look
as if Ford's telegram and letter had been sent—in reply to a request from
Conrad—to make sure he and Conrad were in a tale about the play. Conrad
then adds an odd explanation of why he had put the play forward as entirely
his own.

> And *à propos de tout cela*, if I inquired what you wished done, re
> Play, it was mostly from the feeling that you did *not* like the thing
> anyhow. And as I feel also it's going to fail in the end, I could not
> without your distinct authorization associate you with what I be-
> lieve will be a sort of 'four'[.]

When he got back to the Pent, Conrad kept Ford informed about progress of rehearsals and invited him to join them in their box for the perfor-

mance on the night of June 27, though Ford did not do so. Apparently *One Day More* was—like *The Mirror of the Sea*—one of Ford's attempts to help Conrad by writing something for him; the two attempts were made at the same time, in the early weeks of 1904.[11]

William Rossetti, who had in April asked Ford if he would like, for a fee, to assist Rossetti in revising his articles for the new edition of the *Britannica*, now wrote to offer to let him off if he had more remunerative work available to him, adding with his usual generosity, "It looks as if this year were destined to rid the memory of all the horrid tribulations of last year." But Ford was now ready for anything, including articles for the *Britannica*, even though Pinker was pressing him to write *The Fifth Queen* and "the story of the man who went back to the 13th century," that is, *Ladies Whose Bright Eyes.* "All this," he told Elsie, "encouraged me so much that I came back and wrote 2,500 words straight off."[12]

He must have continued to write at that pace, judging by the amount of work he got through during the summer and fall of 1905. He completely revised his book on Holbein for Duckworth and selected and arranged the illustrations for it; in July he finished *The Heart of the Country,* the first of the two sequels to *The Soul of London;* in September he sent Alston Rivers about half of *The Fifth Queen.* The results of this burst of work showed up during the next year. *Hans Holbein* was published in December, 1905; an artist friend later told him that his career as a writer "shall not certainly be justified by that alone," a judgment he agreed with. But the book had kept him going through a dark period and his research for it was invaluable to him when he came to write *The Fifth Queen,* which was published in March, 1906, and was followed only two months later by *The Heart of the Country.* In December, 1906, there came, finally, *Christina's Fairy Book.* "Hueffer's work," Conrad wrote Norman Douglas, "was kept off for 3 years and now it is all going as easy as can be."[13]

In July Elsie moved to Hurst Cottage in Aldington, possibly because she had just found out about Ford's affair with Mary Martindale. This may also have been her reason for going to the Continent with Mrs. Hueffer and Christina in July; they went to Boulogne and stayed at Etaples and Montreuil-sur-Mer until late September. In August she urged Ford to join them at Etaples; she was anxious about Christina, who was now eager to become a Catholic. Ford found it impossible to go at once: "Graham is starting weekly dinners of the Academy staff and wants me to attend them," he wrote, adding that Graham had given him carte blanche to write anything he wished for the *Academy.* Late in August, however, he managed to pull himself away from these seductions long enough to run over to Etaples.[14]

When Elsie returned to Winchelsea, Ford left Tebb's house in London and came back to Hurst Cottage, though he continued to spend much of his time in London. He was, as always, short of money. He tried to get Pinker to sell "the Country book" (presumably *The Heart of the Country*) though he admitted the justice of Pinker's objection to trying to sell unfinished work and there were only four and a half chapters of the book written: "Do you think [Alston Rivers] c^d be got to stand £ 75 advance for it? I sh^d be gladdish of a small sum." When Alston Rivers refused to make this advance, Ford tried Pinker himself: "I am rather in want of ready money. Could you advance me, say, £ 75—at your usual terms—on The Heart of the Country & such sales as there may be of *The Benefactor?* . . . I sh'^d *imagine* the security is good enough. I spent a couple of days with Conrad & read *Chance*. I think it's really like to do . . . the trick of popularity—this time."[15]

In October, Brown, Langham brought out *The Benefactor*, the novel Ford had completed some two years earlier. It is a far more professional piece of fiction than anything he had yet written. The social background, the Edwardian age's mixture of belated Victorians and unscrupulous new men, is skillfully represented. This was a world in which the country abounded in idealistic Victorian girls like Ford's heroine, Dora Brede, and clergymen like her father, who was trying to adjust himself to new ideas of reform by organizing societies for keeping the peasants on the land in which the main activity is the competition for office among the wealthy patrons. In London it was a world where the new rich struggled to be recognized by the aristocracy and the cunning climbers struggled to attach themselves to the rich.

It was an age of social reform; the ideas for the welfare state were worked out over the next decade of Liberal government. It was also an age of unprecedented extravagance, and of the relaxation of barriers which, if they were partly a matter of snobbery, were also partly a matter of moral posture: if Queen Victoria's conduct was absurd, that of her son Edward was both vulgar and a little ominous. Edward made a practice of extending his patronage to bankers who would make him a profit in the market, and something like that is the reason the rich Mrs. Moffat of *The Benefactor* takes up the clever climber, Hailes, who has a plan for selling cheap Spanish paintings in London for high prices. Hailes is a man almost comically baffled when he is confronted with anybody not wholly motivated by greed; Mrs. Moffat has captured Hailes by deliberately playing on his greed, though she yearns to find in him affection and loyalty. Ford's "artist," Thwaites, has a small-minded passion for money concealed beneath a romantic exterior that completely deceives the book's romantic hero, George Moffat, and its innocent heroine, Dora Brede, both products of the world of Winchelsea and Glebe Cottage, in which the novel is set.*[16]

In November Ford succeeded in selling the serial rights to *The Heart of the Country* to Philip Gibbs, the editor of a new paper, the *Tribune.* Meanwhile, however, he had to call on Pinker for another loan of £40: "W^d you believe it," he asked indignantly, "those vampires [the London & County Bank in Ashford] actually insist on more blood?" In their incredible way they kept on doing so; when Ford sent in the manuscript of *The Heart of the Country* the first week of January, he asked for another £50: "I would not bother you but this morning my Bank Manager informs me amiably that my account is overdrawn. . . . "[17]

*For a discussion of *The Benefactor,* see pp 466–68.

Chapter 11

𝒬

The publishing firm of Alston Rivers (the name was an invention) was created by L. J. Bathurst and René Byles. Shortly after it came into existence, Pinker, unable to place a novel by Archibald Marshall elsewhere, got Alston Rivers to take it. Marshall liked Bathurst and Byles and decided to join the firm; he and Bathurst put up the money and Byles became the managing director. Byles was a diminutive, energetic, stubborn man of Huguenot descent; Ford claims that his family name was originally Boileaux. Everyone seems to have liked him except Pinker. Byles made successes of Ford's *The Soul of London* and *The Fifth Queen* by advertising them so heavily that there were almost no profits for the firm. After a couple of years, Marshall grew discouraged and dropped out, and after another year or so Bathurst and Byles also gave up, and Byles went out to Japan to run a mineral-water business; he did not return to London until 1909.[1]

During its short existence Alston Rivers bulked large in Ford's life. In some part of his mind he knew, as he put it about *The Transatlantic Review*, that "You cannot write and conduct a [business], at least, you cannot write well." But he loved to feel that his hands were on the reins of power. With his offhand way of talking about the great writers of the past and present, he impressed Marshall and Byles; Bathurst did not like him. He was soon in and out of Alston Rivers' office daily, advising, recommending books, and giving at least himself the impression that he had an influence on the firm's policies. By the spring of 1906 he was even trying to do them a good turn with Pinker, who had all but brought them into existence.

> By the bye: I wish you'd dine with me one day & meet Byles [he wrote Pinker]: he's really beneath a thorny exterior an amiable creature: I believe he treats you with, let us say, asperity wh. it's rather

silly to introduce into business matters and it's worrying me because I see a good deal of Marshall and Bathurst.[2]

In February he persuaded the firm to undertake a poetry series under his editorship. The only volume that appeared was Nora Chesson's *Dirge for Aoine*, which Ford himself put together after her death to help provide for her children; his reward was to have her widower address "a circular letter to the press abusing me, [Alston] Rivers and everyone else concerned." Galsworthy put in a word for his friend R. H. Mottram, and Mottram remembered afterwards how, as he and Galsworthy were having tea in Addison Road, "a tall blond man in a grey frock-coat and trousers was ushered in. . . . We sat down to a genial dinner, enlivened by Jack's champagne, and listened to Hueffer's comments on Henry James and other contemporary figures. On returning to the drawing-room he, Jack and Ada went through the poems of mine that had been selected for publication and I learned great deal. . . . "[3]

Ford was now living with his mother at 90 Brook Green in Hammersmith. Elsie was with her mother, and the girls at La Sagesse Convent in Rye. During their vacations Ford would go to Winchelsea to be with them. He enjoyed his weekends in Winchelsea; "one certainly appreciates Winchelsea after London," he said to Elsie. With the understanding that he could spend his weekends there, he lent the Conrads the Bungalow when they got back from Montpellier, to which they had gone to escape the worst of the English winter. Conrad had been working on *The Secret Agent*, which he completed during this summer of 1906, and perhaps there was some idea in his mind that Ford could help him with it; Ford had encouraged him to write this story.[4]

In a circuitous way (Ford ascribed it to Conrad's desire to preserve Ford's respectability by not identifying him too closely with anarchists) Conrad tells in the Author's Note to *The Secret Agent* how the subject "came to me in the shape of a few words uttered by a friend in a casual conversation." Of Martial Bourdin's attempt to blow up the Greenwich Observatory, this friend—Conrad says—"remarked in his characteristically casual and omniscient manner, 'Oh, that fellow was half an idiot. His sister committed suicide afterwards.' " In *Joseph Conrad* Ford observes that this passage is curiously revealing of the intensity with which Conrad's imagination worked on a subject, since Winnie's suicide is entirely his own invention but became so real to him that he was sure Ford had mentioned it. What Ford actually said, according to him, was, "Oh that fellow was half an idiot! His sister murdered her husband afterwards and was allowed to escape by the police.

I remember the funeral. . . . " Ford had heard "the inner story of the Green-wich Observatory outrage" years earlier, he says, from Helen Rossetti in the "office" of *The Torch* in William Rossetti's basement. He also says that Conrad put one of the Rossetti girls and their anarchist press into *The Secret Agent*, though it was actually into "The Informer," written just before *The Secret Agent*. "A little of *The Secret Agent*," Ford says, "was written by me, sentences here and there, mostly about the topography of Western London —which Conrad did not know at all—and details about policemen and anarchists."

Ford certainly knew more about these things than Conrad did, and it would have been typical of the way they worked together for Ford to have inserted a detail here and there. It is impossible now to say whether he actually did so, though it must certainly have been from him that Conrad got the idea of having Verloc sell "obscure newspapers badly printed, with titles like *The Torch.*" It is a curious fact, too, that on the reverse of the original half title of *A Set of Six* (1908) the list of Conrad's previous books describes *The Secret Agent* as a collaboration with Ford M. Hueffer. In any event, there is no question that Ford helped Conrad with *The Secret Agent* in much the way he had helped with *The Mirror of the Sea*, *Nostromo*, and "The End of the Tether"; in all these cases Ford's significant contribution was morale-building, the stimulation of Conrad's will to work.[5]

The joint occupancy of the Bungalow by the Conrads and Ford did not work out happily. Trouble began when Ford washed his Panama hat and put it in the oven to dry above the Sunday joint Jessie had cooking. " . . . there was too much grease inside the lining for my liking," she says. "I removed it to a chair . . . and resolutely closed the oven, voicing my displeasure in as few words as possible." Undaunted by these "few words," Ford next requested that Jessie provide a new black ribbon for this hateful Panama. Jessie acceded to this "fantastic request" and "dutifully sewed" a ribbon on the hat. The next morning at breakfast Ford noticed a small cut in the tablecloth and remarked that Elsie would be upset by it. Jessie recalls her retort with great delight:

> I paused in the act of pouring out his coffee and said indifferently: "I don't suppose she will ever see it." F.M.F. jumped to his feet . . . "Not see it, what do you mean? . . . " I rose quickly to my feet and hastily turned another corner of the cloth towards him, saying slowly and distinctly: "I said she most probably would not see it. You see my name is on the corner. I brought my own linen, and I shall take it home with me. Are you satisfied?"

He uttered a short vexed laugh and stalked out of the house. . . .

After Ford left the next weekend, the maid came downstairs "with a miscellaneous collection of masculine garments crumpled out of all recognition in her arms." These turned out to be Conrad's frock coat and striped gray trousers, his "robes of ceremony" that it was Jessie's special pride to keep carefully pressed. Ford, wanting to sleep late and finding the morning light troublesome, had hung the blanket over the window and then, to keep warm, had grabbed the first thing he could find in the dresser drawer and piled it on the bed. Conrad, said Jessie with triumphant but perhaps misplaced satisfaction, "could not blame me for this calm appropriation and misuse of his wardrobe. . . . F.M.H. was in his own place and any responsibility for the dearth of covering was his own, not mine." "Conrad and Jessie go on Wed.," Ford wrote Elsie, "—and I've not pressed them to stay: they're rather exhausting."[6]

After the Conrads left, Ford spent his weekends more happily. He went over to Rye with Mrs. Hueffer and Caroline Marwood to visit the girls at La Sagesse, where he found "B[abbs] radiantly happy" and offered the Mother Superior some good advice about how to treat her. He lunched and had tea with Henry James and "walked to the sea with Marwood and enjoyed it." One night James and Claude Phillips carried Ford off to Lamb House for dinner and entertained him "with anecdotes not at all fitted for my youth and innocence until a very late hour"—"conversations between [James] and a queer tiny being who lay crumpled up on the stately sofa in James's magnificent panelled room in Lamb House . . . that made the tall wax candles seem to me to waver in their sockets and the skin of my forehead and hands to prickle with sweat."[7]

The realities of literary journalism were turning out not to be so glamorous as he had anticipated. He told Elsie he was planning to "give up" his connection with the *Academy*, where the attention paid him a few weeks earlier had seemed so exciting, and he began once more to suffer from dyspepsia, for which he undertook a course of "electric treatment."[8]

But he was much too happily occupied to be really ill or to work up much sympathy for those who were. "I'm sorry," he wrote Elsie, "you continue to get so tired but of course you can't expect to pick right up all at once." When Elsie complained of neglect, he said, "Believe me, my dear thing, you aren't in the least left out by anybody. . . . Yesterday I lunched at the Mont Blanc with Edward. Juliet is going to St. Petersburg. . . . [I] think I shall begin on the Fifth Queen II [*Privy Seal*] and Spirit of the People. Rivers very anxious for one or the other."[9]

The Soskices' trip to Russia made Ford think he ought to go there too. He proposed that Pinker finance him, so that he could write "a book rather of impressions than statistics, of course," on Russia. He felt he was admirably equipped for this venture:

> ... I have, for a number of years, been connected with most of the Russians who are now prominent in the revolutionary movement. Father Gapon who organized the great movement which led to the January massacres, was actually hidden in my mother's house for a considerable time.
>
> I should, I suppose, run a good deal of risk—but I don't fancy that I should shirk that, as far as I know myself.

It was an exciting enough time in St. Petersburg. In the confusion that accompanied Witt's suppression of the St. Petersburg soviet, David Soskice got arrested, but though he must still have been under indictment in Russia, his credentials as a British journalist (he was the editor of *Free Russia*) were enough to get him released. Father Gapon was murdered in April.[10]

Elsie too began to plan a trip, to Rome, a plan that was thrown into confusion by Mary Martindale's proposal to come to Rome too. "I think," Ford wrote Elsie, "you should see Mary if she comes to Rome"; he was perhaps more ready to have Elsie forgive Mary than Elsie was. But it is not easy to make out what sort of terms Elsie and Ford were on at this time. Perhaps the narrator of *The Nature of a Crime*, which Ford was at work on, throws some light on them. He begins his first letter to his lady by describing how he has imagined himself standing on a hill in Rome and seeing her walking toward him from "a grove of silver poplars. . . . You had, I think, a parasol behind your head." He begs her forgiveness for never having told her that he has been robbing Edward Burden and gambling wildly (to take his mind off his longing for her) and that the ring he wears contains poison so that he can kill himself when he can no longer endure being without her. It is possible this story reflects Ford's way of explaining his conduct to Elsie, with the robbery and gambling substituted for Mary Martindale.[11]

While Elsie was abroad, Ford bombarded her with reports of his triumphs; he had "definitely contracted with [Alston] Rivers for The Spirit of the People and two other Kath[arine] How[ard] books, and another agent has written asking for another soul of London sort of book. . . . Saturday to Spade House. Sunday over to the children. The cover of Kath Howard [*The Fifth Queen*] is gorgeous." With a transparent effort to appear depressed by her absence he concludes, "Walking about 5 miles about London one sees little incidents which keep one from glooming."[12]

On March 14 *The Fifth Queen* was published. Ford took advantage of the

occasion to touch Pinker for another £ 100. He was now operating on the
theory that "it was of the essence of the contract I signed with you [Pinker]
that you would let me have an advance against manuscript to the tune of
about £ 2 per 1000 words. . . . I *must* have money at about this rate. . . . "
Pinker replied that there was no such understanding.

> The sales of the V Queen ought to amount to that much [£ 100]
> for me [Ford said]. C^d you advance me £75 on that amount & send
> it down to my bank?—My wife is clamouring for money in Rome
> & in spite of y^r very opportune £25 I have more to send—because
> my account was already overdrawn. . . . Do as much for me as you
> can & as quickly.—because when I worry I can't work & when I can't
> work I can't make pennies.

He had got himself into this pickle in his usual way. Hearing that the first
edition of *The Fifth Queen* had been sold out before publication, he wrote Elsie:

> The Fifth Queen first edition is sold already. I am going to motor to
> Rye; it is extravagant but I deserve a small spree. . . . [Alston] Rivers
> says 6000 is certain and 12000 probable. The latter would mean £ 900
> which is very cheering. . . .

Shortly after he was telling her that he expected to get £ 50 for the American
rights to *The Fifth Queen* and £ 400 apiece for its two sequels. In prosaic fact, the
total sales of *The Fifth Queen* were 2,850, worth £ 128.5.0 to Ford, and none of the
three novels of the trilogy was sold in America. Ford's overconfidence not only
made him reckless about money; it made him unrealistic in his dealings with
publishers. "I should not object," he told Pinker, "to [Fisher Unwin's] having
my name. . . . if I could have the gratification of screwing a large sum out of
him."[13]

In February Ford had joined the Fabian Society in order to help Wells
drive out "The Old Gang" led by the Webbs and the Blands and Shaw, who,
Wells thought, had too little imagination to share his dream of turning the
Fabians into samurai who would lead a mass socialist movement. It was a quixotic gesture on Ford's part. He knew that he was "a member of a [political]
party that never was on land or sea but that may rule the world when Arthur
shall come again." But he intensely disliked statistically minded reformers like
the Webbs; he thought their attitude "a curious thing, made up of socialism,
free thought, the profession of free love going hand in hand with an intense
sexual continence that to all intents and purposes ended in emasculation, and
going along, also, hand in hand with lime-washed bedroom walls and other
aesthetic paraphernalia. It . . . really frightened me out of my life."[14]

Nevertheless Ford tried to help; he read through the Fabian tracts in preparation for an attack he delivered in March. At the time he was convinced his speech had "materially accelerated the split in the society"; "I fancy," he said later, "I did more harm than good at that Fabian meeting. . . . I must have imagined statistics or something." Wells's politics were no more practical than Ford's, though they had a more plausible air. The Old Gang, as Ford said, "wiped the floor" with Wells, and after a couple of years he gave up his attempt to take over and remodel the Fabian Society. Meanwhile, however, Ford and Wells worked together closely. Rushing through Winchelsea early in March on his way to Spade House for further plotting with Wells, Ford was waylaid by Henry James—"who commanded it over the telephone"—for lunch. He managed to get to Spade House for dinner, and the next day, with characteristic extravagance, he hired a car and took Wells to Rye, where they picked the girls up at the convent, and on to Winchelsea for lunch, "where H.G. had a fine argument with the great Marwood." Motorcars were an irresistible status symbol to Ford; at one point he even proposed motoring to Italy to join Elsie.[15]

Since nothing had come of his proposal of a book on the Russian Revolution, he now began "a new book which Pinker wants to publish anonymously. A series of letters from a man about to commit suicide. I think it will go. It's awful piffle." This is the first mention of *The Nature of a Crime*, which Ford himself eventually printed in *The English Review* under the joking nom de plume of Ignatz (for Conrad) von Aschendrof (for Ford). During the summer of 1906, when Ford and Conrad were again seeing a great deal of each other, they began to work on this story; "C. and I are doing a rather larky collaboration," Ford wrote Elsie in May. In July he wrote Pinker, "I've just heard from Conrad that you haven't had that anonymous m.s. You ought to have had it on the 1ˢᵗ of July. There isn't any reason why you shouldnᵗ for there was practically nothing for C. to do." Still the manuscript did not come in; on July 27, just before he sailed for America, Ford told Pinker again that "I sent Conrad the final pages of that anonymous book some time ago." Finally, when Ford got back from America in the fall, he managed to get hold of the manuscript—still almost untouched by Conrad—and sent it to Pinker. Like Pinker, he had great hopes of its success; it was piffle, deliberately written to sell. But he did not want to spend any more time on it without some assurance of publication.

> The m.s. [he said in his covering letter] can be extended to any length by the insertion of matter between chapters v. and vi. (where the division in the m.s. is). This additional matter only awaits Conrad's revising & can be had at once—but the thing is complete in itself. . . . I really think that this might have such a selling chance that it is worth taking a little trouble over.[16]

The "division" Ford refers to in his letter comes at the point where the narrator drops the story of Edward Burden and returns to his own plan to commit suicide. What Ford means is that the story of Edward Burden might be expanded until it became the central interest of the book and the narrator's situation merely a dramatic device that allows him to observe Edward. The minute we consider this possibility, we see how like *The Good Soldier The Nature of a Crime* is, or might easily have become. The narrator's relation to Edward Burden is very like Dowell's to Edward Ashburnham. They have the same attitudes toward their audiences too. Dowell imagines himself talking to a sympathetic soul beside a cottage fire; the narrator of *The Nature of a Crime* has hours and hours to write the woman he loves: " . . . you cannot understand how immensely leisurely I feel . . . I can put down my thoughts desultorily and lazily." He has Dowell's concern for precise dates and times (" . . . all the years we have known each other—seven years, three months and two days"). He also has Dowell's—and Ford's—conception of the nature of real passion: "For the union with you that I seek is . . . hardly at all, I think, a union of the body, but a sort of consciousness of our thoughts proceeding onwards together"; this is precisely the idea of Edward Ashburnham, who can be happy so long as Nancy loves him, however widely they are separated. If Ford had expanded Edward Burden's story, it would have been like Edward Ashburnham's; Burden has Ashburnham's romantic conscience, his gallantry to the narrator, even his extramarital affair.

The narrator of the novel, who is the object of some irony, would like to think that he and his lady "suffer, not because their [conventional people's] rules bind us, but because, being the finer spirits, we are forced to set ourselves rules that are still more strict in order that, in all things, we may be the truly gallant." In *The Good Soldier*—and also, indeed, in *A Call* before it and in *Parade's End* after it—the heroes have this same romantic gallantry, but they exercise it in the service of a code that is at least nominally the code of their society, so that they appear humble rather than arrogant, as this man does. In his polite way, Conrad criticized *The Nature of a Crime* for being fantastic; "No doubt our man was conceived for purposes of irony," he said, "but our conception of him, I fear, is too fantastic." Since "our man" is almost wholly Ford's, this is Conrad's way of disassociating himself from a hero he thought Ford took too seriously. Ford was certainly being ironic about this narrator's imagining himself a "finer spirit" while he was busy robbing Edward Burden, but he was not being ironic about the narrator's superiority to conventional rules of conduct and his banal speculations about God and the after life and the need for poets, with their superiority to mere businessmen, to be false to their women; these were Ford's own views.[17]

In April Ford was reporting to Elsie that the circulation of the *Tribune* went up 3,000 on the days installments of *The Heart of the Country* ran, but by May—though he caught a man reading it in the library of the National Liberal Club—he recognized that the book was not going to be the success *The Soul of London* had been. This disappointment was not much assuaged by the success of Galsworthy's *Man of Property* ("Galsworthy is almost more than I the coming man," he reported to Elsie) or by Methuen's turning down a proposal he had confidently described to Elsie as "a rather good offer for a book from Methuen about literary technique." He then discovered— to his usual astonishment—that he was overdrawn by some £17. It was not a good moment for poor Dr. Tebb to choose—as he did—to try to borrow £50. Then Levin Schücking, whom Ford had so greatly admired when they met in Germany in 1904, landed on his hands. To the newly distinguished Ford, busy with the larger life of London journalism, Levin was hardly the man he had been in 1904. "He's moderately presentable," Ford told Elsie, "so as I have to pay several lunch calls at the Protheros, the Granbys, and the Watts-Duntons I shall take him with me." He had taken Schücking to lunch with Swinburne and Watts-Dunton earlier and found it "a tiring operation." Schücking's romantic corduroys did not look quite so splendid at the Pines as they had before the great log fire at Telgte while Ford was reading his own poems aloud.[18]

Ford was inclined to put some of the blame for the comparative failure of *the Heart of the Country* on Sir Alfred Harmsworth's *Times* Book Club. The *Times* Book Club sold used circulating-library books at a fifth of the retail price. But now Ford began to think better of Sir Alfred, who, as Ford tells it, suddenly called him in and ordered him to buy the *Academy* without revealing that Harmsworth was putting up the money. "For the first time in my life," Ford let himself "be swayed by prudence"—by Harmsworth's reputation for squeezing young men dry and then dropping them—and "did nothing about the matter." Harmsworth wanted to start a rival to the literary supplement of the *Times* because some of the dislike stirred up by the *Times* Book Club scheme was rubbing off on the literary supplement and he needed to provide a less offensive medium for publishers' advertising. He and Ford had a number of meetings between April and June in which they went into this plan for taking over the *Academy*. Ford devised an unworkable arrangement according to which Child, the present editor, would handle the day-to-day chores of the magazine while he determined its policy. Harmsworth was offering him £ 6,000 for the first year's expenses and he optimistically calculated that "it can be done for this, so as to leave a margin of £ 1500–2000 for me but [I] don't feel *quite* certain." That Harmsworth should have taken Ford so seriously is a measure of his reputation at this time; there was soon to be more such evidence. Exactly what happened to this plan to buy the *Academy* is not clear. It seems unlikely that Ford decided against it; it would have been very unlike him to turn down the chance to be an editor. Apparently Harmsworth decided to take a different tack.[19]

Harmsworth eventually hired Edmund Gosse to start a literary supplement to the *Daily Mail* with Archibald Marshall as his assistant. Gosse's editorship lasted six months; then he was quietly dismissed, with generous severance pay, and Archibald Marshall took over. Gosse had been too literary for Harmsworth, though his name had given the supplement prestige. Marshall was at this time a great admirer of Ford and he quickly involved Ford in the supplement's affairs.

> He took no part in the editing of the paper [Marshall recalled], but he was in my room almost every day, and wrote most of what he did write for it there. I consulted with him about most things, and deferred ... to his skill and knowledge as a writer. ... Hueffer's chief contribution, and it was perhaps the best regular feature in the paper, was a weekly character sketch of some contemporary writer.

Ford's conception of the situation was quite different. Marshall had taken Ford with him when he went to see Harmsworth about his editorship of the supplement and Ford left with the impression that Harmsworth had asked Ford "to assist ... Marshall in editing ... [the] literary supplement [and] I consented to this. It meant that I could pretty well set the pace of that periodical myself." When the *Times* Book Club trouble died out and Harmsworth, no longer needing a rival to the *Times* literary supplement, decided to drop the *Daily Mail*'s, Ford threatened the *Daily Mail* with breach of contract, on the grounds that Harmsworth had hired him for two years. Marshall then told Ford he would testify to the falseness of this claim and Ford replied that, if his action against Harmsworth would inconvenience Marshall—an idea that had never entered Marshall's mind—Ford would drop it. At the same time he told Pinker that Marshall had pleaded with him to persuade Harmsworth to keep him on the job and that, as Harmsworth had yielded to Ford's pleading, he had decided to drop the action. Long after, meeting Conrad at the Arts Club shortly before Conrad's death, Marshall got Ford's conduct during this affair cleared up for him by Conrad's explanation of Ford's character.

This episode was revived in an unpleasant way when Ford published his version of it in *Return to Yesterday* in 1931. By that time he had further improved his story by making his interest in a group of "admirable but needy writers" the reason he protested the closing of the literary supplement, and by making Thomas Marlowe, who had been the editor of the *Daily Mail*—and was, unluckily, still alive in 1931—look a great fool. Marlowe and Marshall were quick to show that Ford's story was "fantastically untrue."[20]

However fanciful Ford's conception of this affair, his indignation when Harmsworth closed down the literary supplement was real. There may have been a quite simple reason for this; in his life of Northcliffe, Reginald Pound says that Marshall and Ford between them "added to Northcliffe's increasing boredom with the supplement"; perhaps he made this boredom clear to Ford. In any event, when Scott-James, the editor of the *Daily News*, wrote to inquire why Ford had not offered his literary portraits to the *News*, Ford wrote him:

> ... the exact circumstances were these: I was helping Marshall with the Mail Supplement, for fun more than anything else. Soap however had shut the Supplement down—the Mail seeking to gain respectability by abandoning its only respectable feature, after the manner of its kind.
>
> ... I should actually have preferred [to do further portraits for] the News; but because I wanted to put the Harmsworthian nose out of joint I wanted to let the series go on in the Saturday of the suppression. (A[lfred] H[armsworth] I mean wanted me to write in the Mail itself whereas I wanted to show him that I'd rather appear in a paper even of the Smallest Advertised Circulation! ...)

He had therefore transferred the series to the *Tribune*—or, as he put it, "the Tribune snapped [it] up before I could communicate with [Scott-James]." The nickname "Soap" was intended as a sharp cut; the *Daily Mail* was being sued for a very large sum by Lever Brothers. Ford's implication that the *Tribune* had snapped up the portraits before he could offer them to Scott-James is a polite fiction; as the successful serializers of *The Heart of the Country*, they were the people Ford naturally turned to when he was bent on showing Harmsworth he did not need the *Daily Mail*.[21]

In September, 1908, however, he began writing a series of weekly articles for Scott-James's *News*, which he continued until he began editing *The English Review*. Thus, from the moment *The Heart of the Country* had begun to run in the *Tribune* in February, 1906, until December, 1908, when Ford became too busy with *The English Review* to continue, he was regularly featured in the London press. Except for the period from May, 1906, until the spring of 1907, during most of which he was out of the country, he appeared at least weekly in one newspaper or the other. This gave him some prominence as a literary arbiter and convinced him he had even more.

Meanwhile, in the spring of 1906, he decided to make a trip to America in the hope of creating a new market for his books. "Incite [Ford] all you can," Conrad wrote Elsie when they were in America, "to astonish the unpainted savage of the Great Republic. What he wants to get there (where you are) is a *succès d'ebahiss[e]ment.*" Ford planned to bring the girls out to Germany, where Elsie would meet them, for July; they would go to New York for August, come back in time to spend September at Winchelsea, and then settle into a flat in London for the winter. The prospect of going to America stimulated Ford to invent a host of writing projects in the hope of obtaining advances to pay for the trip. He got Pinker to press *The Fifth Queen* and *The Spirit of the People* on Dodd, Mead and submitted to Brown, Langham a novel called *Love the Ploughman,* which is otherwise unknown. He proposed to Methuen "two or three volumes" about the south coast of England, along the lines of *The Cinque Ports,* and a book about caravanning. None of these proposals found favor, and he was reduced to planning the trip on the £ 250 he could squeeze out of Pinker, which seemed minimal even to him.²²

On July 2, Ford and the girls and the Martindales' retired maid, Miss Etheridge (who came along to care for the girls) sailed for Germany, where they met Elsie for Christina's birthday (July 3) at Mannheim. During the spring Ford had decided that the girls should become Catholics, and they were received into the Church in Germany, where their relatives were all devout Catholics. Afterwards Tante Emma found, through a convent in Bonn, a good Catholic governess for them named Edmée Van der Noot, and she took the girls back to England, where they stayed with Miss Etheridge, when Ford and Elsie sailed for America on the third of August, aboard the *Kaiserin Augusta Victoria* from Hamburg. At the last minute Ford had worked Pinker up to £ 350 by turning over to him the deeds of Hurst Cottage in Aldington, on which Pinker let him have £ 150. The other two hundred pounds were advances against *The Spirit of the People* and *The Nature of a Crime.*²³

Ford later told many improved stories of his experiences in America— stories of working whole summers on farms near Merion, Pennsylvania, in Canaan, New Hampshire, and Charleston, South Carolina; of attending dinners of "the famous Gloucester Massachusetts [fishing] fleet"; of being "wined and dined" as a literary celebrity in Philadelphia; and of visiting the plantation of his *oncle d'Amerique* in Lexington, Virginia. In prosaic fact they first spent a couple of weeks in New York, where Ford tried to sell his books to McClure.

His great supporter at McClure's was William Bradley, who was to become Ford's agent and friend in Paris in the twenties.

> I left McClure's the proofs of several things & the first vol. of the V Queen[Ford wrote Pinker]. . . . What I have proposed to them to do is to publish the Soul of London, the Heart of the Country, & the Spirit of the People in one vol. called say: *The Anglo Saxons*. . . . And of course there is the Vth Queen—3 vols. I tell you this because S. S. McClure has started for Yurupp. . . .
>
> Bradley is very amiable & well disposed—but I don't know what his powers are.

Only the first of these projects ever came to anything; McClure published *England and the English* the next year.[24]

At the end of August they moved on to Boston. It failed miserably to live up to their expectations; they found America hot, dusty, dull, and uninspiring; the expenses were, Ford reported, "*appalling*," and they succeeded in meeting nobody of interest—"*everybody* being away in hills & woods where it seems impossible to follow." By September 1 Ford had completed about 12,000 words of *Privy Seal* and rushed it into the mail for Pinker as security for an additional loan of £ 50. After a week or ten days in Boston they started back for New York, spending a couple of days in Waterbury with a pair of spinster ladies named Hurlbird whom Ford got to know in Germany in 1904, who would become Florence's aunts in *The Good Soldier*. Except for a few days in Philadelphia, where the heat was overwhelming and Elsie was "quite ill," they remained in New York for the rest of their time. Ford had sent Pinker another 10,000 words of *Privy Seal* from Philadelphia and borrowed another £ 50 on the strength of it. Even so they were able to sail for home on a cattle boat, the SS *Minnetonka*, at the end of September only after Pinker had responded to a desperate cable from Ford: "Impossible return unless you wire sixty."[25]

Before he left New York Ford made an agreement with McClure. He had asked McClure for an advance of £ 250 on *London* and the *Fifth Queen* trilogy and for £ 1,500 apiece on the three books about America. What he got was $350, $150 of which was a loan and $200 an advance on the American trilogy to be called *The Three Ships*, only one volume of which (*The 'Half*

Moon') was ever written—and it was turned down by McClure. When Ford got back to London, he claimed McClure had promised a great deal more than this, but nothing more was forthcoming.[26]

Chapter 12

ℰ

When they got back to London, Ford and Elsie took a flat in Holbein House on Sloane Square; they spent their weekends at Winchelsea. Ford tried to convince Pinker that he would be completing *Privy Seal* within a week of his return and *An English Girl* very shortly thereafter, though in fact *Privy Seal* was not finished until November (and not published until February, 1907), and *An English Girl* was not finished until May, 1907. But he was in even deeper financial trouble than usual and needed to borrow from Pinker.

He had hardly got back to London before "a whole flight of cheques" that surprised him as much as if someone else had written them came "in from America (God damn the day ever I went there)"; he was overdrawn and a check for £35 McClure had cashed for him in New York had been dishonored. He already owed Pinker over £600, and during the remainder of the year he continued to borrow from him—to pay school bills, rent, income tax—until his debt had climbed over £800. This crisis was, of course, only comparatively more severe than Ford's permanent financial difficulties.[1]

Through the fall of 1906 and the following winter he struggled to complete *Privy Seal* and *An English Girl.* He was also writing his articles for the *Daily Mail* and helping Marshall with the book supplement. The Conrads had gone to the Continent for the winter again, and from Montpellier Conrad wrote Ford, " . . . every day as I go about entranced [by the "beauty of this land"], I miss you more and more. . . . I am certain that with no other man could I share my rapture." At the end of January, 1907, he dispatched to Ford a cookbook Jessie had been working on—"130 Recipes and Preface by Yours truly. . . . [Jessie is] . . . very grateful to you the 'Onlie Begetter'. . . . " Ford must have suggested the book to Jessie, doubtless in his role of unofficial adviser to Alston Rivers.[2]

Ford had started "the Hudson book for McClure"—that is, *The 'Half Moon'*—at the beginning of February, as soon as he completed *An English Girl* for Methuen; *The 'Half Moon'* was finished by June. They had given up their flat in Sloane Square the first of the year and Elsie was now back in Winchelsea; Ford was living with his mother at 90 Brook Green and going to Winchelsea weekends. During the early summer Ferris Greenslet, the editor of *The Atlantic Monthly*, stayed with them at Winchelsea; Ford and Greenslet had met the previous fall in Boston. He advised Pinker of this advantageous association at once. We can catch a glimpse of how he dealt with Greenslet in Greenslet's own recollection of the occasion:

> I weekended at Winchelsea, where Ford Madox Hueffer... free-holder of the Cinque Ports, who could wear his hat in the presence of the King, was advising both Conrad and Galsworthy in their early efforts.... We drove over the marshes to Rye to pay respects to Henry James [who was not, however, at home].[3]

In June Borys Conrad fell ill at Montpellier, and Ford and Elsie at once offered to go out to help. Conrad replied, "With our greatest love and thanks for your touching offer; we should not ask you to come unless things were much worse.... One has complete faith in you and Ford." In July Alston Rivers published *From Inland;* apart from half-a-dozen new poems, this volume was a selection from Ford's earlier volumes, made by Edward Garnett. On September 6, 1907, Methuen published *An English Girl*, the first of the three Ford novels they would do. The title was probably theirs; Ford had called the novel *The Reformers*, which gives a much better idea of it: "We're going out [to America] as reformers," the young American hero says to the English heroine.[4]

An English Girl is a hasty piece of work in what Ford called "the manner of Mr. Henry James, written... as a variation on a book of essays to give the effect of a tour in the United States—an international affair." It is Jamesian at least to the extent that it has a neat tripartite structure (1. In Canterbury; 2. On the transatlantic liner; 3. In New York) and that it contrasts an English girl named Eleanor Greville and an idealistic young American with the "American" name of Don Collar Kelleg (though his father, who is alternately called Charles and John Collar Kelleg, had been born in the Rydale workhouse in Yorkshire and named after two of its guardians). Otherwise it is a calumny on James to call the book Jamesian. Its action is merely a peg on which to hang Ford's impressions of his transatlantic crossing and of New York, and we can probably even get some idea of what Ford and Elsie's return on the cattle boat, the *Minnetonka*, was like from Don

Collar's account of stowing away on an American cattle boat called the *Minnehaha*. Some of Ford's impressions of New York have by now a mild period charm, but most of them are the popular clichés of contemporary British satires of America. He gets nearly everything wrong when he tries to be knowing about America; what one of the British reviewers sniffily called his "Transatlantic idioms" are almost always misused. His Americans talk about "British rubber-necks with Baedekers," "Jersey State," and "On the Shady Side of Broadway." The book's speculations about America are scarcely more reliable; they are either excessively obvious or ostentatiously paradoxical in an 1890s way.

Regardless of plausibility, Ford makes his American hero a William Morris socialist so that he can explore his own dilemma by showing Don Collar torn between the idea of social reform and love of picturesque feudalism. As Don contemplates the steerage passengers during the Atlantic crossing, he sees the truth that Ford had seen in *The Soul of London*, that the poor have a heroism of their own that is beyond the understanding of upper-class reformers. Only the book's Tories—Mr. Greville and Eleanor—can accept this, and Mr. Greville recognizes that there is not "in active England or elsewhere any room for what *he* called a decent man; the place of such men was gone from the world." There are only Fabians now. At moments, then, Don Collar's dilemma resembles George Moffat's in *The Benefactor*, he becomes "a nineteenth-century European Altruist," and at these moments he acquires a faint tinge of the kind of interest George Moffat has, and his problem, like George's, becomes the problem of discovering what his own realities are. But this interest quickly fades; the "American" in Don triumphs and he settles down to a life of reform. Otherwise the book consists of characters that exist largely to make obvious comments on the differences between the Americans and the English of 1906.[5]

Ford now decided that he needed a permanent establishment in London; " ... the country," he said firmly, "is not the place for intellectual contacts ... " and he had long since become convinced that Winchelsea was a place to which " 'genteel families' come ... in search of health and quiet, which they find in abundance." He moved to a set of rooms at 84 Holland Park Avenue. They were over the shop of a poulterer and fishmonger named Chandler; you entered by "a side door which gave on to a dark flight of stairs." Goldring, who was Ford's secretary on *The English Review*, had "an impression of almost pushing my way through the suspended carcasses of rabbits, fowls and game birds to get to the door, and of standing in a mixture of blood and sawdust as I rang the bell." Mr. and Mrs. Chandler were fond of Ford and provided him with the luxury of a daily supply of ice for the tiny icebox that stood on his landing. This set of rooms was to remain Ford's home—and the office of *The English Review*—until he moved into South Lodge with Violet Hunt. It consisted of a large drawing room and a bathroom on the first floor and, on the second, the landing with the icebox, two small bedrooms, a minute kitchen and dining room, and the W.C. Ford thought his drawing room very pleasant with its "Chippendale chairs and bureaus that had been in my family for several generations; the portrait of myself as a child by my grandfather [*William Tell's Son*], and his long drawings for stained glass"; it also contained Christina Rossetti's desk (which ended up at South Lodge) and an inlaid Spanish cabinet in which *English Review* manuscripts would later be stored. One of the drawing-room windows, Ford pointed out, looked on a pleasant view of trees. The other, Violet Hunt noted, looked onto "Mr. Chandler's rubbish yard."[6]

Ford loved London and the business of literature and wanted to be a part of it. "Why," Violet Hunt asked, "did he abandon [Aldington] for the mud flats of Notting Hill, the rows of Victorian villas turned into shops, the stress, financial and otherwise, the many-peopled office, the agitating coming and going . . . ?" But Ford liked these agitating comings and goings, and for him there was inexhaustible glamor in "the shop fronts, the artificial stone façades, the electric light standards and the faint smell of horse-dung and dust of the centre of a town." He knew, as Ezra Pound said long afterwards, that "Kensington 1908 to '20 [offered a] pretty useful profile of the life of the literary part of the Brit. mind (when any) of that period." Ford never lost his love of the country but he would also, from now on, be a city man. Down at Aldington, he delighted as always to tell people who did not know him very well that he had "been made, in his cradle, a knight of the Order of the Holy Spirit," a reward to his German relatives for service to the Papacy, that his hunting cost him £ 300 a year, and that his golf handicap was three. Up in London he played the role of the influential literary man who "could pretty well control the policy" of journals like the *Daily Mail* literary supplement, and made and broke authors with his articles.[7]

Elsie never liked the city for long; it exhausted her. "I remember her as a dark, tall, 'formidable' woman, stern, implacable, of rigid principles," Goldring says in *South Lodge*, and adds that she reminded him of Mary Tudor—no doubt the Mary Tudor of Ford's *Fifth Queen* trilogy. Elsie particularly disliked the cosmopolitan women of London; she thought women like her sister, Mary Martindale, and Violet Hunt were "demented." She was not at all sure she wanted her girls exposed to such people.[8]

Then, early in September, Elsie became ill again. Her brother Harri did a urine analysis and failed to detect any sign of the tuberculosis of the kidney that was the real cause of her trouble. Instead her illness was diagnosed as ulcer of the bladder and kidney stones, and she was operated on.

> Death & despair dog me [Ford wrote Pinker]. When is the English Girl coming out? I want the money badly because my wife has to be operated on for stone tomorrow & we are so short of time that I haven't enough to pay her transport to Town let alone the surgeons. ... I suppose the Eng. Girl will be paid for within the next day or two?

After Elsie's operation she went to Dr. Tebb's house in Warrington Crescent to recuperate, and Ford devoted himself to her with anxious sympathy: Elsie always remembered the hours he spent reading James's *American Scene* to her. When she had recovered from the operation, she came back to Holland Park Avenue, but she did not get better and the life there was too strenuous for an invalid; more and more she stayed in Winchelsea, where Ford came only weekends.[9]

Late that fall she decided to give up the Bungalow. Winchelsea was, she thought, becoming artificially fashionable. Her first idea was to move somewhere near the Conrads, who had left the Pent in September, 1907, for Someries on the Luton Hoo estate in Bedfordshire. But Conrad was unable to find a place for her there, and she decided to put Hurst Cottage at Aldington in order and move there. Her motives for this decision are unknown, but some of them are easy to guess. She was unwell and the social life of Holland Park Avenue was a strain for her: she was simply not up to it. She did not like life there anyway, and liked it no better because it consisted largely of friends Ford had made apart from her. Goldring spent a weekend with her and Ford at Aldington that summer and "although I was ... far too inexperienced to understand the meaning of what I observed, I did not get the impression that Ford's was a happy home."[10]

Ford's own feelings about all this can be read between the lines of a letter he wrote his mother in December:

> We have definitely unfurnished the Bungalow & stored the furniture —so there's an end of Winchelsea. I'm sorry myself but E. never liked the place & was always more or less ill there. We are going to tidy up the cottage at Aldington & use that as our country abode.

Elsie continued to make an effort to be with Ford in Holland Park Avenue, much as she hated it; "if Mʳˢ J. w.ᵈ take a train here-wards," Ford wrote Jerrold from there during the fall of 1907, "it w^d delight E. who lies upon her back & groans thro' the heavy hours."[11]

While Hurst Cottage was being got ready, Elsie went to Sandgate in the hope that the sea air would help her, taking Katharine with her (Christina was at school). By this time Ford—no doubt encouraged by Harri's analysis —had decided that Elsie's illness was imaginary. "I got a D[octor] to pretend that he had discovered something the matter with her that no other D. had discovered," he told his mother, "—and to pretend to cure the evil & that really does seem to have proved effectual." This attitude, since Elsie was genuinely very ill, could not have made her happier.[12]

Both girls came with Edmée Van der Noot to Holland Park Avenue for their vacation, and Christina, now eleven, sent her mother a Christmas present from there with a letter saying she hoped her mother would "find [it] very usefull for your bath-chair when you go out by the sea." Elsie came to Holland Park Avenue for Christmas itself and Ford gave several parties. But it was not a happy time: Elsie quarreled with Ford at their Christmas tea party.[13]

At the beginning of March Elsie moved into Hurst Cottage. She had rented a thatched cottage next door, and there the girls, to their immense delight, slept when they were home from school. In 1912 this thatched cottage was reclaimed by its owner and, to compensate for its loss, Elsie sold the Bungalow and used the money to make extensive improvements at Hurst Cottage, which she then renamed Kitcat. Meanwhile, her illness was making Ford's financial situation more than usually difficult. Around the first of November he had written Pinker:

> The £ 300 . . . has gone . . . into the pockets of doctors, nurses, chemists & specialists. . . . My wife gets steadily worse & worse & I'm pretty well at the end of my tether. . . . I'd ask you to lunch but my wife takes up so much of my time.[14]

Partly out of financial desperation, partly out of an inflated estimate of his popularity, Ford then got into a row with Alston Rivers over their handling of his books. Just as he was likely to be made excessively optimistic by the mere suggestion of a success, so he was driven to despair by disappointment or the discovery—always a surprise to him—that he had run up debts. "I do," he wrote Pinker, "quite seriously need the sum I mentioned & can't get on without it. . . . I *must* have money at about this rate &, altho' I haven't the least wish to appear unfriendly—or even to complain—I shall be simply forced by necessity to find someone who will make some such arrangement." This is a cry of despair, but it sounds like a threat and Pinker took it as one, to Ford's pained surprise. "Y^r letter distresses me," he wrote, "I wish you'd reread mine & you'd see that I didn't in the least wish to irritate you & certainly not to threaten you—or even to complain." But one can hardly blame Pinker for being offended at Ford's suggestion that he needed a new agent.

Ford wrote in the same vein to Alston Rivers, taking the line that if Rivers could not sell more of his books he would have to look elsewhere, and he told Pinker to hold up *The Fifth Queen Crowned* until he had a chance to see how well Rivers did with *The Spirit of the People*, to be published October 25, 1907. Since Rivers had advertised Ford's previous books generously, it seemed to Bathurst reasonable to think their lack of success at least as much the fault of their writer as of their publisher. He therefore wrote Pinker:

> We quite recognize that in view of the failure of our strenuous and lavish attempts in the past to make Mr. Hueffer's work popular, you have every right to await the results of "The Spirit of the People." Still when we feel that an author has not perfect confidence in us we should prefer that our relations with him should cease, and therefore beg to withdraw from our offer . . . for the publication of [*The Fifth Queen Crowned*].

He added the sensible observation that if they had to wait till the last minute for *The Fifth Queen Crowned*, as Ford proposed to make them, they would have no time at all to advertise it. Ford thus found himself with the last volume of the *Fifth Queen* trilogy back on his hands; and, he was outraged to discover, Alston Rivers was not working itself to death to sell *The Spirit of the People*. "If Bathurst calls what he's doing with The Spirit of the People publishing," he wrote Pinker, "he has weird ideas. He's not had a single advertisement of it in the London papers."[15]

Though Ford never believed it, Pinker worked hard to get him more money; when *The Fifth Queen* came out he tried to sell *Privy Seal* to other publishers at better terms. One of them, Edward Arnold, asked if *The Fifth Queen* actually had sold the 4,000 copies Pinker's proposed terms for *Privy Seal* assumed. Since *The Fifth Queen* sold (up to December 31, 1908) only 2,850 copies, Pinker's maneuver failed. Failures like this cost nothing so long as Ford had Rivers committed to publishing the trilogy. But when he put Pinker in the position of trying to sell *The Fifth Queen Crowned* without Rivers to fall back on, he made Pinker's task far more difficult. Pinker finally succeeded in persuading Eveleigh Nash to "commission a new historical novel by Mr. Hueffer." Nash was unpleasantly surprised when, at the end of December, he received the third volume of the *Fifth Queen* trilogy. " . . . sequels are rarely a success," he wrote Pinker, "and I could not possibly sell 'The Fifth Queen Crowned' to the same extent as I could a new historical novel by Mr. Hueffer." "I am sorry Nash is recalcitrant," Ford wrote Pinker when he heard this, "& sincerely think he is mistaken. Tell him that the whole Literary World not only of England but of Europe are anxiously awaiting the 3ᵈ V Queen and show him the Revue des deux Mondes to back up the statement." It did not help; the terms of the book's sale to Nash were another installment on the price of Ford's unfortunate quarrel with Alston Rivers. Nash published *The Fifth Queen Crowned* on March 26, 1908.[16]

The *Fifth Queen* trilogy, completed with this volume, is a remarkable achievement, especially when we consider that it was written amid the distractions of a busy journalistic career, of a trip to Germany and the United States, and of nagging worries over money and Elsie's illness. "Ford's last *Fifth Queen* novel is amazing," Conrad wrote Galsworthy. "The whole cycle is a noble conception—the swan song of Historical Romance— and frankly I am glad to have heard it." The ambiguous conclusion of that remark is apparently meant to imply that Conrad is glad to see the end of the historical romance; there is a similar ambiguity, somewhat more deeply buried, in the letter he wrote Ford: "There is a singular fascination about this last volume of the trilogy . . . and I am as far as ever from discovering a sufficiently precise formula of my admiration." It is a curious attitude for Conrad to have taken. He was certainly not averse to the historical romance: like Ford, he greatly admired *Salammbô;* he had stressed the historical character of *Romance;* and some of his own novels, like *Nostromo,* are variations on the historical romance, novels that distance events in space rather than in time, but distance them for much the same reasons the historical romance does. Perhaps he was playing up—as he often did when writing Galsworthy —the idea that his respect for Ford's work was not unbounded.[17]

The trilogy is in fact "a noble conception." Ford had thought through his conception of these historical events carefully, and his knowledge of the period was such that he thought it through, not in abstract terms but in terms of the actual events and people of the period. Even as early as the synopsis of his unwritten book on Henry VIII, perhaps about 1901, he had begun to think of Katharine Howard as a significant figure. "Herewith," he wrote Pinker then, "I forward you a synopsis & a sort of introductory chapter of the Henry VIII. . . . Later on I will forward you a more considerable chapter dealing with Katharine Howard who is certainly one of the most startling of Henry's wives." For years, then, he had brooded over the story of Henry and Katharine, with the result that the realized life of the trilogy is adequate to its idea.[18]

After a momentary hesitation of conception in the first volume of the trilogy, Katharine Howard is consistently the earnest, energetic, essentially simple idealist like Edward Ashburnham of *The Good Soldier*. She is for the old faith in the old way, and her classical studies have taught her to believe that it is possible for men like Henry to be truly magnanimous. She means to settle for nothing less than the reestablishment of the old faith in England, which she innocently believes will be indistinguishable from the rule of God and His Son; and she is assured that Henry has the greatness to establish this heaven on earth, that "his Highness distilleth from his person a make of majesty; there is no other such man in Christendom. His Highness culleth from one's heart a make of pity—for, for sure, there is not in Christendom a man more tried or more calling to be led Godwards." She is half right about Henry, but, alas, only half.[19]

For if there is indeed in Henry "a make of majesty" and a longing to commit himself as wholeheartedly as Katharine does to the old faith, there is also in him a man who loves power and the craft of kingship. " . . . daily," says Cromwell, "have I seen this King in ten years, and I do tell ye no man knoweth how the King loves kingcraft as I know." Cromwell, too, is half right about Henry. Henry is a man profoundly divided between Katharine's love of God and His church and Cromwell's love of an ordered society and the secular state that represents it. Cromwell is a man as dedicated to his vision as Katharine is to hers, and each of them answers to a half of Henry's nature. In a beautifully ordered way, Ford shows us the complex possibilities of both these elements of Henry's divided nature in the novel's minor characters. Mary, Cecily Elliott, Margot Poins, and Udall on one side, and Norfolk, Wriothesley, and Lascelles on the other represent less magnanimous forms that they may take. In Throckmorton, the novel's most brilliant character, Ford creates another Henry, but one who fully understands his own dilemma, reconciles himself to it, and so finds a way—a wholly self-sacrificing way—to live with it.[20]

This conflict, embodied in Henry and Throckmorton and split into opposed characters in Katharine and Cromwell and their followers, is the basic conflict within Ford's own nature translated into the religious and political terms that governed men's minds in the time of Henry VIII. *The Fifth Queen* is the most complex and in some ways the most searching image Ford ever made of his nature. In the deaths of Cromwell and Katharine and in what is perhaps worse, the living despair of Henry when Katharine chooses to die rather than endure the compromise between the two sides of his nature he asks her to accept, Ford faced squarely the only possibilities of life open to a man constituted as he was.*

Ford completed *The 'Half Moon'* at Winchelsea over the weekend of June 8, 1907, very nearly at the same time that he completed *The Fifth Queen Crowned.* The subject had been suggested to Ford while he was in America by William Bradley, to whom he dedicated the book. Bradley was obviously looking for subjects that would attract an American audience: Ford had in mind the *Mayflower* as the second of his three ships. But McClure never published anything of Ford's except *England and the English;* in his gloomier moments Ford could be very bitter about it: "Methuen's must wait & be particularly damned to them. And be particularly damned to the U.S.A. too: there's nothing to be got out of *them."* Ford also intended to use *The 'Half Moon'* as the second of the series of novels for which he had made a contract with Methuen, the first of which had been *An English Girl.* Methuen, however, rejected *The 'Half Moon'.* Ford was incensed. "There can be no question of trouble," he wrote Pinker, "they must either pay & publish or pay & pay damages for breach of contract. . . . One of the inducements to me to sign the contract [with Methuen] was that they undertook to put up the sales of my books. They have not done this. How c^d they, considering how they handled the books? Please be absolutely peremptory in the matter. I will allow of any statement whatever in the freezing them." But the contract with Methuen allowed them to reject *The 'Half Moon'* and Pinker noted on this letter that he returned it to Ford April 30, 1908. It did not in fact appear until March, 1909, the tercentenary of Hudson's voyage, when Eveleigh Nash, who had published *The Fifth Queen Crowned* a year before, brought it out.[21]

The subject, Hudson's voyage to America, had not at first greatly appealed to Ford; "a voyage," he said, "is not a very inspiring thing to write about—even when it is a voyage to a new world." Then it occurred to him that he might focus on the motives that attracted men to such voyages and, by this means, study the "under selves" of modern men at a slightly later point in history than he had been examining in the *Fifth Queen* trilogy. He discovered that the first European to die on the shores of the Hudson River came from Rye, and this made it possible for him to explore this subject in a place he knew something about, the seventeenth-century Rye he had investigated for *The Cinque Ports,* where the practical Anabaptists from Holland

---

*For a discussion of the *Fifth Queen* trilogy, see pp. 469–77.

and Münster, who had settled there after the great plague, came into conflict with the wealthy heirs of Rye's medieval seamen. Ford had earlier suggested to Conrad that they collaborate on an Anabaptist novel, no doubt with this idea in mind. Here was a group of sceptical, practical, modern men brought directly into conflict with a once great but now moribund medieval community.[22]

The result of this idea is, unfortunately, another of Ford's too carefully thought-out novels in which the realized life is insufficient to embody the abstract ideas. The care he took over the precise signification of the events and over the ingenuities of the novel's construction is deadening. It smothers the action in quaint historical details and in long, undramatic speeches in which the characters explain their own historical significance. None of this is helped by the brummagem seventeenth-century style in which Ford has written the book.*

*For a discussion of *The 'Half Moon,'* see pp. 477–78.

Chapter 13

Late in May, 1908, a distinguished surgeon named Fenwick finally diagnosed Elsie's illness correctly as a tubercular kidney. He was appalled that the disease had been allowed to progress so far. Elsie's doctors had practically given up on her case and were pretty sure she was going to die. Fenwick was confident that he could save her, but the infected kidney and the infected part of the bladder had to be removed at once. On May 30 he operated at the Bungalow, with the help of two trained nurses and Edmée Van der Noot. "My wife," Ford wrote Pinker, "has to be operated on again tomorrow & it is now just touch and go with her. . . . I don't know why I treat you to this information except that it obsesses me & is the only thing I can think of." To pay for the operation Ford borrowed £440 from Arthur Marwood.[*1]

When Elsie began to recover from this operation, Ford pressed her to come back to Holland Park Avenue. But Elsie's objections to London were as great as ever. Moreover, she had been told by the doctors that she ought to live in the country and sleep out of doors, and she had a thatched hut built for the purpose at Hurst Cottage. It had sailcloth sides that could be raised or lowered according to the weather; here she spent most of her time until she recovered.

During the months of Elsie's convalescence Ford was rushing about London as busily as ever, arranging important conferences at the Mont Blanc restaurant, where he lunched regularly, or turning up for the monthly meeting of the Square Club in Fleet Street, where Chesterton presided over a group of literary people that usually included Galsworthy, Masefield, Algernon

*In 1913, when Marwood was putting his affairs in order in anticipation of his death, which occurred in 1916, he asked Ford to repay this loan. According to Goldring, whose information presumably came from Ford, Ford did so; according to the Marwood family, he did not.

Blackwood, and E. C. Bentley. He had the air of an influential man of affairs. "My first impressions of Ford," says Goldring, "are of a tall thin man with fair hair and a blonde moustache which imperfectly concealed defective front teeth. He wore a grey-blue swallow-tail coat of uncertain cut, carried a leather despatch case of the kind the French call a *serviette* and had an 'important' manner which in some ways suggested an Under-Secretary of State." Elsie worried greatly over his leading this life; she thought that sooner or later it would upset him badly, as had the strain of their life in Airlie Gardens four years before, and she was sure he could never get any serious work done amid such distractions. Conrad was equally sure Ford should not live in this way if he meant to be a serious writer.[2]

Nonetheless Ford had completed *Mr. Apollo*, his second novel for Methuen, in April, and it was published August 20, 1908. As usual, he was sure it would be a success unless some foolish publisher hindered it.

> Everyone tells me that the Apollo is good [he wrote Pinker] & I daresay it is. I am pretty certain that it ought to sell if it is properly managed. W[d] you give the following message to Methuen: that to atone for the miserable bungle they made with the advertising of the English Girl I consider it their duty to give me special ad[vt] for the "Apollo." After all publishers contract to publish with due care & diligence & in the case of the E.G. they did not begin to use either.

Presumably Pinker was wiser than to convey any such message to Methuen. But Ford usually managed to write a letter of this kind directly to his publishers just about the time they had begun to think that Ford was a very poor risk. Thus when the sale of *Mr. Apollo* (including the colonial sales) barely exceeded 1,700 copies, Methuen was not pleased to have Ford demand an expensive rush job on its successor in the fall of 1909. Desperation for money made Ford sit up nights to finish his novels and he could not understand why publishers would not get them out at once and sell them widely; he was sure he could devise an advertising program that would sell any book of his at any time. This was not the publishers' view.

> I have your note about Hueffer's new novel for the autumn of 1909 ... [Methuen wrote Pinker in December, 1908]. Unless it is really a novel I shall not be able to accept it. The last book [*Mr. Apollo*] has been a terrible frost, chiefly because it is not a novel but a series of essays.... P.S. The first of the three novels—[*An English Girl*]—published last year—was also an absolute failure.[3]

When Pinker attempted to defend Methuen against Ford's charges, presumably in the hope of preventing Ford's starting another damaging quarrel with a publisher, Ford was adamant:

The point about Methuen & the English Girl is not that they advertised it insufficiently but that they advertised it all wrong. . . . You might remind M. that one of the inducem^{ts} that they held out to me was that they were going to push my work.[4]

In *Mr. Apollo* Ford experimented with a new kind of novel. He had been greatly impressed by H. G. Wells's *The Sea Lady* (1902). Its special appeal is indicated by Violet Hunt's response to it. "I adore it," she wrote; "I think it the most passionate poetical piece of work of his hand there is. He [Wells] was scornful. I honestly don't think he thinks it good. It is too poetical for him—A poetical lapse." *The Sea Lady* suggested to Ford the idea of presenting as a pagan divinity the aspect of human experience that always mattered to him most. It may also have been Wells's example that led him to shift the emphasis away from the nature of his divinity to a satiric analysis of society's conventionalized blindness to his distinction. To this shift of focus Wells's earlier novel about a supernatural visitation, *The Wonderful Visit* (1895), probably contributed, though *The Wonderful Visit* is a much more trivial affair than *Mr. Apollo:* its dim angelic visitor represents an early and unusually silly version of Wells's modern Utopia, a paradise of the nineties, where unicorns, exquisite improvisations on the violin, a total lack of social conventions, and an indeterminate love of "Beauty" flourish. "The Angel of this story," Wells says, "is the Angel of Art . . . of Italian art, polychromic and gay." Ford's Mr. Apollo is a much tougher and more genuinely awesome divinity than that. Nevertheless, having chosen a pagan god peculiarly suited to his conception of the god who walks in men's gardens—"a prince, a composer, a musician, an actor"—Ford then devotes little time to Apollo himself, using him mainly—as Wells used the angel of *The Wonderful Visit* —to satirize the fools who have said in their hearts, there is no god, and to detect saving virtues of devotion in unlikely people such as downtrodden Mrs. Todd and the "bovine" poetess, Mrs. Milnes, who is the only person in the book capable of praying, "that you will stay with us for ever, and that we may be your servants till we die."

There are moments when the contrast between Mr. Apollo's divinity and the impenetrable conventionality of the people he encounters is exploited very effectively, as when Police-Constable 742L is forced to deal with the impeccably dressed gentleman who disturbs the peace of Anglesey Square by descending from the air. Occasionally, too, Mr. Apollo makes

Ford's point about the irrationality of conventional rationalism with real dramatic force, as when the stupid clergyman, Mr. Todd, says, "I am the most tolerant of men," and Mr. Apollo replies, "Then you betray your office." Most of the time, however, Ford is debating against rationalism—in the elderly Mr. Clarges, with his devotion to Huxley and Wallace; in the advanced young people with their arid Fabianism, who "deny the evidence of your senses in order to explain along lines purely natural that which to a man of reason would appear a phenomenon purely divine"; in the Harms-worth-like Lord Aldington, who would rather publicize a mind reader than print Mr. Apollo's assertion of his divinity. The result is that the book falls apart into a series of disconnected satiric scenes and the essential idea of *Mr. Apollo*, the divine dimension of experience that only gods and poets grasp, is largely ignored.[5]

By this stage of Ford's career it is possible to see a pattern in his work. He was using these early novels to try to discover his real commitment, and the process was slowed down by his extraordinary talent. Not knowing what he believed, Ford had no way of determining what kind of novel would best serve his purpose except experimentation; and the technical challenge of each new form he tried tended to divert him from the search for a sense of reality that was the main purpose of the experiments. The novels of this period are technically skillful, but they are serious efforts to express his sense of life only in flashes.

The craftsman in him set out in the *Fifth Queen* trilogy and the aborted three-ships trilogy to master the possibilities of the historical romance; the main defect in these romances is that Ford loaded them with more meaning than the form could support. At the same time the nature of the historical romance required him to define this meaning in historical terms, and these terms—he eventually came to feel—were not satisfactory. He does everything he can in the *Fifth Queen* trilogy to use seriously the contrast between Katharine Howard's devotion to the old faith and Thomas Cromwell's devotion to the new. But though Ford's sense of the essential character of life would always have a historical component, so that Dowell sees Edward Ashburnham as a feudal landlord and a chivalric lover, and Christopher Tietjens' secret ambition is to be a seventeenth-century Anglican saint, Ford's full understanding was too complex to be contained by the historical romance.

The Wells novel of fantasy he tried in *Mr. Apollo* must have appealed to him as a chance to define his sense of life in other terms than the historical romance's, as must the third kind of novel he experimented with, Henry

James's; there is some James influence in *The Benefactor;* there is somewhat more in *An English Girl.* But the most Jamesian of all his novels is the next one he would write, *A Call.* Here, too, was a form he imitated skillfully that did not finally serve his deepest purpose, as we can see from the way he forces the limits of the form in *A Call* in order to say what he thinks—or at least to discover in the process of writing the book exactly what that was. The novels of the next seven years of his career are a repetition of the pattern he had established by 1908. Some of these novels, like *A Call* and *Ladies Whose Bright Eyes,* come tantalizingly close to doing what he would finally see he wanted to; none of them quite does it. Ford did not try— because he did not know how to try—to put into a novel all he could feel until he wrote *The Good Soldier* in 1913.

Ford's life was brought to a climax in the latter part of 1908 by two major events. The first was his desire to edit a literary magazine, which was realized in *The English Review;* the second was his affair with Violet Hunt. Violet Hunt's father was a don at Oxford who had been persuaded by Ruskin to give up the academic life for a career as a watercolorist. He came of a prosperous family; when his daughter Silvia married in 1890, he was worth something like £ 25,000. He became a well-known watercolor painter; at the same time Mrs. Hunt became a popular novelist. In her girlhood Mrs. Hunt was the model for Tennyson's "Margaret," whom Tennyson begs to

> Rise from the feast of sorrow, lady,
> Where all day long you sit between
> Joy and woe, and whisper each.
> Or only look across the lawn
> Look out below your bower-eaves,
> Look down . . .

This faint shadow of the shadowy figure of the "Lady of Shalott" is difficult to reconcile with the figure the elderly Mrs. Hunt cut as Valentine Wannop's mother in Ford's *Parade's End,* that "frightfully inaccurate" old lady who had "written the only novel that's been fit to read since the eighteenth century." The Hunts lived in Tor Villa, a comfortable house on Campden Hill, and moved in a circle of well-bred artists and writers, of whom the best known were Tennyson, Browning, and Ruskin. If this society "had a certain bohemian flavour, it nevertheless dressed for dinner, while its daughters were often invited to dances at almost the best houses." The Hunts also knew most members of the Pre-Raphaelite circle in which Ford grew up. Mrs. Hunt's diaries show them exchanging frequent dinners with the Ford Madox Browns, and

Alfred Hunt supported Brown when Brown was an unsuccessful candidate for membership in the Old Water-Colour Society.[6]

The Hunts had three children, Isobel Violet, born September 28, 1862 (and thus eleven years older than Ford); Venice; and Silvia. (Venice was given her odd name at the insistence of her godfather, Ruskin, who compounded her difficulties by calling her "Ice"; he left her £ 200, perhaps as a compensation.) Violet's two sisters made eminently respectable marriages. Silvia married a country gentleman named John Walton Fogg Elliot, who enlivened their marriage by insisting on having his mistresses live in the house (perhaps because the first of them had been their maid and he found it convenient); he became righteously indignant at Silvia for attempting to chase one of them out of his bedroom when she succeeded in catching her there. He was even more indignant when Violet, ever ready with advice in affairs of this sort, urged Silvia to divorce him and succeeded at least in persuading Silvia to "repulse" him. Venice Hunt married William Benson, who was in trade in a way that could not be concealed: his shop was in Bond Street. "I never thought," Violet exclaimed in her diary when the engagement was announced, "I should have a sister in trade!" Willie did not help matters by innocently proposing to borrow money from Alfred Hunt to expand his business.[7]

Violet Hunt was an odd combination of snobbery of the kind that made her dislike having a brother-in-law "in trade," of shrewd curiosity, and of uncontrollable impulsiveness—a middle-class Moll Flanders or Molly Bloom. She talked practically continuously, in an amusing, inconsecutive way that entertained—and sometimes startled—people. "Chattering with sublime disregard for practically everything, distraught golden hair, obviously a beauty of the Edwardian era, Violet Hunt often proved disconcerting ... for the way she pounced," Iris Barry remembered; mixed up in that endless flow of talk there were a good many acute observations—no sooner perceived than delightedly expressed. "She said sharp things about people," as one of her old friends put it, "but it was like a bird chirping." She was a generous and loyal friend and mistress; at the same time she must have been a difficult woman to live with, especially as she got older and her indiscreetness increased. But there is something very appealing about her, an innocent honesty, a directness that is hard to resist.

She liked, as she said herself, "to pitch things dramatically," and described with approval how her friend Ménie Dowie, the author of an advanced novel called *Gallia*, "got a friend to ask her to tea" with her ex-husband's new wife, just for the excitement. "Miss Dowie," H. G. Wells observed, "or, shall we say, Gallia, would be a pioneer even in a society recruited solely from the club in Bruton Street [the Writers' Club, headquarters for the advanced intellectual women of the day]." Violet pursued a similar policy with her two most important lovers, Oswald Crawfurd and Ford. After she became Crawfurd's mistress, she cultivated the acquaintance of his invalid first wife; when he left her, she haunted his flat in Queen Anne's Mansions and wept with his neighbors over his betrayal of her. After she became Ford's mistress, she sought out Elsie Martindale, and when he left her for Stella Bowen, she tracked them down in Bedham and hung over the fence of their cottage watching them.[8]

Whether because she was naturally so or because it was the style of her age, her love of excitement was focused particularly on sex, though her interest seems to have been as much in the drama of the occasions as in the sex itself. "I am," as she put it, "a sensualist of the emotions." What she meant by that is clear in her description of *La Femme Nue* at the Moulin Rouge, to which her old friend Edward Heron Allen took her in October, 1907:

> It was for me a great experience a revelation of the . . . sanctity of the human body *sans voiles* of tights and sashes and maillots[.] The little actress . . . advanced from the back [of the stage] naked except for a sort of gold lace with huge reticulations from her neck to her knees. She was naked except for this network which allowed the brown hair to show very faintly. . . . She had a vast circumambient cloak of gold tissue as she came forwards which she opened and threw off gently. . . . There was no suggestion of meretriciousness about her and yet as I have said she had absolutely nothing on under the wide diagonals of the gold netting—three inches square I should have said[—]and she had not shaved anywhere.

This passage is typical of Violet. The occasion appeals strongly to the sensualist of the emotions in her. At the same time her perception of it is surprisingly innocent. It is not easy to imagine a woman of her experience —she was thirty-five years old and had had several lovers—being quite so struck by the actress's not having shaved "anywhere," as if she still half expected that even at the Moulin Rouge La Femme Nue would look like the nudes of Bouguereau or Albert Moore, whose elegant seductiveness is as smooth as marble—or soap. The girlish emphasis on the fashion aspect of the occasion is also typical; Violet was always acutely conscious of clothes, ready to break off in the midst of describing the most exciting experience to specify exactly what she wearing. And there is the childish solemnity of that intellectual cliché about the sanctity of the human body; Violet was anxious to give an air of superior significance to her sexual interests in order to distinguish them from the merely vulgar sensuality of ordinary people. "On the way home," she reported of a weekend party at a great country house, "I was in the car with Olly and her fancy man. . . . We had a big rug over all our knees and for miles and miles I had to sit under my bit of it watching it heave and wrinkle and the lewd smile on both their faces. . . . I was disgusted."[9]

About her essentially unintellectual nature and her reliance on impulse she was always disarmingly frank. "Violet plays [cards]," she reports someone saying of her as a girl, "like a baby, with flashes of intelligence & no head at all," and she carefully records Arnold Bennett's opinion that she is "just clever and modern without much knowledge or interest in any traditional matters—my walk in life being too purely sexual for him." Nevertheless, there was a persistence in her nature that made her, however whimsical and irrational, formidable. "I am," she said, "a jelly, wellstayed with a Northcountry corset of grim whalebone" (Mrs. Hunt came from Yorkshire).

This last aspect of her character comes out in her pursuit of Henry James. James much admired Violet's tales of the supernatural such as "The Coach" (which Ford selected for *The English Review*), and she deliberately sought to fascinate James by shrewdly exploiting her own natural character when he invited her to Lamb House for a weekend. Up to a point James enjoyed it; he called Violet "his 'Purple Patch.' "

Saturday November 2nd Henry James met me with the dog Max whirling all round us with that immensely long lead and we walked up to the house. . . . there [was] nobody else there and good thing for the *bisque* soup very good disagreed with me and after dinner I had to rush up to me room and be violently sick. I didn't know what to do for my pink new Goupy chiffon[—]two shades of red and white embroidery[—]was the only dress I had[.] About nine I decided . . . to put on my white liberty Chinese dressing gown . . . very pretty and drifted as I know how, into the drawing room where he was all solicitude and I do believe pleasure and we discussed Mrs. Humphrey Ward's books of which he has a row over his writing table, till eleven, I scolded him for admiring them and he said he didn't—that she would keep sending them and even the typed M S for his corrextions[.] I said that he never did as much for me. . . . He always wants my news but never more than half of it always getting bored or delicate.

Sunday Nov 3rd I was pretty ill ... although I managed to be there at breakfast ... and watched him Fletcherizing[,] masticating rather disgustingly[.] He has a plateful of cereals in the form of a bird's nest and an egg poached on it! ...

... We "got talking" about affairs of the heart and I discussed the character of O[swald] C[rawfurd] whom of course he knew[.] He spoke with a *sous entendu* of wonder of how anything so vamped-up such a thin mentality, could have absorbed any of the women wh[o]m common report gave to him for conquests ... I suppose it annoyed [me] and woke my fierce desire for recognition of his value ... I said in reply to some depreciatory remark "I loved him!" and poor H J got up from the table like a dog that has had enough of his bone and closed the discussion. For it was becoming too intimate too little academic for him. He 'skoots' from passion as if he had been once bitten by it and yet I am sure that in *my* sense of the word he never has. ... he is incapable ... a glance at a photograph I once saw in a drawer in my room at The Lamb House convinced me of that[.] It was the face of a lad sealed in eternal ignorance of one side of emotion ... and yet a powerful head ... of the type that goes Nap on passion, if the physical nature had been according ... I don't know how to put it[.]

It is typical of Violet to have contemplated a sexual conquest of James, and equally typical of her to have quickly seen that it was futile to attempt it.[10]

As a girl Violet was almost a Pre-Raphaelite beauty; she was auburn-haired, with large, liquid eyes and an expressive mouth that gave her a properly melancholy look. As an older woman she was "Rather like a handsome witch ... brilliant and caustic; [but] an aura of Pre-Raphaelite glory still flickered about her." When she was a girl, her sharp tongue seemed merely pert and lively, and it is easy to understand how Oscar Wilde was charmed by her to the point of describing her as "the sweetest Violet in England" and half seriously proposing to her, and even the notorious Marc-André Raffalovich, a wealthy, ugly young man who dabbled in the arts and also, in Wilde's euphemism, "feasted with Panthers," pursued her. By the age of twenty she had also been involved in a number of more conventional but sufficiently fervid romances, and was deeply thrilled when one young man wept bitterly over her rejection of him.[11]

Her first serious lover was the painter, George Boughton. Boughton, though born in Norwich, had been brought up in America and made his reputation as a landscape painter in New York. He moved to London in 1863 and had a successful career there, becoming an associate of the Royal

Academy in 1879 and R. A. in 1896. He lived at West House on Campden Hill, near the Hunts; he was a much older man than Violet, fifty-one to her twenty-two, when their affair began in 1884. They became lovers when one day at Tor Villa "George kissed me so wildly and passionately ... and I kissed him and threw my arms round him."

Then, after a little more than two years as her lover, Boughton married, in July, 1887, and "Mrs B made an awful row, and this was the beginning of the end. I did not see George for 2 weeks." On August 3 "George came to say goodbye, as I knew since. I cried and he almost did"—a splendidly dramatic occasion. Violet then retired with her mother to her sister's place at Robin Hood's Bay, in Yorkshire, where unfortunately several tender passages of her affair with Boughton had occurred, so that she "landed at the station all tears, I was completely knocked down by it all." She soon consoled herself, however, with an Etonian named Eustace Strickland with whom she kept up for some months, until one day "poor little," fond Euty became "merely the commonplace, tongue tied young Briton with far too much ... jaw." Meanwhile, she had had, on October 21, a fine scene with poor Boughton. "Met George, and oh, how bitter! I reviled him for being a slave to his wife, and for treating me so badly, and *left* him." But in May of 1888, *"Si heureuse!* George came and our reconciliation was complete." But George was too hopelessly enslaved by that unreasonable wife of his, and by the fall of 1889, the drama of their affair was in its final stages. "George," she noted on November 28, "is growing coarse and jovial, while I stand with tears in my eyes. Perhaps though, he laughs that he may not weep." Still, she felt she had learned something from George about the sacredness of the female form divine, noting years later that she was not disinclined to "drop her dress to the waist" for a painter because "George stopped me being shy of *artists* because he never profited." *"Artists,"* she observed grandly, *"do* care for the form"; and then the shrewd Violet added, "they are used to models, too."[12]

Almost before her affair with Boughton had run its course, she found herself under siege from another older married man named Walter Pollock, who set out quite openly to seduce her. He did not attract her; she thought him a mere libertine. "Mrs P[ollock] has got the gout," she noted on April 21, 1889. "Walter [Pollock] something worse—after a debauch at the Globe Theatre last night. I can hardly speak to him, it is so disgusting...." Still, it was exciting. "I called on the Walter Pollocks," she noted on December 21, 1890. "... I longed to have a reconciliation with him but it is so difficult with a man who can't be in the same room with one alone without wanting to kiss one! A nice habit."

At the same time she had a recurrent awareness that all this could not last forever and that she ought to make some provision for the future.

Tomorrow is my birthday [she wrote September 27, 1890] and 28, and it is rather a dreary prospect. At present I am happy enough. I have plenty of Lovers, of a sort, enough to amuse me but looks, such as they are, cannot last for ever, and then, where am I? Othello's occupation gone!

This matter of her looks was a deep anxiety to her and she consulted a doctor about it. He suggested she take arsenic. "I know well enough," she remarks, "that arsenic *se paye de retour* and that general flabbiness follows it's [sic] disuse"; nevertheless she began taking it and felt that it was "freshening me up wonderfully."

Her anxiety about what might become of her as she grew older was reinforced by her very real desire for respectability. "She had," as Douglas Goldring puts it, "inherited and built up . . . a 'position in Society' which to a Victorian woman, even one as advanced and emancipated as herself, was of immense importance to her life and happiness. . . . She was in no sense a Bohemian and dreaded being ostracized by all the solid and respectable people who formed her real background. . . . " She had plenty of opportunities to make such a life for herself; at least twice during her early twenties proper young men asked her father for permission to propose to her, and during her late twenties she twice engaged herself to similar young men. Until she was well into her forties a very respectable man named Dr. Cholmeley pursued her with stubborn persistence. But these "Lovers, of a sort," were finally too bland for her; "I have not," she wrote longingly in her diary September 22, 1890, "looked into the eyes of a man I love since George [Boughton] . . . " who "initiated me into the secret of what I *could* feel and has now left me—*inassouvie.*"[13]

Restless, and bored with the eligible Dr. Cholmeley, she was easily fascinated by another married man who began to woo her that summer. This was Oswald Crawfurd, a man of "good family," as Violet characteristically liked to remind people. His father had been a diplomat who ended his career as governor of Singapore. Oswald was educated at Eton and Merton College, Oxford. In 1857 he entered the Foreign Office and in 1869 became the British consul at Oporto, where he served for twenty-four years, receiving the C.M.G. in 1890. It was not an onerous post, and Crawfurd managed to spend the six summer months of every year in his flat in Queen Anne's Mansions in London, where he lived the life of a "cultured amateur" of literature. He wrote sketches of Portuguese life, "thoughtful" personal essays, and a number of light popular novels of which the best-known in its day was *Sylvia Arden*. He also dabbled in editing and publishing, being at one time the editor of *The Novel Magazine*, in which Violet appeared; at another a director of *Black & White*, for which Violet wrote a column; and at yet another the chairman of Chapman Hall. These were the accomplishments of a gentleman; "in London literary life," as *The Athenaeum* put it at his death, "Mr Crawfurd was well known and deservedly popular. He was an excellent talker, full of ideas and suggestive fancies.... " His serious interests included "shooting, fishing, polo, fencing, golf"—and women.

He was a handsome, dark-complected man, "an Italian bandit," as Violet said, who looked "like a foreign Count in his black coat and astrakhan collar." He was, she felt, "fascinating, kind, talented, susceptible to the charming[ly] gowned and talented women who threw themselves at his head while affecting to be his wife's devoted companion[s]." His first wife, Margaret, the daughter of the British envoy at Madrid, Sir Clare Ford, was a long-time invalid. At least two of Violet's friends had thrown "themselves at his head" successfully before she became involved with him.[14]

Crawfurd began to pursue Violet in earnest early in the summer of 1890; he was fifty-six years old and Violet twenty-eight. In her indiscreet way she openly sought him out whenever they were at a party together; frequently she persuaded him to walk her home across Kensington Gardens, enthralled by the way he always "discours[ed] of exceedingly delicate matters." She talked about him to everyone. Even Crawfurd himself—to her vexation—felt it necessary to lecture her over her habit of rushing "in—where even angels would fear to tread—into any every conversation. In short, [he said] that I talk too much. So I do and thus I 'give myself away' continually. But if one is born and made passionate and impulsive—there is an end of tact." It was all too true.[15]

Crawfurd took a masterful, Byronic line with her, talking of "the gift of his love" and how she could trust his honor and at the same time advocating "wild notions of free love" of so advanced a character that even Violet confessed she "couldn't find my way about in them." An atypical feeling that "there would be something very ridiculous in my being engaged for a second time in an intrigue with a married man" kept her from falling into his arms at once. "I am," she said unhappily, "walking in the paths of virtue with a vengeance and great dullness." Crawfurd alternated skillfully between anger, penitence, resignation, and indifference, until Violet, always too impatient to play these games successfully, felt "I have never been so prevented from having my own way in my whole life! As far I mean as flirtation goes."

Yet even she must have known that her eventual capitulation was inevitable, for as she wrote with her startling honesty, "sometimes I desperately [want] OC out of sheer *ennui*—as well as great liking for him."[16]
They became lovers sometime in 1892. It lasted until 1898, when Violet began to weary Crawfurd with her possessiveness and her indiscretions. She made frantic efforts to get him back, rushing to Paris to consult her old friend, Agnes Farley (and perhaps in the hope of seeing Crawfurd, who was there). She called assiduously on friends in Queen Anne's Mansions and, when she was at last rewarded with the knowledge that Crawfurd was in the building, "gave myself dead away, crying." She wrote Crawfurd long letters she knew were futile. "I have written three times already altogether like the fool I am. He has not replied like the —— he is!" In 1899—just too late for Violet—Crawfurd's invalid wife died, and after at least one further affair with a friend of Violet's, Crawfurd married Lita Brown, another of Violet's friends, and disappeared from her life. But she never forgot him. When he died on January 31, 1909, she pasted his obituary into her diary, despite the fact that, as Goldring put it, "he did her an injury from which she suffered until the end of her life." It is just barely possible—though unlikely—that she did not know he was responsible for this injury.[17]
She did not discover it until 1905. In August, 1936, six years before she died, she described what that belated discovery had been like.

There was a day when poor dear Cholmeley came to the club at ten Adelphi Terrace (gone) and with tears in his eyes told me to my face and of my face (and my wrist) that I had a disgraceful illness in fact tertiaries only he did not name it or do more than hint. But I had had warnings. Archie Propert looked at me at the Monds and my spots on my forehead and said "You ought not to be out["] ie going about [(] He said "you ought to be in bed" actually) Then Cholmeley clinched it and sent me to a very distinguished doctor Dr. Stephen Paget. Paget looked at me and spoke to me as to something unclean I never went again. All Propert had said at the Monds, was that I ought to be in bed. Propert did not tell me what was the matter and I did not guess it but said I would not go again to C [That is, she said to Cholmeley that she would not go again to Dr. Paget], as he looked upon me with disgust and loathing, as I could see It was the most inglorious moment of my life And of course Archie Propert, being a doctor did not propose, as everyone then thought he would. . . .

"Now," she scribbled at the end of this typed description, "I know what fallen women may feel." This is remarkably honest and at the same time naïve. "Fallen women"—the socially superior and personally charming, if not morally impeccable, company of Pinero's Paul Tanqueray, of Wilde's Lady Windermere and Rachel Arbuthnot, of Violet's own autobiographical heroine in *Sooner or Later*. She has transformed the drab and humiliating life of venereal disease's slow dulling of the mind and destruction of the body into the romantically interesting situation of some Dame aux Caméllias.[*18]

During the years between the end of her affair with Crawfurd and 1907, Violet wrote six books, and in 1904 made a great success with a fictionalized account of her affair with Crawfurd entitled *Sooner or Later*. She also did a great deal of literary journalism, including a regular column called "Ware of Autolycus" for Harry Cust's *Pall Mall Gazette* and reviewing for the *Daily Chronicle*. When *White Rose of Weary Leaf* came out in 1908 she became widely recognized as one of the leading women novelists of her time. *White Rose of Weary Leaf* is dedicated to Somerset Maugham; her work was admired by other writers so diverse as W. H. Hudson and Kipling, W. J. Locke and Reggie Turner, Henry James and D. H. Lawrence (who characteristically added that she was "too devilishly clever for a man ever to want to marry"). As an intellectual woman and a supporter of women's right to the vote and other less openly discussable freedoms who was indubitably a lady, she was taken up by such people as Austen Chamberlain and Lady Houston. One ambitious Oxford undergraduate meeting her at this time thought her "one of the most exciting figures of the Edwardian capital . . . 'fast,' fashionable, brilliant, daring; leading spirit, as we imagined, in a circle of metropolitan celebrities of both sexes. . . . She was glamour personified."[19]

In 1902 she and her mother took a forty-year lease on South Lodge, at 80 Campden Hill Road, which she finally succeeded in buying in the summer of 1908. There she began to figure as a hostess. She gave an annual garden party, which everyone of any literary pretensions attended, but she also entertained steadily throughout the year, and she was a frequent guest at the weekend parties of the Alfred Monds and their friends. In spite of her gloomy forebodings, at the time of Silvia's marriage, over becoming an aunt, she developed into a devoted one; indeed, she became very possessive about her niece Rosamond, now sixteen. She wanted to take over Rosamond's life, have her live at South Lodge, and "bring her out" properly. She did not hesitate to tell Silvia that country people like the Fogg Elliots were not up

---

*It is not clear just when Violet recognized her condition or how fully she understood its consequences. She consulted Stephen Paget sometime in 1905 and his brutality appears to have made her try to forget the whole thing. Ultimately she seems to have understood her condition enough to feel that what she had to fear most was bearing a child, for she added in longhand a note to her typed summary of 1936 to the effect that she had not been "afraid with my displacement."

to such a task, and the whole affair led to serious quarrels between them, which Violet's imprudent conduct, when Ford came on the scene, intensified.[20]

Sometime in 1906 she discovered that her old friend Marguerite Radclyffe Hall had fallen passionately in love with her.

> I had the room next to Marguerite [she remembered later] and she used to come and sit on my bed in the clearest coldest Japanese kimono from Liberty with a streak of blue on the collar and her fine sandy auburn hair in a plait. Marguerite *avant la faute* as I called her. . . .

A little later she noted that "I wear the pearl necklace [Marguerite] gave me and C. G. twits me and says I am wearing goods unpaid for, not the wages of sin." When she went to visit Marguerite in her new house at Malvern, she "gave myself the airs of a Sultana. It is her fault for being so at my feet, poor dear! . . . shows how easily one is corrupted by adoration." Interesting as she found the situation, however, it was impossible to keep it going on these terms; at lunch with Marguerite, she noticed that "there is a coolness only because she loves me so hotly, poor darling . . . [and] because my heart had *never* been full of her!"[*][21]

Early in 1907 she had a very brief affair with Somerset Maugham. At the same time she found her old friend Edward Heron Allen suddenly showing signs of amorousness. Edward Heron Allen had started out as the secretary of Edward Fairfield, at the Colonial Office, and quickly became a prosperous lawyer. He was a bibliophile and a member of the Sette of Odde Volumes, a conchologist and a F.R.S., and an authority on the manufacture of violins. Violet had known him for years, and was taken aback by this sudden attack. She blamed it on the hansom cab they were in: a hansom cab "I say and think breeds all the evil passions in the other sex. But I can manage Edward."[22]

In the fall she found herself interestingly involved with H. G. Wells. She was quick to get herself to Sandgate for a visit. It was very hot and—daringly— she took off her shoes and stockings when she played tennis and lay on her stomach on the grass (staining, she noticed with disapproval, her "fawn voile skirt") when Wells played with his secretary instead of her.

> Jane [Wells] [she noted] does look overworked and she is no longer so pretty, for to save trouble she does her hair in a knot on the top of her head which doesn't suit her[,] makes her look scanny . . .

*Marguerite Radclyffe Hall later made herself well known by the publication of a widely read novel of Lesbianism, *The Well of Loneliness* (1928).

Violet did not hesitate to point out these interesting facts to Jane and concluded from Jane's response that "I don't think she likes me," adding with her characteristic shrewdness, "I don't see, all things considered, why she should." Among the things Jane had to consider was the continuation of Violet's involvement with Wells.

> I hardly see H.G. alone[.] He sometimes wiles me into a tool shed which he calls his study, a place with bare boards and all window and a trestle table with a type writer on it. . . . The buzzing flies on the pane are paralysing . . . I have a funny French Goupy dress . . . white with little green tiny spots on it. The effect is green very pale and demure, I am demure the moment I go into the house and the flies begin to obfuscate me[.]

The situation was reversed, however, when they got outside Wells's study.

> . . . outside near the *taillis*, of bushes encompassing us but not quite [H.G.] is in continual terror of Dorothy's sharp eyes [Dorothy Richardson, the novelist, was staying with the Wellses at the time and—Violet was convinced—hotly pursuing Wells] and I am such a devil that I am only nice to him *outside.*

"[H.G.]," she concluded, "is getting very cross with me." Nevertheless, when she left, he took her to the station, where she borrowed a pound from him for her fare and "he bought me a six penny of The Sea Lady and autographed it with his stylo. I adore it. I think it the most passionate poetical piece of work of his hand there is. He was scornful."

Not long after, Wells sent her the letter of some importunate female Violet had urged to write him; Wells had written across the top: "Damn you Villit!" The exclamation no doubt had general application. Later he told her that Beatrice of *Tono-Bungay* was modeled on her.[23]

But despite her delight in the drama of sexual intrigue, her longing for the security and standing of marriage grew more and more importunate. She was "beginning to think as Mamma says that I have 'run my rig' and want something kind and strong." Her best prospect appeared to be that Dr. Propert whom Angela Mond had in mind for her. On August 10, she wrote:

> To stay with the Emile Monds at Broadstairs[.] Dr Propert whom I do seriously think of settling down with and Angela knows it and thought he liked me but was, like me, not in love—*revenu de tout* went down [to dinner] with me. I was wearing. . . .

Dr. Propert nevertheless had his attractions; for one thing, he was a man of such distinction that many of Violet's friends thought it unrealistic of her even to consider trying to marry him; for another—and one probably more important to Violet—he looked, as she said, "like Mephistopheles in a black bathing suit." But, whether because he never seriously considered marrying her, or because he was not attracted by her this weekend (as she thought) or understood better than she the meaning of the spots on her face (as she later believed), he never proposed to her. This disappointment intensified her fear that she had put off for too long settling down; she was a woman of forty-five, "coarse and plain," as one unfriendly witness described her, "with a skin like leather," who was attempting "the difficult feat of being both spinsterish and intolerant of others, while living openly with [married men]." She still wanted to marry someone she could feel wildly in love with. But above all she wanted to marry; it was becoming almost an obsession with her. Such was her state of mind when she found herself once more in touch with Ford, whom she had hardly seen since children's parties in the eighties, where she "often had to rap the fingers of the two high-spirited Hueffer boys for playing ball with the penny buns."[24]

Chapter 14

§

In later years, Ford told several different stories about how he came to start *The English Review*. In *Return to Yesterday* he says, "It has been alleged that I started *The English Review* in order to print a poem by Thomas Hardy that had been refused by every magazine in England." Ford sometimes alleged this himself. He then says,

> It would be more just to say that that was the suggestion of my partner Arthur Marwood. My own most urgent motive was to provide some money for Conrad by printing the *Personal Record*, and other things which I extracted from him.

Both these statements are misleading.[1]

A magazine like *The English Review* had been discussed during 1908 by a group of writers that included Ford, Conrad, Wells, and Edward Garnett. They were convinced that no existing magazine properly supported the best writers. Ford repeatedly said that *The English Review* was created "with the definite design of giving imaginative literature a chance in England," and whatever other motives may have been involved, this was the most important one. The leading spirit in planning the *Review* was Ford, and it was taken for granted that he would be one of its editors. According to Ford, Wells had originally agreed to do half the editorial work and to find half the money and was exceedingly apologetic when he had to back out of this agreement. But at the start he helped with his usual energy, and there was much running back and forth to Spade House. The Wells's German governess particularly remembered Ford's visits. "With his blond hair, which was rather long, and his black, braided, velvet jacket that he wore most of the time, all he needed was a long corps pipe and a gay corps hat to complete the picture [of a German student]." "Dear Hueffer," Wells would write,

I enclose two letters, one from Lady Elcho, and one from Lady Desborough ... I do not fail to pursue these ladies with subscription forms. Tell me shall I write to Lady Tennant? ... Tell me also what you think of the Evan Charteris proposal. He is, by the bye, a great friend of Gosse, whom you are, I submit, rather an ass not to propitiate.*²

In his less practical way Conrad was equally concerned. At the end of August the Conrads had moved to Aldington, to "rooms in a farmhouse not very far from the Hueffers." Conrad had an idea of looking "for something permanent down that way. ... I have a positive horror of this place [Someries]. ... " They stayed a few weeks, returned to Someries briefly, moved into a cottage in Aldington at the end of September, were again forced back to Someries, and finally, in January, moved into a house "just at the foot of the Hill" in Aldington for an indefinite stay; the whole process is typical of Conrad's management of his affairs. Conrad wanted to be at Aldington so that Ford could help him with the reminiscences they were planning to print in the new review. Thus he was close at hand for conferences with Ford and Arthur Marwood, who had been drawn into the enterprise.³

In the fall Ford gave up writing his weekly article for the *Daily News*, hired Douglas Goldring as his secretary, and set to work enlisting the support of distinguished authors. He wrote twice to Henry James. He asked Galsworthy for short stories and a selection of poetry and Bennett for stories. He also wrote Hardy, who replied:

> I am quite in sympathy with the object you have in view in proposing to launch such a magazine as you describe. But I have not been able to find anything that I can send. ...

Then Ford heard that no editor in England would print Hardy's poem "A Sunday Morning Tragedy" and wrote again to offer to print the poem in *The English Review*. Hardy had actually tried the poem on only one magazine and then kept it by him with the intention of using it "to open a volume of poems ... when I issue another." But he had had enough trouble with pecksniffery to appreciate Ford's sympathy, and he answered:

> Since you write so appreciatively I send it on. ...
> The editor of the review, who returned it, merely said that he would have personally liked to print it, but that his review circulated amongst young people. Of course, with a larger morality, the guard-

---

*For emotions, Ford had the memory of an elephant. "There can," he wrote nearly thirty years later, "have been few literary figures that I more disliked—or who more disliked me— ... than ... Mr.—afterwards Sir—Edmund Gosse."

ians of young people would see that it is the very thing they ought to read, for nobody can say that the treatment is other than moral. . . .

"A Sunday Morning Tragedy" held the place of honor in the first number of *The English Review*.[4]

It was apparently the rumor that "A Sunday Morning Tragedy" had been suppressed that brought Marwood into the enterprise. Arthur Pierson Marwood was a member of a Yorkshire county family that had lived at Busby Hall, Stokesley, since the Domesday Book had been compiled. He and his brother, Sir William Francis Marwood, inherited a strong feudal sense of rights and duties. The behavior of Christopher Tietjens when, at the start of *Some Do Not . . .* , he runs along the station platform, pitches "his enormous kit-bag through the carriage window," and swings on the footboard is typical of the Marwood brothers. Macmaster reflects that "if he had done that, half the station would have been yelling, 'Stand away there.' " Equally typical was Arthur Marwood's sense of responsibility for the proper ordering of society. He published in *The English Review* a remarkable "Actuarial Scheme for Insuring John Doe against All the Vicissitudes of Life," and it would have been characteristic of him to have been outraged by what he believed had happened to Hardy's poem.[5]

He was educated at Clifton and Trinity College, Cambridge, and was a talented mathematician. But he was never a well man and was incapacitated for a career. He lived quietly in the country at Winchelsea and later Aldington with his wife, who had been his nurse, making only occasional trips to London, where he was, however, according to Violet Hunt, a dandy whose "tortoiseshell brushes and trouser-presses used to electrify the editor's charwoman when he came to stay at 84 Holland Park Avenue." Marwood died of cancer, May 1, 1916. Ford profoundly respected what he imagined Arthur Marwood to be, the responsible, hardheaded Tory gen* ;- man.[6]

"My friend the late Arthur Marwood," Ford said, " . . . possessed, upon the whole, the widest and most serene intelligence of any human being I have yet met. . . . [He] was a man of extraordinarily wide reading, of a memory so tenacious that he appeared to be encyclopaedic in his knowledge, and of singular wisdom. . . . " "There are three people," he added, "in whose deaths I have never been able to believe. They are Conrad and Arthur Marwood and Mrs. H.G. Wells. It seems to me impossible that I shall never . . . listen to Marwood encyclopaedically and brilliantly laying down the English Tory law on something or other. . . . He possessed the clear, eighteenth century mind which has disappeared from the earth, leaving the earth very much the poorer. It was not merely that his mind was encyclopaedic, it was that his information was all arranged. [He had a] peculiar, scornful, acute quality of . . . mind."[7]

Violet Hunt believed that personal admiration for Ford, not the Hardy incident, had led Marwood to take a part in *The English Review;* whatever his motives, there is no question about his close involvement, and it was probably through it that he became acquainted with Conrad. They met in Aldington and quickly became friends; when Marwood and Ford quarreled, it was with Marwood that Conrad sided.

"The *English Review,*" Violet Hunt said, "was . . . a Forlorn Hope led for the supremacy of the Kingdom of Literature gone derelict. . . . A Jacobite laird, turning out with his clansmen, could not have spoken of the object of the fight more earnestly and solemnly than did Joseph Conrad." When Ford worked up one of his empire-building schemes for persuading S. S. McClure to finance the venture, Conrad, who disliked Americans anyway, was shocked at the commercialism of the scheme. "Any coalition with McC," he wrote Ford,

> . . . could only mean the debasing of those ideals which, on your own declaration, were to guide your Editorship of the Review. . . . Did he perchance offer you to buy up the E.R. including the Editor, lock stock and barrel including the shop downstairs and the Tube Station, transplant the whole show to the U.S. whip creation, break things etc —etc. *pantoufle?* [8]

He was very angry when Ford, ignoring his feelings, undertook to introduce Willa Cather, who was in England in search of material for *McClure's Magazine,* in the hope that she would return the favor by persuading McClure to support *The English Review.* Confident everyone would play the role he had assigned him, Ford sent Miss Cather off to Aldington with a note for Elsie, who was to introduce her to Conrad. Afterwards Conrad complained sharply to Elsie, and Ford told her she had bungled a perfectly simple move in his campaign to use McClure.[9]

The English Review lost a great deal of money during the eight or nine months Ford was in control of its financial affairs. He was capable of haughtily refusing to pay more than standard magazine rates if he thought a writer was taking a commercial attitude rather than dealing with him as a gentleman. Arnold Bennett offended him by offering him stories through Pinker after Ford had written him personally. Ford—though he had "volunteered [to Bennett] that he would pay 'a good price,'" which Bennett interpreted

to mean £ 40 or £ 50—wrote Pinker: "I think I am not disposed to pay
much more than my regular rate of £ 1.1.0., a page—about £ 2.2.0., a thousand, for Arnold Bennett. . . . That is about the price I should pay for anything . . . unless it is by somebody very special" (at this rate he was offering
about £ 25 for "A Matador of the Five Towns").[10]

Where money was concerned, Bennett stood for no nonsense; he told
Pinker the facts and insisted Pinker collect a proper price for the story. This
insistence produced a long explanation from Ford, about which Bennett
wrote Pinker:

> What Hueffer says is an absolute lie. He wrote me *twice* asking for
> a story. . . . It is entirely untrue that he suggested a short story
> because he could not accept my suggestion for a serial. I have all
> his letters at home, and they . . . prove beyond any possible question
> that the overtures came from him, that he was urgent and insistent,
> and that he offered the inducement of a good price.

Ford as good as admitted the truth of this statement in a letter to Bennett
that at the same time gave warning that the enthusiasm with which he had
begun *The English Review* was fading as he discovered that most of the
writers he dealt with were not idealists like him but fellows who insisted on
his paying them as much as they got from commercial magazines. He had
begun with the idea that he was sacrificing himself for the good of literature,
in return for which he expected a grateful response to his proposal that,
instead of " £ 2 a 1000 words . . . [contributors] take a sporting risk which
might be estimated as a two to one chance against you, as . . . shareholder[s]"
in the magazine. Now he was discovering that only Wells and Galsworthy
were willing to take the sporting risk—and even Wells tried to back out
when he saw the odds were even worse than Ford had estimated. Instead,
then, of eager cooperation and praise, Ford was met with complaints and
demands for payment, exactly as if he were an ordinary commercial editor
instead of a gentleman working for the benefit of fellow writers. As he
usually did in such circumstances, he hastened to say about himself what he
had expected others to say.

> Oh hang! [he wrote Bennett] If you negotiate thro' Pinker what
> can you expect? . . . I am running a philanthropic institution for the
> benefit of the better letters: I am perfectly resigned to bankruptcy.
> . . . I stand here to be shot at: shoot!—But not thro' Pinker. . . . If the
> Review were a business concern it w^d be a different matter. But it
> isn't, it is a device by wh. I am losing £ 300 a month. . . . And *all* you
> chaps: all, do you understand are clamouring for this dissolution.

Very well . . . I won't fight you: I pay any price *any* author asks: no more: no less. But I fight anybody who has what appears to me the indecency to employ an agent, to the bitter death.

I apologise if I misrepresented you to Pinker. . . . It was how the facts presented themselves to my mind. . . . I grew vindictive & no doubt distorted the facts. Let it go [at] that and prove yourself the first generous-minded Author that ever existed. Do come in to dinner with Violet Hunt on Monday . . . [11]

"I got on excellently with Hueffer," Bennett told Violet Hunt, and in a literal sense he probably did, nursing no rancor once he had his £40. But he knew it was hopeless for him to pretend—as Ford probably could have —that nothing had happened. He did not accept Ford's invitation to dinner. "The fact is," he wrote, " . . . that the feeling that I have something against you would impair the naturalness of my demeanour." Ford took this refusal in good part. In his way, he understood the position of practical men like Bennett and Garnett. "Thank God you consent to bury the hatchet," he wrote Bennett: "I didn't really deserve it because my letter to Pinker was silly."[12]

When Ford felt writers were treating him as a gentleman, he was in-clined to be unreasonably generous. He had looked at publication from the writer's point of view much too long not to feel that writers were underpaid, and he loved generous gestures as much as Edward Ashburnham and Chris-topher Tietjens did. He certainly paid a good deal more than a guinea a page for Conrad's *Some Reminiscences*, for James's "The Jolly Corner," and for a number of other stories—including "A Matador of the Five Towns." In general, he paid so generously that it became a kind of nine days' wonder of the London literary world. Reporters noted "the rumors . . . as to the volume of rare and expensive utterance by which the first number of the *English Review* is to be introduced to an astonished world." Late in his life Ford came to recognize, quite unrepentantly, just how impractical his busi-ness methods were. "If I had a million dollars," he said, "I would start a magazine and print all the real talent from here to Baton Rouge and back. . . . What a six months that would be!"[13]

Even at his minimum rate of a guinea a page, Ford was spending £210– £270 an issue for the material he printed; at one point he estimated the actual cost of contributions at "about £300.0.0" a number, a figure that is, if anything, conservative. But like Count Macdonald of *The New Humpty-Dumpty*, Ford had to "brace himself . . . to the trouble of keeping accounts, which . . . appeared to him to be an almost indecent proceeding." His method of keeping accounts is revealed by a letter he wrote Wells in March when Wells inquired anxiously about the *Review*'s affairs.

> Roughly speaking . . . the circulation, of the first two numbers has been 2,000 copies, or a little more, bringing in £ 200.0.0. The revenue from advertisements has been about £ 140.0.0. for the four numbers. The costs of printing, paper, distribution, etc. have averaged about £ 200.0.0., per number. The costs of contributions, agents' commissions, salaries, etc. have averaged about £ 300.0.0., per number. It will thus be evident to you that the net results of the first four numbers is a loss of about £ 1200.0.0.[14]

The magazine received 1/10 per copy. If the first two numbers sold a total of 2,000 copies, they returned approximately £ 200, or £ 100 per number. If production costs averaged £ 200 per number and the cost of contributions £ 300, then the loss on four numbers was £ 1,600 less £ 140 in advertising revenue, or £ 1,460 rather than £ 1,200. It is difficult not to believe Ford reached that figure of £ 1,200 he gives Wells by calculating that the revenue from the sales of *two* numbers (£ 200) offset the production costs for *one* number (£ 200) and that the cost of contributions (£ 300 per number) constituted the loss. This may seem improbable, but Ford's capacity for being unrealistic about money was very great. At the same time that he was planning *The English Review* he publicly offered to guarantee " £ 40,000 [for a National Theatre] from various papers in France and Germany on condition that the National Theatre set aside a week each for the classical theatres of each of these countries. . . . "[15]

Even if we accept Ford's own figures, the *Review* lost about £ 365 a number; the actual loss was probably at least £ 500, which makes Ford's later estimate that the total loss was £ 5,000 very close to the truth. At that rate, Ford was incurring a loss that, as Goldring put it, "must have staggered even a Northcliffe." Little wonder that Wells came to doubt that one-fifth of the profits of the *Review* was an adequate return for the serial rights to *Tono-Bungay*. But Ford, viewing the whole enterprise as a cooperative effort in the service of literature, could not understand the attitude of writers like Wells who worried about whether they would be adequately paid. The attitude he expected them to take is well represented by the plan he worked out for financing the *Review*.

> The Publisher [Duckworth] was to bear all expenses of printing, publishing and everything except advertising and was to receive in exchange one-fifth of the gross receipts; a capitalist was to be found by Mr. Hueffer to find money for advertisement and such contribu-

tors as took their payments in money. To him a share of one-fifth in the proceeds was also payable. The share of Mr. Hueffer was to be one-fifth. The remaining two-fifths of the gross receipts was to be divided among the as yet unpaid contributors in the proportion of the space filled by them.[16]

When Edward Garnett tried to warn him about the awkwardness of this arrangement, he replied,

> I quite realize what you say as to the awkwardness of the profit-sharing idea, but the only people who come into it are very intimate friends of mine and I have put the matter very plainly to [each]. ... I am an idealist and my ideal is to run the "English Review" as far as possible as a socialistic undertaking.

The problem of where the money to do so was to come from was temporarily solved by Arthur Marwood's involvement. When *The English Review* was registered as a company on January 22, 1909, Ford was listed as the general partner, Marwood as the limited. Each then put up £500. Ford asserted that, before they were through, Marwood had invested a total of £2,200 and he £2,800. This sounds a little high, since the liquidator of the magazine found it owing considerable sums to contributors, but it is possible.[17]

Ford's share of this investment did not of course come entirely out of his own pocket. "The money of cohorts of relations—German Hueffers, Dutch Hueffers, Paris Hueffers . . . all agog, and pleased to be called on to foster the English nephew's adventure with some sinews of war—was forthcoming," Violet Hunt said. Forthcoming it was, if not with quite the enthusiasm Violet implies. Ford also borrowed from Elsie despite the uneasiness of their relations. He asked her for £250; she offered him all she could get together without selling fixed assets, £150. "I am glad," Ford wrote her, "you will let me have the money as I should have felt hurt otherwise. £150 will be quite sufficient for the ER—I wanted the other hundred . . . for my own account. However, it's all right. . . . I have plenty coming in . . . " a statement that was certainly not literally true, since he was borrowing small sums about London at the time.[18]

Ford had told Edward Garnett before *The English Review* began that he expected his profit-sharing idea would lead to "quarrels and recriminations"; he had probably not expected anything quite so explosive as the quarrel that now erupted with H. G. Wells. As late as October, 1908, he and Wells were on excellent terms. Shortly after that, however, Wells wrote to say he was afraid the sales of *Tono-Bungay* would be damaged by the remaindering of copies of the *Review* in which it would run serially.

Why this excitement? [Ford replied]Is there no one you can trust?

It must be obvious to you that I shd. not have gone forward with the matter [of the *Review*] except on the terms agreed on—or rather, the terms dictated by yourself. . . . Not a single copy of the first four numbers of the review will be sold as a remainder & I propose to delay publication so that the last number shall appear after the publication [of *Tono-Bungay*] in book form.

Wells accepted this explanation, not attempting to make clear the real grounds of his anxiety, which would have led to an open quarrel. Unaware of Wells's feelings and full of the sacrifice he was making in editing the *Review*, Ford took Wells's reluctant acceptance as a tacit admission of Ford's magnanimity. "Thanks," he wrote Wells. "It's alright and I don't 'grumble!' "[19]

When Wells and Ford had been planning the *Review*, Ford had estimated that each number would sell about 5,000 copies and have an advertising revenue of £300. If this estimate was correct, Wells would then receive £600 for the serialization of a part of *Tono-Bungay*, a satisfactory price. Very early, however, he began to have doubts. Writers were not accepting Ford's profit-sharing idea, which meant they would have to be paid outright, and Wells was beginning to think Ford's estimate of the *Review*'s sales unrealistic.[20]

In the fall he tried to get out of serializing *Tono-Bungay* in the *Review*. But again he was not willing to be frank and once more left Ford feeling that Wells was nagging unreasonably and that Ford himself was being generous. "I hope," Wells wrote, "you understand clearly that I do not consider that things are yet arranged for the use of 'Tono Bungay' as a serial. We have not defined terms. . . . " By January, 1909, Wells had become convinced that Ford not only had overestimated the *Review*'s income but also was, as editor, spending money like water. Before he acted, he consulted Arnold Bennett. "I don't know yet about Hueffer," Bennett replied, "but I'm sure the *English Review* won't last unless he alters it considerably."[21]

Wells now finally told Ford his real feelings about the *Review*. Ford was astounded. He was too deeply offended to send his reply to Wells; he sent it to Mrs. Wells. He begins by asserting that in January, 1908, "Wells asked me to start the Review, saying that *Tono-Bungay* was not marketable & the Review would advertise him & do him good." This seems unlikely on the face of it, but it is possible that Wells did agree with some remark of Ford's about how much such a review could do for real writers; this was one of Ford's favorite claims for the *Review*. Ford then goes on to say that Wells had originally undertaken to share the editing and to find half the money for the *Review*, that he almost immediately "back[ed] out of the Editing" and, a week later, out of finding the money, apologizing abjectly for both defections. Nonetheless, Ford points out, he not only accepted the additional burden Wells had thrown on him but also remained silent about Wells's receiving one-fifth of the *Review*'s profits (one of Ford's characteristic muddles: as Wells's memorandum shows, Wells had talked from the start about gross receipts, not profits). He reminds Mrs. Wells that he had accepted without demur Wells's demand that no copies of the *Review* be remaindered and had never complained about the constant changes in the date of book publication for the novel, though these changes had cost the *Review* money which he felt honor-bound to make good, since "I regard myself as being responsible for having introduced into the affairs of the Review a person whom I ought to have known, & indeed did know, could hardly be expected ever to keep his engagements." He ought, he adds, to have foreseen how Wells would behave because "Wells, as you must know, has behaved again & again most treacherously to me." He concludes by saying that he "would not write to Wells in any circumstances at all," although Wells's "opinion of myself is of no consequence whatever, to me."[22]

Having announced that he "would not write to Wells in any circumstances at all," he promptly did so when he discovered that Wells was offended by his writing to Mrs. Wells. "I am really exceedingly sorry," he said, "if, by writing to Mrs. Wells, I have annoyed you. Nothing else wd. make me re-open the matter: but if in that way I have annoyed you I feel that I owe you an apology—as full as you like."*[23]

Thus, as Wells grew more anxious to minimize the loss he feared he would suffer from serializing *Tono-Bungay* in *The English Review*, Ford became more convinced that he had personally saved *Tono-Bungay* from extinction and had put up with treacheries from Wells while doing so. In the end, Wells attempted to close the matter with a letter in something like Ford's own grand manner.

I should have no objection . . . to waive any golden anticipations I may have formed of the sale of the goodwill of the Review. You will then have your mind and conscience cleared . . . altogether and you will be relieved from such quaint, but I should think irksome, necessi-

*Ford very much admired "Jane" Wells and seems never to have suspected that she did not like him. It was not unreasonable of him to address her in a business matter of this sort if he was too hurt to write Wells. As Wells himself later said, "She transacted and invested for her unhelpful and uncertain husband, and she was wise and wary in his affairs and a searchlight of honesty and clear but kindly illumination in his world"; "no literary agent," he added, "could better" her work. Wells's friends took it for granted that "Jane" managed his affairs.

ties as you impose on yourself at present, of pretending not to be yourself when speaking through the telephone to me. . . . All these antics have been totally superfluous from the outset. I never expected anything from your review, and I was quite willing to help it as I have done.[24]

But in grand manner, anyhow, Wells was no match for Ford. Ford had Miss Thomas, the *Review's* secretary, answer this letter, thus giving his reply almost the air of a royal communication. It was not, Miss Thomas reported, in Ford's power to waive Wells's share of the good will of the *Review*; he would have to consult his partner, Marwood. He wished, however, to assure Wells that, if Marwood accepted Wells's waiver, "Mr. Hueffer will pay you his share of any price received for the Review. . . . " "Mr. Hueffer," the letter concluded, "is not aware of having spoken to you over the telephone in any voice, either feigned or unfeigned." Wells got what may perhaps be considered the last word by putting in a claim for £250 for the serial rights to *Tono-Bungay* when the *Review* went into liquidation.[25]

By the spring of 1909 Ford had been driven by the troubles of the *Review* and the confusion of his private affairs to the edge of a breakdown, and he became extremely irritable. He got into a violent row with Stephen Reynolds, whom he had befriended and had even taken on as a secretary for a short time, about the payment for *Holy Mountain*. He enraged Frank Harris by telling him over luncheon at the Savoy that Marwood thought Harris's story, "The Miracle of the Stigmata," "a piece of blasphemous profanity." Ford says with considerable complacency that, when a story was salacious—"it is the only [case]—I can be adamant" and that he turned Harris's story down; Harris says he did too, adding "the man's an ass." It is therefore somewhat puzzling to find "The Miracle of the Stigmata" in *The English Review* for April, 1910.[26]

Ford also got into knockdown rows with both Garnetts. He burst out at Edward for something Edward had said at dinner one night, saying that, though he minded nothing Edward said about him personally, he "resent-[ed] intensely" and thought "in distinctly bad taste" Garnett's criticizing him in a way that would hurt *The English Review*, "wh. I am doing absolutely for the love of Literature & without any idea of advancement or profit at all for myself." He got into a serious quarrel with Robert Garnett about which he wrote Pinker a long letter that reveals the fantastic idea of himself as a well-to-do gentleman writer that ruled his imagination.

You once wounded me exceedingly by telling me that I had obtained money from you by misrepresentation—the misrepresentation being that I had private means [this alludes to Ford's assertions to Pinker that he does not wish to disturb his investments]. You said that you had been told that I had no private means, by my solicitor [Robert Garnett]. . . .

I am not complaining of this: it does not worry me to be called untrustworthy because, though I do at times outrun the constable [(] & for that reason yʳ occasional loans were a convenience to me) I am perfectly assured of being able always to meet my disabilities wh. are confined to tradesmen. Now however conditions are changed. . . . In the capacity of proprietor of the English Review I am responsible to many other people. . . . It would therefore be exceedingly disastrous if you continued to call me untrustworthy & I wish to acquaint you with the circumstances of my position.

My private means consist in an allowance from my aunt, Frau Geheimrattin Laura Schmedding whose heir I am & who lets me have elastic sums pretty much as I desire them. . . .

What follows must be absolutely private: many years ago I detected, to my own satisfaction [(] tho' I may have been mistaken & do not make it an accusation) that Robert Garnett did not respect his client's confidences. . . . Now . . . I have detected him in what I consider a flagrant breach of confidence—or rather an attempt at it. I have had a very violent scene with him in the course of which he absolutely denied that he had ever told you that I had no private means. And the purpose of this letter is simply to ask this question: "Did Robert Garnett or did he not assure you that of his knowledge I had no private means?" You will be aware of the gravity of the question as I am now, I am very much afraid, forced to bring the whole matter into court. . . . ²⁷

He thus saw himself as an eminently reasonable though little understood man. When he concluded a sharp letter to Scott-James, "if you can not see the matter in [my] light I would really much rather not see you," and Scott-James answered amicably with a little joke about Ford's notorious quarrelsomeness, Ford wrote back:

I wonder if it is true that I am troublesome and quarrelsome to such a degree. I daresay it is. But you see, I am a troublesomely solitary nature without the least desire for the companionship of my kind. . . .

Nothing could be more obviously untrue of Ford than the assertion that he did not desire companionship.²⁸

None of these troubles, however, arose during the planning stages of the

Review's life, and Ford spent a happy time that fall of 1908 with Wells, Conrad, and Marwood arranging the first numbers and dreaming of the revolution in English literature they would bring about. He was pleased to find himself once more working closely with Conrad over Conrad's *Reminiscences*, which were to run serially in the *Review*. "Voilà," Conrad wrote of the first installment, "the thing ran itself into 6000 words I fear. I am sorry for the stress under which you suffer.... I do long to see you. I am losing my grip on everything again." Conrad dictated much of the second installment of the *Reminiscences* to Ford as he had dictated *The Mirror of the Sea* five years before. In October he issued an invitation to Ford to come to Someries for a final great consult over the first number of the *Review;* he was, as Goldring says, acting "in a sense [as] Ford's co-editor." Early in November, then, Ford descended on Someries, Conrad's "gloomy old Farmhouse" surrounded by damp and menacing trees. Ford was "now very much the medieval baron travelling with his 'retinue' " of sub-editor, Goldring, and secretary, Miss Thomas, who were loaded down with packages of manuscripts and proofs. "Each took possession of a separate room" for the night, Jessie complained ("How, otherwise, she expected us to pass the night is too embarrassing for conjecture," Goldring remarks), and "the consumption of lamp oil and candles was prodigious."[29]

Conrad and Ford discussed the superiority of the French novel and Flaubert and assured each other that the *Review* would at last start an English movement dedicated to serious writing. They went over Ford's statement of the *Review*'s editorial policy, that "sweet and fatuous circular," as Violet Hunt called it. "The E[nglish] R[eview] may have to stop," Conrad asserted grandly, "but it mustn't fail." This was the argument of Ford's circular.

> The only qualification for admission to the pages of the Review will be—in the view of the Editors—either distinction of individuality or force of conviction ... the criterion of inclusion being the clarity of diction, the force or the illuminative value of the views expressed.

The only thing Ford and Conrad seem not to have done that evening was edit.[30]

But it was always something of a mystery how Ford got *The English Review* edited. It was his habit to lose manuscripts; when he managed to lose one of Sidney Olivier's that Wells had got, Wells was beside himself, and even William Rossetti was nettled when Ford lost a group of Rossetti-Brown letters he had been planning to print. The "garden" behind 84 Holland Park Avenue, Violet Hunt said, "grew nothing but empty packing cases and reams of discarded packing paper, and—the moment the Review was really started—priceless manuscripts that the rabbits of Mr. Chandler browsed upon." The rest of the manuscripts were stuffed into the splendid but shabby Spanish cabinet that had, Ford liked to say, once belonged to the Duke of Medina-Sidonia.[31]

Ford's drawing-room office was always full of people. Very often they had been invited, for Ford was an incorrigible party-giver, but he left the door of the flat open at all times and anyone—invited or not—could wander in and, if necessary, track him down in his bath. As a result he could obtain even the small amount of privacy he needed to look over manuscripts only by running away. It was therefore his

> singular practice to attend the "second house" at the [Shepherd's Bush Empire]. At least once a week . . . after dinner I [Goldring] went out and stopped a hansom and editor and "sub" drove down to Shepherd's Bush with the MSS which had accumulated. . . . During the performance, or rather during the duller turns, Ford made his decisions and I duly recorded them.

By that time the coast would be clear at 84 Holland Park Avenue and he and Goldring would return and work into the earlier hours of the next morning. Ford assumed that others worked in a similar way and, as a consequence, "drove both printers and compositors wild" with his irregular practices and his astonished impatience with the delays caused by their regular ones. To the end of his life, Ford never really reconciled himself to the fact that editors and compositors could not decipher his handwriting, though it was fantastically illegible, and never completed work as quickly as he felt he could have. About the management of the *Review*'s office, Goldring observed, Ford "was more childishly incapable than any man I have ever met."[32]

He was also an exceptionally gifted editor. For all his quarreling with contributors, he knew exactly what writers were the best and he fought tenaciously to get them. He could measure the quality of an unknown writer almost at a glance without personal or social prejudice. When Violet Hunt, at H. G. Wells's suggestion, brought him her stories, he gave her an agonizingly leisurely tea.

> After tea, and not till then, [he] took my manuscripts all together between his two hands, and, opening and shutting them, flirted the pages. . . . There were three long-short stories. . . .
> He said suddenly, pausing at the middle one: "I'll take this."
> I said, "But you haven't read it!"

Nevertheless, he had seen all he needed to; he had chosen "The Coach," certainly the best of all her "Tales of the Uneasy." When Wyndham Lewis, mute but intense, arrived and "produced crumpled . . . rolls" of manuscript from all over his person as if he were a sleight-of-hand artist, Ford was amused by his own start at Lewis' appearance in an "immense steeple-crowned hat . . . one of those Russian looking coats that have no revers . . . [and] an ample black cape of the type that villains in transpontine melo-drama throw over their shoulders when they say 'Ha-ha!' " It was, he learned later, "the usual uniform of the Paris student of those days." This at least is the way Ford later remembered the episode. The evening after it occurred he told Goldring that, getting no answer to his ring, Lewis had marched straight upstairs to the bathroom, found Ford in the tub, and—after announc-ing that he was a man of genius—read Ford "The Pole," straight through. Ford recognized instantly the merit of Lewis' work; he printed three of Lewis' pieces and at one point hoped to commission a monthly piece from him. There was the same instant recognition of talent when Jessie Chambers sent Ford a batch of D. H. Lawrence's poems.[33]

The best illustration of how Ford performed this editorial feat is his account of coming on Lawrence's "Odour of Chrysanthemums." He says that, because his eyes were tired, he read only the first paragraph and then "laid it in the basket for accepted manscripts"; he knew by then all he needed to know.

> "The small locomotive engine, Number 4, came clanking, stumbling down from Selston" [the Lawrence story begins], and at once you know that this fellow with the power of observation is going to write of whatever he writes about from the inside. The "Number 4" shows that. He will be the sort of fellow who knows that for the sort of people who work about engines, engines have a sort of individual-ity. . . .
>
> "It appeared round the corner with loud threats of speed. . . . But the colt that it startled from among the gorse . . . outdistanced it at a canter." Good again. . . . anyone knows that an engine that makes a great deal of noise and yet cannot overtake a colt at a canter must be a ludicrously ineffective machine. . . .
>
> "The gorse still flickered indistinctly in the raw afternoon. . . ." Good too, distinctly good. This is the just-sufficient observation of Nature that gives you, in a single phrase, landscape, time of day, weather, season.
>
> Your mind does all this for you without any ratiocination on your part. You are not, I mean, purposely sleuthing.

*Ford Madox Brown as he appeared in 1899
when Ford was living with him.*

Elsie Martindale.   *Mary Martindale.*

Christina, Katharine,
and Elsie Hueffer,
ca. 1903.

Elsie, Ford,
and his cousin
in Germany,
ca. 1904.

Edmée Van der Noot, the Hueffer girls' governess, and H. G. Wells playing at being married, Aldington.

Dr. and Mrs. Martindale, Elsie Martindale's parents.

Elsie and Katharine, Christina and Ford.

Elsie at a German cathedral, ca. 1905.

Wells and Conrad, ca. 1906.

The Edwardian man-about-town, ca. 1909.

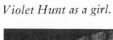

Violet Hunt as a girl.

The LIBRARY: *WEEK by WEEK.*

By FRANK A. MUMBY.

A Link with the Past. Messrs. Chatto and Windus have in the press a book which forms an interesting link between the modern school of fiction and that of a generation or so ago, in the waning days of the three volume novel—those good old days as they are now regarded in the book trade, though the three volume novel, be it remembered, had just as many critics in its own time as the six-shilling novel of to-day. The forthcoming book is a romance entitled "The Governess," by Mrs. Alfred Hunt, one of the popular novelists of the old days, and her daughter, Miss Violet Hunt (now Mrs. Ford Madox Hueffer) one of the successful of the modern school.

Hills and Saunders.

Elliott and Fry.

On the left, Mrs. Alfred Hunt, who is joint authoress with her daughter, Miss Violet Hunt (Mrs. Ford Madox Hueffer) (right), of a forthcoming novel, "The Governess," which links the modern school of fiction with the old three-volume days.

The notice of The Governess, *in which the* Throne *called Violet Hunt "Mrs. Ford Madox Hueffer."*

MRS. HUEFFER WINS HER LIBEL SUIT

Verdict for Wife of Novelist with £300 Damages.

BOOKS SHE NEVER READS.

Judge Declines to Hear Statement Concerning Miss Violet Hunt.

A wife's claim to her name was vindicated yesterday when £300 damages were awarded in Mr. Justice Avory's court to Mrs. Elsie Hueffer, the wife of the novelist, Mr. Ford Madox Hueffer, who brought an action against Illustrated Journals, Limited, the proprietors of the "Throne" newspaper.

Stay of execution was granted, subject to the usual terms.

Mrs. Hueffer brought the action in order to assert her right to the title of being the lawful wife of her husband.

According to counsel for the defendants, Miss Violet Hunt, the distinguished authoress, claimed the name of Mrs. Hueffer as a "courtesy" title.

After the jury had returned their verdict, Mr. Storry Deans rose and said:—

"I am instructed by a lady whose name has been mentioned with great frequency—Miss Violet Hunt—to state that she wishes it to be known that she believes herself to be Mrs. Ford Maddox Hueffer, and intends so to call herself.

Mr. Justice Avory: I have nothing to do with this belief or any of her beliefs.

Mr. Storry Deans: Statements have been directed against——

Mr. Justice Avory: I cannot hear you any further. I am not in a position to decide, and it is useless for you to make an ex parte statement. I decline to allow this Court to be made a medium of advertisement.

The Daily Mirror's *story of Elsie's suit against the* Throne.

Violet Hunt, Anthony West, Rebecca West, and Ford.

*Ford and Violet Hunt
at the Selsey Hotel,
1911-12.*

... And if you are an editor ... you can pitch the story straight away into your wicker tray with the few accepted manuscripts. ...

Ezra Pound summed up Ford's editorial gift by remarking that "the quality of *The Eng. Rev.* [under Ford's editorship] then depended, I think, very largely on the sort of personal touch between the office and writers."[34]

Thus, if Ford's commitment to the highest standards together with his complete lack of business sense pretty well assured financial disaster, that same commitment, with the support of his remarkable powers of selection, made it certain that as long as the *Review* survived it would be a great magazine. That it would, in Conrad's terms, stop quickly was almost inevitable; but it would not fail. The first issue illustrates what Ford could do. It opens with Hardy's "A Sunday Morning Tragedy," followed by two short stories, Henry James's "The Jolly Corner" and John Galsworthy's "A Fisher of Men." Then come W. H. Hudson's "Stonehenge," the first part of Constance Garnett's translation of Tolstoy's "The Raid," and the first installment of Wells's *Tono-Bungay*. At the back of the book are Ford's editorials, brief essays by Cunninghame Graham, W. H. Davies, and Henry W. Nevinson, reviews by Conrad and Levin Schücking "of Gottingen University," and the first installment of "A Complete Actuarial Scheme for Insuring John Doe against all the Vicissitudes of Life," by A[rthur] M[arwood]. The most obvious measure of Ford's editorial skill is perhaps the fact that, even today, none of these writers except Schücking and Marwood needs identifying.

First numbers of magazines are notoriously easier to put together than later ones, but the succeeding numbers of *The English Review* are nearly as impressive as the first. The second, for example, besides the three continuations from the first number, has an unpublished ballad by Rossetti (illustrated with a facsimile of the manuscript that shows Miss Thomas did not transcribe the poem very accurately), an article by Cunninghame Graham, a story by Vernon Lee, and the first installment of Conrad's *Reminiscences*. Another way of suggesting the quality of *The English Review* is to notice that over a span of a year and a half, in addition to serializing two books by Wells and one by Conrad, Ford put into the magazine four poems by Hardy; four James stories; nine poems and three stories by Galsworthy; a complete play (for which he printed a special supplement), a story, a poem, and two essays by Bennett; thirteen poems and a short story by Lawrence; three essays by Wyndham Lewis; nine poems (including "Sestina: Altaforte" and "The Ballad of the Goodly Fere") by Pound; and three poems by Yeats. He also printed Chesterton, Belloc, Hudson, George Moore, C. E. Montague, G.

Lowes Dickinson, Norman Douglas, E. M. Forster, H. M. Tomlinson, Sturge Moore, Rupert Brooke—and President William Howard Taft. Ford's *English Review* would have been an extraordinary achievement at any time; before the literary revolution conducted by "The Men of 1914" it was astonishing.*

*It is a little difficult to know just how long Ford's editorial influence lasted. Apparently the last number of the *Review* he put together was that for February, 1910. On the other hand, much of the material published later than that had obviously been bought by him; for example, he bought D. H. Lawrence's "Odour of Chrysanthemums," though it did not appear until June, 1911. The summary given in the text is perhaps conservative; it covers the issues from December, 1908, through July, 1910.

Chapter 15

As the astonishing quality of *The English Review* became evident, Ford became a prominent figure around London. He went everywhere, carefully dressed for the part. "He was arrayed in a magnificent fur coat;—wore a glossy topper; drove about in hired carriages; and his fresh features, the colour of raw veal, his prominent blue eyes and rabbit teeth smiled benevolently and patronisingly upon all gatherings of literary lions." We catch glimpses of him at Lady St. Helier's advising Bonar Law to have the Conservative party take up Marwood's social-insurance scheme or sitting at dinner at the Pall Mall restaurant with Chesterton, Belloc, Wells, and Maurice Baring, with Wells shouting ebulliently, "Hurray, Fordie's discovered another genius! Called D. H. Lawrence!"[1]

Ford had indeed discovered a new genius and had quickly won both Lawrence and Jessie Chambers. Jessie had sent Lawrence's poems to Ford—at Lawrence's suggestion, she says, though Lawrence later denied that. Ford recalled that Jessie sent both poems and "Odour of Chrysanthemums." Ford saw at once how good Lawrence was and got him up from Croydon, where he was teaching; Lawrence liked Ford. "He is fairish, fat, about forty, and the kindest man on earth," he wrote Jessie; a little later he told her Ford was "really a fine man, in that he is generous, so understanding, and in that he keeps the doors of his soul open, and you may walk in. . . . " Ford set out to publicize Lawrence, talking of him everywhere and taking him about London, not only on literary but on social occasions, which, Jessie Chambers suggests, Lawrence quite enjoyed. Brigit Patmore remembered Ford's bringing Lawrence "to tea with some friends of mine." But she had no great impression of Lawrence; "as usual, Ford talked most of the time in that

fluffy, swallowed voice of his, and one strained one's ears to listen...."
Perhaps he did so out of kindness; he knew Lawrence was shy.[2]

Ernest Rhys also remembered Ford's bringing Lawrence to a party, in
December, 1909.

> They made a curious contrast, for Ford always had the air of a
> man-about-town, well used to town occasions, while Lawrence
> looked shy and countrified; perhaps a little overwhelmed by the
> fanfaron of fellow poets heard in the room, with W. B. Yeats and Ezra
> Pound dominating the scene....
>
> The plan of entertainment on these occasions was... [that]
> every poet [brought] an original poem and read... it aloud. Willie
> Yeats was a capital opener of the feast.... In his turn... Ford read
> us a witty burlesque, after which we persuaded... Lawrence, who
> had been sitting silent in a corner, to read us some of his verse. He
> rose nervously but very deliberately, walked across to a writing desk
> whose lid was closed, opened it, produced a mysterious book out of
> his pocket, and sat down, his back to the company, and began to read
> in an expressive, not very audible voice....
>
> Lawrence's reading went on and on, seemed as if it might go on
> the whole evening, and the other poets became restive, and chattered
> *sotto voce....* [My wife] appealed to me....
>
> "Tell him he must want a little rest."
>
> This I did, adding that if he felt so inclined he might resume
> at midnight! He... [got] up with an awkward little bow, shut up
> the book and desk, and retired to his corner.... As the night grew
> late we tried to get Lawrence to give us one more lyric out of his
> black book... but Madox Ford took him under his arm and
> marched him off murmuring wickedly, "Nunc, nunc dimittis."[3]

Early in November, at Ford's request, Lawrence sent him the manuscript of *The White Peacock*. "He read it immediately.... and in his queer
voice, when we were in an omnibus in London, he shouted in my ear: 'It's
got every fault that the English novel can have.... But you've got GENIUS.'
I always thought he had a bit of genius himself. Anyhow, he sent the Ms.
of *The White Peacock* to William Heinemann, who accepted it at once."[4]

In November Jessie Chambers came up to London to meet Ford and
Violet. As she and Lawrence and Ford were walking from 84 Holland Park
Avenue to South Lodge for luncheon she began to feel "the charm with
which Hueffer was talking to me." At South Lodge she met Violet and "a
young American poet [Pound] who startled me by springing to his feet and
bowing from the waist with the stiff precision of a mechanical toy. There

was also a quiet man named [René] Byles." Jessie was charmed by South Lodge, by the delicious food and the good conversation and, above all, by "the genial warmth of Hueffer's personality." She thought Pound "an amiable buffoon."[5]

But Ford was too harassed by *The English Review* and by his affair with Violet Hunt during the winter of 1909–10 to give Lawrence all the attention Lawrence felt he deserved, and when Ford left for Germany in August of 1910, Lawrence felt deserted. He quickly transferred his loyalties to Edward Garnett, to whom Ford had introduced him. "Ford Madox Hueffer discovered I was a genius—don't be alarmed, Hueffer would discover *anything* if he wanted to," Lawrence said later. ". . . and left me to paddle my own canoe. I very nearly wrecked it and did for myself. Edward Garnett, like a good angel, fished me out."[6]

Besides discovering geniuses and taking them to parties from one end of London to the other during the early months of *The English Review*'s life, Ford did a great deal of entertaining of his own. The company was a mixture of the socially prominent, elder statesmen of the arts like Hardy, Ford's protégés like Stephen Reynolds and Violet Hunt's friends like May Sinclair, old friends like the Garnetts, editors, and publishers. ". . . we grown-ups," Violet Hunt remembered, "were made to play the most childish of games—Clumps, Honey-pots, not stopping short at Hunt-the-slipper. I know we all seemed to be sitting on the floor. . . . There was no one to curb the editor and his German instinct for games."

> At one [of these parties], all those who were invited were poets who had to compete for a crown of bay-leaves by writing *bouts-rimés*. . . . They certainly included Ezra Pound, who had just appeared in literary London, wearing one ear-ring, which was considered very scandalous. . . . Dollie Radford won the first prize and looked very much like an Italian painting in the crown of bay-leaves; Hilaire Belloc won the second prize. . . . [7]

But, concealed from everyone by Ford's intense dislike of any public discussion of his private affairs and by his talent for appearing at ease in public whatever his private feelings, things were not going well with him. In addition to his anxiety about the *Review*, his personal life was in confusion, and he was often lonely. As Violet Hunt said,

> . . . like Cinderella's pumpkin carriage and its mice footmen, all this glory vanished at dusk, and the editor was left . . . sitting by his dying fire . . . or thumping his piano and shouting "Madam, will you walk?"

for his own dreary amusement and company. Mrs. Chandler, in her room below, who pitied him, has often told me this.

Elsie was an invalid, slowly recuperating in her shanty—as she called it—at Aldington. He would go there weekends, when he could break away from London, but there was not much of a life for either of them in that.[8]

Elsie was not a sexually cold or ungenerous woman, and in matters like marriage, where she had some experience to go on, she was intelligent and realistic. She had been ill for over two years now, and with the best will in the world, she could not have been much of a wife to Ford. She was quite aware that he had been having casual, insignificant affairs, and during the spring of 1908, when she felt herself wholly incapable of marriage, she offered Ford a temporary separation. It is very touching that almost the first thing she asked the surgeon after her operation was about the renewal of sexual relations with Ford.[9]

But in other respects Elsie was remarkably unworldly. After Ford left her, she would never have a man stay in the house alone with her because she had been told that to do so would give grounds for a divorce; and she somehow got the idea that if Ford could get the girls away from her he could obtain a German divorce and lived in terror of their being abducted by him. She had almost no sense of what the great world of London in which Ford now lived was like; she knew only that it was endangering his career as a writer and taking him away from her and the girls. It was very late in her life, in the 1920s, before it seriously occurred to her that she might have been damaging Ford's career by fighting in the courts for her right to his name. When it did, she told her lawyer "to give up standing out for [her right to the name of] Mrs. H[ueffer]."

But where she had experience to go on Elsie was quick enough to understand. The seventeen-year-old girl who had married Ford in 1894 had clearly looked to him to explain the world to her. But the woman of thirty-two whom Ford confronted in 1909 had not only a will but a mind of her own, and about the realities she understood she was far more practical than he. During her long illness she no doubt became preoccupied with herself, and she may well have attacked Ford for his neglect of her more fiercely than was wise, not quite recognizing that beneath the assured person he presented to the world—in whom she herself had so long believed—was an uncertain and unhappy man, longing for tenderness and "rest." That was too much to expect from anyone in her circumstances. She was ill, neglected, and anxious about Ford's life in London, and she knew only what he told her—and the stories that friends were quick to report to her.

Ford's London life certainly had its unusual features. Sometime during that spring, with the romantic's "lust for rescue-work," he picked up in the Empire lounge a girl named Gertrud Schlablowsky, the daughter of a tailor in Königsberg. She had, Violet Hunt said, a "white, heavy moon-face . . . [a] short Calmuck nose, wide red mouth, and loops of black hair falling over a rather brutish forehead." Nevertheless, she had her charm; once when she appeared at a party at 84 Holland Park Avenue in a dress "of grey mock fur made tight and plain in the new mode" (it was one of Violet's best dresses, which she had borrowed), May Sinclair very much annoyed Violet by asking her "who the beautiful, pale, Russian princess was." Ford was bent on saving Gertrud; he set aside a half hour, every night at midnight, for talk with her and insisted on her being put forward as much as possible. Violet Hunt was not an irrationally jealous woman. She took her niece Rosamond's passion for Ford with remarkable good nature; "I have not told her anything," she wrote Ford after she and Ford had become lovers, "except that you are *not for her.* . . . And she tosses her head and says she knows that!" But even Violet seems to have had her doubts about just what was going on during those nightly conferences with Gertrud. In March she submitted to the *The English Review* a Browningesque dramatic monologue about it under the pseudonym of George Angel.

> Stir up the fire, draw out your chair:
> Kick off the shoes: let down the hair:
> Your white kimono, now. . . .
> Then snuggle down and let us doze. . . .
> And both with a most ancient work to do,
> You selling worthless love: I modern rhyme,
> Sitting beside your hearth in wintertime
> Cheer on, I know, each other. Yes. I know. . . .

Like most girls of her kind, Gertrud was "bored, pining, discontented, dying to get away, with nowhere else to go . . . wanting luxury, gaiety, new clothes . . . always leaving paper patterns and powder-puffs about the room. . . . " She called Ford "Păpă." When Violet Hunt took charge of Ford's affairs, she made short work of Gertrud, shipping her back to Germany and eventually providing her with the money to emigrate to New South Wales.[10]

But the most serious complication in Ford's life was Violet Hunt herself. She and Ford met one night—it was March 21, 1907—at dinner at the Galsworthys; they walked quietly home together along the Kensington Road talking of the Pre-Raphaelite memories they had in common. About a month later Violet was in Heinemann's office and Pawling suggested to her that she should get Ford to write one of his articles for the *Tribune* about her new book, *White Rose of Weary Leaf.* As she stepped out of the office "I met the man I hadn't seen . . . since we met at the Galsworthys. He looked very red and golden against that dark grey wall in [Bedford] Street and I asked him to notice my new book." Ford told her that he could, indeed, "boom" authors and pointed to "the succéss fulgurante of William De Morgan's novel owing to his article in 'The Mail.' " "He smiled down at me—he is very tall—and . . . was awfully amused at my 'brass.' "[11]

From this time on, she was thinking about Ford, noting in her diary, for example, that he came to her annual garden party on July 20, "alone." But she was very busy in 1907 and 1908 marching in suffragette parades, attending meetings, and having herself photographed "begging" for the cause along with May Sinclair at South Kensington Station, and she did not really see Ford again until Wells suggested that she take her stories to him for *The English Review*, and they had that tea together where he selected "The Coach" for publication. It was October 16, 1908.[12]

They saw each other again three days after that tea and Ford came to South Lodge for luncheon the next week. From then on, they met regularly and Violet—after being taken on a walk and inspected by Marwood—was more or less incorporated into *The English Review* gang. " . . . a woman at a loose end of life," as she could later see, "with a visiting list of notabilities as long as your arm . . . " could be useful. By December Ford was bringing her to the notice of his imagined Maecenas, S. S. McClure, and signing his invitation to her to join him and McClure at the Empire, "Yours until death and after." A month later, although he was still addressing her as Miss Hunt, he was saying, "Certainly I will come to lunch with you. . . . But why don't you come & see me? I am much nicer & more amiable at home than at this sort of pow-wow, to which I would never go for the sake of anyone but yourself. Yours in extremis, F. M. H." The idea of Ford's never going to such a pow-wow except for Violet was, however comically remote from the facts, no doubt an expression of his feelings.[13]

In another month they were seeing each other two or three times a week. Ethel Clifford, Lady Dilke, was still enough in the dark to ask Violet if she would mind coming to dinner with Ford. When Violet said, "Id like it," Lady Dilke said, "Lots of people wouldnt." By the end of another month, everyone was aware of what was going on. In her ill-advised way, Violet consulted Wells about Ford, and when she had dinner at the Ritz one night with Raffalovich and Ford came to pick her up, "Raff observed . . . was so sorry to hear he was married." By early May Ford was telling her that she had made him abominably in love with her, and at the end of that month he followed her down to Selsey, where she had a summer cottage, with a trumped-up excuse that amused and flattered her. Then out of the blue, he said, "Will you marry me if ever I am a divorced man?" She brushed this proposal aside as not serious; "much later I subscribed to his plans." It could not have been very much later, for her diary shows that she took Ford around to her lawyer, Humphreys, at the end of June "to ask him to arrange a divorce."[14]

Ford was worried and lonely. He felt his heroic idealism in founding *The English Review* was completely misunderstood by hard, practical men like Bennett and Garnett, and he was not finding in Elsie the tenderness and comfort—say nothing of the romantic excitement—that he longed for. What he needed was sympathy and consolation; what he dreamed of was a grand passion into which he could fling himself at the same time that he was confounding his enemies by making a splendid success of the *Review*—for in spite of the *Review*'s huge losses he was still, at times, able to persuade himself that "just a very little more would make it a paying proposition."[15]

He stressed for Violet what she called "the extreme need of the artist-egotist for an Egeria—any number of Egerias." That concluding irony is the Becky Sharp in Violet speaking; she did not see the matter that way at the beginning, nor did Ford. Like all men of his romantic temper, he was highly susceptible to women, especially to the promise of unknown women.

A turn of the eyebrow, a tone of the voice, a queer characteristic gesture . . . all these things are like so many objects on the horizon of the landscape that tempt a man to walk beyond the horizon, to explore.

To this kind of appeal he was most susceptible when he was unhappy. He found the excitement of sexual exploration irresistible; he found the sympathy of an attractive woman necessary to the dramatization of himself as the unjustly suffering man.[16]

It would have been completely out of character for Ford to take sex as mere appetite requiring periodic satisfaction or even to elevate the sexual act itself into some sort of mystical experience. But his constantly renewed belief that the last woman who had attracted him was the ideal woman he was seeking, his need for a sympathetic feminine audience, and the unique intimacy the sex act creates worked together to involve him sexually with many women. These impulses can be seen during the development of his most serious relations with women, with Elsie Martin-dale, with Violet Hunt, with Stella Bowen, with Janice Biala. They are equally evident in his less serious relations, with Mary Martindale and Jean Rhys.

They are also evident in the considerable number of transient sexual episodes that occurred with the greatest frequency during the busiest years of his life, from the founding of *The English Review* in 1908 until 1916 and during his years in New York in the middle twenties. It would be easy to look on these episodes as casual encounters, particularly as Ford sometimes did things—like taking money from women—that look almost unscrupulous to the disenchanted view. Just occasionally Ford seemed to see that such a view was possible, but it always seemed to him a shocking distortion of the truth.

Like Edward Ashburnham "when he kissed the servant in the train" and precipitated the Kilsyte case, Ford always believed "he was driven to it, by the mad passion to find an ultimately satisfying woman." Edward Ash-burnham's view of the Kilsyte case was that "He was most desperately unhappy himself and it seemed to him the most natural thing in the world that [the weeping nursemaid and he] should pool their sorrows. . . . He felt quite half-fatherly when he put his arm around her waist and kissed her." He was, to be sure, a little disturbed at the way the Kilsyte case awakened him to the possibilities of women. "He began," as Dowell says, "to indulge in day-dreams in which he approached the nursemaid more tactfully and car-ried the matter much further." But Edward, Dowell knows very well, thought of such approaches wholly "in terms of tactful comforting, ending in absorption." He could think in that way even about La Dolciquita; when he could not, he was miserable: when he found himself pursuing Maisie Maidan, "It made him suspect he was inconstant." No doubt the Edward Ashburnham in Ford occasionally suspected the same thing; no doubt the Dowell in him sometimes made his voice heard. But most of the time Ford, like Edward, felt that in even his most casual affairs he was exploring the horizon, was driven by his passion to find an ultimately satisfying woman.[17]

At least at first Violet found Ford's appeal to her hard to resist. There he was, "Tall, haggard, patient, and urbane, coughing and eating his heart out"; and he asked her for her help. He added a nice touch of daring, comparing himself to her fierce cat Puck and telling her "that I ought to keep [him] in a shed in the garden as a 'dangerous male' as I have to do [Puck]." When Violet thought of things like this, she confessed, "shivers run down me." She was in a particularly susceptible mood, for Oswald Crawfurd had died at Montreux on January 31, 1909, and her romantic heart was filled with memories of the glories of passion. "I had just heard," as she put it, "of the death, far away in Switzerland, of such a one as we women, roughly, and tenderly speaking, choose to call 'the only man we have ever loved.' " She and Ford, then, "had got some idea of comforting each other for the slings and arrows of literary fate, at least that is the way we used to speak of it."[18] There began to be long evenings at 84 Holland Park Avenue.

He was by way of himself preparing little dinners . . . *à la Russe.* One evening . . . I found him upstairs in the little kitchen, with his nice Japanese silk dressing-gown over his shabby morning suit to preserve it from the grease of the frying-pan. And, after all, the cutlets were burned. Some meringues from the confectioner's next door followed. . . . Then we went down, and he began to tell me the plot of his new book [*A Call*]. . . . As he read I looked at him critically. He was no longer so dreadfully thin, since the cough had gone, but he was white like a stick of asparagus grown in a cellar; at any rate, rather pasty. He smoked incessantly, and it made his teeth black, His cuffs wanted "trimming". . . .

It was rather cold. The light was not good. Shadows were encroaching on the little oasis of light in which we sat, he on a hideous red plush Victorian arm-chair . . . and I on a *chaise-longue.* . . . The depression was . . . so thick you could cut it with a knife.

On one such occasion Ford talked of suicide and then abruptly left the room. What was she to do? When he returned, she stood close to him, one hand pressed against his chest, the other reaching into the pocket of his brown-velvet jacket from which she drew forth a bottle marked "POISON."

"Were you?" I said; and he answered, "I was."
"Donkey!" I said, and, keeping the bottle in my hand, sought for my cloak and shouldered it . . . and, for the first time after one of our dinners, he walked home with me—and it was only half-past ten when all was said and done.[19]

It may seem a little hard to understand why, if Ford was serious about suicide, he went so ostentatiously to fetch the bottle of poison and put it where she could easily find it. But as Violet observed long afterward, "I am sure that . . . [he] had brought himself to the point of believing. Wheedlers . . . do invariably possess inordinate powers of self-deception." Her own love of dramatic scenes was as sure to create conviction in her. She could not refuse him after this, and on June 10, 1909, they became lovers and Ford thanked her for "the tenderness that has saved one's reason and one's life.

. . . " He was sincere enough in this profession, but there were other factors in the situation. By this time, with the irritability and bad judgment he always showed when he was anxious and overwrought, Ford had piled up a good many troubles for himself that he hoped Violet might help him with.[20]

Trouble began with his deciding that Arthur Marwood was taking all the credit for the *Review* and giving it out that Ford was responsible for all the failures.

> I wrote M[arwood] on Monday night [he told Elsie in March] saying that upon reflection my own position appeared so open to misre-presentation that I must put the matter upon a proper financial basis —and a formal one. I did not say that any misrepresentations had taken place—but merely that it was possible and that, what with a number of things and seeing how, situated as I was, I get all the discredit of the Review's failures, bear all the liability and all the responsibility, whilst *all* the credit was claimed by various other persons, that I was not in a state to be very companionable and that, in consequence, I thought I had better not see him till I felt more composed.

"I think," he summed up, "I have without any offensiveness let M[arwood] understand that I do not want to see him." Marwood shared—and possibly talked about—the anxiety people like Wells and Bennett felt over Ford's extravagant management of the *Review*. But that he was in any way disloyal to Ford or made any such claims as Ford implied is difficult to believe.[21]

No sooner had this situation developed than Elsie reported to Ford that Marwood had for some time been making advances to her. She asserted that he kept reminding her he had saved her life by paying for her operation the year before and that she had incriminating letters from him. It is impossible now to determine precisely how far Marwood went with Elsie, but that something happened there can be no question. There really were letters; Robert Garnett read them. But there is no way of knowing how incriminat-ing they were. Certainly Elsie made as much of this affair as she could, in the hope that it would persuade Ford to return to her.[22]

Elsie was in a disturbed mood at this time; she even developed a pa-thetic suspicion that Galsworthy's *Fraternity* was based on her and Ford. Galsworthy's heroine, Bianca, though she loves her husband, Hilary, deeply, has deliberately destroyed their relation because of his momentary interest in a model.

> Her pride had kept her back from Hilary, till she had felt herself a failure. Her pride had so revolted at that failure that she had led the

way to utter estrangement. Her pride had forced her to the attitude of one who says: "Live your own life; I should be ashamed to let you see that I care what happens between us." Her pride had concealed from her the fact that beneath her veil of mocking liberality there was an essential woman tenacious of her dues, avid of affection and esteem . . . —this ungovernable itch to be appreciated, governed by ungovernable pride . . . this tragedy of a woman, who wanted to be loved, slowly killing the power of loving her in the man, had gone on year after year.

Elsie did behave something like that, though with a good deal more provocation than Bianca. The Countess Macdonald in Ford's own novel, *The New Humpty-Dumpty*, takes a similar attitude, which Ford explains—shockingly when one remembers that he is more or less describing his own wife—by making her a lower-class woman whom Macdonald had married in his naïve Fabian days and is now committed to by his saintly aristocrat's sense of obligation to the lower orders. Countess Macdonald sees Macdonald as dangerously mixed up with "the dissolute and idle Smart Set" because he knows a duke; she seeks "to drag him from his vicious courses" and takes the view that "it doesn't matter what he likes and dislikes. If he wants to have to do with me, he's got to consider what I approve of." At the same time—like Leonora with Edward Ashburnham in *The Good Soldier*—she loves Macdonald passionately.[23]

The Countess Macdonald is a viciously unjust portrait of Elsie, but it rests on an understanding of her pride, her passion, and her ignorance of the world. She persisted during this period in attacking Ford, in a gloomy and violent way, about the life he was leading in London and in asserting her ill-directed but justified jealousy of the women he was seeing. With his rooted belief that specificity, however irrelevant or even imaginary, would always create conviction, Ford would write her: "Here is a list of the people I have seen this week," and then append a list of fifty-nine innocent names. It is pathetic that, however like Galsworthy's Bianca Elsie was, she should have been so aware of the way her pride was destroying Ford's love that she supposed Bianca was actually modeled on her. Galsworthy was deeply distressed.

> I received with much amazement [he wrote Elsie] a letter from Ford saying that you seemed to think 'Fraternity' is founded on your and his domestic affairs. I can only say with great solemnity that I know nothing of your domestic affairs, that [Ford] has never said a word to me or to my wife about them. . . . Hilary is a skit on half of

my own character, and Bianca was suggested by the sister of a certain actor.[24]

When Ford heard Elsie's story about Marwood, he wrote her:

Dearest E;
I must confess that your letter—as far as it affects Marwood —rather astonishes me. If it be true that he has attacked yr virtue and my honour (which is what it amounts to) I cannot for the sake of business have any friendly relations with him. Besides it's obvious that if I see him he will try to persuade me that your accusations are untrue—so that to have to do with him must mean breaking with you.

With regard to your sending his letters to Robert: I think ... you ought to do it, for he is certainly inclined at present to consider that yr views are hallucinations. ... It is a horrible and very ticklish matter for me. On the one hand I do not like you to be misjudged: on the other certain very ticklish negotiations are just being consummated, involving Marwood, Soskice, Robert and my-self. R. is very anxious that I shd attend a meeting on Monday and make it up with M.—this I do not intend to do: but Robert and Soskice are so exceedingly jealous of each other that any new friction wd, I feel sure, upset the apple cart. ... That is the position:—but such a nightmare as all this is! ...

However: I plug along. "I think I ought to tell you" (as the friend of yrs puts it) that Violet Hunt is coming to dinner. She's really doing her best to get the Monds to take up the Review. If they wd, there wd be an end of all these worries.

And, so far I cannot observe in the lady any signs of desiring more of a quid pro quo than the material desire to keep going a magazine in which she hopes to "appear."

Well goodbye old thing—Preserve Yr tranquillity
FMH

This is ambiguous enough: Ford seems to want to stand by Elsie and at the same time to have serious doubts about her story. Nonetheless, he eventually came to believe Elsie's story about Marwood.*[25]

Elsie sent her letters to Robert Garnett, and Ford apparently wrote him about his decision to have nothing to do with Marwood; Robert's reply to Ford is an attempt to persuade everyone to be reasonable.

*We know he did because, in the analogous episode in the *The New Humpty-Dumpty*, Pett spitefully spreads the lie that Kintyre is trying to make Countess Macdonald his mis-tress. At first Macdonald believes this story, but finally, like Ford, he is convinced of its falseness.

To decline to see M[arwood] would be a very great mistake for you to commit. . . .
I perfectly well appreciate the value of V[iolet] to you but M[arwood] is your partner.
V[iolet] means absolutely well by you but so does M[arwood].
I have read those letters: they tell me nothing I had not divined. E[lsie] forgot that not only M[arwood] was flesh and blood but a highly impressionable & *unhappy* person upon whom her confidences [about her unhappy relations with Ford] were certain to make the greatest mark. You and E[lsie] both make the same mistake: in your troubles you become self-concentrated & oblivious of how you affect others. Your letters to me showed this.
I have written to E[lsie]. I believe she will be reasonable: she is really devoted to you.
Count upon me to do my best.[26]

Devoted Elsie certainly was, and she was fully prepared to follow Ford's advice in this affair; whether that made her conduct reasonable is less certain. As soon as she got Ford's letter, she went up to London to see him; their discussion led to a reconciliation of sorts and an agreement about how to handle the Marwood situation, Elsie wanted above everything to bring Ford back to her and the girls—to be sure, on her terms, in Aldington, rather than on his, in London. "That," as Dowell says of Leonora, "was her sad and modest view of matrimony." But she was uncertain of her power; she did not quite dare press Ford to come down to Aldington and stay at Kitcat.
Instead, on her return from seeing Ford in London, she stopped at the Conrads' to ask their help.

. . . your wife [Conrad wrote Ford] . . . informed me that all your differences were happily settled and warned me against the plots and intrigues (vulgo, lies) of certain people. I confess I was literally shocked by the nature of her communication. . . . We, that is Jessie and I, had been aware for a week or so that there was some tension the nature of which of course was not our affair. . . . For the rest I told Elsie with every consideration which is due to her in my house that I could not believe these people [the Marwoods] were as black as they appeared to her. She seemed to take but little heed of my protest. Later on she proposed that you should come down and stay *with us* for a week. . . . But I said at once, No. That cannot be. If you are reconciled so completely, Ford's place, when he is in Aldington, is in the cottage.
What is the end of such a proposal, what object, what purpose can be served by re-creating an equivocal situation? By such jug-

gling with the realities of life, an atmosphere of plots and accusations and suspicions is created. . . . This evening [the Marwoods]
have called. The man, when we were alone, said he felt bound to
inform me that he had just dispatched a letter to you, breaking off
your intimate relations. He told me he was very unhappy and in
truth he looked ill. As he is of good birth and upbringing and has
always seemed to me a gallant *homme* I can't give him up for a
ruffian. . . . In this case, if it is any satisfaction to you, you have done
some crushing . . . but it strikes me, my dear Ford that of late you
have been visiting what might have been faults of tact . . . in men
who *were* your admiring friends, with an Olympian severity. . . . Is
[it] worth while? . . . You will find yourself at forty with only the
wrecks of friendship at your feet. . . . [27]

Conrad put the same view more bluntly to Galsworthy.

We have fallen here into a most abominable upset the execution
of Marwood by Ford and Elsie. I have seen a man guillotined 30 years
ago but it hasn't made me feel half as sick as the present operation.
For weeks poor Marwood looked as if after a severe operation. My
view of *M* is that he is a galant-homme in the fullest sense—absolutely incapable of any black treachery. We couldn't keep the horrid affair off us anyhow—what with E coming with horrid details
and revelations (I told her plainly I could not believe what she said
—and she only smiled) which it was impossible to silence and the
poor M's whom we *had* to listen to out of common humanity. A
beastly affair. . . . [28]

Ford was not much moved by Conrad's admonition. "I have had a long
letter from Conrad pointing out the evil of my ways," he told Elsie a week
later. Perhaps he had become overconfident of his hold on Conrad. They had
certainly been close during the early months of 1909. When Ada Potter, who
—Violet said—adored Ford, put on a dramatization of *The Fifth Queen
Crowned* in March and it failed badly, Conrad wrote him in the old vein:
"M'wood imparted to me horrid news of '*The Vth Queen*' . . . but may be he
exaggerated his account of utter disorganisation of the production. No good
talking I suppose—but you are a prodigal of your toil and your talent. Yet
one would like to see your largess used respectfully."*[29]

*Ford later claimed that he "spent the time [of the performance of *The Fifth Queen*] underneath the bar in the pit refreshment saloon" out of shyness. He also said that "He had had
nothing to do with the play. It had been extracted from his novel by a dramatist" and that "The
Press . . . was livid with rage at the writer for daring to write a play without having studied the
technique of the drama." But there is an all but complete dramatization of *The Fifth Queen* in
Ford's hand at Cornell.

Nevertheless, Ford would have been wise to take Conrad's letter seriously. Conrad's feelings about Ford were permanently altered by this episode. He was convinced that Ford's personality had undergone a drastic modification for the worse, and he began to talk of Ford in quite a new way. At first he was mild enough. "The fact is that H. loves to manage people," he told Norman Douglas. "No doubt he helps too but his assistance has an obverse side." This feeling rapidly grew fiercer.

> We are looking forward with great delight to seeing you [he wrote his doctor, Mackintosh] . . . —or I should say we have been looking thus forward till about 6 pm today. At that hour Hueffer turned up in a car just for a moment and told us confusedly of a new arrangement. . . . In the course of that interview Ford uttered an unlucky phrase which left me no option but to say that till I heard from you I could take no account of what he had told me. . . . I had really to make a stand against that mania for managing the universe, worse even in form than in substance. . . .

"My attitude," he concluded unconvincingly, "is perfectly consistent with a friendship [with Ford] now of so many years' standing."*[30]

Within a month or so he was telling Galsworthy that "I have been fed up on that connection of late till my gorge rises at the thought of it"; and he wrote Pinker:

> [Ford's] conduct is *impossible*. . . . He's a megalomaniac who imagines that he is managing the Universe and that everybody treats him with the blackest ingratitude. A fierce and exasperating vanity is hidden under his calm manner which misleads people. . . . I do not hesitate to say that there are cases, not quite as bad, under medical treatment.
>
> Generally he is behaving like a spoilt kid—and not a nice kid either.

Conrad continued to hold this view of Ford for the rest of his life; when Violet Hunt tried to patch things up between them, he replied, "Dear Mrs. Hueffer . . . I am glad Ford has forgiven my apparent crimes and transgressions . . . and looks kindly on my timid gifts." "I hear Ford is enraged with

---

*According to Jessie Conrad, Ford announced that he and Elsie were entertaining the Mackintoshes and that they would eat all their meals at the Conrads'. She then "said very quietly: 'Oh, wait one minute, if you please, Dr. Mackintosh is also a friend of ours. This being so, my idea is, that if they are paying a visit to you to-morrow you will do all the entertaining yourself. When they visit us, we shall do the same without involving you or your wife in any way. I decline absolutely to fall in with your suggestion.'" This sounds as implausible as most of the speeches Jessie ascribes to herself in her books, but the story is probably substantially true.

me for not giving him more of my Rems.," he wrote Galsworthy in September. "He says I made a fool of him. I don't see how that can be." A little later he reported to Norman Douglas that "the very echoes of the great upheaval have died out. Hueffer goes about lying exuberantly about everything and everybody. His wife is apparently going to sue him for restitution of conjugal rights and then proceed further. But there is some plot under that and at any time they may get reconciled and turn together on some one or other. However we are out of all that and see very little of her. In fact 'everything is over but the stink' as they say after fireworks." Conrad's attitude was soon widely known and damaged Ford's reputation considerably.[31]

Having put himself in a position where he could no longer count on Marwood, his principal backer, at a time when even he was forced to recognize *The English Review* was in serious financial difficulties, Ford had now to find money for it promptly. As his letter to Elsie about her charges against Marwood shows, negotiations that involved his brother-in-law, David Soskice, were already under way. Ford was also negotiating with a wealthy man named Lyons. He began with high hopes of Lyons. "I have a fair chance to sell the English Review at a price that will show a profit on the outlay," he wrote Elsie April 7, 1909." . . . I think I can retain the editorship too and that would be gratifying." But a month later this plan fell through. "I have seen Lyons today," he wrote on May 5, "alas, he is the worst type of large cigar-smoking Jew and he means to skin me clean and clear. . . . There remains the Soskice project."

Meanwhile he had borrowed a further £500 from the Münster Hüffers which he said would "help me to carry on for a month or two." In these desperate circumstances, Elsie offered him every cent she had, about £600, but Ford said, "As to borrowing money from you that is out of the question for many reasons. For if anything happens to me you would certainly need all you can get and keep. Go on gardening." This is a covert reference to his idea that he might commit suicide.[32]

Conrad had decided not to write any more of his reminiscences for the *Review*. At first he said merely that he was not well and was unable to keep up with the installments, but when Ford announced in the July number that "We regret that owing to the serious illness of Mr. Joseph Conrad we are compelled to postpone the publication of the next installment of his Reminiscences," Conrad was furious and told Ford plainly there would be no more reminiscences. Ford replied with one of his "crushing" letters. Conrad then demonstrated the truth of what he had said to Ford in his letter about the

Marwood affair, that "if you start out crushing people, you will discover that they don't 'crush' so easily as all that."

> If you think I have discredited you and the Review [he began]—why then it must be even so. And as far as the Editor of the *E. R.* is concerned we will let it go at that—with the proviso that I do not want to hear anything more about it.
>
> But as writing to a man with a fine sense of form . . . I wish to protest against the words—*Ragged condition.*
>
> It is so little *ragged* to my feeling, and in point of literary fact, that in the book (if the book ever appears) the *whole* of the contribution to the *E. R.*, as it stands now, without the addition of a single word shall form the Part First.
>
> . . . Nothing on earth would induce me to spoil the thing as it stands now by an irrelevant instalment. . . . If I have discredited the *E. R.*, well, I must bear the disgrace.
>
> Yours,
> J. Conrad[33]

This is evidently disingenuous. There was no reason for Conrad's reminiscences to cease to appear in the *Review* at the end of Part First, and originally—as Ford knew—Conrad had not intended them to. After Conrad's death, Ford wrote bitterly to Edward Garnett, "it has been reported to me by a great many people that a great many people, yourself among the number, had told them that Conrad refused to have anything more to do with me because of my relationships with women." These relations cannot have been to Conrad's liking, and Ford was certainly sensitive about them in his later dealings with Conrad. But they were not the essential trouble; that was Conrad's fixed belief that "a fierce and exasperating vanity is hidden under [Ford's] calm manner."[34]

"The Soskice scheme" was David Soskice's plan for forming a group of men with similar political interests who would take over the *Review,* keeping Ford as the editor but controlling the political content. An interim arrangement, according to which Soskice became the business manager and Ford attempted to hold the balance between the political views of Marwood and himself and those of the Soskice group, was to be maintained during the time it took the Soskice group to find the money to buy the *Review.* This interim arrangement dragged on into December, leading to endless quarrels between the two groups that eventually convinced Ford of what everyone should surely have seen from the start, that the arrangement was impractical.[35]

This compromise arrangement, which was set up May 16, 1909, was a bitter blow to Ford, who could now no longer write his cherished political editorials ("I fancy," he had told Edward Garnett, "that my political articles will astonish even you") or control the contents of the *Review*. After the meeting on May 16, he rushed off to the country. He arrived in a downpour, in his evening clothes, not very sober, and, having warned no one he was coming, was not met at Smeeth. He walked to Aldington and arrived soaked to the skin and in a rage: here was a final injustice heaped on the injustice of the *Review*'s fate.[36]

Characteristically he set out to forget his defeat by concentrating on a new interest, and it was on the station platform at Smeeth, when he was returning to London the next morning, that he asked Elsie for a divorce, alleging that he would love her all the more if they were separated. Elsie's response to this proposal was to argue even harder that Ford should leave London for Aldington and return to his writing. But it was too late for that.

The loss of *The English Review* had merely been the precipitating factor in this decision; Ford had long since committed himself to Violet Hunt. As always, he dreamed of finding peace with her. "Don't you see all it means to me to be certain, only, of knowing one can talk to you for the rest of one's life! That, alone, would be Heaven. And then there's you in addition." She too was committed. "Dined FMH," says the note in her diary for the day they became lovers. "The threatened suicide." This last phrase is then crossed out and replaced by "Final," to which she later added "?"

Violet was scheduled to spend the next three days in Oxford with W. P. Ker. On the train she wrote Ford:

> What happened last night made me know that I loved you. Never regret it, and always believe in me, and I won't fail you. I know this with my soul. . . .

> There's a witch upon the hill
> *Give me a kiss*
> There's a dragon I must kill
> *And there's this.*

> The danger signal's up
> *Give me another kiss*
> There's poison in the cup
> *But there's this. . . .*

Later Violet was to feel that "I should have left the salvation of F.M.H. alone. . . . The male must not depend on the female, even in business." But at the moment she was overwhelmed by Ford's flattering intensity.

Ah [he wrote] but we do make a goodly couple, you know. If it isn't already too late [for her to love him wholeheartedly] mightn't we knock the world. . . . Because—tho' H. J. once called me "*le jeune homme modeste*", I am not, really modest when I measure my possibilities against the wits of my fellows. My dear, all of the Shaws, Galsworthys [,] Grahames and fine noble creatures [are] slow witted, fools when it comes to real brain work beside you and me—and you—well, Helen of Troy and Semiramis [,] The Blessed Damozel and Becky Sharp, St Catherine and Christina of Milan could not, all together extract from me the emotion and devotion that are yours.

When Ford sent her some poems, she commented, "I am not a jealous woman but those poems make me jealous. I don't feel that you wrote them to Elsie somehow—and yet?—if you did, it was her due, for you *did* love her." If he had not really loved Elsie then, did he really love her now? She was facing the perennial problem of the woman late chosen. Then Becky Sharp added, "They are all of them beautiful, most of them[—]meaning, I think, that if anything, you have too much facility. *You won't make* the thought tight and packed . . . because then it would be Browningesque and not Impressionist?"[38]

When she returned from Oxford Monday evening, Ford and the two girls came to South Lodge for tea. "I am a little afraid of them both," she wrote him. But she was determined to make their relation a respectable family one—a marriage—as soon as possible. At the same time, she was happily repeating to Ford the words of a popular song of the day, "You shall have all you wa-ant and a little bit mo-ore," and telling him with period daring that "I've got your letter between me and my stays. Do you like that? I wish it was you—or even your hand. The thought does make me thrill. . . . " ("It-was, literally, the hardness of her [Eleanor's] clean drawn figure, her stays beneath his hand" that moved Don Kelleg in *An English Girl*.) She also hustled him around at once to see her lawyer, Humphreys, about his divorce.[39]

Early in July Violet and Rosamond visited Edward Clodd at Aldeburgh. Ford insisted on following her there, with his "secretary" Gertrud in tow, to the scandal of the congregation, though Violet insisted it was only "a reckless instinct for kindness. . . . a desire to give that poor pathetic victim of life a short good time." At the same time she was concocting with Ford what seemed to them a clever plan for using the pathetic victim of life. Ford had early offered Elsie £ 400 a year—presumably to be guaranteed by Violet since he could hardly have produced that sum himself—if she would divorce him. Harri Martindale had told Elsie to ignore this offer and she had. Violet and Ford now had a new plan. Ford would write Elsie a description of the way Gertrud had been living at 84 Holland Park Avenue and traveling about with him. This description would infuriate her and also provide her the evidence of adultery needed for a divorce. On July 18, Ford met Edmée Van der Noot at Tonbridge, took her—for some obscure reason—on the river, and handed over his letter. As a reward Violet slipped over early to Holland Park Avenue with Annie Child, her maid, to prepare a little supper. When Ford returned, they celebrated. "... when the traveller returned ... we [drank] wine together in the good German fashion. ... The refrain of the Italian song from last night ['You shall have all you want and a little bit more'] was still in our ears."[40]

At first everything looked well. In a burst of rage at Ford's letter, Elsie went up to London to see Robert Garnett about a divorce. Robert felt too involved with Ford to act for her and sent her to another lawyer, William Sturges, who composed for her the necessary letter to Ford with which a petition for restitution of conjugal rights has to begin; "the letter ... means," Violet told Annie Child, "it will be perhaps only six months or eight months hence. So we are both very happy." But then she added, "We took a turn in the shrubberies to read it[.] Ford was very quiet about it—*I* was shy. I could not somehow express my gladness and I don't quite feel that he felt any. ... " He may well not have, for it meant the end not only of Elsie and home but of Christina and Katharine, who were very important to him.*[41]

Violet was also busy trying to get Ford accepted by her relatives. While she was off visiting the Monds at the end of July, she sent him to take her mother, whose mind was now too far gone to permit her to travel alone, to visit her sister, Silvia, at Bedburne. The visit was a disaster. In the first place Rosamond revealed all too openly her schoolgirl passion for Ford, sitting "on a stool at his feet—as it were—and adoring him," as her mother said in disgust. Nor was Ford so insensitive to Rosamond's adoration as he wanted Violet to believe; there is a good deal of what Ford felt about her in Edward Ashburnham's feelings about Nancy Rufford of *The Good Soldier*. Silvia discovered after Ford arrived that he was not, as Violet had led her to believe, already divorced. It was a final complication that Ford found the Fogg Elliots

---

*Child watched—or tried to watch—over Violet like a mother. To quiet her suspicions Ford had to give her a written statement of his "intentions." "Dear Child," he wrote, "This is just to tell you that it is certainly my intention—as it is the most earnest desire that I have—to marry Miss Hunt as soon as my wife divorces me. ... So do not have any doubt about it."

excessively dull ("*how* they bore me!" he wrote Violet) and showed it. "Either Mr H found it restful to rest his brain & rather play the fool," Silvia said tartly, "or he tried to adapt himself to *our* intellects. He was really very dull. . . . " Violet foolishly persisted. "Suppose you told [Silvia] you wanted to marry me," she wrote Ford, "and were taking steps but that I was a little half hearted about it all, because of my being nearly eleven years older! And that you would be grateful if she would ask us up there together. . . . " "I think," Ford said with masterly understatement, "it was really a mistake my coming here . . . and I fancy I have made your sister dislike me. . . . I don't wonder, seeing the character of the country [County Durham] and its inmates that 'Wuthering Heights' was written."[42]

When they were together again in London, they were exasperated by the usual troubles of unacknowledged lovers. They had tried a hideaway in John Street but it was not very convenient; neither was anything else. "I like [your room] so much better than my own at South Lodge," Violet said. "I am a little apprehensive there all the time and I do believe that I prefer it to be me to get up and go! I feel it for you—isn't it absurd of me!" There were troubles of other kinds. There was already gossip about them. Doubts about the practical possibility of Violet's marrying Ford were one thing. "There was not even then," she saw at least afterwards, "the slightest chance of things falling out as he—as I, too, came to wish." But doubts about her intention to marry him, if a logical consequence of her earlier affairs, were a denial of her present passion for marriage and respectability and she wrote her lawyer for details of her efforts to arrange a divorce for Ford. "What I mean to do is to leave a record of my bona fide efforts to unite myself to Mr Hueffer in a business like way. The Hueffer relations are spreading tales."[43]

The Hüffer aunts and uncles, being devout Catholics, were urging Elsie not to divorce Ford but to treat the Violet Hunt affair as a passing fancy. Their word carried a good deal of weight with Elsie, and they made it very clear that they thought good Catholic daughters would be seriously compromised by divorced parents. In addition to that, Harri Martindale foresaw a terrible scandal if Elsie divorced Ford and he openly took up with Mary Martindale, who was as eager as Violet to marry Ford. "Oh dear," Elsie said years after, "if people had not stepped in. . . . Of course it would have been better for me if I had divorced him." In the end these family pressures would persuade Elsie to abandon divorce proceedings, though they could not stop her from beginning them with her petition for restitution of conjugal rights; while she was arranging that, the views of the Hüffers and of Harri Martindale—that the Violet Hunt affair was only a temporary lapse from grace on Ford's part—were, to Violet's indignation, noised abroad.

That people should say such things about him astonished and outraged Ford, who had, as usual, convinced himself of the purity of his motives and the dignity of his conduct.

> The thing really grows worse and worse [he wrote his mother] and there is nothing left for me but an action for slander. . . . Abso[l]utely the only thing that she [Elsie] could allege against me with any shadow of proof and absolutely the only wrong I will admit having done is having a housekeeper [Gertrud] younger than convention demands. And that is all. Yet really, without exaggeration Elsie has ruined me so that I am mentally a wreck. My work is going all to pieces and I cannot even place the last book but one that I wrote [*The 'Half Moon'*] incredible as that seems.

There is little doubt that he was mentally a wreck. These troubles, as Violet said afterwards, produced in Ford "a fresh attack of neurasthenia that lasted three whole years, and was responsible for many things, and much private and particular misery." Experiences such as these "gave him such severe shocks as to render him really ill. His mind was too sensitive to stand it, and for the time being he would be deprived almost of his senses and his power to control himself."[44]

It was a last straw when Edward Heron Allen told them that "Mrs. Hueffer [that is, Elsie] may at any time seize the *furniture* at the flat . . . under her present judgment." Violet quickly arranged for an appraisal and deposited money to Ford's account to cover any demand that Elsie might make. She and Ford even persuaded Ford's mother to write a letter declaring that practically everything at 84 Holland Park Avenue was her property. Ford was, as usual, broke; " . . . it is no exaggeration to say that I am practically at starvation point," he wrote Pinker. Thus, while Elsie was worrying her heart out that Ford might abduct the girls and—she believed—thus make a divorce possible on his own terms, Violet was worrying that Elsie might steal the furniture.[45]

These harrowing troubles, their desire for a "honeymoon," and the approach of Violet's birthday—September 28—became too much for them, and they slipped off together to France to visit Violet's old friend, Agnes Farley, and her husband. In his attempt to conceal what he was doing Ford so confused poor David Soskice that Soskice, eventually discovering Ford had gone off with Violet, concluded they had absconded together—when there was not "sufficient copy for the November . . . number" of the *Review*, too! He thereupon appointed Galsworthy temporary editor, and Ford was enraged to find Galsworthy firmly esconced when he returned after two weeks in France.[46]

Chapter 16

Ford and Violet had their "first quarrel about the fly to the station," but they had a happy time at the Farleys' cottage at Beaumont-le-Roger. Ford dictated *The Portrait* to Violet and Agnes in the mornings and Violet reported to Child that "he is *much* better."

> In the afternoons we walked in the woods. . . . Or we would take a rickety *calèche* and visit Lisieux Cathedral, or some old, mediaeval château ruined by the Revolution, where, on the ground floor, old black-robed peasant women pottered about among dressers covered with bowls of pale primrose-coloured cream. . . . Or we would walk among high hedges, across marshes, by straggling, forgotten paths, to this or that old ruined *manoir* that would not let. *A cause des revenants!*[1]

A price had to be paid for this happiness. The trouble began absurdly enough; Violet had forgotten to bring with her a pair of stays she particularly wanted because she had promised to get a similar pair for Miss Thomas, the *Review*'s secretary, to whom she injudiciously wrote from Paris about the matter. Unluckily, the day she and Ford were on their way back to London —October 14—Elsie and Edmée chose to appear at 84 Holland Park Avenue with Elsie's lawyer and there pressed Miss Thomas for information ("insulted her," Violet says). Miss Thomas admitted she knew where Violet was and under further cross-examination produced a telegram from Ford announcing that he was arriving from Paris at Charing Cross at 10:45 P.M. Edmée then called South Lodge and inquired when Violet would return; on the 10:45 train at Charing Cross, she was told.

As a consequence, when Ford and Violet descended from the train at Charing Cross, "There on the sort of rostrum where it seems passengers stand to await the porters with their baggage through the Customs" stood Elsie, Edmée, and William Sturges. "We were," said Violet in *The Flurried Years*, "so good we were careless and I, so neatly chaperoned while I was in France, *tant soit peu* relaxed when I set foot on the shores of England. One of us surely ought to have got out at Hither Green. . . . " (This sudden appearance of the shrewd woman of experience at the shoulder of the Edwardian lady is typical of Violet.) "It's all up, old girl!" Ford said to her when he saw Elsie. "You will see. There'll be no divorce."[2]

From this point on their troubles multiplied rapidly. Ford quarreled with David Soskice, finally working himself up to the belief that Soskice and his friends were "revolutionary extremists" who must, at all costs, be got rid of. He and Violet sought to persuade Sir Alfred Mond to buy the *Review*. For a man of Sir Alfred's means the sum involved was "derisory"—Ford estimated it at £ 200. He clearly thought that if Mond bought the *Review* he would regain control of it and have his revenge on the Soskice group.

> I do wish [he wrote Mond] you would buy "The English Review." I have given such enormous labour to it that it would really break my heart to see it go to ruin, as it will if it passes into the hands of [the Soskice group]. . . . it is really rather a grave public matter. . . . authors will write for me for almost nothing—I could reduce the losses to very nearly nothing if I had someone to work in sympathy with.

Mond did buy the *Review* and, instead of giving Ford a free editorial hand, fired him and put Austin Harrison in. "And we walked as usual in the Park," Violet remembered, "treading the dead leaves like faded hopes under our feet, in silence. For a week of mornings he did not address more than three words to me."[3]

After the disastrous incident at Charing Cross Station, he and Violet locked the barn tight. Violet never went near *The English Review* office, and Ford spent his evenings at South Lodge playing piquet with Mrs. Hunt, always departing at eleven sharp. This ostentatious decorum did not prevent the rapid spread of the news about their trip to Normandy. H. G. Wells, having heard rumors from Pinker, wrote Violet that he hoped she "wasn't going to get into another mess." Violet's only known comment on this letter was, "Dear H. G.," but it elicited from Ford a letter to Pinker which clearly illustrates what Violet meant when she spoke of the misery his neurasthenia could cause.

> Wouldn't it be better [Ford asked Pinker], don't you think, to tell my overt enemies, rather than people like Wells, silly and untrue

stories about my private life? . . . I have, though I very bitterly regret it, allowed him the run of my house in the past. The result is that he now pretends to a past intimacy which he never possessed and spreads ingenuous inventions which amuse him and tickle his vanity. This would be all right and I am so entirely indifferent to people's opinion that I would not think of protesting. But if you . . . start his fertile mind upon a new track with regard to a third party [Violet] it seems to be a distinct hardship to that third party. . . .

In the future tell these stories—and limit them please to those that damage me—to an avowed enemy. . . . But if you would really like to know who the lady is—and I make no secret)) why not dine with me here [84 Holland Park Avenue] and go over the house. You could then tell everybody everything.

You will observe that I do not mount any high horse of rage, you are so much too off the mark and I know how inveterate a gossip you are. But don't bring me—and still more don't bring third parties—up against little animals like Wells. I don't know him; I don't want to know him and I try to forget that I ever made the mistake of knowing him. When he seemed to be in a bad way I and the third party whom you have libelled did our bests to get reputable people to call on his wife. That was the decent thing to do but I don't want, now . . . to have to think of him.

He wrote Galsworthy a similar letter "declining the honour of [his] future acquaintance on the score that [he] was humanitarian, stole F. M. H.'s thunder, etc.—a mad letter," as Violet summarized it, and, judging from Galsworthy's reply, asserting that his work would outlive Galsworthy's. Galsworthy answered with his usual generosity.[4]

But the worst disaster of this fall was with Henry James. In October, after a hint from Violet, he invited her to Lamb House for a weekend. She and Ford then confided to him that Elsie was about to sue Ford for divorce, perhaps with some ill-judged hope of enlisting his sympathy. James wrote Violet asking her not to come to see him:

. . . I . . . received by the same post which brought me your letter, one from Ford Madox Hueffer. . . . I deeply regret and deplore the lamentable position in which I gather you have put yourself in respect to divorce proceedings about to be taken by Mrs. Hueffer; it affects me as painfully unedifying, and that compels me to regard all agreeable or unembarrassed communications between us as impossible. . . .
Believe me then, in very imperfect sympathy,
Yours
Henry James

Violet protested "that my relations with F. M. H. have never been of such a character as to warrant my being dragged in to Elsie's petition" and freely asserted that "as you know, F. M. H. and his wife have been separated a number of years. And he has only lately allowed divorce proceedings[,] which are merely formal . . . in order that he may marry me." But James was not prepared to listen to Violet having it both ways in this fashion. When Ford wrote him a second time, he said "Very pressing occupation has to this moment prevented my writing you these few words. . . . What I wrote to [Violet] that I deplored or lamented was the situation in which, whatever it had or hadn't been, her general relations with you had landed her."[5]

On January 11, 1910, Mr. Justice Bargrave Deane issued an order in response to Elsie's petition for restitution of conjugal rights. Mr. Le Bas, who represented Elsie, put it that in 1908 Ford "came once or twice to see her" in the country, where she "was obliged to go . . . in compliance with doctor's orders," and that "in July, 1909, he sent a message . . . that he never intended to live with her again, and that it was only due to her to have the custody of the children." "Mrs. Hueffer . . . corroborated, and his lordship made a decree for restitution of conjugal rights, with costs, to be complied with within 14 days." The newspapers—to Violet's dismay—made much of this little story; the headlines said: "Novelist and His Wife. Mr. Hueffer Ordered to Return to Her within Fourteen Days." When Violet saw them, she was not sure she could go home and face the servants; and "who would let in the man whose name was 'up,' as [the maid] put it," when Ford called as usual that night? She need not have worried over that, for Ford never appeared, that night or for many after. When he finally did, he said nothing, "so that I never, to this day, knew how he was taking it." It was all very unsatisfactory. So too was the conspiracy of silence among her friends. "Time passed . . . months . . . well into May-time! No stones—weighty —not even a pebble—dropped into the silent pool of our fates."[6]

Violet continued to hope that Elsie would divorce Ford. For the moment Elsie hesitated, so that despite the court order, she did nothing when Ford did not return to her in the specified fourteen days. At the beginning of December, Ford—or perhaps Violet—had begun paying Elsie £ 3.10.0 a week for her support. When the court, by ordering him to pay Elsie a small sum, created the impression that he had not been paying her anything, he refused to obey the court order, "a plan such as would naturally occur to a romanticist, and commended itself to a reader of Grimm like me," as Violet said. He also had an idea that the thought of him imprisoned for contempt of court might touch Elsie's heart and persuade her to go on with the divorce and give him his freedom.[7]

But, above all, going to prison would bring home to all those who had failed him in the crisis over *The English Review* how small-minded they had been, for he was possessed by the feeling that he had been shamefully betrayed by people he had sacrificed himself to help. "Acquainted as you are with so many of my friends you must know," he wrote Pinker, "that their province is not to help me but to be, perpetually, sponges"; and a year later he was saying to Edgar Jepson with Lear-like irony:

> . . . I see no reason why you should desire to cut my throat, blast my reputation, reveal what you think to be my secrets, or throw vitriol upon me. I never discovered your first work, offered you shelter, food, clothing or encouragement when you were starving. I never lent you money, wrote in praise of your writing or committed against you any of the twenty-seven Nonconformist Deadly Sins.

In due course he was summoned to the Marylebone Police Court and sentenced to ten days in Brixton Gaol. Two days of this sentence were commuted, since they fell on a weekend, and when he came out, Violet persuaded him to give up his defiance of the court.[8]

Before Ford went to jail, Violet had decided to move him to South Lodge as a paying guest at £ 3 a week ("ample in those days," as she is at pains to specify). While Ford was in jail, she and Mary Martindale dismantled 84 Holland Park Avenue—except one room which was to be occupied by René Byles, now back from Japan and starting on a career as a literary agent. They sold most of Ford's books to get money for him, returned the innumerable borrowed books they found, and moved such furniture as was his to South Lodge. While they were busy as this task, Harri Martindale came in. The sight of Mary thus intimately involved in Ford's affairs upset him, and his report of this incident was another factor in Elsie's final determination not to go on with the divorce. Thus ended the last hope that Elsie would free Ford.[9]

Ford had keyed himself up for his stint in prison, and when he came out, Violet took him—along with her mother and, oddly enough, Gertrud Schlablowsky ("whom I found I could tolerate because she was going back to Königsberg")—to the quiet little village of Fordingbridge for a rest. There Ford began his next novel, *Ladies Whose Bright Eyes*; Violet found a name for its heroine (who is modeled on her niece Rosamond)—The Lady Dionissia de Egerton de Tamville—on a tablet in the porch of Salisbury Cathedral. Ford's devotion to work had persisted through all these months of confusion. He had had about half of *A Call* (then named *On the Telephone*) finished by January, 1909, and he had sent the completed manuscript to Methuen on March 7. Methuen turned down *A Call* and so did Hutchinson; they said it was too short. This delayed its publication, by Chatto & Windus, until February 3, 1910; by that time Ford had completed a safe historical novel called *The Portrait* for Methuen, and Methuen published it only five months after *A Call* appeared. "I think it is rather soon," Ford wrote Pinker. "But I suppose Methuen's know their own business best." By March 30, 1910, he had completed and sent to Pinker the manuscript of *The Simple Life Limited,* though it was not published until a year later, and was ready to start on *Ladies Whose Bright Eyes.*[10]

A Call: The Tale of Two Passions is a serious effort to define the theme Ford had been slowly working toward in his earlier books: Ezra Pound thought it the equal of *The Good Soldier.* The fact that it was written for serialization in *The English Review* may have led Ford to make a special effort with it. The limiting defect of *A Call* is that, despite its skill, its image is inadequate to its idea, as if the author had got so interested in the novel's technique that he ignored the need for plausibility in the kind of novel he had committed himself to.*[11]

The Portrait, which followed so quickly on the heels of *A Call,* is a historical romance set in the age of George I. As a piece of light fiction it is thoroughly successful. It begins with a wager over the beautiful model for a painting called *Celia in her Arbour* by a Hogarth-like painter. This wager sets in motion a lively plot that provides plenty of opportunity for colorful period details of upper-class London, rural Kent, and the stinking Ashford gaol. The novel's hero is a large, blond man like Ford. *The Portrait* is a spirited and professional performance. Ford always remembered it with satisfaction and later called it "an eighteenth century pastiche for which I have rather a tenderness." The surprising thing is that it did not compete more successfully than it did with the popular romances of writers like Anthony Hope.

The Portrait was the third and last novel Ford wrote under his agreement with Methuen, but Pinker had already arranged another three-novel contract with Constable, which Ford signed on March 17, 1910, in spite of his fear that "I shall have to stick to historical novels for the Constable Contract, though I hate writing them." Nevertheless, he worked steadily that summer on one of his best historical novels, *Ladies Whose Bright Eyes.*[12]

Tante Laura had died in Münster and the legacy Ford had always supposed was coming to him from her turned out to be contingent on his good behavior, a condition he had already made sure he could not meet. In

*For a discussion of *A Call,* see pp. 478–82.

his overwrought state he got it fixed in his mind that the news of his imprisonment had killed Tante Laura. Meanwhile, Violet was embroiled with her relatives—over her handling of her mother's affairs as well as over Ford. Silvia refused to allow Rosamond to remain at South Lodge; "Nothing you say," she wrote Violet, "will make me change my mind. I consider it *most* harmful in every way for R to be with you in town—& you know quite well *why*. . . . " When Violet persisted stubbornly in trying to get Silvia to countenance Ford and her by having them to Bedburne, Silvia flatly refused. "I regret I cannot ask Mr. H here. Walton [Fogg Elliot] & he are miles apart, & *never* would get on, & naturally this prevents me, but I should of course be glad to have you—later on. . . . How is he going to get a divorce? It is an ambiguous position at present."[13]

No one knew this better than Violet and Ford, but they could see no way to solve their problem, though Violet, full of fighting spirit, did her best. They persuaded Mary Martindale and later Mrs. Hueffer to come to live at South Lodge to lend them respectability. Violet hired an open carriage and dragged Ford about on calls, he in tailcoat and top hat, she "all veils and tocque and parasol." David Garnett was taken along on one of these expeditions during which they called on Adam Sedgwick, Professor of Biology at the Imperial College, and Netta Syrett, the novelist; he noticed they were stared at, as if everyone knew all about Ford and Violet.*[14]

Then Violet decided she would like to visit Ford's relatives in Germany. It would get them out of their difficult situation in London and spare Ford serious financial embarrassments—as usual, a problem for him. Violet ostentatiously provided herself with a chaperone. By the oddest quirk, this was that Lita Brown who had replaced Violet in the affections of Oswald Crawfurd and become his second wife. Mrs. Crawfurd was now living at Bad Nauheim; perhaps Violet felt she would understand Violet's situation better than most, having been through something like it herself with Crawfurd. So they set off up the Rhine for Tante Emma Goesen's. It was a slow journey, and Violet was soon bored, especially when she discovered that Ford could sit endlessly over games of patience while he worked out the day's stint on his current novel and, once he was buried in such work, was impervious to any outside force, "refusing to be confronted with any of the problems that beset an author unfortunately doubled with a man." It seemed to her that the

---

*"These ladies of the upper middle classes rolled along in handsome carriages as they paid afternoon calls. Their white kid gloves were of an immaculate quality. Over one wrist they carried a small, square gold mesh bag containing a gold pencil and a flat gold wallet that held their cards. If the lady of the house was 'not at home,' the visitor handed the servant two of her cards with the corner turned down to indicate that she had 'left cards' in person."

social and financial burden of their awkward situation was being entirely thrown on her. This feeling was not just; Ford made over his considerable profits from the Constable contract to Humphreys for payment to Elsie.[15]

Violet and Ford stayed at Assmanshausen and were assiduous in their attentions to Tante Emma. When David Garnett arrived in Boppard, Ford took him to tea at Tante Emma's imposing Italianate villa and he was much impressed: "[Ford] was exquisitely turned out in a summery tweed suit, with a mourning band [for Tante Laura] on his arm, thoroughly well brushed and shaved, with grey spats and a scented handkerchief." The next day, in Assmanshausen, he and David had their picture taken together with Ford dressed exactly as Garnett describes him. Ford showed him around the town, waving casually to "My dear friend, Prince Metternich," and amusing him with tall stories about his German ancestors. When David later ran out of money in Freiburg he got in touch with Ford, who immediately sent him a hundred marks.[16]

Early in September Mrs. Crawfurd grew anxious to return to what Violet calls "the hectic joys of her cure at Nauheim." The two ladies settled into a smart hotel—Bittong's—where Ford "called . . . every morning . . . for one or the other of [the] ladies" and "was inducted into the bedroom of either— announced by a smart *chasseur* in blue." Violet was fascinated by the romantic young German officers at Nauheim and by the visits of the Tzar and Tzaritza of Russia, who came every day from Freiburg to take the waters. The Tzaritza she thought, "looked stupid, incompetent, haughty, dejected . . . a lovely fool" in "black with pearls." Nicholas seemed to her "a disconsolate figure" "marked down for destruction." She was clearly in her element at Nauheim; it was during this visit that Ford collected the impressions of the place he used to such good effect in *The Good Soldier*.[17]

When they got back to Boppard, Tante Emma suggested to Ford that he might become a German citizen and get a German divorce from Elsie. Tante Emma, Cousin Hermann reported to Elsie from Paris, "deeply feels your having exposed the [Hüffer] name to such comments in England. . . . [She] can furthermore not realize how a woman, once having loved a man, can grow so indifferent in his regard, as not to mind his going to prison." Ford was evidently making good use of the story of his days in Brixton Gaol. When Harri Martindale asked Cousin Hermann what Elsie could do to stop Ford's trying to get a divorce, Hermann said, "The only one [of the Hüffers] who could even attempt that would be my aunt [Emma], and you will find her very loyal if you can convince her that cousin Elsie was under the necessity of opening proceedings against Ford in July 1909."[18]

Unluckily, Mrs. Crawfurd knew of a clever German lawyer in Giessen, Herr Dr. Rechtsanwalt Ludwig Leun, and Ford rushed off to consult him about a German divorce. It was an idea that naturally appealed to him—"something," as Violet said long after, "foolish, the madder the merrier—or the sadder! Something justifiable but not as the world goes, for poetic justice." It would be one in the eye for all those who had gossiped so unjustly about him and Violet and destroyed his reputation in England; it would make him an intimate part of the dignified life of his German relatives and give him all the prestige of his baronial German inheritance. The only difficulty Ford could foresee was the problem of establishing his German citizenship; Francis Hueffer had started to take out naturalization papers in England, and it might take some time to undo the effect of that. Leun left him with the impression that "The dear conceited Germans . . . do not allow a whimsical father by one rash act to deprive his children of the inestimable advantage of German citizenship. . . . They have only to *se donner la peine* of acquiring domicile and getting the burgomasters of some particular German town to accept them as persons likely to be good townsfellows and rich enough to pay their rates regularly. . . . " Ford was full of optimism and, for the moment at least, prepared to give to the task the six months or so Leun thought it would require. He and Violet both recognized that they would have to become Germans, and *The Desirable Alien*, their joint book about their German experience, was largely written—as its title suggests —to show how delighted they were to do so. "Some persons," Violet wrote, "are, of course, born Germans; some achieve citizenship of that great and good nation. Others, again, have the honour thrust upon them. And one fine day I found myself in the last category of all, with no reluctance, but through no fault of my own." She took to calling Ford Joseph Leopold, the German Catholic names he had added when he was received into the Church. In his Preface to *The Desirable Alien* Ford referred to Germany as "my beloved country," and talked of "My august Sovereign, Ernest Ludwig Grossherzog Von Hessen-Darmstadt und bei Rhein"—to the amusement of Ezra Pound, who took to addressing Ford as "My dear ole Freiherr Von Grumpus ZU und VON Bieber-stein." Ford and Violet had visions "of a villa on the Rhine . . . where money . . . would be his for the asking and a little deference and kowtowing to an ancient and influential relative [Tante Emma]."[19]

Once the plan for a German divorce was settled, Ford and Violet set themselves up at Ford's favorite German hotel, the Hotel zum Ritter at Marburg, for a vacation. There Ford became an enthusiastic patron of the cinematograph, and they greatly enjoyed the parades in celebration of Sedan Day (September 2) and their leisurely evenings over ices and coffee at Marchesi's, the town's most popular café. Most important of all, they visited the castle to see Luther's Protest. Full of renewed Catholic enthusiasm as a result of his new attachment to Germany, Ford had already been berating Violet for the way she and the rest of the "Prots" had stolen all the beautiful churches of Germany "from us." Then, "finally, having drunk the Protestant cup of bitterness to the dregs at Joseph Leopold's hands," she was carried off to the source and fount of all her villainy, in a "clumsy, old-fashioned landau" to a castle filled with "the usual suits of armour, made presumably for dwarfs," to see a great many dirty pieces of parchment with "great fat seals ... depending from them by unpleasant-looking strings." With a certain calculated malice she "went hither and thither [in the Ritter Saal], saying nothing, but peeping into this case and that case, and listening to [Ford's] instruction." Finally Ford pointed out the wicked document itself. "There," he said, " ... That is what you mean when you say you are a Protestant!" " 'But I don't say it,' I remarked helplessly. ... Useless! A 'Prot' I am, and seemingly must remain so in the eyes of this black Papist." Here is the actual occasion out of which Ford was to make the climactic scene of *The Good Soldier*, when Florence lectures on the glories of the Protest with her hand on Edward Ashburnham's arm and her eyes on his, until even Dowell "was aware of something treacherous, something frightful, something evil in the day." Violet's description of the actual occasion leaves one feeling that there may have been more to say for her than Ford was willing to allow when he created Florence.[20]

Then Violet fell ill and they had to give up these activities. Ford made the best of the situation by dictating the last of *Memories and Impressions* to Violet while she lay in bed recuperating. "I suppose," she said years later,

> I was cantankerous, for I fell foul of a phrase in the last chapter, when the Author, "a little mad about Good Letters"—a little, good Lord!
> —fancies himself arrived in his author's heaven at last, wandering among green trees and coloured lamps, listening to the whisperings of a happy crowd—his eternal desideratum—blest I, as well as him, wandering with their beloveds—"And too, will have on my arm someone I like very much. ... "

It is difficult not to feel some sympathy for Violet's cantankerousness about this well-meant but condescending inclusion of her among the saved. This is the first sign we have of the scrappy fierceness with which Violet would always meet what she thought—rightly or wrongly—Ford's unfairness to her. Though not unattractive in itself, it was a peculiarly unfortunate characteristic in anyone who hoped to live with Ford, who could not endure even the hint of a scene, especially over what he was convinced was a kindness and a compliment.[21]

When Violet was up and about again, they walked through windy autumn afternoons for their tea to "a little, sad, stale café set down in a stony garden of gravel," where they ate "Sand Küchen, that seemed made of the gravel of the walk and ran out of the corners of our mouths." It was time to leave. In any event it had become necessary for Violet to get back to England; her sisters had taken legal action against her over her handling of their mother's affairs and she had to defend herself. It was time, too, for Ford to get to Giessen and begin persuading the authorities that he was a substantial citizen capable of paying his rates. At the end of September, he saw Violet as far as Cologne on her way to England and went to Giessen.[22]

When Violet got home she began to describe Ford's plan to everyone, and two of her good friends, Dollie Radford and Ethel Colburn Mayne, consulted an expert, R. Ellis Roberts. According to Roberts, they explained that Ford

> would go to the Grand Duchy of Baden. He would acquire citizenship there. He would then secure a divorce from his wife—oh! yes, he could manage *that*. His dear love would then join him: her scruples would be set at rest: they would be married. "What," asked my friends anxiously, "did I think of the plan?" I told them. . . . No doubt in Baden the pair would be married. For one thing it might—though here I was doubtful—leave Ford open to a charge of bigamy in England. Anyway there was no question that under English law the lady would be Mr. Hueffer's mistress, not his wife. . . . Would I speak to the lady? Unwillingly I consented. I told her the facts. . . . Nothing availed. Ford, she insisted, must be right; he was as anxious for marriage as she; it was his plan; after all, he was very clever. The plan was wonderful.

And Violet set to work making notes on *The Life and Letters of Sir Hubert Herkomer*, a royal academician who had resumed his German citizenship in order to marry his sister-in-law.[23]

At the same time, Ford wrote to Elsie's lawyer, Sturges, to say that he was going to become a German citizen and divorce her. His letter frightened Elsie; like Violet, she believed in Ford's cleverness. She consulted Robert Garnett, who first refused to be involved and then, touched by her panic, wrote her, "The idea if there is one that Ford is a German subject is absurd. . . . Of course I would not help against you." Cousin Hermann's advice was equally sensible. "How should Ford be able to call himself a

German citizen, never having claimed such rights before, that I know of, or having fulfilled the military or other duties incumbent on a person claiming German birthright?" "Why not," he concluded reasonably, "wait quietly till Ford serves a writ on you and proves he has the right to do so as a German citizen?" "I do not see," he added, "how Ford should desire to become a German, and thus possibly ruin his career as an English author."[24]

In theory, Ford now settled down to entrenching himself with the local authorities of Giessen, but as Violet observed, "It wasn't [he felt] really his job, and he was up against clever, shrewd people who had spent their lives at it and had not novels to write. . . . And I sometimes think that in disgust at the obvious disparity he took a sort of pride in sticking to—in putting all his wits into his profession, and making the other his hobby. Just playing at law was a relaxation from the stern professional necessity" of writing. He was quickly bored by Giessen; children set off percussion caps outside his window and shouted "*Tag! Englander!*" His two rooms at 29 Nordanlage, with "about two hundred and fifty ornaments, ranging from bits of coral like human brains, to gilded busts of Lohengrin," were depressing; the food was terrible (in spite of it he managed to grow fat, getting up to 224 pounds). There was only the occasional relief of going to Jena to lecture to Levin Schücking's students on the Pre-Raphaelites.[25]

Violet's illness in September necessitated an operation—"a little flutter," she called it—and the day before she went into the nursing home, Mary Martindale surreptitiously wired Ford; he arrived "incognito" in London in time to be with Violet when she came out of the anesthetic. He stayed for the ten days, sneaking off one day to the school at St. Leonard-on-Sea to take the girls a pair of necklaces made by Violet out of amber she had bought in a Marburg pawnshop. He also dedicated *Memories and Impressions* to them. "My Dear Kids," he wrote, "Accept this book, the best Christmas present that I can give you. You will have received . . . the amber necklaces . . . that are the outward and visible sign of the presence of Christmas. But certain other things underlie all the presents that a father makes to his children. Thus there is the spiritual gift of heredity." That, he tells them, is what *Memories and Impressions* is about.[26]

Memories and Impressions is Ford's tribute to his grandfather, a far better one than his earlier biography. He uses his personal experience with Brown without obtrusive vanity and, apart from a few quite deliberate exaggerations for comic effect, with little romancing. William Michael Rossetti, who knew the circumstances Ford was describing and was a comically literal stickler for accuracy, could find nothing more significant wrong with *Memories and*

Impressions than Ford's ascription to Brown of some colorful language. According to Ford, Brown shouted, "God damn and blast you, William, can't you be more careful?" when Rossetti knocked over the fire irons. "I remember this petty circumstance," Rossetti says solemnly, "and I assert in the most positive terms that Brown did not use any such violent or profane language."[27]

Nevertheless, in *Memories and Impressions* Ford was already beginning to develop the defensive air about factual inaccuracy that would eventually become a whole theory of literary art, which he would call "Impressionism." He says of *Memories and Impressions* that "there have been many things written about these facts, [but] no one has whole-heartedly and thoroughly attempted to get the atmosphere of these twenty-five years. This book, in short, is full of inaccuracies as to facts, but its accuracy as to impressions is absolute." The logical blur here is one he would never face: what Ford is guaranteeing is the accuracy with which *Memories and Impressions* represents his impressions of those twenty-five years, not the accuracy with which it represents the atmosphere of those years.[28]

On this matter of inaccuracy, Ford became more and more vehement as the years passed until, by *Provence* (1935), he was going out of his way to attack scholarship itself. "Scholarship," he said, "is a quality for which I have always had a great contempt. . . . The best scholar of his day would have interrupted and destroyed the flow of the Sermon on the Mount by cavilling at the Preacher's use of the enclytic *de.* . . . " The interruption of the flow of Ford's impressions by objections such as critics raised to the inaccuracies of *Provence* is not quite the same thing as an interruption of the Sermon on the Mount by a grammatical complaint. A minute concern for facts may become pedantic, but that hardly proves that facts are contemptible. To Ford, however, they were; he was interested in his own thoughts and feelings about the world and it seemed to him perfectly reasonable to change the facts to suit the needs of his impressions. No matter what kind of book he was writing, it was always, as he said of his book on Conrad, "a novel, not a monograph; a portrait, not a narration; for what it shall be worth, a work of art, not a compilation."*[29]

---

*Throughout his life Ford attacked scholarship in this way, often without the slightest concern for the facts. In *The March of Literature* he condemns Sainte-Beuve who, he says, "sanctified and perpetuated that process" of "disinterring . . . *ana* about littérateurs which has been the secular preoccupation of all the universities of the world . . . " (p. 685), and remarks that "the academic critic despises Jane Austen because her subjects are merely domestic." Nothing could be further from the truth than this, but Ford chooses to take it for fact because he wants to believe that the academic critic "despises the novel as he dislikes most forms of art" (p. 717).

Thus Ford sought to make a virtue out of his habit of representing his memories and impressions of an experience rather than the experience itself.

My brain, I think, is a sort of dove-cote [he said]. The thoughts from it fly round and round, seem about to settle and circle even further than before and more and more swiftly. I try in the end to let them come home with the velocity and precision of swifts that fly at sixty miles an hour into their apertures that you would say could not let them through. I hope thus to attain a precision of effect as startling as any Frenchman.... [30]

This inclination grew on Ford with the passage of time. His fiction became more and more concerned with "the mind wrestling to comprehend the object" rather than with the object itself; "What the individual sees or comprehends [in Ford's novels] depends always upon the kind or number of tribulations besetting him, and he is only rarely in a condition sufficiently detached to see things as they are or for themselves." In Ford's novels, the individual who sees or comprehends, moreover, is always Ford, never an objective, impersonal consciousness. Ford's novels are never reliable representations of reality. Their value depends on the amount of authenticity he can give the imaginary life he creates in them. What Ford did in his novels was to make myths out of his personal experience; that was, Pound believed, his special gift. Looking back over his own career in Canto LXXIV, Pound remarked that

Lordly men are to earth o'ergiven
these the companions: . . .

and the first companion he lists for his own odyssey is "Fordie who wrote of giants." The risk for Ford was always that he would indulge his fancy too far and turn his imagined giants into evidently imaginary ones or that his vanity would lead him to spoil his story with self-pity and self-congratulation.[31]

In Ford's reminiscences, written or spoken, the risks of his impressionism were even greater. He regularly defended himself against what appeared to him an obvious, even malicious misunderstanding by pointing out that he was not trying to collect facts and then establish a just generalization of them; he was trying to represent his personal impression. Objections to his inaccuracies were beside the point. He became particularly aggrieved when, as often happened, he had persuaded himself that his improved version of an occasion was what had literally happened so that it seemed to him his critics were inaccurate, and not he.

But this was the extreme case, and the extent to which Ford recognized the differences between what had actually happened and his version of an affair varied—depending on the extent to which his version was necessary to his emotional well-being—all the way from a failure to recognize any difference to a perfect understanding and controlled exploitation of the difference. One of the subtlest examples of such exploitation has been inadvertently provided by Hemingway, who has described how Ford pointed out to Hemingway that he had just cut Hilaire Belloc, who then turned out to be Alistair Crowley. Ford had known Belloc since his teens, and there is not the remotest possibility that he actually mistook Crowley for Belloc. This little display of British snobbery with its characteristic carelessness about the literal fact was surely intended as a parody of what Ford knew to be Hemingway's idea of him. It is unlikely Ford was unaware of Hemingway's need to think badly of anyone to whom he was indebted, as he was indebted to Ford for his kindness during the *Transatlantic Review* days, and Ford may well have wanted to see if that need would blind Hemingway to what he otherwise could hardly have missed.[32]

Chapter 17

A s soon as Violet recovered from her operation, she went to Spa to recuperate. There Ford, pretending to everyone that he was still in Giessen, joined her. He found Spa "the quietest place . . . that God ever forgot to finish." On New Year's Eve, with the snow "on the trees in a solid wall of white over the red roofs of Spa," they went to Alighans's for supper, where Ford made a punch for which he was famous. "And when day dawned on what was to prove a year of bitter, continuous litigation," they took the train to Aix-la-Chapelle and, "kneeling painfully on the stones of the Cathedral . . . over the tomb of Charlemagne, in the company of other godly Germans, in the coloured darkness of the great rose window, smelling the bitter-sweet of the incense, heard Mass." Violet felt herself rapt. But she thought that Ford, "kneeling at my side —misliking his attitude, the cold stones, or suddenly appalled perhaps, by all this ceremonial [that so solemnly committed him to Violet]: envisaging the enormity of the task he had set himself—was in a sense unsympathetic to me. A cold, patient man, without fire, lazy of habit [about practical affairs]: his heart, dull-beating, was perhaps more faint about it all than he was willing to let appear."[1]

Her conviction that Ford was not being as energetic as he should be about putting their marriage on a solid footing only roused Violet to greater efforts of her own. She "made up my mind to go and beat up the Paris relations for myself," perhaps not realizing how much committed to Elsie's cause Cousin Hermann already was. She got Ford to write Hermann; his answer was not encouraging ("Be more correct in your expressions," he told Ford). But Violet would not give up without a fight; she and Ford went to Paris for a weekend with the Farleys and Violet went to call on Cousin Hermann. "He approved of *me*," she reported; she clearly had not succeeded in getting him to approve of Ford. They retreated to Spa and there parted, Ford to return to Giessen and Violet to England.[2]

In Giessen there were endless delays and Ford grew more and more bored. He did not like the figure he was cutting in his two cheap rooms, and he persuaded himself that if he was to impress the Giessen authorities he must live more grandly, on the hill near the university. Violet, who was financing all this, grew frightened and they had one of the arguments over money that were to become more and more frequent in their lives. Belatedly, she tried to give in, but by this time Ford was on his high horse and refused to take anything but furnished rooms. He compromised, however, by making it a quite impressive flat in a new and imposing building; he hired a man and his wife to care for him. He moved into his new quarters at 15 Friederichstrasse in March. But, bored or not, he was getting his usual amazing amount of work done. *Ladies Whose Bright Eyes* and *Memories and Impressions* had been finished in the fall; a large part of *The New Humpty-Dumpty* was written by February, 1911, and in March he sent Pinker "the first two chapters" of a projected book to be called *Women & Men*; Pinker succeeded in interesting Constable in this book, of which Ford said that "whilst it is deeply serious it is also wildly amusing and it will be bought in large quantities by my large following of suffragettes." But for some reason no more of *Women & Men* was ever written.[3]

He was also involved in his usual complicated quarrels with publishers. Constable claimed that part of the manuscript of *Ladies Whose Bright Eyes* was missing; Ford indignantly asserted that this was impossible unless they had lost it—until Violet turned it up among the things that had been moved from 84 Holland Park Avenue to South Lodge while Ford was in prison. In December, he asked his old friend, Thomas Seccombe, to read *Ladies Whose Bright Eyes* and suggest changes. Seccombe was Constable's regular reader, and when Constable heard what Seccombe wanted the manuscript for, they told Pinker that they would wait to print the book until Ford had made the revisions. Ford then accused Seccombe of having betrayed him: whether he thought Seccombe could get the manuscript without Constable's knowing it or wanted to make his revisions in proof, at Constable's expense, is not clear. Harper, he thought, was illegally withholding the advance they owed on the American edition of *Memories and Impressions*—"if I don't receive your cheque for the amount [50 guineas] less commission by return of post," he wrote Pinker, "I shall tell my solicitors to take proceedings against Harpers, since, apparently, you will not put pressure upon them." Pinker then sent the money—in pounds instead of guineas.[4]

His boredom made another holiday necessary and he slipped back to England again; Violet took him for a visit in the country with Lady De La Warr. There he played endless bridge with his hostess, her daughter, and a Catholic priest, whom Violet calls "Father Consett" to suggest that Ford used this experience in describing Father Consett at Lobscheid in *Some Do Not....* When Ford went back to Giessen, Mrs. Hueffer went with him. Violet joined them for Easter, very pleased with herself because she was able to dazzle the provincial German ladies with the new "harem skirt, that Joseph Leopold had begged me to buy and bring." But Mrs. Hueffer took her duties as chaperone so seriously that "I don't think," Violet said irritably, "that ... I was alone with Joseph Leopold for more than ten minutes" all the time she was in Giessen. When she returned to England, Ford came with her, as did Leun and another friend; they wanted to see the coronation of George V and Violet was happy to have them see her chatting amiably with Lloyd George, who did not, however, really know who she was.[5]

Violet could not have these German visitors at South Lodge; her sisters came regularly to see her mother and it was as much as she could do to keep them from running into Ford and rowing with her about him. When Ford returned to Germany he reported to Violet that Leun "seems to think it is all right now about the naturalisation.... Isn't it jolly?" Violet asked him for "a quite formal statement" and he made one. But when she asked to see the naturalization papers, Ford told her Leun had them; when she pressed him to get them, he said he did not want to call on Leun until he had got his new set of false teeth; when that reason no longer existed, he told her Leun could not lay his hands on the papers. In 1927 Ford wrote the *Herald Tribune,* with injured dignity, that "I never became a German for legal or illegal reasons or for any reason.... I always was and shall always be a British subject."[6]

Ford's naturalization was purely imaginary. He had become intolerably bored with Giessen, but he could not get away from there unless Violet would pay for it; and she had invested too much in this project to let him leave until she could represent herself as his wife. She must have known that Ford's "formal statement" was not worth much, but she could not resist the temptation to deceive herself; "it was," she said, "like the coming out of chloroform to find the tooth out and in the waste-paper basket"—not a very flattering description of Elsie, but one suggested by the fact that Ford was about to have Agnes Farley's dentist husband in Paris pull his teeth and give him a set of false ones. She was appalled when she discovered that the job was costing her eight pounds a tooth; "it seemed to me," she said, "that he could have inserted diamonds at that rate." In spite of a railway strike, Violet reached Paris April 20; Ford met her, "toothless and feckless," and "attempted," as she put it, to see her through customs. She had even less patience than most women with masculine inefficiency, of which Ford had his fair share, and never seemed to suspect that Ford's masculine vanity was even more sensitive than most men's. This was in any event a difficult time for Ford; he was embarrassed by his toothlessness and tried to hide from everyone. On April 29 they left Paris, with Ford still toothless, for "what was now—so [Violet] believed—his country," and Violet, feeling for the first time that she was really Ford's wife, busied herself with the management of his affairs, writing Mrs. Hueffer long daughterly letters about family matters and even dedicating to her her current novel, *The Doll*.[7]

Ford had now persuaded himself as well as Violet that he was a German citizen. They were convinced they no longer needed to fear scandal, and they went off together to Hildesheim for a week of sightseeing and on to Münster to visit the Hüffer relatives. Then Violet returned to London so that Ford could go back to Giessen and complete what they now treated as the mere formality of getting his divorce. So confident was he that he wrote Conrad to announce he was "at peace at last," as if he were already divorced and married to Violet. He also wrote Elsie to arrange the terms of his support for her and the children. But Elsie somehow failed to grasp the idea that Ford's divorce was assured and instead proposed that Ford support her separately, beginning with an immediate down payment of £250.[8]

With his newfound confidence, Ford had no intention of continuing to suffer the boredom of Giessen. "I shall," he wrote Scott-James, "be returning to town for the season on the 27th or 28th [of June]." There was a large party for him at South Lodge on the 29th, both to welcome him home and to celebrate the publication of *Ladies Whose Bright Eyes*, the first book he had published under his own name since *The Portrait* over a year before, though *The Simple Life Limited* had appeared under the pseudonym of Daniel Chaucer in February, 1911. The pseudonym was not pointless—though it was all too quickly penetrated—because *The Simple Life Limited* is a satire on Edward Garnett's circle and the Limpsfield Fabians.[9]

The Simple Life Limited is a group of silly fanatics filled with ideas borrowed from Tolstoy, Edward Carpenter, William Morris, and H. G. Wells, who have chosen to live the life of vegetarianism, handicrafts, and dancing on the green at a place called Frog's Hole. These people have been organized into a corporation (hence the "Limited"); the corporation pays a dividend of 10 percent, and it turns out that the secretary owns 3,494 of the

3,500 outstanding shares: the other six are held by dummies. They have a guru named Simon Bransdon (an anglicization of Simeon Brandetski) who had begun life as a tough colonial administrator, discovered he could write, and made a hit with something called *Clotted Vapours*, and then had an accident that affected his mind, so that he now can be persuaded to sit at a hand loom and recite illiterate 1890's poetic prose: "Nevermore, oh girl of the snowy forehead and shell-like breasts, nevermore shall thy grey gown rival the tender mists of Oysium—Lo, I have begotten me to the waste places of the sea. Black and bitter is my bed. Black and bitter is my companionless bed. . . . "[10]

These people are contrasted with people who live, directly and without theorizing, exactly the way their natures require and thus truly lead the simple life. There is Hamnet Gubb, the son of the Simple Life's secretary, who turns out to be happy living, like Thoreau, in a hut in the woods. There is George Everard, the shrewd cockney who has worked himself up to being a leading producer of musical comedies and remembers the wife who had helped him do it as perfect: "She died with her hand in mine, and her last words were, 'George, I've had a happy life. See that the headbills at Manchester have Harry Peto's name starred.' " There is Simon Bransdon, when he regains his sanity, who goes about dressed too loudly because he likes it and makes a fortune writing bad plays. There is Mr. Luscombe, the Tory radical landlord, a further development of the Marwood-Ford hero, who says of the peasants who complain with comic eloquence about the model cottages he has built for them, "It's one form of the Simple Life. It depends on how it takes you, you know."[11]

The plot of *The Simple Life Limited* is designed to maximize the occasions when the plain good sense of these characters exposes the foolishness and self-deception of the doctrinaire simple-lifers. This plot is merely a convenience, but like the plots of Shaw's intellectual farces, it provides some wonderful satiric moments, such as the one when Ophelia Bransdon, who has been stuffed with the theories of the simple life, arrives in her handwoven, misshapen garments at the Luscombes in the pouring rain. Mr. Luscombe's aged mother, who had sacrificed her respectable life for an heroic love affair and now, an old lady, has married her lover and is living in quiet happiness with him at Coombe Luscombe, provides Ophelia with dry clothes from the wardrobe of her very smart daughter-in-law. She stands watching with delight as Ophelia dresses herself, "in that position that one woman always adopts when she has just 'turned out' another woman—mute, contemplative, attentive, but at the same time very much as if she expected her hairpins to fall out." With innocent arrogance Ophelia assures Mrs. Melville that she defies convention and is free, whereas Mrs. Melville is one of those "people who have never done anything and have led sheltered lives all your days. . . . " "My dear,' Mrs. Melville [says] admiringly, 'you do speak like a book. I wish I could.' " Ophelia ends by falling in love with the contentedly vulgar George Everard and throwing herself dramatically before him, like some heroine of one of George's musical comedies, when a mad Russian tries to shoot George. *The Simple Life Limited* is a witty farce, and it is a pity that the specific conditions Ford is satirizing have so completely passed from men's memories that much of the novel's satiric fun is lost today.[12]

Ladies Whose Bright Eyes was no doubt inspired by the visit Violet and Ford paid to Fordingbridge (and Ford's feelings about her then) after Ford got out of Brixton Gaol. Ford's hero, Mr. Sorrell, is an innocently enthusiastic businessman, a publisher of cheap encyclopedias and sensational biographies of people like Ninon de Lenclos. He is without historical sense; seeing a nun, he thinks that modern countries like the United States "with its salutary laws against undesirable emigrants" surely exclude such creatures. The fast train that is taking him from Southampton, where he has just landed from that admirably modern country, is a great pleasure to him; he is proud to remember that he knows Mr. Makover of Pittsburgh, who made it. It crashes at Salisbury and knocks Mr. Sorrell back into the year 1327, in the valley of the Wiley near Tamworth and Stapleford castles; he is carrying the Tamworth-Egerton crucifix, an object he characteristically thinks of as "about the size of a dog biscuit . . . " and the fourteenth-century people of the novel, quite as characteristically, think of as "fashioned by Joseph of Arimathea, who picked up secretly the gold that had fallen from the tables of the money-changers that our Lord upset."[13]

The general idea for this story was certainly suggested to Ford by Mark Twain, but his purpose was the opposite of Twain's, whose *Connecticut Yankee* he thought "a wilful anachronism . . . where dummy knights in armour are discomfited by electrified barbed-wire fencing, and a modern American perturbs King Arthur by preaching down chivalric ideals to the tune of nineteenth century morality." Ford wanted to show Mr. Sorrell slowly discovering that the fourteenth century was better than the twentieth. That was not so because people were intrinsically superior then, or because they lived in some kind of Utopia. Ford's considerable knowledge of the times would have prevented him from imagining a prettified Middle Ages; he knew too well that "more than half of the northern year was given over to an intensity of boredom such as can have distinguished no other times or places.... The northern knight... could not adventure himself on horseback on his winter roads or pastures simply because his charger would sink in to its belly in deep mud. So he used to find intensive fun when the roads opened themselves in the late spring and early summer and he could ride a-murdering." Mr. Sorrell's introduction to the medieval world is the sight of three corpses hanging from an oak, "Trèsmeschiants gents, voleurs," the nun he is with cheerfully observes. The book's title ironically echoes Milton's vision of "towered cities"

> Where throngs of knights and barons bold
> In weeds of peace high triumphs hold,
> With store of ladies whose bright eyes
> Rain influence and judge the prize. . . .

The Lady Blanche de Coucy D'Enguerrand is a stupid, egotistical, sexually predatory female; the young Knight of Egerton is, like Mr. Sorrell, an innocently illiberal provincial of his time. (" 'Miracles!' the young knight wondered. 'Shall one write letters about miracles! Miracles will keep, and letters are nasty things to have to do with.' ")[14]

These people are ordinary enough, and their life has plenty of drawbacks. Its superiority consists in the values by which even the worst of its people are conditioned. The best of them such as the Knight of Coucy (Ford's vision of himself as a medieval knight) and the old knight, Sir Ygorac de Fordingbridge, with his delight in the art of knightly conduct, show us how much better life can be when people have the benefit of a fine culture.

> Is it [says Dionissia] that we are merchants who must have goods stored up in our houses where we shall live for the rest of our lives? ... Gentle friend, is it a new thing that a great knight, putting upon himself the garb of a minstrel, and accompanied by a page or two and a few men of arms to give him sufficient state and respect, should journey through the world and sing of the high things of love, or of great adventures in arms? ... And so we should travel. ... And our lives shall be very pleasant and restful, and you shall not ever be sad.

Here is Ford's ideal existence which he imagined for a moment he was going to live with Violet Hunt.*[15]

At the end of July Ford and Violet went back to Germany, where they were almost immediately joined by Ezra Pound. They took Pound up to the high, terraced convent of Schiffenberg, where he climbed the ancient

*For a discussion of *Ladies Whose Bright Eyes,* see pp. 482–84.

wooden stage and declaimed his own verses from the "heaven"—which presently gave way and dropped him into "hell." Pound stayed several days; he had apparently come to read his poems to Ford, probably those in *Canzoni*, which had just appeared. According to Pound, Ford rolled on the floor in agony at the academic artificiality of his style, and Pound was forever grateful to him for the lesson. "I would rather," he said shortly after, "talk about poetry with Ford Madox Hueffer than with any man in London." Ford insisted on the living language. "What we want," as he said to Wells very early in his career, "is to use our vernacular so skillfully that words, precious or obsolete, will not stick out & impede a reader." Back of this theory of the effect to be sought there lay, Pound saw, Ford's concern for the thing itself—the object, the experience, the atmosphere—as distinguished from the words.

> and for all that old Ford's conversation was
> better [than Yeats's] consisting of *res* not *verba*,
> despite William's anecdotes, in that Fordie
> never dented an idea for a phrase's sake
> and had more humanity.

As late as *The March of Literature*, Ford compares Vergil's "grandiloquent facility" with the exquisite plainness of Homer's style, taking the trouble to translate his illustration from Homer himself in order to show just how "down to the ground" it is, despite "Homer's breath-taking verse." It was, he thought, typical of the Renaissance and its heirs in the modern world to "applaud the [bourgeois] gentlemanly adiposities of the pious Aeneas as against the hardbitten feverish-eyed spectre of the cunning Odysseus."[16]

Years later, when Pound undertook to criticize Ford for overloading his work with "torabiscotage, Sancte Foi Catholique, Tory party . . . suppressed forsooths and gadzooks of ideation . . . " he began by saying, "In return for the blessings conferred upon me in 1911 by your lecture of, let us say, Aout 7th of that year, these presents."[17]

Ford showed Pound both the theory of diction and the way of thinking about experience that Pound needed. Ford once described himself as "an ascetic *prosateur* of empirico-mediaeval leanings and one inclined in any case to be impatient of the tricks of verse writers." That is to say that, in rejecting the Victorian Great (including the Pre-Raphaelites) who had made a nightmare of his childhood, what he was rejecting was their *kind* of medievalizing and their taste in diction. He and Pound were as romantic as the Victorians in their belief that it is possible to realize the ideal and in their inclination to find that ideal in a heightened vision of the past. But they disliked, as only cultural cousins can, the Victorian version of this attitude, entangled as it was in the subtle web of feelings peculiar to Victorian times and offensive to theirs.[18]

No one could have formulated their attitude more precisely than Ford did when he had Christopher Tietjens scornfully reject Rossetti.

> Leave the furniture out! Or leave me out at least. I tell you it revolts me to think of that obese, oily man who never took a bath, in a grease-spotted dressing-gown and the underclothes he's slept in, standing beside a five-shilling model with crimped hair, or some Mrs. W. Three Stars, gazing into a mirror that reflects their fetid selves and gilt sunfish and drop chandeliers and plates sickening with bacon fat and gurgling about passion.

Here is the idealizer of the advanced Edwardian's "realistic," unadorned sensuality scornfully condemning the idealizer of the advanced Victorian's richly adorned sensuality. Ford hates the excessive decorative detail and the lush verbal effects that dominated poetic visions of passion and of the past from Tennyson's "Lady of Shalott" and "Mariana"—perhaps even Coleridge's "Christabel" and Keats's "Eve of St. Agnes"—to Swinburne and Rossetti. He rejected them most violently when they achieve the superiority of Morris' medievalism or Swinburne's classical learning, kinds of superiority that Ford and Pound also laid claim to. Ford hates the décor and the poetic style of these poets because they so successfully express a life-style he hates. But it was the style that he and Pound rejected, not the romantic idealization of sensuality and the past.[19]

By an accident of timing Ford had early worked out the style Pound was looking for, one that rejected all he thought false in the late Victorians without rejecting either Aphrodite ("Venerandam, in the Cretan phrase") or an idealized (but not prettified) past. Ford began experimenting with this style in "On Heaven," developed it in his war poems, and brought it to his own kind of perfection in the *Buckshee* poems. Pound gave it his kind of perfection in the *Cantos.*

By the beginning of September Ford and Violet were back in Paris for Ford to have Dr. Farley do the final work on his new teeth. "He has his new front row (4 false porcelain ones)," Violet wrote Mrs. Hueffer,

> and they work so nice. I believe the German business is all right but the naturalization did not come in time for the divorce to be pronounced before the courts rose for six weeks holiday. So that would make it deferred till they "set" again in October. Anyhow, no one will see me or Ford again till we are married.

After their separation, Violet wrote Ford that "I have lived with you as your supposed wife for eight years, counting from the fifth of November 1911," and sometime shortly after that date, according to her, they were "married" by a priest.[20]

After a quick trip home, Violet rejoined Ford and they went on to Trier for a rest; there Violet became ill ("Three years of constant agitation had done their work") and they went back to Spa, where she had another operation. As they were starting out one day for a drive to Montjoie, a reporter from the *Daily Mirror* turned up. Violet was all for discretion; though "we both of us had new books out," she thought advertising interviews "an odious literary 'wheeze' unworthy of either of us." But the reporter hung around, and that night he caught Ford at Houtermans, "where Joseph Leopold went most nights to play billiards." The *Daily Mirror* had been on the scent of scandal for some time; a reporter had already questioned Robert Garnett about Ford and Violet. Ford played straight into their hands.

AUTHOR WEDS
Mr. Ford Madox Hueffer married aboard
to Well-Known Lady Novelist

The Daily Mirror is able to announce that Mr. Ford Madox Hueffer, the famous novelist, has been married on the Continent to Miss Violet Hunt, the well-known authoress. . . .

Mr. Hueffer was seen at the Red House, Spa, Belgium, yesterday, before starting for his daily motor-car ride with the second Mrs. Hueffer.

"I don't want to advertise myself," he told The Daily Mirror, "but it happens that both my wife and myself have books appearing today. . . . I married her in Germany after divorcing my former wife on a technical ground, desertion, as I had a perfect right to do, being domiciled in Germany.

"I am heir to large entailed estates in Prussia, and have therefore retained my German nationality. . . . I offered myself for service with the German army, but was not required to serve, and I attended Bonn University.

"My former wife brought an action against me for restitution of conjugal rights. Then we agreed upon a separation order, she having the custody of our two daughters. . . . "

Mr. Hueffer further said that he was now lecturing in German universities upon history. . . . [21]

They returned to England early in December. Violet's friend, Lady Byron, lent them her house, Sunnyside, at Littleston-on-Sea, and they settled in, eager to renew relations with the world. Ford attended a *Bystander* dinner at the Trocadero and Violet got into a fight with Chatto & Windus over whether she might not be called "Violet Hueffer" on the title page of *The Governess.* "Of course it is very important," Chatto told Pinker, "that her maiden name shall appear"—thus sparing themselves a lawsuit. Ford and Violet sought out the Conrads and the Marwoods. Things were, as usual, in a mess at the Conrads. "I don't know if I ought to encourage you to come into a house full of 'flu,' " Conrad wrote Ford. "I too may be down by to-morrow. . . . Jessie's throat is awful. . . . I know you like what I write, but you have an ever-fresh and encouraging way of saying it to me—Thanks."²²

Then Violet's maid, Annie Child, returned from an errand in London with the news that she had seen what Violet calls "an Implacable Face." They knew Ford had put his foot in it with his interview for the *Daily Mirror* because in January Elsie had threatened to sue the *Daily Mirror* and it had run a "Withdrawal and Apology" to placate her. But they had committed themselves to carrying through the bluff that Violet was Mrs. Hueffer and could hardly start now avoiding the use of the name; Violet, with her passion for the respectable position of the married woman, was inclined in impulsive moments to insist on its use. They had thus put themselves in a trap that Elsie could spring at any moment; no wonder that Implacable Face made them nervous.

Annie enlarged on her experience while she was serving dinner that night, with the result that later in the evening Ford, imagining he had heard the front doorbell pealing violently, tied up all the doors with odd straps, strings, and dog leads, and blocked the front door with a bicycle; he came to bed with a white, scared face. "It was the beginning of a fresh attack of neurasthenia that lasted three whole years, and was responsible for many things, and much private and particular misery," Violet said.²³

A few days later Lawrence saw them together in London and wrote Edward Garnett one of his brilliant descriptions.

> I found Hueffer getting very fat. . . . But he's rather nicer than he was. He seems to have had a crisis, when, dear Lord, he fizzed and bubbled all over the place. Now, don't you know, he seems quite considerate, even thoughtful for other folk. But he *is* fat.
>   . . . Do you know, I rather like her—she's such a real assassin. . . .
>   She looked old, yet she was gay—she was gay, she laughed, she bent and fluttered in the wind of joy. She coquetted and played beautifully with Hueffer: she loves him distractedly—she was charming, and I loved her. But my God, she looked old.

Perhaps because she wore—she was going to some afternoon affair of swell suffragettes—a gaudy witch-cap stitched with beads of scarlet and a delicate ravel of green and blue . . . and she peeped coquettishly under the brim—but she looked damned old. . . .
I think Fordy liked it—but was rather scared. He feels, poor fish, the hooks are through his gills this time—and they *are*. . . .
They sport a carriage now—have one on contract, I believe.

Violet's cure for Ford's "subdued state," his neurasthenia, was perhaps as good as any; she provided company. René Byles was had down to Selsey; the Conrads, now recovered from their flu, were invited in as frequently as possible; Marwood was called on. Marwood offered the most practical sympathy; perhaps he now blamed Elsie rather than Ford for the famous quarrel at Aldington. In any event, he advised Violet to get Ford away, perhaps to Paris, at least to some place where writs did not run. Even Jessie Conrad tried to warn Violet that catastrophe was impending. Violet thought this fanciful, but clearly the Conrads and the Marwoods knew something of Elsie's plans.[24]

Whatever those plans were, they were certainly changed by the publication on April 18, 1912, of *The Governess*, Mrs. Hunt's unfinished novel that Ford and Violet together had completed. It had caused Violet trouble from the start. Her sisters, who had already been suing her for mismanagement of their mother's affairs, had attempted to get an injunction preventing the book's publication, on the grounds that Mrs. Hunt had not been in her right mind when she authorized Violet and Ford to complete it. Ford ostentatiously referred to Violet—certainly with Violet's approval, perhaps at her insistence—as "Mrs. Hueffer" in the introduction he wrote for the book. René Byles, at the moment the business manager of a somewhat shaky magazine called *The Throne*, had *The Throne* run a little publicity piece about it in the April 3 issue of the magazine. It carried photographs of both Mrs. Hunt and Violet, which Byles obtained from Violet herself, and borrowing from Ford's introduction, it said, "The forthcoming book is a romance . . . by Mrs. Alfred Hunt, one of the popular novelists of the old days and her daughter, Miss Violet Hunt (now Mrs. Ford Madox Hueffer) one of the successful of the modern school."[25]

"Sulky, top-hatted, loathing it," Ford had been accompanying Violet to the hearing about her mother's estate. Now he was confronted by a suit at which he would be no mere spectator. Elsie sued *The Throne*; the threat which had, when it was only a possibility, driven him to imagine pealing doorbells had become a reality. The strain was not eased by the knowledge that he would have to wait six months for the case to come to trial, and he had a serious breakdown. Violet wrote Lawrence that he was not allowed even to dictate a letter unless it was absolutely unavoidable; he did in fact write a few, mostly letters of complaint to Pinker about the way Constable was handling *The Panel,* the novel he had written hastily the previous winter. "You worried me in their interests until I wrote the novel in about a month," he said in June, "and induced a very severe nervous breakdown from which I am still suffering."[26]

Ford dedicated *The Panel* to Ada Potter, who had produced the dramatic version of *The Fifth Queen* in 1909. He began by reminding her of that occasion ("Since it was historic tragedy which, as you might say, brought us together ... ") and went on to say that she was responsible for "inspir[ing] me to a task so obviously frivolous" as this novel. Frivolous it is, a frothy Edwardian drawing-room comedy with all the usual ingredients—a dashing Lady Mary disguised as a maid in order to rescue a lover caught in an unhappy engagement; a string of silly reformers, including a farcically bad-tempered old gentleman who is president of the First Church of Christ Quietist; the pretty, tough-minded authoress of *Pink Passions,* or *Crime in a Nightgown,* and the good-natured star of a musical comedy called *Pigs Is Pigs* that might easily have been written by P. G. Wodehouse. These people are all gathered in an old country house, where they rush in and out of one another's rooms through sliding panels and secret doors like characters in a French farce. Only a brief courtroom scene, where rural justice is satirized, and an almost wholly irrelevant one in which booksellers, publishers, and intellectuals who buy secondhand books ("It's ... only *quite* intellectual people who know how to be really mean") take us away from Basildon Manor. The action is carefully divided into three "acts."[27]

Ford obviously wrote *The Panel* with dramatization in mind and deliberately kept it what he called "confoundedly bad silly stuff," though it is often quite amusingly silly stuff, as when the hero closes scenes by remarking, "So that there, in a manner of speaking, we all are." This hero, a simple, honorable soldier has, he feels, become the youngest major in the British army by reading the novels of Henry James, in which one has to work very hard to find out where the characters who are always saying, "there we all are," in fact are. Behind an impenetrable surface cheerfulness, he is subject to extreme shifts of feeling from optimism to despair; he is innocently given to elaborate fabrications—he calls it tact—that make a good deal of trouble for him. He is Ford's image of himself, a little younger than usual and reduced to the conventional circumstances of drawing-room comedy.[28]

The Panel was an attempt to profit from the literary situation Ford had analyzed shortly before in *The Critical Attitude*. He satirized the publishing trade and the public that was responsible for "The Two Shilling Novel" and the general state of "English Literature Today," the ignorant materialism that made cheap salacious fiction like the novels of Marie Corelli or Juliana Kerr Howe of *The Panel* sell 40,000 copies while Henry James's work languished. But this pill was, he hoped, concealed in a popular novel designed to sell almost as well as the work of these ladies. Having tried and failed to live by "the critical attitude" with *The English Review*, where six chapters of *The Critical Attitude* originally appeared, he tried in *The Panel* to write, with tongue in cheek, a successful popular novel. This alternation was characteristic of Ford. He saw that the heroic conception of culture to which he was dedicated did not arouse wide interest; he saw the forces that were inimical to it; and—at least since he had written *The Inheritors*—he had been trapped between a romantic commitment to the ideal and a desire for success. He wanted to be both a great writer and a famous man, but he was so outraged by the world's indifference to what he thought it ought to be that he could not—though he tried—effectively accept what it was. It is sad that a man who so longed to have it both ways at once was temperamentally incapable of having it either.

Chapter 18

A t almost exactly the time Elsie sued *The Throne* for calling Violet Hunt Mrs. Hueffer, Ford published, under the pseudonym of Daniel Chaucer, a novel called *The New Humpty-Dumpty*. It contains devastating portraits of Elsie, H. G. Wells, and David Soskice, and heroic ones of Ford and Violet. It is one of those romances in which an insouciant, aristocratic hero undertakes to restore the deposed king of an imaginary country; it is often entertaining in its *Prisoner of Zenda* way. But *The New Humpty-Dumpty* only sporadically exploits the adventure-story element. It is mostly taken up with its hero's character and his personal difficulties.

The cause for this displacement of the novel's attention is Ford's concern to make his story a disguised account of the cultural counterrevolution he had attempted as editor of *The English Review* and of his personal experience as the lover of Violet Hunt. The story's hero, Count Sergius Mihailovitch Macdonald, the spoiled child of the Russian court (as Ford thought himself the spoiled child of the baronial Hüffers), is a large, blond, blue-eyed man with an easy, charming way that allows him to rule men effortlessly, and a high-minded generosity that makes him forgive them all for their mean-minded betrayals of him. He is both a brilliant manager of affairs and "an idealist with fifty [ideas]" who puzzles ordinary humanity by refusing to take any reward for what he does. "He was forced to regard himself—if he was to regard himself as anything at all—as something of a crusader in life. After all, he was trying to key things up—to key up the whole world."[1]

All this, the cockney Herbert Pett explains, is no particular credit to Macdonald; it is as natural to him, the aristocratic gentleman, as it is "for the sun to shine or for vines to grow grapes." To illustrate this point, Pett tells a story of how Macdonald once stepped from a London bus to awe a set of vicious policemen into treating a poor girl kindly, while Pett, with his lower-class fear of the police, watched in wonder. The original of this episode is in *Return to Yesterday*, where Ford describes how he did exactly the same thing, and "When I got back to the bus there was Arnold Bennett. He was standing on the top of it with his jaw hanging down. He said: 'You dare to talk to the police like that?' I said: 'Why not? Aren't the police there to do what you tell them to do?' " This episode reminds Ford of another occasion, when he had been startled by a policeman and said, " 'God damn and blast your something eyes what do you mean by startling me?' He said: 'Beg pardon, sir, I did not know that you were a gentleman.' "[2]

Early in his life Macdonald had come to London, where he first joined up with the anarchists, to whom he gave his entire fortune; then he became a socialist under the influence of Herbert Pett, to whom he gave a second fortune, just then inherited from his mother; Pett used it to get himself started on a career as an economic journalist. During these early years Macdonald married the socialist daughter of a London tailor. She turns out to be hopelessly limited; "whereas his own views had completely altered, his wife's had remained exactly the same. She still dressed [as did Elsie Hueffer] in clothes of sage green, her sleeves still swept the floor; round her neck was a rope of amber beads, each one as large as a duck's egg. Her dark hair was elaborately waved with curling irons, and because she passed the greater part of her life in the open air, she had a startlingly high colour." She is bitterly determined either to dominate or to destroy Macdonald—a "fierce and arrogant spirit," bent on making Macdonald desire her and then live in misery. She finds it easy to torture him for, despite his gracefully casual manner, he is intensely sensitive to vulgarity and cannot bear scenes. He finds unendurable the "intolerably vulgar" imagination that leads her to think of him as "liv[ing] with the smart set [and] plung[ing] into a whirl of dissipation."[3]

As the novel opens, Macdonald has decided that the right kind of society is a truly Tory one, and he undertakes to use his great personal powers to restore the King of Galizia to his throne. At the same time he meets Lady Aldington, an enormously rich beauty who is unhappily married to a brutal husband and has devoted herself to the dull life of a political hostess and never known what happiness is until she meets Macdonald; both of them are so instinctively honorable that they hardly admit to themselves that they love each other until the Countess Macdonald's jealousy forces the knowledge on them. This is Ford's improved version of Violet Hunt and her suffragette activities and his affair with her; Count Macdonald woos Lady Aldington in almost exactly the same words Ford has used with Violet: " ... there's the blessed warmth, and there's you!" As Violet did Ford, Lady Aldington provides Count Macdonald with large sums of money. Macdonald believes this money has been supplied by the Duke of Kintyre, who is so in awe of Macdonald's high sense of honor that he does not dare tell Macdonald the truth. This sense of honor has also made Macdonald turn over his whole personal income to the Countess Macdonald; nonetheless he will not use for himself a penny of the money he thinks Kintyre has provided; it must all go to the support of the counterrevolution. He survives by living in a cellar and pawning his personal possessions. This reflects Ford's belief that he had impoverished himself in order to be generous to Elsie at the time of their separation, only to be accused by her of leaving her and the girls to starve.[4]

The Duke of Kintyre is the Arthur Marwood of the story. He is very much attracted by the extraordinary vitality of the Countess Macdonald. "He imagined her pacing up and down like one of the great caged cats waiting for [Macdonald] whose presence she passionately desired, and whom she would overwhelm with outrages the moment he appeared." He persuades himself that it will take the Countess Macdonald off Macdonald's hands if he flirts with her, but Macdonald, understanding the whole situation perfectly, persuades Kintyre that "He can't have me philandering with his wife. I did it in order to help him. But I see that it was a sort of suspect— an unpleasant position." He therefore offers the Countess a choice: she can divorce Macdonald and marry him or he will withdraw entirely. The Countess is attracted by a ducal coronet, but in the end she cannot give up her revenge on Macdonald. Presumably this is the way Ford explained to himself Elsie's story of Marwood's attack on her and justified his renewed relations with Marwood.[5]

While Macdonald is intolerably harassed by these personal difficulties, Herbert Pett begins to make trouble for him over the counterrevolution. Pett is an egotistical little man. He is reduced to screaming hysterics when he discovers that Lady Aldington actually prefers Count Macdonald to him. "In his public utterances Mr. Pett would have declared that it was the duty of Lady Aldington to admire—even to adore him for his eminence and wisdom. . . . In private he had the feeling that his physical charm and the brilliant bitterness of his wit ought by now to have forced her to become his mistress." Then he quickly forgets her for "a very pretty, pert, and vulgar lady's maid." He alternates between immense admiration and murderous hatred of Count Macdonald. In the first flush of enthusiasm he had agreed to help run the counterrevolution and to find a large part of the money for it. He later backs out of both commitments with some embarrassment, but

Macdonald accepts the additional responsibilities thus thrown on him with generous casualness. "Oh, it's all right," he says. "I'll attend to the money. Don't bother." The extravagant malice with which Pett talks about Macdonald when he is angry is largely responsible for Macdonald's death. This is Ford's portrait of H. G. Wells, who had had a brief affair with Violet Hunt, had promised to help edit and finance *The English Review* and then backed out, and had, Ford believed, gossiped maliciously to Pinker and others about him and Violet Hunt. Wells's portrait of Ford as the Bulpington of Blup is mild by comparison with Ford's portrait of him.[6]

But the heart of *The New Humpty-Dumpty* is its representation of Elsie Martindale as the Countess Macdonald and of Ford himself as Count Macdonald, a noble, long-suffering, selfless man tormented by his wife's uncomprehending accusations. The passion of their scenes comes directly from Ford and Elsie's actual quarrels. Macdonald is, the Countess tells him, "a man who leaves his wife when she is ill to go and revel in the luxuries of the smart set," who insists on living in town near his job when she "can't and won't live in town," who values "things that I don't stand for ... things that are despicable."

> "What does it all mean?" she asked. "I don't understand it! ... Why don't you think as I think any more? ... You *ought* to think as I do. ... Why have you changed? ... "
>
> "It's impossible that we should go on living together!" she exclaimed; and from a faint smile, full of hatred, that was round the corners of her mouth, he knew that she was setting a trap for him. He did not, however, care to temporise, and he replied simply:
>
> "I think that I must agree with you at last. ... I can't stand these continual discussions. I am at this moment at the end of my tether."
>
> "You're always saying that," she retorted contemptuously. "If you were a man instead of what you are, you would show some signs of excitement. I simply don't believe that you are feeling any sort of excitement at all. You are incapable of feeling." ...
>
> And she knew him well enough to recognise that though his voice was ... low ... he was certainly labouring under intense excitement. Indeed, she knew that, with what she called his effeminately excitable nature, he was probably on the verge of being so unmanned as to risk an illness. ...
>
> ... his wife's tongue, her mannerisms, the flow of her voice, acted with an enervating physical effect. It seemed at the same time to stop his heart, to set an immense weight upon his skull as if for

many nights he had been deprived of sleep, and to render his limbs numb and heavy.[7]

When Macdonald befriends a naïve girl from Hamburg adrift in London and, secure in his own innocence, writes the Countess all about it, the Countess immediately concludes that he means to get rid of her "in order to plunge into a whirl of dissipation." This is the novel's improved version of Ford's involvement with Gertrud Schlablowsky and of the letter he and Violet concocted about her. In the novel, however, it is the Duke of Kintyre who suggests to the Countess that she use Macdonald's acquaintance with this girl to get a divorce. "I shall bring a divorce action against him," she answers, "so as to show to the whole world what an abominable, dissolute creature he is. . . . And then when I've got the decree I shall never apply to have it made absolute. He'll never be free." She applies for restitution of conjugal rights and is triumphant when the story makes headlines, but her scheme for keeping him in her power is defeated by Macdonald's getting a Russian divorce from her (Ford's German divorce from Elsie). She then follows him and Lady Aldington to Galizia, comes aboard their yacht with a gun in one hand and a bottle of vitriol in the other, and is prevented from using them on Macdonald only by his being killed before he can return to the yacht. Herbert Pett, now full of repentance, because "Macdonald's the noblest and finest soul I ever came across," sums her up for us.

The difference between you and gentlefolk like Macdonald—Good God!—the difference between both you and me and him is that we haven't got a spark of generosity in us. We've both conspired to injure that fine gentleman mortally. . . . All you've ever thought of in your life is the forty pieces of silver, of your own dirty personal vanity. We aren't either of us fit to loosen the shoe latchets of Sergius Mihailo-vitch.[8]

In his dedication Ford says he wanted to call this novel *The Dark Forest*, a title which directs the reader's attention to the crucifixion of Count Macdonald, to "the pilgrimage of our good Mac—into the Dark Forest." This title is derived from what Ford describes as a Russian proverb, "The heart of another is a dark forest." The phrase occurs frequently in the novel, and it is the last thing Count Macdonald says to Emily Aldington as he "turn[s] his head into her lap" and dies. What he means by it he has earlier made clear.

And his depressions came from that essential dark forest which is the heart of another. He had to come across so many basenesses, little and big, and so many mere selfishnesses, big or little, and whether these affected himself or merely other people, they troubled him beyond all reason. . . . That sort of thing gave him such severe shocks as to render him really ill. His mind was too sensitive to stand it, and for the time being he would be deprived almost of his senses and his power to control himself.

Such was Ford's conception of his experience in editing *The English Review* and in leaving Elsie for Violet.[9]

That summer of 1912 was not an easy one for Ford to get through, and it was made no easier by Violet's absorption in the legal battle she was fighting with her sisters. "I became," as she said herself, " . . . a woman of one idea . . . antithetic to socibility [*sic*], to the lure of sex, and to the production of good literature." She had some reason to be: she was in danger of losing a good deal. Ford nonetheless found her preoccupation with this battle absurd; how could a woman of her intellect, he complained, worry about money? He then found himself forced into bankruptcy. Marwood added to the unpleasantness of things by quarreling with Ford over what seemed to him the bad taste of the satiric portraits in *The New Humpty-Dumpty*. Then Mrs. Hunt died.[10]

Tebb put them both on what Violet calls "that nice new German drug," Adalin—Ford was taking four Adalin pills a night—and they went about in a dream. They did their best to divert themselves. They had the Patmores down for company; Ford played so much golf with Masterman that Violet wrote Mrs. Hueffer a little irritably, "Ford is out in the *pouring* rain playing golf with Masterman & improving his views (M's views) on the political situation. . . . [He] talks of coming back here *alone* to this cottage for a fresh bout of golf with Masterman but I don't know if that will come off. One never knows anything with a raging fiend like Elsie hanging about. I am getting a mixture of desperate & philosophical." In the evenings Ford lost himself in parlor games "like an adventurous schoolboy." They sought out new young friends like Katherine Mansfield and Middleton Murry. They looked up the author of a brilliant review of *The New Humpty-Dumpty* who turned out to be the eighteen-year-old Rebecca West, with her great eyes and her enchanting voice and her fine mind. They saw a great deal of Pound and Wyndham Lewis. "These intellectual Hosts," said Wyndham Lewis, "were of that valuable kind of human, who shuns solitude as the dread symbol of unsuccess, is happiest when his rooms are jammed with people (for preference of note)." He thought they entertained people like him and Pound "as a concession to 'les jeunes', but [Violet's] spirit dwelt with the Pre-Raphaelites, as did half of her husband's." Ford, as always, worked steadily; he also began to drink heavily.[11]

In October they took a couple of weeks' vacation in the north and Violet insisted on calling on Silvia at Bedburne; she got short shrift—a cup of tea from Rosamond and a message from Silvia that they had better leave their differences to the lawyers. At Christmas they borrowed a cottage at Farnham Common, near Burnham Beeches, and took down Ezra Pound, Mary Martindale, Ford's nephew, Frank Soskice, and the Compton Mackenzies. On Christmas Day Ford retired to his bedroom and locked himself in, possibly because even with his remarkable self-control, he could not trust himself in company that day: he had wanted very badly to spend Christmas with Christina and Katharine. Elsie had refused, saying that she would not put the girls through the suffering of his appearing and then disappearing all over again. His absence from the house party on Christmas Day, said Mrs. Mackenzie, "gave a spice to the party [at Farnham], since Violet was continually running upstairs to entreat him, speculating loudly as to why he was up there at all . . . " and Pound talked without ceasing from dawn till dusk. On St. Stephens Day, Ford reappeared, benevolent and lively; Violet was flushed with excitement at his return; Pound went on talking. "It was," Mrs. Mackenzie concludes, "a really notable Christmas. . . . "[12]

This was all a way of trying to avoid the knowledge of what was likely to happen at that trial that was gradually working its way to the top of the court calendar. It put *The Throne* in a peculiarly difficult position. René Byles, *The Throne*'s business manager, was their close friend and they were acquainted with its editor, Comyns Beaumont. They must have known that *The Throne* had been in serious financial difficulties and was only just beginning to see daylight. Beaumont and Byles were ready enough to print an apology to Elsie for calling Violet Mrs. Hueffer, as the *Daily Mirror* had, to avoid damages, if they could be sure that what they had printed was libelous; if not, to apologize might lay them open to a suit from Violet. Byles consulted Ford and Violet and they assured him that Ford had really divorced Elsie and had married Violet in Hanover; both of them promised to testify on behalf of *The Throne* if the case ever came to trial, but they assured Byles it would not. The loyal Byles never questioned any of this; he and Beaumont determined to defend the case.[13]

The case came to trial before Mr. Justice Avory in the Court of King's Bench on February 7 and 8, 1913. Elsie told the court that in August of 1908 Ford had said he had no intention of returning to her and she had told him she "had objections to seeking a divorce, as it would be detrimental to my children and myself." Ford always deeply resented it ("the rest," said Violet, "didn't matter much [to him]") that, when Elsie's counsel asked her if she had not been awarded £3 a week at the time of her separation from Ford, she said only that she had but that Ford has ceased to pay it after May, 1912. On the strength of this, counsel then asked the jury if Elsie "had not suffered enough in being left to keep and educate two children on £ 3 a week?" But in fact Violet was spending something over £ 200 a year, according to her calculations, in various ways for the girls.

Elsie then described her proceedings against the *Daily Mirror* and said that it had paid damages and apologized; she had also complained to the *Lady*, which had apologized; and she had complained to the Postmaster-General about Violet's being listed as Mrs. Hueffer in the telephone directory and he had "promised to have the matter attended to." She had never been served with any divorce papers and, so far as her solicitor could determine, there had never been any divorce proceedings in a German court. The defense was extremely feeble, since, as Beaumont put it, "Hueffer and his lady friend" had simply disappeared. After the case was settled, Mr. Storrey Deans, Violet's solicitor, rose to say a word for her; he got only as far as "Miss Violet Hunt . . . wished him to say she believed herself to be Mrs. Ford Madox Hueffer and intended to continue—" when the judge interrupted to say "he declined to allow this court to be made a medium of advertisement." The jury, without leaving the box, awarded Elsie £ 300; with costs, *The Throne* paid out about £ 1,000, and it had to cease publication. Such was the publicly humiliating end of Violet's pretense that she was Ford's wife.[14]

With his passionate hatred of scenes, Ford probably could not have stood the experience of testifying in *The Throne* suit. Even on social occasions he would go badly to pieces under determined cross-examination; one vigorous old lady who cornered him about Violet Hunt reported that "He behaved like a jelly at bay." Tebb, who understood Ford's problem, gave him a letter asserting that he had been attending "Mr. Ford Madox Hueffer for neurasthenia during the last six months," that he had forbidden Ford to work during that period, and that "to have to appear in a Court of Law at the present time would be most injurious to him. . . . " There is a certain ambiguity here: Dr. Tebb must have known Ford had not ceased to work during these months, and he avoided certifying Ford unfit to appear in court, saying only that "I should in all probability feel myself obliged to certify that he was unfit to attend" if he were called.[15]

A few days before the trial, Ford and Violet slipped away to France. Literally ill with anxiety, Ford stayed in Boulogne, but Violet returned to England for the trial. She could not, of course, attend; she could only wait nervously for the verdict, first at Venice Benson's house and then at Mrs.

Hueffer's. During the first day Mr. Storrey Deans called to tell her that "dreadful things were being said" and to ask her if she would authorize the statement he was to try to make at the end of the trial. This was very frightening. Late the second day she crept back from Mrs. Hueffer's to South Lodge. On her way she tried without success to find a newspaper that would tell her the verdict. Back at South Lodge she "sat still for a long time in the dark, in the empty dining-room. . . . The servants, shamefaced, pretended they had not heard me come in, and did not come near me." At six-thirty she rushed to the telephone and tried to find someone who could tell her what had happened. Finally she learned. The verdict staggered her: "I realised that I had not for a moment supposed that the *Throne* would lose —not for one moment!" Now she had to recognize that the social position that had always meant so much to her had been completely destroyed, largely as a consequence of her ill-conceived efforts to consolidate that position by becoming a married woman.[16]

The morning after the trial, a hysterical Mary Martindale, "her large white face like a rock with the rain running down it," saw Violet off for Boulogne, and Violet sat in the compartment wondering if the other passengers could recognize her from the photographs of her that stared out from their newspapers. She arrived in Boulogne late at night in the pouring rain to find Ford tired and upset, his voice gone completely; *"la poitrine légèrement atteinte,"* the doctor told her later, more from nerves than from serious infection. The next morning at breakfast, "a large, important" English woman she had been friendly with before the trial addressed her coldly as "Miss Hunt." Until Ford was well enough to move they lived in their Boulogne hotel "in Coventry." Violet's nightmare of social ostracism was coming true.[17]

They got away as soon as they could, going to Montpellier because Conrad had loved it. They found it "ugly and ordinary" and quickly moved on to Carcassonne, where they found an epidemic of rabies and—against every probability—snow. While the icy mistral blew, Ford struggled to write. His study was the bathroom, his desk the lid on the bathtub. "We forced a calmness that spoke less of emotion controlled than an utter atrophy of all the springs of feeling," Violet remembered. "We hardly spoke to each other that month. . . . " For Violet the terrible thing was the loss of her reputation. Ford wept "as only a German can" at having been publicly accused of neglecting his children. To them it seemed the final irony when Ford got a letter from Elsie asking him to begin once more to pay the £ 3.10.0 a week the court had originally ordered him to pay. "No apology,"

Violet said bitterly. *"Quelle vie!"* Marwood chose this moment to ask Ford to repay the £ 440 he had borrowed to pay for Elsie's kidney operation. Conrad hastened to explain to them that Marwood had nearly died that winter and wished to put his affairs in order. But Violet had talked over this debt with Marwood the year before and he had assured her he would not ask for its repayment until her "ship came in." This convinced them that his sudden demand was a result of his believing that Ford really had neglected his children.[18]

Violet's north-country toughness of spirit made it possible for her to rally more quickly than Ford. Five days after the trial she wrote Mrs. Hueffer from Carcassonne:

> One must put ones back to the wall & let "Egypt stand where it did."
> ... The only thing for Ford & me to do is to wipe the unjustifiable mud Elsie has thrown off our faces, make ourselves presentable & go on as if nothing had happened. I have heaps of nice letters—making light of it & invitations . . . expect to see me with a very stiff upper lip—knocking about as usual. After all Ford did divorce Elsie. . . . And Ford did marry me—& we spent nearly £ 500 on it & I've got all Leun's bills[.]

When Mrs. Hueffer replied rather sharply that Violet should think of what she and Ford had done to others, she wrote,

> Dear Mother
> Don't write to me so severely—I mean I do remember that I am not alone in this awful time to feel. . . . Of course you were sad. I can't forget your eyes on that awful day when Elsie was swearing away all my reputation & I could do *nothing*. . . . I only know what your son tells me of the German business[.] I mean the divorce—that is his affair. Of course the marriage is mine & no one contested that, for of course Elsie wants to try and get Ford for bigamy. That is why I did not insist on going into court—for I might have been made to give date & place & witnesses. Now—nobody, not even you knows them[.] So she cant even begin to. . . . Oh, thats all right & we shall go on as before but such continual attacks make life hardly worth living.[19]

They tried to compensate Byles for the harm they had done him. When *The Throne* ceased publication, Byles had joined a couple of young men to start a new publishing firm, Howard Latimer, and Ford gave him his next book, *Mr. Fleight*, "for nothing: that is to say without an advance." Pinker wired him to know if he could really mean it and Ford replied: "Please give

Byles his own way.... Both Violet & I want to do Byles a good turn vis a vis the people he is working with." "It is," he added in another letter, "rather more in the nature of a present to him than anything else." But he was optimistic about Byles' chances, remembering how successful Byles had been in getting *The Soul of London* publicized when he worked for Alston Rivers; "I suggest," Ford wrote Pinker from Saint-Rémy, "that [Constable] should publish all the historical novels that I write [he was already halfway through *The Young Lovell*], leaving the modern ones to Byles who is very enthusiastic and will spend a great deal of money on advertising them." No doubt Byles would have done so if he could have, but the two young men, who had represented themselves to Byles as having a large capital available, turned out to have none and Howard Latimer failed before *Mr. Fleight* could be properly published.[20]

For two months more, unable to face returning to England, Ford and Violet drifted about the south of France. It was May before they could nerve themselves to return to South Lodge. Ford's instinct was, as always, to act as if nothing unusual had happened and to offer no explanations. "I hold very strongly," he said, "the view that friends are people before whom one does not need to justify oneself and, personally, I am absolutely determined to speak to no-one about these matters." This was not only a matter of principle with Ford but a matter of temperamental necessity. On this occasion, it was also the most practical policy. But if Ford could remain silent, Violet could not. It was her nature to rush into action and to argue her case, however bad. She was a fighter, and a very unwise one.[21]

Violet's difficulty was not only that she had a weak case but that the feelings of the people she cared about, the upper-middle class, were very fierce about scandals of this sort. The rapid spread of sexual irregularities among the upper classes in Edwardian times had increased their feeling that they must maintain an appearance of propriety: if they did not behave, it was, they thought, all the more important for them, as the class that set an example for the country, to look as if they did. They accepted Edward VII's many mistresses and his gambling; Arthur Balfour might live with a woman not his wife; and gentry like Valentine Baker (on whose disastrous exposure Ford based an episode in *Parade's End*) might make advances to serving girls in railroad trains. What they would not accept was Edward VII's being involved in a public scandal over Lady Aylesford or taking the witness stand in a trial, as he did in the Mordaunt divorce case and in the Tranby Croft case.

Ford and Violet had had no serious social difficulties before Elsie sued

The Throne, though it was an open secret among those who knew them that their story of the German divorce did not hold water. The trouble began when this fact became public knowledge; then everyone felt obliged to express horrified surprise. May Sinclair wrote Violet, "Personally, I don't care two straws whether your marriage holds good in this country or not, (and should *not* care if it had never taken place)"; but, she added, "the absurdly strong feeling this case has roused" made it necessary for Violet and Ford to remain out of England for at least six months. Another close friend, Mrs. W. K. Clifford, wrote her:

> ... I don't think you know *how strong* the feeling about you is, and it would be *impossible* for you to go about and be received without first asking what sort of reception you would get or whether you would get any at all. I would do a good deal for you but I simply should quake if you came here on Sundays, and I believe other people would walk out.—*Go away for three years!* and trust to your old friends to smoothe things as far as they can for you.

These pleas only stimulated Violet to further argument. She wrote Mrs. Clifford:

> The mud flung at me in the course of the attempt to ... drag me [i.e., my name] into a Court, where I was prohibited by the law from putting in an appearance, was of course disagreeable enough to bear but it did not alter the situation for people who had accepted the fact of the legality of my German marriage. ... I should expect all my real friends to accept my version of the affair naturally and easily—and if other friends walked out, let them!

But Mrs. Clifford could see as well as the next person that Violet should have provided proofs of her marriage, "that *no* solicitor [for *The Throne*] would have withheld them—that no Court would have given a verdict against that paper till it had made sure the proofs were not forthcoming." She cut firmly through Violet's verbiage by urging her to have her solicitor publish a statement giving the time and place that Elsie had been served with the divorce papers; the court, date, and place of the granting of the divorce and the date it became absolute; and the date and place of her marriage to Ford. No amount of rhetoric about how Henry James and Masterman and her relations were backing her up or about how she had saved Ford from "a state far worse than death, which indeed he did contemplate," could conceal the fact that this Violet could not do. Nevertheless Violet was determined to return and fight her battle.[22]

Meanwhile, Byles had begun to advertise *Mr. Fleight* by having cards engraved

Mr. Fleight
Palatial Hall
Hampstead N. W.

and leaving them on people; it embarrassed Ford, especially as, in the end, the book was not published at all but "was seized by the Sheriff's Office because Byles' firm could not pay its printer's bill." This sounds exaggerated; *Mr. Fleight* was reasonably widely reviewed. On the other hand, the assertion on the verso of the title page that this is the "third impression" is no doubt another of Byles' publicity maneuvers.[23]

Mr. Fleight is the most powerful of Ford's satiric attacks on the contemporary world, as the historical novel he followed it with, *The Young Lovell*, is the most serious of his romances. Heretofore he had been committed to an impractical Pre-Raphaelite daydream. This attitude was beginning now— perhaps as a result of his personal experience—to seem to him irresponsible. He now began to try seriously to imagine what stance a man who committed himself to a medieval conception of life and a feudal order of society should take in the modern world.

> ... the constitutional theories, such as they were, of the Commonwealth and the Stuart age, have disappeared; the Whiggism of Cobden and Bright, the bourgeois democracy of the first and third Republics and the oppressive, cruel, ignorant and blind theorising of later Fabianism have all died away. . . . We have a sort of vague uneasy feeling that the old feudalism and the old union of Christendom beneath a spiritual headship may in the end be infinitely better than anything that was ever devised by the Mother of Parliaments in England, the Constituent Assemblies in France, or all the Rules of the Constitution of the United States.

In the weekly series of articles he wrote for *The Outlook* between April and July of 1913, he set out to demonstrate that "the feudal system [was] the most satisfactory form whether of government or of commonwealth" and used D. H. Lawrence's *Sons and Lovers* to show that only the natural life of the lower classes retained any of the quality of feudal existence. The extent to which he was personally committed by his own unhappy experience to a hatred of the world created by the Elementary Education Act of 1870 is evident in "Süssmund's Address to an Unknown God," a poem he first published in *High Germany* in 1911. There he describes himself as a man who will not

tear his hair to tatters in the cause
Of garden suburbs or of guinea pigs

Injected with bacilli . . .

and therefore has

No share in fruity Progress or the wrongs
Of market porters, tram conductors, pimps,
Marriage-reforming divorcees, Whig statesmen
Or serious Drama.

What he wants is a heaven of "simple drunken knights" and

high-breasted ladies
Beauteous beyond belief and not one better
Than you would have her be—

where life would be made real in a human way by the right kind of treachery

—Adultery, foul murder, pleasant things,
A touch of incest, theft, but no Reformers.

Mr. Fleight has the loose, episodic structure of Ford's earlier satiric novels of modern life. It is meant to show, at any cost to the coherence of the story, that every aspect of modern life suffers from a common degradation, "democracy and education and that sort of sneakiness being the coin of the realm." Ford drags in the episode of the *New Review* in order to show the degenerate condition of modern journalism; without pretense he has his central character lecture the reader on the shoddiness of modern life ("Now I'm going to tell you the absolute truth about Society as it is, and the life we lead"). *Mr. Fleight* often states eloquently Ford's feelings about a plutocratic liberalism and its unworldly reformers, who are put into office by the dirtiest kind of political corruption and there babble "the great, fine truths" and about the way modern society has made the average man into "An almost incredible chatterer with a head full of snippets and a mouth that [is] a perfect geyser of democratic balderdash." When these feelings are embodied in the action, the story becomes impressive. Few novelists besides E. M. Forster and Evelyn Waugh have killed a character off with such terrifying casualness as Ford shows when he kills off Gilda Leroy; a lower-class girl whose head has been stuffed by cheap novels with romantic notions about dukes and serving girls, she is casually reported to have committed suicide on the steps of Palatial Hall when she discovers Mr. Fleight is not for her.[24]

This judgment of the modern world is mainly expressed by Mr. Arthur Blood and his brother, Reginald. Arthur Blood is driven to sardonic despair by a groom who would cheerfully have given his life for Mr. Blood—"His people had been in my village for four hundred and fifty years"—but nonetheless drugged Mr. Blood's show horses for a bribe of a thousand dollars from an American gambler. Mr. Blood would not have objected to traditional corruption; that is what life has always been. But he could not stand the idea of a family servant who would "betray . . . horses that ought to be like his own children" for "a nasty sum" like a thousand dollars; the groom "should have taken a five pound note or twelve thousand pounds." Mr. Blood strangles the groom with his own hands and then turns himself in for punishment; he is hurried onto a boat and out of the United States. "Oh, that was the most extraordinary fun," he says. "The sort of fun that makes you vomit. . . . Isn't it the moral of the life we lead?" Arthur Blood's brother, Reginald, has been driven into neurasthenia and Catholicism by being made to look a fool rather than a villain during a love affair; he develops a set of neurotic habits very like Ford's own when he was neurasthenic.[25]

Then Arthur Blood meets Mr. Fleight, a gentle, immensely wealthy Jew who thinks that "Society being what it is," it is not right for so rich a man as he to be nobody. "I feel that I ought to be Prime Minister . . . " he says, and Mr. Blood answers, "By Jove, you are right!" and undertakes to make him so. His doing so allows Ford to show us the earnest silliness and the corruption of the Edwardian world. All that keeps Mr. Blood from being driven mad by his vision of that world as "an extraordinarily cruel and disordered machine" is his conviction that others are, as Mr. Fleight puts it, "so inestimably below [him] that it would be utterly impossible for [him] to quarrel with us." Mr. Blood is an eighteenth-century Tory gentleman driven by the cheapness of modern society to a radical despair that he is too proud to express as anything but a tough honesty. "I don't object to crime, and I don't object to robbery, and I don't even object to sanctimoniousness or to hypocrisy. But I like a hypocrite to know that he's a hypocrite and a criminal to know that he's a criminal." Mr. Blood is Ford's image of a modern hero, partly what he wanted to be (and perhaps believed Arthur Marwood truly was)—the tough-minded heir of a long line of Tory squires—partly what he believed himself to be, the brilliant, impressionistic thinker who is devoted to medieval Catholic values and committed to political ideals far too radical even for the radicals of the day. Mr. Fleight is what Ford knew himself to have been in most of the actual crises of his life, a gentle, romantic, impractical man. Mr. Blood is the first clearly recognizable precursor of Christopher Tietjens, and Ford so admired him that he used him on and off for the next three years as a spokesman in his journalism.[26]

The instant Violet got back to London, she went into battle. She had cards engraved for Ford that read:

Ford Madox Hueffer

South Lodge
Campden Hill Road, W.

The Knap Cottage
Selsey
Sussex

She had stationary printed for herself: "From Mrs. FORD MADOX HUEFFER, (VIOLET HUNT)." She sent out engraved invitations to her garden party for July 1. "... never so well attended," she said of it. "Cabinet Ministers, by Jove." But the cabinet ministers must have been Masterman, Ford's old golfing companion, and perhaps John Burns, neither of whom set social precedent. Most of the people she really wanted did not come; a few had the candor to write and tell her why. Violet continued to give parties at South Lodge, with Ford in tails dispensing his special punch. But from now on she would entertain those who, like May Sinclair, did not care two straws whether she was married to Ford or not and the people Ford liked to call *les jeunes*—Ezra Pound; Wyndham Lewis; Rebecca West; the Compton Mackenzies; W. L. George; Brigit Patmore; the young American poet, Skip-with Cannell, whom Pound had discovered, and his wife, Kitty.[27]

"The Hueffers held open house at teatime," Kitty Cannell wrote later.

We sat down at a large, beautifully appointed table. . . . Authors on every rung of the literary ladder were apt to drop in, from Lady Gregory to Frank Stewart Flint, who spoke 10 languages, and his surprising Cockney wife who practically spoke none. . . . Famished beginners were sustained by the lavish crumpets and sandwiches, nut bread and plum cake. . . . [Ford's] almost huge, pink roundness, his silky straight, canary-colored hair and moustache and very pale blue eyes gave him the air of an English country squire. . . .

Pound used South Lodge as a headquarters for the bewildering series of demonstrations by which he and Lewis undertook to blast the establishment from the seat of power. He was also quick to see the advantage of the tennis court in the communal garden across from South Lodge, and a daily game there became customary. Only the young Kitty Cannell could put up with Pound's tyrannous ways on the court. The others took revenge on him by teaching Violet's parrot to shout imperiously "Ezra! Ezra!" when they came in from tennis. Violet prowled up and down the sidelines muttering about Ford, who had conceived a passion for Brigit Patmore. She specially re-sented the jeweled pectoral cross Ford claimed Brigit had given him; she said it dangled in her face during their most intimate moments like an insulting reminder of his unfaithfulness. She also found it hard to put up with Ezra's green velvet shirt and his trick of tipping his chair onto its back legs:

when he succeeded in breaking one of the "very beautiful cane and gilt chairs" she and Ford treasured she had a kitchen chair brought in for him to use.*[28]

"I never had any pity on [Ford]," Pound said later, "not realizing the effect of his earlier breakdown/ maH H H H/ It was POSSIBLE to discuss a serious idea with him. . . . " Ford never resented anything Pound said: he loved Pound and found him endlessly entertaining.

> When I first knew him his Philadelphia accent was comprehensible if disconcerting; his beard and flowing locks were auburn and luxuriant; he was astonishingly meagre and agile. He threw himself alarmingly into frail chairs, devoured enormous quantities of your pastry, fixed his pince-nez firmly on his nose, drew out a manuscript from his pocket . . . and looking down his nose would chuckle like Mephistopheles and read you a translation from Arnaut Daniel. The only part of that *Albade* that you would understand would be the refrain:
> "*Ah me, the darn, the darn it comes toe sune!*"

In return, Pound remained loyal to both Violet and Ford to the last. In his nostalgic correspondence with Brigit Patmore during the St. Elizabeth days he says of Violet, "glad of confirmation re/ V's virchoos. alZO the number and quality of her friends OUGHT by any logik prozess to prove she warnt totally 'that VIper.' " He is equally firm in his defense of Ford: "You prob/ can't ADmire Fordie's damNuvvls/ but PARTS of 'em/ and that he had all his faults, like his moustache, out in front where everyone cd/ see Yum. au fond a serious character as J. J. the Reverend Eliot and even ole Unc Wm/ the yeAT were NOT."[29]

Ford and Violet were also kind to Wyndham Lewis, but with different results. When Lewis moved into Augustus John's studio in Fitzroy Square, Violet gave him most of the furniture for it and they made Lewis as welcome at South Lodge as they did Pound. But Lewis was incapable of Pound's warmth. Hueffer, he said, "was never a favourite of mine"; but with his brilliant, dehumanizing vision he saw very clearly what was, like Ford's moustache, "out in front where everyone could see."

> Hueffer was a flabby lemon and pink giant, who hung his mouth

---

*Brigit Patmore did not much like Ford though she was devoted to Violet. She flatly denied giving Ford the pectoral cross and was indignant when, in the twenties, Ford went about New York saying, "Well, I am not quite sure he [Derek Patmore]'s not my son." Pound's destructiveness was notorious. "[He] was so muscular & agitated & throwing himself about he would be sure to break . . . gilt chairs which were meant to sit on cautiously & not to lean back on," Iris Barry said. Gertrude Stein never forgave him for breaking the leg of one of her antique chairs.

open as though he were an animal at the Zoo inviting buns—especially when ladies were present. Over the gaping mouth damply depended the ragged ends of a pale lemon moustache. This ex-collaborator with Joseph Conrad was himself, it always occurred to me, a typical figure out of a Conrad book—a caterer, or corn-factor, coming on board—blowing like a porpoise with the exertion—at some Eastern port.

What he *thought* he was, was one of those military *sahibs* who used to sit on the balcony of a club in Hindustan with two or three other *sahibs*, *stingahs* at their sides. . . . He possessed a vivid and theatrical imagination. . . .

These were his failings, irritating to me (though Ezra Pound, who referred to him as 'Fatty,' appeared to accept him—amused but impressed—as the *Sahib* . . .).[30]

Thus Ford and Violet began their new life together in London in 1913, and Ford began his long private struggle to keep abreast of the present without being false to the past. As he was to put it later,

We used before 1914 to have the simple old view

> "Que toutes les joies et tous honneurs
> Viennent d'armes et d'amour."

But upon those lines one could scarcely now conduct a life. . . . For how can a man conduct the delicate affairs of his fellows . . . if he have no acquaintance with the psychology of his time, and how can a man have acquaintance with the psychology of his time if he be unacquainted with the works of art of his day.

This position laid him open to much brutal comment from the young. "Ever so little belated, in spite of his intense and resolute modernity," Middleton Murry wrote, "Mr. Hueffer unbuttons his heart [in *Thus to Revisit*] . . . in two hundred pages of shocking garrulity . . . [with] a poetic that would be renounced by every single one of the poets whom he affects to champion." Almost as if to illustrate this view, Ford published his *Collected Poems* that November. Even the poems from *High Germany*, written in the fall of 1911, though some of them deal with remarkably elusive states of consciousness, are Victorian—Browningesque—rather than contemporary.

> It's an odd thing how one changes . . .
> Walking along the upper ranges
> Of this land of plains,
> In this month of rains,
> On a drying road where the poplars march along,

Suddenly,
With a rush of wings flew down a company,
A multitude, throng upon throng,
Of starlings. . . .

The *Collected Poems* was, in fact, an accident; Douglas Goldring had taken over a derelict publishing firm named (quite arbitrarily) Max Goschen; he owed Ford money and, to repay him, published this handsome collection of Ford's poems, giving him a £ 30 advance.[31]

During the summer Ford also dashed off the book that was his tribute to Henry James; it was, as Dixon-Scott said, "garrulous, slap-dash, untidy." Ford obviously hoped to get it out for James's seventieth birthday; in the event it did not appear until January 1, 1914. Ford thought James a very great writer of exactly the kind he most respected, a writer in the tradition of Turgenev, Flaubert, and de Maupassant, who held an undistorting mirror to the world. At a time when men stood, "in the matter of political theories, naked to the wind and blind to the sunlight," only novelists like James, he believed, could "give us the very matter upon which we shall build the theories of the new body politic." "Mr. James," he said, "is the greatest of living writers and in consequence, for me, the greatest of living men." The only way he knew to praise James was to describe James as a writer of what he thought the perfect fiction, the kind of novel he himself strove to write. But he did it so extravagantly that, as one reviewer remarked, "Any novelist might well pray to be spared from the humiliation of such exalted praise. . . . " James probably was spared it; at least he claimed never to have read Ford's book.[32]

As usual, Ford followed the modern satiric novel, *Mr. Fleight,* with a historical romance, *The Young Lovell,* which appeared in October, 1913; most of it had been written while he and Violet were roaming the south of France the previous spring. *The Young Lovell* is another of those slow-moving, tapestrylike stories that gets its best effect from Ford's detailed descriptions of the life of the times and a representation—at once serious and amused—of the way medieval men's minds worked.

So . . . Adam Swinburn and the others . . . went with courtesy, saying that they would come again and defend those towers if there were need of it. But the truth of the matter was that all of the fresh meat was eaten, which is a thing very unbearable in summer; the best wine was all drunk . . . they had tired of all the serving maids that there were in the Castle. . . . So they had neither desirable wine nor women; not much prospect of meat nor gold, and what else should keep them? Therefore they rode away.*[33]

*For a discussion of *The Young Lovell* see pp. 485–86.

Chapter 19

❧

In September, 1913, Ford and Violet took a trip down the Rhine with the Mastermans. Masterman had been largely responsible for the Insurance Act the Liberals had just put through and the nominal purpose of their trip was to allow him to study the working of Germany's act. But Masterman wanted to see the battlefields of the Franco-Prussian war. When they got into the German border country they found it very unpleasant—soldiers everywhere, the people sulky, plainclothes policemen following them around. Ford thought Lucy Masterman's camera had been tampered with because all her photographs were spoiled; Violet became convinced that the Germans believed Masterman was Winston Churchill. Violet was reading her own *The Desirable Alien*, with its extravagant expressions of love for Germany; when she had written the book, Germany had been Ford's newly acquired native land. But now this enthusiasm of the previous year was badly out of date. "Do you want me to be shot or forced to fight against France?" Ford asked when Violet wanted to visit the Hüffer relatives. "If you're prepared to risk that, dear, we'll go."[1]

Back in London, they found Pound had quarreled with Harriet Monroe and had "resigned from *Poetry* ... in Hueffer's favour." But Ford knew better than that. "If I tried to help you," he wrote Harriet Monroe, "that energetic poet would sit on my head and hammer me till I did exactly what he wanted. . . . " But if he was not going to get caught between Pound and *Poetry*, he was still anxious to help these young rebels and to be accepted by them; there was a great deal of tennis and discussion of the nature of poetry at South Lodge. If nothing else, it would have taken Ford's mind off his troubles, which seemed to him to have reached a crisis.[2]

He would be forty in December, he had worked very hard at every kind of writing, and he had little to show for it: he was more deeply discouraged about his career than he had been at any time since 1904. Since then he had written seven books of nonfiction, three volumes of poetry, and sixteen novels, and they had brought him neither fortune nor fame. "The slump," as he said to Pinker, "has been going on for years." He was seriously considering "taking a contract with one of the more ancient firms on a basis of 20% royalty on sales and no advance." In his eyes this was defeat, the acceptance of a financial arrangement far inferior to what he deserved; in fact, he found it impossible to make any such contract.[3]

He had met Stanley Paul, the publisher, at luncheon in November and thought Paul would agree to an extended contract, "say six novels at £ 250." But Paul talked merely of "several novels," at a lower figure. At this disappointment Ford exploded with rage at the insolent ignorance of people like Paul who failed to recognize his eminence.

> The view I like of it [he wrote Pinker] is that I don't want to deal with Stanley Paul at all, & if he wants my name he must just pay for it.
>
> I have worked damned hard for many years to establish my name as a good-will & that's all there is to it—conceit or no conceit. I don't need money &, unless I can get a good price, I won't sell my immortal soul to any of your blooming devils.
>
> . . . If Paul wants to attain to respectability by publishing me, he must give me my own terms. He must pay me £·300 on receipt of the manuscript of a first novel & after that what any book earns on subscription, & must make up accounts & pay them on the 1st of each subsequent month. He must contract to publish twelve novels from me on these terms & I must be at liberty, if I want to oblige a friend, to give an occasional novel to someone else. . . . [4]

What kind of society was he living in—he asked himself—if it was possible for an innocently idealistic man to be crucified by pharisees who treated genuine passion such as his and Violet's as if it were libertinism? What kind of social system was it that would allow self-righteous people to carry a public attack on a man just far enough to make their case against him, and then drop it before he could have his day in court? What kind of a world was it in which a gifted writer who had worked very hard could get neither recognition nor a decent income? The question for Ford was how a gentleman of Tory predilections, for whom the clear eighteenth-century mind was a model, who believed the feudal system of social relations the best mankind had ever devised, and who had an heroic sense of personal honor, would conduct himself in such a world.

This was the question his imagination faced in *The Good Soldier.* In the dedication he wrote for Stella Bowen when the book was reissued in 1927, Ford says that he sat down on his fortieth birthday (December 17, 1913) to start it. But there can be little question that he began *The Good Soldier* immediately after finishing *Henry James.* During the summer of 1913 Violet asked a beautiful friend of hers to stay with them at Selsey. "Intermittently, when she was well enough—like all the other pretty ladies she played secretary to Joseph Leopold." He dictated *The Good Soldier* to her. "To see his happy face when she came down to breakfast next morning," Violet said later, "ought to have told me" what was going on.[5]

Gradually during the winter of 1913–14, Ford succeeded in inventing a conception of himself and his motives that explained his recent conduct in a way that satisfied his imagination. During the time when he had been thinking of himself as the heir of an ancient and noble south German family, his romantic Catholicism had taken on new life. Now, as his feelings about the contemporary world from which he felt he had suffered so unjustly became more bitter, he began to see himself as a medieval Catholic astray in the modern world. "I am aware," as he put it, "that I write a little as a black Papist and . . . a Tory mad about historic continuity." " . . . in a Papist sort of way," he told Lucy Masterman, "I am a tempestuously religious sort of person and I do not think any clearness of thought is possible unless one either is or has been intensely religious."[6]

Perhaps a little irritated by this assertion that "clearness of thought" is possible only to the "tempestuously religious," Violet said to him one day at Selsey, "You say you believe in a heaven; I wish you'd write one for me. I want no beauty, I want no damned optimism; I want just a plain, workaday heaven that I can go to some day and enjoy it when I'm there." A few days later in the dark little drawing room of the Selsey cottage Ford read to her and the beautiful "play-secretary" "*con amore, sans façon,* tactlessly evincing his honest joy in his work"—his best-known poem, that modernized "Blessed Damozel" called "On Heaven. *To V. H., who asked for a working Heaven.* "It is a vision of a Provence in which God makes everything satisfactory for Ford, and Violet comes to join him in a "swift red car" and God says a kind word to them, and Our Lady promises them a son if they will make a pilgrimage to Lourdes, and they lie in each other's arms undisturbed by all the complications they have left behind them forever in Mrs. Grundy's England. In her peppery, impatient way Violet thought it an expression of "Love without breadth, depth, or thickness, without dimension. Subjective, purely. . . . Not . . . the love that moves mountains, faces the seven deaths of

boredom, but the mild, watery variety that . . . sits down in front of ["opposition"] and repeats the great word Agony three times, taking up all one
line!"[7]

Violet's continuous entertaining, Ford's literary engagements, and the
energetic activities of Ezra and Wyndham Lewis kept them busy during the
summer of 1914. Ford once noticed that there had been only six days in May
and June that he did not have at least three dinner and after-dinner engagements. Many evenings had to be spent at the Cave of the Golden Calf, the
nightclub run by Strindberg's third wife. Mme. Strindberg was a Viennese
woman of eccentric ideas and—judging from the way she pursued Augustus
John—considerable persistence. The Cave of the Golden Calf became, for a
time, very popular. It had been "hideously but relevantly frescoed by . . .
Wyndham Lewis"—almost his first job—and supplied with white wooden
pillars like caryatids by Epstein; "All had scarlet details, the heads of hawks,
cats, camels. . . . " The food and wines were excellent and well served, and
there was an orchestra, "with a frenzied Hungarian gypsy fiddler to lead it,"
to which everyone could "dance those obsolete Vorticist dances, the Turkey
Trot and the Bunny Hug." Madame, chalk white, with "wonderful dark
hair, a hooked nose, and eyes that blazed out and then went in again, brown,
like a hawk's," drifted about among her guests, wrapped in a fur coat. Between dances there were entertainments, usually what Edgar Jepson called
"violent, Vorticist assaults on the drama." Ford wrote a shadow play to be
performed there. Everything, of course, went wrong and it ended with
Ford's having to act it himself.

> The shadow play was imbecile in a silly class of thing—a burlesque
> of Romance. A man is attacked by a cobra and an assassin at the same
> moment. The cobra bites his little finger—which of course is irrevo-
> cable death; but at the pain he starts aside, and the descending yata-
> ghan of the assassin cuts off the little finger. So the hero is saved from
> his oriental adventures—the assassin was, of course, a Deceived Hus-
> band—and returns to Europe with a heroine from behind the grill of
> a harem, to open a tobacco shop.

Such, at least, is the plot of the shadow play performed at the Night Club
—which is closely modeled on The Cave of the Golden Calf—in *The Marsden Case*.[8]

Then Marinetti "brought off a Futurist *Putsch*" at the Doré Gallery and
a counterputsch had to be organized. *Blast* was being planned and "by
August 1914 no newspaper was complete without news about 'vorticism' and
its arch-exponent Mr. Lewis. . . . " "Those young people," Ford said, "had

done their best to make a man of me. They had dragged me around to conspiracies, night-clubs, lectures where Marinetti howled and made noises like machine-guns. . . . So they pranced and roared and blew blasts on their bugles and round them the monuments of London tottered." Thanks, no doubt, to Pound, the first number of *Blast* included the opening section of *The Good Soldier;* Ford even lectured, in a tailcoat, at Lewis' Rebel Art Centre in Great Ormond Street. In his more cheerful moods, he believed he was making a success of this career among the young. "I used to be everyone's Dutch uncle in those days," Ernest Jessop (who represents Ford in *The Marsden Case*) says of his position in the literary London of 1914, "that, I suppose, is why I have gathered no moss." But in his more realistic moments, especially when Wyndham Lewis found time—as he so often did— to tell Ford what he thought of him, Ford was under no illusion about these young men. " . . . my Great Auk's Egg, they called it [*The Good Soldier*]," he said. "The Great Auk lays one Egg and bursts. That bird was no louder than a thrush in the pages of *Blast*."[9]

It was a blast from Lewis, apparently remarkably bad-mannered even for Lewis, that convinced Ford his day was past and determined him to say farewell to literature with the completion of *The Good Soldier.* It is typical of Ford's generosity with young artists that he repaid Lewis' attacks by persuading Harold Monro to have Lewis do the designs for Ford's *Antwerp* when the Poetry Bookshop published it in January, 1915. In print Ford made a joke of these attacks. " *Tu sais, tu es foûtu! Foûtu [sic]!* Finished! exploded! Done for! Blasted in fact. . . . Get out or get under." But his private feelings about Lewis' judgment of him were not so philosophical; as late as *The March of Literature,* he was remembering it, and when Pound discouraged Stella by telling her what was wrong with her painting, Ford wrote her: "[Ezra's] *criticisms* of yourself . . . arise sole[l]y from a frantic loyalty to W. Lewis . . . gramaphonic records of Lewis's dicta (in wh. Lewis himself doesn't for a moment believe). . . . " He then proceeded to demolish Lewis' dicta for her.[10]

Violet had given Ford the right front room on the first floor of South Lodge as a study. When John Gould Fletcher saw it in 1913, it was, with "its innumerable pipes on a table, its special machine for cutting tobacco, its books, its air of comfort," a conventional enough room. Violet now decided to make it a "Vorticist Study." She commissioned Lewis to do a large painting that turned out to be almost entirely crimson; on her own she supplied "three brick-red coloured tapestry window curtains." The room also contained, however, some less Vorticist decorations—Ford Madox

Brown's painting of Ford as William Tell's son and watercolors by Violet's father—and was, as Iris Barry put it, "a very typical [room] of the period & class." With her incurable passion for clothes, Violet also made an effort to dress in what she fancied to be a Vorticist style, which she thought ugly. Lewis consoled her by telling her she looked better in her inelegant Vorticist garments than if she were going about like a "dying stag or a virgin in Greek dress picking daisies."[11]

In the spring Amy Lowell had written Pound that she was thinking of starting a magazine. Pound promptly offered her the services of Ford and himself to run the London part of the magazine and, when she arrived in London, included her in the Vorticist circle; she was present at the dinner at the Dieudonné restaurant in Ryder Street that was held to celebrate the publication of *Blast* the night of June 20. She and Ford got into a fierce row that evening; nevertheless, she included Ford in the *"Imagiste"* dinner she gave at the same restaurant two nights later; there Ford created an embarrassed silence by saying that he really had no idea what an imagist was and suspected nobody else did. It was, Ford said later, " . . . a disagreeable occasion of evil passions, evil people, of bad, flashy cooking in an underground haunt of pre-war smartness. . . . There were also speeches—and one could not help knowing that the speeches were directed at [Amy Lowell's] breeches pocket. [She] leaned heavily sideways at table, devouring the bad food at once with gluttony and nonchalance."[12]

Late in July Mary Borden, the American novelist, then married to a Scotsman named Turner, invited Ford and Violet to come to Duns Manor, near Berwick, which the Turners had rented for the summer. Ford always remembered that weekend as a charmed occasion, a last, magical Edwardian pause before the crash of the war.

> . . . the turf of the Scottish lawns was like close fine carpeting and the soft Scottish sunshine and the soft Scottish showers did the heart good. . . .
>
> We sat on the lawns in the sunlight and people read aloud— which I like very much. [Lewis] had brought the proofs from *Blast* of my one novel [*The Good Soldier*]. I read that. Mrs. Turner . . . read from some magazine the instalments of the work of a writer of whom I had never heard. His name was James Joyce.

They argued, too, about the possibility of war. According to Wyndham Lewis' recollection,

Mrs. Turner was emphatic. . . .

"There won't be any war, Ford. Not here. England won't go into a war."

Ford thrust his mouth out, fish-fashion, as if about to gasp for breath. He goggled his eyes and waggled one eyelid about. He just moved his lips a little and we heard him say, in a breathless sotto voce—

"England will." . . .

"England will! But Ford," said Mrs. Turner, "England has a Liberal Government. A Liberal Government cannot declare war."

Ford sneered very faintly and inoffensively: he was sneering at the British Government, rather than at us. He was being omniscient, bored, sleepy Ford, sunk in his tank of sloth. From his prolonged sleep he was staring out at us with his fish-blue eyes—kind, wise, but bored. Or some such idea. His mask was only just touched with derision at our childishness.

"Well, Ford," said Mrs. Turner, bantering the wise old elephant. "You don't agree!"

"I don't agree," Ford answered, in his faintest voice, with consummate indifference, "because it has always been the Liberals who have gone to war. It is *because* it is a Liberal Government that it *will* declare war."[13]

Ford's feelings about the war were complicated. He had strong emotional commitments to France and to southern Germany—or at least to his private conceptions of those places; he was also devoted to his idea of England. But more powerful than any of these feelings was his intense dislike of liberal democracy with—as he thought—its shady capitalists, venal politicians, and an electorate stuffed with fatuous ideas of its own wisdom by a shoddy system of universal education. His commitment was to a feudalism he imagined had been gallantly chivalric. In one of his weekly articles for *The Outlook* written just as war was declared he poured out these feelings:

. . . what is senseless, what is imbecile, are the ideas for which people are dying. . . . I should feel intensely any mortification to Germany; almost more intensely any mortification to France; and any blow to this country would cause in me emotions more horrible than any others. . . . What effects me even more depressingly is the want of chivalry in expressions of nationality. . . . It is simply an indictment of the Parliamentary system and of democracy. For the present war, as I see it, is simply a product of the indefinite, mysterious, and subterranean forces of groups of shady and inscrutable financiers working their wills upon the ignorant, the credulous, the easily swayed electorate. . . . Men have not rights—they have only duties.[14]

But despite his disapproval of liberal democratic ideas, he believed in his own democratic right to express freely his opinions of the Liberal government and his sympathies with the southern Germans, views bound, in a time of superpatriotism, to make trouble for a man who had so extensively advertised his Germanness. He was nonetheless astonished that anyone should question his loyalty to England. By August 2 he was back in London, where he managed to get hold of Masterman—according to him, in the Foreign Office itself—to try to discover what England was likely to do. That afternoon, he descended on Edgar Jepson to give him an account of this conversation.

> He told me that he had had a hard morning, and I gathered that both Asquith and Grey had spent a couple of hours with him, laying the facts of the situation before him, and reiterating the question: "Shall we fight, Hueffer, or shall we not fight?" . . . I have always wished that he could have seen his way to forbid them to fight.

He and Violet went down to Selsey, and when England entered the war, he again sought out Masterman to inquire anxiously about his status. Masterman assured him there was no question he was a British subject in good standing.[15]

Things were not at all comfortable at Selsey. Edward Heron Allen, an old friend of Violet, lived close by. He had become obsessed by the idea that there were likely to be German landings, from submarines, in the neighborhood (Selsey is only eighteen miles from Portsmouth). "Allen *did* go frightening girls about a German invasion & Ford remonstrated in a friendly way with him," Violet said. Allen had never liked Ford and he deeply disapproved of Violet's association with Ford; it is easy to imagine how he responded to being remonstrated with "in a friendly way" by Ford. Then, in November, 1914, Ford published in *The Bystander* a story called "The Scaremonger" that is an obvious satire on Allen. "I did not," Allen wrote Violet, "believe that even a German journalist would sit at one's table, make one's house a sort of Inn for the entertainment of his friends, and use one's time, money, and brains in his service for years, and then perpetrate an outrage of the kind." Ford "apologised," in Violet's words, " ' on the wrong side of his face.' " Allen understood well enough what Ford was doing. " . . . the execrable taste displayed in your study of myself and my friends in 'The Bystander,' " he wrote Ford, "is equally conspicuous in your letter. . . . " None of this could have been very pleasant for Ford, who thought of himself as an English gentleman of impeccable taste.[16]

At Allen's suggestion, as Ford always believed, in any event at someone's, the Chief Constable of West Sussex wrote Ford officially that "I have been requested to prohibit your residing in the area of the Chichester Division. I therefore give you notice that you must leave this county." This order was quickly canceled, doubtless at Masterman's request, but it left Ford feeling very bitter. He saw himself as a man of reason urging people to consider "that the reports of German atrocities were probably a good deal exaggerated, and that if we could fight the war in terms of the 'gallant enemy' it would be better for all parties," only to find that "if I walk down the village street [of Selsey] I am apt to be insulted every two minutes— because of my German descent." He could not see that he did not have the reputation and authority that would allow him to combat this attitude effectively but, indeed, was in a peculiarly awkward position for doing so.[17]

Masterman had been given the job of countering German propaganda in the United States; the whole operation was highly secret and was never referred to except by the name of the building where Masterman's office was, Wellington House, the headquarters of the National Health Insurance Commission, which Masterman had headed before the war. Copies of the books Wellington House secretly sponsored were sent to influential Americans accompanied by tastefully printed cards announcing them to be the gifts of this or that distinguished British professor. Masterman enlisted Ford's assistance and in September he began writing the first of the two books he did for Wellington House, *When Blood Is Their Argument: An Analysis of Prussian Culture.* He took on Richard Aldington as a secretary.

> We worked every morning. I took down from his dictation in long hand. . . . He was a great worker. He did a long literary article every week and at the same time he was engaged on a novel, *The Good Soldier,* and his propaganda book, *Between St. Dennis and St. George.* During the months I worked with him I believe he turned out 6000 to 8000 words a week.

This is, to be sure, somewhat inaccurate. Ford had completed *The Good Soldier* in July and he would have been writing *When Blood Is Their Argument* rather than *Between St. Dennis and St. George* at this time. But there is no doubt about the amount of work he was doing.[18]

When Blood Is Their Argument—"For how can they charitably dispose of anything, when blood is their argument?" as Williams says in *Henry V*—was published in March, 1915. It is a lucid, informal, man-to-man argument that with the triumph of Prussia over the other German states the "gentle, simple, rather sentimental" southern Germany, from which all the important art of Germany has come and where culture has always flourished, came under the control of Prussia, with its passion for *Kultur*—for commercialism, applied science, philology, and war, instead of idealism, pure science, humane learning, and peace. The argument is conducted with intelligence and restraint; due credit is given to the German achievement and to the merits of Wagner and Nietzsche and Bismarck, a rare thing in such works. This argument peculiarly suited Ford, since it allowed him to contrast a southern Germany he could describe as almost feudal—"cultivated, spendthrift, and gay, good-humoured and quite as much concerned with the workings of the next world as with the workings of the Customs Union"—with the Prussia that had imposed the Customs Union and all it implied.[19]

Ford's other propaganda book for Masterman, *Between St. Dennis and St. George, A Sketch of Three Civilisations*, was published six months later. It is a much less careful, more heterogeneous affair. "I am afraid," Ford said in his dedication of it to Lucy Masterman, "that this book will present the aspect of a number of essays thrown together"; and it does. This is so partly because Ford wanted to answer the anti-British arguments of men like Shaw and had to range over considerable ground to do so. In the process he hung himself up on some dubious distinctions, as when he attempted to show that German military dominance was a menace but that British naval dominance had always been a fine thing. Another difficulty is created by Ford's belief that an extended discussion of how to translate *Un Coeur Simple* is the best way to define French culture. But Ford always remembered this book with deep satisfaction because it was translated into French and got him a certain amount of attention from the French government.[20]

Meanwhile, on March 17, 1915, what Ford frequently called his "one novel," *The Good Soldier*, was published. Ford always said that he had finished it by July, 1914, and the evidence suggests that date is substantially correct. In the 1927 dedication to Stella Bowen, he says he had refrained until he was forty from trying "to put into any novel of mine *all* that I knew about writing" and then, on his fortieth birthday, had "sat down to show what I could do—and the *Good Soldier* resulted." This is evidently an improved version of the facts, but it probably represents an impression that is based on the truth. Everyone was aware in those months before August, 1914, that western Europe was in a state of crisis, and Ford had had a growing conviction, at least since *Ladies Whose Bright Eyes*, that there was something radically wrong with the part of that civilization he knew best. These feelings had been brought to sharp focus by his personal experience in the years between the collapse of *The*

English Review and his gradual recognition, in 1913, that his affair with Violet Hunt no more satisfied his "mad passion to find an ultimately satisfying woman" than his marriage to Elsie had.[21]

"For personal reasons," he said long afterward, "I thought about the subject [of *The Good Soldier*] at intervals for ten years before beginning on it. When I did begin on it I had almost every word of it in my head, and I dictated it very quickly.... " In his dedicatory letter to Stella he hinted that the story was very familiar to him ("the story is a true story ... I had it from Edward Ashburnham himself... "). It was, he said, "a work over which I sweated real drops of sweat and shed real drops of tears." Because he felt deeply and directly about the subject of *The Good Soldier*, the marvelous skill with which—as so often—he deploys its story is purposeful. One may question, as with any novel, the wisdom of its occasional generalizations, but one cannot doubt the genuineness of its dominant attitude, that life is an inexplicable horror, "all a darkness."[22]

He worked hard to remove from *The Good Soldier* the evidence that it was based on personal experience; in the manuscript he has even cut a passage that describes Florence as chattering volubly about "the expression on the face of the wife of the Czar of Russia as she drove in [to Nauheim] from Friedberg"; he feared people would recognize that as Violet. But there is really no concealing the fact that Florence is based on Violet; it was impossible to cut the crucial scene in the Schloss at Marburg from *The Good Soldier*, and it echoes their visit to it that Violet describes in *The Desirable Alien*. The conduct of the Grand Duke, described by Violet as "so popular ... that he only dined once at his own expense ... and that once was when he, as in duty bound, returned all this hospitality in the lump"; those "fine fellows," the favorite officers of the Emperor—including Count Lelöffel— who are at Nauheim with heart trouble caused by "excessive attention to and prowess at polo"—these things have obvious echoes in *The Good Soldier;* they show clearly that Florence's inhuman, Vassarish learning and her complacent, amoral moralizing are based on Ford's vision of Violet.[23]

Less obvious but equally pervasive is the influence on Leonora of Ford's view of Elsie Martindale, to whom by this time he was ascribing the same feeling for status, the same dislike of impulsive generosity, the same willingness to disregard traditions and obligations that Leonora shows. A good many other, less significant details of the novel also come from Ford's personal experience—for example, the "saturnalia" at Nancy's convent, the Misses Hurlbird from Stamford, and the incident that was the source of the novel's plot, Edward's drive to the station with Nancy, which is based on a personal experience Ford had had many years before and described as an example of a British "national characteristic that is almost appalling"—that is, the determination of the best people to "play the game to the very end" with a "Spartan repression," a determination he thought at once magnificent and terrible.[24]

[Ford's purpose in *The Good Soldier* is to realize his eerie insight into the tortured condition of a society in which the life of men's feelings no longer flows into the beautiful, refined ritual of the society's most cultivated life. "Someone has said," Dowell warns us, "that the death of a mouse from cancer is the whole sack of Rome by the Goths, and I swear to you that the breaking up of our little four-square coterie was such another unthinkable event." It is possible to see now that for at least a quarter of a century, since the Pre-Raphaelites rebelled, the arts had been moving toward some such insight, and the remarkable thing about *The Good Soldier* is not so much the character of its insight as its genuineness and its earliness.[25]

Superficially, the response of Edwardian writers to the new affluence and the breakup of Victorian values was twofold. There were the aesthetes, like James and Conrad, deeply concerned about private experience but apparently untouched by the social movements of their time; and there were the reformers like Wells and Shaw, deeply concerned with changing the world and apparently impatient of psychological subtlety. James and Wells had a famous argument about the novel that turns on this disagreement, and Conrad, finding no analysis of inner reality in Wells, asked him plaintively, "My dear Wells, what is this *Love and Mr. Lewisham* about?" Yet the two groups were more alike than these disagreements suggest. Conrad was as concerned for society's problems as were Wells and Kipling and as emotionally dependent on his solution for them. Henry James told Wells that he would not have been Boon (Wells's caricature of him) for anything and spent his middle years writing about social problems. Nor was it for nothing that James thought the young Wells the most gifted novelist of his generation and that Shaw had a weakness for the gratuitous imaginations that could hear Beethoven in the destruction of the world, even while he was saying savagely, "Do you think the laws of God will be suspended in favor of England because you were born in it?" They all foreshadow the need for a form of fiction that would represent in a single image the public and private senses of reality and the exacerbating conflict between the two. Ford was the first good writer to bring that conflict into sharp focus and to find a form for it: *The Good Soldier* was completed seven years before *Mauberley*, Pound's first wholly modern poem, and eighteen years before *Ulysses*.[26]

In *The Good Soldier*, Ford made, for the first time, a success of the method of narration that was to be peculiarly his own, toward which he had been struggling in novels like *A Call*. It is possible he was helped to do so by having to distinguish his own position from that of Pound and Lewis; at least he tried hard to define that position in the farewell to literature he wrote for *Poetry and Drama* in 1914 and called "Impressionism."

For the rest of his life, Ford liked to think of the "Impressionistic Novelists" as a "group, who since the days of Flaubert have dominated the public mind," and to say that "the modern 'impressionist' novelist . . . [has] stretched technique almost as far as it could go." This group he said included James, Conrad, and Crane ("Those three . . . were, almost equally, the protagonists of literary Impressionism in Anglo-Saxondom")—and, of course, Ford himself. Impressionism was, he thought, "a world movement" that had become during his lifetime "all-pervading." But Ford's theory is, like most writer's theories, a rationalization of his own practice as a writer rather than a description of any actual historical movement. It focuses on the determination of the author's subject and his method of communicating this subject.[27]

Ford often spoke as if the whole theory and practice of Impressionism consisted of the second. "It is to be remembered," he would say, "that a passage of good prose is a work of art absolute in itself and with no more dependence on its contents than is a fugue of Bach. . . . " He could see that writing too much too quickly had its dangers. " . . . though a man in [his sixties] may still write good prose," he said when he was struggling to complete *The March of Literature*, "the odds are that he will not be able to do it incessantly, untiringly and to earn a scanty living. Or he may pray to be defended from such a fate." Even here, however, he is considering the damage to the expression rather than to the substance of the work. His proud conviction that, along with the other "Impressionists," he had for the first time made the novel "a conscious art" convinced him that to "put . . . *all* that I know . . . about the way writing should be done . . . how words should be handled and novels constructed" into a book was the whole duty of the novelist. This conviction led him to overrate merely skillful work, like *The Rash Act*, to ascribe the whole merit of books like *The Good Soldier* to technical triumphs, and, above all, to write too much.[28]

In this mood he would dwell on the various literary devices he believed he and Conrad had worked out for making a narrative lifelike and speak almost as if what the writer had to say was of no account. " . . . the purpose of a technique is to help the writer to please, and . . . neither writing nor the technique behind it has any other purpose.... You must have your eyes forever on your Reader. That alone constitutes ... Technique!" Because he could not conceive a reality that was not the reality of his own conception, he never doubted that the way to please the reader was to represent a person perceiving a set of events ("imaginative ... literature is that writing which most reveals the personality of its author").

> That we [Conrad and Ford] did succeed eventually in finding a new form I think I may permit myself to claim, Conrad first evolving the convention of a Marlow who should narrate, in presentation, the whole story of a novel just as, without much sequence or pursued chronology, a story will come up into the mind of a narrator, and I eventually dispensing with a narrator but making the story come up in the mind of the unseen author with a similar want of chronological sequence.[29]

He would then set forth the various devices he and Conrad had worked out to refine this form of presentation—the time-shift; the treatment of dialogue both as elliptical (as it so often literally is) and fragmentary, as a narrator may plausibly be supposed to recall it; a diction so artfully simple that it would fix the reader's attention on the impression rather than the narrator; and, finally, what Ford called *progression d'effet*, the slow building of the narrative from a quiet start through a gradual speeding up and intensification of the reader's impressions to a climax of his involvement in the feelings of the narrator.*[30]

At the peak of his career, Ford also kept in mind the first and most significant aspect of Impressionism. When he was writing *The Good Soldier*, he said, "Impressionism is a frank expression of personality.... The Impressionist author is sedulous to avoid letting his personality appear in the course of his book [that is, letting himself speak in his own person, as Thackeray does]. On the other hand, his whole book, his whole poem is merely an expression of his personality"—that is, of his personal "impression" of the circumstances he is dealing with. The impressionist's subject, then, is always himself, *his* personality, usually—in Ford's own case, in any event—as the writer imagines himself to have felt during some important experience of his own. The nominal subject is an objective correlative, a set of circumstances which, though different from the actual circumstances of his own experience, allows him to express his feelings about these actual circumstances in exactly the pattern they have taken for him.[31]

---

*It was W. H. Hudson's unobtrusive diction that made Ford admire him so greatly, particularly because, despite his theory, Ford himself found it difficult to avoid using a dramatically personal style that draws attention to itself and thus to the narrator.

At his best, Ford had an unmatchable gift for conceiving objective correlatives of this kind. They are never perfectly convincing as representations of the world: the pressure of his feelings required them to be too radically altered from everyday experience for that. But they are rich in precise if not actual details of life, organized into an imagined whole that has a remarkable inner consistency. As a reviewer put it of Ford's vision of England in *Some Do Not . . .*, he describes "an England that Englishmen generally will have some difficulty in recognizing. . . . This country and people . . . are made astonishingly real to the reader. . . . It is really a triumph of mind over matter. The mind is always there, acutely observing even when most grotesquely misunderstanding; a distinguished mind that molds everything to its will. . . . Given its premises its argument is almost flawless." Something very like that is true of *The Good Soldier*.[32]

Chapter 20

༖

The Good Soldier has been the subject of a great deal of controversy that depends ultimately on the ambiguity of fictions narrated in the first person by a participant. In such fictions there is no way for the author to provide us with a reliable judgment of the narrator so that we can determine how to take what he tells us. We can know how to take a dramatized narrator only if we share the author's values. The author cannot tell the reader what these are; each reader must guess; and what each reader usually guesses is that the author has the same values he has.

As a result critics have seen John Dowell, the narrator of *The Good Soldier*, as everything from a man "incapable of passion, sexual and moral alike," who suffered from "the dull hysteria of sloth . . . the sluggish insanity of defective love" (as Mark Schorer says) to a "narrator [who] fits the [Conrad-Ford] ideal better than Conrad's Marlow, being even less of an idiosyncratic observer" (as Robie Macauley says). The first kind of critic takes what Dowell tells us as a systematically "distorted understanding" of what really happened, dictated by the narrator's need to defend his own sexual inadequacy. For him *The Good Soldier* is—like Edmund Wilson's version of "The Turn of the Screw"—an ironic portrait of its narrator, "a comedy of humor." The second sort of critic sees *The Good Soldier* as a tragic story of mismatched lives in which—"his preservation com[ing] from having understood more of the story than any of the other people in it"—the narrator alone survives intact. The only recourse for criticism confronted by disagreement so radical as this is to such evidence of the author's intention as can be discovered outside the novel.[1]

Critics who share Professor Schorer's Lawrentian conception of human nature may well be right that in real life men who demonstrate the "fantastic [sexual] failure" of Dowell's life with Florence inevitably have "mind[s] not quite in balance," that the judgments of such men are the "weirdest absurdity, the final, total blindness of infatuation, and self-infatuation." For better or for worse, however, Ford did not hold this view. From his marriage to Elsie Martindale to his final union with Janice Biala, and from his telling Elsie that "du bist die Ruhe" to his telling Janice Biala that

> Your Dante's aura was unmerited
> Till he met his Béatricë . . . So he says
> And the tale is good enough. Thus set it down
> For us. . . .

everything he did in his life and everything he said shows that what Dowell says about passion is not intended as ironic exposure of Dowell's neurotic personality but is what Ford thought true.

> Of the question of the sex instinct I know very little [Dowell says, not meaning he understands less than most men about it but that no man of intelligence pontificates on the subject] and I do not think that it counts for very much in a really great passion. . . . I don't mean to say that any great passion can exist without a desire for consummation . . . that must be taken for granted, as, in a novel, or a biography, you take it for granted that the characters have their meals with some regularity. But the real fierceness of desire, the real heat of a passion long continued and withering up the soul of a man, is the craving for identity with the woman that he loves. . . . There is no man who loves a woman that does not desire to come to her for the renewal of his courage, for the cutting asunder of his difficulties. And that will be the mainspring of his desire for her. We are all so afraid, we are all so alone, we all so need from the outside the assurance of our own worthiness to exist.[*2]

The belittlement in Dowell's comparison of the sexual act with eating is a considered expression of Ford's own judgment in the matter. He thought the romantic deification of the sex act was nonsense. This was also Edward Ashburnham's view. For his declaration of love to Nancy Rufford, he "was very careful to assure [Dowell] that at that time there was no physical motive. . . . No, it was simply [a matter] of her effect on the moral side of his life. . . . " In his blunter way Christopher Tietjens takes the same view of the sex act. "You seduced a young woman in order to be able to

---

[*]"To put the matter exaggeratedly for the sake of clearness," Ford says of Dante in *The March of Literature*, "the serious Italian writer considered that spiritual love alone could be dignified by the name of that passion, the sexual act having no more to do with it than eating or drinking."

finish your talks with her. You could not do that without living with her. You could not live with her without seducing her; but that was the by-product. The point is that you can't otherwise talk ... [can't have] the intimate conversation that means the final communion of your souls." "[Ford] made Dowell proper, extremely proper," Harold Loeb says. "And Ford was like that."[3]

There is a certain dramatic exaggeration about the representation of the innocence that allows Dowell to play the role of male nurse so earnestly for the twelve years of his marriage with Florence. Part of this exaggeration was Ford's alone—a miscalculation, if one pleases. Ford wanted to suggest how fantastic the private lives people lead, behind the orderly appearances of their public lives, really are. People "will talk about rain, about the opera, about the moral aspects of the selling of Old Masters to the New Republic, and those conversations will convey to your mind that the quiet talkers are living in an atmosphere of horror, of bankruptcy, of passion hopeless as the Dies Irae"; a modern novel, he thought, must somehow convey that curious "balancing of the mind between the great outlines and the petty details" that characterizes modern life.

> In the afternoon [as he once put it, clearly thinking specifically of how he himself played golf with Masterman while Elsie destroyed his reputation in *The Throne* trial], whilst the Courts or the Stock Exchange or some woman up in town are sending you to the devil, you play a foursome.... The sky is blue; you joke about the hardness of the greens.... You ... make the approach shot of your life whilst you are joking about the other fellow's necktie ... though he knows, and you know, and they all know you know, that by the second of next month not a soul there will talk to you or play with you. So you finish the match three up and you walk into the club house and pick up an illustrated paper [called, perhaps, *The Throne*].... [4]

For the dramatic exaggeration Ford used to emphasize this point he had more excuse than many critics grant him. Unconsummated marriages were not unknown to the Edwardian world and it was not merely Ford's opinion that "Americans, you know, can envisage such unions without blinking." No one then supposed such marriages proved the participants hopeless hysterics. Sylvia and Christopher Tietjens, for example, "lived for years" together "in conditions of chastity," after Sylvia's fling with Perowne. All through that time Sylvia nursed "a madly vindictive passion for [Christopher's] person. A physical passion at any rate." Nevertheless, "They hadn't slept together." The model hero of American Edwardians, Richard Harding Davis, lived with his first wife in an unconsummated marriage. Ford believed with some reason that he was making this dramatic detail more plausible by making Dowell an American. In any event, it is absurdly unhistorical—like a rigid Marxist's interpretation of *Pride and Prejudice*—to assume that Ford believed conduct like Dowell's showed a man was blindly neurotic.[5]

Part of this dramatic exaggeration is, however, Dowell's. By the time Dowell came to write down his story he knew how ludicrous his marriage with Florence had been, just as he knew how ludicrous it was that Edward and Leonora did not know "for perhaps a couple of years after [their marriage] ... how children are produced." He sums up the view of his marriage that he held when he began telling his story by saying: "Well, there you have the position, as clear as I can make it—the husband an ignorant fool, the wife a cold sensualist with imbecile fears. ... " But because he had himself once been that fool and was far from certain he was better off for having now ceased to be, he could sympathize with him. Though his judgment of his own foolishness and of Edward's is always clear-cut, he treats himself and Edward—and all the rest of the decent people in the book, all of whom are also made fools of between their passionate unconscious selves and their idealistic conscious selves—with a delicate mixture of pity and amusement.[6]

This is the governing feeling of the novel, exactly as it was of Ford's view of his own life whenever he looked at himself disinterestedly.

> From the earliest times that I can remember the first maxim that was impressed upon [me] was that of *Mens sana in corpore sano*. My second maxim was *Fiat justitia, ruat coelum*. Armed, in fact, with these two guides to life, as if the one had been a shining spear and the other an impenetrable buckler, I was prepared to face journeys into an unknown Berwickshire and explorations of the precipitous Cheviots. On the one hand, as long as I got myself into condition, neither the steepest crags nor the longest rides need have any perils for me; on the other hand, as long as my attitude to every human vicissitude that could arise was that of an absolute "correctness," I had nothing to fear from life.[7]

This is precisely the tone of Dowell's treatment of all the admirable characters in *The Good Soldier*. The conditioned, conscious self of each one of them puzzles over the recalcitrant facts of experience in a way that is at once pitiful and absurd, trying to explain these facts according to his training. Thus Nancy's conscious self, reading the account of the Brand divorce in the newspaper, found the whole thing ridiculous; "she could not understand why a chart of the bedroom accommodations at Christchurch Old Hall should be produced in court."

And yet the whole effect of that reading upon Nancy was mysterious, terrifying, evil. . . . She asked God how He could permit such things to be. And she was more certain that Edward did not love Leonora and that Leonora hated Edward. Perhaps, then, Edward loved someone else. It was unthinkable.

If he could love someone else than Leonora, her fierce, unknown heart suddenly spoke in her side, why could it not be herself?[8]

Or there is the way Dowell brought disaster on himself by becoming so preoccupied with getting Florence down that rope ladder the night they eloped that he "received her advances [in the bedroom] with a certain amount of absence of mind"; the result was that Florence, the experienced sensualist, decided to stick with Jimmy. This was not just a grim joke on Dowell; it was also a joke on Florence, who soon learned to scorn Jimmy and to see that, next to Edward Ashburnham, Dowell was about the most attractive man around. By the time she did, she was inescapably committed to her lie about her heart, but she still could not resist flirting with Dowell; "I think, perhaps, the enigmatic smile with which she used to look back at me over her shoulder when she went into the bathing place was a sort of invitation. . . . It was as if she were saying: 'I am going in here. I am going to stand so stripped and white and straight—and you are a man. . . . ' " When that happened, Dowell was still too innocent to recognize the invitation. But when he told about it he was not.[9]

Dowell was an American—that is, a very naïve—version of Edward Ashburnham. " . . . I loved Edward Ashburnham," he says, " . . . because he was just myself. If I had had the courage and the virility and possibly also the physique of Edward Ashburnham I should, I fancy, have done much what he did." Ford had experimented before, less successfully, with this doubling of his hero, with Robert Grimshaw and Dudley Leicester in *A Call* and with Mr. Blood and Mr. Fleight in *Mr. Fleight.* In both cases, we have one active, decisive, confident man and one passive, indecisive, unsure one. The second does not differ from the first in essential nature, but, like Dudley Leicester, he is naïvely upright and at the same time unconfident enough to be easily governed by strong natures like Etta Stackpole; or, like Mr. Fleight, he is dreamily impractical and easily maneuvered by clever ladies like the "Baroness" into situations he would not have chosen but feels obliged to accept. Ford saw that a single hero could not easily be made to display the characteristics of both Mr. Blood and Mr. Fleight, but he knew himself to be, at one time and another, both.[10]

The Good Soldier depends for its "heart" on the fact that Edward Ashburnham is the "hallucinated" Ford's passionately sympathetic, idealized conception of himself, of the simplicity of his motives, the goodness of his intentions, the "seriousness" of his conduct. Many of the things Edward does Ford only dreamed of doing or imagined he had done. But there is nothing in Edward's nature that Ford did not believe part of his own. There are occasional traces in the novel of the actual circumstances of his life that he is translating into the terms of its story, notably in the case of Florence. Much of the time, however, as in so many of Ford's anecdotes, the facts of Edward's situation have been changed, but the conception of Edward's self is an exact representation of Ford's conception of himself.

Ford saw himself as an innocently idealistic, well-intentioned English gentleman, too well-bred to enjoy ostentatious luxury but with a gentleman's instinctive sense of the right thing, whose only pleasure in life was to show feudal generosity to his inferiors and chivalric gallantry to the women whose sympathy was a necessity to him. But he knew he alternated between extremes of self-assurance and self-doubt. In the first mood he was sure of his ability to live heroically, and then he plunged eagerly into difficult projects like *The English Review* or daydreamed of making a brilliant political success like Mr. Blood's getting Mr. Fleight elected to the House.[11]

In the second mood he felt he was "the patient but extremely stupid donkey" of his father's judgment, hopelessly incapable of meeting H. G. Wells in repartee, reduced to a kind of cataleptic incompetence by scenes, and all too likely to meet the cross-examination of old ladies "like a jelly at bay." In this mood he was uncertain of his talent and easily convinced that a cruel world was ready to treat him as an old horse. At worst, he would collapse into neurasthenia. He would then be filled with all sorts of paranoid suspicions and obsessive anxieties, as Dudley Leicester was after he received the mysterious telephone call. At best, he would see himself, as does Mr. Fleight, driven by passions he did not understand. "I was as timid as you will," as Dowell says, "but in that matter [of Florence] I was like a chicken that is determined to get across the road in front of an automobile."[12]

Like Mr. Fleight, who unaccountably finds himself committed to the Baroness di Sonnino, this unconfident Ford regularly found himself in situations incongruously unlike anything he had anticipated; out of a combination of conscience and hatred of scenes, he would meet these situations stoically, proudly anxious to take what he got for doing what he had wanted though clearly aware of what a fool he looked. Then, instead of sharply snubbing anyone who doubted that *The English Review* would be a *succès fou*, he behaved as David Garnett and D. H. Lawrence described when he awoke from his dream of love in a Provençal heaven and found himself living the petty social life of South Lodge with Violet Hunt.[13]

This second aspect of Ford's nature was evident only to those who knew him well because he concealed it beneath his apparently self-possessed, off-hand manner. Even when he was most tortured by neurasthenia, he could appear, as he said in discussing Conrad's impression of him, "large, blond, phlegmatic *on the surface*." Stella Bowen saw clearly what lay beneath that surface:

> He was all too ready, anyhow, to feel discouraged when things went wrong, and he found so many reasons for feeling frightened. . . .
>
> Poor Ford! There was something about the sight of his large patient fingers tapping at the keys, that I always found infinitely touching. He was a writer—a complete writer—and nothing but a writer. And he never even felt sure of his gift!
>
> He needed more reassurance than anyone I have ever met.

Harold Loeb saw it too:

> . . . the impression that never left me was of a sensitive, emotionally tumultuous spirit hiding behind an impassive gentle face and an imperturbable manner. . . .
>
> Ford . . . [concentrated] in Dowell his own weaknesses, in particular his ineffectiveness and ingenuousness. . . . [He] attributed to Ashburnham . . . his generosity and altruism. . . .
>
> When I read "The Flurried Years" . . . it seemed to me quite a matter of course that [Violet Hunt] should suppose as I had that Dowell and Ashburnham were two aspects of Ford's own character.[14]

Dowell's conscious self, then, is like Edward Ashburnham's—high-minded, innocent, idealistic. Edward was fairly promptly awakened—by the nursemaid he kissed in the third-class railway carriage—to the realities of the unconscious self that underlay his conscious self. Dowell was not. But Dowell's unconscious self, if he "had not the hot passions of . . . Europeans," and was, "because of my American origin . . . fainter" than Edward's, was perfectly normal. Until he ceased, sometime before she died, to care for

Florence at all, she was to him an "unattained mistress" for whose sake he flashed out in rage at his beloved servant Julius and struck him because Julius dropped Florence's medicine case. He hated Florence "with such a hatred that I would not spare her an eternity of loneliness" when he discovered that she had tricked him into "twelve years of the repression of my instincts." "Perhaps," he says with quiet bitterness, "she thought that I should not mind ["the part of a male nurse"]," for, deeply as he had hated that role, he could see how Florence, the experienced sensualist, might have misread his character in much the way some critics have. He hated Leonora, too, when she lost that passion which made it impossible for her to become Rodney Bayham's mistress just to have "a good time." He sympathized with Edward's extravagant outbursts of passion as no passionless man possibly could have. When Leonora just failed to expose Florence after the scene in the Schloss at Marberg, he expressed great relief—not because he had been spared a confrontation with a passion he was not equal to but, on the contrary, because he feared the power of his own passions. "If my suspicion that Leonora was jealous of Florence had been the reason [Leonora] gave for her outburst I should have turned upon Florence with the maddest kind of rage." "Forgive me for writing of these monstrous things in this frivolous manner," he says to the reader as he looks back at the events he has lived through. "If I did not I should break down and cry."[15]

As a participant in the events of *The Good Soldier*, Dowell has his limitations and blindnesses, just as the rest of the characters do. But the Dowell who is telling the story knows everything that Ford does and thinks all the things that Ford did about human affairs. The ironic wit of *The Good Soldier's* style depends, not on a discrepancy between the narrator's attitude and Ford's, but on a discrepancy between Dowell's attitude as a participant in the events and Dowell's attitude as a narrator of them. All the perception, the tolerance, the humility that recognizes the limitations of its own understanding; all the poetic wit of the book's figures of speech; all the powerful ironies of the narration; all these things are Dowell's.

It is he who notes "the profusion of [Edward's] cases, all of pigskin and stamped with his initials" and remarks that "it must have needed a whole herd of the Gaderene swine to make up his outfit," because, by the time he tells us this, he has learned that these cases are the money-oriented, Nonconformist Leonora's idea of the right thing, not Edward's. Edward hated status symbols and thought of even the D. S. O. as "a sort of a thing they give grocers who've honourably supplied the troops with adulterated coffee in wartime." It is Dowell who tells us, without the italics that emphasize his irony, "I believe that for the twelve years [Florence's] life lasted, after the storm that *seemed* irretrievably to have weakened her heart—I don't believe that for one minute she was out of my sight, *except when she was safely tucked up in bed . . .* "—with Jimmy. It is he who tells us—apparently apropos of nothing but Florence's ghastly dehumanized culture-chatter—the story of "that fellow Peire Vidal" that displays so perfectly the precise mixture of absurdity and sadness that Dowell realizes is displayed by the story he is about to tell, "the saddest story I have ever heard," as he calls it in his very first sentence (which is what Ford wanted to call the story too). The affair Dowell is describing in *The Good Soldier* was "half-jocular and altogether merciless," and the story of Peire Vidal, as he says, is at once "funny" and "full of love" and terrible; and that is the way he tells it. "So, out of compliment to [La Louve]—the things people do when they're in love!—[Peire] dressed himself up in wolf-skins and went up into the Black Mountains" where he was torn to pieces by the shepherds' dogs, much as Edward Ashburnham is torn to pieces by Leonora and Nancy. "Isn't that a story?" It is, just as is Edward Ashburnham's, except perhaps that Nauheim and Branshaw are not Provence, "where even the saddest stories are gay," not just horribly absurd.[16]

It is surely a mistake to set down as a victim of "sluggish insanity" the man who could say of himself, when bad roads disturbed Florence, that imaginary heart patient who was disturbing the real hearts of all of them with her monkey-like sexual meddling, that "I would grumble like a stockbroker whose conversations over the telephone are incommoded by the ringing of bells from a city church." It is not the "dull hysteria of sloth" that makes Dowell say, with bitter amusement at the fool he was to believe Florence when she locked him out of her bedroom at ten at night, "And at ten o'clock of the next morning there she would come out the door of her room as fresh as Venus rising from any of the couches that are mentioned in Greek legends." It is only by ascribing the wit of such figures to Ford and assuming he means us to think Dowell fell into it by accident that anyone can suppose Dowell the narrator is unaware of the realities of his story.[17]

Of this narrator Ford makes very remarkable use. As Robie Macauley has said, "[Ford] ranges over the whole field of memory, selecting events or sequences of events from all the tenses of memory—the past, the perfect, the pluperfect and the 'novelistic present'—and fits them together so that they will supplement and comment on each other as images in a poem do." Later, Ford liked to say that he and Conrad had invented this method of narration years before solely to give their narrative verisimilitude.

We wanted the Reader . . . to be hypnotised into thinking . . . that he was listening to a simple and in no way brilliant narrator who was telling—not writing—a true story. . . .

And it is in that way that life really presents itself to us . . . dallying backwards and forwards, now in 1890, now in 1869; in 1902—and then again in 1869—as forgotten episodes came up in the minds of simple narrators. . . . Your Phraseology will be the Real thing in *mots justes,* for just so long as they remain within his probable vocabulary. There will be no jewels five words long. . . .

It is more than likely Ford and Conrad discussed narrators and diction in these terms, especially in relation to "Youth" and "Heart of Darkness." But the fact is that Ford struggled along through the whole period of his collaboration with Conrad and for five years afterward trying to express his sense of life without either narrator or time shift; it is only in 1913, with the writing of *The Good Soldier,* that he begins to use them. This theory about the narrative method of *The Good Soldier* was developed after he had worked it out in practice; if his talks with Conrad contributed something to both the practice and the theory, they determined neither.[18]

Broadly speaking, *The Good Soldier*'s story comes to us in chronological order; that is, Dowell focuses on three "acts" (some of which are subdivided into scenes) that he describes in temporal sequence—the meeting of the Dowells and Ashburnhams at Nauheim and the visit to Marburg on August 4, 1904; Florence's suicide at Nauheim on August 4, 1913; Edward's refusal to seduce Nancy and his putting her on the train in the second week of December, 1913. But within that chronological frame Dowell ranges backwards and forwards, ostensibly in the easy way of a man telling things as they come into his mind while he sits "at one side of the fireplace of a country cottage, with a sympathetic soul opposite me" ("From time to time we shall get up and go to the door and look out at the great moon and say: 'Why, it is nearly as bright as in Provence!' And then we shall come back to the fireside, with just the touch of a sigh because we are not in that Provence where even the saddest stories are gay"). Dowell's casualness is Ford's means of bringing the significant particulars into dramatic relation. The most obvious effect of this procedure is the surprise with which we learn the shocking facts of the story and are made to feel unexpected sympathies, as when—before we have learned anything about Edward and Florence—Dowell says: "But just think of that poor wretch . . . I, who have surely the right, beg you to think of that poor wretch. . . . There is no other way to think of it. None. I have the right

to say it, since for years he was my wife's lover, since he killed her.... "
This effect can be reversed, as when—after we have known it for some time
—Dowell the narrator shows us Dowell the participant learning the truth
about Florence because Leonora assumes he has known it since the scene at
the Schloss and says, "And isn't it odd to think that if your wife hadn't been
my husband's mistress, you would probably never have been here at all?"
and then adds, "I think it was stupid of Florence to commit suicide."[19]

But the most pervasive form of irony Dowell the narrator uses is to
speak in such a way that we can take what he says as he would have meant
it at the time the event occurred and also as he means it now that he
understands what really happened. That is how he is speaking when he says
Florence was never out of his sight "except when she was safely tucked up
in bed." This kind of irony is pervasive because it is Dowell's means of
keeping before us the double perspective of the novel, the simultaneous
awareness of what the experience was like for a participant as it was actually
occurring and of what the full knowledge of hindsight shows it to have been.
Dowell is aware of the comedy of this discrepancy; but he knows too its
sadness, and often suggests it, as when—at the start of the novel, before we
know the story—he tells us how beautiful life at Branshaw was and then
suddenly adds, "And that poor devil [Edward] beside me was in an agony.
Absolute, hopeless, dumb agony such as passes the mind of man to imagine."[20]

Finally there is the irony that results from Dowell's having written
down his story over a considerable period during which he was thinking
hard about its meaning. In order that we may grasp this irony, Dowell is at
some pains to make clear to us how long he has been writing. Halfway
through the book (with what is, on Ford's part, an ironic apology), Dowell
says, "I have, I am aware, told this story in a very rambling way.... [But]
you have the facts for the trouble of finding them.... " The facts are that
Dowell began to write down his story at Branshaw Manor approximately six
months after his arrival there. Since he reached Branshaw about December
1, 1913, this means he began to write about May 1, 1914.[21]

By the time he reaches the composition of Part IV it is October, 1914,
and during the six months he has been thinking over his story he has come
to see Florence more clearly: "I may, in what follows, be a little hard on
Florence," he says, "but you must remember that I have been writing away
at this story now for six months and reflecting longer and longer upon these
affairs." Between the writing of Parts IV and V, Dowell then tells us, "a full
eighteen months" passed; Part V was therefore written about May, 1916.

During those eighteen months Leonora has settled in with Rodney Bayham, and that rabbity fellow has, according to his kind, got her pregnant. Leonora has thus declined into a "perfectly normal, virtuous, and slightly deceitful heroine," and Dowell, who had said in May, 1914, when he started to write, that "I loved Leonora always and, to-day, I would very cheerfully lay down my life, what is left of it, in her service," now says, "I cannot conceal from myself the fact that I now dislike Leonora."[22]

It is by gradually increasing these shocks to the understanding as the narrative progresses that Ford creates his *progression d'effet.* Since Dowell, the narrator, knows from the beginning everything that has happened, what he tells us is less a gradual revelation of what happened, the emergence in time of events that show the meaning of the novel, than the gradual uncovering of a meaning that has been there from the start. What the novel involves the reader in is not so much "what happens" as "what it means." "The action," as Mr. Hynes puts it, " . . . is not the sequence of passionate gestures which in another novel we would call the plot, but rather the action of the narrator's mind as it gropes for the meaning, the reality of what has occurred." We circle the situation more and more tightly, as in a whirlpool or —as Ezra Pound would have called it—a vortex, until we reach the blank center. This pattern is deliberately broken at the very end by the false-naïve device of Dowell's saying "It suddenly occurs to me that I have forgotten to say how Edward met his death," and then going on to tell us how he did, so that the book's most grimly comic disaster (that "quite . . . small penknife"!) can come after the contrasting pictures of Nancy sitting in blank perfection at the dinner table and Leonora—"to cheer you up"—discovering Bayham can save money by buying his clothes ready-made.[23]

Ford had wanted to call *The New Humpty-Dumpty* *The Dark Forest,* because in it he was fumbling toward the view of both society and the individual life that he succeeds in defining in *The Good Soldier,* the view that beneath the conscious, social self of everyone there is a "mysterious and unconscious self," "as if one had a dual personality, the one being entirely unconscious of the other." The "inner soul" breaks through into the conscious mind only in moments of great stress, when it takes over and directs men's lives in ways that are by no means all good. Perhaps the most striking instance of this kind of eruption is when Dowell hears himself saying, "Now I can marry the girl." His conscious self had not had the faintest inkling that he loved Nancy Rufford until that moment when he was shocked into knowledge by Florence's death.[24]

In much the same way Edward is astonished to find himself declaring his love for Nancy. "He had missed her when she went away to her convent-school; he had been glad when she had returned. But of more than that he had been totally unconscious. . . . The real point was his entire unconscious-ness. . . . It had not even come into his head that the taboo which extended around her [as his 'daughter'] was not inviolable. And then, suddenly, that —." Nancy's love for Edward bursts through when her conscious belief that marriage, being a sacrament, makes love eternal is disturbed by the news-paper's account of the Brand divorce. Leonora cracks when she ceases to go to confession "because she was afraid her spiritual advisers would blame her for deceiving [Dowell]." "You may put it that, having been cut off from the restraints of her religion, for the first time in her life, she acted along the lines of her instinctive desires" and tortured Edward and Nancy.[25]

Here Dowell makes one of the novel's crucial points. "I do not know whether to think that, in that she was no longer herself; or that, having let loose the bonds of her standards, her conventions, her traditions, she was being, for the first time, her own natural self." Dowell's sympathies, like Ford's, are with genuinely passional under selves—Edward's, Nancy's, his own. "Well," he says ironically of Florence's claim to be the victim of an uncontrollable passion, "I always say that an overmastering passion is a good excuse for feelings. You cannot help them." He means what he says of passion, though he does not believe Florence capable of it. Nevertheless, he also believes that people go to pieces, "deteriorate," when the unconscious passional self overrides the conscious self's conception of right conduct. It cannot be helped, but it does as much damage as does the inhibition of genuine passion by an inhuman conception of right conduct. "Pride and reserve are not the only things in life; perhaps they are not even the best things. But if they happen to be your particular virtues you will go all to pieces if you let them go. And Leonora let them go"—and ended up a conventional woman in the bad sense. But Edward, "drunk or sober . . . stuck to what was demanded by convention and by the traditions of his house," and died a conventional man in the heroic sense.[26]

Dowell can now see the absurdity of his own high-mindedness; he knows well enough it allowed Florence to make a fool of him. But that does not persuade him it is good to live without such high-mindedness; "surely, surely," he says, "these delusions are necessary to keep us going." There is grim comedy in Nancy Rufford, who has been tossed like a shuttlecock between her conscious mind's convent-trained view of things and her uncon-scious passion for Edward, sitting like a well-behaved child at the dinner table and saying, "*Credo in unum Deum Omnipotentem.*" But Dowell is not suggesting Nancy would have been better without that faith. "Even when she was mad Nancy could behave herself" is true irony; it cuts equally sharply both ways.[27]

Ford makes the same point about society as a whole; "that long, tranquil life" the Ashburnhams and the Dowells lived at Nauheim "was just stepping a minuet. . . . The mob may sack Versailles; the Trianon may fall, but surely the minuet—the minuet itself is dancing itself away" forever in some heaven, because it was so beautiful. At the same time he knows all too well that, because of their passional under selves, that life at Nauheim "wasn't a minuet . . . it was a prison—a prison full of screaming hysterics. . . . "

This is the divided world in which, carefully conditioned to ignorance of themselves and one another according to the traditions of their society, Ford's four noble characters are set to make their ways. Edward Ashburnham, who is Ford's image of his successful self, was the only one who might have made a go of it. Exactly as Ford believed himself to be in his own essential nature, Edward "was really a very simple soul—very simple." "He was just a normal man and very much of a sentimentalist." His natural impulses coincided with the highest standards of his society almost too well, so that "He did nothing for fun except what he considered to be his work in life." Edward's work consisted primarily in protecting his tenants at Branshaw as if he were their feudal lord and caring for the men who served under him in the army as if he were their father; for him the bonds of sentiment, not money and status, were the essential things. In his relations with women he was very simple and very serious. Emotionally he was deeply dependent on them. "He imagined that no man can satisfactorily accomplish his life's work without [the] loyal and whole-hearted co-operation of the woman he lives with." He felt a chivalric obligation to them which his idealistic nature would never allow him to think was inapplicable. This feeling often drove him to act with great seriousness in ridiculous ways.[28]

If he indulged himself in "long conversations of an intimate kind" with Florence it gave "that woman an irrevocable claim—to be seduced," and for Edward "to enjoy a woman's favours, made him feel that she had a bond on him for life. . . . Psychologically it meant that he could not have a mistress without falling violently in love with her. He was a serious person," as well as a very simple one—so simple that he even tried to convince La Dolciquita, a good-natured, completely unsentimental courtesan, "that he regarded it as . . . his duty . . . to cherish her and even to love her—for life. In return for her sacrifice [of her virtue] he would do that. In return, again, for her honourable love she would listen forever to the accounts of his estate. That was how he figured it out."[29]

Their parents married this man off to the daughter of an impoverished Irish Catholic family. Leonora was a woman of real distinction, of nobility of a kind, but it was not Edward's kind. He immensely admired her, but she had "not for him a touch of magnetism." To her, with her "Nonconformist" Catholic temperament and her girlhood experience of poverty, Edward's performance of the "dut[ies] of his rank and station," which was all that made life meaningful to him, was simply feckless extravagance. She became sure he "was riding hot-foot to ruin" and "it worried her dreadfully; she lay awake nights." His attitude was as incomprehensible to her as hers was to him, for "whereas his own traditions were entirely collective, his wife was a sheer individualist." Leonora loved Edward passionately but his conduct seemed to her "megalomania." Edward thought Leonora admirable—self-disciplined and wonderfully efficient—but "physically and mentally cold . . . even . . . actually wicked and mean."[30]

Edward, though nominally an Anglican, had the temperament of those heretical Catholics who are descended from "the Troubadours and . . . the Albigenses" of Roman Provence that was "salutarily latitudinarian . . . without prejudices as without puritanism." Leonora was Irish Catholic and so had the quintessential Nonconformist temperament. Florence Dowell, who thinks it is Luther's Protest that has made Edward "honest, sober, industrious, provident, and clean-lived," insults Leonora by saying the Irish Catholics lack these qualities; she could not have done so had Leonora not been more Protestant than Catholic in temperament. By what is for Ford a happily ironic coincidence, Luther and his friends had met to sign their Protest under the protection of "Ludwig the Courageous [who] wanted to have three wives at once—in which he differed from Henry VIII, who wanted them one after the other, and this caused a good deal of trouble." "I'm not," Dowell remarks, "really interested in these facts but they have a bearing on my story," an indirect one not unlike that of Peire Vidal's career. The Lutheran view of humanity makes no provision for the impulse Dowell recognizes is in every man, including himself as well as Edward Ashburnham, to have several wives. "In my fainter sort of way," he says, "I seem to perceive myself following the lines of Edward Ashburnham. I suppose that I should really like to be a polygamist; with Nancy, and with Leonora, and with Maisie Maidan, and possibly even with Florence." It is part of the comedy of idealism's anxious irrelevance that men should seek to justify their polygamous impulses by some sort of hairsplitting distinction between whether you have all the women at once or one after the other and so cause "a good deal of trouble"; Dowell notes with amusement that Ludwig the

Courageous and Henry VIII in the end became allies. In *The Good Soldier* neither the trivial Protestantism of the dominant ethos nor the Nonconformist Irish Catholicism of Leonora takes the workable view of the Provençal Catholic God in Ford's "On Heaven," that jovial fellow who claps unhappy lovers on the back with a "great laugh," or stops by the café tables of happy ones to speak a kind word. Neither does because neither has any conception of the sentiment that governs truly Catholic temperaments like Edward's.[31]

With her unconquerable conviction that Edward, in his heart, saw life as she did, Leonora set out "to rule with a rod of iron" "the man whom she loved passionately," to destroy in him the very qualities that made her love him. Edward's financially ridiculous conduct over La Dolciquita gave her her opportunity. She took over the management of his affairs and began recouping Edward's losses so that he could return to Branshaw and live in the manner she believed becoming to his position in life—"and there was an end of Edward as the good landlord and father of his people." She set Edward's land steward to squeezing every penny out of his tenants; she got Edward transferred to Burma and rented Branshaw Manor; she sold two Vandyke portraits of Edward's ancestors. "They were," she thought, "just frills to the Ashburnham vanity. Edward cried for two days over the disappearance of his ancestors . . . but it did not teach her anything. . . . " " . . . she could not see that he could have anything against her. She left him his liberty; she was starving herself to build up his fortunes; she allowed herself none of the joys of femininity—no dresses, no jewels—hardly even any friendships, for fear they should cost money."[32]

She tried hard to be magnanimous, for there was nothing mean-minded about Leonora. "Indeed, in a way, she did him very well—but it was not his way." Thinking that he would delight to see how the estate was recovering, she "imagined the cheerful device of letting him see the accounts." It was torture to him, especially when he discovered that old Mumford—they had first quarreled over Edward's generosity to old Mumford—had been ejected from his farm and given a rent-free cottage and ten shillings a week. "Leonora considered that she had been unusually generous to old Mr. Mumford"; Edward was so disturbed that he fell for consolation into the sympathetic arms of Mrs. Basil, to Leonora's uncomprehending grief. "Why, she asked herself again and again, did none of the good deeds that she did for her husband ever come through to him, or appear to him as good deeds? By what trick of mania could not he let her be as good to him as Mrs. Basil was? . . . She could not understand how Edward could go on and on maundering over Mrs. Basil." Nor could she understand his heroism in jumping overboard from the troopship to save private soldiers; she could only imagine he was trying to commit suicide. "Leonora ought never to have been on that troopship; but she got there somehow, as an economy." She would not let Edward get himself transferred to the Transvaal. "It would," as Dowell says ironically, "have done him a great deal of good to get killed. But Leonora would not let him; she had heard awful stories of the extravagance of the hussar regiment in war-time."[33]

Leonora's great moment came when she was able to tell Edward that the estate had been brought back to its original condition. "She thought that he cared very much about the expenditure of an income of five thousand a year and that the fact that she had done so much for him would rouse in him some affection for her.... He hated her when he found that she proposed to set him up as the Lord of Branshaw again—as a sort of dummy lord, in swaddling clothes." Leonora "saw life as a perpetual sex-battle between husbands who desire to be unfaithful to their wives, and wives who desire to recapture their husbands in the end. That was her sad and modest view of matrimony.... The lot of women was patience and patience and again patience—*ad majorem Dei gloriam*—until the appointed day, if God saw fit, she should have her reward.... She would show, in fact, that in an unfaithful world one Catholic woman had succeeded in retaining the fidelity of her husband. And she thought she had come near her desires." Then Florence came along.[34]

Florence was a being wholly incapable of passion; the nearest she could come to it was the shriveled commitment of a primitive superstition that "forced her to certain acts, as if she had been hypnotized." For her, sex was not the consummation of passion; she had no passion to consummate; it was merely the physical lust of a "cold sensualist." In place of the pride of Edward and Leonora she had vanity, the vanity that made her long "to get to Fordingbridge and be a county lady in the home of her ancestors" and "to leave this world a little brighter by the passage of her brief life" by working up the textbook information and the recommended moral poses with which she filled her endless chatter.

> She would tell [Edward] the story of Hamlet; explain the form of a symphony, humming the first and second subjects to him, and so on; she would explain to him the difference between Arm[i]nians and Erastians; or she would give him a short lecture on the early history of the United States. And it was done in a way well calculated to arrest a young attention. Did you ever read Mrs. Markham? Well, it was like that....[35]

She liked, of course, to combine this display of her elevated nature with the satisfaction of her lust in a way flattering to her vanity, that is, with the most presentable man available. So she went after Edward Ashburnham.

She cut out poor dear Edward from sheer vanity; she meddled between him and Leonora from a sheer, imbecile spirit of district visiting. Do you understand that, whilst she was Edward's mistress, she was perpetually trying to reunite him to his wife? She would gabble on to Leonora about forgiveness—treating the subject from the bright, American point of view. And Leonora would treat her like the whore she was.

To Leonora, this seemed like the end; "she could not see how, after that, Edward could return to her—after a vulgar intrigue with a vulgar woman"; "she so despised Florence that she would have preferred it to be a parlourmaid. There are very decent parlour-maids."[36]

Because Florence had no natural feelings, she could not know for herself the kind of man who would do her credit and allow her to play the role of the great lady swept away by an overmastering passion. All she really felt was lust, and for that Jimmy was quite satisfactory. But when, with her shrewd sense of how to look like a lady and satisfy the needs of her vanity, "She had arrived at figuring out the sort of low-down Bowery tough [Jimmy] was," she lived in real terror that her affair with Jimmy might become known—partly because of her overmastering vanity, partly because of her primitive fear of Dowell, whom she had seen fly at Julius in a rage for a trivial offense. So, when her vanity was struck the double blow of discovering that Edward truly loved Nancy Rufford and that Dowell had learned the truth about her and Jimmy; and when she was struck this double blow on August 4, the day she had learned superstitiously to feel was crucial in her life, she killed herself. She was careful, before she did so, to lie "quite respectably arranged, unlike Mrs. Maidan, on her bed," "because of course she was always play-acting," even in death. Play-acting at being human was the nearest she could get to being so. "Florence was a personality of paper . . . she represented a real human being with a heart, with feelings, with sympathies, and with emotions only as a bank note represents a certain quantity of gold. . . . She wasn't real; she was just a mass of talk out of guide-books, of drawings out of fashion-plates." When she died "She just went completely out of existence, like yesterday's paper."[37]

What *The Good Soldier* is showing us is that both within the private selves of people and in the relations between them that make a society there is a terrible division. " . . . to me, living [at Branshaw Manor]," says Dowell, "enveloped with the charm of the quiet and ordered living ... to me who was hourly with them they appeared like tender, ordered, and devoted people, smiling, absenting themselves at the proper intervals; driving me to meets—just good people! How the devil—how the devil do they do it?"— for he knows all too well now what was going on beneath that beautiful surface. It is this conflict that makes Edward's drive with Nancy to the station at once heroic and appalling to Dowell—that makes, indeed, all heroic lives seem to him appalling. One may live in innocent ignorance of what goes on beneath the surface of life, and then one is likely to be maneuvered into being the male nurse for a cold sensualist who pretends to be an invalid; or one may understand everything and be maneuvered into being the male nurse for a well-behaved idiot. No wonder Dowell says in all seriousness that as long as you do not know the apple is rotten you possess a goodly apple: he understands very well that knowing which apples are rotten changes nothing. "Is there then," he asks at the end, "any terrestrial paradise where, amidst the whispering of the olive-leaves [of Provence], people can be with whom they like and have what they like and take their ease in shadows and coolness? Or are all men's lives like the lives of us good people ... broken, tumultuous, agonized, and unromantic lives, periods punctuated by screams, by imbecilities, by deaths, by agonies? Who the devil knows?"[38]

Dowell has no doubts, as Ford had not, about the ordered refinement of upper-class Edwardian life. "Mind," he says, "I am not saying that this is not the most desirable type of life in the world; that it is not an almost unreasonably high standard." But even he finds its rituals irksome; very rare roast beef is nauseating, he thinks; brandy is disagreeable when what you really want is Kümmel; cold baths are nasty. And the whole ritual might have been designed to prevent people's ever knowing more about one another than that they live this ritual: "you never really get an inch deeper than the things I have catalogued." "But these things have to be done; it is the cock that the whole of this society owes to Aesculapius."[39]

There was certainly, in the Edwardian world Ford was contemplating, some radical discontinuity between what Dowell calls the "natural inclinations" of people's unconscious selves and the trained habits of their conscious selves that made them "good people" and that made their society "the proudest and the safest of all the beautiful and safe things that God has permitted the mind of men to frame." Perhaps there always has been such a discontinuity; perhaps there always will be. Perhaps the more beautifully ordered and successfully disciplined the "parade" of civilization becomes, the more destructive of men's natural inclinations it also becomes.

> O what if gardens where the peacock strays
> With delicate feet upon old terraces,
> Or else all Juno from an urn displays
> Before the indifferent garden dieties;
> O what if levelled lawns and gravelled ways
> Where slippered Contemplation finds his ease
> And Childhood a delight for every sense,
> But take our greatness with our violence?[40]

Chapter 2 I

In the dedication of the 1927 edition Ford says that *The Good Soldier* was not published until he was "engaged in other pursuits" (that is, in the army), but he was still in London when it appeared and missed none of the reviews; they contributed to the state of mind that led him to enlist several months later. Except for a few of them like Rebecca West's, which recognized the book's quality, they said it had a "sordid theme" and (taking Dowell's comment quite literally) that it was written "in an odd, rambling sort of way." There was also a mean-minded personal attack on Ford by "J. K. Prothero" in Chesterton's *New Witness*. It described Ford as a Jew, a stallion, and a coward. This brought Wells charging to Ford's defense. "This business ... in the *New Witness* makes me sick," he wrote Chesterton. "Some disgusting little greaser ... has been allowed to insult old F.M.H. ... His book [*The Good Soldier*] is a great book and ... the whole outbreak is so envious, so base, so cat-in-the-gutter-spitting-at-the-passer-by, that I will never let the *New Witness* into my home again."[1]

Meanwhile, Ford's relations with Violet were becoming strained. "Although [they] continued to keep up appearances by giving parties at South Lodge until ... Ford left to join his regiment, it had become apparent ... that a split was inevitable." "I found," Ford said afterwards, "that she had been entertaining at Selsey the various gentlemen whose chief claim to patriotic activities, as you know, had been the denouncing of myself to the police as a German agent & I also found that various gentlemen were stating, on her authority, various other untruths to my disadvantage.... Altho' I am entirely indifferent to what anyone says about me, Violet's course seemed to me to be so radical a disloyalty to any form of joint life that I saw no other way open than to retire from the scene."[2]

In spite of the intellectual's habitual skepticism about the dominant attitudes of his society, Ford was always subject to the influence of his environment, and the patriotism of the early years of the war worked on his Tory sense of obligation to his country to make him uncomfortable as a civilian despite his doubts about the war both as a national enterprise and as a personal career.

But Ford Madox Hueffer [Wyndham Lewis said of him at this time] looked at me with his watery-wise old elephant eyes—a little too crystal-gazing and claptrap, but he knew his stuff—and instructed me upon the very temporary nature of this hysteria. . . .

"When this War's over," he said, "nobody is going to worry, six months afterwards, what you did or didn't do in the course of it. . . . Within a year disbanded 'heroes' will be selling matches in the gutter. No one likes the ex-soldier—if you've lost a leg, more fool you!" . . .

This worldly forecast was verified to the letter.

Nevertheless, Ford told his mother, "I cannot imagine taking any other course [than enlisting]. If one has enjoyed the privileges of the ruling class of a country all one's life, there seems to be no alternative to fighting for that country if necessary." His work for Wellington House had eased his conscience for a time, but like George Heimann of *The Marsden Case,* who was also offered a propaganda job, he "was romantic. . . . It had for him to be enlistment or nothing. . . . "³

Ford also wanted to escape from a literary career that seemed to have become hopeless. He had, he thought, had his chance and failed, and the world now belonged to younger men. If he joined the army he could give up the struggle. It would be a blissful relief to do so: "I have never felt such an entire peace of mind as I have felt since I wore the King's uniform," he wrote his mother shortly after taking his commission. "It is just a matter of plain sailing doing one's duty, without any responsibilities except to one's superiors & one's men." He even expressed this feeling in print, "If not to-day, then tomorrow, I hope to be up and away to regions where I shall be precluded from uttering injunctions to find le mot juste."⁴

Early in the summer of 1915, then, he made up his mind to seek a commission. On July 30 he wrote Lucy Masterman: "You may like to know that I went around to the W[ar] O[ffice] after seeing you and got thrown into a commission in under a minute—the quickest process I have ever known." In later years he often said that everyone expected to be killed in the war and that he had given his all in *The Good Soldier* because he believed it would be the last book he would live to write. This cannot have been literally true; *The Good Soldier* was finished before he decided to enlist. But it may well reflect his feeling, at the time he did enlist, that he had found an honorable way of putting an end to his literary career. His later belief that when he returned to London after the war he was completely forgotten is to some extent a result of his having enlisted with the idea that that would be the result. The deep discouragement of finding himself a middle-aged writer who had missed his chance and was now barely tolerated by the young, the oppression of his situation at South Lodge, his Tory feeling of obligation to his country thus combined to make him enlist.[5]

Up to the moment of his being "thrown into a commission," Ford had concealed the whole business from Violet, but that evening, as he and his secretary got into the car with her on their return from London, he said, "I have got my commission." Violet's comment on this maneuver shows why he had not previously mentioned that matter to her. "Then, as now," she says, "he sheltered behind the presence of a third person that precluded cross-questioning." Infuriating as this was, however, it was a temporary expedient that did not protect Ford "later, when I was lying on my bed crying"; she continued to cry—and no doubt cross-question—for three days. "I wanted," Ford wrote his mother, "to get a commission without talking about it [Violet would certainly have talked to everyone about it], & a commission in the regular army, not in any of the fancy services [such as Violet would have argued for] which are only a form of shirking. . . . V. takes it rather hard, poor dear, but I hope she will get used to the idea."[6]

That hope, as he probably knew, was doomed to disappointment. Under any circumstances, Violet would probably have seen in Ford's enlistment only a selfish disregard for the misery he was causing her. Her natural impulse to do so was intensified by her belief that Ford's decision was partly motivated by his desire to escape from her.

> This is what you have brought on me, dear Ford [she wrote him in imagination after he had left, and her beloved Rosamond, now married, refused to have her for a visit], and you are happy in Cardiff and leaving me to bear it alone. It is this sort of thing all the time—and loneliness. . . . And this is the last straw, more than I can bear. Don't write to Rosamond on any account. You have done me enough harm already.

Absurdly self-centered and exaggerated though that is, Violet was right in thinking Ford no longer cared for her. Behind all her unreasonable demands lies her knowledge of that fact; they are desperate and pathetic efforts to

force Ford to love her again. About this time, in a copy of D. H. Lawrence's
Love Poems that Lawrence had given Ford with the inscription, "Remembering that he discovered me," she wrote: "Ford gave me this when he loved
me."⁷

In her usual way she showed her feelings to everyone. She published
poems like "Merciful Aphasia," which describes how her passion fought a
war to keep Ford.

> When you are with me it is Life.
>
> Réveillés, alarms
> The thrust, the parry, the séance in the trenches . . .
> Feints of passion
> Too starved, too ill-equipped to succeed. . . .
> But still we are washed and laid out, and our eyelids closed.
> At peace. . . .
>
> It is a merciful dispensation.
>
> Yet you'll come back?⁸

Ford, then, got his commission in late July; though the appointment was
not gazetted until August 13, he got into uniform immediately and took what
he calls "the Chelsea Course" with the Irish Guards at their London barracks.
"He was then always in uniform—impressive with all that rosy colour and
blue eyes, moustache, drooping lip." It was apparently during this interval
that he had an unhappy encounter with the Lawrences. According to Ford,

> . . . Authority—in the shape of the Ministry of Information—was
> afraid that [Lawrence] was being persecuted and I was sent down to
> see what could be done for him, Mrs. Wells . . . kindly driving me the
> thirty or forty miles into Sussex where Lawrence had been lent the
> house of Mrs. Meynell, the poetess. . . . The moment we arrived at
> that pleasant place, Mrs. Wells, who was very small, and Mrs. Law-
> rence, who resembled the Germania above the Rhine at Rüdesheim
> —fell into a discussion as to the merits of the Belgians. And, as Mrs.
> Lawrence saw fit to address, on the side, unfavourable remarks to the
> uniform I was wearing, I thought it was better—because I *was* there
> to report to Authority—to retire to an outhouse and await the close
> of the discussion. So that the last image I have of Lawrence is his
> standing there, a little impotent, his hands hanging at his side, as
> if he were present at a dog fight in the beautiful, white-walled,
> shady, aesthetic room of Mrs. Meynell.⁹

When this passage first appeared in *The American Mercury* in 1936, Frieda Lawrence wrote indignantly to say that Ford had not been in uniform, that Violet had spent the whole visit trying to suggest that Ford was of Russian descent in order to free him of the disgrace of being German, and that Lawrence had not been present. Later she dropped the second of these claims but added that Ford squirmed when she said, "Wir sind auch Deutsch," and that there was no outhouse for him to retire to. Violet further complicates the puzzle by claiming it was she and not Mrs. Wells who got into the row with Frieda; according to her, Frieda said, apropos of Ford's then famous poem, "Antwerp," "Dirty Belgians! Who cares for them!" "It came," Violet says, "to a regular mill between me and the Valkyrie." About all that seems certain about this occasion is that a row occurred that prevented Ford and the Lawrences ever meeting again and that, the minute it started, Ford got as far away as he could—a detail too characteristic of him not to be true.[10]

Ford was ordered to report to Tenby August 15, 1915, but that was a Sunday. Violet gave a farewell party for him at South Lodge the night of the 16—"Not a party—only whisky, and sandwiches and a few old friends," as she said in her invitation. According to Violet's secretary, Ford stayed on after the other guests to finish the whiskey, he and Violet quarreled violently, and Ford "was finally ejected to find his way to bed as best he could." Before he left London, he officially changed his name. He had already quietly dropped the Joseph Leopold of his German days. Now he got rid of the middle name on his baptismal certificate, Hermann, and became Ford Madox Hueffer.[11]

At first he found army life the enormous relief he had hoped it would be. It made him feel "fit [mentally] and with a place in society. Low enough, but still a place." "Hueffer up in town on leave yesterday," Ezra Pound wrote Harriet Monroe a month later. " . . . he is looking twenty years younger and enjoying his work." His only complaint was that he was lonely. "I am really quite happy," he wrote Masterman, "except for an absolute lack of social life. I suppose you or Lucy don't know anyone hereabouts to whom you cd. give me an introduction?" By the end of the year, having been transferred to Cardiff Castle, he was beginning to complain more seriously. "I am . . . pretty hard at it from 6.30, every morning, until five & then hopelessly stupid till bedtime. . . . I get too much work in the Coy. offices filling up returns about absentees & the like all the time, to be altogether fit & Cardiff is so relaxing that one is half asleep most of the time." This description of an overworked company officer was written from the Royal Porthcawl Golf Club "where I go . . . every Sunday to play golf with an old major who is a soothing person." He also took frequent weekend leaves, visiting the Wellses, Rebecca West at Leigh-on-Sea, and the Mastermans in London, as well as Violet at Selsey.[12]

He very much enjoyed the companionship of the young officers of the battalion and was his usual kindly self with them. "We [younger men] all liked him in the mess, and for my own part I always found him . . . like an elder brother or senior boy at school. . . . The thing that struck me most perhaps, was the 'softness' of his voice. He always spoke very quietly. . . . " Occasionally he found the paper work amusing, as when a girl named Violet Heyman was "introduced by Lance Corporal Plant, 5th Welch" into "enclosed premises the property of H.M. the King for the purpose of committing prostitution" and "was chased round and round . . . over the men's beds and the like. . . . " "They lived—these desperadoes—in a tumble-down skating rink . . . a great cavern of a place that was laid out in stalls like a cattle market. . . . " Miss Heyman was then, quite improperly, turned over to the civil authorities, and Ford took delight in proving that the charge against the girl would not lie because she "had not come into the Rink *proprio motu.*" He was entertained when the "forcible document" he had composed was returned to him by the garrison commander as not only illegible—which it no doubt was—but illiterate.[13]

Violet continued to be unreconciled to his absence: she was sure he was up to no good. She may have had more than imagination to make her think so, for Ford had some kind of sentimental experience during these Cardiff days.

> In Chepstow stands a castle;
> My love and I went there . . .

> The sun was high in heaven,
> And the perfume on the air
> Came from purple cat's valerian . . .
> But her footsteps on the stair
> Made a sound like silver music
> Thro' the perfume in the air.

In a companion poem written after he reached the front, he says, "For it's just nine weeks last Sunday/Since we took the Chepstow train." Yet another poem, "What the Orderly Dog Saw," was dedicated to a Mrs. Percy Jackson when it first appeared in *Poetry,* and Ford gave Mrs. Jackson the manuscript.[14]

Whether Violet knew of this episode or not, she busied herself enlisting the help of all her friends in the good work of keeping Ford faithful to her; it was the worst thing she could have done. When Wells, at her insistence, wrote Ford about their problems, Ford answered with a polite suggestion that it was none of Wells's business and a strong hint that it would be a good idea for Violet to shut up.

> I am much touched by your letter—tho I do not really know what to make of it. I hadn't the least idea that there was any difference between Violet & myself—or at least anything to make her face the necessity of talking about it. I, at any rate, haven't any grievance against her & want nothing better than to live with her the life of a peaceable regimental officer with a peaceable wife. Of course that is not very exciting for her & her enjoyment of life depends so much on excitement. But one's preoccupations can't, now, be what they were in the 90's—or even three or two years ago. . . . At any rate, if you see V., do impress her with the fact that . . . I have the greatest possible affection & esteem for her; there isn't anyone else (but I don't know what she has got into her always romantic head). . . .

That last sentence sounds suspiciously as if Ford did know what Violet was worrying about.[15]

As early as the first of June Ford's battalion was advised to hold itself in readiness to depart for France, but there were the usual maddening delays, and it was another month before they actually left. During the interval Ford said his farewells. Ever since he had joined Violet he had been seeking to get back on the old footing with Conrad. Conrad, though always polite, kept his distance. But Conrad was very patriotic. He could not refuse Ford's request that he serve with Violet as Ford's literary executor when Ford left for the army, and when, with characteristic and rather appealing sentimentality, Ford wanted to carry Conrad's old binoculars into service, Conrad had to tell him they had long since disintegrated. "Yes, *mon cher!* Our world of 15 years ago is gone to pieces." Conrad even announced himself as planning to call on Violet after Violet had been kind to Borys when Borys passed through London on his way to his post. In July, before Ford left for France, he had a farewell meeting with Conrad.[16]

He also asked his daughters to come to London to say good-by. He took them to luncheon at a Lyons cafe. Katharine, who was fifteen, was mute with shyness at the unaccustomed surroundings of the restaurant and Christina, seventeen, distressed by her need to deny her father's earnest request that she put off entering a religious order until his return from France. Ford and Elsie had both fought to delay this decision, but she told Ford that waiting would make no difference. A few days after, she had a letter from him saying, "I took the communion and prayed for you both." This was the last time Ford's daughters ever saw him.[17]

As usual, after all these farewells had been said, their departure was delayed.

> You have rushed around to get your money.
> To get your revolver, complete your equipment;
> You have had your moments, sweeter—ah, sweeter than honey;
> You have got your valise all ready for shipment:
> You have gone to confession and wangled your blessing,
> You have bought your air-pillow and sewn in your coat
> A pocket to hold your first field-dressing . . .
> And, like a ship that floats free of her berth,
> There's nothing that holds you now to the earth,
> And you're near enough to a yawn. . . .

Ford found the waiting nervewracking, especially as he was so broke "that I can't stir out of the Castle." On July 13, however, they finally left Cardiff for a base camp at Rouen. Three days later he was attached to the 9th Welch Battalion, a part of the 58th Infantry Brigade of the 19th Division which fought the battle of the Somme as part of III Corps. He did not go into the line then or at any time, nor was he ever wounded or gassed, but he was under constant fire with the first line transport of the battalion, which was stationed behind Bécourt wood at the bottom of what was known as Sausage Valley, the depression that ran at an angle from back of Bécourt wood through the front lines to Contalmaison wood behind the German lines, along which most of the attacks on Boiselle were made.

> We are [he wrote Lucy Masterman] right up in the middle of the strafe, but only with the 1st line transport. We get shelled two or three times a day, otherwise it is fairly dull—indeed, being shelled is fairly dull, after the first once or twice. Otherwise it is all very interesting —filling in patches of one's knowledge & so on, but it isn't more than interesting, because one gets no news.[18]

This letter, with its effort to strike the proper note ("being shelled is fairly dull," "all very interesting"), is appealing; it suggests what must have been true for everyone, that, dull as shelling may grow, it grows no less terrifying; interesting as filling in patches of one's knowledge no doubt ought to be, it is not so diverting as one could wish. A number of companies from the 9th Welch had suffered through the terrible battle of Mametz wood during the early days of July and the several attempts to advance up Sausage Valley on Boiselle. Many of these companies, after a short rest, went back into the line before Mametz wood when Ford was with their transport on July 21; they were finally relieved and sent back to train new drafts on July 29.

On top of all this there was the torturing ignorance of what was happening at home.

I used to think [says Ernest Jessop of *The Marsden Case*] that, once out there, we should be surrounded by a magic and invisible tent that would keep from us all temporal cares. But we were not so surrounded and it is not like that. The one nail does not knock out the other. There is that never ceasing waiting about; and the cold; and the long depressions. Now and then there is terrible noise—wearing, lasting for days. And some pain. All that is bearable. But what is desolating, what is beyond everything hateful, is that, round your transparent tent, the old evils, the old heart-breaks and the old cruelties are unceasingly at work.

Christopher Tietjens felt this anxiety too. It was obviously Ford's own. "I wonder," he wrote Lucy Masterman from Bécourt, "what is happening to [Violet]. I have not had a line from her since I started; I don't know what psychological vagary or manoeuvre it implies. But it is a queer way to set to work." Things were not—any more than they were for 09-Morgan of *Parade's End*—much improved when he did begin to hear from home.

Why does *no*body write to me? Does one so quickly become a ghost, alas!

I have had nothing for a week but notes from V deploring the fact that I have lost my bicycle & the like—wh. of course takes one's mind off oneself. . . . [19]

Though this period on the Somme lasted only ten days, the accumulated strains were more than Ford's delicate nervous balance could sustain, despite his stubborn determination not to give way. The truth was that what he was doing was too much for him; it meant, as he wrote Masterman, "getting wet thro' & coming in to write for a couple of hours in a stifling room, often getting wet through some more & then sleeping in a dripping hut." When he was knocked down by the concussion of a near-miss and damaged his front teeth, he went to pieces. He was sent to Corbie to have his teeth attended to and found he had lost his memory; for thirty-six hours he could not even recall his own name; for at least a month after, he could remember very little, and he later said that he did not get "over the nerve tangle of the war" until 1923. This was a peculiarly horrible experience for him; he had always prided himself on his memory which was, if not always precise, extremely vivid and detailed. "When I consider," he said, "that I wrote the whole of the Fifth Queen series without a single note more than went on the back of one visiting card. . . . "[20]

He had a very bad time of it at Corbie.

At any rate [he wrote later], after I was blown up at Bécourt-Bécordel in '16 and, having lost my memory, lay in the Casualty Clearing Station in Corbie, with the Enemy planes dropping bombs all over it and the dead Red Cross nurses being carried past my bed, I used to worry agonizedly about what my name could be—and have a day-nightmare. The night-nightmare was worse, but the day one was as bad as was necessary. I thought I had been taken prisoner by the Enemy forces and was lying on the ground, manacled hand and foot. . . . Immense shapes in grey-white *cagoules* and shrouds, miching and mowing and whispering horrible plans to one another! It is true they all wore giant, misty gas-masks. . . .

Out of these horrors he made Christopher Tietjens' nightmare of forgetting.[21]

"Using a good deal of determination," he wrote Lucy Masterman shortly after, "I have got out of the nurses' hands & back to duty, after an incredibly tortuous struggle across France"; while he had been at Corbie, the 19th Division had been relieved (July 30) and sent to the comparative quiet of the Ypres salient; the 9th Welch were stationed "in front of Kemmel Hill, facing Wychaete," and he had to make his way there to report for duty by whatever means he could. He was far from recovered. "During the worst phase of the first battle of the Somme . . . " he wrote later, "at night, when one had a long period of waiting, with nothing to do, in pitch blackness, in the midst of gunfire that shook the earth I did once pray to the major Heavenly powers that my reason might be preserved." He prayed, indeed, more than once; on September 6 he sent his mother "A Solis Ortus Cardine" with its plea for the prayers of all the living and all the dead. After the shock of that first breakdown, he lived in terror of going mad, though he somehow managed to appear perfectly phlegmatic to those around him. His fellow officer, Thomas Sugrue, who met Ford just as he was going into the hospital (as Sugrue was coming out of the line on July 29), remembered Ford as "a big, florid, heavy, unhealthy looking man" who behaved quite normally.[22]

Nevertheless, he remained frighteningly tense. "Things are exciting & the firing all day keeps me a little too much on the jump," he told his mother; and he apologized to Lucy Masterman for his handwriting by saying, "We are in a h-ll of a noise, just now—my hand is shaking badly—our guns are too inconsiderate. . . . " This excitability made it difficult for him to do his work efficiently and he got into a row with his commanding officer, Colonel Cooke.

> ... the C.O. [he wrote Lucy Masterman]—an ex-Eastbourne Town
> Councillor & the adjt., an ex-P. O. clerk—annoy me—the C. O. says
> I am too old & the adjt. thanks me all day long for saving the H. Q.
> Mess 2 frs. 22 on turnips & the like. I don't know which I dislike most.

"... they can worry me a good deal in details," he added in a letter to
Conrad, "—there are almost endless openings for the polite taquineries
called 'strafing' in a regiment...." He therefore began to hope he could be
transferred to a staff job. He was encouraged when Major-General G. T. M.
Bridges, who commanded the 19th Division, rode up to him one day and
talked about *Entre St. Denis et St. Georges* and he picked up a rumor from
Bridges' staff captain that Bridges had recommended him to General Plumer
as a staff officer. Nothing, however, happened, and he was soon writing
Lucy Masterman again with his characteristic combination of bravado and
anxiety.

> With the labour of 184 men I have today drained a considerable
> portion of this country & I have also marched 12 miles to bring up a
> draft. So I have not been idle. But the C. O. continues to impress on
> me that I am too old for this job. I think he wants to force me to
> relinquish my commission. I suppose you do not know anybody who
> cd. impress on Gen¹ Bridges the desirability of having me in his
> Intgce Dept? ... I am sure I deserve better—even in a military sense
> —than to be harassed by a rather doting Lt. Col. of C. A. who
> cherishes a special dislike for the Special Reserve.²³

During the first week of September, he wrote Conrad three long letters
about the queer effect of the sounds of battle—of shells bursting, of rain on
tin roofs, of screams. "I wonder," he said, "if it is just vanity that in these
cataclysmic moments makes one desire to *record.*" But in this instance, at
least, it was a desperate need to exorcise the terror of these sounds, to steady
himself by confessing indirectly—to the one man in the world he believed
would understand his difficulties. "In hot, dry weather, sounds give me a
headache—over the brows & across the skull, inside, like migraine," he says
—like the "gout in the eyebrows" he had suffered during his breakdown in
1904. He read avidly; "lying awake in a tent in the moonlight towards four
of a September morning in 1916 [he suffered badly from insomnia], on the
slopes behind Kemmel... I was reading the *Red Badge of Courage.*" He
wrote a preface for Violet's *Their Lives* under the pseudonym Miles Ignotus,
reading the proofs while watching "the gas shells bursting in Poperinghe."
He also wrote a considerable number of poems. How desperate the demons
he tried in these ways to hold at bay really were can be seen in the descrip-

tion of them he wrote for the hero of his unpublished novel, *That Same Poor Man.*

> To him fighting had been very terrible because of mental tortures rather than physical fears, though of course he had known fear. But he had been filled with acute dreads that his self-control might give way even now after peace had been declared. It did give way whenever he was vividly reminded of the brown turmoil, the distorted limbs, the sweat and the clay. . . . He had for long been desperately excitable—so excitable that when one of his fits [was] on him he had terrible desires to strangle. He had . . . a desperate memory of shouting and unbelievable mental pain; arising out of nothing, in a perfectly quiet Mess. . . . [He] did not want to come into contact with mad, or even with highly excitable people. He had, for too long, been too much afraid, himself, of going mad.[24]

At this moment his quarrel with Colonel Cooke reached a climax. He summarized it to Masterman in his own terms in a letter that was—though he could not bear to say so outright—a plea for help.

> Att[d] 9/Welch
> 19[h] Div.
>
> My Dear C. F G,
> Eight weeks ago next Monday I arrived at the first Line Transport of this Bn. where I remained a week. the Bn being in the trenches. We were shelled pretty consistently every evening, six shells at a time. the distances of the shells from us ranging from 40 y[ds] to 250. I was twice knocked down by the percussion from these shells, on the second occasion damaging my mouth & loosening my teeth wh. became very bad, affecting my whole condition. When the B[n] went into rest camp I applied to the M.O. for treatment. He sent me in an ambulance to a Field Ambulance the F.A. sent me to C.C.S. 36; C.C.S. 36 had no appliances for treating me & ordered me to report to H.Q. of the 4th Army. I thought it better to report to B[n] H.Q. There the C.O. of the IX Welch sent for me & read me a comm[n] he had sent to my home address—to the effect that I was an inefficient officer; could not inspire the men with confidence. that he requested me to resign my commission & that he could not recommend me for employment at home. At that date the C.O. had seen me only once. . . . I was too ill to protest—& indeed I had no wish to protest. I returned to my Coy. & wrote a letter to the Adjt.—as per form—requesting, on account of my knowledge of French, German & Flemish, to be given some employment of a non-regimental nature in H. M. Army in this country.

Later General Bridges caused me to be informed that he had written G.H.Q. recommending me for employment in the Intelligence Department. Yesterday—6.9.16—the C.O. sent for me & told me—or rather partly read to me—a comm? from G.H.Q. to the effect that my record was so bad that the app? c? not be entertained. He then ordered me to return to the 1st Line Transport where I now am, awaiting further orders.

I thought you ought to know these details wh. I present to you without comment, simply asking you to believe that I have certainly committed no military offense of any kind; that I have carried out punctually & exactly any military duties I have had to perform & that, at the time of his writing his first comm? to me the C.O. had not so much as shaken hands with me. nor had the Adjutant & that neither of these officers or any other had seen me in contact with the men—simply because I had not been in contact with the men, but only in the 1st Line Transport wh. is composed mostly of mules.

There are improvements here; Ford's correspondence shows, for example, that his hopes of a staff or intelligence job never got beyond hopes. But the "comm?" from Colonel Cooke saying he found Ford hopelessly inefficient and would not even recommend him for home service was exactly as Ford describes it; it still exists.[25]

When he heard that *Entre St. Denis et St. Georges* was about to be published by Payot, he immediately applied for leave to go to Paris September 9–11. "My financial affairs," he told the adjutant, "having become exceedingly embarrassed owing to my having done this [book] & other work, without pay, for H. M. Government, it would be of the greatest advantage to me...." At the same time he wrote the M.O. requesting an "order on a dental artist" in Paris so that he could have his teeth attended to. "I only know that I am beastly bad—with rheumatism & agoraphobia—wh. w? all go if my (literally) bleeding teeth c? be pumped out." In Paris he was formally congratulated for his book by the Minister of Instruction. He used his conversation with the minister and a discussion with a group of French officers during the entr'acte of *Lakmé* that evening as two of the major images in *No Enemy*. These scenes have a marvelous, dreamlike verisimilitude, but they are, of course, impressions; they do not describe what actually happened. In fact, Ford collapsed during that weekend in Paris, owing, he wrote Masterman, to his strenuous work on *Entre St. Denis*—"cutting it down & writing into it in French—a rather pretty epilogue wh. pleased Payot. The writing rather exhausted me—& indeed I collapsed & was made to see the M.O. who said I was suffering from specific shell-shock & ought to go to hospital. However, I wdn't. & got back here [to the battalion]." There is, in fact, neither cutting nor epilogue in the French translation of *Between St. Dennis and St. George.*[26]

Masterman finally succeeded in freeing him from Colonel Cooke, and he was sent back to the 3rd Battalion's home base at Kinmel Park, near Rhyl in northern Wales. This assignment does not appear anywhere in his official service record, which, instead, shows him wounded October 16, 1916. He disliked the assignment to Kinmel Park; he thought it a waste of his talents, and, deprived of the extra pay for service abroad, he found himself in financial difficulties.

> I seem to be destined to be stuck down here [he wrote Masterman from Rhyl] & am posted to a Coy—wh. does seem to be a waste of my abilities—otherwise I wd. not worry you. Moreover I can't afford it—wh. is also a motive—whereas in France I c'd. be really useful in a dozen ways and could just live. So if [General] Braid [at the War Office] wd. play Perseus to this Andromeda it wd. be what the French call une bonne action.

Masterman tried, but when he inquired two weeks later, Ford wrote him, "No: I have not heard anything at this end. . . . I wish you cd. have done something —but never really expected that you cd. My luck is too much out. As things are I see nothing for it but to relinquish my comm[n]—wh. I shall do on 1.11.16—& to disappear into a decent obscurity."[27]

Despite these forebodings, however, he was ordered back to France at the end of November. Now his main worry became how to avoid Colonel Cooke. "Wd. it be too much to ask you to ask Genl. Braid," he wrote Masterman, "to suggest to Col. Dickinson at the Base Camp at Rouen" that Ford not be sent back to the 9th Welch? When he reached Rouen, however, he found himself assigned to the 9th Welch. He protested, "rather vigourously, though unofficially." Then he hung about Rouen "writing proclamations in French about thefts of rations issued to H.B.M.'s forces & mounting guards over German sick." Before anything was settled, he fell ill. " . . . my lungs intervened . . . with extensions at the bases & solidifications & all sorts of things. . . . So they shoved me in here [that is, No. II Red Cross Hospital at Rouen]." His nerves were also bothering him again. "I lie awake & perceive the ward full of Huns of forbidding aspect," he wrote Masterman, " . . . I am in short rather ill & sometimes doubt my own sanity—indeed, quite frequently I do. . . . I find myself suddenly waking up in a hell of a funk—& going on being in a hell of a funk till morning." He meant that "hell" quite literally.

Red Cross Hospital No. II at Rouen . . . was in the old priests' semi-
nary. . . . We occupied small white priests' cells, two to a cell, a camp
bed in each corner. Diagonally opposite me was a Black Watch
second lieutenant—about twenty, wild-eyed, black-haired. . . . As
soon as the last visit of the V.A.D.'s was over he would jump out of
bed and rush to a wall-press with sliding doors. He took out a kilt and
a single shoe. His face assumed a look of infinite cunning. He would
fix his black, shining, maniacal eyes on me and, stealthily stretching
out an arm, would extract from the press a *skene dhu*. A *skene dhu* is
the long, double-edged dagger that Highlanders carry in their socks.
From the creasing of his lips you could tell when he had put a sufficient edge on that instrument. He would be sharpening it on the sole
of his single shoe. He never removed his eyes from mine. He would
run his thumb along the edge of the blade and with a leering, gloating
look he would whisper

"We know who this is meant for."

I never ascertained. Delirium would then come. I was delirious
most nights.[28]

Real or imaginary, that Black Watch lieutenant is a measure of Ford's
condition. Little wonder he wrote Masterman he was "a bit dotty" and said
quite simply to his mother, "It w^d be really preferable to be dead—but one
is not dead. . . . " The day before he left Rouen, he wrote a poem for the
Welch Regiment's dead:

> The rain drips down on Rouen Town
> The leaves drip down
> And so the mud
> Turns orange brown . . .
> A Zeppelin, we read, has been brought down.
> And the obscure brown
> Populace of London town
> Make a shout of it,
> Clamouring for blood
> And reductions in the price of food . . .
> But you—at least—are out of it . . . [29]

H. G. Wells was convinced that Ford was permanently changed by this
breakdown. "[Ford's] extraordinary drift towards self-dramatization," he
said in *Experiment in Autobiography*, " . . . became conspicuous only . . . after
the stresses of the war." He put this view a good deal more vigorously in
correspondence. "In the 1914-18 war he was a bad case of shell-shock from
which he never recovered. The pre-war F.M.H. was tortuous but under-

standable, the post-war F.M.H. was incurably *crazy.* He got crazier and crazier." Wells was thinking mostly of *Thus to Revisit,* which Ford wrote immediately after the war when he was, as he himself recognized, seriously disturbed. *Thus to Revisit* bulked large in Wells's mind because he and Ford had had a public row about what Ford said in it about Wells.[30]

What Wells meant about Ford is made clear in his novel *The Bulpington of Blup,* in which the hero, Theodore Bulpington, though his life parallels Ford's only in a general way, gets his character from Wells's conception of Ford. From childhood Theodore lives much of the time in an imaginary world of heroic virtues and slightly old-fashioned romantic values of which his imaginary self—The Bulpington of Blup—is the hero. As he grows older, his imaginary life becomes more sophisticated but no less discontinuous with the actual world, and Theodore is forced to more and more desperate expedients to convince himself that he has lived in the way his imaginary self requires him to have.

The war brings him to a crisis. He denies that he turned tail and ran during a battle and insists that he was stunned by a shell burst. He persists in seeing the love of his life, Margaret Boxted, as the humble worshiper of his heroism that his fancy requires her to be. When he meets the doctor who had examined him when he was shell-shocked, the doctor says, "I examined you. After the last German push. . . . They wanted to shoot you. Voluntary shell-shock. I lied. Anyhow I bent my report to save you. And here we are again!" With almost perfect sincerity, Theodore answers,

> Never. I was knocked out by a shell and poisoned by the fumes. I was unconscious for a long time. . . . It's on record. You've made a mistake. I've never set eyes on you.

When Margaret Boxted rejects him, he becomes obsessed with his relation to her.

> And after his habit of mind he dramatized it and told himself stories about it. He became a brain-storm in narrative and literary form. His imaginations welled out in letters. . . .
> . . . He remembered only her refusals, her disbelief in him and this crowning outrageous fact that she could think of another lover.
> . . . He could not persuade because he was so desirous of putting her in the wrong, solacing his chagrin and self-reproach by charges of instability and treachery on her part, denouncing the baseness of her motives, the coldness of her blood.[31]

Just as Ford always convinced himself that, in his love affairs, he had behaved unusually well, so he quickly convinced himself that he had been a good soldier during his service in France. Probably only a man with Ford's romantic need to see himself as a hero could have imagined in the first place that a man with his habits of life could at forty-two turn himself into a first-class officer. He clearly did not become such an officer; but needing, when the war was over, to believe he had been, he worked up an improved and improbable account of his war service. *The Bulpington of Blup* shows that Wells knew this account in some detail and doubted all of it.[32]

Ford's vision of himself as a responsible upper-class Englishman imposed a very high standard on him and contributed a good deal to his ultimate collapse. In any realistic sense he was behaving with some heroism when he continued on active duty after his first breakdown in July. It was not until he had his second breakdown, in December, that he gave up the struggle and openly admitted that "I . . . sometimes doubt my own sanity— indeed, quite frequently I do." But Ford could not live very long with a self that was heroic only in this way; he needed to see himself, and to believe others saw him, as the conventional upper-class officer-hero. He quickly improved his war experience with this end in view and thus obscured the very real if homelier heroism of his actual conduct.

Chapter 22

The medical board that examined Ford when he was released from the hospital at Rouen first suggested he be sent home; when he objected, they assigned him to limited service in France. Then, on Christmas Eve, he had a serious relapse. When he recovered, the doctors sent him to Lady Michelham's convalescent hospital at Menton. "Ah, but we lived like gentlemen in that Red Cross Hotel on Cap Martin," he wrote later. " ... one of those great gilded caravanserais that of my own motion I should never have entered.... We ... sat at little tables in fantastically palmed and flowering rooms and ... ate *Tournedos Meyerbeer* and drank *Château Pavie* 1906 ... *1906*, think of that."[1]

He left Menton on February 2. It was intensely cold and the ground was covered with snow from Marseilles north and his lungs were, he thought, "in a terrible condition still." When he reached Rouen he was put in command of a Canadian casual battalion for a month; then he was moved to Abbeville, where he was in charge of prisoners of war. He hated this "bare, cold & trampled North, with nothing but khaki for miles & miles ... Bare downs ... & tents ... & wet valleys ... & tents ... & AAc guns ... & mud ... & bare downs ... & huts ... & bare downs ... & RFC ... & mud ... & motor lorries ... & mud ... & bare downs."[2]

In March, 1917, this climate became too much for his lungs, and he was invalided home on the fifteenth. He never got out to France again, though for financial reasons he tried to, and at one point even got himself applied for by the colonel of the labor battalion with which he had served briefly at the beginning of the year ("just as dangerous as a service [battalion], yet the credit is less. However, I don't mind that"). But the doctors would not pass him fit. He was officially hospitalized until May 11, though in fact he was given "light duty" as captain of a company of the 23 King's Liverpool Regiment at Kinmel Park in April. There he fell under the benevolent command of Lieutenant-Colonel G. R. Powell, to whom, in gratitude, he dedicated *On Heaven*. Colonel Powell wrote a recommendation for his service record: "Has shown marked aptitude for grasping any intricate subject and possesses great powers of organization—a lecturer of the first water on several military subjects—conducted the duties of housing officer to the unit (average strength 2800) with great ability." But managing without overseas pay made Ford's situation difficult. By November, he was in such desperate straits that he wrote to ask Jepson to help him "impignorate" the copyrights of his books with the Royal Literary Fund for a loan of £ 50 to £ 100. He was, he told Jepson, too ill to supplement his income, as he had before he went out to France, by occasional writing.[3]

Nevertheless Ferris Greenslet met him on the London train to Liverpool that spring, looking "a fine figure of a fighting man." Greenslet's innocence always tempted Ford and he informed him that he was reading the proofs of "an erotic novel in French that he had just completed." When he had first got back to England he had spent his leaves with Violet at Selsey, but by the first of the year he was inquiring of Lucy Masterman if she could find him cheap lodgings in London as "South Lodge does not seem to be available."[4]

Among other things, Violet was angry about *On Heaven and Poems Written on Active Service*, the volume Ford was putting together for publication that spring. Around the first of the year he had been moved to a job with a training command at Redcar in Yorkshire. There Violet joined him. They got on very badly: according to Violet, Ford greedily ate up all the cream she ordered for herself and insisted on going on duty instead of staying to protect her when there were air raids. Then she discovered he was selecting the poems for *On Heaven* with the assistance of the colonel's wife. "I only saw Ford for 3 days before the matter" of the volume's content was decided, she told Harold Monro, "and as he arranged and collected the poems with the help of the wife of the Colonel of the Welch Regiment my influence was at a discount. I objected very much to the inclusion of some cheap silly pieces & above all, to the preface which is going to play old Harry." The "cheap silly pieces" were doubtless the poems written for Mrs. Jackson when he was at Cardiff, and the preface belittled "On Heaven," which was dedicated to Violet.

Ford first tried *On Heaven* on the Poetry Bookshop which had published *Antwerp* two years before and when they offended him by not answering his letter, sold it to John Lane. Pound, busy as ever—"I have now got Hueffer's best ms. for 1918"—got *Women & Men* published in *the Little Review.* Ford had begun *Women & Men* seven years earlier on the theory that it would sell widely among the suffragettes, but this fragment was all he ever got written.[5]

He was now beginning to benefit from his new view of himself as a soldier-writer. "After all," he wrote Pinker, "few poets—& *no* man of letters of my standing—has been twice out to France, actually on service & in the trenches, without wangling any sort of job on the staff, but just sticking it in the Infantry for love of the job." "So," as he put it in "Footsloggers,"

> . . . in the Flanders mud,
> We bear the State upon our rain-soaked backs,
> Breathe life into the State from our rattling lungs,
> Anoint the State with the rivulets of sweat
> From our tin helmets.

His morale was so improved by this view of himself that he suggested Pinker get him a commission for a novel, though only two months earlier he had felt unable to write anything. Then in March he was declared fit and got a new appointment that paid him better and was to last for the duration of the war; he was "attached to the staff and [went] all over the North of England inspecting training and lecturing" "on the Ross rifle—which was a beast of a thing—or on the Causes of the War. . . . " He also got an inspiriting check for his share of the advance on Nelson's new edition of *Romance.*[6]

On April 11, 1918, *On Heaven and Poems Written on Active Service* was published by Lane. In his Preface Ford emphasized the poems that were written during the time he was with the 9th Welch in the Ypres salient, and insisted on the merely "local" (that is, war) interest of the book "since I am no longer a writer and have no longer any place in the world of letters." Two of the three important poems in the volume—"Antwerp" and "On Heaven"—were written before he enlisted and the third, "Footsloggers," after his return from France. But the poems actually written in France, such as "The Old Houses of Flanders," "Albade," and "Clair de Lune," were among the earliest expressions of the Edwardian soldier's feelings; Harriet Monroe compared them with Rupert Brooke's war poems; she might better have said Siegfried Sassoon. The idea that, as an ex-soldier, he no longer had a "place in the world of letters" was gradually to develop into the theory that there was a special malevolence in the literary establishment directed against him.[7]

On one of his leaves in London during this spring of 1918, Ford was introduced by Pound to Stella Bowen, a shy, energetic Australian girl who

298] THE SADDEST STORY

had come to London in 1914 at the age of twenty-one to study painting at the Westminster School of Art. During her first years in London she fell in with girls like Mary Butts and Phyllis Reid, who took her to hear Marinetti "reciting his zoom-bang poetry in Italian" and introduced her to the G. D. H. Coles and the Raymond Postgates. In 1916, she and Phyllis Reid took a flat in Pembroke Studios. One night Ezra Pound came to a party there, and they quickly became friends. "Ezra was a dear. . . . All the features [of his face] would gather together in the kindliest twinkling movement whenever he was amused, which was often. He would then make a rhythmic, hooting noise which represented laughter." "He desired us to teach him to dance, and quickly evolved a highly personal and very violent style, which involved a great deal of springing up and down, as well as swaying from side to side, which caused him the greatest satisfaction. . . . " Pound soon had Stella and Phyllis attending his weekly dinners at Bellotti's and there they got to know T. S. Eliot, Wyndham Lewis, May Sinclair, and Violet Hunt.[8]

Ford was well known to Stella "by reputation because he was one of the writers whom Ezra allowed us to admire," and they had heard "Footsloggers" and "The Old Houses of Flanders" discussed and admired at the Poetry Bookshop. Ford appealed to her immediately, "He was quite the most enthralling person I had ever met."

> He was very large, with a pink face, yellow hair, and drooping, bright blue eyes. . . .
> When I got to know him better, I found that every human quality could be found flourishing in Ford's make-up, except a respect for logic. . . . But he could show you two sides simultaneously of any human affair, and the double picture made the subject come alive, and stand out in a third-dimensional way that was very exciting. What he did not know about the depths and weaknesses of human nature was not worth knowing. . . .
> The stiff, rather alarming exterior, and the conventional, omniscient manner, concealed a highly complicated emotional machinery. It produced an effect of tragic vulnerability; tragic because the scope of his understanding and the breadth of his imagination had produced a great edifice which was plainly in need of more support than was inherent in the structure itself. A walking temptation to any woman, had I but known it![9]

By June Ford, though still addressing her as "Dear Miss Bowen," had established his image of himself as a simple soldier who had quite fallen out of the sophisticated literary world that Ezra dominated.

Of course you may call me Ford if you like [he wrote her]
...I am much touched by your triple letter and my thirsty lips
grow thirstier at the colours [of the Selsey countryside, where she
was staying with Violet] it calls up. . . . I am going to lecture to 3000
WAC's and VAD's this week. Imagine it! It is a job for Yeats or Ezra
rather than for poor old me. . . . How you gifted people with all the
talents frighten me!

"He began," as Stella put it, " . . . filling me with pride by confiding all his
troubles and weaknesses. . . . [He] revealed himself as a lonely and very tired
person who wanted to dig potatoes and raise pigs and never write another
book. Wanted to start a new home. Wanted a child. . . . "[10]

Ford was convinced that this longing had developed during the strain
of his participation in the battle of the Somme.

... it was on the whole such a relief to be [in France] out of contact
with one's civilian friends at home ... that he was more contented
than perturbed. Nevertheless, the strain was a long strain, even if it
was impersonal, since it was a strain concerning itself with the English Country and not at all with one's regiment or one's self. . . . And
suddenly, at that point it came—the castle in the air; the simulacrum;
the vision of the inviolable corner of the earth. . . .

Possibly that little vision of English country, coming then, was
really a prayer, as if the depths of one's mind were murmuring:
"Blessed Mary, ask your kind Son that we may have the peace of God
that passes all understanding, one day, for a little while in a little
nook, all green, with silver birches, and a trickle of a stream through
a meadow, and the chimneys of a gingerbread cottage out of Grimm
just peeping over the fruit trees."

In "Footsloggers" he recalls how vivid the English country was to him as he
rode the train down from Cardiff on his way to France,

In the long, light, gently swaying carriages
As the miles flash by,
And fields and flowers
Flash by
Under the high sky
Where the great cloud towers
Above the tranquil downs
And the tranquil towns.[11]

When he found himself again in London, poor, forgotten, persecuted—he
believed—for having fought for his country in the war, he became the simple
gentleman philosophically committed to the pastoral life, "Captain Ford,"

"Gallophile, Veteran, Gardener, and, above all, Economist, if not above all Poet," one of those who could say gently to less perceptive men,

> Who doth ambition shun
> And loves to live i' th' sun,
> Seeking the food he eats,
> And pleased with what he gets,
> Come hither, come hither, come hither.
> Here shall he see no enemy
> But winter and rough weather.

To the economy of this dream, some Rosalind was necessary. "I don't think it matters much," Stella said afterward,

> from whom the artist gets his nourishment, or his shelter, so long as he gets it.
>
> In order to keep his machinery running, he requires to exercise his sentimental talents from time to time upon a new object. It keeps him young. It refreshes his ego. It restores his belief in his powers. . . .
>
> I happened to be the "new object" at a moment when Ford needed to be given a new lease of after-the-war life.

"What I got out of it," she added, "was a remarkable and liberal education, administered in ideal circumstances. . . . [It] was a privilege, for which I am still trying to say 'thank you.' "[12]

Ford's assertion that he never wanted to write again did not represent a practical commitment. From the beginning he was ready enough to think about a new book; the only cause for hesitation he took seriously was his mental condition. "As soon as the war was over," he said later, "I wrote a novel. But when I came to read it over I found that I had been writing like a madman. The book was not readable. I suppressed it." In fact, at the very moment he was telling Stella he would never write again, he was writing Secker,

> Do you think you would care to try a collected edition of my novels?
> . . . In that case I would write you a new one called "G. C. M."

He was, in short, ready to start *True Love & a G.C.M.* even before he was out of the army; on September 18, 1918, he told Stella he had begun to write it, and a good deal of it was done by March, 1919, when Stella read it.[13]

In August Ford was assigned the task of defending a man at a court martial, but before he could do so the man went mad, "rushed into my tent, having escaped from his escort: tried to strangle his father, bit me, and has just been carried off to an asylum." "If there is anything of that sort going," he added, "I am usually in it!" By September the note of his relation with Stella had changed considerably. "Of course you may disappoint me as often as you like, with impunity! That is the privilege of your share of our relationship. . . . " he wrote her. He then begged her to stay in London rather than going to Berkhamstead while he was in town for his next leave, for which he was careful to send her the exact dates. This meeting produced another distinct change in their relation; after it Ford wrote her,

My dear darling:
I am afraid I made you rather a painful scene last night and I am very ashamed of myself and mortified.[14]

But perhaps, he added, it was as well for her to learn early that, under a placid surface, he had very strong feelings.

In October Stella came to Redcar and together they watched what they believed was the last convoy for France to sail from Tees Bay; later Ford sent her a "silly little poem: I daresay you will understand it." It was called "Peace."

The black and nearly noiseless, moving, sea:
The immobile black houses of the town,
Pressing us out towards the noiseless sea
No sounds. . . .
And, Thou of the Stars! beneath the moving stars
Warm yellow lights upon the moving sea . . .
Moving. . . .

" . . . yes," he wrote her, "we will have quite a *little* cottage and a few acres if you prefer it, as long as you will be there."[15]

Just before the armistice, Ford had a violent row with Arnold Bennett. Bennett had been one of the writers who worked for Masterman at Wellington House. In the spring of 1918, he became director of British propaganda in France in Beaverbrook's Ministry of Information, and in September he was put in charge of the whole operation. According to Ford, Bennett called him in and asked him to write about the English terms for a peace settlement. Ford had a plan of his own that included making Alsace-Lorraine an independent neutral republic. When Bennett objected to using the resources of his office to propagate Ford's terms, Ford lost his temper, first at Bennett and then at Sir Walter Tyrrell of the Foreign Office, who supported Bennett. According to Ford, Bennett nevertheless agreed to publish what Ford wrote. Then, Ford adds, "It was lost in the post. There are things we manage more smoothly than they do in France. Immediately afterwards the colonel in chief of the regiment reminded me that as a British officer I was forbidden to write anything. . . . " This quarrel with Bennett is transmuted in *Last Post* into Mark Tietjens' quarrel with Lord Wolstonmark over the occupation of Berlin.*[16]

On Armistice Day Stella rushed around to Church Street and routed Pound out. They spent the day on the top of a bus, "Ezra with his hair on end, smacking the bus-front with his stick and shouting to the other people packed on the tops of other buses jammed alongside ours." "Darling," Ford wrote her that day from Easton: "Just a note to say I love you more than ever. Peace has come, and for some reason I feel inexpressibly sad. I suppose it is the breaking down after the old strain." Stella came north to be with him for his birthday (December 17), and during Christmas week he came to London for a party at the French embassy for the English writers who had supported France during the war. He recognized no one at the party but Arnold Bennett, and no one recognized him. He had expected as much. "It was seven years," he said with superb impressionistic inaccuracy, "since I had written a word."

> A long black figure detached itself from Mr. Bennett's side and approached me. It had the aspect of an undertaker coming to measure a corpse. . . . The eyes behind enormous lenses were like black pennies and appeared to weep dimly; the dank hair was plastered in flattened curls all over the head. . . . His hollow tones were those of a funeral mute:
> "You used to write," it intoned, "didn't you?"[17]

During these months Violet had been pressing him to appear at South Lodge. But whenever he did, she berated him violently. Ford told her plainly she did not "realise how you hurt me. How you drove me out of the house by insults—saying I only lived with you for the sake of your money. I will not, I will not sleep in the house again. . . . " Her rejoinder to this complaint was to "let out" with more insults.[18]

When Ford was "gazetted out of the Army" on January 1, 1919, and returned to London, he was as good as his word about not living at South

---

*Ford's belief that there had been a concerted effort to suppress his peace terms increased his belief that the writers who had cunningly climbed to power while he and his like were sacrificing themselves for their country in France were determined to persecute him. Shortly after this he claimed that he was refused a passport to France because "Mr. George's government . . . were determined that no Briton should speak for France" by suggesting, while the Peace Conference was going on, that France should be given "both banks of the Rhine from Basel to the Dutch frontier." He also found it very suspicious that he was not asked to stay on in the army permanently as Education Adviser to the Northern Command with the rank of lieutenant colonel. His lectures on "The Causes of the War" and his theories about preserving peace had, he believed, made that appointment almost inevitable.

Lodge. He took a "studio," a single room, in a tiny house at 20A Campden Hill Gardens. He was so poor that he dressed most of the time in army leftovers to save what few clothes he had; "his dressing gown was his [officer's] overcoat. Beneath this . . . a blue-grey army shirt and a pair of khaki slacks . . . blue-grey woolen socks and scarlet, heel-less Turkish slippers." Like Christopher Tietjens on a similar occasion, he slept on a "camp-bed for use of officers, G. S. one." During these months two small checks of his were dishonored: "A friend [this can only be Violet] had drawn out the whole of my £ 72 on two forged cheques! . . . For a man of English public school training there is nothing left when faced by such discreditable bits of paper—nothing left but to leave the world." Ford was as deeply humiliated by this experience as if he really had been "a man of English public school training." The whole business seemed to him a carefully planned conspiracy to persecute him, like the calculated dishonoring of Christopher Tietjens' check and Sylvia's deliberately drawing all the money out of his account when he was at Rouen.[19]

Violet continued to insist on his attendance and criticized him bitterly. In order to supply herself with information for this purpose, she had Annie Child open his mail, which he continued to receive at South Lodge in order to create—for her benefit—the appearance that he lived there. Mary Martindale, now Violet's intimate friend, meeting him one day in Campden Hill Road, followed him up the street cursing him loudly and vigorously for his falseness. One day, on an impulse, he went down to Charing, where Elsie and Katharine were living, presumably to find out how Katharine was; he never got beyond talking to their landlord, Hickman.*[20]

His only happiness was an occasional day with Stella at Berkhamstead, where Stella had found a cottage; after one such day he wrote her: "It was a lovely day—one of the loveliest I have ever had—and I hope it was for you too. . . . [This morning] I got up all right—but monotonously and wetly and longly—which last isn't a word. Today I seem to have spent entirely in

---

*After Dr. Martindale's death in 1902, Mary Martindale moved to London; for a time, in 1909, she shared a flat with Mrs. Hueffer in Hammersmith. Gradually she made her way into the world of women like Violet Hunt and May Sinclair who were interested in the arts and in liberal political causes. Sometime during the twenties she went to Germany to live. In the early thirties, her younger brother, Leonard (of whose children she was very fond), was beaten up in a back street of London and died, and Mary returned to England. Shortly after, she and Elsie set up housekeeping near Harri and his wife, in Icklesham. This arrangement was not a happy one; Mary wished continually to discuss their past, which Elsie wanted to forget. When Harri and his wife both died in 1933, they gave up the house in Icklesham. Elsie bought a house called Frithfield for herself, in Aldington, and a house called Belmont for Mary, in Appledore. Mary outlived her sister by some years.

shopping and O-Cedaring my floor.... Darling. I feel in ever so much better spirits after yesterday." He had, he said, been very low in spirits before that day with her. "... you know, you're very brave about saying you don't really mind V's rows," Stella wrote him, "& it gives her satisfaction, when you're not in the middle of them. But you know they kill you really." She decided they had to find a cottage to which they could retire together, as Ford had been dreaming of doing ever since they had met. She finally found one called Red Ford Cottage, near Pulborough, Sussex, for five shillings a week.[21]

> The fact that it had a big hole in the roof, and that water had to be carried in a pail from a "dip-hole" down the garden, did not disturb us unduly in the month of May. Nor did the long and muddy lane which was its only connection with the high road, nor the damp that soaked into the back wall and on to the wavy old brick floor. It *looked* all right, and that was the main thing. It looked like home.
> It was built of old red brick and old red tiles, all greened over with mossy stains, and it was tucked under a little red sandstone cliff, and faced over a lush meadow which sloped downwards to a little stream, and upwards to a wood on the opposite side. The garden was bounded by a hedge thrown like a loop into the meadow, within which it stood, a proudly cultivated peninsula, above a sea of waving grass.

Ford went there alone April 6 because they felt they had to conceal their relation until Stella's brother, Tom, was demobilized and "out of earshot," on his way back to Australia. Meanwhile Violet—not the easiest person in the world to deceive—had to be kept in the dark until Ford could set in motion an elaborate plan to have Ethel Mayne explain the situation to her after he and Stella were safely hidden at Red Ford. As a result of these complications Stella got to Red Ford only one weekend during the whole of April and May.[22]

"My first feelings of dismay at the dilapidation of the house," Ford wrote her the night he arrived at Red Ford, "have given way to comparative complacency after a meal of fried chicken and beans and oranges—but *no* drink." The ceilings were down and the laths rotten throughout the house and the roof was a ruin; you could, Herbert Read said later, see the stars through it.

> The haven from sophistications and contentions
> Leaks through its thatch;
> He offers succulent cooking;

The door has a creaking latch,

as Ezra Pound put it; the garden was "more over-run by rabbits than any Horstralian ever imagined." But Ford was determined to think well of it. " . . . we shall be very happy here—I saw the new moon looking very beautiful. It *is* a quaint cottage. . . . You are a clever dear Australian thing to have found it. It is exactly what we want."²³

Ford had once more begun to dream of becoming the Small Producer. The idea of growing his own vegetables and raising his own pigs and chickens and not having to eat poisonous tinned foods was once more a prime consideration with him. He busied himself at Red Ford getting the rabbits fenced out and the garden turned over almost before he had swept out last autumn's leaves and O-Cedared the floors. But he was not very good with his hands, and his additions to Red Ford were, according to Stella, untrustworthy. It was the pride of his life that he was able that year to show his potatoes at the annual Pulborough Flower Show, and he began to fancy himself an expert on the Sussex Large Black Pig. With his alert mind and vivid imagination, he quickly impressed others as well as himself with his image of himself as the skillful Small Producer. But it was what he imagined rather than the reality that mattered to him, as is evident from the fact that he began—in *Mr. Croyd*—to write about what he imagined he was doing before he attempted to do any of it.²⁴

Early in June Stella was finally able to join him. As soon as she did Ford changed his name to Ford Madox Ford: he was not going to risk another lawsuit by having Stella called Mrs. Hueffer.

> Yesterday [he wrote Pinker] I changed my name by deed poll from Hueffer to Ford, partly to oblige a relative & partly because a Teutonic name is in these days disagreeable & though my native stubbornness would not let me do it while the war was on, I do not see why I shd. go on being subject to the attacks of blackmailers indefinitely.²⁵

At the same time he got Ethel Mayne to inform Violet of the situation. He was prepared—at Stella's urging—to continue to make occasional appearances at South Lodge if Violet wished him to, but he was very anxious to conceal from Violet where he and Stella were. "Will you please," he said to Pinker, "not let the [Red Ford] address go to anyone outside your office— I mean to *anyone whatever.*" When Violet heard he was living with Stella she sought out Mrs. Hueffer and Juliet and told them exactly what she thought of Ford. "I was so frightfully exasperated with him," she explained afterwards, "—2 months without a letter!—that I was quite reckless about myself

& exceedingly thoughtless for you. But do forgive me." She then took to her bed and summoned Ford to appear. When he left, she wrote Mrs. Hueffer:

> I have been in bed since Friday—and I believe I have broken a small blood vessel. Now Ford has come up at another woman's petition. . . . We have agreed to stay together without love. It is a very trying proposition for me, and we . . . argu[ed] it out by my bedside all Monday morning. . . . He left for four days at 12 o'clock that day and returns tomorrow Friday about lunch.

It is impossible to say whether she really believed Ford's offer of occasional appearances meant they were "to stay together without love" while he carried on with "the other woman" some hole-and-corner affair or whether she was only pretending to believe this for pride's sake.[26]

As soon as Ford and Stella were settled at Red Ford, he sat down to give his mother what he hoped would become the official version of the whole business.

> In January of this year [1919] I heard that a gentleman, an intimate friend of Violet's [probably Edward Heron Allen], had said in a drawling voice, to a friend of mine on Violet's authority, that I was living on Violet. I also heard that Violet was constantly associating with two people who during the war denounced me to the police as a German spy. When I heard the first statement I gave Violet an opportunity of contradicting it; she refused to & I left South Lodge for the studio [20A Campden Hill Gardens]. When I heard the second I told Violet that if she did not give up altogether the acquaintance of these three gentlemen & two others whom I regard as my bitter enemies I should break with her for good. She chose them. . . . I therefore left London. . . . It seemed to me . . . that no man could be expected to stand treachery of that particular nature. . . . I believe no other created being wd have stood it as I have done. . . .
>
> In June I set up house with another lady. . . . We are in pretty poor circumstances but not starving & at any rate no one can say that I am being kept—tho' I suppose they will. I appear at Violet's parties at this lady's request. She wishes to save Violet the mortification of appearing officially deserted. . . . only it does not make things easier that Violet turned up & made a scene at my Club on the afternoon of her party. . . . If you consider how I did stick to her during all the years when I knew perfectly well how she was calling me drunken & dirty & parasitic to everyone in London. . . . At any rate that is why I have disappeared & am determined to remain hidden.[27]

While he had waited for Stella to join him, Ford had thought of himself as making a living "as a jobbing gardener" and putting Red Ford into first-class condition with his own hands.

[He] distempered the living-room and whitewashed the kitchen until the whitewash ran down into his armpit.... [He] bought a job-lot of old oak boards of which he was inordinately proud. "We'll have nothing but oak here," he said, and proceeded to build a cock-eyed lean-to outside the kitchen door to accommodate the oil stove on which we cooked, and which had a habit of belching smuts all over the tiny kitchen which was also the pantry and the scullery. When Ford's oak cook-house was finished, there was just one spot where you could stand upright as you tended your stew pots. When it rained, the floor became a puddle bridged by an oak plank.

No sooner had she arrived than Stella came down with "septic tonsilitis" so severe that it was first diagnosed as diphtheria; Ford promptly caught it from her. The pig, for which Ford had constructed a sty with some of his precious oaken boards, died of a chill.[28]

But nothing could prevent them from having guests. The Herbert Reads came, the Raymond Postgates, Mary Butts and her new husband, John Rodker, Phyllis Reid, Francis Meynell, and Margaret Postgate, now Mrs. G. D. H. Cole—"a greedy girl," Stella said, "[who] said she would have preferred a snack at seven-thirty to a banquet at—she alleged—eleven o'clock."[29]

Despite this stream of visitors, Stella persuaded Ford to go back to his writing; he even began to complain that "as we have so many people staying with us, I don't get as much done as I might"—always a good sign with him. While he had waited for Stella to come to Red Ford he had started writing the landscapes that eventually became Chapters II and III of *No Enemy*. Now he went to work in earnest to get himself reestablished as a writer; he pressed Pinker to sell these landscapes and they soon appeared in *The New Statesman* as "English Country." His idea was to make a whole book about the country, giving it the added poignance of a soldier in France remembering home. This book was to be "like the 'Soul of London' in tone ... about 40,000 words.... " He was also at work on a novel, *Mr. Croyd*, which had by this time replaced *True Love & a G.C.M.*[30]

No Enemy is a realization of the feelings that slowly converged to make Ford's dream of inhabiting "in tranquillity with the most charming of companions a rural habitation so ancient, frail and unreal that it is impossible to think of it otherwise than as the Gingerbread Cottage you may read of in the tale of 'Haensel and Gretel!' " It was written at and about Red Ford, though it was not published for another decade. It is marred by a certain amount of literary penny-pinching, by the patching in of bits and pieces of work written at other times and for other purposes, and occasionally by self-congratulatory descriptions of Gringoire, the "poet and Gallophile" who represents Ford. Nonetheless it is Ford's first successful attempt to dramatize his narrator's consciousness in a way that would express everything he felt.*[31]

*For a discussion of *No Enemy* see pp. 487–89.

Chapter 23

Ford cared very much for the idea of the Gingerbread Cottage; and so did Stella.

> I even loved the pigs [she wrote afterwards]. I loved everything I did, inexpert and unaccustomed as I was at first, because it was all real, immediate and useful, and had to do with living things. And I loved being with someone with the same tastes and who lived through his eyes in the same way that I did. We took such perpetual and unanimous pleasure in the *look* of everything, the sky and the weather and the view and the garden and the arrangement of our cottage. . . .
>
> You can live upon a view. Almost.

But the practical disadvantages of Red Ford were considerable, and they soon began to plan a change. In June Pinker had sold the movie rights of *Romance* for $5,000, Ford's half of which—he was surprised to discover—came to only £429 when what he owed Pinker had been deducted. With this sum in hand, he felt rich. "His whole system," as Stella said, "rejected any knowledge of money matters. . . . On the other hand, the smallest unexpected cheque would inspire a mood of ebullient optimism which led to an immediate orgy of spending . . . and a new bill to arrive at the next awkward moment." "Lately," he told Masterman, "I have made a good deal—indeed, a great deal—of money, quite unexpectedly, by the sale of various cinema rights in the U.S.A. & in other ways." It was, he thought, "enough money to keep [me] going for the next four or five years at the rate at wh. I live contentedly. That gives me the chance of a good rest, wh. I need & I can then go on writing. . . . My nerves . . . are a bit jumpy."[1]

But in June Ford asked Pinker to put £400 of the payment for *Romance* in the war loan until he could find a new cottage to buy. With the remainder Pinker was to "open an account for me at the Pulborough branch of the London & County Bank—for Capt. F. M. Ford." In August they purchased Coopers Cottage in the tiny village of Bedham with Ford's £ 400 and an addition from Stella's inheritance. But it was not until March, 1920, when the tenant "paid the debt of nature," that they were able to take possession, and it was fall before they had put the house in order. They therefore spent a quiet, muddy winter at Red Ford, where Ford started "two immense Novels that look like being seven million words long each, and I am sick and tired of writing immense novels, and anyhow, I don't seem to get well enough to write much. So I am rather thinking of going for the laurels of de la Mare or Masefield."[2]

Ford was finding it difficult to write. "I haven't written another word of that Nuvvle and precious little of owt else," he told Herbert Read the next spring. Then, as frequently happened when he had settled into a new romantic relation, he found himself writing verse. "I am getting back into work again," writing "a long poem—between 7, and 800 lines of a Fairy Tale type. Beautiful! A sort of (relatively) Jazz Patmore, Angel in the House Affair." This was "A House," to which Monro would devote an issue of his *Chapbook* the following March. "A House" is yet another embodiment of Ford's dream of country life in which Red Ford ("I resemble/The drawing of a child/That draws 'just a house' "), all the farm animals, and the human inhabitants contribute to the history of the struggle against winter and rough weather. Even the unborn child of the house (for by this time Stella knew she was pregnant) contributes his share: of course it was going to be a boy. Herself, as Stella is called, cries out that everything must be done "For my son; my son; my son; my son!" And they are rescued from financial disaster by the unexpected windfall from the sale of *Romance. Poetry* awarded Ford its annual prize for the best poem of the year for "A House."[3]

This success made him feel much gayer that spring; "I have just got a new typewriter," he told Monro, "and it carries me away . . . but it does not seem to possess any accents)) at least, I have not found them yet"/2-£ &'()¼ ⅛ ⅜ :!%?. No, they aren't there." The spring weather also revived the Small Producer. He purchased a Black Sussex sow and what he believed a champion Angora goat, which he named Penny, "because he facially resembled (but was not) POUND, Ezra."[4]

But for all his cheerfulness Ford was not a well man. "As for me," he told Flint, "I am not done in and am gradually recovering physical fitness; and mental, too, I hope. The only thing that seems to have gone is my memory—and even that comes back slowly! . . . In patches it comes quite vividly." But this letter ends with a passage typical of Ford when his mental control was shaky: "It is true I am a great writer . . . probably the very greatest! And you just wait, my dear; Give me three years to get all the bits and poison out of my poor old carcase and lungs. . . . " His memory was still very unreliable. "I have," he wrote Herbert Read, "lacerated [Flint], I don't know how"; he would have known had he remembered he had called Flint's friend Amy Lowell "an unpleasantly obese Neutral." Ernest Jessop, the narrator of *The Marsden Case,* whose war experience is closely modeled on Ford's, "was not, after [being bombed], much good until . . . 1921. . . . "[5]

The strength of his fantasy that he was a great writer shockingly neglected is revealed by a poem called "Immortality: An Elegy on a Great Poet Dying Abroad."

> Heaven knows, you may well prove Immortal
> So consummate, consummately handled your prose is,
> And your poems the summit of Poetry. Only,
> Your death might so well, had you chosen,
> Have silenced some brutes
> Who deem that the odour and soul of the rose is
> Matter to cozen
> And barter about. . . .
> Yet here, at home, you could not find one hearth
> To crave your shadow falling from the ingle
> Towards the curtains. This is your own land
> And your face forgotten![6]

At the end of July, he and Stella left Red Ford and moved into rooms at Scammell's Farm in Bedham. Their plan was to spend August and September putting Coopers Cottage in shape—"up to [their] eyes," as Ford put it, "in painting, papering, plastering and bricklaying"—and then "during October and November [to rest] from our labours in one Metropolis or other, supposing us to have the car-hire left to go. . . . " Ford had hoped to finish *Mr. Croyd* before they left Red Ford, but the work dragged on into October, so that it began to seem to him "an Immensity—a sort of Literary Via Dolorosa." He was also working on the series of articles for *The Dial* and *The English Review* that were to constitute *Thus to Revisit.* When these articles began appearing in *The English Review,* Alec Waugh of Chapman & Hall wrote to ask if there were enough of them to make a book. This was flattering but also troublesome. "I am at the moment," Ford wrote Pinker, "hideously busy, building here, onto the place I bought so as to get it weather-tight by Xtmas—but Waugh could have either the novel [*The Wheels of the Plough*] or the other [*Thus to Revisit*] in a month or six weeks."⁷

Early in August Pound had come down for a night and a couple of weeks later Ford wrote him,

> I am getting along with the Dial articles [*Thus to Revisit*]—with interruptions from Violet who has planted herself in the neighbourhood & runs about interrupting my workmen and generally making things lively. I fancy she had you followed by a detective when you came down & so got the address.

Three weeks later he reported that "I have been too much cluttered up what with getting a novel [*The Wheels of the Plough*] corrected for the typist and the continuing activities and incursions of Violet & her agents—which are really bad for Stella—to write. . . . " Violet and May Sinclair greatly annoyed Ford by hanging over the gate peering at him as he fed the pigs, like Sylvia spying on Christopher and Valentine in *Last Post*. One time, however, Ford and Stella had the pleasure of seeing "a whole car-load of uninvited London busy-bodies coming to peep at Ford in his new retreat" "gently rolling backwards down" Bedham hill.⁸

But even Violet could not stay forever in Bedham. Instead she hired the wife of the local carpenter who was doing the repairs on Coopers to spy for her. Violet was an importunate employer, and Mrs. Hunt's reports regularly begin, "In reply to yours of today. . . . " Often, too, she found Violet's requests difficult. "I received safely yesterday the parcels, & gave them myself to your Husband. . . . Surely they must think I am a fool excuse me Although I myself have never told them than [*sic*] I understood you were the wife. I suppose that accounts for it all being taken so calm[.]" Ultimately she balked. "I am returning the Stamps as I am afraid of getting myself into trouble in sending you a wire [presumably about when Stella's child was to be born], & in Mrs Ford's condition I do not think it fair to her, to worrie her so much. . . . " "I should," Wells wrote Violet about her campaign, "leave the whole business alone & go on being called & calling yourself *Violet Hunt*. If Ford will go on behaving like an ass there is no reason why you should follow suit."⁹

Violet then decided to call on Elsie in Charing. Suddenly, while Elsie was sitting at the little outdoor fireplace where she liked to make tea, a voice behind her said, "Is that Katharine?" and she turned to discover Violet. Violet did not herself very well understand why she made this visit, and she was so absorbed in her own feelings that she brought up the awkward question of who was Mrs. Hueffer in the letter she wrote Elsie afterwards.

Dear Mrs. Hueffer:
 You will think it very strange of me—but I felt a great peace after
I had seen you. Your wonderful attitude towards F. made me feel
how strong a virtue self-control is, and your dignity, when you spoke
to me, brought out the best in me—who am still storm-tossed. I hope
I shall see you again. . . . Thanking you for your reception of me—
                                        Yours,
                                        V. H.

I will be seeing Mary [Martindale] soon—but I will not tell Ford's
mother I saw you, shall I? . . .
 Dreadful things have been happening, and I wish I could see you
with regard to the disposition of my legacy to your daughter. [It]
needs some sort of trust, I think.
 Will you write to me, as Miss Violet Hunt, of course, now.[10]

Early in September Ford and Stella moved into Coopers.

Bedham [Stella wrote] was an extravagantly beautiful and quite
inaccessible spot on a great wooded hill. . . . There was an immense
view, and lovely paths winding through beech woods all over the
hillside. Our cottage, white plaster and oak beams with a steep tiled
roof, was about three hundred years old and had settled well down
into its hillside. There was an orchard full of wild daffodils running
up to the hard road at the top of the hill, a small wood full of bluebells
lower down behind the cottage, and below that, a big rough field.
Ten acres in all, sloping towards the view.

They had an old man, Bailiff Standing, and a little girl, Lucy, to help them.
Six weeks before the baby was due, Stella sprained her ankle and was laid
up—perhaps fortunately, for she had been overworking badly. The baby,
Esther Julia, was born in a London nursing home on November 29, 1920.
They stayed on in London until the new year. Ford adored the baby despite
her perversity in being a girl; she "gave him a big new stake in the post-war
world where he still felt pretty lost."[11]
 In the winter Bedham was not so beautiful. "It was the rain we minded
most. There was mud all around the back door, and the path down the
orchard from the road was a long, perilous slide. The pipe which brought
our water from the spring would freeze and burst, the kitchen was damp and
draughty and it was always cold upstairs." It soon became clear that Ford
was conducting a very uneconomical operation—"Two litters of pigs, thirty
hens, twenty ducks, three goats and the old mare" were eating them out of
house and home. Ford "imagined that the possession of ten acres was a

guarantee of monetary profit and talked grandly and reassuringly about [their] becoming self-supporting," but in fact they were operating at a loss. The worst of this for Stella was that she had to bear it alone; Ford's vision of himself as the skillful Small Producer was so important to him that if he was forced to contemplate the truth "he would collapse into such a misery of despair that [their] entire lives became paralysed." He put it to Stella "that he could not finish his book if his mind was upset, and that I must manage to keep all worries from him . . . [which] meant that I must not let him know how overdrawn we were at the bank, nor how big the bill from the corn mills had become, nor how badly we needed a paraffin tank." "I was in love, happy, and absorbed," Stella said. "But there was no room for me to nurse an independent ego"; Ford was too "great a user-up of other people's nervous energy."[12]

Ford understood their situation better than Stella allows. His way of dealing with it was to write more and to press Pinker and his publishers with more unreasonable demands for money. He sent the Northern Newspaper Syndicate a story about which the editor wrote Pinker, "I feel sure . . . you have not read this story yourself or you would not have sent it to us for publication in 1921. It is purely and simply a war story and, I imagine, has been typed for some considerable time. We could not possibly use it. . . . " Ford also rushed the manuscript of *Thus to Revisit* to Chapman & Hall with only a small part of it typed, and when Arthur Waugh said they could not pay the sum due on delivery of the book "until we can read it," Ford, who wrote one of the most illegibile hands in the history of literature, replied that "I can assure you printers will have no difficulty with my handwriting." He tried to get Lane to take *The Wheels of the Plough* by submitting it as the work of Daniel Chaucer. He dug out a six-months-old offer from Orage to write a literary page for *The New Age* and was upset to discover Orage had given the job to Herbert Read. He suggested that Pinker get him a commission—"about £150 and expenses"—to go to Oberammergau and write a couple of articles about it. None of these ideas helped; they only damaged him with editors and publishers, though he never understood why: "I always get into mysterious rows and misunderstandings with publishers if I deal with them direct," he said. These efforts to increase his income were not helped by the sudden death of J. B. Pinker in New York in January, 1922.[13]

Discouraged by these rebuffs in England, Ford took comfort in the idea that he was highly regarded in America. A number of American admirers appeared at Bedham that summer of 1921, including Glenway Wescott and Monroe Wheeler and Professor Lawrence M. Price of California. Ford began to believe he was "setting the Hudson on fire with various articles and poems" and that "articles about me have been appearing in the heavy monthlies." There were admiring English visitors, too—the young novelist Anthony Bertram, Dyneley Hussey, who reviewed music for the *Times*, Alec Waugh, David Garnett, Edward Shanks. "He needed," Stella said, "more reassurance than anyone I have ever met. That was one reason why it was so necessary for him to surround himself with disciples.... In exchange for the help that he gave [them] Ford received something very valuable and without which he could scarcely live. He received the assurance that he was a great master of his art."*[14]

Thus to Revisit: Some Reminiscences was published that spring by Chapman & Hall; it was Ford's first postwar book. It was both brave and foolish of him to publish it. Neither his memory nor his judgment had sufficiently recovered for him to control the fantasies by which, in the privacy of his imagination, he explained the unjustified neglect from which he believed he suffered. Also, he had widely advertised his determination never to write another book. About this he was a little apologetic. "It is all very well to ape Cinna and, planting one's cabbages, to ignore all public omens. But once one is tempted from green tranquilities, it is not easy to close one's ears to the groans of the Body-Politic." These groans were in fact his own angry complaints that creative literature had been destroyed by the sterile pedants who had taken over the literary establishment during the war. "... Creative Literature—Poetry—is the sole panacea for the ills of harassed humanity," it alone can serve as a foundation "for the study of psychologies," and it is being stifled. In this crisis, he, "an insubstantial ghost revisiting the glimpses of a moon" to which he had said farewell in 1914, set himself to make a survey of the contemporary literary scene.[15]

He begins with his theory that all scholars, critics, and reviewers are unmitigated fools, busy proving from a study of poets' laundry bills what is not of the slightest significance. This is a mild version of what he felt; in his unpublished *Toward a History of Literature* (1922), he describes a bibliographer as a "fellow... not content to let a poem remain a poem: it must become a sort of cheese in which innumerable maggots must pullulate." He then goes on to describe in the same way all the "Intelligentsia" who write for the *Saturday Review* and the *Times Literary Supplement*. This "Intelligentsia" is now in complete control of the literary journals of the day. "... to the war went the Futurists, the Cubists, the Imagistes, the Vorticists

*Ford's total publication in American magazines during 1921 consisted of one chapter of *Thus to Revisit* and "A House." Nothing but reviews of *Thus to Revisit* was written about him.

—even the poor old Impressionists. The Eminent Middle-Aged remained in undisturbed possession of the fauteuils of Parnassus ... a serried phalanx of metricists, prosodists, young annalists, young commentators. And there they still remain, controlling all the Sources of Information." These people devote themselves to lowering "the standard of civilization towards the most una-shamed materialism," with the result that in "Anglo-Saxondom [art] has died." "If you wish for wars, civil commotion, revolution, outburst and outcry one very good way to assure this is to build within your state a caste of Intelligentsia." He runs into a slight difficulty with this argument when he comes to his own theory that narrative art grew up with Flaubert; in demonstrating this point he finds himself arguing for a minute analysis of "tautologies, inexact phrases, repetitions, or a too great indulgence in per-sonal idiosyncrasies" and speaking with considerable scorn of the popular writer who thinks such analysis pedantries.[16]

From there *Thus to Revisit* drifts off into meandering reminiscence. Ford's instinct was to produce a book of criticism on the model of *The Good Soldier*, a piece of easy talk that mixed critical theory and anecdotal illustra-tion in an apparently casual way to bring out the essential meaning of the literary situation in the postwar world. This is the kind of book he would write with much greater success in the thirties: much of the material in *Thus to Revisit* is reused more effectively in *Return to Yesterday* (1932). But in 1920 his control was not firm enough and *Thus to Revisit* is, as *The New Statesman's* reviewer said, "a muddled, miscellaneous book," full of random personal history improved to fit Ford's thesis—accounts of his own career as a pioneer writer of *vers libre* and of famous writers he had known. ("And there was Mr. James! For many years he came to tea nearly every other winter after-noon at my house in Winchelsea and used to talk in sentences—the lovable, glamourous sentences!")[17]

Reminiscence, with its temptation to self-justification, was particularly dangerous for him. In the course of discussing how he "used to be alone among English-born writers in worrying ... about the 'how' of writing," he describes how he listened "respectfully to a certain delightful Novelist whilst he lectured me on how to write. . . . " He then describes his own over-whelming retort to this "delightful Novelist." When this first appeared in *The English Review,* Wells wrote the editor angrily, "Why does [Ford] make capital out of the friendliness and hospitalities of the past to tell stupid and belittling stories of another man who is, by his own showing, a very inferior and insignificant person? This childish nonsense about my lecturing him, or anyone, on how to write a novel is particularly incredible." It is made less incredible by Wells's going on in this very letter to lecture on the nature of literature.[18]

Ford thought of his anecdote as poking gentle fun at Wells. He could not see the extent to which it took for granted his own kindly superiority and the Dickensian absurdity of Wells. He was surprised and hurt by Wells's response and hastened to explain.

> You speak much faster than I do [he wrote Wells]; I daresay you think much faster than I do. Many people do. . . . When that happens I think I am being lectured. . . .
>
> . . . You must remember, too, that you guyed me in Boon and that might seem to give me a certain prescriptive right to poke a little fun back at you. . . .
>
> I am perfectly and absolutely sure that I have never to any living soul reported—or even hinted—that I had worsted you in conversation. . . . I couldn't, you know, think of myself as getting the better of you in repartee!

This is an obviously genuine apology, made in spite of Ford's inability to see what had given offense in the first place.[19]

Despite his unhappy experience with *Thus to Revisit*, Ford retold this anecdote a decade later in *Return to Yesterday*. There Wells is "an eminent politician" (this was when Wells told Ford his plans for taking over the Fabian Society). He takes Ford to the Reptile House of the Regent's Park Zoo and lectures him on the protective coloration of birds; he then gives his version of "a disagreeable affair" and begs Ford to spread this version around. Ford does so, only to be accused by the politician of "relating unthinkable things about him." Ford then writes him "a mild letter, more, as the saying is, in sorrow than in indignation. . . . He never answered my letter." This revised version of the anecdote shows the way Ford's fancy worked, substituting the protective coloration of birds for the novel, "a disagreeable affair" for some personal confidence, a political speech for Wells's letter to *The English Review*, an admirably "mild letter" for his letter of apology. The significant values of the experience as Ford had arranged them in his own imagination are carefully preserved; the insignificant facts are all changed.[20]

Both versions of the anecdote show the extent to which Ford's fanciful impression of events governed his conception of reality. The cause of his difficulties remained incomprehensible to him.

> My life through I seemed to have been mixed up in terrific rows with people who appeared singularly touchy. That is probably my own

318] THE SADDEST STORY

fault. I suppose I have always rather liked teasing public characters and public characters must dislike being teased more than I imagined they did.

Thus it was that Ford stirred up the enmities that seemed to him so undeserved.[21]

Ford's view of the English literary establishment in *Thus to Revisit* delighted Pound. Pound's dependence on Ford's critical judgment slowly faded during the late twenties. Though affectionate as ever, the tone of his letters changes in these years. "Thank god," he would write, "I was born ten years later than you were. Escaped a lot of god damned nonsense. Not sure that beastly word gentleman hasn't caused more trouble in yr/ bright l'il life than all the rest of the lang. (lang=langwidg). . . . That bloody minded nurse. . . . " His respect for Ford's judgment, however, was as strong as ever during these early years of the twenties. He was still addressing Ford in his old teasing way—"My deah ole Freiherr von Bluggerwitzkoff"—and was careful to speak tactfully of the parts of *Thus to Revisit* that seemed to him not serious ("You have done a very charming book"); and he called Ford's attack on the literary establishment of London "several pages of the only criticism that has been in England."[22]

How genuine Pound's respect for Ford was at this time is illustrated by an exchange between them about the canto Pound was at work on (the original Canto VIII, the present Canto II). Pound had sent Ford the manuscript of *Mauberley*, with its poem about Ford and Stella at Red Ford ("Hugh Selwyn Mauberley," X), with a hint that Ford was to take the poem about himself as a compliment. "Will send you my new versicul-opus to yr. new address [Scammell's Farm]," he wrote Ford; "believe it contains an 'advance'; by no means as rich as 'Propertius' but has form, hell yes, structure, and is in strictly modern decor. J. R. thinks both he and I will be murdered by people making personal application of necessary literary constructions verging too near to photography. My defense being that 'Mr. Nixon' is the only person who need really see red. . . . " (Mr. Nixon is an obvious and very uncomplimentary portrait of Arnold Bennett).[23]

Shortly after this he sent Ford Canto II.

I wish [he wrote] . . . your infinite patience could persuade you to go th[r]ough the enclosed with a red, blood-red, green, blue, or other pencil and scratch out what is too awful.

I've done fifteen or more versions . . . Dido and the, 'elenaus, 'eleptolis, have to stay, they are the links with the preceding canto. . . .

Ford's comments on the canto produced a fascinating reply from Pound.

Dear Hesiod:

Thanks orfully. It is only the minute crit. that is any good, or that prods one. First to rebuttals. Ox is slung. At least my recollection is that I saw in Excideuil a sling and wondered wottell it was until I actually saw an ox in it. D[orothy] also thinks I told her at *THAT* time of seeing the ox. I don't believe this is an hallucination born of seeing the sling and building hypothesis that it was for ox. . . .

Thank heaven the points that worried ME, have got by your eagle optic; that is some relief. Now Snipe?, arent they the damn longlegged barstards that scurry along the sand in N. J.? I can hardly go in for reed-birds or more scientificly differintiated orniths. I wuz told as a kid that the damn things were snipe. BATH-IAN BRIMFUGL BRAEDAN FAETHRA, is the general text.

I tried a smoother presentation and lost the metamorphosis, got to be hurley burley, or no one believes in the change of the ship. Hence mess of tails, feet, etc. . . .

Re the double words, and rep. of cadence. The suffering reader is supposed to have waded through seven cantos already: MUST bang the big-bazoo a bit, I mean rhythm must strengthen here if he is to be kept going. KHRRIST, To make a man read forty pages of poetry, and with prospect of 300 to follow?????

As to Gargoyles, some one has got to make the plunge, decide whether the Epic, or wotell of cosmographic volcano is extinct or not. It will take me another thirty years at least. . . . Surely one speaks of "receding wave". It may be a technical looseness of phrase, but it is certainly "english". "Wash" is impos. Homophone with laundry. (which is used both of the institution and of the wash). . . . Re/ pulling. Surely, you must have been at sea in a storm and known how the bloody wave pulls the whole boat. Boat makes a heave at wave, cuts in a bit, then gets dragged off course. . . .

Thanks eturnully, for going over thing. Snipe, long legs, long beaks, certainly on Jersey shore, leaping about pools left in the sand. Fond memory of cheeildhood. . . . I dare say it wd. be easier to cut the preceding cantos & let Acoetes continue=only I dont see how I cd. get *him* to Bayswater.[24]

The summer of 1921 passed pleasantly for Ford.

Uncle Ford [Mrs. Hueffer wrote her grandson Frank Soskice]

has a hut in which he writes—when not working on his ground as
a labourer—it is a big place and they have . . . two *huge* pigs who to
me are hideous but your Uncle stands by them with a bland smile
& a straw in his mouth & says they are "beautiful." . . . The cottage
is very pretty & *very* simply furnished & cosy. They have . . . very
pretty china and silver: but it is really the end of the world. . . .

A constant stream of visitors compensated Ford for that. "I go about in filth
all day," he told one of them, "& put on a cricket shirt & very old dress
things at night—not for swank but because I have only one other respectable
suit which I have to save for the metropolis." But it was for swank too. "In
those days [before the war]," says the narrator of *The Marsden Case*, "we
dressed for dinner every night: to think of it!—and there would be wax
candles and silver dishes." Ford provided his own version of that at Coopers.
When he needed to escape their guests he could retire to the leaky hut he
had built himself at the top of the orchard.[25]

Stella, who had both the baby and the house to care for, was not so
lucky. " . . . it seems to me," Ford said, "that Stella leads a fairly idle &
luxurious life—but she says she doesn't." "Ford," said Stella, "never understood why I found it so difficult to paint whilst I was with him. He thought
I lacked the will to do it at all costs. That was true, but he did not realise
that if I *had* had the will to do it at all costs . . . I should not have been
available to nurse him through the daily strain of his own work. . . . " Stella
got only "a few little portraits, and . . . some illustrations for Ford" done at
Coopers, but she "nursed" Ford so well that in September he was able to
start *The Marsden Case*, his first publishable postwar novel.[26]

At the end of February, 1922, he sent *The Marsden Case* off to Macmillan
in the hope of salvaging something from Pinker's plan for making Macmillan
his permanent publisher. Samuel Roth, the owner of a New York magazine,
Two Worlds Monthly, and a friend of Pound, managed to trap him into being
the British editor for the magazine and he spent a good deal of time that
spring enlisting writers for it, only to discover it was financially untrustworthy. In July Macmillan turned down *The Marsden Case*. Ford then tried
unsuccessfully to persuade Liveright to buy *The Marsden Case*, a volume of
poems, and *Toward a History of Literature*, which he was now working on.
Duckworth finally took *The Marsden Case*. According to Ford, they did so
as part of an arrangement for republishing Ford's old books as quickly as
their copyrights reverted to him, thus fulfilling his dream of a collected
edition. Duckworth's records were destroyed in the war, but if they ever
agreed to such an arrangement, nothing came of it.[27]

The winter of 1921–22 at Bedham had not been any pleasanter than the previous one: "We have a household of neuralgics, due to this hideous east wind," Ford reported in March. As the summer of 1922 drew toward its close, therefore, they began to make plans "to winter abroad" ("How dazzled I was by that phrase!" Stella says). *The Marsden Case* was to provide the money, and Harold Monro offered to lend them his tiny villa at Cap Ferrat. There was a great deal to do before they could go; the livestock had to be sold off—at shocking prices; their possessions had to be stored; the cottage had to be rented; and they had to have clothes. "We simply had nothing fit to be seen," as Stella said, "and no money to re-stock our wardrobes; yet we were planning to stay a month in Paris before going south." She spent weeks refurbishing their shabby clothing.²⁸

As so often happened with Ford, this project built up to a climax like that of an old movie; would Duckworth's acceptance of *The Marsden Case* arrive in time to save them? The suspense was sustained to the last moment.

> . . . in our usual foolhardy fashion [says Stella], we went right ahead with our plans, trusting that the Lord would provide. The luggage was packed, the passports obtained, and we were actually piling into the dog-cart to drive to Fittleworth station, when the postman delivered the manuscript—returned! This caught us hard in the pit of the stomach. As we stood on the windy station platform . . . I managed secretly to undo a corner of the parcel in case there was a letter inside.
> . . . The letter said that Duckworth would like to publish the book if Ford would make certain minor alterations. . . .
> So we had a happy journey after all.²⁹

Just before they left, Ford completed a long poem which expressed his reasons for leaving England, *Mister Bosphorus and the Muses or a Short History of Poetry in Britain. Variety Entertainment in Four Acts . . . with Harlequinade, Transformation Scene, Cinematograph Effects, and Many Other Novelties, as well as Old and Tried Favourites.* Ford has three main counts against England: the climate, particularly in the winter at Bedham; the insensitivity of critics to the kind of art he admired; and the middle class's stupid disapproval of real love.

> But how is it possible that men hold dear
> In these lugubrious places,
> This dreary land; the clod-like inglorious races,
> The befogged, gin-sodden faces,
> The lewd, grim prudery; for-ever-protracted chases
> After concealed lechery; hog-like dull embraces

> Under a grey-flannel sky; un-aired and damp
> Like poems a-stink of the lamp
> And the learned bronchitics that camp
> Hodden-grey thoughts all to stamp
> Craving tenpence for fourpence
> And grudging us our pence.

The Southern Muse then makes Mr. Bosphorus immortal and places him in Ford's heaven:

> Warm sands to write on, and a yielding breast!
> A thousand years to write in! Say ten thousand!
> A million years to write in; and no cold!
> No hindrance! Just to write! And kiss! And write!
> Why, on the surface of these blanched sands
> In characters legible in Orion's belt
> I'll write such love and wisdom![30]

The Marsden Case: A Romance is Ford's first self-possessed postwar work. In *True Love & a G.C.M.* and *Mr. Croyd* and *No Enemy* he had produced only implausible daydreams in which an incredibly high-minded hero triumphed over malicious persecutors in a revised version of Ford's own career. *The Marsden Case* more nearly resembles the related parts of *Parade's End*. Ernest Jessop, the narrator, still feels some of the uncertainties of the "newly recovered nerve patient"; his imagination is working again, but he still does not trust it completely. Ford allows the novel to fade away into an unlikely happy ending that is only slightly qualified by the heroine's fears for George Heimann's sanity and by the narrator's surprise that he has sufficiently recovered from his neurasthenia to get "through the evening perfectly well" at a formal dinner; even this slight qualification is largely destroyed by the casual brilliance with which he writes a series of dispatches for an incompetent American newspaperman.[31]

The difference Ford's newly regained self-possession makes is evident from the first words of the novel, when Jessop describes the books in the office of Podd, the publisher. Podd is Ford's revenge on Lane for having said he lost money on *The Good Soldier*, when Ford chose to believe that Lane had profited heavily at his expense.

> In such a place books are at their most sinister and their most forlorn. . . . They appear wearisomely old, with the oldness of a last week's daily paper. Upon them there will be always a film of dust, and they fit too rigidly into the white deal shelves. A limbo of books! A place where the Unborn float pallidly in dimnesses![32]

Ford uses a great deal of his own experience in *The Marsden Case.* The most striking example is the long scene at Madame Strindberg's Cabaret Club, but there are dozens of lesser ones, some of them almost private jokes. The old earl spends his evenings in a German hotel modeled on the drawing room of the Shückings' house at Telgte. Jessop is told by a Spanish diplomat that "he had been recommended to read one of [Jessop's] books—in order to acquire the purest English style," as Conrad said he had been recommended by Henley to read Ford's. George Heimann dresses exactly like Wyndham Lewis: to complete the joke Ford hangs Wyndham Lewis paintings in a restaurant—"slate-green men with . . . cylindrical, dirty blue limbs ministered to each other in scarlet landscapes." He gives Sir Arthur the characteristics of Arthur Balfour—"that pose of the blandly idiotic," the long liaison with Lady Ada.[33]

The process by which Ford transformed the actuality of his own experience into the life of George Heimann is easy to trace. Marie Elizabeth's steely determination to be recognized as "Lady Mary" and her blindness to the suffering she is causing George with his hatred of public exposure is a transformation of Violet's insistence on being recognized as "Mrs. Hueffer," and of her disregard of Ford's feelings. Marie Elizabeth's eager supporter, Miss Jeaffreson, Ford's portrait of the intellectually advanced woman as pure bitch, is his conception of the self-righteous intellectual women who egged Violet on. Marie Elizabeth and Miss Jeaffreson have the same effect on George that Violet and her friends had had on Ford during the *Throne* suit. George's feeling that he is being made a fool of during his internment in Germany echoes Ford's feelings during his long wait at Giessen for citizenship and divorce. The *Evening Paper*'s persecution of George combines Ford's feelings when he was accused of being pro-German and his feelings about the publicity given his private affairs by Elsie's suit against *The Throne.* This list could be extended.*

---

*For a discussion of *The Marsden Case,* see pp. 489–94.

Chapter 24

&

Ford and Stella got to Paris in the middle of November. They put up at the Hôtel de Blois, a small *hotel meublé* in the rue Vavin; "The lowness of the franc makes this just possible even to persons of our exiguous means." "We were tired, jumpy and overworked, and I can remember both of us almost sobbing under the nervous strain of being buffeted along the narrow pavements of the clattering and screaming streets of the Left Bank." Ford was nonetheless pleased to find himself back in the thick of things. "I had not been ten minutes in Paris before I was invited to a *lunch d'honneur* at the Paris branch of the Pen Club," he said happily. "Ezra is here, going very strong; Joyce going rather weak; my brother Oliver enormously fat & prosperous." He elected himself "a representative of English letters" to attend Proust's funeral. " . . . it was lovely," Stella said. "Whole groves of candles, the church draped from top to bottom in black and silver, masses of flowers, rows upon rows of black-veiled widows, and Bach upon the organ." Afterwards Ford liked to think Proust's death stimulated him to begin *Parade's End*: "it was his death that made it certain that I should again take up a serious pen. . . . I think I am incapable of any thoughts of rivalry. There is certain literary work to be done. . . . Proust being dead I could see no one who was doing that. . . . "[1]

Then winter began; "rain," Ford remembered, "fell for three days. It became cold with the cold that Paris alone knows as winter sets in." Reluctantly they set off for Harold Monro's tiny villa in the Chemin des Moulins at Saint-Jean-Cap-Ferrat. After sitting up all night in a second-class carriage, they woke next morning at Avignon to "that great radiant floodlight [of sunshine], which hits the ground and reflects upwards, to fill the shadows with a bubble-like iridescence. . . . " It was the country of Ford's heart. The Villa des Oliviers seemed magical to them.

You climbed to it by a rough mule-track, or alternatively by long flights of stone steps of a giddy and exhausting steepness. . . . The garden terraces which overhung Villefranche harbour appeared to have been levelled and stoned up . . . since ["the dawn of history"]. . . .

The villa had three microscopic rooms in front and two behind. The only provision for cooking was the usual peasants' charcoal contraption, but . . . there was electric light and the water was laid on. . . . The front windows opened wide on to a great luminous sky with a Saracen fortress on the skyline opposite. . . .

Behind the villa . . . you looked over Beaulieu towards Monte Carlo and Italy. . . . ²

There Ford began *Some Do Not.* . . . It took courage. He was still very much afraid that his memory and his creative powers "might have deteriorated." "There remained then for me, under Munro's olive-trees, a final struggle with my courage." " . . . one day I sat down at Munro's grandfather's campaign-secrétaire—it had been on the field at Waterloo—I took up a pen: saluted St. Anthony who looked down on me, in sheer gratitude for his letting me find my pen at all and I wrote my first sentence." If this is impressionistic—for this was not the first time Ford had "found his pen" since the war—it nonetheless represents his feeling that he was about to face up to his own most harrowing experiences. *Parade's End* is not merely Ford's largest single work; it is also, in a very personal sense, his profoundest.³

In March the Pounds offered to take Stella on a fortnight's trip about Italy to look at some "real pictures." "Vous avez quand même une certaine honnêteté," Tchelitcheff was to say of her work; such was her nature. But the way she fulfilled it was marked by that visit to Italy. This was the first time she had been separated from Ford and Julie and she missed them greatly. Nonetheless, when they moved in late April to the Hôtel Terminus in Tarascon, she took a fortnight in Paris for some painting lessons while Ford plugged away on *Some Do Not* . . . and *A Mirror for France.* From now on Stella would be a serious painter; three or four of the pictures she did that summer were hung in the Salon d'Automne that year; in her honest way she judged them not very good.⁴

In the luxuriant spring of Tarascon "life seem[ed] to run more freely in its channels than elsewhere. . . . There [was] gaiety and leisure . . . and always someone in the café, with whom to pass the time of day."

We used to pass it . . . with the local avoué and avocat. . . . He and Ford would discuss at length the proper use of the subjunctive, in elaborate French prose. Ford really knew French perfectly but he spoke it badly because he never moved his lips enough.

They went to a bullfight at Nîmes, and Julie ate quarts of cherries with the avocat's children. But as May drew on the heat became severe. Then a provincial fair moved in "and settled under the four rows of great plane trees . . . outside our bedroom windows. . . . The shouts and howls and mechanical music . . . were death to the functioning of the creative mind . . . so that it became necessary to perform the always difficult operation of transplanting the writer in the middle of a book." On the advice of the avoué, who described it as "un petit coin qui mérite d'être mieux connu," they decided to go to Saint-Agrève in the Ardèche. They found it a grim, stone-built village, still bitterly cold. Ford came down with bronchitis—"my old lung trouble"—and "almost lost all chance of dying in Tarascon." Then the cold suddenly went and "in a moment the corn was golden, in the next the rays of the sun [were] white, like magnesian light. . . . The streets, the houses, the fields [were] filled with holiday-makers. . . . " Ford worked in an annex of the hotel and Stella painted out-of-doors, "between-whiles . . . being further educated by Ford on the subject of the Albigenses and the bitter religious wars that had once shaken the part of the country we were in." Phyllis Reid and her husband joined them for some sight-seeing, and "then suddenly it was September, and going to be cold again. We made tracks for Paris."[5]

On one of their first days in Paris, they bumped into a "large, pink-faced blue-eyed gentleman" in the Place Médicis, Ford's brother, Oliver. It turned out Oliver's wife was just off to America and they would be glad to rent their place for a song. Ford and Stella began to dream of being able to afford Paris for the whole winter. Oliver's cottage, behind a row of crumbling studios at 65 Boulevard Arago, was picturesque, *style rustique*, with a little walled garden and Virginia creeper growing around the French windows of the living room. It was also damp, shabby, and without gas or electricity. But during the autumn it was delightful, especially for parties. "Les 'parties' données par Ford et Stella, quoique anglaises, étaient dans le goût américain, c'est-à-dire très bruyantes; on y buvait beaucoup," Alice Halicka remarked. Harold Loeb attended a typical one.

> . . . the main room was full of dancers, expounders, strollers, music, and smoke. . . . I could not see Stella, our hostess, but heard her voice in the stairwell which led down to the kitchen. As I started down to her, Silvia Goff kicked Mary Butts' behind.
> At once Tommy Erp and Wheeler Williams began to fight up above on the main floor. A ring formed about the fighters. Stella

roared up from below. "Miserable man, he's spoiling my party by committing suicide."

The crowd deserted the fighters and tumbled down the stairs. There was blood but no body.... I ... was dancing with a tall, elegant Swedish girl when Berenice Abbott fell on her back in the middle of the floor.

Waldo Pierce looked at her tersely. Some of the guests seemed confused but Ford was quite calm....

Everyone in the Quarter said it had been a good party.[6]

In that walled garden, Ford put the finishing touches to *Some Do Not.* ... It was the best novel he had yet written and he must have known it; "he knew," as Stella says, "that his power was coming back to him." "I've got over the nerve tangle of the war," he wrote Wells, "and feel able at last really to write again—which I never thought I should do." With this renewed confidence he began to participate in the literary life of the Left Bank; there were long evenings at the Dôme and the Deux Magots, where he was to be seen "sitting on the very edge of a chair, gasping ... and emptying one tall glass after another as though they held naught but water, showing no effects, talking endlessly, tirelessly, but never boringly...." He "moved ponderously," another observer noticed, "with his feet at right angles to each other. His hair was white, his teeth imperfect. His head resembled Humpty-Dumpty's except for the walrus moustache and the rosy complexion of a retired officer of the Indian Army.... He spoke with a slight, sibilant hesitation, as if he suffered from asthma."[7]

It was a pleasant life of aperitifs at the Closerie des Lilas and Sunday dinners *en famille* at Ford's special restaurant, the Nègre de Toulouse, in the Boulevard Montparnasse. As they walked home one such Sunday afternoon, with Julie prancing and laughing and "our bosoms [swelling] with pride at the sight of ourselves as *bons bourgeois* and *gens sérieux* amongst so many other *bons bourgeois* in this exhilarating town," they suddenly realized that the life of the Small Producer had lost its magic and that they did not want to go back to Bedham. The new vision of themselves as *gens sérieux* called for an establishment of their own; besides, they were beginning to discover the disadvantages of Oliver's cottage. "We shall probably sell our small place in Sussex," Ford told Wells, "and with the proceeds buy a small house here [in Paris] and one almost smaller in Provence." So Stella began "those hopeless journeys in suburban trains, those trampings in the rain from one *agence de location* to another ... the ignorant struggle with the most astute rogues in the world, gérants, propriétaires, and concierges...." She found nothing. At the new year they moved temporarily into one of the studios on the Boulevard Arago. It was immense, without gas or electricity and with the kitchen underground. But at least it was heated, "by an ancient and leaky anthracite stove," the fumes of which caused Stella endless anxiety.[8]

They did succeed in selling the cottage at Bedham for what it had cost them. This meant they had what was for them a large sum of cash; it was always very dangerous for Ford to get his hands on cash. Ezra Pound had been agitating for a new literary journal: Paris had been filling up with writers he approved of and they needed a forum. He was, as Ford noticed with amusement, very busy himself. "He had ... persuaded Mr. George Antheil ... to practise his latest symphony for piano and orchestra in [his] studio.... Mr. Pound fiercely struck blocks of granite with sledge hammers. ... It was not to be imagined that, with all this on his hands, Mr. Pound could be expected to give time to the conducting of a *Review*...." Coincidentally, according to Ford, Oliver offered him the editorship of a review. "He mentioned names which were dazzling in the Paris of that day and sums the disposal of which would have made the durability of any journal absolutely certain." This project came to nothing, but not before word that Ford was starting a new review had been so widely circulated that he felt embarrassed to give the idea up.[9]

At this point John Quinn, a wealthy American lawyer with an interest in the arts, arrived in Paris. Pound, the tireless entrepreneur, arranged a meeting at his studio that included Quinn, Joyce, Ford, and Pound himself. Quinn agreed to put up 35,000 francs, approximately $2,000 (the franc was then about 18 to the dollar), if Ford would do the same. Thus Ford put up about £ 435. Only £ 400 of this was strictly his; the remainder was Stella's, as was the money he used to pay contributors when the original capital ran out in May, 1924. Stella understood the dangers of this project from the start: "I was profoundly alarmed. We had the money in hand from the sale of Bedham.... Meanwhile Ford was more and more absorbed in his scheme. ... " But she was a generous woman: "I could not help seeing how lovely it would be for [Ford] if he could have his review"; "We never had any arguments or difficulties about money at all. When necessary, I withdrew small slices of my capital from Australia, and considered that I was investing it in a promising career."[10]

Ford persuaded William Bird, who published so many of the expatriate writers, to allow him to install himself in the shop of Bird's Three Mountains Press at 29 quai d'Anjou; in gratitude Ford dedicated *No More Parades* to Bird. "At the rear," Bird says, "accessible by a flimsy flight of stairs, was a sort of gallery running the whole width of the shop, say 15 feet, and perhaps 6 ft. deep. There Ford . . . installed a desk, an editorial chair and a chair for callers, and there he edited the review." Pound promptly produced a White Russian prince to be one of Ford's sub-editors and Basil Bunting, "a dark youth with round spectacles, in a large trilby hat and blue trench coat with belt," to be the other. Bunting lived—if it can be called that—"in a damp little store-room beyond [the] kitchen" of Ford's apartment; the Russian prince promptly disappeared, taking the manuscript of Ford's first editorial with him. Fortunately Pound also turned up a really efficient secretary, Marjorie Reid, who produced such order in the affairs of *The Transatlantic Review* as there was; it was not a great deal. "I had," as Ford said quite as if he had not contributed his share to making it necessary, "to edit [the *Transatlantic*], put it to bed, see it packed in boxes, and delivered. The problems of running a magazine in Paris are certainly numerous. There are no efficient young men to manage things . . . ": one of the comic aspects of Ford's relations with the American expatriates was the combination of his assumption that they would be delighted to do the magazine's boring chores while the Master designed its policy with their assumption that Ford existed to produce a magazine for their benefit; they could not imagine what other use the old man could have, as Ford in the end ruefully recognized. "I really exist," he confessed to Gertrude Stein, "as a sort of half-way house between non-publishable youth and real money—a sort of green baize swing door that everyone kicks both on entering and on leaving."[11]

Ford wrote everyone he knew to solicit contributions, to young friends like A. E. Coppard and Anthony Bertram, to established writers like T. S. Eliot, to elder statesmen like Thomas Hardy—important to Ford as the man for whom, he sometimes remembered, he had started *The English Review.* He also wrote Conrad and, as a sign that he was eager to let bygones be bygones, he suggested Conrad produce more personal reminiscences; Conrad replied that "I am afraid the source of the Personal Record fount is dried up."[12]

But Ford's greatest triumph was Joyce. Shortly after their return to Paris that fall they had had dinner together and, despite Ford's tendency to lecture Joyce on his pernicious habit of drinking white wine, got on well. A month or so later, at a party of Lloyd Morris's, Morris "found them irately pacing the garden path in the darkness. It developed that the presence of an unfrocked priest was an affront to their piety, and the venom of their indignation left Morris stupified." A few days later, he came on Joyce and Ford lunching amicably with this same unfrocked priest. Ford urged Joyce to let him have a piece of *Finnegans Wake* for the section of the *Review* he proposed to call "Work in Progress" (Joyce liked the name so much he adopted it). Joyce finally consented. "Ford has come so often to the well and talked about support given me in the past that I have consented to give him the four masters bit (which is only a sidepiece) for his next number," he wrote Robert McAlmon in the spring. Later he told Harriet Weaver that Ford was, by virtue of supplying the temporary title for *Finnegans Wake*, the book's godfather, in return for which he agreed to stand up as Julie's godfather at a Catholic christening, no small concession for a man of his rigid principles.[13]

In December the first number of *The Transatlantic Review* appeared under its lower-case title, which was an accident. Its essential character was determined by Ford's Utopian vision of a world in which all writers would welcome good writing from any quarter, without regard to politics or power, literary or otherwise. "The aim of the REVIEW," he said in the prospectus, "is to help in bringing about a state of things in which it will be considered that there are no English, no French—for the matter of that, no Russian, Italian, Asiatic or Teutonic—Literatures: there will be only Literature." He had, to be sure, his own ideas of Literature; he did not care to think that the great writers of his own young manhood were not still as significant as they had then seemed to him, and he was very loyal to the young men like Bertram and Coppard with whom he had made friends at Bedham. At the same time, he was keenly aware of the rising generation, mostly Americans, who were beginning to cause a stir in Paris. For their approval he was willing to pay a considerable price. In his final editorial for the *Transatlantic* what he congratulated himself on was his success in providing "a place for publication for commencing authors."*

But there was one thing Ford would not do to win over the young.

He had genuine pride in his own achievement; he spoke of himself as the greatest master of English prose after Meredith, Hardy, and James. . . . Through his career, he felt that he had strengthened the great tradition which nourished him, and which he sought to transmit to youth.

The one thing he would not do was to deny that tradition. This refusal exasperated the young expatriates, who felt little respect for the past: when

*" . . . the reason the review came out without capitals was not from any desire to be 'arty,' " Bird told Professor Poli. " . . . the problem seemed to be to get the distinguishing word TRANS-ATLANTIC into the largest size possible. It turned out that the word would fit exactly into the measure of in 36-pt the page provided it was not capitalized."

Ford put together a "Conrad Supplement" immediately after Conrad's death, for example, Hemingway felt it was the proper occasion to point out that his generation disliked Conrad's work. They did not see Ford as a "master of English prose"; to them he was "like Bairnsfather's Old Bill, or like a friendly walrus, obese, stertorious, heavily comic." Robert McAlmon, to whom Ford was one of a large company that insufficiently admired the work of Robert McAlmon, said:

> He wheezed and talked in an adnoid manner . . . I found it difficult to understand . . . and not necessarily to be believed when I did. It is quite impossible to talk of a place or a person without Ford topping your story and knowing more about that place or person than anyone else possibly can know. . . . [He] is a Mythomaniac . . . [who] could step into the Moon Mullins cartoons and double for Lord Plushbottom."[15]

These young writers were also offended by Ford's manner. When he had been young, manners had been formal; he himself had been happy to express his admiration for Henry James by listening to him respectfully and calling him "Cher Maître." Now that he had become an elder statesman of letters, he expected to be treated with similar respect, and "Cher Maître," as Stella said, "filled his heart with simple pleasure." But to the young, to whom "he seemed like a Sir John Falstaff, large, bibulous, bulging with impossible tales, a very cutpurse," this expectation seemed absurd. " . . . his spirit, courage, and generosity came through" to very few of them, though when it did, they would say,

> I have never known a man of letters who was more genuinely eager to be helpful to newcomers with any promise whatsoever, or who had more of a passion for literature as a great and fine art and was more desirous of furthering it through the uncovering of new talent.[16]

The Transatlantic Review was aimed at a very mixed audience, one that, as Professor Poli says, "accurately reflected Ford's personal tragedy of re-adaptation to a new literary world and a new Bohemia of which he was no longer a part." But Ford went to work with enthusiasm, partly because he greatly enjoyed playing the role of the Master and partly because he would never face the fact—often as he found himself up against it—that the marketing of magazines requires qualities other than a devotion to good literature.[17]

The first number of *The Transatlantic Review* illustrates the consequences. Conventional readers would certainly find E. E. Cummings and Pound too advanced for their taste; yet these were writers little calculated to attract the Young Turks, for whom they would seem elder statesmen of the modern movement. Neither group was likely to be charmed by the memoirs of Luke Ionides, a friend of William Michael Rossetti now in his eighties. (In fairness to Ford it should be said that Pound, too, was an Ionides enthusiast.) Ford miscalculated in the same way when he reprinted his own collaboration with Conrad, *The Nature of a Crime*, from *The English Review* of a dozen years earlier; this work could hardly attract even Conrad specialists—or, for that matter, Conrad himself, who "declared it to be too trivial to be reprinted, and ... only yielded to Mr. Hueffer's request to be allowed to republish it in the Transatlantic, 'because,' as he said, 'he was tired of argument.' " Its republication only created a suspicion that the editor wanted to flatter Conrad's collaborator, a suspicion greatly increased by his adding a minute account of the Hueffer-Conrad collaboration on *Romance*, which nearly everyone but Ford had long since forgotten. Nor is it comforting to imagine what the Left Bank must have thought of Ford's editorial "Communications" with their display of genteel expertise about French food and wines. Yet apart from the unfortunate effects of Ford's loyalty to the great tradition and of his evident pleasure in advertising his own share in creating it, his selection is critically admirable. Its fatal defect is its superiority to the power politics of publishing, its confident disregard of the prejudices of both writers and readers.[18]

This defect would get Ford into serious trouble when Hemingway returned to Paris and became the *Review*'s sub-editor. But for the moment, it caused no crises. Meanwhile Ford was enjoying himself. *Some Do Not...* was at the printer's and he was well along with *No More Parades*. His relations with publishers seemed to be improving and he began to think that his future was secure. "For once in a way we're flourishing," he wrote Jepson. "I have fixed up a contract in U.S.A. for all my work as in England...." As editor of the *Transatlantic*, he was in the thick of things.

> On Thursdays the *Transatlantic Review* was at home, and I made tea for all and sundry at the office [Stella remembered] ... Ford would first be observed aloft at his desk, narrowly framed by the semicircle of the arched roof, and talking to a new contributor. Presently he would descend and spread geniality amongst the faithful.
> He really enjoyed himself superbly.

There were "lots of cafés and restaurants and parties and good talk"; in January, McAlmon invited all the right people to a big dinner for the William Carlos Williamses at Le Trianon—Joyce, the Fords, Antheil, Duchamp, Bill Bird, Man Ray, Mina Loy, Sylvia Beach, Louis Aragon, Harold Loeb, and Kitty Cannell.[19]

Stella had some difficulty adjusting to this world; "It took me a little while to get used to living amongst people who, on the whole, had replaced all their moral prejudices by aesthetic ones." She often unintentionally offended, as Hemingway's portrait of her in *The Sun Also Rises* shows. When Jake arrives for dinner with the *poule*, Braddocks (Ford) asks him to join them for coffee. " 'And bring your friend,' said Mrs. Braddocks laughing. She was a Canadian and had all their easy social graces." When he returns with "my fiancée, Mademoiselle Georgette Leblanc," Mrs. Braddocks asks if she is related to Georgette Leblanc, the singer.

> "Connais pas," Georgette answered.
> "But you have the same name," Mrs. Braddocks insisted cordially.
> "No," said Georgette. "Not at all. My name is Hobin."
> "But Mr. Barnes introduced you as Mademoiselle Georgette Leblanc. Surely he did," insisted Mrs. Braddocks, who in the excitement of talking French was liable to have no idea what she was saying. . . .
> "Did you hear that, Henry?" Mrs. Braddocks called down the table to Mr. Braddocks. "Mr. Barnes introduced his fiancée as Mademoiselle Leblanc, and her name is actually Hobin."[20]

In January it was discovered that Mrs. Hueffer, now seventy-three, had diabetes. "She has seen a doctor," Juliet Soskice wrote her son, Frank, "who tells me that she is very ill . . . and will not be long with us. *She knows nothing* and is very happy, at staying here now. . . . I have written to Uncle Ford and am going to write to Oliver." Not that she ever counted on much from either of them; "I often wish Dadla's sons had been different," she wrote Frank soon after. "I think she must have suffered horribly over them." Ford came over from Paris to see his mother that weekend.

> Uncle Ford [Mrs. Hueffer wrote Frank] came to England on business, & looked in at Girdler's Road & brought with him a portrait of himself as a present—painted by Stella—a very clever but *hideous* as a likeness exactly like him and also looking like a Frenchman with a past.

As that peppery comment suggests, Mrs. Hueffer was not so ill as they had feared; she lived for more than three years longer.[21]

Early that spring Ford and Stella's lease on the studio in the Boulevard Arago came to an end and they "moved into a poky little apartment in the Rue Denfert-Rochereau. There was of course no bath, and one of the beds was in the kitchen." It was so small that Julie and Madame Annie, her nurse, had to spend most of the time in the "old stone labourer's cottage with four rooms" that Gertrude Stein had helped Stella find at Guermantes as a weekend retreat. Ford and Gertrude Stein had met years before; Hemingway had now reintroduced them and immediately involved them in one of his elaborate intrigues. Hemingway had returned in January, 1924, from Canada, where he had been since September. He met Ford almost at once, at Pound's studio, and Pound recommended him to assist with the *Transatlantic*. Ford was never comfortable with Hemingway; "he comes and sits at my feet and praises me. It makes me nervous," he said. Hemingway was determined from the start to run the *Transatlantic* his way, which meant printing his friends, and he had, if possible, even less consideration for Ford than the other young Americans.[22]

His first move was to insist the *Transatlantic* print Gertrude Stein; he "wanted The Making of Americans to be run ... as a serial and he had to have the first fifty pages at once." "Ford," he said, "alleges he is delighted with the stuff." "Hemingway when he first handed me your manuscript, gave me the impression that it was a long-short story that would run for about three numbers," Ford later told Gertrude Stein. "It was probably my fault that I had that impression." In the end the *Review* ran nine installments of *The Making of Americans*.[23]

The first installment appeared in the April number, along with an excerpt from *Finnegans Wake*. Ford was worried that Joyce's contribution might be censored, an anxiety Joyce shared. Sisley Huddleston of the *Times*, whom they called in for advice, suggests Ford's fear was silly and that Joyce was hurt by it, but Joyce himself wrote Harriet Weaver with evident relief that "the correspondent of the Times here [that is, Huddleston] was appealed to and, having examined it, gave his opinion that it would not lead to prosecution for blasphemy." With this issue Ford's effort to make the *Review* international by balancing contributions from English, American, and French writers ended, and the *Review* became in effect the magazine of the Left-Bank writers: "it was," as Professor Poli says, "no longer entirely readable by a cultivated gentleman of the pre-war period; it was becoming part of a movement which tried to destroy old values and accepted ways of writing to create a new literature, even though Ford had always wanted to launch movements deeply rooted in the past, in a tradition." The Young Turks, under Hemingway's command, were beginning to have their way.[24]

Some Do Not ... had appeared in April and received enthusiastic reviews. One reviewer called it "the biggest novel of the century as surprising [after the disappointment of *Thus to Revisit*] as it is delightful"; the *Manches-*

ter Guardian said, "there is no need to worry about the state of the English novel while books like this are being produced." Ford made ineffective use of the power this success gave him. For the May number of the *Transatlantic* Hemingway had submitted a letter to the United States in which he made what Professor Poli calls a "childishly vulgar" attack on critics that was clearly meant for Ford; as if to defy Ford to print it, he said, "If this letter is accepted [by the editor] . . . ." Ford did accept it, and then wrote, under the pseudonym of R. Edison Page, a reply in which he argued that there were four contemporary English novelists who counted, Conrad, Wells, Douglas—and Ford; of Ford he said, "The only recent novel of vigour and charm and truth to English life is . . . " a remark that everyone would recognize as a reference to *Some Do Not. . . .* This display of vanity reinforced the Young Turks' belief that Ford was simply impossible. The fact remained that if there was anyone connected with the *Transatlantic* who could command additional money to subsidize it, he could, and by May additional money was badly needed.[25]

It is not now possible to discover just why the *Transatlantic* was in financial difficulties. "I am," Ford said at the time, "a pretty good writer and a pretty good editor and a pretty good business man but I find it difficult to be all three at once"; but if the first two claims were true, the third was not, as the history of *The English Review* had long ago demonstrated. Ford was inclined to blame these difficulties on Thomas Seltzer, the magazine's agent in New York. He also blamed John Quinn, who was supposed to watch out for the *Transatlantic's* interests in New York but was dying of cancer and unable to attend to business. "Over twenty thousand copies of the review have vanished into the American scene," Ford said. It seems unlikely that difficulties over the American sales alone could, by May, have made a considerable addition of capital necessary if the magazine was not immediately to cease publication.[26]

In this crisis Ford resorted to his favorite idea of shares. Pound caused him trouble by not bothering to answer his letters about this plan.

DEAR EZRA,
 Would you please signify to me as director of this company that you agree to the following motions and empower me to act as your proxy in voting for them?
 1—That the capital of the company be raised to 150,000 francs by the issue of 115,000 francs of further shares.
 Or in the alternative
 2. That the publication of the Transatlantic Review be discontinued from 1st. prox. . . .

Do please answer this at once as this makes the third time I have written to you on the subject and having these matters held up all this time is mentally very harassing besides being absolutely ruinous.

Ford then sent out a letter to subscribers and contributors asking them to buy these shares and announcing that 470 of them had already been subscribed for, presumably by Stella. There were a few small contributions from people like Gertrude Stein, Natalie Barney, William C. Bullitt, Nancy Cunard, and Mrs. Romaine Brooks; Ford then decided he would have to go to America and either collect the money he was convinced was owed the *Review* or use his new-won prestige to get fresh backing.[27]

Meanwhile, he had gotten involved in negotiations with Conrad over the book publication of *The Nature of a Crime*, the material about their collaboration on *Romance*, and the French translation rights for *Romance;* he also complained about Dent's refusal to put Ford's name on the covers of its reprints of their collaborations. When Ford had been in London in February to see his mother, he had also seen Conrad. "We met," Conrad wrote Eric Pinker, "as if we had seen each other every day for the last ten years. ... As we talked pleasantly of old times I was asking myself, in my cynical way, when would the kink come. ... " Ford, he added, "wants to be friendly in personal relations with me. In fact, *entre nous,* too friendly. ... " Ford's devotion to Conrad was as great as ever, and whatever Conrad's feelings might be—however much Ford's past conduct may even have justified them —Ford eagerly accepted Conrad's superficial friendliness as evidence that they were back on the old terms. He poured out his troubles to Conrad in a way that is touching when one knows how unsympathetic Conrad really was. He even confided to Conrad that "I am quite determined not to have anything to do with [Eric] Pinker in future: he having treated me with gross insolence ... " at the very moment that Conrad was confiding to Pinker his scorn of Ford (Ford, Conrad told Pinker, "seems to be suffering from the idea that everybody in the world has insulted him").[28]

Personal affection, not admiration of what Conrad was now writing, determined Ford's feelings in all this. With his customary critical penetration, he had seen at once the decline in the quality of Conrad's later work. " ... to tell you the truth," he wrote Jepson in 1921, "his later work appeals to me so relatively little that I don't want to write any more about it. I mean, it's difficult to do so without appearing, and for all I know, being, ungenerous."[29]

In order to get rid of Ford, Conrad made him a proposal for settling all the questions Ford had raised. "After sending you the copy of the letter I wrote to Ford," he told Pinker, "I received a further communication from the man.... One would think it a mania if one did not suspect that there is a purpose in it.... If you agree with my point of view that a small sacrifice is worth getting rid of the damnable 'incubus' of that rotten 'Crime' embroglio then you will just post it for me.... In fact it is cheap, and what a luxury it would be to get rid of his nonsense.... You will admit that I have dissembled my rage successfully [in his letter to Ford]." Conrad's proposal agreed to everything, including Ford's right to put their collaborations in any collected edition of his work. *"This stipulation,"* Conrad told Pinker, "... is inserted in order to conciliate the swell-headed creature who seems to imagine that he will sweep all Europe and devastate Great Britain with an eventual collected edition of his own works. I humour this strange illusion being anxious to have the matter settled." Early in May Ford went to London, where he saw both Conrad and Pinker, to complete the arrangement. This meeting fixed Ford's belief that he and Conrad were once more intimate friends.[30]

A problem arose for Ford when he imagined he and Conrad were once more friends. Gossip had convinced him that Conrad's main reason for shying off in 1909 had been Ford's "relations with women," and he knew that at this very moment Elsie was planning yet another suit against Violet for having signed a letter to the *Weekly Westminster* "Violet Hunt Hueffer." He therefore wrote Conrad:

'You ought, I think to be advised of this: Mesdames Elsie and Violet Hueffer are about to burst into new and even more violent litigation as to their right to use my abandoned patronymic. As, in the course of this a good deal of mud is certain to be showered over me I do not know whether you ought to associate your name so intimately with mine as these joint prefaces [to *The Nature of a Crime*] would seem to connote, so that I should be perfectly ready to have you drop out my contribution....

I'd like by the bye to make one comment that, though I'm determined never to utter anything in the nature of an apology for my existence, and still more never to indulge in anything like polemics, when I look back on my life I can see nothing to regret except mistaken—or miscalculated, generosities. These are of course as flagitious as crimes or any other form of dishonour.[31]

So strong was his sense of renewed comradeship with Conrad that as his ship approached Plymouth on his way to America he had a sudden impulse to write Conrad. "When, late at night, the *France* [*sic:* the *Paris*] touched at its English port, I was seized with an overwhelming conviction that I should never see Conrad again. I got up and desperately scrawled to him a last letter assuring him of my forever unchanging affection and admiration for his almost miraculous gifts." This passage was written with hindsight, with the actual knowledge that he never saw Conrad again. But he did write Conrad that night, telling him that he was not resigning the editorship of the *Transatlantic:* "at a shareholder's meeting of the T. R. last week I was unanimously requested not to resign. . . . It will be run while I am away by young Hemingway. . . . Let me know how Jessie fares. My address will be The Columbia University Club, New York till the 21st."[32]

Chapter 25

In New York Ford tried to talk to John Quinn, but Quinn was too ill to see him, nor could he find anyone else to help. He spent a day with Burton Rascoe, who admired the *Transatlantic* and, being far from the scene of battle, was prepared to believe Ford was making it what he wanted it to be. "I am amazed," he said, "at Ford's mental resiliency and receptivity, by which he keeps abreast of his time in three countries and brings a sympathetic appreciation to new work of merit among the younger experimenters." At that very moment "young Hemingway" was busy making sure the *Transatlantic* was not that kind of magazine. Rascoe also took Ford to one of those publicity affairs of the New-York twenties, a luncheon given by Gilda Gray in honor of an albino monkey. Ford sat next to Miss Gray "and seemed to enjoy himself greatly, though at times he looked a little bewildered."[1]

As soon as Ford left Paris, Hemingway began chopping up the August number of the *Transatlantic*; he omitted the usual installments of Luke Ionides (of whom Ford had been boasting to Rascoe in New York) and of Ford himself. By the time Ford got back it was too late to do anything about these changes; Hemingway had skipped off to Pamplona. All Ford could do was put a few words in the editorial he had already written in New York. "[The August] number," he said ironically, "is entirely of Mr. Hemingway's getting together. It must prove an agreeable change for the Reader and it provides him with an unusually large sample of the work of that Young America whose claims we have so insistently—but not with such efficiency—forced upon our readers." He promised that in the next number Mr. Ionides would reappear "and, should any large body of readers so demand, some more of *Some Do Not. . . .* Other works of English and French writers will also be again allowed to creep in."[2]

But ironies like these were not for Hemingway. When he got back, Ford

339

asked him to write an article on Pamplona, saying he really owed it to the magazine for having done what he wanted to while Ford was away. Instead, Hemingway wrote an article about this conversation with Ford. To Ford's claim that he owed the magazine an article, he reports, "I said, 'Well I don't look at it that way,' and came home." He then went on to belittle as "journalism" what he—and by implication Ford—wrote for the *Transatlantic:* "When I write journalism I like to be well paid for it. That is the only reason for writing journalism. And when you destroy the valuable things you have by writing about them you want to get big money for it. . . . It is only by never writing the way I write in a newspaper office, though, that I make you believe that I can write." Ford answered this with an indirect comment on Hemingway's bad manners by printing immediately after Hemingway's article the last paragraph of the article he had written at Conrad's death for the *Journal Littéraire*, in which he describes himself as the Sancho to Conrad's Don Quixote, to whom Conrad used to say, "Mon cher, c'est, notre métier, le vrai métier de chien . . . Vous écrivez, et vous écrivez . . . Et personne, personne au monde ne comprendra. . . . "3

In July, after a long period of ill health, Conrad had had a heart attack; on August 2, when he was trying to show his friend Curle a house he was thinking of buying, he had another; on the morning of August 3, after waking up and announcing he was better, he died. Ford started at once to put together a "Conrad Supplement" to the *Review* and asked Hemingway to write an article for it.

> What is there [Hemingway began] you can write about him now that he is dead? . . . It will not be hard for the editorial writers . . .

CONRAD, OPTIMIST AND MORALIST

> Admirers of Joseph Conrad, whose sudden death is an occasion for general regret, usually think of him as an artist of the first rank, as a remarkable story teller and as a stylist. But Mr. Conrad was also a deep thinker and serene philosopher. In his novels as in his essays etc.

> It will run like that. All over the country.
> And what is there that you can say about him now that he is dead?

Fortunately, Hemingway knew the answer to that rhetorical question. Conrad, he said, was a writer that Ernest Hemingway could not reread but whose books, nonetheless, had given Hemingway something that he had got "from nothing else that I have ever read." His fashionable friends told him that Conrad was a bad writer and T. S. Eliot a good one, but if Ernest Hemingway, who was able to report that he had read *The Rover* in Sudbury, Ontario, "knew that by grinding Mr. Eliot into a fine dry powder and sprinkling that powder over Mr. Conrad's grave Mr. Conrad would shortly appear, looking very annoyed at the forced return and commence writing, I would leave for London early tomorrow morning with a sausage grinder." He concluded by wishing "to God they would have taken some great, acknowledged technician of a literary figure and left him to write [Conrad's] bad stories," as it no doubt seemed to him Ford often enough claimed to have done.[4]

Ford's principles would not allow him to censor this attack on Eliot, but he felt obliged to apologize for it. "Two months ago," he said in the November number, "one of ['our chroniclers'] made an attack on Mr. T. S. Eliot. ... We hesitated a long time over the ethics of the matter. ... [But] we had invited the writer to write, we had indicated no limits to his blood thirstyness: our hands fell powerless to our sides." If he imagined he would get any credit with Hemingway, he misunderstood his man: Hemingway was outraged at Ford's apologizing to Eliot.

On Bastille Day Ford and Stella gave an elaborate party at the Dôme; then they gave up their "nasty little flat" in the rue Denfert-Rochereau and retired to the cottage at Guermantes. On his return from the United States on the *Majestic* Ford had made friends with a young American named Markham Harris. When he heard that Harris was leaving for England, he commissioned him to put flowers on Conrad's grave in Canterbury together with a card on which Ford had written a phrase from the dedicatory poem in *Romance:* "C'est toi qui dors dans l'ombre, ô sacré Souvenir." At Guermantes he dropped everything to concentrate on the writing of his "Personal Remembrance" of Conrad; he completed it in the incredibly short time of two months. It was, as he said, "an offering In Memoriam constructed solely out of memory," on Ford's lifelong principle that mere biographies were outrages and that it was only when "the time comes ... for some creative artist to have a try at re-breathing life into [a writer's] dead bones" that he lives again.[5]

The reception of *Joseph Conrad* was excellent. Christopher Morley remarked that "to those who have any inkling of the kind of man Conrad was, or of the kind of furious inward life such a man must lead, this book will prove enormously valuable." There was, however, almost universal complaint that "Mr. Hueffer insists on telling us a great deal about himself that we don't the least want to know," and an occasional complaint about the book's obvious improvements ("Anything more unlike the style of [Conrad's] conversation than the nebulous, sensational, highly coloured anecdotes, retailed by Mr. Hueffer as droppings from Conrad's lips, cannot be imagined"). Then, on December 4, 1924, Jessie Conrad published in the *Times Literary Supplement* a letter in which she asked, "If Mr. Hueffer intends a personal remembrance as a tribute to the dead friend . . . why endeavour on every page to show the vast differences between himself and his friend, and always to the detriment of that friend." One of Ford's statements, she concluded, "is, like nearly everything else in that detestable book, quite untrue." Ford's displays of vanity laid him open to this kind of attack, but William McFee was right when he said, "The theory that a writer's wife is necessarily an infallible guide in matters concerning her husband's literary activities . . . is . . . amazing. . . . What I want to protest against is the *embalming* of Conrad in a grand tomb. Ford shows us the living man." But Jessie's attack fixed permanently the idea that Ford's vanity was not just a weakness but a mania that destroyed the value of everything he wrote.[6]

By August the *Transatlantic* was in desperate straits. McAlmon referred casually to "the expected death of the T. A." in a letter to Gertrude Stein and Hemingway remarked that "the review was dead . . . [and] Ford was returning subscriptions in August. . . . " Hemingway was in a state of muddled resentment about the *Review*, asserting that Ford was trying "to use the death of Quinn as an excuse to kill off the Magazine," that Ford was trying to turn it into a quarterly, and that Jane Heap was trying to get "Major Elliot and Lady Rothermere," the backers of the *Criterion*, to support it. He gave himself full credit for coming to its rescue at this point, though his main object seems to have been to see it fall into the hands of people he could control. He found a man named Krebs Friend to guarantee Ford $200 a month for six months, with an option to continue thereafter for another six months or to buy the *Review*. What followed, as Hemingway describes it, sounds all too likely.

> That of course was not good enough for Ford, who had hitherto stayed up all night writing pneumatiques and spent 100s of francs on taxis to get 500 francs out of Natalie Barney and that sort of business. Once the grandeur started working Ford insisted on 25,000 francs down in addition and then as the grandeur increased he declared he wanted no money at all till October if Krebs, this guy, could guarantee him 15,000 francs then! . . . Now Ford's attitude is that he is selling Krebs an excellent business proposition and that Krebs is consequently a business man and the foe of all artists of which he Ford is

the only living example and in duty bound as a representative of the dying race to grind Krebs, the natural Foe, into the ground.[7]

By the middle of August, Friend had taken over the financial responsibility for the *Transatlantic* and had been elected president. According to Hemingway, "He has breakfast every morning at Ford's and things are going smoothly." Friend was a badly disturbed veteran who had been married by a rich woman forty years his senior who was trying to make him want to live again; her support of the *Transatlantic* was part of the program. Hemingway quickly found the Friends even less congenial to work with than Ford had been; like many very wealthy people, Mrs. Friend was possessed by the fear that people were using her, and she insisted on getting her money's worth.

> ... Mrs. Friend [Hemingway wrote Gertrude Stein] conceived the bright idea of reducing the expenses of the magazine by trying to drop everything they would have to pay for. ... Krebs' latest idea is to have all the young writers contribute their stuff for nothing and show their loyalty to the magazine by chasing ads during the daylight hours.

It went without saying that this was all Ford's fault: "Ford ruined everything except of course himself, by selling the magazine to the Friends instead of taking money from them and keeping them on the outside as originally arranged [by Hemingway]." By November, Ford was asking subscribers to let him know if they intended to continue their subscriptions. By the middle of the month he had given up and called a meeting to wind up the affairs of the *Review*, though in his last editorial he expressed the hope that it could be restarted; he also said that it had fulfilled the objective, set forth in the prospectus, of treating literature as international, despite the fact that it had been captured by the Americans of the Left Bank and turned into a little review.[8]

This was the summer that Ford and Stella began giving their weekly party at a small working-class dance hall called the Bal du Printemps in the rue du Cardinal Lemoine; this establishment was usually closed Friday nights and Ford got the proprietor to open it for him and his friends. Nathan Asch says Ford started these parties to entertain the Krebs Friends, but if he did, he soon found himself entertaining practically everyone on the Left Bank.

> We enter to the high whining moan of an accordian and the measured thump of a drum. The music resolves itself to the eternal tune of Parisian *bal[s] musettes* this season as we press by the tiny zinc bar

> *Valencia!*
> *Terre exquise*
> *Où la brise*
> *Effeuille les fleurs d'orange!*

... the small square of dancing-floor ... is now crowded with figures hopping up and down in a peculiar rhythmic fashion. Above these syncopating puppets is a small balcony fastened like a bird's nest to the wall and in it are seated two perspiring nonchalant musicians. . . .

We notice what at a first glance appears to be a behemoth in gray tweeds. He turns in the dance and we recognize him immediately. The blue eyes, the blond hair, the bland cherubic expression, the open mouth. . . .

It is the Leviathan of the Quartier Montparnasse, the gentle Gargantua of Lavigne's. . . . He plods happily and with a child-like complacency through the dance, his partner swaying like a watch-fob before him. . . . And then, at another table much nearer the dancing-floor, we see Stella and Olga and Jean and Ernest and Bill and realize that this is Ford's Night at the *bal musette.*

However, the chances are that "Ernest" and Ford were not speaking that night, or at least that Hemingway was not speaking to Ford.[9]

The "Jean" who is sitting with Stella and Hemingway is Jean Rhys, who described an evening at the Bal du Printemps.

> Somebody said to somebody else: "It's all very well to talk about Jew noses, but have you ever tried to paint your own mouth?"
> The artist addressed burst into tears.
> "He's only trying to be modern and brutal and all that, poor dear," said her friend. . . . "Don't mind him."
> "Fine a l'eau," bawled a tall dark gentleman immediately into Mr. Rolls's ear.
> "Don't shout in my ear," said Mr. Rolls irritably.
> "Well, get out of the way," said the tall dark gentleman. "Always blocking up the bar."
> "It's my bar," remarked Mr. Rolls with majesty.
> "Then you ought to give your clients a chance," said the other.

According to Nina Hamnett, these parties came to an end because of "a disturbance between the intellectuals who wanted to talk and the dancers who wanted to dance and to drink." Stella says it was also because journalists who wanted to write the place up "would bring Englishwomen in evening dress, who thought it fun to go slumming in Paris, to see how the artists amused themselves in their lairs," and because some "clean-living Americans wanted to organize the whole thing as a club."[10]

With the collapse of the *Transatlantic,* Ford went back to his own work. He began *No More Parades* on October 31, 1924, just a few days before *Joseph Conrad* was published. At the same time, he got himself involved in an unfortunate affair with Jean Rhys. Jean Rhys was the daughter of a Welsh doctor and a Creole mother and had grown up in the West Indies. At sixteen, she was sent to acting school in London, became a chorus girl there for a short time, and then married a Dutch poet and went to live in Paris. She lived, according to Stella, in "an underworld of darkness and disorder, where officialdom, the bourgeoisie and the police were the eternal enemies and the fugitive the only hero." But she had talent, as her novels show, "a needle-quick intelligence and a good sort of emotional honesty." This is essentially the girl, Marya, that Jean Rhys herself portrays in *Postures,* the novel she wrote about her affair with Ford. " . . . she was reckless, lazy, a vagabond by nature"; "she spent the foggy day in endless, aimless walking, for it seemed to her that if she moved quickly enough she would escape the fear that hunted her. . . . She had always known that it was there—hidden under the more or less pleasant surface of things. Always. Ever since she was a child. . . . " "And what was there to catch on to in life? . . . A dark river that swept you on you didn't know where—nobody knew where. What was the use of worrying, anyway?"[11]

This is a consciousness that exists entirely in the present, hardly aware of yesterday or tomorrow, governed by the self-generated mood of the moment. Sometimes it is a "longing for joy, for any joy, for any pleasure. . . . It was like some splendid caged animal roused and fighting to get out. It was an unborn child jumping, leaping, kicking at her side. . . . " And sometimes it is an equally powerful grief that makes her seek out her husband, whom she has betrayed, when her lover deserts her "because I thought it would help me. . . . I was awfully unhappy. . . . " "She was," Stella thought, "a doomed soul, violent and demoralised."[12]

Struck by the "sordid novel of great sensitiveness and persuasiveness" she showed them, Ford and Stella asked her to come live with them so that Ford could help her with her work. It was a dangerous thing to do. Ford was depressed by the slow collapse of the *Transatlantic* and looking for emotional excitement. "Oh, God, I am so utterly sick of myself sometimes," says Heidler in *Postures.* "D'you ever get sick of yourself? . . . And yet it goes on. . . . One knows that the whole damn thing's idiotic, futile, not even pleasant, but one goes on. . . . One's caught in a sort of trap, I suppose." He tells Marya, dishonestly, that he and Lois (that is, Stella) have agreed to go their own ways, though Lois has told Marya that she loves him hopelessly. "I was singularly slow," Stella says, "in discovering that she and Ford were in love." When she did, she accepted the situation. She appears to have taken her usual generous attitude throughout. "Une de ses [Ford's] ambitions était de se faire passer pour Don Juan," said Halicka. "Sa seconde femme . . . Stella Bowen, avait vingt ans de moins que lui . . . [mais elle] est l'être le moins égoïste que j'ai connu. Jamais elle n'a peu un mot amer pour Ford dont le conduit envers elle n'avait pas toujours été irreprochable."[13]

> Ford's girl was by no means without generous instincts [Stella said] and her world had its own standards of *chic*. . . . Yet here I was cast for the role of the fortunate wife who held all the cards, and the girl for that of the poor, brave and desperate beggar who was doomed to be let down by the bourgeoisie. I learned what a powerful weapon lies in weakness and pathos and how strong is the position of the person who has nothing to lose, and I simply hated my rôle! I played it, however, until the girl was restored to health and [a] job materialised, since we appeared to represent her last chance of survival.

Needless to say this is scarcely the view of Stella and Ford taken in *Postures*, where they work together to keep up bourgeois appearances at all costs and whenever Ford is not present, Stella snipes nastily at Jean, whose view of the case is represented by the epigraph of *Postures:*

> . . . Beware
> Of good Samaritans—walk to the right
> Or hide thee by the roadside out of sight
> Or greet them with the smile that villains wear.

As a wooer, Heidler sounds very like what we know of Ford: "I'm dying with love for you, burnt up with it, tortured with it. . . . Don't you know that I wanted you the first time I saw you? . . . I knew that I could have you by putting my hand out, and I kept off you. . . . I thought it wouldn't be playing the game. . . . But there comes a limit, you see"; "I love you, my dear, I love you. . . . And I wish I were dead. . . . For God's sake, be a little kind to me." "He wasn't a good lover, of course. He didn't really like women. She had known that as soon as he touched her. His hands were inexpert, clumsy at caresses. . . . " She also discovers that he is habitually evasive; Lois points out to her that whenever he is involved in a scene, he pretends afterwards to have been too drunk to remember it. Watching him evade her demands, she thinks, "He'd take any advantage he could—fair or unfair. Caddish he is." Her simple view of the matter is that, as one of her friends says to her, "You're a victim. There's no endurance in your face," and that Heidler is, as Cairn (Hemingway) says to her violently, "a humbug."[14]

After six months or so, Heidler tires of Marya and sends her off to the Riviera (which is where Stella and Ford found a job as ghost-writer for Jean Rhys). He offers her a sum of money to leave him alone, but she clings to him. If we can take literally Miss Rhys's next novel, *After Leaving Mr. Mackenzie*, Ford remained firm. She is convinced this affair has destroyed her. "He sort of smashed me up. Before that I'd always been pretty sure things would turn out all right for me, but afterwards I didn't believe in myself any more." Whether Ford was wholly responsible for her smash or not, he had, as Stella said,

> cut the fundamental tie between himself and [Stella]. . . .
> After being quite excruciatingly unhappy for some weeks, I found on a certain day, at a certain hour, that for the first time, I was very tired—not to say bored—with personal emotions, my own no less than Ford's. This feeling recurred with greater and greater frequency, until it became perpetual.
> . . . When Ford had disengaged himself from what he called "this entanglement," he announced that . . . nothing could ever upset us again. But of course he was wrong. The desire for freedom was already beginning to work in me, and what he really needed was another mate.[15]

Thus, the decisive change in Stella's feelings began, though she did not quite recognize it for another three years. "[Ford's] personal atmosphere," she said, "was always charged with a highly emotional egotism. He also had a genius for creating confusion and a nervous horror of having to deal with the results. . . . It was a constant strain because he never allowed me to escape from it, even for a moment. It meant being on duty twenty-four hours a day"; and little by little she realized she was tired of it. "During the winter of 1926–27, and also the following winter, Ford made two visits to America. . . . For me, these periods alone in Paris served as dress-rehearsals for the time when I should be permanently alone."[16]

In May, 1925, Ford finished *No More Parades* in the cottage at Guermantes and then, throughout the summer and fall of 1925, took things comparatively easy. In January, however, he did finish up *A Mirror to France*, which he had begun in 1923 and then dropped. He wanted to dedicate it to Gertrude Stein, who had been generous to him about the *Transatlantic* and very kind to Stella, whom she frequently had in after dinner for what Stella calls "a spot of cosy low-brow conversation" beneath the Picassos; and she was devoted to Julie.

> ... then we went to see some one [Gertrude Stein remembered], just after The Making of Americans was printed, and Hemingway who was there came up to Gertrude Stein and began to explain why he would not be able to write a review of the book. Just then a heavy hand fell on his shoulder and Ford Madox Ford said, young man it is I who wish to speak to Gertrude Stein. Ford then said to her, I wish to ask your permission to dedicate my new book to you. May I. Gertrude Stein and I were both awfully pleased and touched.[17]

A Mirror to France is not a very good book; parts of it are taken word for word from earlier books; the rest consists of the unfocused comments and unpersuasive anecdotes Ford produced when he was forcing his imagination. The effect is that of a man asserting arbitrarily that his subject has the qualities he admires and that whatever facts about it he has happened to observe, however unlikely the connection appears to the reader, prove it. Thus he tells us that France is the home of Thought and Art because the French despise vacuum cleaners and canned foods; and, because he himself "really ask[s] nothing better of life than to be walking home peaceably along the rue d'Assas late at night," the Left Bank is the height of civilization. The main interest of A Mirror to France is that in it Ford begins to transform his early Pre-Raphaelite feelings about Provence into the theory that "chivalric generosity, frugality, pure thought and the arts are the first requisites of a Civilisation" and that these virtues originated in Provence—the theory that he began to work out in Mister Bosphorus and would elaborate in Provence and Great Trade Route.[18]

When their summer at Guermantes ended, Nina Hamnett found them an enormous studio in the rue Notre-Dame-des-Champs. It had an electric light, a water tap, and a zinc sink, but the only privacy was provided by some movable screens. They build an enclosed balcony to make a bedroom for themselves and a cabinet de toilette; Julie and Madame Annie had to sleep on divans behind the screens. Despite these difficulties, Stella set to work enthusiastically to make the studio a home. " ... it had immense windows and a lovely light," she said, "and a small outside balcony and it overlooked the trees of a convent garden." They moved in while the workmen were still constructing the new balcony and had to camp for some time. The great advantage of the studio was that it made parties possible. "The nice thing about most of the scallawags of Montparnasse," Stella said, "was that they had no respect for people of importance.... Nobody suffered bores gladly because they were rich or well known. . . . " "All English-speaking Montparnasse crowded into [Ford's flat], drank his hospitably offered libations, and paraded its secret inhibitions in much confused talk, much strenuous dancing, much hearty alcoholic laughter, horseplay and petting." Not that these parties were very wild. Jean Rhys thought them stuffy.

> ... everyone seemed so efficient, so up and doing, so full of That Important Feeling and everything—even sin—was an affair of . . . proving conclusively that you belonged to the upper classes, but were nevertheless an anarchist.... The women were long-necked and very intelligent and they would get into corners and say simple, truthful things about each other.[19]

Juan and Josette Gris, whom they had met at Gertrude Stein's, then persuaded Ford and Stella to come to Toulon for the winter of 1925–26 (Ford, Gris remarked, was "middle-aged, rather drunken and quite witty"). They waited until after Christmas to go, since Christmas was a special family occasion for them.

> ... on Christmas eve, half a dozen of us [spent] an ecstatic afternoon with Julie, doing the decorations [of the Christmas tree]. I can remember Pavlick [Tchelitcheff], more serious and concentrated than any child, stepping backwards and announcing critically, "Il faut un peu plus de mystère à gauche." He would then proceed to create the *mystère*, with *cheveux d'ange*, silver snow, fairy lights and a little ballet-dancer doll on an elastic who pranced every time the old floor shook....
> The Père Noël always arrived by the roof and entered via the balcony. The children of our friends and of all the *concierge's* [*sic*] and *femmes de menage* with whom we had ever been connected would be seated around the lighted tree ... until the Père Noël cracked his whip, and they looked round and discovered [Ford] gazing benevolently down ... and preparing to descend the stairs with a sackful of presents for everybody.

Ford "spoke French, as nearly all the children spoke French better than they spoke English," Nina Hamnett said, "and Ford's child did not speak English at all. Gertrude Stein nearly always came."[20]

They reached Toulon on December 30, just in time for a New Year's Eve celebration." [Ford] absorbs a terrifying quantity of alcohol," Gris reported. "I never thought one could drink so much." Both Ford and Stella fell in love with Toulon; "Il y a cinque cinémas et deux dancings," Josette Gris exclaimed when they arrived. "Ça fait juste la semaine!" Each night they would gather at a café to decide which cinema or dancing deserved their patronage. When the dancings were overrun by British sailors, Ford, the Tory gentleman, told Stella she might dance with a seaman but not with a petty officer. There was interesting companionship for them both; besides Gris, there were the painters Louis Latapie and Othon Friesz. Francis Carco, the author of *Perversity*, which Jean Rhys would translate, came to stay with Friesz, and Georges Duthuit was there. Gris did a pencil sketch of Ford that was duly reproduced in *The Saturday Review.*[21]

The lively, talkative life of Toulon appealed to them so much and they found Cap Brun so attractive when Friesz took them out there that they decided to buy a house there. "We never admitted," said Stella, "that having financed the *Transatlantic Review*, we had nothing left to buy a house with, nor that it would have been an act of folly to jeopardise my small but precious Australian income by blueing the remainder of the available capital. Neither would we face the fact that, given Ford's temperament, his earnings would never, by any conceivable chance, be set aside and saved." But Ford stuck to this idea with all his monumental stubbornness, and it was eventually carried out.[22]

They went over to Rapallo to see the Pounds, who had been settled there since 1925. Ford pressed Pound to visit America to publicize his work, but Pound hated the whole idea. This was the first evidence of Ford's developing conviction that his future lay in the United States. He began to think so with the American success of *Some Do Not . . .* and the even greater success of *No More Parades* during these early months of 1926.

By March the little society of Toulon was beginning to decline into quarrelsomeness. "Toulon's 'Rotonde' is breaking up," Gris wrote Kahnweiler. "Duthuit is charming, but Ford is always giving himself airs for some mysterious reason and Latapie is a worker-type like Braque but boring." At Easter Ford and Stella started north for Paris, stopping in Castelnaudary to eat the cassoulet at the Hôtel de la Reine Jeanne. The splendor of the meal called for two bottles of wine, after which Stella got loose in an antique shop and bought eight hundred francs' worth of furniture for their studio in Paris.[23]

By the time they left Toulon, Ford was committed to the idea of America. He sent off a batch of what he called "American literature" (reviews) to Gerald Duckworth and told him that "last Thursday a deputation of American citizens from a liner came over from Nice to shake me by the hand and thank me for existence. I mean my existence, not theirs: yesterday by the same post I had two contracts from Lecture Agencies asking me to lecture. . . . " But the prosperity of his American success had its drawbacks. It threw him in the way of wealthy people like the William Bullitts; "When you sank on to a divan [at the Bullitts'']," as Stella put it, " . . . you really sank completely in, until you found yourself looking up at your own back teeth reflected in a ceiling mirror."[24]

These people were a challenge to Ford's pride. "At the least hint of patronage, his pride would flare up, and he would metaphorically double the stakes." " . . . bitterly aware that his best suit was nothing but a poor old has-been, and that standing his share of the drinks meant that he could not have the shoes he needed, [he] nevertheless talked the jargon of the rich as to the manner born," Stella said. "He was not conscious of any incongruity." With his strong sense of his own gentility and his powerful imagination, he played himself into this role completely. "He presented a wonderful appearance of a bland, successful gentleman whose shabbiness was mere eccentricity and who regarded a preoccupation with the relative merits of Foyot and Larue, Vionnet and Poiret, the Ritz and the Hôtel George V, as very natural and necessary."[25]

The modest prosperity that came their way with the success of *No More Parades* would not support this life, particularly as they now had a good deal more freedom for it, with Julie and Madame Annie living almost continuously in the cottage at Guermantes (Ford and Stella went there only weekends). There were more parties than ever in the rue Notre-Dame-des-Champs. Mary Bromfield remembered one of them, perhaps not very accurately.

Ford had a vast and dismal studio. . . . He was a great fat Englishman . . . [who] took into his home a series of mediocre and respectable women who took care of him and were all called Mrs. Ford. . . . Studios are nearly always uncomfortable, and this one of Ford's was no exception—a vast room badly heated by a very small oil stove and furnished with all sorts of uncomfortable chairs and day beds, most of them too far from the stove to be reached by its faint glow.

I found their parties very exciting, however. . . . I remember . . . making conversation with Ford, who for some occult reason fancied himself as a lady-killer, but in spite of this was witty in the best manner of the English and really fun to talk to. Around and about me was greatness and fame . . . the Hemingways, the F. Scott Fitzgeralds, the Archie MacLeishes . . . the Ludwig Lewisohns . . . and oodles of others.[26]

Ford had got himself into another tangle with publishers, this time in America, where his greatest hope of profits lay. He had made a contract with Seltzer for *Some Do Not...* , which Seltzer published in October, 1924. Meanwhile Ford quarreled with Seltzer over the payments for the *Transatlantic* and began to hear rumors—accurate enough as it turned out—that Seltzer was financially shaky. He therefore persuaded Albert Boni to buy *Some Do Not...* from Seltzer, who was Boni's uncle, and Boni also published it. Unfortunately, there was something wrong with the copyright on *Some Do Not...* , and Seltzer went on publishing it without paying Ford royalties. This trouble was not finally cleared up until the fall of 1927, when *Some Do Not...* became Boni's exclusive property and Ford sold him the rest of the tetralogy. While this quarrel was going on he finished *A Man Could Stand Up*—, which he had started in Toulon.[27]

In August Ford and Stella went to Avignon for a vacation and then, on October 20, Ford went to America for a lecture tour. The prospect greatly excited him.

> ... to my adventures [he wrote Stella]. I got thro' the passport here splendidly—being let thro' first of all the passengers with complimentary speeches from the officials. Lots of reporters awaited me. ... *A man could stand up* has started very well—4,000 sold before publication and sales very large.... I've already been asked for articles worth $700.00 and I shall stop here as long as I can keep myself and save a little. It is certainly good for my book market and that is the great thing.... New York is just the same. I really like it very much.

Stella sent him an anxious, wifely letter about his lecturing. " ... I do hope," she said, "you'll manage to remain a mysterious European and tell them rather about Europe than about themselves." It was sensible advice, but Ford could not resist being the visiting expert. *New York Is Not America*, a collection of the essays he wrote during this visit, is full of opinions about America.[28]

Ford put up for a week or two with the Herbert Gormans. He had discovered when he arrived that his lecture agent had got him only one engagement—hardly enough to allow him "to keep myself and save a little." " ... I don't worry about [not having lectures]," he told Stella. "I shall sit down and do some more writing." He found a flat and set to work on his new American career. This was the main purpose of his trip, the application to his own life of the course he had recommended to Pound: in his letters to Stella he discusses almost everything he is doing in terms of publicity and its effect on his sales and constantly reports to her the number of times he has been interviewed, photographed, and invited to meet important people. " ... Bradley and Spingarn ... [and] the brothers Boni ... are all unanimous in saying that it is essential that I shd. stop here for the full ten weeks. ... To go back wd. be a confession of failure and fatal to my book sales."[29]

He had two primary objectives. The first was to negotiate a long-term contract with Boni. He proposed that Boni issue a new edition of *Henry James* and a "novel about two old maids" (no doubt the Misses Hurlbird of Stamford) in the spring of 1927, a volume of his collected poems that Christmas, and a "novel about Ney" (*A Little Less Than Gods*) in the spring of 1928. Later he proposed that they issue these books in a uniform edition which would, he hoped, form the basis of a collected edition. These negotiations went on all through his visit and eventually terminated in a three-year contract under which Boni was to pay him $400 a month as an advance against royalties in return for all his novels.[30]

Ford's second objective was to get publicity by writing and lecturing. He was delighted to be asked to write a weekly article for the *Herald Tribune Books* and took every opportunity he could to appear in magazines; he also accepted Rudge's offer to do a limited, signed edition of a few poems, which Rudge issued in January under the rather misleading title of *New Poems* (of the seven poems in the volume, four were new). He was eager to lecture to clubs like the Brooklyn Ladies Club and the Pen and Brush Club of New York ("378 ladies ... gave me a perfect ovation") or even private groups if the hostess was prominent enough, as he thought Mrs. Harry Payne Whitney was. He went to Chicago to speak to the Arts Club (a group of Gold Coast ladies) and to Boston because a Mrs. Ames who was, he reported, a cross between the wife of the Archbishop of Canterbury and Queen Victoria, had offered to give a luncheon for him. He began to feel that, even if he were dead, he would begin to talk if some one put him on a platform. What he hated most about these public-relations chores was the receptions with their endless handshaking and small talk.[31]

Nevertheless, he felt he was making a great success of his tour; his schedule was "cram full with 'dates.' " This was the best way to build "a steady market for my books—preferably here, because the market is so large. ... Mrs. Foster is working tooth and nail to get me lecture appointments in Boston and Washington. If I could conquer *those* metropoloi I should feel myself quite safe as far as the Eastern half of this country is concerned—and the West must take care of itself. The Middle West I think I have conquered." He also lectured informally at a number of colleges and universities—at Cornell, Columbia, Harvard, Dartmouth, and Williams.[32]

In her letter of advice to Ford about his lecturing, Stella had suggested he ought to be particularly careful not be misquoted. This was her tactful way of saying that he did not speak very clearly, a fact that leaped to everyone's mind at the thought of his lecturing. "I have never heard him speak publicly," Rascoe wrote, "and I was astounded to hear that he had engaged to lecture; for he always speaks with such difficulty and with such a wheeze . . . that in private conversation with him it is very hard to understand what he says." The *Bookman*'s reporter, who interviewed him before he lectured to six hundred members of the American Women's Association at the Plaza on November 10, was not sure he heard anything Ford said to him. As if to prove everyone's worst fears, Ford's first public remarks, a brief speech at the Seaman's Church Institute for the Joseph Conrad Memorial Committee on November 3, produced a report in the New York *World* that he had said Masefield wrote the first part of *Romance;* he had to write the *World* a letter telling them that he had really said Masefield—who had preceded him as a speaker that night—had written the first review of *Romance*, which was quite possibly not true either.[33]

Sometimes Ford tried to meet the interests of his audience; to the American Woman's Association he "spoke without notes, just like that—about the Pankhursts and Votes for Women in England. They nearly went mad with enthusiasm when I paid—a really moving tribute—to Mrs. Pankhurst." But the notes for his all-purpose lecture read like a chapter of *Return to Yesterday;* he talked about his bet with Conrad over the success of *Chance*, his refusal to make a serious effort to write a novel until *The Good Soldier*, and half a dozen of his familiar stories of front-line experiences in World War I. Markham Harris, who got him to lecture at Williams the next fall, remembered that

> Ford . . . began by requesting that if he did not speak loud enough for those toward the back they let him know by raising their hands. At first people good-naturedly complied [but without appreciable effect]. . . . To those down front like myself, the hazy contours of a rambling, soughing, ironic, paradoxical, and blandly egocentric reminiscence gradually took shape. . . .

But it was Ford's only half-jokingly expressed impression that " . . . these people love me when they see me. I have only to appear in a room and smile with my shy modesty and whole cities fall for me—and buy copies of No More Parades."[34]

In December he was, along with Hugh Walpole and Osbert Sitwell, a guest of honor at a P.E.N. Club dinner. Despite this sign of success, he was worried about the effect on his reputation of the American edition of Violet

Hunt's *The Flurried Years*, which had just been published by Boni under the title *I Have This to Say.* "If they are bad," he wrote Stella when he heard Violet's memoirs were to be published, "they will make a pretty good stink and might make Boni's want to draw back [from publishing him]." As if he wanted to increase this danger, he refused to dine with T. R. Smith of Boni; with success he had begun to treat publishers in an old-fashioned Edwardian style, as if they were not quite gentlemen. During these years he built up a reputation for being difficult that would complicate his relations with publishers for the rest of his life.³⁵

He was furious when he heard that Rebecca West, who had always been fond of Violet, had been defending her. "Rebecca," he told Stella, "naturally has sailed in and made matters excruciatingly more disagreeable. She has told several people that V.H. is an admirable and martyrised saint and that every word of the book is true. At the same time, if you please, she has rung up Fanny Hurst and Elinor Wylie . . . and said: 'Do come to lunch or dinner with Fordie and me!' " He was also beginning to understand how much damage Jessie Conrad's letter to the *Times Literary Supplement* about his *Joseph Conrad* had done him. He sent *The New York Times* the selection from *The Cinque Ports* on which "Amy Foster" was based, hoping to minimize the effect of Jessie's letter.³⁶

In January he lectured in Chicago and Harriet Monroe gave a party for him, after which she took him to the *Poetry* office, where he astonished the staff by sitting down and dictating an article they had asked him for. "Harriet," Ford wrote Stella, "is very affectionate and useful but she wrung a two thousand word article out of me to-day and that has left me fairly dithering"; it was not so easy to produce articles on the spur of the moment as he made it look. He pressed Samuel Putnam to drive him out to Oak Park so that he could meet Hemingway's parents and get "the 'feel' of the place from which . . . the new literature was coming." It did not impress him; he thought Oak Park "a particularly Puritan and ridiculous suburb . . . (Hemingway would never forgive you if you let people know that he was born there)." But he delighted the Hemingways. "I am so pleased to write to you," Dr. Hemingway wrote Ernest afterward,

and tell you of our very delightful dinnerparty this Noon with your great admirer present, Mr. Ford Madox Ford. . . . When I learned that he was at the Blackstone Hotel, I phoned to him and invited him out to our home. . . . He came on time and made a very charming guest. He surely does appreciate you and your work. He gave us a wonderfull word picture of you and your boy. . . . Mother was so

pleased with the Englishman. He seemed to enjoy his dinner and the
Tea and all the other eats.[37]

While Ford was dining with the Hemingways in Oak Park, Stella in
Paris was trying to help Hadley Hemingway through her divorce. " . . . she
. . . is quite calm and matter-of-fact," Stella said, "but it's awful to contemplate the situation, because she would so much like not to divorce Hemingway . . . but the other girl is a Catholic and insists on marriage." At
Christmas Stella took Julie to England. They saw Mrs. Hueffer in London
and spent Christmas with Douglas·and Margaret Cole in Oxford, where
Stella discovered she had changed a good deal during her years in France:
"the windows are *always* 9 inches open at the top," she said, and she found
herself quarreling with Douglas Cole for thinking Gertrude Stein was "purest bosh." Ford sent her a Christmas cable that she "loved getting." But
"The wire from 'Jeanne [Foster] and Ford' came 10 minutes later and
thrilled me less!" Stella guessed that part of Ford's excitement about
America was a response to the ladies he found himself involved with, and
Ford only increased her suspicions by telling her far too frequently that he
never saw any of the women he talked about except in crowds of people.[38]

Chapter 26

Ford returned to France at the end of February and he and Stella went to Toulon, where, "owing to the success of *No More Parades*, [they] were able to hire a room [at the Victoria] with a bath." But Toulon was not the same: Juan Gris was dead; there were no longer the "old café gatherings" and the cinemas and dancings. Ford finished *New York Is Not America* there and they went back to Paris, where he began *Last Post*. On June 3, 1927, Mrs. Hueffer died and Ford went to London for the funeral; he stayed about a week trying to improve his British sales. For the next several months he concentrated on the English market, even offering to do an article on the Dempsey-Tunney fight for the *Sunday Express* and assuring them that "I know a good deal about boxing as I am a qualified Army Referee. . . . "[1]

Then Ford heard that Borys Conrad had got himself into serious trouble. Borys had been badly wounded in the war and came home "morose and silent and obviously a changed man mentally." After Conrad's death he "seemed to have lost his head completely . . . and to have become extremely extravagant, taking the view that his expectations would be enormous." By 1927 he was running a garage and was deep in debt. He concocted a scheme for getting money out of a Mrs. Bevan. He told her that if he could get together £ 4,000 he could buy manuscripts of his father's that he could resell for £5,000; he said he had £ 2,900. Mrs. Bevan supplied the rest. Borys had in fact neither a purchaser nor a seller of manuscripts, nor did he have £ 2,900. What he did have was pressing debts, and he applied Mrs. Bevan's money to them. He was exposed and sent to prison for a year. Ford wrote off immediately—to Pinker—to ask if "it would do Borys Conrad's wife and child any service to invite them to come and stop with us at Avignon where we are going on the 1st August. . . . People like to get to France where as a

357

rule nothing is known of their cases." Nothing came of this generous offer.[2]

At Villeneuve-les-Avignon the proprietor of their little hotel cleared a space under a dormer window and set up a deal table and a straight chair; there Ford sat typing *Last Post* on his Corona from seven to ten each morning. They all swam in the Rhone and took long afternoon walks through the fields with Ford naming every flower and herb, like Christopher Tietjens walking Valentine home from the Duchemins' through the Kentish countryside and thinking with pleasure of the technical names of flowers like sainfoin and wild white clover "that the best people must know"; there were excursions to Les Baux and Nîmes; and once Ford led them in a round dance on the bridge to the tune of the nursery song. In the late afternoon they sat on the *terrasse* drinking beer, and Ford talked about world civilization (the theme of *Provence* and *Great Trade Route* was clearly developing in his imagination) or silently meditated the pages of *Last Post* he would write the next morning. His daughter Katharine married the Irish painter Charles Lamb this August, but Ford gave her no sign.[3]

In the middle of September he went back to New York, stopping in London for a couple of days to work on his English market. He crossed on the Canadian Pacific liner, S.S. *Minnedosa*, and by overworking he managed to finish *Last Post* the night before they reached Quebec. To celebrate, he offered at the ship's concert that night to make a limerick on any passenger's name in thirty seconds. In spite of a violent cold he went to work the minute he reached New York to settle his contract for the Tietjens series. He proposed to Harrison Smith of Harcourt that Harcourt buy *Last Post* and *New York Is Not America* for $7,000, pay Ford a monthly sum against royalties on future novels, and buy the previous Tietjens novels from Boni. Smith wanted *Last Post* but "was *not* so mad about taking over the others." But these negotiations worried Boni, and they quickly accepted the terms Ford had proposed to them a year earlier. It was a great relief to Ford. He had worked himself into a nervous state about his future and had even begun to suffer dizzy spells—the agorophobia that had marked his earlier nervous breakdowns.[4]

Then Ford discovered a man named Macy-Masins he believed willing to guarantee the expenses of a new *Transatlantic Review*. It made Stella apprehensive. "You know I don't believe much in contracts and guarantees," she said. "Of course a large sum of money in a bank is a solid sort of fact but there is always the difficulty of getting along with people who own the money." They had recently acquired a tiny flat at 32 rue Vaugirard so that during the daytime Stella could have the studio to herself; it is a sign of her growing independence that she dreaded the thought of losing it.

. . . I *would* like to ask you not to envisage using your bureau here in the studio in any way for the Review. Since I've been working here hard, regularly, I realise how much I count upon being quiet and alone in the studio.

This project for reviving the *Review* came to nothing, thanks (Ford believed) to the opposition of Ben Heubsch of Viking.[5]

> Whereabouts in New York Ford actually "resided" [Goldring said] I never discovered. I called for him once at an address he gave me and found him in a small and dingy apartment which he used as an office. The room into which he ushered me had no furniture at all except a small table, on which a typewriter reposed, and two hard chairs. Ford, who in those days had become rather stout, was dresssed only in his under-garments. Like most New York apartments . . . the place was overheated, and he was sweating profusely. "I just use this place to work in" he explained.

This garret was in West Thirteenth Street, and there Caroline Tate, wife of the poet, Allen Tate, began to work as Ford's secretary. Mrs. Tate soon persuaded him to work at 27 Bank Street, where the Tates lived. The advantage of having someone to take his telephone calls was a revelation to him. He moved into a second-floor flat at 27 Bank Street and began taking his meals with the Tates.[6]

Ford was much distressed by what he imagined the difficulty of the Tates' life.

> The way those people live is something terrible [he told Stella]. They are the janitors in a big apartment house—for wh. they get two rooms and nothing, and have to do all the concierge's work. Then they make $18 a week by letting one room and that is all they have except an occasional dollar or so for a review. And Tate is such a nice fellow and a good poet and she extraordinarily well educated and quite a lady—from the S[outh].

Ford's gift for inventing the lives of his friends is at work here. Twenty-seven Bank Street was a small, three-story building in which the Tates had two and a half basement rooms, the half room being regularly occupied by friends such as Katherine Anne Porter, Robert Penn Warren, and Andrew Lytle. The owner of the building lived on the first floor and Ford's two-room flat was on the second (a third room on the floor was occupied by E. E. Cummings's sister). Besides getting their rooms free, the Tates were paid $50 a month. Mr. Tate earned about $100 a month in addition to what he made as a reader for Minton, Balch. "Never since that time," he once said, "have I felt so well off." Ford's anxiety about what he imagined to be the

Tates' hard life did, however, produce an eloquent letter of recommendation to Henry Moe of the Guggenheim Foundation, and Mr. Tate got a fellowship that took them to Paris the next year.[7]

These were the years of the Tietjens novels. *Some Do Not . . .* was mainly a critical success but it created interest. "All our intellectuals," said Mary Colum when *No More Parades* appeared in September, 1925, "are reading it now. . . . It gets attention for exactly the same reason . . . the work of T. S. Eliot [does]." It even got discussed in news magazines like *The Literary Digest. No More Parades* sold much better than *Some Do Not . . .* , so that Ford and Stella were able to indulge themselves in the forever remembered luxury of a bathroom in Toulon that year. *A Man Could Stand Up*— did a little less well, but *Last Post* was taken by the Literary Guild. The Guild was supposed to be good for about 25,000 copies. Ford—always inclined to impressive round numbers—claimed *Last Post* had sold 50,000 copies "within a fortnight of its appearance"; it probably sold 30,000 to 35,000 in all. The critical success of the Tietjens novels made Ford a prominent figure around New York; their sales made him, briefly, a prosperous one.[8]

No one knew how to enjoy success better than Ford. He made himself very much at home in New York. One day he astonished Burton Rascoe by slipping suddenly into the Guaranty Trust Company on Fifth Avenue and explaining afterwards that though he had no account there, he had discovered that the Guaranty Trust had a *urinoir,* a very useful facility, as he pointed out, in the worst-equipped big city in the world.

He was to be seen everywhere, dining with inflential literary people or attending the parties of the young writers where one drank "home-made red wine, out of tea-cups." In these surroundings, as Goldring remarked, "Ford . . . was perfectly happy. He was the Master, addressing a circle of attentive disciples. In this capacity, he [would discourse] for several hours on French and English prose. . . . As the beloved Professor, expounding his theme to a group of promising students, he was in his element." In his prosperity he was also able to indulge his generosity to the young much more freely. When Goldring was abruptly called back to Paris in November by the sudden deaths of his wife's sister and her husband, Ford took care of everything. He cabled Stella to watch over Mrs. Goldring in Paris, packed for the stricken Goldring, and saw him onto the boat. It was a busy life, as his description of one of his days shows.

> After working [all morning] I went to lunch at the Brevoort—
> I don't know why, except that it suddenly came into my head and
> I wanted to: then I went and sat to Hartmann till five, then to tea at

Mrs. Saxton's. . . . Then I dined with Harrison Smith of H'ct Brace
and went to see Eva Legallienne in Tchekhov's *Three Sisters.* . . .
Then I went on to a party at the Gorman's where we all got
horribly drunk on crude alcohol—tho' I didn't know it till I began
to feel the extraordinary effects. . . . I get up religiously every morning at eight and mostly I don't get to bed till two—I don't know
why.[9]

In November, Burton Rascoe had bought for *The Bookman* the fragment
of a novel called *The Sisters,* which Conrad had—at Edward Garnett's
suggestion—abandoned in 1896 (before he and Ford met). Rascoe was convinced Ford would not have heard of *The Sisters,* but he thought it would be
a journalistic coup to get Ford to complete the story. He figured that if he
took Ford's familiarity with it for granted, Ford would not want to admit his
ignorance. This maneuver worked perfectly and Ford was soon telling
Rascoe that Conrad had discussed the plot with him and that he could easily
describe how it was to have ended. Ford's solution involved what he called
"incest" (the hero has a child by his wife's sister); Ford was himself at this
moment planning a novel—*A Little Less Than Gods*—that turned on incest.[10]

But Ford was kept even busier in New York by an aspect of his life he
could hardly discuss with Stella. This was a romantic relation with a lady
named Rene Wright. Ford dedicated *A Little Less Than Gods* to her ("To
Rene Katherine Clarissa David"). "My dear R.," he wrote, "When you were
in pigtails and adorably starched, stiff little frilly things and I, oh dear, as
slender as a gazelle, we walked in Central Park and you asked me to tell you
a tale. . . . Here it is, then, your Tale." This would have been during Ford
and Elsie's trip to America in 1906. In 1906, Ford was thirty-two and Rene
twenty-eight, which makes the "pigtails and adorably starched, stiff little
frilly things" of Ford's description somewhat misleading.[11]

They met again when Ford was in New York during the winter of
1926–27; Ford was fifty-four and Mrs. Wright forty-eight. Ford wrote a poem
about her that winter called "Winter-Night Song" in which he describes her
as

> My dearest dear, my honey-love,
> My brown-eyed squirrel, my soft dove.

Ford's young friends, in whose eyes Mrs. Wright appeared "a pleasant,
full-bosomed" but distinctly "middle-aged woman," thought this poem very
funny: among themselves they always referred to her as the Brown-eyed
Squirrel. In the twenty years since she and Ford had first met, Rene had led
a busy life. In January, 1914, after the death of her first husband (a man

named Luther), she married Guy H. Wright of a prominent St. Louis family. By 1926, this marriage was beginning to break up; when Rene sued for divorce, in May, 1928, she told the court that Guy had refused to accompany her on trips or to "places of recreation and amusement" and, when she insisted on going, nagged her and was "cold." This explains why she was in New York alone during the winter of 1926–27 and prepared to look with favor on Ford.[12]

She was also in New York to greet Ford when he arrived there in the fall of 1927. In October, a young Yale book collector named James Babb asked Ford to New Haven for the weekend of the Yale-Brown football game and Ford brought Mrs. Wright with him. He was not much taken with the game, but he recognized the social importance of football weekends in the 1920's and from now on would pretend to be a football expert as he had, in the old days, pretended to be a cricket expert. New Haven had the additional advantage of offering Wilbur Cross and *The Yale Review* for him to cultivate.[13]

Ford's involvement with Mrs. Wright affected the tone of his letters to Stella despite his efforts to conceal it. As he did when he was concealing his affair with Violet Hunt from Elsie, he wrote suspiciously long descriptions of innocent activities, such as his visit to Pound's parents ("They are delightful people . . . it was really like visiting Philemon and Baucis"). He observed that "N.Y. is such a whispering Gallery that you might hear that I had taken a whole house and set up an establishment. . . . Please, my dear, do not read any other motive into this but what I say: I mean that exactly." He was full of reasons why it was necessary for him to stay on in New York. "I do not see any chance," he would say in one paragraph, "of my not *wanting* to return to my Julie and you for Xmas," and, in the next, that his maintaining a residence in New York "would pay . . . because it would please my readers and the press. They like, sentimentally, to think that I like America enough to have a permanent pied à terre." He even, occasionally, became the injured party. " . . . your letter enjoins me to stay 'as long as possible'. . . . Does it mean that for some reason you do not wish me to return, or merely that you leave me free not to"; " . . . I suppose you are tired of writing [letters to him] or perhaps don't believe in my anxieties." Stella began to substitute for her expressions of love, "God prosper you my dear," and "I hope you are well and Happy." Ford quickly followed suit with, "God bless you, my dear."[14]

It was Mrs. Wright as much as the demands of Ford's American career that held him in New York, and Stella as good as knew it. At the end of the year Ford wrote her:

Darling:
    I expect this will be the last letter you will have from me this year

so I do want to repeat to you all that I said to you at the end of last year—the assurance of my deep, deep admiration of all you are and stand for—and of all you have given me.... I sent you off to-day the first copy of the *Last Post*—and that represents the end of a considerable labour that I could not even have begun without you and that I certainly could not have finished.

On December 30, he cabled her to take for him a small apartment he knew was vacant across from theirs on the fourth floor at 32 rue Vaugirard.

My dear [Stella wrote him],
    I am very touched by all the tributes in your New Year's letter, and enormously pleased with Last Post.... But your letter and the 'Last Post' together, seem to mark the end of our long intimacy, which did have a great deal of happiness in it for me....

She was sure, she concluded, that they could live in neighboring flats in the rue Vaugirard in peace and amity.

This different and more peaceful life was Ford's idea. "He thought," as Stella put it afterwards, "that our Paris ménage could go on just the same in between-whiles" of his proposed life in America with Mrs. Wright. Fantastic as this proposal was, it was not without its reasonable purpose. Ford knew that Stella was a fundamentally conventional woman and that the appearance of a settled domesticity would be important to her. Much as he had tried to save appearances for Violet Hunt by appearing at her parties after he had begun to live with Stella, so he was offering now to save appearances for her. No doubt he also remembered that this arrangement would keep him in touch with Julie, whom he loved very much.[15]

What Ford did not take into account was that Stella had been gradually worn down by the strain of living with him; for all her admiration and affection for Ford, she had reached the point where she wanted to be alone. When Stella fully understood Ford's plan, she went off to the south of France, ostensibly to think it over.

    I feel I ought to write something definite to you just as soon as possible [she wrote him], so that you may make your own plans and be relieved of the strain of uncertainty.
    I am sure that there must be an absolute and public break between us. You yourself dismissed the idea of a 'half and half' separation and indeed I have come to think that it would not be feasible....
    I shall therefore tell people, when I get back to Paris, that my

absence until after your departure [for New York] was because we had mutually agreed to separate for good. . . .

I want not to be the one to begin any scandal about you and R[ene] and in any case I will not say ill of either of you. . . . And I should like you to remember that you said I might always tell people that we remain good friends. . . . It will be *much* better for Julie that this should be so. . . . You said R[ene] might object to your remaining friendly with me except for the sake of keeping up appearances to protect your reputation. . . . I think R[ene] might be asked to be a sport about this. I am making everything else as easy as I can for her!

Don't let me become a 'bogie' for you both. I should so hate that!

If it ever becomes known that we separated on account of R[ene] I should like it also to be known that you wanted not to break with me outwardly, and that it was I who wished to end it all. . . .

My dear, I really decided all this before leaving Paris, but I thought it would hurt us both so much to discuss it again. But ever since I *did* decide it, all my bitter feelings have gone and I feel so much more sympathy towards you and so much more anxious that you should be happy.[16]

That was the end, though Stella could not stop worrying about Ford, and when he eventually settled down with Janice Biala, wrote her, "I feel all right in my conscience about the rôle I played in Ford's life even if it didn't eventually succeed. . . . But I am tired of looking backwards, & tired of remembering how much things hurt. It doesn't seem important any more. I shall always be grateful to you for relieving me of the habit of worrying about Ford which I went on doing even after we parted, & it didn't do any good."[17]

They agreed that Stella should keep the studio in the rue Notre-Dame des Champs and the original flat at 32 rue Vaugirard and Ford the newly rented one there. Ford acknowledged his debt to Stella for the sum of "2.704 livres sterling, payées par elle . . . pour le compte de [Ford] entre le 1er Juillet 1920 [when she put up a part of the money for Coopers Cottage at Bedham] et le 30 Septembre 1927." In another document Ford agreed to turn over to Stella his British earnings—which had, to be sure, not been large in recent years—until his debt and 5 percent interest had been paid. Thereafter she was to receive £ 200 a year out of his British earnings "destinée à constituer une dot pour Esther Julia Madox." In addition he would pay her half his

American earnings, up to a maximum of $4,800, for the support of her and
Julie. This arrangement turned out to be largely theoretical, thanks to the
Depression and the drastic decline in Ford's earnings.[18]

With the publication of *Last Post* in January, 1928, Ford completed the
series of novels that constitute his major work, the tetralogy now known as
Parade's End. Like all Ford's work, these novels grew immediately out of
personal experience. He began with actual people and events, gradually
shaping them into representative figures of the country of the mind that was
Ford's England.[19]

The story begins in the Kent he knew best. Christopher and Macmaster
are on their way down to Ashford, where they will change trains for Rye
to play golf; they intend to go on to Hythe and Sandwich, though Sylvia's
telegram from Lobscheid spoils that plan. The Duchemins' house is at Pett
and looks out over Romney Marsh, and Campion is staying with his sister,
Claudine Sandbach, at Mountby, near Icklesham. The great ride of Christopher and Valentine to take Gertie to her uncle's twenty miles beyond Tenterden is through country Ford knew intimately. Grays Inn, where Sylvia
and Christopher live after Sylvia's return from Germany, Ford knew from
staying at the Inns of Court with Dyneley Hussey. *No More Parades* takes
place at Rouen, where Ford spent time in the hospital and on limited service.
A Man Could Stand Up—, though it covers a period of the war Ford did not
actually participate in, takes place on a front he knew and is filled with
episodes that occurred there or that Ford had long imagined had. *Last Post*
takes place at Coopers Cottage, Bedham; the only change is that the
"shanty" Elsie lived in at Kitcat when she was recuperating from her operation is set up for Mark in the orchard where Ford's small writing shack was
really located. When *Last Post* was being published in America, Ford got
Stella to send him, for publicity purposes, a snapshot of what he described
as "the corner of [Coopers] that Marie Léonie could see when elle deman-
dait pas mieux!"[20]

One can catch glimpses of how Ford built up his characters. A simple
instance is Stephen Fenwick Waterhouse, the pleasant Liberal minister
Christopher meets at Rye in *Some Do Not....* Waterhouse is basically Ford's
conception of Masterman; he too had to his credit a famous labor act ("his
Labour Finance Act"). " ... over their port [he and Christopher] ... agreed
on two fundamental legislative ideals," which turn out to be the principal
points of Arthur Marwood's "Complete Actuarial Scheme for Insuring John
Doe against All the Vicissitudes of Life." The suffragette demonstration
aimed at Waterhouse by Gertie and Valentine Wannop on the Rye golf

course is a softened version of the demonstration against Asquith at Lympne in 1909.[21]

This process of transformation becomes immensely complex with the major characters. Ford himself was not always aware of all that went on in his imagination when he was creating them. For example, when Stella said she was surprised to find, in *Last Post*, that Sylvia had relented and decided to give Christopher a divorce, Ford wrote her:

> Yes, I suppose the volte face in Sylvia surprised you—but I had thought of it a long time and it occurred to me that, after all she was a 'sport' and it takes a pretty unsporting woman to damage an unborn child. Besides Mark could not have let himself die if something of the sort had not happened . . . And it would have been too melodramatic to kill Tietjens: he could not die whilst any worries remained for him. So I think I have done it right.[22]

But Sylvia is far more complicated that this explanation suggests. Like Edwardian society itself, of which she is so typical a figure, Sylvia has run out her string and, tired, hardly cares any more. Her mind is haunted by Father Consett, brutally hanged along with Roger Casement (whom Ford had known and whose judicial murder had outraged him). She understands that it was what Father Consett "saw of us—the future mothers of England, you know, and all—at Miss Lampeter's—that made him take to the slums[.] Out of disgust and despair[.]" She never forgets his prediction that "her hell on earth will come when her husband goes running, blind, head down, mad after another woman"; when she hears Christina Rossetti's

> Somewhere or other there must surely be
> The face not seen: the voice not ever heard,

it seems to her an expression of Christopher's longing for that other woman. She cannot keep herself from asking him about it. But Christopher is too honorable to have admitted to himself that he loves Valentine Wannop. The only thing Sylvia's quotation does is to set him worrying over his lost memory. He says to her, "I've worried out some of the words of that song," and then quotes them. "I don't know the writer's name. But I hope I'll worry it all out during the day." "Sylvia had gone absolutely white. 'Don't!' she said. 'Oh . . . don't.' She added coldly: 'Don't take the trouble.' "[23]

Sylvia has an almost superstitiously Catholic mind. She has always felt —and resented—the power of Father Consett's saintliness. Reluctantly she submits to being lectured by him at Lobscheid, but she is terrified when he says to her "*Exorciso te Ashtaroth*" and threatens her with holy water. "She erected her body above her skirts on the sofa, stiffened like a snake's neck above its coils. . . . 'You . . . you *daren't*,' she said. 'To me . . . an outrage!' " Her pride depends on her belief that whatever she does is right because she does it, and she fights to escape the power of Father Consett's goodness just as she uses every outrage she can think of to destroy the goodness in Christopher that makes her long for him passionately.[24]

When, in the hotel at Rouen in *No More Parades*, she wants to save Christopher from being seduced a second time by the physical charms she plans to exercise as soon as she can get him up to her bedroom, she offers to make a pact with Father Consett in heaven. She tells him she will "leave off torturing Christopher" and retire permanently to a convent if Father Consett will show her just one presentable man. She knows you do not make deals with heaven, knows that Father Consett will make sure she earns, of her own volition, the freedom of submission to the divine will, and is almost amused "at the ingenuity of " his answer: he empties the room of everyone but General O'Hara, a drunken lecher, and two nondescript men. She is thus doomed by her pride to take Christopher to her bedroom and to sit at her dressing table "with the merest film of clothing on her long, shining limbs . . . humming. Maliciously! . . . She had incredible arms, stretched out amongst a wilderness of besilvered cosmetics. Extraordinarily lascivious! Yet clean! Her gilded sheath gown was about her hips on the chair. . . ."[25]

Thus it is that we are slowly prepared for the situation in *Last Post*. First it comes to her, with a shock so fierce that even Gunning, her arch-enemy, pities her, that in getting Groby Great Tree cut down in order to make Christopher suffer she had really been following the will of God; "in letting Groby Great Tree be cut down God was lifting the ban off the Tietjenses." Then she has a vision of Father Consett. "Up over the landscape, the hills, the sky, she felt the shadow of Father Consett, the arms extended as if on a gigantic cruciform—and then, above and behind that, an . . . an August Will!" It convinces her she must free Christopher to marry Valentine. "It's Father Consett in heaven that has done this," she says to Valentine.[26]

Behind this subtle pattern of motives lies Ford's conception of his personal experience. About this he was inclined to mislead his critics. He once carefully pointed out that at a dinner at Kettner's in September, 1922, he had met "Mrs. [Sinclair] Lewis [who] had a golden sheath-gown and her golden hair coiled over her ears." On another occasion he said:

> And suddenly, in Amiens station, I had my other [female character]. . . . She stood before me in the shadows above the luggage barrack and the waiting passengers as the train ran into the station.

She was in a golden sheath-gown and her golden hair was done in a bandeaux, extraordinarily brilliant in the dimness. Like a goddess come in from the forest of Amiens!

But Sylvia is not either of these ladies; she is Ford's conception of Violet Hunt and her persecution of him, neatly reinforced by Ford's conception of Elsie's persecutions. "I do fancy," Violet wrote when she read *Some Do Not* . . . , "apart from her [Sylvia's] beauty, he has come to look at me as like that. . . . " By the time she read in *Last Post* of Sylvia's peering over the hedge at Valentine and Christopher's cottage, pumping the carpenter's wife, and setting detectives on Christopher, she must have been quite sure. Violet was also very much struck in reading *Some Do Not* . . . by the severity with which sexual offenses are punished in it, and is frank to admit that she and Ford committed such offenses. There was a strong physical attraction between them and perhaps it endured even after Ford wanted no more to do with Violet, as Christopher, after the Perowne affair, wanted no more to do with Sylvia but still, at Rouen, felt the power of her physical attraction. But when Sylvia begins "divorce proceedings [against Christopher] and throw[s] all the mud [she] can over the miserable fellow," she is following what Ford thought Elsie's tactics of persecution.[27]

These details are scattered surface signs of the process by which Ford's imagination built up its image of his life. This process characteristically began as self-protection.

> The truth is [Violet said] that Ford is very soft—he has all the timorousness of the savage living in a civilization that is too much for him, he is panicky like the animal which splashes mud about to hide himself from the understanding eye of his fellow men who don't know a primitive, let alone a genius when they see one. . . . He says he is, and so said Stella once, "a moral coward" who fears nothing so much as the dislocation of his mental attitude and being forced to see the world and men as others mostly see it. . . . Under the influence of the terror of being disturbed mentally he gets flabbergasted and ungrateful. . . .

But the sheer creative energy with which Ford has imagined Sylvia is so great that we can follow every twist and turn by which this proud and beautiful woman is at first irritated by Christopher's justness and chivalry—because she respects and fears them—and then gradually becomes obsessed with trying to break him, more and more wildly "committing herself to the first extravagant action that came into her head—and exulting in the consequences." By *No More Parades* she is aware that her actions are no longer really under her control: "I didn't know I was coming [to Rouen]," she says. "It came into my head to come suddenly. And I came." She thinks of Father Consett as forgiving the men who had hanged him because they did not know what they were doing and adds: "Then have mercy on me, for half the time I don't know what I'm doing." But she cannot recover herself, cannot stop pretending she has cancer, lying in the divorce court, and to Mrs. de Bray Pape (whom she persuades to cut down Groby Great Tree), and to Lord Fittleworth, who, she hopes, will evict Christopher and Valentine. This lie to Fittleworth is, she knows, her last bolt—and it misses. She hardly cares; by that time she is too tired. Sylvia is a creature of the country of Ford's mind; we recognize that she has her counterpart in our world but that no one there is ever quite so completely herself, so systematically and ingeniously cruel. She is the product of a remarkable and fantastic imagination.[28]

One could trace the genesis of Ford's other major characters in much this same way. He said that the leading lady of the original cast of Galsworthy's *The Silver Box*, Dorothy Minto, "sat to me . . . for the subsidiary heroine of a series of my novels," that is, for Valentine Wannop. But Stella sat for Valentine Wannop, as she recognized with wry disapproval: "And poor Valentine! But all that is a bit too near the knuckle. . . . She *is* so beastly normal!" Valentine's brother, Gilbert, is Ford's version of Stella's brother Tom. Mrs. Wannop is Mrs. Hunt. Edith Ethel Duchemin, with her shadowy hair, her dark complexion ("over the cheekbones, a delicate suffusion of light carmine"), her pointed chin, is Ford's last portrait of Elsie. Her dress is immediately recognizable; "it contrived to be at once artistic—absolutely in the tradition [of Pre-Raphaelite taste]! And yet well cut! Very large sleeves, of course, but still with a certain fit. She had worn an immense necklace of yellow polished amber: on the dark blue!" She combines Pre-Raphaelite sentimentality with appalling vulgarity in a wholly convincing way, and she becomes obsessed with Macmaster's debt to Christopher—as Elsie seemed to Ford obsessed with collecting large sums from Violet for calling herself Mrs. Hueffer—in a way that leads her to act almost insanely. With typical Fordian extravagance, she offers to let Christopher sell the love letters of a poet with whom she had had an affair before Macmaster died to pay that debt (an echo of Ford's disapproval when Elsie sold Conrad's letters).[29]

The most detailed instance of this sort of imaginative transformation is Christopher Tietjens. Ford always made much of Christopher's resemblance to Arthur Marwood. He did take a few details from Marwood—the mathematical talents, the habit of checking up on the *Encyclopaedia Britannica* from memory, the actuarial scheme, and the Yorkshire stubbornness. Arthur Marwood's own family has borne witness to the accuracy with which Ford represented both Arthur Marwood and his brother, Sir William Francis Marwood, as Christopher and Mark Tietjens. Nevertheless, Christopher Tietjens is Ford's conception of himself. All the essential characteristics—the commitment of the young Christopher to the ideals of the Edwardian ruling class; his extravagant rectitude in matters of money, of women, of duty; his systematic persecution by the world; his secret longing to be an Anglican saint; his gradual transformation during the war from Tory younger son to Tory radical prepared to go underground to preserve the Tory values ("... if," says Valentine, "a ruling class loses the capacity to rule—or the desire!—it should abdicate from its privileges and get underground")—these are all characteristics of the man Ford imagined himself to be.[30]

Christopher's judgments are Ford's too—for example, his violent denunciation of Rossetti which is the starting point of *Some Do Not . . .* 's contrast between the Macmaster-Duchemin affair and the Tietjens-Wannop one. In his own person, Ford said of Rossetti,

> ... love, according to the Pre-Raphaelite canon, was a great but rather sloppy passion. . . . It was a thing that you swooned about on broad, general lines, your eyes closed, your arms outstretched. It excused all sins, it sanctified all purposes, and if you went to hell over it you still drifted about among snowflakes of fire with your eyes closed and in the arms of the object of your passion. . . . The lovers were protected by a generalized swooning passion that formed, as it were, a moral and very efficient mackintosh all over them. . . . As much as to say that you do not mind the bad cooking of the Brighton Hotel if you are having otherwise a good time of it.
> ... I should say that Rossetti was a man without any principles at all, who earnestly desired to find some means of salvation along the lines of least resistance.[31]

The transforming powers of Ford's imagination were never better illustrated than by Christopher, who—though like all Ford's characters, not strictly realistic—has his own independent existence. If Ford is not exactly —in Stephen Dedalus' phrase—"like the God of the creation ... within or behind or beyond or above his handiwork, invisible, refined out of existence, indifferent, paring his finger nails" (for Ford feels too much compassion for Christopher to be so loftily indifferent), he is protected from destructive identification with Christopher by his awareness of the comic simplicity beneath Christopher's great talents.

The difference made by this awareness is evident when we compare Christopher to Gabriel Morton of *True Love & a G.C.M.*, the unfinished novel Ford wrote immediately after the war. It uses exactly the same materials *Parade's End* does and, frequently, even the same language. But Gabriel Morton remains an exercise in self-exculpation, as we can see if we compare the crucial passage of *A Man Could Stand Up—*, in which Christopher confronts his own nature, with the comparable passage in *True Love & a G.C.M.* Christopher thinks, "Now: what the Hell was he? A sort of Hamlet of the Trenches? No, by God he was not. ... He was perfectly ready for action. Ready to command a battalion. He was presumably a lover. They did things like commanding battalions. And Worse!" But Gabriel Morton thinks:

No interest in himself. Was he a sort of Hamlet, then? No, by God he wasn't. If he had been born to set Denmark right, by God, he would have set Denmark right. But not for himself. His life really, had been spent in putting Denmark to rights. All sorts of Denmarks. ... He had put any number of things right, down to drunk-sodden officers, and the books of the Battalion Quarter Master. But he hadn't ever put himself to rights. Why?

Was it because he had been too self-sufficient, too sure of being the best of the bunch? Was it the result of his public school training? At Westminster ... ?[32]

How disastrously Ford has failed to eliminate here such imaginatively irrelevant but personally consoling details as particulars of Gabriel's self-sacrifices, and of the public-school training Ford liked to believe he had had. Gabriel Morton is an expression of Ford's self-pity. We may question the reality of Christopher Tietjens, for Christopher is not a man of the real world: he is a Tory gentry younger son of Ford's imagined England. But, as such, he exists quite independent of Ford's emotional needs.

Chapter 27

The essential subject of *Parade's End* is the inner process by which Christopher and Valentine are gradually transformed from Edwardian to modern people, and *Parade's End* is designed to dramatize this process. It arranges images according to their significance, as a poem does, rather than events according to their occurrence in time, as history does. At the same time a historical perspective is important in *Parade's End*. One of the marked characteristics of Ford's sense of his own life was his feeling for its public significance, and one of the most obvious things about Christopher Tietjens is his representative character. What is true of him is only a little less true of the other characters in *Parade's End*.

To emphasize this aspect of his characters, Ford limits his story to the climactic moment of Edwardian civilization, from 1912, when the approach of war was evident, to the mid-twenties, when the destruction of the Edwardian world had become clearly visible. By then, *Last Post* had been sounded at the funeral of the world "their class [had] ruled" and men who hoped to go on living had to turn away from its grave, with whatever regrets for that buried land of Hope and Glory, knowing that its customs and ceremonies were now irrelevant to the inner reality of their lives. This was Parade's End, the end of the beautiful social ritual that had once displayed the moral convictions and values by which that class had ruled both itself and its world.

"At the beginning of the war," Tietjens said, "I had to look in on the War Office, and in a room I found a fellow.... What do you think he was doing ... what the hell do you think he was doing? He was devising the ceremonial for the disbanding of a Kitchener battalion. You can't say we were not prepared in one matter at least. ... Well, the end of the show was to be: the adjutant would stand

372

the battalion at ease: the band would play *Land of Hope and Glory,* and then the adjutant would say: *There will be no more parades.* . . . Don't you see how symbolical it was: the band playing *Land of Hope and Glory,* and then the adjutant saying *There will be no more parades?* . . . For there won't. There won't, there damn well won't. . . . No more Hope, no more Glory, no more parades for you and me any more. Nor for the country . . . Nor for the world, I dare say . . . None . . . Gone . . . Na poo, finny! No . . . more . . . parades!"[1]

"Land of Hope and Glory"; Elgar's Edwardian celebration of England perfectly expresses Christopher's confidence in his class and its values as he walks home with Valentine after their breakfast with the scatalogical maniac, Duchemin, and his corruptly aesthetic wife.

"God's England!" Tietjens exclaimed to himself in high good humour. " 'Land of Hope and Glory!'—F natural descending to tonic, C major: chord of 6-4, suspension over dominant seventh to common chord of C major. . . . All absolutely correct! . . . Full grand organ: all stops: special *vox humana* and key-bugle effect. . . . Across the counties came the sound of bugles that his father knew. . . . Pipe exactly right. It must be: pipe of Englishman of good birth: ditto tobacco. Attractive young woman's back. English midday mid-summer. Best climate in the world! No day on which man may not go abroad!"

We last hear this phrase near the end of *A Man Could Stand Up—,* when Christopher has his moment of elation over the achievement of the single command: "It *is* a land of Hope and Glory!" This moment is short-lived; the bitter disappointment of the British refusal to occupy Berlin ends it.[*2]

Christopher Tietjens is an Edwardian saint; it is his secret ambition to become, like his mother, an Anglican saint. He would like to retire to the neighborhood of George Herbert's Bremerton and stand up on a hill with a Greek testament under his arm gazing forever at the English countryside

---

*In *A Man Could Stand Up—* Christopher hears a key bugle remark "with singular distinctness to the dawn":

I know a la ^{dy} fair _{and} kind

Was never face
       so   mind
     pleased my
          y

and exclaims to himself: "Herrick and Purcell!" "Across the counties, etc.," recurs several times. The reiterated title of *Some Do Not . . .* derives from a variation on a couplet that occurs several times in *Mister Bosphorus and the Muses,* which Ford was completing at the same time he was planning *Some Do Not . . . :* "The gods to each ascribe a differing lot:/Some enter at the portal. Some do not!" But the phrase implies a variety of things throughout the novel.

he loves. "How," says Valentine Wannop to him before she knows him well, "can you so hate your country?" "Don't say it! Don't believe it!" Christopher answers. "Don't even for a moment think it! I love every inch of its fields and every plant in the hedgerows: comfrey, mullein, paigles, long red purples, that liberal shepherds give a grosser name . . . and all the rest of the rubbish—you remember the field between the Duchemins and your mother's. . . . " But "it is not a good thing," as he tells General Campion, "to belong to the seventeenth or eighteenth century in the twentieth. Or . . . it is not good to have taken one's public school's ethical system seriously. I am really, sir, the English public schoolboy. That's an eighteenth century product. . . . Other men get over their schooling. I never have."*³

Ford was wholly in earnest about this idealized conception of an early England. In *The March of Literature* he said:

> But having, then, in a Tudor manor's room, in a cool, calm, light, listened to the incomparable fingering of Colonel Hutchinson's lute, giving you Purcell, and turned over at random *The Delights of the Muses* and [such] anthologies . . . you become aware of an England . . . that we may never see again . . . a country Christist, almost more than Christian. . . . It is, perhaps, almost above all, the all-pervasion of music into those cool, bright Laudian days that, together with the fervent, as if domestic love of the Redeemer who came, lightly as a lambent flame leaping upon the hills, gave the note of those matchless years that have never returned.⁴

Christopher loves the graceful parade of Edwardian society, not for its luxury—he hates ostentatious luxury—but for the earned authority he believes it expresses; it is the outward sign of the inner values he has grown up with. He treasures the belief that England will deal with her political enemies as he deals with Sylvia, his sexual enemy, by taking the "gallant enemy" attitude Ford himself had recommended so unsuccessfully at the beginning of the real war. He saw

> the Almighty as, on a colossal scale, a great English Landowner, benevolently awful, a colossal duke who never left his study and was thus invisible, but knowing all about the estate down to the last hind at the home farm and the last oak; Christ, an almost too benevolent

*Much later Valentine, quite spontaneously, does remember that field between the Duchemins' and her mother's. When she meets Christopher outside the War Office and, in a panic of jealousy, asks him if he has had a child by Mrs. Duchemin and he brushes her aside "as if she had been a midge," saying, "I imagined you knew me better," "She was Valentine Wannop again; in the sunlight the chaffinches said 'Pink! pink!' The seed-heads of the tall grasses were brushing against her skirt."

Land-Steward, son of the Owner, knowing all about the estate down to the last child at the porter's lodge, apt to be got around by the more detrimental tenants; the Third Person of the Trinity, the spirit of the estate . . . the atmosphere of the estate, that of the interior of Winchester Cathedral just after a Handel anthem had been finished. . . .

He will learn better than this as time goes by; indeed, even then he knew he was thinking "good-humouredly about his official religion." But at the beginning of *Parade's End* he is so innocently and literally a ruling-class younger son that, though he instinctively reacts against the signs of decay in Edwardian society, he does not really understand what they imply.[5]

But we do. At the middle of *Some Do Not . . .* stand the contrasted pairs of lovers—on the one hand Christopher and Valentine, with their sharp, happy arguments over Ovid and Catullus, their love of the English countryside, their strict sexual self-discipline; on the other Macmaster and Mrs. Duchemin, with their love of the appearance and rhetoric of chastity, of taste, of dignity, of authority—and their lust, their obtaining of a knighthood by cheating, their purchase (with money they owe Christopher) of "a pleasant little place in Surrey . . . to let Macmaster know something of the leisure of a country gentleman's lot" ("As an amusing detail, the villagers there already called Macmaster 'squire' and the women curtsied to him").[6]

These pairs of lovers are contrasted at every moment. Christopher tells Macmaster that the Rossetti pòem Macmaster will presently quote to Mrs. Duchemin is "a filthy picture." He and Valentine walk across their English field to the "admirable luncheon of cold lamb, new potatoes and mint sauce variety," served with silver picked up at sales and old cut glass, and to their conversation with Mrs. Wannop, the only decent novelist since the eighteenth century, leaving Macmaster and Mrs. Duchemin amidst the debris of that incredible breakfast at the Duchemins', amidst the rich paneling, the orange Turners, the Chippendale, the echoes of "Breakfast" Duchemin's scatalogical outbursts, to share their Rossetti and their preparations for adultery. On either side of these contrasted couples stand the sex-obsessed Duchemin and the "man-mad" Sylvia.

Christopher and—later—Mark Tietjens have an assurance of their place and privileges that is tough and unapologetic; they have earned this assurance by their talents and their high standards of duty. In immediate contrast with them are the upper-class characters who have the style of a ruling class without the talents or standards that justify it. General Campion believes Sylvia is "a splendid girl. Straight as a die; the soul of loyalty to her friends. And fearless" because she looks the part. But she is not. General Campion also belies his splendid appearance. He is frightened of Christopher because Christopher is "the sort of Fellow you couldn't believe in and yet couldn't prove anything against. The curse of the world. . . . " He does not want to know the truth of Christopher's situation; he wants only "a plausible story" that "shows you're not flying in the face of society." He thinks Henry VIII's castles are solidly built because—like Sylvia—they look right; they are in fact —as Christopher knows from having really looked at them—mostly rubble. General Campion is a conscientious soldier and the habits of conduct drilled into him by his class are good ones; but he is an unintelligent and self-indulgent man. Part of what makes him believe he can rely on Sylvia is that she rides well, but he himself is quickly seduced by that newfangled means of transportation, the automobile. His vanity persuades him he is a skillful driver, despite his evident incompetence, and he bursts recklessly out of the driveway of Mountby and runs into Valentine and Christopher, who is driving a horse with the superb skill of his old-fashioned Tory understanding of animals. At the subsequent trial Campion unquestionably perjures himself. He and his kind, in what Christopher calls their "muddle-headedness," no longer rule either themselves or their society, as such people must if the parade that is their personal privilege and the public image of their social function is to be justified.[7]

Though born to the upper classes, General Campion is most at ease with self-made gentlemen like Macmaster; his sister, Claudine, is married to Paul Sandbach, "the son of an ennobled mayor of Middlesbrough." Sandbach is not very different from the City men Campion rebukes for loudly discussing their sexual exploits in the Rye golf club. All the men in the family Valentine Wannop works for at Ealing attempt to seduce her. The presence of such people in society, when their manners are as bad as those of the City men in the golf club, is "for these Tories . . . the end of the world. The last of England!" (Ford's ironic adaptation of the title of his grandfather's famous Victorian narrative painting). But such people put Tories like Campion at ease when they display what the fashion magazines and the theater have taught them to suppose are upper-class manners: "steel-blue tie, true-looking gold ring, steel-blue eyes beneath black brows! . . . 'Oh, dear lady!' (And it seemed [to Mrs. Duchemin] to be charming to be addressed thus!)."

The pattern of images Ford slowly builds up by a careful selection of scenes from the lives of these people defines the character and quality of Edwardian society. Christopher sits in the Rye train thinking of the "inso-lent phrases" with which Sylvia has announced she is returning to him after her love affair and concludes it is his duty as a gentleman to take her back;

Macmaster sits opposite him meditating the glories of Rossetti's love poetry. "I stand," says Christopher, "for monogamy and chastity"; the claim has its ironic aspect, considering how Christopher came to marry Sylvia and his condoning of her present escapade. Macmaster quotes Rossetti on chastity and arranges to meet Mrs. Duchemin at the little white gate behind her house. Valentine Wannop says to Mrs. Duchemin, "Look here, Edie. Stop worrying about my mind. If you think that anything I hear at your table after nine months as an ash-cat at Ealing . . . can corrupt my mind, you're simply mistaken," and amidst the luxuries of the Duchemins' dining room, "Breakfast" Duchemin suddenly shouts, "Chaste you observe! What a world of suggestion in the word. . . . " Valentine says to Mrs. Duchemin, "I'd like you to understand that in spite of it all I'm pure! Chaste, you know. . . . " and Mrs. Duchemin says, "There's something beautiful, there's something *thrilling* about chastity." "You mean like an egg-and-spoon race," says Valentine. But Mrs. Duchemin is incurable; "Isn't the real symbol Atalanta, running fast and not turning aside for the golden apple?" "The man with the oily hair [in the Rye golf club says] in a sickly voice that Gertie [is] hot stuff, but not the one for Budapest with all the Gitana girls. . . . " When Gertie Wilson and Valentine risk jail by demonstrating on the golf links, this same man chases them shouting "Strip the bitch naked! . . . Ugh . . . Strip the bitch stark naked!"[9]

In this way the characters of *Some Do Not . . .* are made to suggest the various elements that constitute Edwardian society and the sexual, social, and political attitudes of each. With her mastery of social climbing Mrs. Duchemin stage-manages Macmaster's steady, unscrupulous climb up the social and political ladder. Simultaneously, Sylvia uses Christopher's unconventional behavior to destoy Christopher's reputation and hasten his steady, scrupulous slide down the social and political ladder.

Ford's purpose in the succeeding novels of *Parade's End* is not so much to describe what happens later in the lives of his characters—though he does that—as to explore the meaning of the situation that has been defined in *Some Do Not. . . .* What was implicit there becomes overt in *No More Parades.* Even the appearance of principle and self-discipline in people like Sylvia collapses. Sylvia leaves her retreat at Birkenhead to pursue Christopher to Rouen in a disintegrating passion to seduce and dominate him, now not even with the purposeful if cold-blooded practicality of her first seduction of him, but with uncontrollable longing ("Blessed Virgin, Mother of God, make him take me. . . . "). In an agony of incomprehensible impulses ("Have mercy on me, for half the time I don't know what I'm doing!") she also plays on the lust of Perowne and General O'Hara. This beautiful and imperious Edwardian image of sexual power has become irrationally destructive; the purposeful and self-controlled life of passion is now being led only in obscure corners such as girls' schools by women like Valentine Wannop.[10]

What was potentially dangerous socially and politically in *Some Do Not* . . . —what Christopher called "the muddle-headed frame of mind" of General Campion and his kind that " . . . lets us into wars with hopelessly antiquated field guns and rottenly inferior ammunition"—has become in *No More Parades* literally destructive as the processional figures of the staff— Campion, Levin, Perowne, O'Hara—and the civilians in Whitehall muddle the conduct of the war.[11]

Parallel with Sylvia's self-destroying and socially disruptive sexual attack on Christopher are the sexual confusions in the lives of a series of other characters, all, like Christopher's, complicated by their involvement in the war in France and the collapse of Edwardian moral conventions at home. McKechnie, a young officer driven half mad by his long spell in the lines, gets leave to go home and divorce his wife. However, "acting under conscientious scruples of the younger school of the day," he decides against divorcing her and, instead, spends the money he has borrowed from Christopher in going about with her and her lover. Christopher refuses home leave to one of his men, O Nine Morgan, because he knows O Nine Morgan's wife is living with a prizefighter who will kill O Nine Morgan if he goes home. O Nine Morgan is hit during a shelling of the base and dies at Christopher's feet. Levin, a staff officer, depends on Christopher to get him out of his endless troubles with Mlle. de Bailly, the jealous French girl he has engaged himself to.[12]

Christopher is maddeningly frustrated by the Chinese ritual of army regulations devised for another age and a different kind of war; he is worried to death by the effects of a civilian influence made possible by what had once been the strength of the ruling class, that it is like a club in which the right people all know one another; and he is ultimately defeated by the fact that Sylvia, using her social position and her beauty, persuades her old lover, Perowne, to bring her, without papers of any kind, straight to Campion's headquarters at Rouen. In this way Ford concentrates what he wants to say about Edwardian society at war in Sylvia's sexual war on Christopher.

Exactly as Christopher, the Tory younger son, has a lingering devotion to Edwardian society and is reluctant to recognize its bankruptcy, so he is still subject to the physical beauty that had made it possible for Sylvia to seduce him in the first place; and his Tory gentleman's conception of what

he owes the woman he has married requires him to give Sylvia every opportunity to exercise that attraction. Ford shows us exactly how she does so that
night at the hotel in Rouen, and how nearly she succeeds. At the end of the
evening, Christopher politely asks her to dance: "It was the luck of the
half-drunk." As they start, Sylvia says,

> "You call the compounds where you keep the W.A.A.C.'s
> Venusberg's, don't you? Isn't it queer that Venus should be your
> own? . . . Think of poor [Valentine] Elisabeth [Wannop]!"
> The room where they were dancing was very dark. . . . It was
> queer to be in his arms. . . . You see, father [Consett]! . . . In his arms!
> . . . Of course, dancing is not really. . . . But so near the real thing!
> So near! . . . She had almost kissed him on the lips. . . . All but!
> . . . He had pressed her tighter. . . . All these months without . . . My
> lord did me honour . . . Good for Malbrouck *s'en va-t-en guerre.*
> . . . He *knew* she had almost kissed him on the lips. . . . And that his
> lips had almost responded. . . . As they mounted the stairs she
> thought what a fat tenor Tannhäuser always was! . . . The Venus-
> berg music was dinning in her ears. . . . She said: "Sixty-six inex-
> pressibles! I'm as sober as a judge . . . I need to be!"

Ford interweaves Christopher's battle with Sylvia and his struggle to
do his military job. With him and Sylvia at dinner is Sergeant-Major Cowley. He is celebrating his commission and gets a little drunk, so that he talks
endlessly about his admiration for what Christopher has done for the battalion. In addition, their dinner is constantly interrupted by telephone calls
from the base, by conversations between Christopher and General O'Hara,
by Christopher's constant brooding about his men that includes the sudden,
horrible thought that he saved O Nine Morgan at Noircourt only to get him
killed two years after.

Sylvia is indignant that Christopher should thus "betray her with a
battalion. . . . That is against decency, against Nature" according to her
lights. Yet she is more responsible than Christopher for Christopher's situation. It is she who has set Campion against Christopher. It is she who causes
Perowne and General O'Hara to come creeping down the hotel corridor to
her room late that night. Christopher does not recognize Perowne, who is
in his dressing gown ("looking for the bathroom" he later explains); "I
imagined him to be a French waiter," Christopher says. When he sees
Perowne's face peering around the door at the near-naked Sylvia, he pushes
Perowne across the hall. When General O'Hara arrives in a drunken muddle, Perowne accuses Christopher of having arranged the whole thing in

order to blackmail him, O'Hara accuses Christopher, and, when Christopher pushes him out of the room, puts Christopher under arrest. As a result General Campion sends both Perowne and Christopher to the front.[14]

During the long conversation between Christopher and General Campion the next morning, Christopher's mind nearly gives way under the strain of trying to maintain its commitment to the Edwardian mode of life against which his under self has already rebelled. This conflict comes to a climax when General Campion, in all his shining splendor, "as when a godhead descends," inspects Christopher's cook house.

To Tietjens this was like the sudden bursting out of the regimental quick-step, as after a funeral with military honours the band and drums march away, back to barracks.

Forever. There will be "no more parades for [Christopher] any more. Nor for the country . . . nor for the world, I dare say . . . None."[15]

In *A Man Could Stand Up*— Valentine and Christopher reluctantly recognize that the long battles they have carried on to deny their feelings have been waged in the service of an ideal of conduct no longer workable because the culture that conceived it and provided a world for its exercise has collapsed. Both of them have unconsciously known this for some time— Christopher at least since his conversation with General Campion in January, 1918, at the end of *No More Parades*, Valentine, "for two years . . . oh, *call* it two years" during which she "had been inhibiting—*pro*hibiting— herself from thinking about herself." Both deliberately resign from Edwardian society. Valentine rejects her father's conception of women's role and leaves her girls' school. Christopher refuses to remain the heir of Groby or to touch a penny of its income, refuses to work for the government even in an obscure post in Toulon, and gives up his attempt to treat Sylvia as an Edwardian gentleman should. He and Valentine celebrate their *nuit de noces* and the end of the war in the stripped rooms of Christopher's once splendid flat at Grays Inn along with a motley group of Christopher's damaged and dying front-line friends. They are setting off together on a life that, by denying all the Edwardian rules of conduct and by rejecting all the splendors of its luxurious parade, will enable them to realize anew the fundamental moral values of Edwardian society by which they have always existed.[16]

Last Post shows us, in Mark Tietjens, the deliberate refusal of life by all that is left of the true ruling class of Edwardian society, and the rebirth of its values in the new life of Christopher and Valentine and their unborn child. As Christopher and Valentine struggle to build a new world for their child, Mark is freed, by Sylvia's surrender, to die as he wants to. Before he

does so, he speaks for the last time—and for the first time since Armistice
night—to recognize and bless the life Valentine and Christopher are struggling to create out of the destruction of the Edwardian world.

> "Did ye ever hear tell o' t' Yorkshireman . . . On Mount Ara
> . . . Ara . . . "

He had not spoken for so long. His tongue appeared to fill
his mouth; his mouth to be twisted to one side. It was growing dark.
He said:

> "Put your ear close to my mouth. . . . " She [Valentine] cried

out! He whispered:

> " ' *'Twas the mid o' the night and the barnies grat*
> *And the mither beneath the mauld heard that. . . .* '
>
> . . . An old song. My nurse sang it. . . . Never thou let thy child weep
> for thy sharp tongue to thy good man. . . . A good man! Groby Great
> Tree is down. . . . "

"She [Lady Tietjens]," Valentine says, "would like to have had his last
words. . . . But she did not need them as much as I."*[17]

Chapter 28

When Stella went south to think over Ford's proposal for their separation, Ford was left alone in his three-room flat at 32 rue Vaugirard. Like Henry Martin Smith of *The Rash Act,*

> He went out for most of his meals. Sometimes he found an acquaintance to talk to him. As often as not he did not. He imagined that some people still avoided him—but he might have been mistaken. . . . He sat, most evenings, at the table of Miss Cameron in a café! She had a rather noticeable mustache and occasionally she drank far too many *petits verres.* . . . They sat huddled together for hours in a corner of a rather noisy café. . . .

During the day he worked on *A Little Less Than Gods.* The rest of the time he was at loose ends.[1]

For relief he began to give regular "Thursday afternoons" at which he started to develop his image of himself as the Dean of English Letters and the sympathetic adviser of young writers, especially attractive young women writers—the Ladies Whose Bright Eyes, as his friends called them. These Thursdays were very proper; Ford never served anything but tea and liked things to be decorous.

> As the ladies sat on the divan and smiled up worshipfully, he would mince up and down the floor with a gait that slightly resembled that of an overgrown duckling, would show his teeth through his moustache in a restrained fatherly smile or would give an equally restrained chuckle, and would . . . drop bright little bits of elderly, reminiscent wisdom.

He very much disliked it when rowdy elements intruded. F. S. Flint once arrived filled with aperitifs and a desire to speak nothing but French. "For

God's sake, Flint," Ford finally burst out, "remember that you are an Englishman and a gentleman!" At the same time, Ford liked to think of himself as able to join in the fun when that was appropriate; he told Gerald Duckworth that when he came to Paris he would discover that Ford was "being coerced into learning a number of new Charleston steps, so Mrs. Duckworth will know what to expect," though in practice Ford's dancing never consisted of more than a shuffling walk.[2]

In spite of his good relations with Duckworth, he was aggrieved by the continued failure of his work in England; he was selling—as he told himself—in the tens of thousands in the United States and only in the hundreds in England. He took out his feeling on the first available object, the Inland Revenue Service.

> ... this matter of income tax [he wrote Duckworth]—that is to say a tax on what is not income at all, for royalties on books are as much payment for sales as if one sold a sack of potatoes and indeed much more so, since one is selling a portion of one's brain which is exhaustible ... so that I have quite decided that I will give up publishing in England at all rather than submit to such a pettifogging injustice. . . .
>
> Of course, as you probably know, the commercial side of it has never bothered me much and I should not let it bother me now but for this last straw.[3]

Just before Ford left for New York in May, 1928, Samuel Putnam's *New Review* had a dinner for Pound at which Ford was to eulogize Pound. Instead a surrealist somewhat the worse for drugs pulled a knife on Pound and the dinner broke up in confusion. On Ford's last night in Paris he gave a large party at which—he was happy to claim—all the glasses were broken. When the company had left, he sat down and wrote a farewell letter to Stella.

> I was glad to have your letter of Wednesday [May 9], for it cleared up a few misunderstandings. . . .
>
> As to the religion, pray do not misunderstand me. I *want* Julie to remain at the école Alsacienne as both doctors agree that it is as good for health as any school in Paris. . . . I should also like her to go to Mass with fair regularity and be a real Catholic for as long as it lasts. I should also like her to go later to a convent of Dames Nobles of the Ursulines to which order my family has always gone —and I can assure you that if you find any trace of the nuns influencing her against you as a Protestant I will interfere with the extremest of vigour. . . .

Just before I dispossessed her of this machine Julie produced the beginning of her first short story. . . . She said that she was having a discussion with Mlle Renée and Fannie as to what they would do in heaven and they said that she would look after the little angels. But she said: 'Non! Non! Je taperai à la machine comme Daddy!' . . .

It is now 3.15 in the morning . . . so I shall cut this short. After all there is no need for it to be my last.

But let me say that I esteem you and am attached to you as I have always done and been.

He left Paris for New York the next day.[4]

He was glad to get back to New York and Mrs. Wright, who had, while he had been in Paris, divorced Guy Wright and come on to New York to be with him. With his habit of ignoring the obstacles in the way of anything he wanted badly, Ford had made little of Mrs. Wright's steadfast refusal to consider becoming his mistress. He had assumed that, if he could solve the problem of Stella's presence in his life, all would be well. But Mrs. Wright's romanticism was unconquerably marital. She had divorced Guy Wright in the expectation of marrying Ford, and she was not going to settle for less. The next winter in Paris she was to annoy Ford's young friends by putting it to them that she was "too fine" to live with Ford as his mistress.[5]

During this summer of 1928 Harold Loeb saw something of her and Ford around New York. "She seemed," he remembers, "touchingly fond of what, to my young eyes, was an elderly man. I would call for Ford at her small hotel, to find them sitting side by side in the lobby. On one occasion I escorted her to a publisher's tea. . . . Ford had asked me to take her because he had to be there ahead of the guests. All the way up in the taxi she was on the verge of tears. She told me that Ford could not marry her and that she could not live with him unmarried. I was very sorry for them both. Ford needed desperately the care and love she equally desperately needed to give."[6]

Ford's attitude toward Mrs. Wright may seem naïve, but what always counted for him was companionship, intimate conversations, "identity with the woman." As John Dowell says in *The Good Soldier*, "For, whatever may be said of the relations of the sexes, there is no man who loves a woman that does not desire to come to her for the renewal of his courage, for the cutting asunder of his difficulties. And that will be the mainspring of his desire for her. We are all so afraid, we are all so alone, we all so need from the outside the assurance of our own worthiness to exist." Like Edward Ashburnham, however, Ford was likely to lose interest once he had settled into the routine of domesticity; his imagination would then fix itself on a new woman. Each time he would believe he had found what he always dreamed of, both domestic intimacy and sustained romantic excitement. " . . . for a time," as Dowell also says, "if such a passion come to fruition, the man will get what he wants. . . . But these things pass away. . . . The pages of the book will become familiar; the beautiful corner of the road will have been turned too many times." Then, with undiminished confidence that this time it was the real thing, Ford would move on to a new woman. Thus it was that, like his own Joe Notterdam with Henrietta Felise in *When the Wicked Man*, he was, with Mrs. Wright, "driving . . . towards what he had longed for for years. . . . Well, towards . . . Home." "Sleep after toil, port after stormy seas. . . . " Notterdam thinks as he contemplates Henrietta, exactly as Gringoire had at the end of *No Enemy* a decade before, as he contemplated Madame Sélysette —that is, Stella—sitting in the garden of Coopers Cottage, Bedham.[7]

Ford left New York for Marseilles on the *Patria* on July 27 and, the first night out, composed the dedication of *A Little Less Than Gods* to Mrs. Wright. He was deeply depressed. He could no longer ignore the fact that Mrs. Wright would not have him on the only terms he could offer her. In Marseilles he could get a room only at the Bristol, which was very expensive. He had only 312 francs, less than his bill at the Bristol, and could not leave until he could get more. Brandt, he believed, had promised to send him $200, but had not done so. "I have written," he complained, "over 100,000 words since I left for New York [in May] and have not had a day's holiday and several thousand dollars are owing to me and I am perpetually penniless. . . . I have, naturally, no word from Julie."[8]

Eventually he got out of the clutches of the Bristol and went to Carqueiranne for a month. From there he went to Corsica, perhaps to look again at the place he had described in *A Little Less Than Gods*, and thence through the Jura to Strasbourg. By the end of October he was back in his little flat at 32 rue Vaugirard, in time to read and disapprove of the publicity for *A Little Less Than Gods*, put out by Viking, to whom he had now moved. "For myself," he said, "I should have preferred a little less of dwelling on Conrad . . . for I am a little tired of being tacked onto C's coattails and I don't believe the public cares a damn about it." Already, in the spring, he had "deprecate[d] any championing of my own side of our collaboration" and deplored "the depreciation of myself that I understand has lately occupied the activities of various writers," though he could not resist saying once more that, during the collaboration, he "had been the more popular author in England" and that the "English press was booming" him then. After that, it did little good for him to say what was perfectly true, that "Conrad and I worked together during many years with absolute one-ness of purpose and absolute absence of rivalry." Now, he thought, Viking was stirring up the old trouble again and he feared the reviews would have more to say about his collaboration with Conrad than about "the sterling romantic qualities" of *A Little Less Than Gods*. Perhaps he was sensitive on this point because the subject of *A Little Less Than Gods* was one that he and Conrad had discussed together years before and Conrad had already used in *Suspense.*[9]

He need not have worried; reviewers scarcely mentioned *Suspense*. They treated *A Little Less Than Gods* respectfully, though they thought it inferior to the Tietjens novels. L. P. Hartley, who wrote the most penetrating review, said,

> Of course all artists arrange the raw material of life to suit their purposes; Mr. Ford does more, he cooks it. . . . Conrad would surely have simplified [the hero, George Feilding], made him more obviously the sport of conflicting loyalties, drawn his portrait in firmer lines than those rhetorical flourishes which Mr. Ford weaves.

A Little Less Than Gods sold between five and six thousand copies, barely paying off the advance of $3,500.*[10]

That fall in Paris was less lonely for Ford than the spring had been; in late November the Tates arrived on their Guggenheim fellowship and settled near him at the Hotel de Fleurus. In January, when Stella moved out of their old flat at 32 rue Vaugirard so that Ford could return to it, the Tates and Léonie Adams moved into Ford's flat. The stimulating presence of competing poets led him to revive the sonnet-writing contests he had first introduced in Holland Park Avenue in *The English Reveiw* days. "It was," as Samuel Putnam said, "all very exciting if you cared for that sort of thing, and, contrasted with what commonly passed as amusement in the Quarter, it was innocent enough. . . . These were simply the genial pastimes of a lonely old man. . . . " "The prize," Allen Tate said, "was always a stale cake provided by Ford, which he always won but gave to the runner-up."[11]

Mrs. Wright had now arrived in Paris too—to buy clothes, she was careful to announce. At the end of the year she and Ford returned to New York, and there, on New Year's Eve, he was mugged. With characteristic exaggeration, he described himself as having been "set on by racketeers" and modestly announced that he had "got off rather successfully with a little damage to my teeth and throat." He felt he now knew at first hand the

*For a discussion of *A Little Less Than Gods*, see pp. 515–17.

world of Dot McKeown and the gangsters he would describe in *When the Wicked Man.*[12]

The continued failure of Ford's work in England and the success of the Tietjens novels in America now began to make him feel that he was not merely a British writer with a considerable reputation in America but, in an important sense, an American writer. "The greater part of my life since the war," as he put it later, "has been spent in literary America or in the society of American writers; I pass in that country for an American writer myself and am given credit for having what is called 'discovered' a considerable portion of the better-known post-war American writers." He began to look for some means of settling permanently in America.[13]

He had taken up the problem with his agent, Carl Brandt, before he left New York in July, and Bernice Baumgarten now wrote Bradley about Ford's doing some literary scouting in New York. This was what Carl Brandt thought he and Ford had been talking about. Ford thought otherwise.

> Carl [he wrote Miss Baumgarten] asked me to take up my residence permanently in New York and I said that I was perfectly ready to spend six, or at most eight months of the year there, Carl assuring me that he could find me a lucrative position of a literary kind—as I understood him a position of literary advisor to a consider-able firm.... Your suggestion of my doing "scouting" for any firm would be quite out of the question.... But if Carl wants me to settle in New York I must have some sort of assurance of a settled income. ... What I imagined Carl to be proposing—and what would suit me quite well would be a general partnership in some firm with a control-ling voice in their book list, I being ready to put in some capital on debentures and to receive a salary as apart from shares in the profits.

Since this is the position Ford regularly—and unsuccessfully—proposed to publishers for the rest of his life, it seems likely that the idea was his rather than Brandt's; in any event, Miss Baumgarten could recall no such proposal and pointed out that, unless Ford were employed by his own publisher—which would be awkward—such an arrangement would be impractical so long as he himself was an active author. Ford decided that Brandt had let him down badly in this matter, and they soon came to a parting of the ways. This added another influential New York literary firm to the list of those he had quarreled with.[14]

Ford's belief that he was an American writer also made him want to write a novel about American life, and he felt he now knew Americans well enough to do so. Before leaving New York that summer of 1928 he had made a contract with Viking according to which they advanced him $3,500 on this American novel, to be called *When the Wicked Man*, and an unspecified additional sum for *That Same Poor Man*, the novel he had written immediately after the war and had never been able to sell. He did a hurried revision of *That Same Poor Man* before leaving New York, and was unhappy when Viking turned it down: "I rewrote Poor Man at urgent request of Oppenheimer [of Viking] and also Carl Brandt against my own judgment and wishes." But he must have suggested the idea; Oppenheimer and Brandt could not otherwise have known of the novel's existence. He began writing *When the Wicked Man* when he got back to Paris in October, 1928.[15]

In January, 1929, Ford made a serious effort to persuade Elsie to divorce him so that he could marry Mrs. Wright.

> I would be obliged [he wrote Robert Garnett] if you would suggest to her [Elsie] that the present would be an appropriate time for completing [the divorce] proceedings. For I was recently told—very much to my surprise—for I do not receive newspaper cuttings—that Mrs. Elsie Hueffer had stated in Court that her reason for not completing these proceedings was that she was a Roman Catholic—this being the only reason I ever heard. And I heard it only New Years Eve last. I at once consulted a priest here and he gave it as his opinion that there would be no difficulty whatever in having the marriage dissolved by Rome ... and the Church would not only approve but enjoin a dissolution of the civil marriage by divorce.
>
> I need not point out to you that my present position is one of great hardship and indeed of embar[r]assment that makes life almost impossible for me. ... It is indeed one of my most serious regrets that I am precluded from paying her alimony ... but I solemnly resolved that under no sort of compulsion would I pay any money to Mrs. Elsie Hueffer until she had completed these proceedings and in that resolve I have remained.[16]

This letter was hardly calculated to achieve Ford's purpose: it is too preoccupied with self-justification. It is true that Ford did not subscribe to a clipping service, but he had known from the start about Elsie's suit against Violet in 1924 and her counsel's misstatement that she was a Roman Catholic, and Elsie knew he had. His pretense to the contrary could not possibly have deceived her and must therefore only have annoyed her. The letter's emphasis on the injustice of Elsie's refusal to complete the divorce proceedings may have relieved Ford's feelings but was not likely to conciliate Elsie. Moreover, Elsie knew Ford had prided himself since the days when he was studying Henry VIII's marital difficulties on his knowledge of the Church's views of divorce. She could only have been irritated by his attempt to give authority to his own opinion by ascribing it to an anonymous priest. Ford's regret that his resolve not to pay Elsie money under compulsion prevented him from supporting her was also more likely to soothe his vanity than to persuade Elsie.

This letter is a good illustration of how—and why—Ford so often mismanaged his affairs. He wanted to persuade Elsie to divorce him so that he could marry Rene Wright. Yet he could not resist asserting the moral superiority of his own behavior and the shabbiness of Elsie's. In this instance, at least, it probably would not have done any good if he had been able to; it is unlikely Elsie would have divorced him anyway. Robert Garnett replied that Elsie had not in fact become a Catholic, that "her Counsel's remark was made as we gather by reason of a misunderstanding between him and the instructing Solicitor. . . . Our client tells us that she wishes the matrimonial position to be left as it is. . . . It appears to us that our client's decision above stated has been come to for the sake of the children." If this was not the whole reason for Elsie's attitude, it was certainly a part of it. This was the end of any real hope that Ford would be able to marry Rene Wright. It was his last, indirect contact with Elsie.*[17]

Ford was occupied that spring writing for *The Bookman* the essays that were published by Lippincott in March as *The English Novel*. He was also working on *When the Wicked Man*, which he finished in May. When Viking read it, they decided it was unpublishable. Ford was already angry at Viking because they had rejected *That Same Poor Man*; their decision to reject *When the Wicked Man* offended him even more.

I was trying in the book [he wrote Miss Baumgarten] a technical experiment which seems to me to have been successful and you are, I suppose[,] aware that I have in my time been a good deal praised

*In 1933 Elsie sold Kitcat; it was too large for her and difficult to let. She tried living at Appledore and Icklesham, where Harri Martindale lived, but Harri died soon after she moved there and she returned to Aldington, to a house called Frithfield on Aldington Frith. During her last years she had a bad heart; when she became too ill to be alone, she was moved to a retired nurse's home at St. Leonards-on-Sea, and there she died on January 29, 1949. She was buried in Aldington churchyard in the presence of Mr. and Mrs. Harry Simpkins, who had cared for her during her last years, her nephew, Martin Martindale, and her daughter Katharine. Her grave looks across the valley to Kitcat. Katharine had married, in 1927, the Irish painter Charles Lamb, and gone to live in a house designed for them by Harrison Cowleshaw in Carraroe, County Galway. The Lambs had five children, two sons and three daughters. Christina, Sister Mary Matthew Hueffer, became in 1919 a member of the Society of the Holy Child Jesus, a Roman Catholic congregation founded in England in the middle of the nineteenth century by Cornelia Connelly, an American from Philadelphia. Sister Mary Matthew has been engaged throughout her religious life in educational work, principally with adult students in London and Oxford.

for the technique of my fiction and that I have had a good deal of influence on the technique of the more modern novelists of today. It seems therefore more likely that I am right in the matter than a group of tradesmen who have no literary experience. . . . When you have lived as long as I have you will see that in such affairs the publisher is invariably wrong.

He insisted to its British publisher, Cape, that "The more I think of WHEN THE WICKED MAN the more I feel that it is one of the considerable *moral* books of the world."[18]

The violence of this response to Viking's rejection of *When the Wicked Man* is not simply arrogance. Ford was unusually susceptible to doubts about his own work; he could be made literally ill by them. Any criticism that touched his inner self, whether in "discussions" such as Violet Hunt subjected him to, or conversations about his personal affairs, or questions about the quality of his work, was unendurable to him. He would go to almost any lengths to avoid it, and when he could not, he either collapsed completely or asserted his superiority with the factitious assurance of his letter to Miss Baumgarten. He ended his letter by saying, "I am at the moment extremely unwell and the writing of letters about complicated matters is very fatiguing to me." A few days earlier he had said, "I have been extremely unwell during the past few days and the doctor says it is imperative that I should get away from here [New York] as soon as possible." What he needed to get away from were those demoralizing objections to *When the Wicked Man*.[19]

Viking had sound reasons for rejecting *When the Wicked Man*. It is not a good novel, and the reason it is not tells us a good deal about what was happening to Ford. In *A Little Less than Gods*, he had gone back to the historical romance, a form he had not used since writing *The Young Lovell* fifteen years before, and to a subject he and Conrad had first considered almost a quarter of a century earlier. He now turned, for the first time in years, to the writing of history (*A History of Our Own Times*) and reminiscence (*Return to Yesterday*), and he dug up and tried to publish two ten-year-old books, *That Same Poor Man* and *No Enemy*. He was evidently having trouble finding subjects for novels. Subjects had always been a problem for Ford. Perhaps no writer can, by the mere exercise of the conscious intelligence, discover the subjects that will draw out his deepest feelings. Perhaps they come to him, when they do, by lucky accident, by some process of the subconscious beyond his control that can only be waited for, not commanded.

But there is no doubt that in Ford's case impatience, a belligerent self-confidence that concealed self-doubt, and practical necessity made him more than usually disinclined to wait for such subjects. He needed to be writing all the time, and he had so much natural talent that he found it easy to think he could write a good novel about anything. This inclination was undoubtedly reinforced by his belief that he was an authority on a great many subjects. He had, as Pinker said, a remarkable journalistic talent for writing entertainingly about almost anything; it must have been temptingly easy for him to believe he could do so not merely entertainingly but seriously.

As a result, he allowed himself—when no subject chose him—to choose subjects largely for their convenience. He certainly did so with *When the Wicked Man.* What—he must have asked himself—could be more promising than a satiric novel by Ford about the New York publishing world? Perhaps the example of Sinclair Lewis persuaded him to write a satire; he praised Lewis' *Dodsworth* enthusiastically in the spring of 1929, in a way that shows why he thought he could write a satire, however untrue of Lewis his remark may be; "the superiority of Mr. Lewis as a sociological writer far in advance of others," he said, "lies in the fact that he has a remarkable gift for rendering...." His own recent experience, he felt, had clearly revealed the crookedness of American publishers and it would be a pleasure to show these people up; he apparently did not consider what effect doing so might have on his hopes of making a career of his own in America.[20]

*For a discussion of *When the Wicked Man*, see pp. 517-19.

Chapter 29

However angry Ford may have been at Viking for rejecting *When the Wicked Man*, their refusal must have warned him that the novel was going to be difficult to place and probably not very successful. When it finally did appear, in May, 1931, Burton Rascoe said it seemed "like the collaboration of a genius and a pulp-paper hack ... bristling with gaffes in documentation," and *The Saturday Review* remarked that "Mr. Ford's attempt to probe the nervous system of American business ... begins apprehensively, develops hysterically, and ends with caricature." Possibly because he had some inkling of what was coming, Ford made yet another attempt to rebuild his market in England. When he left New York for Paris in the middle of August, 1929, he stopped off in London and renewed his relations with Pinker's firm, now being run by Pinker's sons, Eric and Ralph. He was no less bitterly convinced that the failure of his work in England was the result of malice. "But no, my dear Walpole," he wrote Hugh Walpole a few months later, "you will find it difficult to make me believe in the esteem of my English colleagues for myself. The heart, you know, knoweth its own bitterness and there are circumstances in my career of such an extraordinary nature that you would hardly believe them." This feeling made him reluctant to turn once more to England, and less tactful than he might have been in dealing with English publishers: publishers were his most active enemies. Nonetheless he tried: a success in England would have done a great deal for his morale.[1]

What he hoped to achieve there is shown by the letter he wrote Ralph Pinker. He urges Ralph to try *The English Novel* on Cape and, if Cape rejects it, on Constable. He tells him Cape has already given him a £ 250 advance for *When the Wicked Man*, but that he is reluctant to have it published in

England because he fears the English, in their anti-Americanism, will see its attack on New York publishers as an attack on America. Pinker is therefore to substitute *No Enemy* for *When the Wicked Man* and to promise Cape that Ford will repay any loss Cape suffers on the advance he has paid Ford. He has told Cape that Cape can have no more of his work unless Cape promises to take all his future work, including *A History of Our Own Times*, the first volume of which is nearing completion, and to put together a collected edition of his work.[2]

As was so often the case, this plan was based on a serious overestimation of his bargaining position. Threats to refuse publishers *No Enemy* were ineffective because none of them wanted *No Enemy* to begin with. Cape would not exchange *When the Wicked Man* for *No Enemy* without getting back the advance that Ford did not have the money to repay. Ford was quick to believe that this refusal was the result of a plot against him. The surprising thing really was that Cape had been willing to gamble on *When the Wicked Man*. How necessary it was for Ford to believe otherwise is clear from the eagerness with which he responded when Hugh Walpole observed that Ford's fine earlier work—the *Fifth Queen* trilogy, *The Good Soldier*, and the Tietjens novels—was beginning to be forgotten. This was not the same thing as praising Ford's current work, but Ford ignored that distinction.[3]

During the autumn of 1929 Ford made a quick trip to New York to try to straighten out his New York publishing arrangements, which were, as always, confused. By Christmas he was back in Paris to play, for the last time, the role of Father Christmas for Julie and her friends. During the spring he helped Richard Aldington with his anthology of Imagist poets, collecting material and writing the preface. Its reception must have seemed a sort of memento mori to him. One of the reviewers said that reading it was "like going up into an attic on a rainy afternoon and dressing up in greatgrandmother's hoop skirts." In their heyday the Imagists had seemed to Ford the daring young men of a new generation who made him feel like an aging uncle; now even they were thought ridiculously old-fashioned.[4]

On May Day, 1930, an anniversary they celebrated for the rest of their lives together, Ford met Janice Biala. She had been persuaded by a friend to come to one of Ford's Thursdays by the promise that she might meet Ezra Pound, whom she much admired. The friend, who did not admire Pound and did not stop to ask herself whether Ford might, told Ford about Janice's admiration of Pound as a great joke. But the joke was on her, for Ford was sure to take seriously anyone who admired Pound. He quickly discovered in Janice a kindred spirit who shared his complete devotion to the arts and his

394] THE SADDEST STORY

scorn of the "tradesmen" who batten on artists. She was as scornful of security and social position as Mrs. Wright had been concerned for them; even better, she was a fighter, ready to fly at anyone who was not ready to give Ford his due, in a way that Ford himself was never able to. " . . . your letters of the 14th to me and of the 18th to Ford," she would tell publishers,

> are in the tone of a person repelling beggars. That is not the way to write to a person of Ford's standing and I should really be grateful if you did not write him again personally. It serves no purpose and only upsets him. . . .

" . . . we both liked and admired her," said Edward Davison, "for her candor and blazing honesty as well as for her unmeasured devotion to Ford"; very few of the people who knew her failed to share this feeling.[5]

This quality must have been all the more moving to Ford because she was very much a woman—small, feminine, young. He could not have been luckier, and he knew it.

> I think God must have been a stupid man,
> To have sent a spirit, chivalrous and loyal,
> Cruel and tender, arrogant and so meek,
> Gallant and timorous, halting and as swift
> As a hawk descending—to have sent such a spirit,
> Certain in all its attributes, into this Age
> Of our banal world. . . .
> A coin of gold dropped in a leaden palm,
> Manna and frankincense and myrrh and balm
> And bitter herbs and spices of the South
> Are you and honey for the parching mouth . . .
> Because God was a stupid man and threw
> Into our outstretched palms, Haïtchka, you!

She gave Ford great happiness for the rest of his life and the support of a fierce loyalty that has continued unabated to the present.*[6]

Almost the first thing Ford did when he discovered he was in love with Janice Biala was to take her around to Stella's studio where—as Stella put it —he "asked for our blessing on his approaching union with her." The plural is probably significant; Ford admired Stella and it would have meant something to him to have her approval, but it was probably even more important to him that this new arrangement should not come between him and Julie.[7]

*Janice Biala was born Tworkov in Biala, Poland. Fearing that her work might be confused with that of her brother, Jack Tworkov, she borrowed the name of her home town. She has had a distinguished career as a painter. She now lives in Paris with her husband, the painter Daniel Brustlein, who may be best known to literary people as *The New Yorker* cartoonist, Alain.

In September Ford made a quick business trip to New York, where he arranged a contract with Liveright for the volume of reminiscences that eventually became *Return to Yesterday.* While he was there, Susan Jenkins of Macaulay showed encouraging enthusiasm for the first volume of *A History of Our Own Times.* Macaulay had accepted *No Enemy,* which Ford had dug out and decided to sell about the same time he had *That Same Poor Man.* On the strength of Macaulay's acceptance of *No Enemy,* Ford had sent them the manuscript of *When the Wicked Man* after Viking had turned it down. Then he became convinced Macaulay intended to make no decision about *When the Wicked Man* until they had seen how well *No Enemy* would do. He could not afford to quarrel with Macaulay until *No Enemy* had been published, but he had Miss Kerr get the typescript of *When the Wicked Man* back on the excuse that he wanted to revise it. He did not return it, and by the fall of 1929 Macaulay realized that he was stalling. As a consequence they were not anxious to take on yet another work of his, especially when they learned— as they quickly must have—that as soon as Ford had established relations with Liveright, he sold them *When the Wicked Man,* and they did nothing about Miss Jenkins' recommendation of *A History of Our Own Times.*[8]

The sale of *When the Wicked Man* made it necessary for Ford to repay Viking's advance, and he agreed to turn over to them 50 percent of what was earned by both *When the Wicked Man* and *That Same Poor Man.* This was a costly arrangement for Viking: *When the Wicked Man* sold only 3,233 copies during its first year and *That Same Poor Man* was never published at all. Ford did not make Viking feel any more friendly by spreading it about that they were deliberately trying to prevent the publication of *When the Wicked Man* because it told the truth about New York publishers.[9]

Ford got back to Paris in December, 1930, and in January he and Janice went to Toulon, to live in the studio that had once been Stella's, on the quai du Parti (William Seabrook had occupied it in the interval). After a few months there they discovered the Villa Paul on Cap Brun. They were enchanted by it; Ford always found it impossible to resist a great view, and the Villa Paul had one.

The Villa Paul stood high above the sea, towards which there sloped a long garden with fig trees and oranges and a water cistern. . . . The shutters of its upper windows were always closed. They concealed the domestic life of M. le Commandant and Madame, who lived a dim but passionate existence on the upper floor, sub-letting the *rez de chaussée* and the garden to Ford and Janice.

The ground-floor shutters were always open. They had once

396] THE SADDEST STORY

been painted palest grey, and were folded back against the pinkish stucco walls whose flaking surface discovered patches of a previous periwinkle blue. Through the windows you stepped into two small rooms with rough grey walls and red tile floors. Behind these, on one side was the kitchen, dark and primitive, and on the other a sleeping alcove and *cabinet de toilette.* . . . Before the house was a wide *ter[r]asse* whose comfortable balustrade served as a sideboard for outdoor meals. There was a shady tree and a fountain with goldfish and a great view right across the harbour to Saint Mandrier. It was indeed a most delectable spot.[10]

In December, 1930, Ford had a heart attack from which he recovered very slowly. By March, 1931, he was nonetheless writing Hugh Walpole (Walpole had persuaded Gollancz to accept *Return to Yesterday*): "I have recovered a good deal of the vitality that I thought had gone for ever with my heart attack last December. And indeed I have got back into complete writing form and have made immense strides with my book so that even if another heart attack *did* carry me off Gollancz would have at least *a* book."[11]

Though he was really grateful to Walpole, he could not control his impulse to complain to him that Gollancz had not sent him a contract promptly and was probably planning to repudiate the agreement. This kind of fretfulness was bad for Ford himself, and it did not improve his relations either with publishers or with helpful friends like Walpole.

His disappointment over *A History of Our Own Times;* his irritation when Liveright sent him a misdrawn check; his impatience at Macaulay's delay in delivering the proofs of *No Enemy*—about such things he could not quite control his feeling of persecution. "I don't think it's much good Miss Jenkins writing to me on business," he told Ruth Kerr for Miss Jenkins' benefit, " . . . she has no authority to speak for the firm [Macaulay] . . . and . . . is of no use or consolation to me because it means nothing whatever." He could not resist telling Miss Kerr that Liveright "may have [misdrawn the check] on purpose so as to delay having to meet it." He announced that Macaulay's delay over the proofs of *No Enemy* had had disastrous consequences for his life, which he detailed at length, and then added, "it is of course all my fault for trusting Macaulays—but it is a rather heavy penalty to pay."[12]

He could no longer throw off the anxieties about money that had always pursued him. His regular explanation for his financial difficulties during these years was the catastrophic effect of the Depression. The Depression made it difficult for writers to place their work and was soon to drive a number of publishers into bankruptcy, to the distress of the writers to whom they owed royalties. These considerations were not, however, Ford's point. His difficulties, he thought, were the consequence of a severe disturbance of his capital position. "The collapse of Australian Securities has hit me even worse than the collapse of [the American] market . . . " he said. This suggestion that Ford lived largely on income from investments is an exaggeration, but he needed to think of himself as a man of means who had seen his wealth disappear in the Wall Street crash of 1929. "Why," he would say, "should I have known the names of streets [in London in his early days]? If I wanted to go anywhere I took a cab and so kept my mind free for matters more necessary than the names of streets. Alas, for '29 on Wall Street!" Ford did do some speculating in the bull market of the late 1920's—who did not—but he did not have much to spare for such purposes and his losses could hardly have been a major cause of his difficulties. The drastic decline in the value of Australian securities created a real problem for Stella, and Ford certainly worried about her situation, but he was not, as he implies, directly affected by it. Stella had been determined to get out of the flat in the rue Vaugirard so that Ford could have it and had taken a much too expensive flat in the rue Boissonnade. When the Australian pound declined, she found she had spent all that was left of her inheritance after *The Transatlantic Review* and was still in debt.[13]

In May, George Keating, the great Conrad collector, offered to pay Ford's fare to New York. Ford would not have that; he proposed that Keating give him an advance of £400 on *A History of Our Own Times* when the first volume was finished (this was what Ford was asking for it in the American market) and reimburse himself from the profits of the *History* when it was published. Even this face-saving arrangement humiliated him. "Consider me," he said to Keating, "who have been at it [writing] for thirty-eight years almost to a day and am forced to beg my bread." Keating, however, did not want to get into the position of having to sell Ford's book. By July Ford's financial position was desperate. " . . . I am," he wrote Wells on July 28, 1930, "really quite penniless: I mean *really:* and am living on credit in a small country pub. . . . " He asked Wells to help him apply for assistance to the Royal Literary Fund. In his generous way, Wells, instead of sending in Ford's application to the fund, sent him his own check for two thousand francs.[14]

But for all their anxieties about Ford's health and their financial situation, he and Janice had much happiness at the Villa Paul. In the mornings Ford would sit over his games of patience while he thought out what he was going to write that day. Then he would write it down.

I usually write [he said] in my home in Provence at an extraordinarily knocked-together table with flanking shelves of walnut bed-
panels, supported by sawn-off chair legs and above me an immense
deal shelf supported in turn by sawn-off broom-handles and nobody
is more contented than I or prouder of his atelier. And when neigh-
bours come in and I show them my contrivance they say: *Tiens, mais
vous avez du goût!*

There is an echo here of Ford Madox Brown's appealing conviction that his
studio was "grandly romantic": it was a conviction not everyone shared
about the Villa Paul. When Ford persuaded Stella and Julie to take it over
during the winter of 1931–32, Stella said that she "had never felt so sharp a
pang of desolation as when . . . I looked around and took stock of the
domestic difficulties which confronted us." But to Ford this lack of bourgeois
comforts was insignificant when there was that splendid view.

> . . . with its long terrace, giving over the foam of the Mediterranean,
> with the shade trees for masts, and the balustrade over which to look
> at the hyacinthine sea and the sparkling island of St. Mandrier—with
> that for taffrail, wasn't the Villa . . . exactly an enchanted ship an-
> chored for ever in the Islands of the Blest?[15]

Then there was the gardening. It was a constant battle against drought,
but that was only a challenge Ford took pleasure in meeting, an image of life
itself. "Do you remember," he asks Janice in his poem, "L'Oubli—, Temps
de Sécheresse,"

> Do you remember what stood where the peppers
>   and eggplants now stand?
> Or the opium poppies with heads like feathery wheels?
> Do you remember
> When the lemons were little, the oranges smaller than peas?
> We have outlived sweetcorn and haricots,
> The short season of plentiful water and the rose
> That covered the cistern in the day of showers.
> And do you remember the thin bamboo-canes?
> We have outlived innumberable flowers,
> The two great hurricanes
> And the unnumbered battlings back and forth
> Of the mistral from the Alps in the North
> And of siroccos filled with the hot breath
> —'Sirocco that man unto short madness hurrieth!'—
> From the sands of Africa, infinite miles to the South
> And, having so, ephemeral, outlived the herbs of the hill

We may, maybe, come through the drouth
To the winter's mouth
And the season of green things
And flowing cisterns and full springs.[16]

There were too, as always, many visitors with whom they lingered far into the evening at the table by the balustrade looking out over the Mediterranean, after one of Ford's special dinners and many bottles of wine. The Tates came from Paris and the Crankshaws from England, and innumerable New York friends traveling in Europe stopped to see them. "I remember," Louise Bogan wrote Janice, "the goat cheese and the casserole full of Ford's magnificent cooking and the *Gaulois Bleus* and the ducks you almost bought in the market and the *Marc* and your Niçois hat and the Rossetti drawing on the wall and the big magnolia flower and your painting of the Tates and Ford's voice and yours singing in the evening, and the garden terraces, mixed with salad leaves and herbs, and Debussy and Bach on the gramophone. . . . "[17]

In August, Duckworth inquired about the possibility of a one-volume reprint of the Tietjens novels, and in his reply to Pinker Ford made his much-debated suggestion that *Last Post* be dropped from the tetralogy. "Please consult Duckworth about this," he said. "I am ready to be guided by them . . . " as if he were not sure this judgment was right. He added that "if the publication goes through I shall have to do a certain amount of work on the books." But the publication did not go through and we shall never know what Ford wanted to rewrite.[18]

He somehow got together enough money to take himself to America in the middle of September. The perfect existence, he once said, consisted of "February and March in Provence and half April; the other half of April, May, June and half July in Paris; the other half of July, August and half September again in Provence; the other half of September on the sea between Marseilles and Sandy Hook; and then October, November, December and as much of January as will leave me time to scurry back to Marseilles by the first of February—in New York." It sounds an expensive program, but Ford made an heroic effort to carry it out this year. In New York he stayed with his friend Dr. Michael Lake on Twelfth Street. "He had," Harold Loeb remembers, "no money to pay his bills. He sent me to Dr Rosenbach, the book collector . . . with one of his manuscripts. I was unsuccessful in getting the doctor to buy it. Ford just shrugged his shoulders." Loeb also offered to take Ford and Susan Jenkins and another friend to Tennessee to visit the Tates in the house they called Benfolly after Mr.

Tate's brother, Ben, who had helped them buy it. While one of the girls was taking her turn driving she tried to pass a car, miscalculated, and started to slide into the ditch on the left-hand side of the road; then she overcompensated so violently that they ended up in the right-hand ditch. Ford, Loeb remembered, remained "ponderous, relaxed and smiling faintly." "Let's stick to the high road," he said. This was Ford's imperturbable front; it did not mean he was not thoroughly frightened. He himself remembered feeling that that high-speed skid from left-hand to right-hand ditch (at what seemed to him "seventy-eight" miles an hour) took, "I should say, eight hours."[19]

He returned to France late in November, 1930, and during the crossing on the *Mauritania* did some rewriting on *When the Wicked Man*. Shortly after his return, he met Joyce for the first time since he and Janice had joined forces. Joyce was impressed by Ford's ability to appeal to attractive women, and presently Harriet Weaver got a couple of stanzas of doggerel to the tune of "Father O'Flynn" about it.

O Father O'Ford, you've a masterful way with you,
Maid, wife and widow are wild to make hay with you,
Blond and brunette turn-about run away with you,
You've such a way with you, Father O'Ford.

That instant they see the sun shine from your eye,
Their hearts flitter flutter, they think and they sigh:
We kiss ground before thee, we madly adore thee,
And crave and implore thee to take us, O Lord.[20]

During the early months of 1931 he and Joyce saw each other often. Ford at once renewed his old argument against Joyce's preference for white wine. "I hope," he told Joyce, "you have given up white wine and prosper.... Le premier devoir du vin est d'être rouge. I am sure the wine of Cana must have been." Joyce was—as he was meant to be—amused by Ford's persistence in this matter. But if Ford insisted on his superior wisdom in the matter of wines, his admiration for the great writer he knew Joyce to be made him extraordinarily untouchy with Joyce in literary matters. He agreed readily when Joyce asked him if he would write the preface for *Tales Told of Shem and Shaun*, supposing Joyce's first choice, C. K. Ogden, refused (Ogden, in fact, accepted). He also agreed, at Joyce's request, to write an introduction for the English translation of Italo Svevo's *Senilità*, a job Joyce himself had turned down. Joyce recommended Ford to Signore Svevo as "perhaps the best known and most successful lecturer among English·authors in the United States."[21]

Ford's health remained uncertain. His heart still bothered him and he felt that the climate and the social life of Paris in the winter were too much for him. He and Janice therefore went south once more to the Villa Paul, Ford's "Islands of the Blest," where,

Amongst the trunks of the planes,
Though they roar never so mightily overhead in the day,
All this tumult is quieted down, and all
The windows stand open because of the heat of the night
That shall come.
And, from each little window, shines in the twilight a light. . . .

Ford was sure that living at the Villa Paul did him a world of good. " . . . though you precious near did lose me in December," he wrote T. R. Smith of Liveright, "my health is immensely improved by staying down here and I hope to finish the book [*Return to Yesterday*] . . . in July. . . . " The friendly tone of this letter does not represent Ford's real feelings about Liveright. "Mr. T. R. Smith," he wrote Dreiser, who had suggested he try Liveright, "has been playing the devil with my affairs which has annoyed me and put me out. How can he expect me to recommend other authors to go to him when he treats me more [inconsiderately] than any other publisher I ever had to do with I don't know." He complained too to Gollancz about the smallness of Gollancz's advance on *Return to Yesterday* and got at cross purposes with them by selling the serial rights for the book to *The Nineteenth Century* without consulting Gollancz, who controlled these rights.[22]

By May, he was so angry at Liveright that he wrote George Keating asking him to talk to them. Keating did so, and then wrote Ford a businesslike summary of Ford's actual situation. He pointed out that Ford had, in 1927, taken an advance of $3,500 from Viking for *When the Wicked Man* and had then agreed "in writing" to reimburse Viking by paying them half the royalties on the book if they would release it to another publisher and that Viking did therefore have a lien on the book that required Liveright to pay Viking money Ford claimed they were illegally refusing to pay him. Contrary to Ford's assertion, he said, Ford's contract with Liveright called for a payment of $500, not on receipt of the manuscript of *Return to Yesterday*, but on publication. He concluded by observing that, despite the earnest advice of all his friends, Ford persisted in dealing with dubious publishers—too often, Keating implied, swayed by flattering enthusiasm for Ford's work and vague promises of large profits of a kind responsible publishers did not indulge in. But it required more than Keating's well-intended severity to convince Ford he was not being treated with insulting injustice, and he involved himself in a complicated feud with Viking and Liveright, during which he offered his New York lawyer copious advice.

If you like to suggest to him [Smith of Liveright] that he is a fool to treat me in an offhand manner because, as he knows quite well, I can make his fortune as a publisher if I want to, you're quite at liberty to do so. It is not necessary to state that per contra I can quite easily stop authors sending any manuscripts to him at all because that would look like blackmail, but it is nonetheless a fact.

But Liveright's royalty statements and payments turned out to have been correct.[23]

When Stella, to Ford's delight, sent Julie south to stay at the Villa Paul with him and Janice, they decided to remain there for the summer. It was, apart from Ford's perpetual financial anxieties and his feeling that he was being badly treated by publishers, a good summer. By early August he had completed *Return to Yesterday* and sent it off to the publishers. He also completed the series of poems he called *Buckshee*, his moving account of all that Janice meant in his life. He sent the series off to his old friend Harriet Monroe at *Poetry*, and after she had with some reluctance accepted the series intact (she first tried to take only six of the poems), he managed to blunder into letting the poems appear in book form in England before *Poetry* printed them. When Miss Monroe protested, he wrote her: "I can only plead ignorance. I never knew that *Poetry* claimed exclusive publication.... If I had I should have sent Buckshee elsewhere. I was meaning an act of friendship in sending it to you." It is inconceivable that a writer of Ford's experience did not know magazines dislike being anticipated by book publication, though it seems likely Ford landed himself in this difficulty rather out of carelessness than calculation.[24]

"*Buckshee*," Ford wrote in a note to these poems, "... signifies something unexpected, unearned—gratifying.... If you have long given up the practice of verse and suddenly find yourself writing it—those lines will be *buckshee*." "In these reveries," as Robert Lowell says, "[Ford] has at last managed to work his speaking voice, and something more than his speaking voice, into poems—the inner voice of the tireless old man, the old master still in harness, confiding, tolerant, Bohemian, newly married, and in France." It is astonishing how Ford conveys the tone of their life—difficult, often anxious, sometimes illuminated, and always something he would have no other way—in his quiet talk about Cap Brun.

> We shall have to give up watering the land
> Almost altogether.
> The maize must go.
> But the chilis and tomatoes may still have

A little water. The gourds must go.
We must begin to give a little to the mandarines
And the lemon-trees.
                    Yes . . . and the string beans.
We will do our best to save
The chrysanthemums
Because you like them. . . .

For this is a corner of France,
And this, the Kingdom of the Earth beneath the Sun
And this, the garden sealed and set apart
And that, the fountain of Jouvence . . .
And, yes, you have a heart.

This quality is even more beautifully realized in "Coda," where the world of the "the hourly repeated shock/Of reverberated panic from Richelieu's old clock" that they could clearly hear at 31 rue de Seine is set against the time when "We are/Again suspended in our velvet blackness,/Floating on velvet fingers, in a haven/of fertilised hours"—from which they are aroused by Janice's "Oh, Hell, I've got to finish this damn canvas!" Ford can even include successfully in the poem a little lecture explaining the nature of eternity ("That is not truly hard to understand") and a number of his most familiar everyday prejudices.[25]

"Coda" is a brooding meditation, a quiet recollection of the small realities of daily life in Ford's beloved Paris, where the "iron tocsin notes" of Richelieu's clock

            pour through the pellitory of the wall that grows
        Over the mouldering stones
        Their droning overtones.

But this meditation takes place during a wakeful spell at two in the morning, when

                the velvety, black
        Night with her myriad fingers floats back.
        She stifles the notes in the bells' throats
        And her velvet silences obliterate
        Their scars on the velvet pall.

("It is," Ford said of Villon, "from male suffering supported with dignity that the great poets draw the greatest of their notes—that sort of note of the iron voice of the tocsin calling to arms in the night that forms, as it were, the overtone of their charged words . . . the note of a church bell beating out the inevitable decree of destiny.") Thus Ford sets the subject that lies beneath the homely, even trivial domesticity of the poem's occasion. Without ever violating the casual, conversational tone of voice in which the consciousness speaks its commitment to the ordinary experience of life, the poem defines the interplay of what Ford calls Time and "Time grown incorruptible" in that experience. It is a beautiful, quiet image of the accumulations of ordinary time that make

> The love of the Arts, knowledge and temperate learning,
> Some sort of just appreciation of life's values
> And pity and moderation naturally grow
> Like pellitory of the wall on crumbling stones

in the Paris he loves, and of the queer "time" of shared thought that is "commensurate and yet not measurable" that he and Janice know as they labor together, day after day, at their arts.[26]

Just as Ford got back to Paris *Return to Yesterday* was published (November 2) and there was an uproar in London. "MONSTROUS STORY ABOUT KING," the headline said. "Indignant Denial of Any Pre-War Threat to Abdicate." The "monstrous story" comes at the very end of *Return to Yesterday*, when Ford describes how, standing on the railway platform at Berwick in August, 1914, he read a disapproving newspaper article in the *Daily News* about King George's Round Table Conference on the Irish question at Buckingham Palace. "I imagined I knew all about that," Ford says and goes on to describe how Charles Masterman had told him that, when the cabinet opposed the King's scheme for an Irish conference, the King had said, "Very well, gentlemen. I am the richest commoner in England. If you wish me to abdicate I will abdicate, supposing that to be the wish of the country. But before that we will have a general election and I have not much doubt as to the results as between you and me." "So," Ford adds, "he had his conference."[27]

This speech, with the King's neat entrapment of his Liberal ministers, sounds improved. But it is hard to doubt that Masterman had told Ford some story of a quarrel between the King and his cabinet over the Home-Rule question. Ford the Tory had no desire to offend his king: a passionate Irish sympathizer himself, he had thought the story all to the King's credit. When he learned the Palace felt otherwise, he wrote Gollancz at once that "of course you may delete that paragraph in subsequent editions. . . . I am quite literally and naively a subject of H. M. and entertain the greatest admiration of him as Head of the State." The official spokesman's comment on his story, he added, was "the lamest piece of denial I have ever seen," and in fact it did not deny Ford's essential point.[28]

Return to Yesterday deals with the golden age when Ford lived in Winchelsea, Wells at Sandgate, Conrad at the Pent, James at Rye, and Crane at Bude. It ends with the First World War. Most of its stories are inaccurate in detail and improved in the way the story about George V appears to have been. Nearly all of them illuminate the character of the man Ford is describing, or at least the character Ford believed the man to have. Ford's "rich and glamorous imagination," as Arthur Waugh called it, makes the reader feel he is being taken behind the scenes, where he discovers that writers are dashing and colorful figures. For a good many readers, however, *Return to Yesterday* is marred by what Morton D. Zabel called "the garrulous self-esteem which can be as ingratiating as Mr. Yeats's or as tedious as Sisley Huddleston's, and which could condone in this book wholesale repetitions from earlier volumes. . . . " *Return to Yesterday* is nonetheless an attractive book, a civilized, generous, and romantic vision of the life Ford had known before the war.[29]

After *Return to Yesterday*, Ford turned back to fiction. He had been thinking further about Americans, now not so much about Americans out of the age of Mark Twain, like the hero of *When the Wicked Man*, as about the kind of Americans he had known in Paris in the twenties. He saw that in some ways the psychological effects of the Depression were most evident among the Americans abroad. Given a hint for his story by what Katherine Anne Porter had told him about Hart Crane, he began to plan a trilogy that would "do for the post-war world and the Crisis what the TIETJENS tetralogy did for the war. . . . " It was to be set largely at and about Cap Brun and in Springfield, Ohio (where he had once lectured). He told Ruth Kerr in December, 1931, that "I am just starting a novel which will probably work out to be in three parts," and by July he was describing the plot of the trilogy to Ray Long of Long and Smith, with whom Bradley had arranged a contract for the first volume. Only two of the three volumes of this trilogy were ever completed—*The Rash Act* (1933) and *Henry for Hugh* (1934)—but it was the most serious work Ford undertook during his last years.[30]

Early in the spring of 1932, he and Janice returned to the Villa Paul to take care of Julie while Stella went for six months to the United States to paint portraits. Katherine Anne Porter and her husband, Eugene Pressly, occupied the Paris flat. Ford was anxious to stay close to Julie, especially as he believed his older daughters had rejected him.[31]

Chapter 30

F ord and Janice got back to Paris at Christmas, 1931, and Ford plunged into another round of negotiations with publishers, this time with the firm of Ray Long and Richard R. Smith. This was a new firm started in September, 1929, by Smith, who had been an editor at Macmillan. A month or so later Long, then the editor of *Cosmopolitan*, became a sleeping partner and the largest stockholder in the firm, but he did not become active in its affairs until two years later. He then promptly established himself at the Crillon in Paris and let it be known that Hearst was back of the firm. Long was ready to spend money freely. He offered to pay Ford $200 a month against royalties as long as Ford produced a book every twenty months. The contract was to cover Ford's next three novels and that *A History of Our Own Times* he had struggled so long to sell. Here, in the depths of the Depression, was $2,400 a year assured to Ford for at least two and a half years; it seemed too good to be true and, as things turned out, it was.[1]

When the contract was finally signed in March, Long made the $200 monthly payments retroactive to February. Nevertheless, Ford had to ask Bradley to borrow money for him against his contract with Long, and when the bank refused to make the loan, Ford's suspicion of publishers flared up. The bank's refusal was, he thought, "incomprehensible.... The only thing I can think is that the bank do[es] not consider Long's signature good enough." It was no use Bradley's assuring him that "the question of the *signature* did not enter at all.... As a matter of fact [Rousseau of the Guaranty Trust] even refused to *look* at the contract and insisted it was a matter of principle only, & an iron rule governing the bank's practice." Ford remained convinced that Long and Smith were a doubtful quantity, and whenever their monthly payment was slightly delayed—as it often was by

the transatlantic mails and by having to pass through Bradley's hands in Paris
—he was sure Long and Smith were insolvent. He partly understood that
this anxiety was unreasonable, but he had so often been reduced to desperation by the failure of money to reach him at the earliest possible moment
that he had worn away such tolerance as he had for the refusal of editors and
publishers to keep track of his constantly changing addresses and to get his
checks on the first transatlantic liner. He was convinced that his publishers
were neglecting their most elementary duties and ascribed the shaken state
of his nerves to the needless trials they subjected him to. "And to be rid of
material worries," as Henry Martin Smith says in *The Rash Act,* "was something in which no one who had not been through them could believe.
... " "I have," Ford told Bradley, "already been made so very ill by the
irregularities of Liveright that I can scarcely hope to survive any further
anxieties. . . . I am unfortunately a very sick man and any additional strain
or further shock might well put an end to me."[2]

Ford's view of publishers is made explicit in his description of the way
Henry Martin Smith's publisher treats his history of gossip in *The Rash Act.*
The publisher gives the book a misleading title, *Be Thou Chaste,* without
consulting Smith (as Ford felt that the misleading titles of *The Good Soldier*
and a number of his other books had been chosen by publishers without
regard for his opinion). They also "decorated the pages with vignettes of
revolting lewdness." The very sight of the book all but makes Smith sick.
The publisher promises to pay Smith $200 on publication and does not.
When his father finally gets a lawyer to inspect the publisher's books (which
give every sign of having been doctored), they show the publisher owes
Smith $1,600 in royalties. Nevertheless, the publisher refuses to pay Smith
a penny, and Smith's father tells him it would gain him nothing to sue them,
since a suit would drive the publisher into bankruptcy, make Smith very
unpopular, and get him perhaps two cents on the dollar. This is an improved
version of what Ford felt he had suffered throughout his life from the un-
scrupulousness of publishers; Smith's father's advice is almost exactly the
advice that Bradley was to give Ford when he wanted to sue Long and
Smith over *The Rash Act* itself and that Pinker had given him more than
once when he had been determined to sue a publisher.[3]

In his distrust of Long and Smith, Ford decided to repeat with them the
maneuver he had tried with such disastrous results a quarter of a century
before, when he had refused to let Alston Rivers have the manuscript of *The
Fifth Queen Crowned* until they had shown what he considered good faith in
publishing *The Spirit of the People.* When *The Rash Act* was completed he had

Janice wire Bradley: "Book finished has remittance come if not Ford proposes not deliver manuscript. . . . " Bradley, who seems throughout this affair not to have recognized the state of Ford's feelings about publishers, saw only the unreasonableness—and the dangerous impracticality—of this maneuver. "It never occurred to me," he wrote Ford," . . . that you could be so distrustful of your new publishers. I really think it is only fair to them—and to me who brought them to you—to assume that they are honest and solvent," as in fact they were at this time.[4]

Since Long and Smith had sent this remittance, Ford's maneuver caused no permanent trouble, but he was quickly at cross purposes with Bradley again for similar reasons. *Harper's* had written inquiring about a series of articles from Ford, about which Ford told Bradley:

> I quite well know that I am in demand in New York. My daily letter bag gives me sufficient evidence of that. But getting paid for my work is quite another matter as I have bitter reason for knowing and I am quite determined that I will not do any more work for America or anywhere else unless I am absolutely certain not only of its appearing but of my getting paid for it.

Bradley thought the self-deception by which Ford was justifying this intransigence very dangerous. He knew that Ford's work was not so valuable a commodity in the New York market as Ford believed it was; by 1932 very few writers could afford to be so peremptory in their demands when a magazine like *Harper's* proposed to buy a whole series of articles from them, and Ford was not one of those few. His reputation in America had declined considerably since the publication of *Last Post* in 1928; in 1931 his magazine sales there consisted of two reviews for *The Bookman*—one a review of Caroline Gordon's *Penhally* he must have suggested himself—and a chapter from *Return to Yesterday* that appeared in *Scribner's*. ". . . *no* offer," Bradley wrote, " . . . is to be turned down casually nowadays—very few magazines in America are buying anything at all. . . . " Ford replied with a few ideas he had already begun to work up for books—a series on travel (*Great Trade Route*), on cookery (a book he proposed without success to a number of publishers), on the twenties (Part III of *It Was the Nightingale*), and on Zionism. None of these ideas seemed to *Harper's* of immediate interest in the Depression-haunted America of 1932. In the end Ford wrote only two articles for *Harper's*; both were excellent.[5]

When Ford sent *The Rash Act* to Long and Smith, he submitted alternate endings for it, as he had done with *Some Do Not . . .* , the first volume of his previous series of novels. The first ending rounded the story off, the second left the reader in suspense. Long and Smith were badly confused by these two endings until Ford explained that *The Rash Act* was the first novel of a trilogy.

> You see the RASH ACT is the beginning of a trilogy that is meant to do for the post-war world and the Crisis what the TIETJENS tetralogy did for the war. . . . Now the chief characteristic of these years is want of courage—physical and moral. We are in the miserable pickle that we are in simply because *no one* has the courage either to spend money, commit suicide, or anything else. Henry Martin is the typical man of this period.

As such, Ford argued, he would not commit suicide at the end of *The Rash Act*, as Long had suggested Ford have him; nor would a second volume of the trilogy be possible if he did. Eventually Ford decided to omit both the conclusions he had written.[6]

Then, in August, there was disturbing news. "Tell Ford," Bradley wrote Janice after a visit to the Villa Paul,

> that I found here a letter from Richard Smith containing an extraordinary piece of news. Ray Long, who had gone to California to rest, was so upset there by the death of one of his oldest and best friends, that he decided he had need of a complete change of air and scene and set sail at once for the South Seas! He said he would be back in about two months, but Smith is still without an exact date for his return.

In October Smith wrote Ford himself that "[Long] has not been in New York since July but it was not until recently that I learned he is not likely to return to New York in the near future." Long's indefinite absence raised questions about the firm's financial stability at a time when the Depression was visibly worsening; it also meant that Ford's work had languished unpublished or unread since July: Ford was Long's writer, not Smith's. Only now, in October, did Smith take Ford's work in hand. He decided to reject *A History of Our Own Times*, which Long had agreed to publish, on the grounds that it had been represented as a book like *Only Yesterday* when in fact it was a textbook. Ford saw these misfortunes as evidence of Smith's incompetence, but he was persuaded by Bradley not to sue Smith over the rejection. Bradley was convinced that an action by Ford would drive Smith into bankruptcy and prevent the publication of *The Rash Act. The Rash Act* was published on February 24, 1933; nine days later President Roosevelt closed the banks. "My RASH ACT," Ford said, "which is more like what I want to write than anything I have done for years came out on the 24th ult. and has naturally been absolutely submerged."[7]

In August, two of Smith's creditors tried to force him into bankruptcy; he succeeded in warding them off by producing an independent audit showing that the firm had had, at the end of the last fiscal year, an excess of assets over liabilities of $251,675.39. This audit showed nothing, of course, of its condition in August, but Ford concluded from it that, at the very time Bradley had persuaded him not to sue Smith for fear of driving him into bankruptcy, Smith had commanded a quarter of a million dollars. He wrote Bradley that they had been "spoofed" by Smith. Not sensing the accumulated rage that lay behind this apparently mild remark, Bradley replied cheerfully that "the fact remains, whether we were 'spoofed' or not, by these people, we got from them an advance of nearly $2000 for a book which has sold little more than 1000 copies."[8]

This unfortunately jaunty remark brought Ford down on Bradley at once.

Your letter of the 2nd inst. [he wrote] seems little less than libellous and to any third party could only seem the composition of a person openly hostile to my interests.

You say that I "got from them an advance of nearly two thousand dollars for a book that has sold little more than a thousand copies." In the first place that advance was on two books not one. Then, if the RASH ACT sold so little it was obviously because Long & Smith had no organization at all for selling novels—a fact of which you should have been aware. . . . they published the book at the very moment of the crisis in March when no one in America had any money at all in their pockets. Even Liveright . . . managed to sell the first edition of WHEN THE WICKED MAN before publication and there was no outside reason for any falling off in my sales. . . .

That I did not try to enforce legally the specific performance of [the contract to publish A History of Our Own Times] was due to your confirmation of Mr. Smith's untrue statement that his firm was on the point of bankruptcy. . . . Yet not only are you paid, but it is your moral duty to assure yourself as to the financial soundness of the houses into contact with whom you bring your clients. Long & Smith's non-publication of the HISTORY has been ruinous to me. You must be aware of that yet no one could read into your letters and your handling of the matter anything but that your sympathies are with the defaulting publishers as against your client. . . . [9]

Bradley weathered this storm, at least temporarily, but Ford was clearly through with Long and Smith, even if they managed to survive, as in fact they did not. In January, 1933, Smith wrote Bradley to explain that he never had thought Long's contract with Ford a practical one and that now, in the firm's straitened circumstances, he could not go on paying Ford $200 a month. If Ford wished to sue, Smith would take his chances.[10]

At the end of July Ford and Janice went to Rapallo to see Pound and Olga Rudge: at last Janice was to get that sight of Pound her anxiety for which had led to her original meeting with Ford. While they were at Rapallo Pound and Ford had themselves photographed in front of the Columbus monument, Pound looking every inch the poet and Ford like a large English gentleman not quite certain what he is doing there. Pound also did a facetious interview with Ford for the Rapallo paper, *Mare.*

From Rapallo Ford and Janice went on to Germany. They made a sentimental stop at Boppard, but "the weather was cold and the state of things [in Germany] depressing" (this was just after the Lausanne Conference, which tried to rescue Germany from financial collapse by setting aside her reparation debt). After that they remained at the Villa Paul until January, when they came to Paris for three months and Ford began writing *It Was the Nightingale*, in which he carries his reminiscence from the end of the war to the death of *The Transatlantic Review* in 1924.[11]

By March, 1933, with the cessation of Long and Smith's monthly payment of $200 and the deepening of the Depression, Ford found himself in another financial crisis. President Roosevelt closed the banks "at a moment when having worked too hard and too long I was in Paris and in desperate need of a long holiday ... Well, no one in Paris had any money ... We had to give a wedding reception, for which we had issued invitations, on frs 60 *pour tout potage* ... It was amusing ... but also a little tiring." He had Stella and Julie to worry about as well. Ever hopeful of profiting from collectors, he first tried to sell the "mixed type-holograph ms" of *A History of Our Own Times.* When this failed, he turned again to Pound. "I have," he wrote,

> wrung £50 out of Cape [for *The Rash Act*] for Stella and Lippincotts have paid [the advance on *It Was the Nightingale*]—with a cheque that cannot be cashed. If you do not mind I will keep your cheque by me till Stella has actually got Cape's money....

He had to use Pound's check, paying him back when he was finally able to cash Lippincott's check. With the cash from this check in his pocket, "relatively large sums of money—we all decided to make straight for Tarascon. ... It was to provide me with a long, long holiday and afterwards a long, long rest." Not trusting himself, he turned this cash over to Janice. The first thing they did when they got to Tarascon was to take a walk along the

Rhone; the mistral was blowing. On the suspension bridge between Tarascon and Beaucaire

> Our treasurer's cap was flying in the air ... Over, into the Rhone
> ... What glorious fun ... The mistral sure is the wine of life
> ... Our treasurer's wallet was flying from under an armpit beyond
> the reach of a clutching hand ... Incredible humour; unparalleled
> buffoonery of a wind ... The air was full of little, capricious squares,
> floating black against the light over the river....
>
> And then began a delirious, panicked search ... For notes, for
> passports, for first citizenship papers that were halfway to Marseilles
> before it ended ... An endless search ... With still the feeling that
> one was rich ... Very rich.

So, tired as he was, Ford went back to work on *It Was the Nightingale* when
they got to Cap Brun.[12]

That summer Caroline and Allen Tate came to Cap Brun, to a villa Ford
had found for them; one day they went to Les Calanques on a picnic organized by some friends of Ford at Cassis. Before the picnic was over—according to Ford—"Sixty-one bottles of wine were consumed by sixteen adults."
Les Calanques, as Ford said, is "unimaginable unless you have seen it.
... Blood-red cliffs into which a blue, shining mirror should have introduced
itself for miles—a fjord of the Mediterranean, a beach only to be approached
in boats, with the dark-green, red-trunked stone- and umbrella-pines, the
multicoloured boats grouped at the landing, the incredible blue of the sky,
the incredible whiteness of the light, the ten-foot flames beneath the caul-
drons but pale beneath the sun. And, beneath the surface of the mirror,
shoals of vermilion, of ultramarine, of amethyst fishes—and octopuses dart-
ing, like closed parasols, through the waving groves of the algae.... " Mr.
Tate thought of Virgil there.

> Where we went in the boat was a long bay
> A slingshot wide, walled in by towering stone—
> Peaked margin of antiquity's delay,
> And we went there out of time's monotone....

This sense of a momentary escape from time's monotone made him think of
Aeneas landing on the northern shore of the Mediterranean and determining
to found Rome, and he wondered

> What prophecy of eaten plates could landless
> Wanderers fulfill by the ancient sea?

With his characteristic generosity, Ford always remembered with pleasure

that he had been involved in the occasion for this fine poem; he dedicated
Provence "To CAROLINE GORDON who chronicles another South and to
ALLEN TATE who came to Provence and there wrote to 'that sweet land'
the poem called 'The Mediterranean' and where we went in the boat was a
long bay. F. M. F. and B."[13]

The drought that summer was very severe. It

destroyed everything in the garden except for the semi-tropical
things like melons and pimento. Even the corn felt the drought. We
went away for about ten days to Juan les Pins, leaving a man to water
and of course he did no watering so when we got back all the straw-
berries and all the string beans and peas and things of a northern
complexion were as dry as paper.

This is the summer he described in "L'Oubli—Temps de Sécheresse":

We shall have to give up watering the land
Almost altogether.
The maize must go.
But the chilis and tomatoes may still have
A little water.[14]

It upset Ford when, that summer, Stella gave up her effort to live in Paris
and moved with Julie to England. "Julie," he told Caroline Tate, "is in
London with her mother who fled before the rising franc—or the falling
pound. I don't like it much—for I should have preferred Julie never to learn
English and certainly not to go to an English school and become the usual
English hobbledehoy." His dislike of England was so strong it often led him
to exaggerate the extent to which England ignored him.

Occasionally [he wrote Horace Shipp] a daring London publisher
puts out one of my books in that city. Five months or so afterwards
he writes to me to say that the volume has sold anything between two
and a hundred copies. . . . It is like dropping things down wells so
deep that even after years of waiting no reverberation comes to the
listener at the well-head.

This was written at almost the precise moment *The Rash Act* was being
published in London, where it sold better than it had in America.[15]

In October, 1933, Lippincott published *It Was the Nightingale*. It was
widely reviewed in America by people like William Rose Benét and John
Chamberlain as a highly entertaining book; the English edition was less
widely reviewed, with considerable emphasis on Ford's unfavorable opinions
of England. It sold respectably, in England as well as America. But none of
the reviewers discussed what gives the book its real power, Ford's eloquent,

inaccurate vision of the England he believed had mistreated and humiliated him because he had fought in the front lines. When Ford created Christopher Tietjens he followed minutely the pattern of feelings and—a good deal of the time—the experiences he describes in *It Was the Nightingale*. Like *Parade's End*, *It Was the Nightingale* is a vision of "an England that Englishmen generally will have some difficulty in recognizing," an England that is, by some strange power of the controlling imagination ("acutely observing even when most grotesquely misunderstanding"), "made astonishingly real to the reader."[16]

This is the last book in which Ford used his special kind of narrative structure purposefully. Even in *The Rash Act*, written earlier, he had begun to use it for its own sake rather than because it was the most effective way to express his meaning. But in *It Was the Nightingale* his passionate resentment of England's imagined persecution informs everything he says and gives the odd order of events a deeply felt meaning. At the very beginning he moves from the thought of how gay the twenties in Paris were (the subject of the book's last part) back to the moment of his demobilization: "I had a year or so to wait before that ambience [of the twenties] was to enfold me." "Naked came I from my mother's womb," he remarks. "On that day [of demobilization] I was nearly as denuded of possessions." Nor was there any way for him to acquire new possessions, for—how quickly he gets to this crucial feeling—everyone was determined to put down the ex-soldiers. Why, only the Christmas before he had been at a literary party at the French embassy, where he much impressed the ambassador's wife with his knowledge of viniculture, but he knew none of the English writers there except Arnold Bennett. Naturally Bennett would be there, dominating the party "like a round sun." Just before the armistice Ford had had an experience with Bennett which had given Ford a clear hint of the way the wind was blowing. He describes this experience before completing his account of the party at the French embassy. "A month or so later," he then adds, "I might, had it not been too dark, have been seen with my sack upon my shoulder, approaching Red Ford. . . . My being there was the result of [his humiliating experience] at M. Berthelot's party." He had told Mme. Berthelot, "to her incredulous delight," of his longing to go to Provence and grow the grapes of Châteauneuf-du-Pape. But when he was demobilized, Lloyd George's government refused him a passport because of his ardent sympathy for France; he had therefore to stay in England. Even there, however, it was necessary to his sanity to grow things.[17]

It takes him eighty pages of similarly organized images of his experi-

ence to make clear what had happened to give him this feeling, to arrive at
the moment when he can say, with full assurance that the reader has also felt
all that had gone to make that moment,

> ... At any rate I saw, standing on that Campden Hill kerb, that as
> far as London was concerned there was nothing [for me] to do but
> to get out or go under!

It takes him another fifteen pages to bring himself to Red Ford Cottage. This
is not merely a demonstration of Ford's skill in managing this kind of narration;
it is a display of his experiences—carefully improved for the purpose—arranged to enforce a powerful and coherent, if fanciful, view of his situation.[18]

The modest success of *It Was the Nightingale* prompted Ford to try once
more to get a collected edition of his work published. The persistence with
which he carried this Edwardian idea into the 1930s is revealing. Wells had had
his Atlantic edition; Galsworthy his Manaton edition; Conrad his Sun-Dial and
Concord editions. Old enemies like Bennett and Archibald Marshall, by staying with the same publishers for long periods, had had their books published in
uniform bindings that looked like collected editions. A collected edition, Ford
thought, made evident a man's acceptance as a writer, as one of those "Deans
of English Letters" that he so longed to be. There was still money in handsome,
uniform editions of writers like Robert Louis Stevenson, who somehow
managed to be both popular and "serious." But Stevenson, "who spent an
immense amount of his time in finding too just words, and jewels five words
long that on the stretched forefinger of Old Time sparkle forever," was just the
kind of writer Ford never could be, or ever wanted to be. In any event, by the
thirties the collected edition of a living writer was no longer a practical idea.
For Ford it never had been; except for a brief period in the twenties, his novels
had never sold well enough to suggest such an edition might pay, and in his case
the cost would have been exceptionally high, since—as Lippincott pointed out
to him—it would take at least $5,000 to buy up the plates and stock of his books
from the many publishers he had been involved with.[19]

One can see how much the prestige Ford believed a collected edition
would have given him meant to him as one watches the increasing pleasure he
got from using his influence to help young writers. Here was a role that allowed
him to satisfy his generous impulse to help the young, his pleasure in being
admired as an old master, and his longing to participate actively in contemporary literary affairs. He began to put more and more energy into helping young
writers like Caroline Gordon and Eudora Welty, as well as a considerable number who never came to anything.

From early in 1933, when Katherine Anne Porter arrived in Paris, she and her fiancé, Eugene Pressly—Pressly was attached to the American embassy—were close to Ford and Janice. Ford was best man at their wedding and Julie bridesmaid when the Presslys were married at the *mairie* of the 16th Arrondisement. Ford gave Miss Porter a bouquet of white heather—for luck. The mayor conducted the ceremony with a flourish and gave the bride and groom a little booklet with directions for the care and feeding of twelve children; "Whoever," said Mrs. Pressly, "dared call the French pessimists." After this ceremony, they retired to the Deux Magots—it was eleven in the morning—and drank champagne.[20]

When Ford and Janice were in Paris they saw much of the Presslys and the Presslys were continually about to come to the Villa Paul for a vacation, though they never managed to get there. Many letters nevertheless went back and forth between the Presslys' flat in the Boulevard Montparnasse and the Villa Paul and there was much discussion of work—Miss Porter was busy with her book on Cotton Mather—and much gossip and a good deal of talk about cooking. Eugene Pressly undertook the formidable task of deciphering the manuscript of *It Was the Nightingale* and typing it for Ford; Ford rewarded him by dedicating *It Was the Nightingale* to him with a letter that sought to invoke their times together in Paris:

> The persons of the transatlantic drama are scattered but all active. You, it is true, are in Paris with Katherine Anne, and Mr. Glenway Westcott [*sic*] is still faithful to the great Faubourg; Mr. Pound is Professor of Economics in Rapallo; Mr. Hemingway is writing a novel in Key West if he is not momentarily shooting lions in Arkansaw or diving to recover bottles of Perrier Jouet from a sunken rum-runner.... And so the city sitteth solitary and the round table is dissolved.... [21]

For young writers, Ford was prepared to read manuscripts, write to publishers, and stir up his friends. In his amused way, Pound summed the matter up.

> Dowbtless yr/ reeward will be great upstairs and by the law of averages you DO discover 97 ducks to every swan and a half.... I never did like NOVELS just as such. an krrist you have spieled about a whole lot of books that never cast any illumination on the waste of a questionable world....

When Greenslet of Houghton Mifflin gently chided Ford for claiming his ducks were invariably financial successes, Ford replied,

> I don't of course seriously mean that every manuscript that I casually recommended to a publisher made good, but I do mean that

all the writers I very specially recommended did so, either very rapidly like Hemingway or gradually like Lawrence.

The difficulty for publishers was that there was no visible difference between Ford's casual recommendations and his special ones. Ford really cared only for writers' interests and never considered the interests of the publisher in making a recommendation.[22]

Ford and Janice had stayed on at the Villa Paul that fall of 1933, having given up the flat at 37 rue Denfert-Rochereau. But early in 1934 they came on to Paris, intending to stay there until the end of March and then "return to Toulon which is our Home." Having finished *Henry for Hugh* in December, 1933, Ford began at once on *Provence.* Then he decided he would like to go to London, perhaps with some idea of showing it to Janice. They got there in the middle of March and took rooms in what Ford described as "the garret of a gloomy, fog-filled, undignifiedly old, London house" at 31 Southampton Street, Fitzroy Square, close to Ford Madox Brown's old house. There Ford settled down to *Provence.* "It gave me a shock," said Goldring, who had not seen Ford since his days of prosperity in New York in 1927, "to see Ford, at his age, in such 'reduced circumstances'. He had, of course, been hit by the Wall Street crash, and a further minor disaster had occurred in ... Tarascon. ... "[23]

In an outburst of ironic patriotism Ford took Janice to see what he considered "the only Great View in London or the British Empire," the view from "the third step of the left-hand entrance-staircase of the National Gallery." From there one could, he thought, look down Whitehall to the "dreaming spires of the Abbey" and of Parliament. But during the twenty years since he had last looked at that view, things had changed; all they could see was the "livid, shuddering and blazing portents" of electric signs around Trafalgar Square; "it gave irresistibly the impression that someone having murdered London's sleep all the witch-doctors of Macbeth were dancing in a *Walpurgisnacht* across the London skies." Janice thought it very like New York, and when she learned there were no cafés in London, she—or Ford —wondered how London could "expect to have any art? ... Or any letters? Or any civilisation? Or any anything?"[24]

It was during this visit that Ford met Edward Crankshaw. Crankshaw was a great admirer of both Conrad and Ford and he was exactly the sort of intelligent, enthusiastic young man Ford liked. They quickly became friends, and for the rest of Ford's life Crankshaw watched over the publication of Ford's work in England, smoothed relations between him and publishers and, in general, acted as an unofficial and very skillful literary agent for Ford. He was a reader for Allen & Unwin, and with some trepidation, he arranged a lunch with Stanley Unwin for Ford. He knew Ford's feelings about publishers, especially British publishers, and he felt some anxiety about how Ford might treat Unwin. But Unwin understood Ford and was a tactful man; to help him, he had his respect for Ford's work, and the luncheon went off well. Unwin became Ford's English publisher beginning with *Great Trade Route* in January, 1937; he published Ford's last five books. He was generous and tactful with Ford and Ford liked him; there were never any difficulties between them. As a result, Ford had a mild revival in England during these last years of his life.[25]

During this trip to England Ford and Janice went down to Pulborough for a weekend with Ford's friend from Bedham days, Anthony Bertram. A chapter of *Provence* takes place on the train to Pulborough. Bertram recalled that Ford took their child ceremoniously in his arms and said, "He will always be able to say that he was held in the arms of Ford Madox Ford."[26]

In the middle of May they said farewell to London at "a sort of bottle-party" got up by old friends, and Douglas Goldring remembered Ford, "a stout and rather stertorious figure [revolving] slowly but majestically round the room, with Biala in his arms." Goldring had been closely questioned about Ford by Violet Hunt. "I wish," she said, "he'd come to see me. Why doesn't he?" Goldring did not remind her that Ford deeply resented her having books and pictures and furniture at South Lodge that he thought his —"stolen," as he once inaccurately put it—or that *The Flurried Years* had not been calculated to make Ford feel friendly. In her now absentminded way, Violet had forgotten these things. She continued to the end of her life to try to write, but, as she told Goldring, "I *can't* get on and it tires me so to try and compose.... " She did not finish anything after *The Wife of Rossetti* (1932). She died January 16, 1942, during the bombing of London, no longer knowing what was going on around her: she thought the bombs were thunder and that she was back in her childhood, on a visit to the Welsh mountains with her father.[27]

When, in June, 1933, Ford had begun negotiating for the English publication of *It Was the Nightingale*, he had sent the manuscript to Stella, remarking that he hoped she would handle its sale herself; she could, he said, "put the mss. into Bradley's hands but I would much rather you did not. Bradley has always got much worse terms out of publishers than I have myself. ... " This had been the first consequence of his anger at Bradley over the business of Long and Smith. Stella succeeded in placing *It Was the Nightingale* with Heinemann. Ford now had her try *Henry for Hugh*, which he had completed in December, 1933, on Heinemann. He also had her try *A History of Our Own Times.* Heinemann rejected both. When Stella suggested that she might let Bradley try his luck with *Henry for Hugh,* however, Janice wrote her that "Ford will not let his future books be handled by Bradley," and *Henry for Hugh* never did appear in England. Fortunately "those good Middle Westerners," J.P. Lippincott of Philadelphia, were ready to follow up the American edition of *It Was the Nightingale* with *Henry for Hugh,* which they scheduled for publication in October, 1934.[28]

Chapter 31

ૐ

What Ford intended to do with his two novels about Henry Martin Aluin Smith is made clear by the blurb he wrote for the second of them, *Henry for Hugh*, which was originally called *As Thy Day.*

> With AS THY DAY Mr. Ford Madox Ford adds another to the lengthening chain of novels, beginning with the pre-war GOOD SOLDIER and going on through the "Tietjens" novels which dealt with the war years to his present group, in which he deals with the Crisis. The whole series thus forms an extended chronicle of our own times. These books thus differ from the more usual novel of the day in that world circumstances impinge on his characters as much as or almost more than their private vicissitudes. AS THY DAY has a certain universality of theme, the private life of Henry Martin [Smith] illustrating a phase of universal desire whilst all around him civilisation quakes....

His first idea had been to make Henry Martin an illustration of the moral defects he believed had brought about the economic crisis of the thirties ("the chief characteristic of these years is want of courage—physical and moral"), and in *The Rash Act* he made some effort to show that Henry Martin was a victim of these defects. But by the time he came to write *Henry for Hugh*, he had identified himself closely with Henry Martin and had come to see him as a basically heroic man struggling with adverse circumstances, about whom it can justly be said, as the dying Elizabeth Freiligrath does say of him at the end of *Henry for Hugh*, "As thy day, so shall thy strength be."[1]*

*The shift in Ford's attitude toward Henry Martin begins toward the end of *The Rash Act*, when Henry Martin starts to speculate in an offhand, omniscient, Fordian way about such

In both novels, Ford exploits his special narrative method with excessive ingenuity. He had recently come to admire the detective story; "its construction is admirable; its style fluid; it will of necessity employ the modern aesthetic device called the 'time shift'. . . . And it gives information as to the workings of life that is certainly of value," he said. This admiration is reflected in *Henry for Hugh*, which "shews," Ford said in his blurb, "the working out of [Henry Martin Smith's] destinies in what is in effect an inverted detective story, the almost innocent misdemeanant, watching the sleuths getting onto his tracks, rather than the functionings of the ministrants of justice being what occupies the reader[']s attention." But the extravagance of Ford's detective-story plot turns it into a kind of *Comedy of Errors*. An impoverished American, Henry Martin Aluin Smith, substitutes himself for a wealthy Englishman, Hugh Monckton Allard Smith; and Ford increases the extravagance of the coincidences that make this substitution possible by inventing a complicated genealogy to show that the two men look alike because they are ultimately descended from the same family, named Faber: *Sine fabro nihil* ("without a smith there is no art") is their motto.[2]

The result is more ingenious than persuasive. As Bonamy Dobrée said in his review of *The Rash Act:*

> If anybody but Mr. Ford had written *The Rash Act* it would be an infuriating book. In his magnificent war tetralogy . . . Mr. Ford proved himself a great novelist; and in this book the great novelist is still apparent, but one is left not quite knowing what the book is about . . . [it] does not 'come off'; and it is only Mr. Ford's style . . . his sinewy twists of mind, that makes the book the continuously interesting and entertaining thing it is.

Herbert Agar made the same point more bluntly when he said the reader "finds himself cheated of any interpretation and with no reward for his pains but a very silly and unimportant fantasy."[*]

Late in November, 1934, Ford and Janice came up to Paris to make

---

esoteric matters as the Pilgrimage of Children and is described by Hugh Monckton as "trustworthy. Exceedingly cultivated! With an immense knowledge of the world. And wealthy. . . . " That Ford should come to sympathize with Henry Martin was probably inevitable from the moment he had Henry Martin think "It would be nice to have . . . on one's tombstone" that inscription to the memory of a Roman boy dancer that was "on the wall of the Roman Theatre" at Antibes: "SALTAVIT. PLACUIT. MORTUUS EST." In *Provence* Ford himself had called that inscription "the most beautiful" "of all the beautiful and mysterious motives and emotions that go to make up the frame of mind that is Provence. . . . "

*For a discussion of *The Rash Act* and *Henry for Hugh*, see pp. 519–22.

arrangements to go to New York for the winter. They somehow managed to book passage on a Nazi ship that sailed from Antwerp and landed them in the mud in Weehawken. They were entertained during the crossing by a German professor who was all for peace when he was sober and all for lining Jews and Communists up against a wall when he was not—which was much of the time. In New York they located an apartment at 61 Fifth Avenue, an old haunt of Ford's. One of his friends observed that he had returned like a dog to his vomit; "I don't really like," Ford said, "people who use my own favourite quotations appropriately." The apartment was "incredibly mouldy"; it was inadequately heated, there was no hot water, the stove was dangerous, and "the refrigerator in the night makes sounds like the Yeth hounds passing overhead on Exmoor." None of this was very good for the gout that was beginning to trouble Ford more or less continuously. Ford amused himself among New York's fashionable Marxists by quoting from his own work of thirty years before to show they were saying nothing new and reading them passages from Lenin about the Small Producer.[4]

They spent Christmas with Dreiser at Mount Kisco and Ford got into a fierce argument with Howard Scott, "the Eminent Technocrat," as he calls him. Like the German professor on the boat, Scott is—in Ford's account—in favor of lining several sorts of people up against walls and ends by shouting that America could be self-sufficient even without tin because it has cellophane. Ford was very angry about cellophane: it was what Americans put around all those foods not grown by the Small Producer for his own consumption ("At least they don't cover [their champagne] corks with cellophane . . . yet"), foods that were in any event poisonous because not grown under natural conditions by the Small Producer. " . . . our intelligences," he said, "are enfeebled by the blood supplied to our brains by artificially grown, chemically fertilized and preserved foods." "You are not a man if your body is built up of long dead meats kept in suspended putridity by refrigeration plus every imaginable coal-tar products [sic] from picric acids to arsenical fruit washes." On the way back to New York the next day Scott's car stalled on the ferry across the Hudson and he was unable to start it. So much for the wonders of technology.[5]

Ford's dislike of the contemporary world's technology, its uncivilized cosmopolitan life, and its disregard of the arts was as great as ever. To it, as always, he opposed a civilization based on the Small Producer. His beloved Provence offered the best example of this life. "Since the last of those Courts of Love ['that the Troubadours held in the little castle of Roumanille in the Alpilles above St. Rémy de Provence five miles or so from Tarascon'] was holden [,] our Western World ... gave up the attempt to reconcile [Beauty and Righteousness,] those necessary concomitants of the existence of a civilisation—and slid towards the Pit. And still slides." Musing on the possible connections between this civilization and the Tory England he had idealized in his earlier years, he slowly constructed a theory that the two were connected by the ancient Great Trade Route "along which went all beauty, all light."

> The route started ... in Pekin, ran level to Constantinople, turned a little North above Greece to reach Venice and Genoa and to skirt the Mediterranean as far as the mouth of the Rhône. It turned north up that stream passing Lyons and then descended the Seine passing Paris. It left Paris still going North and reached the shores of the Channel at Calais. It crossed in dug-outs and rafts to somewhere about Rye, West of Dungeness on the English South Coast, followed the coast, and reached according to legend and worked-out history, the country of King Arthur and the Land's End. As they could go no further the Merchants and civilizers of the Great Route there turned back and returned to Pekin.[6]

It is quite remarkable how Ford manages to make all the favorite places of his own life parts of the Great Trade Route. He even persuaded himself that, since his boyhood days when he and Walter Atterbury had sailed the seas of the world on the inverted kitchen table, his imagination had been haunted by Memphis, Tennessee. "But *that* vision," as he said,

> goes beyond the great oval sweep that is my Great Trade Route one and indivisible. To see that I must place myself in Cathay, or at its Western limit. ... That last is Memphis, Tennessee. But not the Memphis, Tennessee, that you mean. Ah, no, it is the Memphis, Tennessee, of my childhood's imagination. It had immense red-sandstone temple pillars, towering up into the limpid sky, the lotus flower painted below the capitals, the Father of Waters no eye ever saw flowing beside them. And palm trees and the ibis and the hippopotamus for ever on its sands. ...
> Those, then, are the limits of my Great Trade Route: Cathay with the mandarins in flowered silks and jewelled stairs and gilded junks; and a Memphis, Tennessee, of a Golden Age with red pillars and ibis and hippopotamus.[7]

Allen and Caroline Tate were living in Memphis (Mr. Tate was teaching at Southwestern), and Ford and Janice were going to visit them during the summer of 1935. Ford's Tory romanticism and his memories of his oncle d'Amérique in Lexington, Virginia, made him sympathize with the Agrarian conception of the South the Tates so eloquently advocated. He was therefore eager to see the Tates' South as part of his civilized world, and Memphis, Tennessee, became an extension of the Great Trade Route.

The theory of the Great Trade Route is simply the application of Ford's lifelong attitude to a new set of circumstances. His imagination was no longer limited to England and Yorkshire Tory gentry, as it had been in his earlier days; it was now focused on the Mediterranean and the American South. But his attitude remained the same. He was very much in earnest about it. He proposed to devote to it a trilogy of books, a Fordian *Decline of the West* "in which I project—for what it is worth—my message to the world." He completed only two volumes of this trilogy, *Provence* (1934) and *Great Trade Route* (1937).[8]

The value of both these books frankly depends on the value of Ford's views: even their historical information is selected and arranged—and surrounded with personal anecdotes—in such a way as to make it meaningful only as an illustration of Ford's opinions. Both books, moreover, frequently generalize Ford's opinions about such things as the deleterious effects of preserved foods into a plan for saving the world. It is impossible not to be entertained by the inventiveness with which Ford brings the discussion around to these ideas, often against the heaviest odds. He consciously exploits their effect of learned eccentricity.

You see, Biala addressed the New Yorker, that's how his mind works. You'd think he couldn't connect his uncle's hauling tobacco in sleds [at Lexington, Virginia], and Nîmes and Thomas Jefferson and Madeira and indigo and Charles I, all in one sentence. But he will and cite them as instances of the Route being all one civilization.

It isn't, I said, authentically certain that Virginia made the silk for the coronation robe of Charles I.[9]

Provence thus becomes an informal personal guidebook, diversified with accounts of Provençal characters and cafés Ford has known; he is, as he says, "giving you my Provence." His purpose is to show "that Provence is not a country nor the home of a race, but a frame of mind," and that "our great, noisy and indigestion-sick Anglo-Saxondom . . . can only be touched by inspiration from the spirit of Provençal Latinity, frugality and tolerance." In order to enforce this point, *Provence* alternates chapters about Provence itself with chapters that describe unfavorably Ford's experiences in England during the spring of 1934.[10]

Great Trade Route is even more evidently a travel guide, and its style is so personal that it is often difficult for anyone not familiar with Ford's private life to see what he is driving at. It begins with Ford and Janice's crossing from Antwerp to New York in October, 1934, and describes their life in New York that winter and their trip south the next spring. It ends with their return crossing and their arrival back at the Villa Paul.

As in *Provence*, Ford seizes every opportunity to preach, not only on the subjects like New York's ignorance of food and wines that come up naturally, but on the larger ideas that constitute his cure for Western culture. Much of this speculation is harmless enough, as when—having discovered the Merion Cricket Club—he assures his readers that Pennsylvania is "a cricketing state" and the country around Paoli, like the imagined East Kent of his young manhood, filled with "artists, players, hounds, and . . . oh, say, cricket. . . . " But he asks us to take quite seriously his conclusion that Madeira is the lost Atlantis because, unlike Santos to the east but like North America to the west, it was without the wheel in Columbus' time. "Scientific evidence," he says in support of this theory, " . . . should always be suspect; legend destroys science." Much too much of the time he is complacently describing himself as one of the "moderate people who read or write books, visit picture galleries, listen to concerts . . . who are the backbone of our countries, asking nothing of them and giving unceasingly"—the people who are, he assures us, ideally equipped to take over the world and run it sensibly.[11]

As in *Provence*, Ford's ingenuity is entertaining. One is never quite sure afterwards how Thomas Jefferson was shown to be a product of the Great Trade Route's culture or even how Jefferson got into the discussion at all, but as Ford is working round to Jefferson, one is held by his cleverness. But *Provence* and *Great Trade Route* are not meant to be merely entertaining. Ford valued highly the personal opinions he set forth in them and meant them to be taken seriously. As Caroline Gordon acutely observed after his death, "These last few years have been very hard for [Ford]. There was only his work—he had got to the point where it was impossible to communicate with him. He and Janice seemed to inhabit a closed world, a sphere which rolled here or there, from France to New York and back again, but never changed inside." Only the personal views of a very wise and responsible man could have supported the burden Ford asked his to support in *Provence* and *Great Trade Route*, and Ford was neither. His opinions are not the result of a careful contemplation of the world; they are simply the play of an ingenious fancy around the places Ford liked and the activities he was interested in—"my thoughts," as he said, "on faiths and destinies and chances and cuisines and the Stage and music and the fine arts and the neglect of writers and love and honest merchanting and treason and death and strategies." His ideas on these subjects are too cranky to be taken seriously, and the form in which he expresses them, clever as it is, encourages his worst faults, his weakness for dramatic extravagance and for talking too much about himself. *Provence* and *Great Trade Route* are not the fascinating monologues of a wise and mature man that Ford evidently hoped they were. As Graham Greene said of *Provence*, "[Ford] . . . has a personality which calls both for respect and mockery. A fine writer with traces of a most engaging charlatan . . . his style swings like ribboned glasses. . . . As in his fiction he writes out of a kind of hilarious depression. . . . The method has something in common with Mr. Pound's *Cantos.* . . . "[12]

Provence was published in March, 1935. It got favorable reviews, though most of the reviewers treated it simply as a book that "to the reader who knows Provence . . . will bring a nostalgia (and to the reader who doesn't know Provence, a longing) almost insupportable in a New York March." Only one or two, who appear to have been tipped off by Ford, mentioned what he thought important, that *Provence* offered a "new and exciting interpretation," was not only "a magnificent revelation of . . . Provence, but an autobiography, a history and a philosophy as well. . . . " *Provence* sold slightly over 2,500 copies in America and a little over 1,200 in England. On the strength of its reviews Ford tried once more to find a publisher for *A History of Our Own Times.*[13]

In late March they started south to visit the Tates in Memphis, traveling by bus in order to see as much of the South as possible. Allen Tate arranged a lecture for Ford at Southwestern and Robert Penn Warren asked him to speak the next month at the Writers' Conference organized by *The Southern Review*. They hoped to pay for the trip with the fees from these engagements, supplemented by the small sum Ford received for writing a pair of newspaper articles about the trial of Bruno Hauptmann for the kidnapping of the Lindberghs' child. But their financial situation was, as usual, very difficult, and before they left for the South Ford made an effort to obtain money from Lippincott. This effort was unsuccessful.

> The situation is just this [Lippincott wrote]—to date we have published two of your books, IT WAS THE NIGHTINGALE and HENRY FOR HUGH, and our loss on both, without overhead, is in excess of $3000. We have still to publish PROVENCE and LA-DIES WHOSE BRIGHT EYES on which we have already advanced you the sum of $1750. In addition there is the contract for a further novel on which you have received an advance of $375. . . . I

cannot see how we could make you any further advances on your future work.

It is clear from this letter that Lippincott was not inclined to commit itself to Ford beyond that "further novel"*(Vive le Roy)* for which there was already a contract. The feeling was mutual; when Ford sent them *Vive le Roy* he suggested they publish it under a pseudonym. " . . . you have been so uniformly unsuccessful with my books," he said, "that my name cannot be any good to you. . . . "[14]

They reached Memphis April 5, 1935. The Tates took them to the zoo, where Ford observed "a large red sandstone fragment of the other Memphis," "a symbol," he thought, "of the Union and Indivisibility of the culture that flows perpetually between the Blue Nile and the yellow Father of Waters." He observed the "hippoipotamon," also an indication of the continuity of Egyptian and Tennessee culture, and he found it "inevitable that there, at the Western extremity of my travels, both real and imagined, I should be fated to talk about the Isles of Greece" with Caroline Tate. Ford went on to Baton Rouge for the Writers' Conference on April 11 and 12. Huey Long addressed the gathering at a luncheon, speaking, Ford said, "in exactly the dialect, with the vapidity, with the images—even some of the accent—of a Cambridge—England—Head of a College addressing his staff on a not very important occasion." It had become "insupportably hot" by the time Ford spoke, and he felt "too tired to remember where" he was. He fancied that he was offending nearly everyone by defending the concentration of book publishing in New York and arguing that Southern writers got more than their fair share of praise in the New York book reviews—"Caroline Gordon starting with indignation at my every second word; and Mr. Tate looking intently at the ground. . . . And . . . Penn Warren . . . asking me if I could keep it up for another half-hour . . . to fill in the schedule." "My voice is going on talking. . . . I can hear it. . . . What the devil is it saying? . . . I must pull myself together."[15]

After a couple of days of sight-seeing in New Orleans, Ford returned to Tennessee with the Tates (Janice had gone back to New York to prepare an exhibition of the drawings she had done for *Provence*). He did not stay long at Benfolly; he was anxious to be back in New York for Janice's exhibition and to negotiate with Howard Lowry of the Oxford Press for the publication of his collected poems and *Great Trade Route;* he never liked to leave such matters to agents and he distrusted Curtis Brown, whom he was now using, at least as much as he had all his previous agents. These negotiations seemed to him particularly important because he hoped the Oxford

Press would publish him in England as well as in America. The future of Stella and Julie depended on his English sales, and Stella's inability to place Ford works in England was making their situation difficult.[16]

Ford thought he had carried out these negotiations with great skill: "The agreement was all right," he said, and Janice wrote Stella to point the moral. Try, she urged Stella,

> to rub in the eminence of Ford and the value of his name which no agent will take the trouble to do. Ford . . . concluded his own agreements [for *Great Trade Route* and *Collected Poems*] with the [Oxford] Press and [for *Portraits from Life* with *The American*] MERCURY in ten minutes after Curtis Brown had done nothing for seven months. Things are very bad here [in New York] indeed. No other 'best seller' has done any better than Ford's book *[Provence]* . . . and the publishers have formed a regular combine against authors. I thought we should starve too till yesterday, as it is we may just scrape through.[17]

Ford also had luncheon at the Plaza with Paul Palmer, the editor of *The American Mercury*, to settle the last details of their arrangement for the publication of Ford's "Portraits from Life" in the *Mercury*. As often happened, Ford came away from this luncheon with a different conception of what had been agreed on than Palmer. "You are, you know, treating me very badly . . . " Ford was to write Palmer later. "It was . . . quite definitely settled that you would take the Pound and Dreiser at our conversation at the Plaza. . . . Moreover I want the money."[18]

Shortly after these arrangements were made, they started home, taking the *Roma* to Naples. Ford found it a very unpleasant trip. They were traveling third class, and the lack of privacy made it "simply Purgatory." He was particularly annoyed by a large number of young Italians who kept howling "*Giovinezza*"; he never had been able to stand noises. He was also irritated by the staff's failure to treat him as "a member of the governing classes"—"it is we who pay those fellows and they ought to behave as our servants." It disturbed him to see the first-class passengers coming "out on a gallery above—gorgeous cinema stars . . . hair blowing back in the dawn wind, eyes gazing soulfully into the growing luminosity as if into spotlights. . . . They were as far above my head as Pallas Athene when she rescued Athenians from battlefields." After "fourteen nights of complete sleeplessness and dispiritude" and no vegetables, even out of cans, he was delighted to get back to the Villa Paul, where he hastened to plant some fast-growing peas. He was thus able to conclude *Great Trade Route* with a last lesson for the reader on the advantages of being a Small Producer. "The day after the day after to-morrow I shall see a line of untidy, brilliant green things pushing through this lilac-tinted soil above the tideless sea. There is no greater joy. Money for nothing. Think about it, Nordics."[19]

That summer Julie came to stay with them; in *Great Trade Route* Ford represents her as sympathetic to his views, but he calls her "the little English Girl," not, in his vocabulary, a compliment. Ford had never reconciled himself to Julie's growing up in England and taking on the characteristics of a culture he disapproved of instead of growing up in France and adopting his style of life. Janice had suggested to Stella that spring how hurt Ford was by Julie's attitude and Stella had replied that she did her best "but his attitude in general & towards me in particular has made these efforts rather futile, & it is only Ford himself who can remedy the position he has created."[20]

Julie was now fourteen, and she no doubt expressed herself with innocent tactlessness that summer at the Villa Paul. When she returned to London in the fall Ford sat down and wrote her a letter which, however well' it expresses his feelings, was not calculated to persuade a fourteen-year-old to understand and love him.

> You suffer [he said] under various difficulties as regards myself. ... Politics no doubt have a great deal to do with it. You live apparently amongst the middle-class Left in England and I live about the world with no politics at all except the belief—which I share with Lenin—that the only thing that can save the world is the abolition of all national feelings and the prevailing of the Small Producer—and the Latin Tradition of clear-sightedness as to what one means oneself. ...
> ... Anglo-Saxondom is a hybrid collection of human beings all of whose refinements and practical sense comes from the Latin Tradition. ... You can't make a silk purse out of a beefsteak and kidney pudding cooked without condiments. ... French and Latin are the only lifeboats for the maelstrom that is coming. ...
> ... Our sort of *vie simple* is however not merely the product of clear thinking; it is an elected form of life. Clear thinking it is true is the cause of indigence because the immense lower middle class that has latterly defaced the surface of the globe shudders and screams when thought is presented to it—but in spite of that we might have a little more comfort than we have if I had not long ago come to the conclusion that material comfort deadens one's interest in life—and extinguishes self-respect. ...

You see, if you will think of it, I am the kind of person whose truths eventually swim up [to] the surface. They seem silly to you now as they seem to the press and public of your country. But if you think of the persons whose truths, historically, have eventually swum up to the surface of public consciousness and have prevailed you will see that it is the lonely buffaloes, ploughing solitary furrows who have generally produced those truths.[21]

Chapter 32

In October, 1935, "to be a little tranquil," Ford and Janice went to Geneva for a few days, a trip Ford used to enforce the point of one of his most impressive letters to a young author, his criticism of Anthony Bertram's *Men Adrift* for trying to deal with the Christ story without being really Christian.

> ... Christianity isn't you know a Sunday supper with the maids given the evening off; it is eating flesh and drinking blood. ... If you had been—as we've just been for the last few days—in Geneva what I mean would appear to you with startling effect.

This is a characteristic example of the kind of wisdom that Ford could bring to the problems of others: what better way to make Bertram feel the terror and tragedy in Christianity than to remind him of the middle-class Sunday —"Sunday supper with the maids given the evening off." "Dante," as he remarked on another occasion, "was a bitter man who had seen hell; Tasso was a gentleman who had read about Jerusalem." At almost the same time, Ford was giving an illustration of how this wisdom would fail him in his own affairs. By Christmas he had run out of money again. He persuaded himself that, whatever the immediate causes of such crises (the carelessness of publishers and agents, the inefficiencies of banks), they were fundamentally the consequences of his commitment to a way of life everyone would eventually realize was wisdom's choice.

> I can't send you any Christmas present [he wrote Julie] because we have literally no money at all. ... try market-gardening or carpentry. They are both good for exactness of thought and movement and will be useful when, the middle class having been extinguished in a year or so, you have to adapt yourself to proletariate conditions. I do not know where we should be if I hadn't known how to market-garden.[1]

In March they came north to Paris, and Ford, deciding that Edward Crankshaw needed to meet French painters if he was to become a really good art critic, invited Crankshaw to visit them. The 'opportunity meant so much to Crankshaw that, though he was very poor, he rode his bicycle to Dover in order to go to Paris. Ford invested time and energy in Crankshaw's education with typical generosity, taking him about Paris to the studios of a remarkable number of painters, all of whom, Crankshaw was astonished to discover, he was on intimate terms with. Only Picasso seemed to be too much for him; Crankshaw had a strong impression that Ford was relieved not to find Picasso at home when they called or at the Deux Magots when Ford sought him out there.[2]

Ford made this effort in spite of ill health; his heart condition continued to worry them, and Janice became increasingly anxious to protect him from the disappointments he would sometimes fret himself ill over. As early as the previous summer, she had written Stella about a complaint of Julie's that they had promised her a trip to Italy and then had put off going until she had to leave them: "Julie was very anxious to go to Italy. As the heat was very great until the 15th [of August] we couldn't go until then because of Ford's heart. Julie was told this at least a week before she was due at the Marcoussis'.... I am of course ready to have Julie in my house at any time or all the time, but I must at all costs protect Ford from unpleasantnesses." This spring, when Julie decided at the last minute against a trip to Paris to see them, Janice wrote:

> But it is rather important that she should keep to arrangements that she does make. Ford's heart is in a pretty bad state and if we have stayed in Paris it was partly with the expectation of having her here for Easter and he frets a good deal about her health.... We have distresses enough without adding to them.[3]

Early in April Lippincott brought out *Vive le Roy*, Ford's last completed novel. In it he imagines that the conflict of the 1930s between the French Right and Left—between the *camelots du roi* and the extreme elements of the Front Populaire—has produced a civil war. The Royalists have just recaptured Paris and established the young Duke of Orléans on the throne as Henry V. Then the king is assassinated. *Vive le Roy* describes how the Grand Chamberlain, M. Penthièvre, conceals the king's death and substitutes for him an almost perfect double, a young American named Walter Leroy, in order that the regime with its admirable policies may remain in control of the country.

The most interesting thing about *Vive le Roy* is the ingenuity with which Ford arranges the story to represent his idea of his own place and influence in the world of the thirties. He admired the energy and enthusiasm of the young and sympathized with their feeling that the world was a mess. He understood how, given the climate of the times, this feeling made them vaguely Marxist; but, though he hated violent reactionaries like the *camelots du roi* as much as they did, he was confident of his own judgment that their Marxism was the wrong answer.

> Tyranny [he has Penthièvre say] is a necessity to [Marxists] because according to the dictates of their theory of government men must be adapted to their machine not their machine to the tastes and desires of men. Lenin . . . was a very admirable tyrant—but still a tyrant, his machine lopping off heads, arms, feet, where they would not conform or could not conform to the perfect sphere of his governmental theories.

The right answer was an absolute monarchy committed to all Ford's favorite Tory doctrines—the *poule au pot* of the French peasant instead of the "boiled fowls out of a pot that is no pot but a can" of American mass production; the nation "of small hamlets, each self-contained, each potentially self-supported, self-governing . . . almost without central government. . . . Almost without roads even!" and entirely without taxes, particularly on the royalties of writers —"a country of small producers, sitting in cellars, hammering tacks into shoe-soles or exposing outside on the sidewalk small piles of firewood. Or forever bending over plants in vegetable beds. . . . And in the whole of broad France . . . no specimen of the dead and damned, soul-destroying thing known as a factory. . . . "[4]

In *Vive le Roy*, then, Ford is, in all seriousness, crying "*Vive le roi*," showing his young friends the triumph of absolute monarchy in the person of an heir of Saint Louis and Henry IV and setting forth its admirable policies in the disquisitions of cultivated and humane Penthièvre. At the same time he is showing these attractive but youthfully ignorant young Americans that the bulky, middle-aged, wise Penkethman, for all that he may seem to them old and ignorant of the passionate life they know so well, has had a tragic romance with Walter Leroy's mother that is even yet too poignant a memory for him to be able to talk about it. This was Ford's vision of himself as one of the "lonely buffaloes, ploughing solitary furrows" whose truths, as he had told Julie, though they might seem "silly" to the thoughtless and often cruel young, would "eventually [swim] to the surface of public consciousness and [prevail]."*

*For a discussion of *Vive le Roy*, see pp. 522–23.

Vive le Roy was not a success; after the advance had been paid off Ford got about $250, and they had to live as best they could on his journalism. In July they went to stay with the Crankshaws at Penshurst for a month. There Ford worked on his portrait of Swinburne for *The American Mercury*. He also worked on the *Buckshee* poems, the last and finest of which, "Coda" (written after their return to Paris), has a note of dedication to Janice reminding her of the anniversary of their first meeting: "*Written in the rue de Seine for an anniversary between feasts of SS. James & Paul* (Otherwise May Day) *& That of Saint Joan of Arc.* MCMXXXVI."

They got back to Paris August 4 and went on to Toulon, where they remained until late October. Then at last, reluctantly, they gave up the Villa Paul—"the end, alas, of a phase! Life is really so dear here." "We are going . . . [to] go and live in one room in Paris. It's impossible to make a living outside New York, one's agents are always so incompetent and we'd both die if we had to live in the U.S.A. for good"—as they were soon to find they practically did have to.[6]

Despite the brave front Ford puts up, these unhappy necessities were very bitter to him, particularly as he thought the worst of them the quite needless result of the incompetence of others, as he pointed out to Ruth Aley, the new agent he had recently taken on in New York.

> I wish [he wrote her] you would seriously consider the position. I may tell you that we are having to give up this villa—on which my health entirely depends—and go to live in one room in Paris simply because of this uncertainty [about money]. . . . It is not your not placing *[Portraits from Life]* that I grumble at. I could place it myself in a day if I were in New York but I know that agents find me difficult. But it is the continual unnecessary delay [in sending the money she collects] and the never being able to average out what is beneath your optimistic forecasts that has broken my back. . . . Do you not see that, even if you should now succeed in placing the book for a decent price it will be all the more bitter to have had to give up this place . . . and to have had ten years taken off one's life, which is what will happen.

Ford is exaggerating the dependence of his health (though not of his personal happiness) on living at the Villa Paul, but he is not exaggerating the badness of his health itself. In addition to his heart trouble, he was now struggling with increasingly painful attacks of gout. "Gout," he had written the Presslys when he got back to the Villa Paul in August, " . . . has completely crippled me, ever since we got here, leading to as complete sleeplessness—not one wink of sleep last night at all!—the whole being conduced by the really very bad behaviour of the O. U. P."[7]

When Ford had made the contract for his *Collected Poems* with Howard Lowry of the Oxford University Press of New York in June, 1935, he had understood that Lowry would also arrange for their publication by the Oxford Press in England. This turned out to be more easily promised than done. The peculiar relations between the two presses made the negotiations for the English edition drag on in a way that would have wearied a much more patient author than Ford. The Oxford Press of New York finally did publish the *Collected Poems* in October, 1935. The Oxford Press in England delayed for three more years; their edition was in galleys when the war broke out and the project was shelved indefinitely. After the war they claimed never to have heard of the book.[8]

Ford met these exacerbating disappointments by struggling to write enough to keep them alive, working steadily on his essays for *The American Mercury* even when the subjects were uncongenial to him. "Can you imagine," he asked Paul Palmer, the *Mercury*'s editor, "what it is to try for six weeks to read SWINBURNE? to try and try and TRY, like Bruce's spider . . . and to fail . . . I got up at half past five again this morning . . . as every morning . . . to face those printed pages to which the mind will not adhere." Of D. H. Lawrence he said, "I'm not a hell of a lot in sympathy with him and find him difficult to re-read." "We most of us," as he said to Allen Tate, "have so much to overwrite ourselves to get the little thin oatmeal." He felt too that he was becoming isolated.

> Janice said this morning: "It's odd, you know, the Tates seem to be the only friends or family we have in the world" . . . quite out of the blue, like that. . . . I so thoroughly agreed with her that I came straight in and wrote this. It's true that we haven't any more got any real friends—in the sense of people one can talk to . . . and both Janice and I are pretty good at making enemies.[9]

On November 11 they sailed for New York on the *Lafayette*. After staying for a few days with Dr. Lake, they located a flat in Ford's old stamping ground, at 10 Fifth Avenue—"three or four secondhand Quatorze chairs, a poor spindly table, the scantest number of books, a jetty sphynxed cat, several of wife's, Biala's, paintings of Paris rains, or murmurously lighted artichoke-colored buildings along quays or the Seine, all of which was served to you with tea and Sutter's cakes." When Edward VIII abdicated in December, Ford did a radio broadcast about him over WJZ. " . . . *did* you hear my broadcast . . . about the King?" he asked Paul Palmer. "I hear there were few dry eyes amongst those who heard it—but I can't find anyone who did. The N. B. C. were so overwhelmed by it that they have rung me up every half hour since to tell me so. . . . The N. B. C. have just rung up to say that they are cabling my broadcast to the King!"[10]

He was not a well man, though he tried to conceal his illness, refusing to acknowledge, as he struggled "about the New Jersey landscape [with William Carlos Williams] to discover at my request some answer to some of the secret[s] of American truck gardening," that it was a torture to him. When concealment was impossible he gave romantic explanations for his incapacities; when gout made it necessary for him to use a cane, he said, "You see, I was wounded in the foot at Armentières and can't stand for long without a cane for fear of collapsing on the floor." "Ford . . . was really, at that time," Williams said, "a sick man—gasping often for breath on mild exertion—though he'd never if possible let you know it. One night, trying to get into a taxi, I thought his end had come."[11]

When the American edition of *Great Trade Route* appeared in January, 1937, and was followed shortly by *Portraits from Life*, the reviewers described Ford as entertaining but not to be taken very seriously; "Critic and raconteur, he is a British Alexander Woollcott," as one of them put it. This judgment must have hurt Ford, but he went immediately to work to profit from the publicity these two books earned him. He told Stanley Unwin that, despite Houghton Mifflin's publication of *Portraits from Life*, he thought Greenslet "too cautious and canny a Scot, to be much good to me." Nevertheless he once more exhumed *Mr. Croyd* (now called *That Same Poor Man*) and tried it on Greenslet. "It strikes me," he wrote, "as a remarkably spirited performance—like the Tietjens books but more bitterly humorous," though in 1927 he had thought it "unreadable," the work of a madman. But he had guessed right about Greenslet, who thought it "too definitely dated to sell now." However, "old Mrs. Doubleday has asked me to be guest of honor at one of her parties . . . which is as a rule, a sign that they mean to do business." Unwin urged Ford not to get mixed up with Doubleday, but on the strength of "old Mrs. Doubleday's" invitation he set down the terms he would accept. They included $1,000–1,500 on signing a long-term contract, $150 a month against royalties up to the amount earned by his previous book, and a collected edition of thirteen volumes. In return he would produce 150,000 words a year, beginning with the projected third volume of the *Great Trade Route* trilogy, *A History of Our Own Times*, and a novel.[12]

Except for that old dream of a collected edition, this is a very modest proposal; Ford was not, with a "salary" of $1,800 a year, suggesting that some publisher stake him to life on the grand scale. He had calculated what they could conduct their very modest life on, and had asked for that. He had, to be sure, slowly come to recognize that it was more than the sale of his books would justify any publisher's offering him, but he persuaded himself it was nonetheless worth a publisher's while to get him at this price because his name was a valuable commodity. As he told Stanley Unwin, "I am unquestionably one of the most eminently high-brow—I don't say invariably bestselling, writers they [America] have and a great many publishers have paid me quite large sums merely to have my name on their list"—or at least, he was convinced, they should have. He did not now expect the popular audience to accept the ideas of a lonely old buffalo so much in advance of his time, but he believed that the value of these ideas would be recognized after his death. "I have always," he told Unwin—meaning that he had now begun to do so—"staked my all on the plan that my books should sell, if largely at all, after my death. One has, I think, to take one's sales either before or after one's decease."[13]

But, like all Ford's efforts during the thirties to get a livelihood from his books, this one failed, and he had to manage as best he could with an occasional article for *Forum* and some lecturing. In March he talked at a "Round Table luncheon" for the Town Hall Club, offering a suggestion for bringing together as an effective political power the citizens of the Great Trade Route. "Real democracy," he said, "needs a national system of voting devices—some speedy electrical arrangement so that the people [can] register their will directly and immediately." When a worried listener asked if his plan would not involve abolishing Congress, "Mr. Ford appeared surprised that anyone should be concerned about that, but he gave a kindly and reassuring answer."[14]

At the end of March they went to Boston for Houghton Mifflin's publication of *Portraits from Life;* Ford lectured there and was, he claimed, offered an LL.D. and two professorships, one of which he was seriously considering. Dale Warren of Houghton Mifflin lent them his apartment. "Don't you find him a rather messy old thing?" Greenslet asked Warren; Warren did. *Portraits from Life* is Ford's last account of his "fifty years of contacts with the Great in letters." He made some effort to treat these writers critically, rereading them and seeking, in his concluding chapter, to make a critical summary of the period. But as Edward Crankshaw said in his reader's report for Stanley Unwin, Ford's vignettes "are not critical studies . . . the approach is primarily personal; the idea is to make the reader see [the writers] more than their work. . . . The only thing conceivably comparable to them, as portraits, are Moore's portraits of his contemporaries in his autobiographies. ... Ford is not a critic. The [concluding] essay ... is pretty bad—not as writing, of course, but as thinking. . . . I say 'bad,' but I should have said 'silly,' or something like that." This is a reasonable comment, for even when Ford is attempting to write criticism, as he is in that concluding essay, he falls into personal reminiscence. He tells us how oppressed his childhood had been by the Victorian Great, and how, when he was "blown up at Bécourt-Bécordel," his nightmares were conditioned by his childhood recollections of them. He summarizes the history of literature for the last fifty years in terms of the triumph of that Impressionism he believed James, Crane, Hudson, Conrad, and he had worked out and of its replacement by Pound and Hemingway and "the literary Middle West." He justifies this approach to his subject by telling the reader that Paul Palmer kept insisting that "You don't know what it means to Us to know what it felt like to have been in contact with Them! ... That was what it felt like. Now you know!" But it was of course because he found reminiscence irresistible that he wrote *Portraits from Life* as he did. *Portraits from Life* was widely reviewed, and nearly everyone thought it highly entertaining; nearly everyone, too, shared Crankshaw's doubts of its critical value.[15]

Their plans for the summer and fall were a good deal more definite than usual, thanks to the Tates. During the previous summer, the Tates had been to a writers' conference organized by Joseph Brewer, a publisher friend of Mr. Tate who had become president of Olivet College in Michigan. Brewer shared the Tates' feelings about the state of American education and, as Robie Macauley—then a student at Olivet—has pointed out, "for one brief period under [his] presidency . . . Olivet College had an extraordinary life as a center of education in the arts. . . . After President Brewer left, a new reactionary regime triumphantly returned the college to its former level of mediocrity." One of President Brewer's projects was an annual summer writers' conference in which the Tates took part in 1936. Sharing the Tates' admiration for Ford, Brewer was eager to get Ford to Olivet the next summer. "[President Brewer's] brightest idea," Mrs. Tate wrote Ford that fall, " . . . is to create a chair of letters or whatever you'd call it and get you to fill it." Ford and Brewer met in New York during the Christmas holidays and the matter was settled. Ford would hold the position of a writer and critic in residence; ·the salary would be $1,500. He would come to Olivet early enough to participate in the 1937 writers' conference, along with the Tates and Katherine Anne Porter, for an additional fee of $150. "I have," as he put it, "consented to give a course of lectures on comparative literature to a class [at Olivet] until the beginning of December." In their generous way, the Tates invited Ford and Janice to stay with them for the whole summer, and so, on April 30, accompanied by Janice's sister-in-law, Mrs. Jack Tworkov, who went along to act as Ford's secretary, they set off for Clarksville, Tennessee.[16]

Robert Lowell, then a student at Harvard, had met Ford in Boston and been attracted to him; he also greatly admired Allen Tate. It struck him that a summer at Benfolly with the Tates and Ford would be an excellent thing. "Instantly, and with keen, idealistic, adolescent heedlessness," he drove to Clarksville and offered himself to the Tates as a house guest. "The Tates' way of refusing was to say that there was no room for me unless I pitched a tent on the lawn. A few days later, I returned with an olive Sears-Roebuck-Nashville umbrella tent. I stayed three months." It was overwhelmingly hot. "What's the heat like in New York?" Janice wrote George Davis of *Harper's Bazaar.* "It's awful here. In every room in the house there's a typewriter and at every typewriter there sits a genius. Each genius is wilted and says that he or she can do no more but the typewritten sheets keep on mounting. I too am not idle. I sit in the parlor where I paint on three pictures at once in intervals of killing flies. I don't eat them. Neither do I invite them in."[17]

The amount of work done at Benfolly that summer was astonishing. Mr. Tate was writing his remarkable and neglected novel *The Fathers.* Robert Lowell was writing "grimly unromantic poems—organized, hard and classical as a cabinet," as he believed he was learning from Mr. Tate to do. Since Mr. Tate had also told him he believed each poem he finished would be his last, Lowell also "ached for the conviction that each finished poem would be his last." "They were," he added, "very flimsy" poems. Ford was dictating to Mrs. Tworkov *The March of Literature,* the history of literature he had wanted to write for many years. He had at last succeeded in interesting the Dial Press in it the previous December, and as soon as he was free he went to work on it with an energy and enthusiasm that seem almost incredible in anl ill man of sixty-four. In addition to his remorseless dictation of a thousand words a day, he was reading omnivorously over the whole range of literary history. He seemed, Robert Lowell remembered, always to have "armloads of Loeb classics." In sickness and in health, for richer or poorer, Ford's love of literature, his sense of its overwhelming importance, remained undiminished. Within a month of his arrival at Benfolly, he sent Dial the first hundred pages of the book and throughout the summer he kept going at this pace. "Indoors," Robert Lowell remembered, "life was Olympian and somehow crackling. Outside, Uncle Andrew, the calf, sagged against my tent sides. I sweated enough to fill the cistern."[18]

Lowell's figure of speech is no accident. The only cistern at Benfolly ran dry during the summer. Ford undertook to solve this problem by building them a Sussex dew pond. With much ceremony and a full explanation of his expertise for the benefit of Mr. Norman, the farmer, who appeared skeptical, Ford sank an old washtub in the meadow and filled it with a tangle of twigs. No one was more surprised than he when it failed to fill with water. The burden of all these guests on the domestic routine of the house was considerable. Ford found the rich Southern food prepared by the Tates' cook, Ida, too much for him. Closed doors were out of the question in the heat, and there was very little privacy. Always sensitive to noise, the dedicated Small Producer found life in the country disturbing. "This is one of the noisiest spots in the world," he said of Benfolly, "what with children and chickens and birds and cows and steamboats and Tennessean voices and doors slamming in the wind." He was also bothered by the climate. "Here the weather [is] one day ... like July on the equator and the next, being today, is like something in Camchatka."[19]

At the end of May Ford went to Chicago to speak at one of *Poetry*'s fund-raising dinners and lecture at the University of Chicago. " ... a ferocious but relatively triumphant course of lectures and interviews and all the usual ballyhoo," he called it. In June he and Janice conceived the idea of going to New Orleans and doing a portrait of it, as part of a series of portraits of cities that they hoped to sell to magazines and then make into a book that would be the third volume of the *Great Trade Route* trilogy. It would consist of an "introductory section on the outward bound voyage from Naples to Boston in which comparisons will be made between various types of highly cultured civilizations ... quite light in tone with occasionally more pensive passages to forecast the general tone of the book." Then there would be an account of a journey around the United States. This book would require much delightful travel, to be paid for by magazines and publishers. But nobody would buy the idea and they had to drop it.[20]

In the middle of June, when news came that Vanderbilt had failed to meet an offer Kenyon College had made John Crowe Ransom, Allen Tate and Andrew Lytle organized a dinner for Ransom in Nashville, a protest in the form of a tribute. Ford was eager to join the young in protesting against this example of the Establishment's disregard of the arts. He made the main speech, "dressed in white duck trousers, a beat-up dinner jacket, and shod in espadrilles," to a gathering of forty-odd people, and read, "between wheezes," the fifty or more telegrams that had been received. The occasion was, he thought, a "glorious victory for the forces of intellect."[21]

The writers' conference at Olivet was to begin July 15; Ford anticipated it with some anxiety. "As for our activities," he wrote Dale Warren of Houghton Mifflin, "Heaven knows what they will or won't be because consorting with the Tates is like living with intellectual desperados in the Sargoza Sea." He did not relish the prospect of the dramatic conflicts so often produced by the Tates' fiercely uncompromising intellectual warfare. The Tates' style was, as Lowell noted, "stately yet bohemian, leisurely yet dedicated. A schoolboy's loaded twenty-two rifle hung under the Confederate flag over the fireplace" at Benfolly, an echo of the gun that turns up so often in Agrarian fiction and is the symbol of the Agrarians' yearning to

> Turn [their] eyes to the immoderate past,
> Turn to the inscrutable infantry rising
> Demons out of the earth . . .

and to achieve "the vision," "the arrogant circumstance,"

> Of those who fall
> Rank upon rank, hurried beyond decision.

They could not—or at least did not—achieve it. But in the process of seeking to they produced moments of intellectual and emotional violence of a kind Ford had all his life dreaded.[22]

In the middle of July Ford and Janice, the two Tates, and Lowell jammed themselves into the Tates' Ford and set off for Michigan. The first night they got as far as Urbana, and Ford was so worn out by traveling in these uncomfortable conditions that he and Janice went the rest of the way by train. They were at Olivet until the end of July. Ford had also accepted an invitation from the director of the writers' conference at the University of Colorado, Edward Davison, to be there for the last two weeks—August 1–13—of that conference. As soon as he was finished at Olivet, therefore, he and Janice took the train to Boulder.[23]

Ford was unwell when he reached Boulder. His gout had flared up and the air-conditioning on the train from Chicago, together with the altitude of Boulder, had greatly exacerbated his shortness of breath. "He was overweight, out of condition, breathless and in considerable pain." He found their small furnished apartment hot and stuffy. But, as he always did, he made light of his physical difficulties and went staunchly to work, giving a small informal lecture to a group of twenty or thirty people each of the first four days. These lectures were based on the material he had just been working up for the first book of *The March of Literature* and were a good deal too learned and allusive for much of his audience, though those who could follow them were enthusiastic.[24]

These informal lectures alerted Davison to the weakness of Ford's voice and he provided a microphone for the formal lecture Ford gave the night of August 3, even though the auditorium held only 650 people. Ford lectured on "The Literary Life," describing his relations with Conrad, to whom he referred, somewhat bafflingly, as Józef Korzeniowski. He lectured sitting down, paying no attention to the microphone in front of him; at one point a young woman jumped onto the platform and moved it closer to him, but he soon managed to get away from it again. The results were unfortunate; even those sitting on the platform could hear only a word or phrase here and there. The audience behaved with sympathy and respect, but about halfway through, little clusters of them began quietly to slip away until, by the time Ford had finished, very few were left.*25

Though Ford gave no sign of uneasiness during the lecture itself, this unhappy experience made him wish never again to lecture to a large audience and hate the whole idea of the lecture tour the Dial Press wanted him to make that fall in connection with the publication of *The March of Literature*. "Some fellow," he wrote George Keating, "wants me to do a lecturing tour which is a thing I despise and detest, but if he offers me a sufficiently attractive program I shall have to accept it, though I expect the winter travelling will finish me off." In the event, bad health prevented his making this lecture tour he contemplated with such dread.26

Ford spent a day or two after his Boulder lecture in bed. But except for a couple of round-table sessions, his work at the conference was now over and he was soon able to enter with his usual pleasure into its social life, the nightly gatherings with John Peale Bishop, John Crowe Ransom, and Sherwood Anderson at the Davisons' house, where he and Janice were now staying in considerably greater comfort. These were thoroughly congenial occasions. On the last night of the conference, there was a farewell dinner, and Ford undertook to prepare it. The menu announced the fare as

Soupe de Poissons au Cocktail
Chevreuil des Prés Salés
Sauce Poivrade

Salade de Saison
Syllabube la Syrene

The *Chevreuil* was actually much-marinated lamb, and Ford was delighted

*Robert Lowell, who was present at Ford's lecture, thought more than inability to hear was involved in the audience's behavior. "I watched," he says, "an audience of three thousand walk out on him, as he exquisitely, ludicrously, and inaudibly imitated the elaborate periphrastic style of Henry James. They could neither hear nor sympathize."

when Davison suborned a neighbor to burst in and announce himself as the game warden come to arrest Ford for killing a deer out of season. After a few extra days in Denver for an exhibition of Janice's paintings they returned to Olivet, "after," as Ford said, "criss-crossing the whole continent from East to West."[27]

At Olivet, Ford and Janice lived in a tiny house, "not much bigger than a hen coop," Robie Macauley says.

> [Ford] was a large stout man and I was always surprised to see that he actually fitted inside. My impression was that the place was in complete chaos and that Ford was the center of disorder. Some operation was always ponderously, with many interruptions, under way. . . .

Once a week, he served tea in the basement room of the Olivet library that was his office. There he was surrounded by an incongruous collection of books, the overflow from the library stacks—books on theology and the evils of tobacco "that all seemed to have been published in Chicago around 1901"; his desk was deep in the manuscripts of unpublished young writers, pages of *The March of Literature,* and packs of his favorite French cigarettes— "Dust and Dung," he called them.[28]

His method of teaching was characteristic. His memory, as Mr. Macauley says, "had rewritten a good deal of the world's literature. . . . He was the least academic man who ever taught and for him all books, in themselves, were contemporaneous."

> He succeeded in giving the impression for instance that, though he had just missed meeting Marlowe in London, he knew all about him and was very much excited by the young man's work.

As a student Mr. Macauley quickly saw through the fanciful literary anecdotes that were Ford's main resource; he saw, too, how much these anecdotes often revealed about their subjects. But what impressed him most was Ford's conviction of the sacred character of the writer's function, the unqualified dedication it required of anyone committed to it. "This is," as Mr. Macauley rightly observes, "a very subversive idea and, if it were taught clearly enough, it would probably . . . reduce all 'creative writing' classes . . . to a couple of students here and there." Of his special kind, Ford was obviously a fine teacher.[29]

Chapter 33

As soon as Ford completed his work at Olivet, they set off for Paris. It was November and Ford caught a cold that affected his weak lungs and brought on another heart attack. Not until the end of February was he able to attend once more to business and even then, he reported, "I am still very weak. ... hardly able to walk a step or two," and not at all sure what had gone on during his illness. "I have," he wrote Unwin, "been extremely ill for a long time and am still very weak, so perhaps you did not write and I only dreamed the letter" he was trying to answer. He was anxious to have Julie come while he was recuperating but she was unable to.

> It is a pity you could not have been here whilst Janice's exhibition was on [he wrote her], because she had to be at the exhibition most of the day and I had to sit here alone and should have been glad of your ministrations for I am still pretty feeble, practically unable to walk and so on.[1]

During the previous autumn at Olivet Ford had begun to think about a radical reformation of the college's curriculum in the humanities. He was full of ideas on the subject that he had been working out for *The March of Literature*, and visions of what he might accomplish flew about in his mind. "I occupy the chair of Comparative Literature at this college in which I am extremely interested," he said, "because I think that eventually it will revolutionize the teaching of the liberal arts in this country," and, taking the word for the deed as he so often did, he was presently saying that " ... I am in demand for re-organising the literary departments of several universities" in the United States.[2]

These prospects made him think of Pound, the great expert on education. As he wrote Pound, "I don't take myself to be an educational panjandrum and would like to talk the subject over with you." He worried a good deal, anyhow, about how Pound was managing to live. As soon as he left Olivet, he wrote President Brewer suggesting they include Pound in the next writers' conference at a fee of $500, an exorbitant sum for Olivet, and also try to get Pound to come there permanently at the same salary as Ford. President Brewer tactfully turned down Ford's suggestion about the writers' conference but agreed to let him discuss a regular appointment with Pound. "Dear Bertran de Struwwelpeter y Bergerac," Ford wrote, recalling Pound's habit of beginning his letters with teasing allusions to Ford's baronial German ancestry ("My deah ole Freiherr von Bluggerwitzkoff late baron of the Sunk Ports etc"). "It is one of my normal worries thinking about your material prospects." He knew Pound hated the idea of living in the United States, but he thought he could meet that difficulty. "Of course I know that one cannot expect a man of your age to change his habits or renier his material gods," he wrote. "But you have arrived at an age when few men save themselves unless they do change their habits and travel a little." He also suggested that Pound was unnecessarily violent in his refusal to work even with the best of the people who were trying to do something about the disgraceful state of American education.

Here, he pointed out, was "a permanent contract—to fill a job [such as] I'm filling myself and if it's good enough for me it's damn good enough for you, concealed son of the authoress of John Halifax Gentleman though you be." It would, he said, allow Pound "to stroll for eight months of a year—or several years—about the philosophers' groves of Olivet" at a living wage and with no serious teaching responsibilities, and it would give him "a working, model educational machine to play with." But knowing Pound as he did, Ford was under no serious illusion that Pound would be moved by these arguments. "Still I know all this is beating the wind," he concluded. "The main point is that I should like to see you... to talk the subject [of educational reform] over with you."[3]

Pound did not disappoint Ford's expectations.

Dear Fordie
Vurry sorry you have been ill. Does Olivet USE my text books?
Will the clog-dancer [Ford had jokingly described President Brewer as "one of the best clog-dancers in the world"] communicate with me direct and ANSWER a few civil questions?
Will he GET a printing press/ LINO or amonotype/ I.E. practical and not fancy hand arty machine for the DISTRIBUTION of

knowledge and ideas? No use discussing details viva voce unless or until fundamentals can be got on paper.

> you git well.
>
> Yrz deevotedly
>
> Ez
>
> and dont think I dont appreciate yr/ noble efforks on my behalve.
> am perfectly willing to ASSIST Olivet, but not to lay down my life

When Ford replied to this postal card with a repetition of his arguments Pound became more definite, "1. I do NOT want your job 2. If Olivet wants me to do 1500 dollars worth of work or even less in my own way, I am ready to talk. . . . " In his own way, Ford could be as stubborn as Pound and he tried a third time. "Dear ole Fordie," Pound answered. "ONCE you get an idea in yr/ head it is difficult to deracinate it. Let me put it in yet another form. I do not want YOUR job. I do not want the JOB you have got/ whether you keep it or not. I will not go to Olivet and teach."⁴

There was excellent sense as well as affection in Ford's proposal, however much he may—in his anxiety to persuade Pound—have exaggerated the advantages of life at Olivet. He was thoroughly impatient with Pound's stubborn resistance—so very like his own in similar situations—to the suggestions that Pound take what he could get for the chance to work such reforms as he could. In his frustration, Ford came as near as he ever had to writing Pound in his "crushing" manner. "Dear Ezra," he began one of his letters,

> Do exercise a little imagination and try to understand the situation. I am an *extremely* sick man and your incomprehensible scrawls are a torture to me—to read and to have to answer. Get the waiter at your hotel to write your letters for you; he will at least write comprehensible dog-English. Your 1892 O. Henry stuff is wearisomely incomprehensible by now.

In the end, however, Ford had to recognize that Pound was too much for him, and he wrote President Brewer that Pound did not want a job in the United States. At the same time he announced that he would return in April to "take up my professorial duties at Olivet. . . . "⁵

He and Janice sailed for America on the *Normandie* on March 23 and arrived at Olivet early in April—in a blizzard. Whether Ford's health had actually improved or the change—always stimulating to him—made him feel so, he was more cheerful than he had been since his illness and, once the blizzard was over, even began to think the weather "fairly springlike." "I seem," he wrote Paul Palmer, "to be slowly getting a little strength together. . . . If we can ever find something decent to eat I might once more resume my Gargantuan activities. As it is, I can't do much more than crawl about." Nonetheless he was able to put the finishing touches on the first half of *The March of Literature* and send it off to the Dial Press.[6]

When his health failed to improve, however, he began to feel that the "fairly springlike" weather of Michigan was unendurable. "For myself," he said, "I am now so crippled with rheumatism that I can't even dress myself or brush my own hair. It is the cussedly damp climate of this place and I may not suppose I shall ever be even nearly well again until I can get to Provence." His beloved Provence would cure anything, even what was probably by this time in his life incurable.[7]

In June President Brewer persuaded the trustees of Olivet to give Ford an honorary degree. "Should a little bird whisper to you that you will henceforth be able to print L.L.D. after my name on titlepages etc. it will be true," he wrote Unwin; Unwin took the hint; on the title page of *The March of Literature* Ford is "D. Litt." An honorary degree from Olivet College (305 students, 45 teachers) was not an overwhelming distinction, but Ford was delighted with it, contributing information for the citation in his most enthusiastically impressionistic vein. At the Olivet commencement on June 19, Professor Akley, the college orator, found himself telling the assembled company that Ford was "a Dr. of Agriculture of the University of Sorbonne," that he had "known war as a colonel in charge of two regiments in action," that he had been the "first to praise Dreiser in England, first to credit Joyce and Stein . . . first to publish a short story by Arnold Bennett and by Galsworthy" and was the "guarantor of Conrad's first novel, Aylmer's Folly." " . . . my proper style," Ford wrote his daughter, "is now F. M. F., D. Lit.; Professor Emeritus of Comparative Literature &c. &c. So the laugh is on me."[8]

After the pleasures of dressing up in academic robes and hearing himself praised, Ford settled down to the strenuous work of finishing *The March of Literature.* He was anxious to have the book come out that fall; he needed the money. He promised the Dial Press that he would complete his book by July fourteenth and he was as good as his word. "I finished the HISTORY OF LITERATURE with a tremendous rush on Tuesday the 12 inst.," he wrote Unwin, " . . . doing nothing else but write from five in the morning till seven in the evening in order to get it finished." The next day he and Janice went ceremoniously to Battle Creek to express the manuscript to the Dial Press.[9]

Dial, in its turn, promised to rush the galleys, and the first fifteen of them arrived the third week of July. They were a shock; a number of the quotations Ford had laboriously culled from his reading, many of them untranslated because he had included them to suggest nuances of style, had been cut by Dial's editor, Vernon. Ford returned these galleys promptly, "except for the two... in which the quotations are omitted.... I cannot possibly let the book go to press without these," he said, "as the letterpress is incomprehensible without them." It is debatable whether Ford should have included all the quotations he did; what is not debatable is Vernon's deleting them without consulting Ford. In his reply to Ford, Vernon argued only to the first question; in addition he directed Ford to translate the remaining quotations, blithely ignoring Ford's objection to his deciding these questions without consultation. As so often happened when Ford was met with a blank refusal to recognize that his case existed, he fell into angry despair. "Do what you like to book," he wired Dial. "I have lost all interest in it. And there will be an English edition." When he reported his troubles with the Dial Press to George Keating, Keating tried once more to persuade Ford that his refusal to deal with established publishers made such difficulties inevitable. But he refused to believe Keating; to do so would be to admit that his previous complaints against these older publishers had been unjustified.

I appreciate yr. concern in asking me to go to the older publishers [he said] but they are no good for my type of work. Lippincott was a defeat; the Oxford University Press a disaster; Houghton Mifflin complete ruin.... Allen & Unwin... can sell me in England because I am a classic but this country won't buy classics... [10]

The possibility that Ford might refuse to help sell the book brought Dial's president, Burton C. Hoffman, into action. The day they received Ford's wire he wrote a five-page letter in which he attempted to explain Vernon's action.

[Deletions] have... been made to eliminate such difficult untranslated passages as Mr. Vernon, our editorial board and our sales staff felt would hinder the chances of the book's attaining a wide sale.

Ford replied: "Mr. Vernon cut out those extremely essential French passages without consulting me at all—that is what I resent." Nevertheless, he knew that the deleted quotations could, at this stage, be reinserted only at a prohibitive cost—as Vernon no doubt had foreseen when he gave Ford no hint of them until the book was in galleys. He therefore digested his resentment, accepted Hoffman's proposal of a lecture tour to advertise the book, and even arranged on his own a radio talk "about the book on a nation wide and indeed world-wide network. . . . "[11]

After all these concessions to what Dial assured him their commercial wisdom dictated, it turned out that Dial had badly miscalculated the market situation. They were not entirely to blame for this miscalculation. Ford was a new author to them, and they were unaware of his reputation with the bookstores. They began with high hopes of making *The March of Literature* another such success as Van Wyck Brooks's *Flowering of New England* or Will Durant's *Story of Philosophy*. But, in order to get the book out quickly, they hurried their prepublication advertising and sent their salesmen out without any knowledge of Ford's book; the salesmen had to promote it on the reputation of Ford's previous books, and that turned out to be disastrous. As early as August 1, 1938, Hoffman was telling Ford that *The March of Literature*

> is, unfortunately, being only indifferently received by the booksellers to whom it has been presented so far. . . . In the first place, your selling reputation in this country is not a good one. In the second place, booksellers have never been able to dispose of large quantities of your book[s], and in the third place, not having seen the finished book . . . they have felt it was just another book on literature.[12]

Ford's health had not been improved by the strenuous effort he had made to finish *The March of Literature*, but he tried hard to believe that the main difficulty was Olivet's climate.

> I'm still fairly dizzy with finishing [*The March of Literature*] and half crippled with rheumatism. The climate of this place is *cruel!* We hope to leave it for good in the beginning of September & to be in New York on & off till December & then Provenceward Ho!

Considering how important he believed the educational reform he was initiating at Olivet, this eagerness to get away shows how ill he really felt. He even returned the Unwin proofs of *Provence* (published in England in November, 1938) unread, with the admission that "I simply do not feel well enough actually to correct the book." He and Janice made their escape from the "atrocious climate" of Olivet on September 9, 1938.[13]

Ford still hoped that *The March of Literature* would be a commercial success and offered to help in any way he could. He had worked harder gathering material for it than he had for any book he ever wrote: the amount of rereading he had done was staggering, and the strain of writing its nearly 900 pages had cost him much more than he could afford. He had to believe the book was going to be the success he thought it deserved to be and was bound to do everything in his power to help it.[14]

The March of Literature is the final manifestation of Ford's lifelong devotion to literature with all its intense loyalties and its vigorous prejudices. " . . . for him," as Robie Macauley says, "all books . . . were contemporaneous. . . . No good book was ever entombed in the Dewey Decimal System; it had always just been published and most of its career was before it." *The March of Literature* begins for Ford in Babylon and ends with what were for him the most recent "Impressionists"—René Béhaine, Virginia Woolf, and the young Middle Western novelists. He consciously sought "to find as it were a balance between national conceptions, his own taste and the standards of wide-spread schools," but it was impossible for him to look at literature except in the light of the beliefs he had been cultivating for a lifetime. He believed much too deeply that the only true civilization was "a Latin—a Mediterranean—civilization [that] has a definite place for the providers of literature" not to be biassed in favor of the Latin literatures.

> A Cicero can mould the fortunes of an empire, a Lamartine those of a republic; the lightest word of a Victor Hugo will travel to the ear of the remotest peasant in the land. . . . A member of the French Academy has the precedence of a Marshal of France. . . . But . . . look at any time in one or other half of Anglo-Saxondom and you will find our best writers starving.

He was much too devoted to his idea of the Middle Ages not to give a great deal of attention to that "tumultuous, mad, bloodthirsty, sadistic affair with highlights of . . . chivalrous rules for the conducting of single combats . . . [and] mediaevally incestuous, murdering mercenary princes who built the most beautiful palaces and collected Greek manuscripts with the passion of mad misers." He valued too highly the idea of the conscious artist not to favor the craftsman.

> We stand for Homer and the Greek lyricists as against Virgil and the Augustan Romans; for the middle ages as against the renaissance; for the seventeenth as against the eighteenth century; for the realists as against the romantics; and, above all, for the conscious literary artist as against the inspired. . . . [15]

"When you have said the names of the *Odyssey*, of the Bible, of *Oedipus Tyrannus*, of the *Divine Comedy* itself and the great and little testaments of Villon you have almost exhausted the catalogue of the great . . . works of humanity." The omissions from this list are certainly notable. Ford was equally uncompromising in judging later writers: Ben Jonson, Milton, George Eliot, Joyce—to choose at random—he almost wholly ignores. Scott is given a page and a half of denigration, Chateaubriand five pages of praise.

Six pages of quotation are given to Spanish picaresque tales, half a page to Shakespeare's plays. A curious element of prudery occasionally creeps in: he says *The Decameron* consists of "stories rather below the level of imagination that is to be found in any hedgerow inn," pronounces *The Country Wife* a piece of "shapeless bawdiness," and describes *Tom Jones* as "one of the most immoral books ever written." He even persuades himself that Oscar Wilde's personal "excesses . . . as in subsequent private conversations he confessed, used to make him vomit."[16]

His literary prejudices are firmly expressed. He attacks Cervantes as a bad writer because Cervantes destroyed "the gentle ideal of chivalry [that] might have saved our unfortunate civilization" and rendered "the world fit for Big Business." He pronounces the "sticky jewelled" verse of Sidney, Spenser, and Lyly "perfectly unreadable." He says the seventeenth century's great prose style "had, by the eighteenth, deteriorated into a sort of mechanical rhythm" that became, by the nineteenth century, "timid and indefinite." It "came alive again at the hands of W. E. Henley and his group"; meanwhile, however, "between the death of Swift in 1745 . . . and . . . Cardinal Newman . . . almost no imaginative prose masterpieces saw the light. . . . " Goldsmith was, "unconscionably, a literary hack," Pope the voice of "the gross materialism that the Hanoverians brought to Anglo-Saxondom," Sir Walter Scott an "amateur literary hack," and Byron "odious because he writes the thoughts of a city clerk in metropolitan clerical vernacular." The Victorians produced only two great works of the imagination, *Vanity Fair* and *The Way of All Flesh.*[17]

But if *The March of Literature* has the eccentricities of Ford's personal tastes, it also has the advantages of them. His treatment of the writers he admires is vivid with affection. He lingers over the image of Horace "forever prosperous, forever sunny, forever frugally generous." He delights in Ovid's easy way of dashing "off with the maids to gather chromatic blossoms . . . of which Ovid does not even know the names," and then suddenly remembering "that he is really writing about a kidnapping." It is all "very lovely and there is room in the world for that kind of fluidity and grace." Often, as in his accounts of Virgil reading the *Aeneid* to the court of Augustus or of Shakespeare pouring over French with the daughter of the silk weaver of Spitalfields with whom he lodged, the historical novelist in him takes over with striking effectiveness. And sometimes he hits on a striking judgment, as when he says that Shelley "is almost never natural . . . almost never not intent on showing himself the champion of freedom, the Satan of a Hanoverian Heaven."[18]

The March of Literature is very much Ford's history of literature, of the Greek and Latin authors he had learned to love at school, of the troubadours admired by his grandfather and his father, of the minnesingers of his ancestral home, of the modern novelists he thought Impressionists. It has the virtues and the faults of such a history, the virtues of a passionate, lifelong commitment, the faults of deliberately cultivated prejudices.

Ford's health continued to grow worse. Because of his heart condition, the doctors were anxious about his weight, which was by this time better than 240 pounds; they put him on a diet. But Ford's pleasure in society and his habit of hard work made it impossible for him to slow down. His pocket diary shows that in November and December he lunched or dined out a dozen times, attended a half-dozen concerts, ballets, or plays, saw the Cornell-Columbia football game (he was now becoming an expert: the "game was too much of a walkover for Cornell to be very thrilling"), had fifteen or twenty engagements with literary people of various sorts, and lectured half-a-dozen times, not only in New York but in Boston and at Bennington and Briarcliff. No wonder he was obliged to write Stanley Unwin in October that "at the moment I am not very well and am also so extremely busy that I will put off writing . . . until my head is slightly clearer."[19]

He did, however, refuse to take the lecture tour that the Dial Press had been trying to arrange for him. This made certain difficulties for him in his relations with Olivet.

> . . . the doctor says I certainly mustn't travel in order to lecture during the winter [he wrote President Brewer], so I shan't be coming to either Evanston or Kalamazoo. I am very sorry but I keep on being rather ill. . . . This puts me rather in a dilemma as to the many statements I have been making here, there, and everywhere about your literary faculty.

He had advertised widely the revolution in the teaching of literature he was working at Olivet, and since he was also applying for "a permanent professorial permis de séjour" in the United States, he wanted to remain a professor at Olivet. Brewer solved the problem for him by making him "Professor of Comparative Literature on leave."[20]

Meanwhile, his relations with Dial had been steadily worsening. He had proposed that they put him in charge of their fiction list and got the impression they were going to accept his terms. "I must say," he wrote Unwin, "I find them very agreeable people to work with." Dial then turned down Ford's suggestion that he write a book on the international situation and failed to show any enthusiasm for the young novelists he recommended to them. In addition, they tactlessly offered him $100 a month to be their "fiction editor and literary advisor." They thus made themselves distinctly less agreeable, and Ford decided to leave them—"more," as he wrote Stanley Unwin, "because I found them unsupportable as individuals than because they were also rather too skillful in making up their accounts."[21]

Ford found Dial's attitude hard to understand. In the middle of November the P.E.N. Club had given a dinner at the Algonquin in honor of Pearl Buck, Sinclair Lewis, and Ford, and Sinclair Lewis had made a speech in which he praised Ford to the skies; Ford took this praise literally.

> It is very curious [he thought]: I have really an enormous reputation here. I am generally regarded as the Dean of American Letters and I am told that if I were American I should be a certainty for the Nobel Prize. . . . Mr. Lewis . . . if you please . . . styled me not only the Dean of American Letters but the most eminent man of letters not only in English but in the world and the sentiment was received with unanimous applause. In spite of that my books sell very little—

and the Dial Press offered him $100 a month to edit their fiction.

> I think it must be evident to you by now [he wrote Hoffman] that the Dial is not the publishing house for me nor I the writer for the Dial. . . . There would be no purpose in my trying to edit your fiction since what you think you could sell I should not like and you would not think you could sell what I should like. . . . Will you please regard this as final?[22]

This break with Dial made his financial situation once more acute, and he had to borrow £250 from Stanley Unwin. It also meant another harrowing round of negotiations with New York publishers. He began with Quincy Howe of Simon and Schuster, with whom he lunched late in November. He proposed to Simon and Schuster the final volume of the Great Trade Route trilogy, to be called *Forty Years of Travel in America;* this would, as he told Unwin when he proposed it to them, cover "the parts of [the Great Trade Route] which I have not hitherto treated—i.e. the English South Coast, the U.S. deep SOUTH and back by way of the Azores, Tangiers, Jaffa and the Mediterranean shores." He also offered Simon and Schuster a novel, the outline of which shows that it was to be *Professor's Progress,* which he was working on when he died. In addition he wanted Simon and Schuster to publish his completed *A History of Our Own Times from 1895* and "an anthology," presumably of his own work. The terms he suggested were his usual ones; they were unacceptable to Simon and Schuster. "I'm sorry to say," Howe wrote George Bye, "that nobody here feels that Simon and

Schuster should go in on anything like the sort of arrangement [Ford] has in mind, which would call for an advance on each new book to be based on the total earnings of the previous book." It was the following spring before he was able to establish himself with a publisher.[23]

By the end of the year he was again seriously worried about his health. " ... I am rather crippled," he told Unwin, "not so much by rheumatism as by the fierce dopes that the American doctors are giving me to cure that complaint." This disapproval of the treatment he was undergoing led him to look for a new doctor; a week later he was saying, "I shall be beginning a new sort of treatment next Monday that may restore me to some sort of activity," and a month later he reported that

> I am slowly picking up from a bad relapse. I have got pretty well about a month ago [when he changed doctors], then I began to work again and went about and lectured and dined and went to receptions and then had another collapse so that I've only just begun to think of work again—that is to say, I have written slowly the first two chapters of a novel [Professor's Progress]. ...

In a spurt of optimism, he decided that his new doctors had solved all his problems by raising his diaphragm.

> I have really had a miserable experience with my health and doctors for a long time [he wrote Brewer] until at last, more or less by accident, we hit upon a really miraculous doctor who found out after eight others had given wrong diagnosis [sic] that I had something internal displaced and since then I have made—umberüfen—remarkable strides toward physical and mental recovery.[24]

But, though he was unquestionably ill, Ford had not slowed down as much as his accounts of his health suggest. In January he put considerable time into organizing a society he called The Friends of William Carlos Williams. Williams never did make out quite what this was all about, but he was fond of Ford, who reminded him of his father. "I've gotten to like the man," he told Robert McAlmon. "If I can be of use to him towards the finish of his life, and let me tell you it is toward the finish of his life unless I'm much mistaken, I'm willing to let him go ahead." "What he saw in me, an American[,] even though he pretended to be a poet, I could never make out," he added. What Williams saw in Ford, rightly or wrongly, was a man after his own heart:

> Thank God you were not delicate, you let the world in
> and lied! damn it you lied grossly sometimes. But it
>   was all, I see now,
> a carelessness, the part of a man that is homeless here on earth.

Provence! the fat-assed Ford will never again strain the chairs of
                              your cafés,
pull and pare for his dish your sacred garlic, grunt and sweat and
                              lick
his lips. Gross as the world he has left to us he has become a part of
that of which you were the known part, Provence, he loved
                              so well.[25]

Ford talked a number of his friends into joining The Friends of William
Carlos Williams and the society met a few times in various Greenwich
Village restaurants for dinners and speeches. Part of the reason for Williams'
confusion about Ford's purpose was that Williams was only the nominal
object of the organization.

> Between ourselves, but see that it is strictly between ourselves
> [Ford said in inviting Brewer to become a member], I am really
> trying to get a kind of Academie Goncourt in this country for the
> benefit of more thoughtful and read writers . . . and if the funds
> should run to it, we would probably give an annual prize like the Prix
> Goncourt.

Pound saw real possibilities in this idea. "A 'sort of' Academie Goncourt
COULD be used as a prod. to the useless Institoot of Letters. . . . THAT
body IF seriously criticized/ Murry Butler strangled and Canby educated or
drowned COULD be useful. . . . "[26]

As soon as The Friends of William Carlos Williams was organized, Ford
also began making plans to revive *The Transatlantic Review.* Unwin was to
handle the magazine in London and Stokes, with whom he had just completed arrangements for the publication of his own books, in America. He
was feeling a good deal better during these early months of 1939; "I am really
kept in such a continuous whirl making up for the time lost during my
illness," he said with relish to Crankshaw, "that I haven't got the brain to
write anything with even the most minute degree of subtlety." He also
asked George Keating for business advice and financial help with the new
Transatlantic. " . . . the project has," he told Keating, "already taken serious
shape. . . . My success in England has now become so marked that I think
I can afford to give time to this project. . . . " Keating found a lady who
showed some interest in financing the *Review,* but he insisted that it be run
from New York, possibly because he wished to keep an eye on Ford. This
did not, however, suit Ford. "I have had to put off restarting the *Transatlantic,*" he wrote William Bird; "the people who are furnishing the money
. . . would go on if I wished to publish here but that doesn't suit me at all.

... " Allen Tate had meantime suggested there might be some hope of enlisting the aid of his sister-in-law and Ford proposed she advance $15,000. These plans for renewing Ford's "Organ of the Seven Arts and the Three Democracies" had not developed beyond this point when, two months later, he sailed for France.[27]

By the middle of March, Ford had also signed a contract with Frederick A. Stokes for *Professor's Progress* and the third volume of his trilogy about the Great Trade Route. In the fall of 1938, he had proposed to Dial and to Unwin that he "write a book on the international situation from my rather aloof— nowadays distinctly very left—point of view." Unwin accepted but Dial turned the idea down. He then decided not to write this book but to include his new political views in the final volume of his *Great Trade Route* trilogy. His conception of the political situation is suggested by his remark to Henry Goddard Leach that "Governor Cox told me that almost every house in Grosse Point is an arms depot ... the extremists of the Right here would prefer German rule to Left rule even if established at the price of blood." Stokes made him an advance of $750 on the novel. With his publishing plan settled, he and Janice paid a ten-day visit to Olivet, and by the end of April he was telling Stokes that he was "making some progress with the Professor book," perhaps all the progress he ever made, for it remained unfinished at his death.[28]

Ford described *Professor's Progress* to Stanley Unwin as "a kind of projection of the way the intelligentsia of practically all the nations have swung latterly towards the left in politics." But *Professor's Progress* is essentially Ford's improved version of his own life during his last years. It describes the career of Godfrey Havermeyer Bullen, an "internationally known ... Professor of Modern History" at Essex University, some twenty-eight miles "upstate" from New York City. Bullen's main interest is the economic history of the nineteenth century (Ford's *A History of Our Own Times*). As the novel opens, Bullen has just inherited properties worth $1,850,000 from a brother; he has sold these properties and bought annuities in his wife's name. He irritates the bankers who advise him by refusing to stipulate that the annuities revert to him if he and his wife are ever divorced and, because of his "old-fashioned Tory patriotism," insisting on selling out only to firms that have Edward Ashburnham's paternal concern for their employees. "Godfrey," his wife, Mary Juliana, says, "isn't a business man. He's a gentleman." It is a delight to him that he is now "free [to retire and] to occupy his house in Washington Square and to know that no small financial embarrassments would ever again distract his life of tranquil thought"; his intention is to

"The Good Soldier," ca. 1915.

Coopers Cottage in Bedham, with a portrait of Stella at the left.

Ford at the cottage with Penny, his prize goat, 1921.

Brigit Patmore with Michael Arlen, in the twenties.

Stella Bowen.

*Ford and Pound before the Columbus monument
at Rapallo, ca. 1927.*

Rene Wright as she appeared in 1930.
(*C. F. Dieckman*/St. Louis Post Dispatch)

Ford and Julie at Cap Brun, 1930's.

On the terrace of the Villa Paul, 1930's.

Caroline Tate, Janice, Ford, and Allen Tate, Clarksville, Tennessee, 1930's.

Ford and Janice,
Fittleworth in the 1930's.

Ford and Janice on the Riviera, 1930's.

*Ford receiving his honorary degree at Olivet College. At the center,
Joseph Brewer, president of the college.*

spend the next ten years on a life of Freycinet, the nineteenth-century French statesman.[29]

Bullen is "high-coloured; red-golden haired; good humoured; sound [of] wind and limb; happily married; long sighted," all of which Ford either was or wanted to be (Ford described himself at this time as a "platinum blond, rosy-cheeked, six foot one, 240 pound—otherwise 17 stone 2—English gentleman"). Bullen has been revising the Essex University curriculum in the nationally significant way Ford believed he had been changing Olivet's. "It had been a not disagreeable . . . it had been an almost glowing period of his life. It is pleasant and inspiriting as you approach your prime to be not merely popular with, but intimately treated by, the vivid youth of your day"; Bullen had personally taken responsibility for the "morals and probable future careers" of half-a-dozen students a year with striking success. "Time and again students . . . after two minutes' acquaintance . . . would show . . . they would be ready to accept him as counsellor, guide, guardian, inspiration, Dutch uncle! . . . Students and others." Here is Ford's longing to believe that, even at sixty-six, he could be the affable, influential "Dutch uncle" to young intellectuals.[30]

Bullen has always been deeply concerned to understand society, as Ford believed he had been. But now, under the influence of his Marxist wife, he has begun to feel that the institutions he has spent his life studying are instruments of power and that if he, with his profound understanding of them, does not seek to control them, they will be controlled by evil men. He is approached by a Senator Fischauer (roughly modeled on Howard Scott, the Technocrat), "a banal parody of Hitler in terms of the almost forgotten madness called Technocracy." Fischauer's first idea is to arrange to have Bullen's life of Freycinet published "at an extremely handsome rate of honorarium," and then to buy up "a million or more copies" to distribute as propaganda. This idea horrifies Bullen; "Sooner than let my book become the tool of any political party," he says ("gently but peremptorily"), "I would leave it unwritten. . . . I detest all politicians and *all* their enactments. But I should particularly dislike the prospect of a Facist organization . . . in this country." Fischauer then discovers that Bullen has "a great gift of extempore speaking and a really admirable delivery" and tries to get him to stump the country for him. This experience with Fischauer convinces Bullen that he must use his immense charm and his great talents to stop such people. The reflection of Ford's view of himself in all this is obvious.[31]

Under the influence of the Tates' conspiratorial view of the intellectual struggle they were engaged in and the conviction that young teachers were deeply impressed by the reforms he had introduced at Olivet, Ford had become convinced that there was an unorganized underground of young intellectuals fighting the established professors throughout the American academic world, and he has Bullen become—as he no doubt dreamed of becoming himself—the leader of this group.

> It was as if right over his imaginary map [of the United States] there arose, like the castles and abbeys and cathedrals, on the map of Europe, the collegiate spires beneath which, immured and despised by the haughtier dons, sat one or two learned, constructive, clear spirits. The land was lurching like a galleon steered by a drunken helmsman into the Gothic night of materialism and mailed ballyhoo. The humanities were spat upon; the Arts trampled under foot, the historic sense spurned and ridiculed—in all these haunts of Instruction—those whorehouses of the trades and paid sciences.... The literary and historic professoriate were all but starved; but they had specially endowed Window Dressing Faculty with twenty-four branches all of whose professors lived on the scale of Hollywood Stars. It was insupportable.*[32]

If he was to lead these "lonely monks in lost valleys," Ford would have to find some way to make his Tory anarchism palatable to them. In *Vive le Roy* he had tried to make the young Leftists recognize the superiority of his views, and recently he had even gone on record—in reply to one of the endless questionnaires the Communists sent out in those days to "Writers and Intellectuals"—as believing that "universal fascism is now, outside the U.S.S.R., actually in operation." "The world," he believed as passionately as any young radical, "was rotten!" His old sympathy with Zionism, dating back to the time he had advised Charles Masterman about the Balfour Declaration and perhaps increased by his devotion to Janice, who was of Jewish descent, made him particularly sensitive to the horrors of German anti-Semitism; this was a subject on which he could feel himself wholeheartedly in agreement with his young radical friends. But the essential rottenness of the world was for him, as it always had been, "its disdain for Learning and the Arts... its ferocities... its materialisms...." It is Bullen's belief—as it was that of Ford the "genuinely Catholic spirit" and Small Producer—that "the first measure of any Utopian Parliament would rid the world forever of

*The citation for Ford's honorary degree, which he helped compose, says of him that, "as the monks of the early monastic orders stood by the culture of remembered antiquity amidst the undignified barbarities of medieval Anglo-Saxon leisure, so has this genuine Catholic spirit stood incorruptibly by art ... while his race was thinking with its blood, the circulating medium of its barbarous economic system."

the Industrial System." Now Ford thought he had found the way to gain the sympathy of the young for these views. Stressing the cultural evils of a developed capitalist society—something that both the Marxist intellectuals of New York and the stern Agrarians of Benfolly could agree on—he set his professor to overcome these evils with the assistance of the "learned, constructive, clear spirits" beneath the dreaming spires of America's collegiate Gothic campuses. He satirizes his novel's Stalinist, Bullen's research assistant Frenssen, and his royalists, exiled princes of the Ukraine, though Bullen sympathizes with the intellectual Marxism of his wife and the romantic royalism of his secretary, Carol Handy, who is in love with one of the Ukrainian princes.[33]

He feels specially tender toward Commandatore Raymondo Poggio, who is, as Ford felt he was, a neglected and lonely old buffalo. Poggio had been with Garibaldi and still preserves his old-fashioned libertarianism. He believes himself a great composer, but he has been reduced to making a living by playing patriotic songs from Garibaldi's time to bored New York Italians in a restaurant whose proprietor employs him out of pity. When the restaurant is sold, he loses his job; at the same time he is told that the Metropolitan Musem (Ford presumably means the New York Public Library) will accept an artist's manuscripts only after he is dead. Poggio therefore carefully wraps up the scores of his "unsupportably dull violin sonatas," mails them to the Metropolitan, and commits suicide. Ford comments that the death of Austria in the German annexation of March, 1939, and the death of this last surviving Garibaldine coincide.[34]

The manuscript of *Professor's Progress* ends here, but, according to the outline, Professor Bullen would ultimately, like all Ford's heroes, have been defeated by his virtues. His wife, Mary Juliana, ceasing to be a merely intellectual Marxist, would first become the mistress and then—after divorcing Bullen—the wife of Bullen's Stalinist secretary, Frenssen; they would live comfortably on the annuities Bullen had refused to stipulate would return to him if Mary Juliana ever divorced him. Carol Handy, Bullen's secretary, then becomes his mistress, and with the last of the money Mary Juliana has left him, he produces the plays Prince Michael has written for Carol to star in; when this money is gone, Carol leaves him for Prince Michael. Bullen then retires to "quite a small mid-Western college," in Michigan, where he settles down to writing his life of Freycinet.

Chapter 34

🎜

Late in April, 1939, Ford and Janice went to Greensboro, North Carolina, to visit the Tates, who were teaching at the Women's College there.

> Ford [Mrs. Tate recalled] . . . seemed to feel the heat even more than we had feared that he would. [We] debated as to whether it would be safe to let the old man make the talk he was bent on making. When we reached the classroom the next morning and I saw that his veined, rubicund face had gone ashen from the effort of climbing the stairs I wished that I had not accepted his offer to speak. He sat down at one end of a long table, his chair pushed well back in order to accommodate his great paunch, his legs spread wide to support his great weight. . . . I remember thinking that he looked like a big white whale as he sat there, forcing the breaths through his wide open mouth.

But if this occasion was a great physical effort for Ford, his spirit was unflagging. As he sat waiting for the class, he picked up a copy of *The Saturday Evening Post* that lay on the table and, after glancing at a story in it, "Suddenly . . . looked up. The fishlike gaze brightened. He said, with a chuckle: 'I see that our method has reached the *Post.*' " "Our method" was Ford's Impressionism.[1]

This visit revived Ford's interest in the South, and he began planning to spend the summer there; he wrote to a distant cousin of his, Gerald Tetley, in Danville, Virginia, asking if Tetley could find them some place there to live. But by the time Tetley had, Ford's mind had changed. "Our plans for going South on this continent this summer," he told Allen Tate, "have given place to an invincible yen for Europe." He had convinced himself that only European cooking could cure his illness. " . . . my doctor says that a long course of French cooking is the only thing that can finally restore me to health and certainly the idea of never seeing a canned vegetable or meat that has been refrigerated presents attraction that I can hardly describe." They did not dare go all the way to Provence but settled for staying "in the neighborhood of Havre for three or four months simply because Havre is a good jumping off place in case, because of war alarms, we wanted to skip. . . . " If they could, they would stay there until they had to return to Olivet for a fortnight in October for Ford to "deliver a series of lectures covering the whole of modern literary technique."[2]

During May, as they were getting ready to sail for France, Pound turned up in New York. "He seemed," Janice remembered, "irritated at the thought that Ford might think he was in Mussolini's pay because he came over in the royal suite on an Italian boat. (I don't think Ford thought it.)" Pound had come to America primarily to interest influential American politicians in Major Douglas' economic theories. On May 25, when William Carlos Williams stopped by the Fords' flat to say good-by, Ford told him that they had been arguing with Pound in favor of lechery "or anything at all to keep him amused and distracted"—and perhaps off the subject of Major Douglas.[3]

The day they sailed (May 30), Ford started one more, final quarrel with his publishers by writing George Bye that "I am so fed up with Stokes from every possible point of view that if you feel it advisable and could switch me and all my works over to Harrison Smith, I think I should be glad." He was specially angry at Stokes for having "turned down every one of the manuscripts, I have strongly recommended to them. . . . " He had also found them "petty-fogging" about his affairs. Bye urged Ford to stick with Stokes and tried to calm him with the news that he had collected $375 more on the advance for *Professor's Progress,* but the tone of Ford's letter suggests that, if he had lived to do so, he would soon have broken with Stokes.[4]

Ford fell ill during their crossing on the *Normandie.* They went to Honfleur, across the Seine from Le Havre, and when, after a week there, he was no better, Janice became worried enough to write Stella to ask if Julie could come, and Stella brought her. But the end of Julie's last year at Michael St. Denis' London Theatre Studio was approaching and she had to go back to London after a few days, leaving Janice alone once more to bear the burden of Ford's illness.*[5]

---

*In 1946, Julie married a German exile writer named Roland Loewe. Shortly after, Stella became ill with an inoperable cancer, but she was determined to live to see the grandchild Julie was then carrying, and did. Julian Loewe was born October 7, 1947, Stella died October 30. She

Ford was suffering from uremia, and after Julie left he became much iller. When he had remained so for nearly two weeks, it became necessary to get him to a hospital, and on June 24 Janice moved him to the Clinique St. François in the Avenue de la Republique in Deauville, "a pleasant hospital . . . run by the most charming and devoted nuns." There Ford appeared to improve momentarily, but on June 26, he grew worse again.

We were waiting for the clinic doctor to come all day in the hope that he could relieve the nausea [Janice wrote Julie after Ford's death]. He never came. . . . About a quarter to five [Ford] suddenly said he was hungry . . . so I called the sister. . . . After she left . . . he made some movement and fell forward into my arms. I don't believe he was conscious of what was happening. He died almost immediately.

His heart had at last failed.[6]

Janice got in touch with an old friend in Paris, Lucie Le Son, who agreed to let their friends know of Ford's death. With her clear understanding of Ford's feelings, Janice knew that Ford would want to be properly buried by the Church, with some recognition from fellow writers of the kind he had felt had to be given to Proust in 1922. " . . . Though [Ford] was not croyant," she said " . . . he would consider [a proper funeral] convenable."[7]

Only Mrs. Le Son came from Paris; Edward Crankshaw, hearing the news on the BBC, hurried over from England. The three of them attended the mass and the service at the cemetery, where, just before Ford's grave was filled, Janice dropped a *bouquet garni* onto the coffin. Deauville's cemetery stands on a hill back of the town and looks out over the sea. Ford's last home had the great view he had always loved.[8]

---

had arranged to be cremated at Golders Green, and she left Julie a note in which she said, "Darling Julie The time will come when you will have to arrange some sort of service for me at Golders Green or Brompton Cemetery. . . . Anyway don't wait for the ashes or any nonsense of that sort! Go and have a drink somewhere—" (Stella to Julie, March 13, [1947], in the possession of Mrs. Loewe). The Loewes now live in Pasadena.

Appendix

Ford wrote or collaborated on thirty-two novels.

The Shifting of the Fire   1892
The Inheritors   1901
Romance   1903
The Benefactor   1905
The Fifth Queen   1906
Privy Seal   1907
An English Girl   1907
The Fifth Queen Crowned   1908
Mr. Apollo   1908
The 'Half Moon'   1909
A Call   1910
The Portrait   1910
The Simple Life Limited   1911
Ladies Whose Bright Eyes   1911
The Panel   1912
The New Humpty-Dumpty   1912
Mr. Fleight   1913
The Young Lovell   1913
The Good Soldier   1915
The Marsden Case   1923
Some Do Not...   1924
The Nature of a Crime   1924
No More Parades   1925
A Man Could Stand Up—   1926
Last Post   1928
A Little Less Than Gods   1928

No Enemy   1929
When the Wicked Man   1931
The Rash Act   1933
Henry for Hugh   1934
Vive le Roy   1936

Of these novels a number are discussed in the text; the rest are discussed here.

❧ The Inheritors

The Inheritors is unconvincing, especially in its motivation, an effect that is emphasized by the author's insistence on the psychological conflict within the central character. This defect is partly due to Ford's decision to make *The Inheritors* "An Extravagant Story," as the title page calls it. The success of H. G. Wells's science-fiction stories may have suggested to Ford the idea of putting a "fourth Dimensionist" into his novel. In theory at least this was also a useful device for the allegory of the novel. But it had the fatal defect, for a realistic novel, of forcing the author to sacrifice verisimilitude to allegorical implication.[1]

The Inheritors is the story of a young man, Etchingham Granger, torn between a love of the old and the fascination of the new. He is drawn to a younger generation that is "clear-sighted, eminently practical, incredible; with no ideals, prejudices, or remorse; with no feeling for art and no reverence for life; free from any ethical tradition"—"a menace to the institutions which hold us to the past, that are our guarantees for the future." "You are . . . for me," as the heroine says to Granger, " . . . only the portrait of a man —of a man who has been dead—oh, a long time; and I, for you, only a possibility."[2]

How better to show "the destiny" behind this conflict than to introduce a fascinating, quasi-supernatural girl dedicated to the destruction of the traditional way of life? Her plan is to convince the public that "all the traditional ideals of honour, glory, conscience, had been committed to the upholding of a gigantic and atrocious fraud" like Leopold's in the Congo. Her cunning way of doing so is to exploit with cold inhumanity the human virtues of established society, particularly its capacity for love and loyalty. Ford's hero falls hopelessly in love with this girl of the future and struggles to choose between her and the traditional world he also loves. From the allegorical point of view, this struggle is very cleverly represented. The novel begins, for example, with Granger and the girl looking down from a high hill at the glory of Canterbury Cathedral, "the place of martyrdom of Blessed Thomas," and when the girl utters some incomprehensible sound, "It all looked contemptible. One seemed to see something beyond, something vaster—vaster than cathedrals, vaster than the conception of the gods to whom cathedrals were raised." And the girl says simply, "We are to inherit the earth."[3]

Etchingham Granger comes of an ancient county family and is the heir to a country estate that he loves "not from any sense of prospective ownership but from the acute consciousness of what these things stood for." He has buried himself in the country in "the hope of one day . . . putting greatness on paper." He is devoted to Churchill, a statesman and writer and a man of casual aristocratic greatness. But Granger is acutely aware that greatness does not succeed in the world: the crotchety, neglected genius, Jenkins, shows him what the achievement of artistic greatness comes to. We know Ford was haunted by the possibility that a man might devote his life to becoming a great artist and yet remain obscure, as he believed Ford Madox Brown had. Before he and Conrad had made their decision to aim at a best seller with *Romance*, they had contemplated a book about "an old and famous painter, and the base, wicked intrigues surrounding a great man who has been successful but just because he was a supreme artist remained misunderstood." "H[ueffer]," Conrad said, "has a well founded knowledge of these problems . . . de visu for he had been a close friend of Ford Madox Brown during the last six years of his life." Ford's longing for fame and fortune and his fear that the better he wrote the less the chance he had to achieve them went deep. His attacks of melancholy when his work failed, his constant efforts to write popular books, his extravagant delight whenever he was noticed all show it. These feelings are the source of Granger's corroding doubts about devoting himself to the realization of his gifts.[4]

His doubts are reinforced, as were Ford's, by his journalistic talent. Granger longs for success and also finds the unfeeling brutality of the younger generation, especially the Dimensionist heroine, curiously exciting, "a stimulant . . . [that] set me tingling somehow," much as Ford found tempting sophisticated women like Violet Hunt. Both Granger and Ford think of themselves as essentially artists and bohemians—in a rather grandly county-family way. But both find the life of the successful journalist a standing temptation, just as both find stimulating what seems to their conservative natures the hardness of young and beautiful women of the world. They found this temptation nearly irresistible because they both believed that the old, honest, responsible world was as certainly—if unjustly—doomed as the *ancien régime* in one of whose Paris houses *The Inheritors'* Dimensionist girl plants herself, under the nominal protection of the English county *grande dame* who is Granger's aunt, in order to carry through her scheme for destroying Churchill and his world.[5]

Etchingham Granger is "on the one hand . . . 'one of us' [in the company of the Churchills], who had temporarily strayed beyond the pale; on the other . . . [when he writes newspaper articles about famous writers] a sort of great author's bottleholder." He is set "tingling with desire, with the desire that transcends the sexual; the desire for the fine phrase, for the right word—for all the other intangibles"; but because he is sexually in thrall to the girl, he writes journalism and, in the end, uses his power as a journalist to destroy everything he loves. "I had co-operated with the powers of the future, though I wanted no share in the inheritance of the earth." Such is the allegorical ingenuity of *The Inheritors'* plot that like some *belle dame sans merci*, the girl—the corrupting image of the future that Granger (and Ford) love—becomes Granger's sister, his mistress, and his destroyer.[6]

❦ The Benefactor

In *The Benefactor* Ford began to find his true subject and his own voice. The book's major characters, though still only sketches, represent types that were going to dominate his later fiction. Clara Brede has many of the characteristics of Valentine Wannop of *Parade's End*; her father, the mad clergyman, anticipates "Breakfast" Duchemin. George Moffat's wife resembles the Countess Macdonald of *The New Humpty-Dumpty* and Ford's other possessive women. George, the novelist's "altruist," is the first of Ford's many attempts to deal with his own idealism: George's ultimate successor is Christopher Tietjens.*

The disastrous consequences of George's altruism accumulate with nightmarish plausibility. His last-minute good fortune, which looks for a moment as if it would lead to a happy ending, turns out to be the perfect occasion for George to insist, with destructive pride, that he must live up to his gentleman's conviction that "some do not," an insistence that requires him to desert the novel's heroine. He is acting in a way more consistent with

---

*Ford wanted to call *The Benefactor* *The Altruist* but discovered that Ouida had preempted that title. By altruism he meant "that form of imagination which implies a sympathetic comprehension of the hopes, fears, and ideals of one's fellow-men" (*When Blood Is Their Argument*, p. vii).

his represented character than Ford appears quite to realize, reinforcing a judgment of him that is frequently suggested by his conduct though not by the novel's comments about him.

Clara Brede, the novel's heroine, urges George to take her with him when he leaves England to live out his life on the Continent, even though he cannot marry her. But George, thinking of what people will say of him if he does that, decides that it "would be a calamity for us all." When he tells Clara so, she is overwhelmed by "a violent passion," not, as we expect, against George for his refusal to have her, but "against the universe." "Self-sacrifice," she says. "Doesn't that ever end?" Ford evidently means us to think that George's decision is not an act of selfish pride but the inescapable act of a man committed to the moral code of his society: he cannot in conscience act otherwise, however much personal suffering his act costs him. We are meant to feel that George has sacrificed his selfish desires for "a point of honour," and that Clara blames society, not him, because she recognizes and accepts this view of his decision.[7]

The difficulty about this interpretation of the action is that Clara has already considered and rejected the demands of society's code in favor of the demands of their passion. She is already committed to seeing George's anxiety about society's judgment as a refusal to risk public disapproval for the sake of their love. Clara's considered commitment to passion rather than duty makes it difficult for the reader not to feel that George is acting selfishly, satisfying his conventional conscience without regard for Clara's feelings. Ford did not intend this impression, and when he came to deal with a similar situation in *Some Do Not . . .* , he took pains to make Valentine Wannop feel as deeply as Christopher the wrong of acting against the public code.

The Benefactor's conception of George Moffat is, in fact, its greatest weakness; it is as if Ford could achieve enough psychic distance from George to describe him accurately but not enough to judge him. George is a gifted writer who is always discovering how profoundly he is admired, despite his own indifference to his talent and his refusal to extend himself. Princes arrive from Moldavia to thank him for patriotic songs; distinguished French writers address him as Cher Maître. He gives lavish help and brilliant advice to protégés. His "fatal weakness," as one critic says, is meant to be "his goodness"—his altruism. But George never recognizes that this altruism is the product of an unconscious and perhaps self-protective arrogance; and it is not clear that George's creator recognized it either, though he provides the evidence for it. George admits that he does not understand himself. Like so many of Ford's heroes, he has the habit of watching himself to discover his feelings: "He was ruined. He was penniless.... He wondered a little how he was taking it. How *was* he taking it? What *did* it mean? He couldn't tell." His arrogance is so innocent that he explains it quite openly, the protégé who betrays him is to him like "a porter or a guide [who] tries to do you out of an extra franc or so ... it's his whole life to him; it's nothing to you."[8]

Ford limits himself to George's point of view, as if he had no better understanding of George than George himself has. Perhaps the reason he has not is that George Moffat is Ford Madox Hueffer.

> Seeing always, clearly enough, the ends and aims of others; never having had any very conscious goal of his own, he had always been content to step out of the way, and to supply the immense incentive of applause. It was as if, recognizing very fully the futility of human strivings, he were content himself to strive not at all, and had attempted to be, in a small, practical way, a tutelary of good fortune.

Ford can see there is something distinctly odd about this attitude and that it is dangerous; but he cannot understand why George adopts it.

> With him it was like drink—and he knew it. He came across men, vivid, real, with strong outlines, with intense hopes, and he entered into their desires and hopes, and made them more than his own. ... He did not want to do something for them so much as to set them in the position of their ideal as they represented it, or as he figured it.

Years later a friend was to say to Ford of the young people of that time, "They're suffering from what we—H. G. and the rest of us, used to say was the matter with you, years ago.... They don't know what to think.... About anything.... " And Ford thought she was quite right about how he had been then. As a representation of himself Ford's description of George Moffat is a remarkably honest if sincerely puzzled one. Ford never hesitates to show how much George harms himself and everyone else. But something—perhaps "the subtle veneration ... [the] author" feels for George noticed by one of the reviewers—drives him to make George an immensely talented and glamorous man deeply loved by all the good characters in the novel, and keeps him from seeing what made George act as he did.[9]

❧ The *Fifth Queen* Trilogy

The remarkable moments of Ford's *Fifth Queen* trilogy are its dazzling historical scenes. The night scene of Chapter II of *The Fifth Queen*, in which the Lord Privy Seal moves down the winter Thames "beneath a tall cresset in the stern of his barge," watching thoughtfully the flare of the King's barge a quarter of a mile ahead "in a glowing patch of lights and their reflections" with "nothing else visible in the world but the darkness and a dusky tinge of red where a wave caught the flare of light further out"; the entertainments Cromwell and Gardiner give for Anne of Cleves—the luxurious banquetings, the allegorical displays of wild animals, the interludes with their Renaissance neoclassicism and their elaborate political implications—these are the things that stand out.[10]

These scenes are dazzling reconstructions, paintings in the tradition of Ford Madox Brown's *Cromwell, Protector of the Vaudois* and Ingres' *Molière at the Table of Louis XIV at Versailles* (or of Leighton and Gérome, for all of that), historical occasions represented with painstaking accuracy, painted with a care for representation and a glow of color that is more "real" than experience itself, at once historically accurate and romantically exaggerated, and loaded with moral implications for the artist's own age. Much the same thing is true of the trilogy's narrative method. This is, in the Jamesian sense, scenic. Ford picks out moments that reveal the inner meanings of the action, which he emphasizes by making the characters acutely conscious of the implications of their situation. We seldom see the story's scenes of violence —the torturing of witnesses, the brutal trials, the deaths of Thomas Cromwell and Katharine Howard; these events occur off-stage and are reported to us.

What we do see are the scenes of pageantry which reveal the complex political purposes that cause these events, and the scenes of plotting and planning that bring them about. The *Fifth Queen* trilogy is a historical novel of manners performed in a setting painted with Pre-Raphaelite minuteness of detail and jewel-like brilliance of color. Its "academic" paintings of "Thomas Cromwell in his Barge on the Way to the Palace at Greenwich" or "Henry VIII at the Bishop of Winchester's Palace" are both metaphors and occasions for analyses of the motives that led these men to make the history of their times, and these motives are carefully traced back to what the author believes are the permanent natures of men, the final causes of conception and act in any time. As Ford said when he first thought of writing about the times of Henry VIII:

[Henry] represents the modern world being born out of the medieval. As a ruler at home he had to face almost exactly the social problems we are still facing, even to the relations of capital & labour & the question of agricultural depopulation. As a foreign politician he is one of the first & certainly one of the most portentous of the type of Bismarck.

In this Tudor trilogy we are meant to see the life of our times reflected in the life of Henry VIII's.

It was this aspect of the trilogy that led Ford to say later that "a historical novel even at its best is nothing more than a *tour de force*, a fake more or less genuine in inspiration and workmanship, but nonetheless a fake." This comment has had the unfortunate effect of encouraging critics like Mrs. Ohmann to make seriously distorted judgments of the trilogy. Like the condemnation of the Pre-Raphaelite and academic paintings analogous to this kind of historical novel, these judgments fail to recognize the serious purpose the "genuine . . . inspiration," that led men to produce them—their need, as Yeats put it, to hold in a single thought the "reality" of man's historical experience in time and the "justice" of his vision of life's permanent possibilities.[11]

A little later the writers who mainly determined the form of twentieth-century literature would discover—as Joyce did in *Ulysses* and Pound in the *Cantos*—that by making the mind of a protagonist and not the actual world the stage of the fiction they could include within their fictions both senses of the past. They could show the past as remote and so simplified to the point where the horror and the glory of experience shine through the boredom and make the past heroic instead of, as the present is, a grubby and insignificant tangle of contingencies; and they could also show the past as life lived and actual. It became, for the protagonist's mind, what the mind needs it to be, something at once meaningful and immediate, "not," as Pound said, "as land looks on a map/ but as sea board seen by men sailing." Only then did it become possible, in the phrase of Pound's disciple, Eliot, to grasp at once both the pastness of the past and its presence.

The *Fifth Queen* trilogy does not achieve that breakthrough into a new form, though *The Good Soldier*, five years later, does. In the *Fifth Queen* trilogy Ford is, in Mr. Kenner's words, "a little anachronistic [compared to Pound, Eliot, and Joyce], writing from a basis a little closer to the time in which the novels are set than to that in which they were conceived." Given Ford's choice of realities in the trilogy, this limitation was unavoidable. As long as he committed himself to a third-person narration and the reality of time and space, he could present the past in only one way—either as more or less idealized period pastiche like Hardy's *Woodlanders* or as contemporary history of the kind Shaw turns poor Joan's life into.

Inevitably Ford gained something by thus limiting himself that Pound, Eliot, and Joyce lost. In Ford's fiction the events of the past occur in a "real" world (that is, in the world of historical time that is the ordinary "reality" of most readers) where familiar rules of cause and effect operate. He did not have to risk throwing the reader into that phantasmagoria that any direct representation of the consciousness, however superior its reality may be, always seems. This in turn allowed Ford to emphasize the simple, comforting, and powerful fact that the past—however different from our time in the physical conditions and the social customs of its life—is essentially like the present. Effective, however, as this truth was, it involved Ford in an infinite regress. A major motive for turning to the past was to find an image of a golden age, a time when the essential meaning of human experience, its permanent values, had been able to realize themselves in action. This purpose cannot be fulfilled by a realistic image of the past, in which hard, practical, politic men like Thomas Cromwell clash with idealists like Katharine Howard, who is for the Old Faith in the old way and sees the political life of Henry VIII's court through a mist cast over her mind by the New Learning, so that "mazed with reading of books in the learned tongue," as she says of herself at the end, she sees Henry as "such a man as was Pompey the Great, or as was Marius, or as was Sylla." In this realistic image of the past, Katharine herself is looking back to a yet remoter past which had, she believes, realized an ideal she dreams of recreating in her own time, and Ford's image of the past thus becomes, not an image of justice, but an analogy of the present.[12]

All that can be shown us in the *Fifth Queen* trilogy is the pastness of the past. Ford does his best—and it is an astonishing best—to give what he shows us a full and convincing relevance to our experience. Much of the time he succeeds, perhaps most remarkably in a figure like Throckmorton. Throckmorton is Thomas Cromwell's chief spy, a man who understands his world completely and has used his understanding to achieve success. When he meets Katharine with her beauty and her idealism, he begins to see that his idea of himself has been a self-deception; seeing that helps him also to see the self-deception of his master, Thomas Cromwell.

> . . . it is in the nature of profound politicians [he says to Katharine] to love women [like Katharine Howard] that be simple as it is the nature of sinners to love them that be virtuous. Do not believe that

an evil man loveth evil. He contemns it. Do not believe that a politician loveth guile. He makes use of it to carry him into such a security
that he may declare his true nature. Moreover, there is no evil man,
since no man believeth himself to be evil. I love you.

Feeling this way, he at first tries to persuade Katharine to use the weapons
of worldly intrigue to win for her ideals a victory in the world. "It is," as
he rightly says, "a folly to be too proud to fight the world with the world's
weapons."

Yet he quickly sees that for Katharine to use the world's weapons—even
if she had the gift for it—would be to betray the very cause she fights for.
He therefore separates himself from her in order to fight the world for her
cause without involving her, knowing that if her cause triumphs the best he
can hope for is retirement; the worst is death. He is the good machiavel, the
selflessly cunning man, and nobody sees the irony of his position more
clearly than he does.

"It is a good doctrine of the Holy Church," he said [to Katharine],
"to call no man evil until he be dead." He looked down at the ground,
and then, suddenly, he seemed to mock at her and at himself. "Doubtless, had such a white soul as yours led me from my first day, you
to-day had counted me as white. It is evident that I was not born with
a nature that warped towards sin. For, let us put it that Good is that
thing that you [Katharine] wish." He looked up at her maliciously.
"Let that be Good. Then, very certainly, since I am enlisted heart and
soul in the desire that you may have what you wish, you have worked
a conversion in me."

It is one of the many nice ironies of the trilogy's action that it is primarily
he who does win Katharine's battle for her—who brings down by his machiavellian cunning the Lord Privy Seal, Thomas Cromwell, Katharine's
great enemy, and puts her into the position, as Henry VIII's wife, where she
can influence Henry and attempt to bring back the Old Faith. Throckmorton sees quite clearly that he can use the world's weapons either to win a
place for himself in the world or use them to help Katharine at the cost of
losing for himself the rewards of the world. His position is the intelligent
man's equivalent of Katharine's, for Katharine, too—though she does not in
her impractical idealism see it—can either live according to her idealistic
virtues and be destroyed by such cunning men as Cromwell's successor,
Lascelles, who does in the end destroy her, or she can fight the world with
the world's weapons. But she cannot, any more than can Throckmorton,
love virtue and triumph in the world too.[13]

The novel thus counterposes two faiths. On one side is Katharine's faith in a virtue that she believes was manifest in the Old Faith and in the great men she has read of in Plutarch's *Lives* and which she at first imagines is also embodied in Henry VIII, who has at least his magnitude of character—if not real virtue—to help her believe it. On the other side is Thomas Cromwell's equally profound faith in his Utopia. As Throckmorton sees clearly, Cromwell uses guile only to reach a security in which

> He would be perpetually beside the throne. . . . He would be there by right; he would be able to give all his mind to the directing of this world that he despised for its baseness, its jealousies . . . for kingcraft, solid, austere, practical and inspired, should keep down all the peoples, all the priests, and all the nobles of the world. . . . His eyes became softer in the contemplation of this Utopia. . . .

His devotion to kingcraft, to the belief that men, by the exercise of reason, can govern their world, is absolute. He is, as Ford said elsewhere, "the founder of modern England." He floats through the benighted world of men's passionate irrationality in the little pool of light cast by the cresset of his barge, dedicated, skillful, selfless. For him "before all creeds, and before all desires, and before all women, and before all men, standeth the good of this commonwealth, and state, and King, whose servant I be."

In the great central scene of *Privy Seal,* Katharine comes to Cromwell to suggest in her straightforward way that, because she now realizes his profound loyalty to "his master's cause," he stay the King's man when she has persuaded Henry to return to the Catholic faith. This, they both see, is the only possible grounds for an alliance between the only two unselfish people near Henry. But an alliance between them is not possible because Cromwell's faith is as firm as Katharine's: "If ye have faith of your cause," he says to Katharine, "I have the like of mine." Katharine says, "Shall not God and His Son our Saviour have their part of the King's glory?" and he replies:

> "God is above us all. But there is no room for two heads of a State, and in a State is room but for one army. I will have my King so strong that ne Pope ne priest ne noble ne people shall here have speech or power."

In her idealism Katharine cannot see the difference between the secular, ecclesiastical power of the Bishop of Rome and the power of God. In his realism Cromwell cannot see that God should have any power at all in the affairs of men. They are both wrong, Katharine to believe it is possible to fight the world deprived by virtue of the world's weapons and to establish the kingdom of God on earth, Cromwell to believe that it is possible to make the kingdom of Henry VIII perfect and to substitute guile for virtue.[14]

Behind each of these major characters is a group of minor ones who represent the variations that insight, confusion, weakness, or selfishness may work in the attitudes they represent. Throckmorton is a Cromwell incapacitated for success in the world by his clear understanding that guile is not virtue and the good of the state is an evil. Behind Cromwell, too, stand the Catholic prelate Gardiner, the Catholic lord Norfolk and the Lutherans Wriothesley and Badge, the printer—people who imagine they are dedicated to a cause but are, in fact, driven by their own selfish interests—Gardiner for Cranmer's office, Norfolk and Wriothesley for the retention of the wealth of the dispossessed monasteries they have acquired, Badge for his land. They are all fanatics, unscrupulous men unaware of their own real motives. Faintly visible behind them is the mass of common men who take delight in their own fanaticism, whose happiest passion is to hate, for whom no rumor of evil in their enemies is too absurd to be believed.

Behind Katharine stands a similar group. Her Throckmorton is Mary, the daughter of Henry by Katharine of Aragon. Mary's insistence on right and virtue is qualified by her Spanish arrogance and her unforgiving hatred of her father. In the end she risks her neck and subdues her pride to support Katharine, observing with sardonic wisdom that "well I know—since I saw my mother die—that virtue is a thing profitless, and impracticable in this world. But you—you think it shall set up temporal monarchies and rule peoples. Therefore, what you do you do for profit, I do it for none." Behind Katharine, too, stands Cicely Elliott who, having seen her family killed off by Henry for political reasons, insists on viewing life itself simply as a great joke: "God hath withdrawn Himself from this world," she says. "All mankind goeth a-mumming." Here too stands Nicholas Udal, with his passion for classical learning, his commitment to the Old Faith, his lechery, his cowardice, his devotion to Katharine. Beside Udal stands Thomas Culpepper, Katharine's childhood sweetheart. He is a very simple man, arrogant, drunken, violent, passionate almost to insanity, and he loves Katharine with all the lack of calculation of his simple nature. He is man who, like a child, acts directly on his feelings; these feelings are usually silly and destructive. Nonetheless Culpepper is the same kind of person that Katharine, with her ineradicable dedication to her feelings, is. She is right to think at the end of her life that to have married him would have been to marry one of her own kind of people, though wrong to think that that would have been a solution to her life. Katharine believes to the end that to love "without regard, without thought, without falter" is enough. Perhaps nothing is enough without such love, but by itself such love is not enough. That is her tragedy, and by setting beside her, in the figure of Thomas Culpepper, a kind of reductio ad absurdum of her idea, Ford has shown us that. Margot Poins, Katharine's maid, loves her with a similarly thoughtless and unqualified devotion. No torture will persuade either her or Udal to bear false witness against Katharine. They represent the common people who, when they can know Katharine for what she is, are devoted to her.[15]

Ford shows astonishing skill in subduing all these actual people, with their recalcitrance to imaginative revision, to his scheme, and represents their parts in the scheme with a richness of historical particularity that is remarkable; it is a triumph of the historical imagination. The single exception is perhaps Katharine Howard herself, whose historical character—as far as we know it—offers no grounds at all for what Ford has made her. It is remarkable how cunningly he twists the best-known details of Katharine's story to his purposes: he can even make that dying defiance of hers—"I die a Queen, but I would rather have died the wife of my cousin Culpepper"—serve his turn. But in the end his romantic need to turn her into an impossibly ideal figure makes her unconvincing, just as his romantic need to idealize the figures of his literary anecdotes so often carried them—for all his cleverness in managing them—beyond human possibility.

At the center of Ford's action, the source of power and the person who must be controlled by Cromwell and Katharine if they are to succeed, is Henry VIII. He is proud and passionately devoted to power; he is a master of the kingcraft that Cromwell so well understands, and he practices it with the heavy cunning of a peasant. But he is also a cultivated man with a powerful and by no means ignoble desire for happiness who is now growing old. He wants Katharine Howard because she is beautiful; he wants her even more because her conversation gives him much pleasure: she is at once innocent as a child and almost as learned as he is. But he wants her most of all because she promises him the salvation of his soul, for which, as he has grown older, he has become more and more concerned. He is both the head of the state and the head of the Church in England, and there is not room, as Cromwell understands, for both of them. Cromwell pulls him toward one mode of life, Katharine Howard toward the other, and though Katharine temporarily triumphs and Cromwell is killed, Cromwell's disciple, Lascelles, carries on Cromwell's fight until he drives Henry to condemn Katharine, though he knows she is innocent, on trumped-up charges in order to maintain his power over a populace that has been convinced by Lascelles' lies that Katharine is a whore.

With a last display of guile, Henry devises a scheme for deposing Katharine and keeping her alive in private as his mistress. She will have none of it, though she had once offered to be his mistress. But not now,

> "But once you offered it!" Henry cries.
> "Then you appeared in the guise of a king!" she said.

Then she adds:

> Very truly you say when you say that once I made offer to be your leman. But it was when . . . I did see you such a one as was Caesar Julius who, as you well wot, crossed a Rubicon and set out upon a high endeavour. But you—never will you cross any Rubicon. . . . I came to you for that you might give this realm again to God. Now I see you will not—for not ever will you do it if it must abate you a jot of your sovereignty, and you never will do it without that abatement. . . . I was of the opinion that in the end right must win through. I think now that it never shall—or not for many ages—till our Saviour again come upon this earth with a great glory. . . . And this, I will add, that I die a Queen, but I would rather have died the wife of my cousin Culpepper or of any other simple lout that loved me as he did, without regard, without thought, and without falter.[16]

This closing speech of Katharine's makes a magnificent rhetorical conclusion to the novel. That is its fault as well as its virtue, for Katharine, who had been at the beginning of the trilogy ambitious of shows, of power and success, and the lover though not the mistress of her cousin Culpepper, has gradually turned into an impossibly ideal figure, and Henry has become almost wholly a worldling. This reduces to the black and white of melodrama the genuine drama that is implicit in Ford's original conception of his situation and characters. It solves the dilemma posed at the start by making one major character all good, the other all bad, though it has been made clear by Throckmorton at the trilogy's start—and recognized even by Katharine herself—that neither was she all good nor Cromwell all bad. Ford did not simplify the conclusion of his trilogy in this way in order to court popularity; his motive was something more dangerous—namely, the seductive appeal of pretending that ideal virtue is humanly possible. Katharine confesses to crimes she has not committed in order to save from torture her imperfect but loyal servants: she dies for them; the intended analogy is all too clear, and it makes her divine, not human, and her end not a rounding off of the novel's vision of reality but an apotheosis. This is the price Ford has to pay in order to get an image of "justice" into a fiction wholly committed to "reality." Having committed himself to this kind of ending, he wrote it eloquently. But it is impossible not to wish that he had not ignored the full implications of the human situation he so beautifully imagined in the body of the novel.

ஐ The 'Half Moon'

Perhaps because Ford was tired of historical novels and had to hunt around for an idea for *The 'Half Moon,'* the book's theme and its carefully worked-up historical details never really fuse; the historical details never become expressions of the characters' natures: they remain abstractions, types rather than people. The wealthy barons of Rye exemplify aged and somnolent conservatism; Anne Jeal, for all the paraphernalia of seventeenth-century witchcraft with which she is surrounded, is a conventional image of passion corrupted by possessiveness; Edward Colman is the practical modern man; Henry Hudson—skillful, demagogic, humanitarian rather than humane—is a humors character, a man obsessed by a single interest, "sailing over unknown seas." Ford's characters are much too obviously and exclusively what his theme requires them to be, and the historical detail about them, though it is interesting in itself, is merely décor.

This failure is doubly unfortunate. We know from Ford's later work that his imagination responded to the conflict between the practical, efficient, businesslike man and the man whose sense of the past gave him an understanding of the fragile structure of custom that supports human values. For Ford this conflict stood at the heart of human experience. There are moments in *The 'Half Moon'* when we can see his imagination beginning to respond to this conflict, when Edward Colman finds himself frustrated by the mindless traditionalism of his society, or Henry Hudson's passion for exploration makes him treat his men with inhuman brutality. This conflict between operational control and physical possession on the one hand and understanding and spiritual intimacy on the other troubled Ford's feelings in his actual life and stirred his imagination most deeply when it was raised by the relations between the sexes. It is there in his contrast between the tiny, dark, passionate Anne Jeal, who will kill Edward Colman rather than lose possession of him because her love for him is inextricably entangled with her desire for power, and the large, blond, devoted Magdalena Koop, whose love will survive even Edward's death because "it is not the corporeal presence of him that can make him more mine, for I have his heart and he mine...."[17]

But this conflict is never allowed to develop imaginatively in *The 'Half Moon'*; it disappears beneath a heap of archaeological detail. The one serious effort Ford made to realize his meaning is a failure, a supernatural image in a Pre-Raphaelite style that is, ultimately, as irresponsibly quaint as Tennyson's Middle Ages or Rossetti's heaven. Ford sympathized with practical men like Edward Colman and understood the corruption that long possession of wealth and power slowly works in the conservative representatives of an old belief in the mysterious forces that underlie human experience and are beyond the control of man's intelligence. At the same time he believed in the reality of these forces and felt that those who could evoke them would in the end dominate men like Edward Colman who trusted to their merely human powers. He chose, however, to show the reality of these mysterious forces by making Anne Jeal's seventeenth-century witchcraft real: she makes a figure of wax and of blood from her breast and melts it before a fire, stabbing it with a knife; and Edward Colman dies on the remote shores of America. Thus it is that Ford's awareness of the mysterious, subrational realm of men's under selves and the powers that operate there is frittered away by a merely prettily romantic, period image.

৵ A Call

A Call is at once a tribute to Henry James and a declaration of independence from him, the first of Ford's novels that is explicitly "An Affair" with Ford's typical *progression d'effet*, the slowly accelerated revelation of motive and meaning in a series of carefully dramatic scenes. This method is explained in the novel's "Epilogue," addressed to Violet Hunt. Ford had read *A Call* aloud to Violet when he was courting her, as she later explained.

> Hypnotised by the voice . . . I was able to think, *sub rosa*, of my own affairs. . . . No discourtesy to the author was involved; I had discovered that his reading was purely subjective, independent of his listener. Also that he disdained criticism or comment of any kind; criticism ran off him like water off a duck's back; comment, even praiseful comment, merely interfered with the psychic flow between himself and the medium of the moment—me.

But Ford did hear her criticism: he reproduces a detailed though exaggerated version of it in the "Epilogue" and even attempted, in the book version, to meet her objections by making much explicit that had been only implicit in the serial version.[18]

A Call is the story of Robert Grimshaw, who has loved faithfully, for years, Katya Lascarides. Katya insists that she will not marry Robert; he must live with her unmarried, as her father had lived with her mother. Robert is equally determined that she shall marry him properly. Robert then falls in love with Pauline Lucas and she with him. Feeling he is obligated to Katya, he marries Pauline off to his friend Dudley Leicester, so that she will be cared for and he may remain honorably faithful to Katya. When Katya's sister, Mrs. Langham, says that what he has done is horrible, he says, "What have we arrived at in our day and class if we haven't learned to do what seems proper and expedient—and to take what we get for it?" Then slowly he learns that the real meaning of his deepest belief—"Do what you want and take what you get for it"—is exactly the opposite of this. He discovers what, as "a man of many knowledges, [but] a man of no experiences at all," he had missed, that

> the traditions—traditions that are so infectious—of his English pub-
> lic-school training, of his all-smooth and suppressed contacts in Eng-
> lish social life, all the easy amenities and all the facile sense of honour
> that is adapted only to the life of no strain, of no passions; all these
> habits were gone at this touch of torture . . .

he has to endure because of his passion for Pauline Leicester.[19]

Pauline now knows this too, but she has no more intention now than Robert Grimshaw had earlier of betraying her commitments; she will stick by her obligation to her husband as firmly as Robert stuck by his to Katya. "You do not love Katya Lascarides," she tells Robert quite truly, "you are as cold to her as a stone. You love me, and you have ruined all our lives." Realizing this is true, Robert decides to take Katya on her own terms, and she, seeing he loves Pauline, says, "I think, my dear, as a precaution . . . I think you had better marry me."[20]

A Call conveys feeling with a Jamesian minimum of dramatic gesture, the faintest of smiles, the simplest of words, the slightest gesture. As with James, the central situation, well known to the characters and only alluded to by them, emerges very slowly for the reader; even Robert Grimshaw's responsibility for the telephone call that drives his friend Dudley Leicester insane and forces Robert himself to face his hopeless passion for Pauline is not revealed to the reader until the end of the novel. This last concealment is not justified by the dramatic method of the novel or the character of Robert Grimshaw; it illustrates Ford's inability to stick to the rules of his chosen game, his tendency to use dramatic effects he has not earned. The same tendency is shown by the semiprivate jokes by which he declares his independence of James, as when he gives unlikely characters Jamesian names like Moddle (*What Maisie Knew*), Brigstock (*The Spoils of Poynton*), and Etta Stackpole (who is, in her sexual predatoriness, a satiric comment on Henrietta Stackpole of *The Portrait of a Lady*).

This tendency shows most strikingly in Ford's handling of his characters. Katya Lascarides, for example, is a passionate, possessive, stubborn woman; as such, she is thoroughly convincing, as are all the women characters who represent Ford's conception of Elsie Martindale. Katya loves Robert Grimshaw desperately, and she refuses to have him. But the situation Ford invents to cause her to refuse him is hopelessly fantastic. Her devoutly orthodox mother, she had learned after her mother's death, had never been married to Katya's father because no Greek Orthodox priest had been available at the moment, though the Lascarides go to Athens regularly. Then, with wildly romantic idealism, Mrs. Lascarides decided that the great thing was to "trust each other; then you will become perfectly to be trusted," and took to exhorting her children to take the same view of life. Katya insists on doing just what her mother did.[21]

Throughout the novel, Ford's exuberant fancy provides similar absurdities, not so much of motivation as of the circumstances which cause the motives to come into play. "I may say," Arnold Bennett observed in his review of the book, "that I consider 'A Call' to be profoundly and hopelessly untrue to life. . . . But regard [it] as an original kind of fairy tale, and it is about perfect." "[Ford] doesn't," he added in his journal, "get down to the real stuff." When Violet Hunt wrote this remark into her copy of *A Call* she added: "Nor I think, does in life." "He was determined," as she shrewdly observed, "to get—he could not help getting—the fierce ancestral colours—Brunonian madder red and vandyke brown—always into his plots, schemes, and books. For he was the grandson of the painter of 'Parisina,' who . . . came to see all life, even still life, like matter in a rage. . . . The passions of [Ford's] puppets are set forth with a reasonable, yet cloudy violence."[22]

But taken as "an original kind of fairy tale," *A Call* is "about perfect." Its impressionistic picture of the life of London's upper classes, though vague, is vivid. Its action, however unlikely its circumstances, is closely articulated. The stubbornness that makes Katya Lascarides balk Robert Grimshaw also makes her able to cure her niece, Kitty, who, out of a similar Lascarides' stubbornness, refuses to speak though she is six years old; and this parallel is enforced by showing us young Kitty wrestling with a stubborn pet lamb: "Against its obstinacies Kitty's [were] valiant but absolutely useless. . . . She would be dragged across the moist earth, and left upon her back like a little St. Lawrence amongst the flames of the yellow crocuses."²³

Mrs. Ohmann thinks Ford has mistaken the point of his own story in making its central problem Robert Grimshaw's struggle between personal desire and public responsibility. But this objection is based on a disbelief in public responsibility that Ford did not share. Robert Grimshaw is like George Moffat of *The Benefactor* and, as Violet Hunt tactlessly reminded the author, like Ford Madox Ford. Like Ford, he is only half English; the foreign half of him "makes you have what no Englishman has—a sense of responsibility," he says. "I can't bear to see chaps of my class—of my clan and my country—going wrong." Ford clearly means us to admire this attitude. The order and design imposed on life by the acceptance of responsibility is beautiful to him, though the sacrifice of people's real feelings it demands is very destructive. Robert Grimshaw, watching four sparrows by the Albert Memorial, thinks that "they were going ironically through a set of lancers, and the smallest of them, a paler coloured hen, might have been Pauline Leicester"—and the other three Dudley Leicester, Katya, and Robert. Like the minuet to which the life of the Ashburnhams and the Dowells in *The Good Soldier* is compared, the dance of this society has an ordered beauty, but the human beings who try to move through its graceful figures are, with their uncontrollable passions, about as suited to it as these lustful sparrows.²⁴

The outcome of the story is the result of Robert Grimshaw's initial inability to recognize that he is not strong enough to fulfill the responsibilities he believes his position in society impose on him, to do what honor, as he conceives it, requires of him. Passion is far stronger than he had been able to imagine when he decided to remain loyal to Katya and to make Pauline marry Dudley Leicester. But Ford clearly means us to see this conflict between personal passion and public duty as a genuine one. For Ford civilization and the responsibilities it imposes on men are not absurdities, nor is devotion to civilized values merely the rationalization of a "man who shies away from passion" and the Lawrentian life of "impulse." Mrs. Ohmann, whose phrases these are, believes them so firmly that she invents a "second story within the frame of the first" story in *A Call*, which, she argues, is the true story of *A Call*, even though Ford does not know he has written it. The dilemma of *A Call* is not, however, to be resolved by any such recourse to doctrines of "Life." What happens in *A Call* is a necessary disaster. "Look at the misery of it all!" Pauline says to Robert at the end. "That's it. We can make a day and a class and rules for them, but we can't keep any of the rules except just the gross ones like not making scandals. . . . We haven't learned wisdom: we've only learned how to behave. We cannot avoid tragedies."

That is not a recommendation that, for passion's sake, they learn how not to behave, it is a recognition of their lack of the wisdom that will reconcile behaving and passion. Rightly or wrongly, Ford believed both that the passions are irresistibly powerful and that the social order, sustained by honor and responsibility, is necessary and beautiful. *A Call* is an expression of the essential idea of both *The Good Soldier* and *Parade's End*; it fails, to the extent that it does, because in place of that "felt life" on which Henry James said the moral of a fiction depends for its reality, it too often gives us what Arnold Bennett called "a fairy story."[25]

❧ Ladies Whose Bright Eyes

It suited Ford's imagination perfectly to conceive himself as the practically effective, idealistic Knight of Coucy living in the fourteenth-century world of *Ladies Whose Bright Eyes*. He had gradually worked it out that he was an English gentleman of country-gentry character committed to a quietly unostentatious existence and holding social views "of a Tory kind so fantastically old fashioned as to see no salvation save in the feudal system as practiced in the fourteenth century—or in such Communism as may prevail a thousand years hence." The essential consideration was that "Nothing could be less bourgeois than the Middle Ages with their Gothic comfortlessnesses, their grim gargoyles, their starvation-wrinkled faces"; instead of bourgeois comfort, the Middle Ages loved "the high things of love, or of great adventures in arms," and gave its admiration to the "great knight," garbed as a minstrel but traveling in "sufficient state," who sang of these things. The fourteenth century was therefore a time when a man like Ford or the Knight of Coucy —large and physically powerful, skillful in practical affairs, scornful of bourgeois comfort, and devoted to the poetry of courtly love—could flourish. The present was not; only the British public school that produced men like Arthur Marwood or Colonel Blood made men of this kind possible in the twentieth century, and as Ford's imagination committed itself to this ideal, it became necessary for him to have attended an "ancient public school and [a] school preparatory for it," a fiction that angered the more snobbish of his enemies more than any other improvement he made on his life history.[26]

Ford's conviction that life in the fourteenth century was superior to life in the twentieth century was strongly reinforced by his special interest in what he considered the Church's practical skill in handling unsuccessful marriages. In *The Good Soldier*, Dowell points out that Leonora with her

"Nonconformist temperament" "quite seriously and naïvely imagined that the Church of Rome disapproves of divorce . . . [and] could be such a monstrous and imbecile institution as to expect her to take on the impossible job of making Edward Ashburnham a faithful husband," whereas, in fact, the Roman Church "would have had her marriage dissolved in six months for two hundred dollars paid in the right quarter." In the letter Ford wrote Edward Garnett in 1929, when he made his final attempt to get Elsie to divorce him, he pointed out that if Elsie had become a Catholic, as had been asserted in court, a divorce could easily be arranged. Ford, in short, was convinced the Church held the views he did on this subject. He first began to suppose so when he was trying to find some way to get free of Elsie in order to marry Violet Hunt—that is, when he was writing *Ladies Whose Bright Eyes.* This interest dictated the long scene during which Mr. Sorrell and the Dean of Salisbury work out the arrangement for freeing the Lady Dionissia from the Young Knight.[27]

Ford put this demonstration of the fourteenth-century Church's wisdom in the context of the age. The scene begins with Mr. Sorrell riding into Salisbury through "narrow streets" lined with "houses [that] appeared to him to be indescribably squalid," along roads that were "indescribably filthy" and filled with a noisy crowd of subhuman creatures. "He observed only noise, dirt, nauseous smells, and great crowds of importunate and ugly people." He then enters the gaudy blue-and-scarlet interior of the newly created Salisbury Cathedral, which was in fact less than seventy years old at the time Ford is imagining. From there Mr. Sorrell passes into the lovely garden where the Dean's house stands. Here is the fourteenth century, with its violent contrasts of squalor and elegance, its lurid taste and its genuine beauty, its churchmen who are at once devout and worldly, like the monk Francis in *The Young Lovell,* who "loved God and considered the world," and were therefore, unlike Katharine Howard, willing "to fight the world with the world's weapons."[28]

Mr. Sorrell's discussion with the Dean is nothing if not practical. They are both skillful businessmen who take pleasure in these negotiations: this is, evidently, the right way to handle affairs of this sort. It would be foolish not to regard the world and to deal with it effectively. Nevertheless both the Dean and Mr. Sorrell are devout men; the Dean truly loves God and Mr. Sorrell the Lady Dionissia. His aim is to wander the world with her in due state, as lover and poet like one of the *trouvères* or minnesingers Ford so greatly admired; this will be "life and peace." But he means to do so in the most serious and responsible way, "respectably," as he puts it to the puzzlement of the Dean, who imagines he understands Mr. Sorrell only when Mr. Sorrell glosses this adverb as "with the sanction of the Church." There is nothing cynical in any of this, and if there is a comic incongruity in the enthusiasm with which Mr. Sorrell and the Dean, with their sincerely idealistic purposes, arrange their bribes, it is only the comic incongruity of all human affairs. After a happy session of close bargaining, then, they settle the problem to their mutual satisfaction—as Ford no doubt dreamed that, if only the modern world were as sanely Catholic as the fourteenth century, his marital difficulties would have been arranged.[29]

At the end of *Ladies Whose Bright Eyes*, Mr. Sorrell recovers from his injury and finds himself back in the twentieth century. Having come to understand the values of the fourteenth, he can now see—as he could not at the beginning of the novel—how silly modern values are. He sees that business is childish. "If you took a potman or a cabman or a Board School teacher, or anybody who could keep sober," he says of his publishing firm, "they could run this show or any other show in the City." The skills required to operate the machinery of life, Mr. Sorrell now understands, are trivial. What is important is to use that machinery for some admirable purpose. To run a publishing house "in order to do something for literature" is worthwhile; so too will be the revival of fourteenth-century ways of life that Mr. Sorrell can bring about by reconstructing the castle he had been given in 1327 and finds himself once more in possession of in 1910. To these things Mr. Sorrell settles at the end of the novel.[30]

Ford was able to make the medieval world of the novel so vivid because he knew a great deal about it—perhaps too much. The novel contains a good many scenes like the one in which Mr. Sorrell is given a medieval bath that are more archaeological than narrative. It is saved by Ford's ability to make not only his scenes but his characters medieval: they think with amusing and yet impressive unconsciousness according to the ideas of their times. He imagines himself completely into a world where the manners are radically different from those of his own time. Moreover, he uses this image of fourteenth-century life for a serious purpose. The needed changes in the values of the twentieth century suggested at the end of *Ladies Whose Bright Eyes* are, in their Pre-Raphaelite way, insignificant; Ford revised them completely for the 1935 version, without, however, making them much more impressive. But the action of the novel does show us a medieval world that is both convincingly real and radically different from our world, in which men no better than we in their essential natures lead lives of magnanimity.*[31]

---

*When Ford revised *Ladies Whose Bright Eyes* for republication by Lippincott in 1935, he did so extensively. Besides bringing the modern parts of the novel up to date and moving passages about

ക് The Young Lovell

The events of *The Young Lovell* occur in June and July of 1486, during the reign of Henry VII, near Bamburgh in Northumberland, country Ford knew well, thanks to Violet. There a handsome, serious, sensitive knight, the Young Lovell, much traveled in Italy and unusually cultivated for these wild northern parts, is put into a trance for three months by a goddess who smiles "at him with the mocking eyes of the naked woman that stood upon the shell in the picture he had seen in Italy." When he comes out of his trance, he finds his castle and all his possessions in the hands of his bastard half brother, who has also trapped the girl he had loved into a betrothal. He undertakes to put the situation right, but "he desired none of these things for his intimate pleasure. It was all for decency and good order in his lands that he did it, and to punish evildoers." The world has become unreal to him, for "ever since [he] saw that lady's face this world has seemed as a mirror and an unreality to [him] so that [he] cannot cease from sighing and longing."

His ideal of conduct is a cultivated version of the old chivalric attitude; for him too

> toutes les joies and tous honneurs
> Viennent d'armes and d'amour.

He cherishes the independence of this northern country, though he disapproves of the careless illegalities of those red-headed Swinburns and their like. His greatest worldly enemy is the king, who would bring the whole country under his power, and the king's men such as the Percies.

> I do not like your kind [he says to Henry's man, Sir Bertram of Lyonesse], for I have seen some of them about the courts of princes, here and elsewhere and you are the caterpillars upon the silken tree of chivalry that shall yet destroy it.

(the original Chapter V, for example, becomes Chapter III), he made—at least in the first hundred pages or so, before he got bored—extensive verbal changes to bring the style into accord with his prose of the thirties. For example, in 1911 he wrote: " ... great bees buzzed sleepily above his head. The sound of the singing died away, and in his intense weariness Mr. Sorrell dropped asleep. He was always very dizzy and stupid upon awakening, so that when he was gently shaken he had not the least idea where he was" (p. 67). In 1935 this became: "The place smelt of thyme; great bees buzzed sleepily just above his head. The sound of singing died away.... He was gently shaken. He did not know where he was" (p. 70). Most important of all, he had Mr. Sorrell suggest to Dionissia at the end of the novel that they go to live in a remote ruined castle "on the side of a valley in the Russian Caucasus." " ... it would be a ruin now ... " Dionissia says, "But of course *they're* beginning" (p. 349). This reference to the Soviet Union was perhaps more romantic in 1935 than it is today.

Therefore, out of his sense of duty, he organizes an attack on his castle and recaptures it from his brother. Then he quietly disappears; only the monk Francis knows that he is the mysterious stranger who has had himself walled up for the rest of his life in the hermit's cell near the castle. There he lives "in a very high valley of Corsica" with "the mistress of the world."

During the course of the story, Venus keeps appearing, surrounded by a great company of ladies-in-waiting, like some medieval dream of fair women; nearly everyone, at one time or another, sees her following the Young Lovell. But he alone understands her full powers and can say to the medieval explanation of her (that this is all witchcraft and magic) as he could have said to the modern explanation (that she is a figment of the imagination) "All that is a child's tale!" It is not easy to write a modern fiction that will make the reader see what Pound said Ford "saw quite distinctly[,] the Venus immortal crossing the tram tracks"; but in a medieval romance, where the author's own vision can be half-concealed behind the vision of characters whose superstition the reader takes for granted, it can be done, though at a cost of appearing fanciful that Ford eventually came to feel was too great. Because of that cost the historical romance, Ford knew, did not do the job that Pound and Eliot, Yeats and Joyce, would do—that is, make men see once more the bright gods and Tuscan that floated in the azure air before ever dew was fallen. But *The Young Lovell* comes as near to doing it as any historical novel Ford ever wrote. " ... if it is anything at all," Ford said, "it is really literature and I have spread myself enormously over it. ... "[32]

He did so because *The Young Lovell* is another of his attempts to explain his own nature to himself. He thought himself a man who, having begun life as an energetic reformer and socialist, had early come to feel, in some way he could not quite understand, that the practical affairs of the world were not really serious. He had a good many views about them and imagined that, if he could bring himself to take the trouble, he could handle them with skill and success; but he did not really care enough about them to involve himself. He was, he thought, a man with no serious ideas of his own. Why was this so? Perhaps it was because he had had a vision of a world of ideal beauty— had been entranced, as it were, by the goddess of a pagan heaven—and could not any longer feel the actual world was quite real. The "very high valley of Corsica" in which the Young Lovell's spirit dwells is only sketchily treated at the end of the novel, but so far as it goes, it represents, in the medievalized classical terms the novel is committed to, an existence not unlike that of Ford's poem "On Heaven."

❧ No Enemy

In *No Enemy: A Tale of Reconstruction*, Ford for the first time let feelings and attitudes rather than chronology determine the structure of his fiction. This is impressionism of a more radical kind than he had ever attempted before. His primary concern here is to represent the tenuous but—in its way—intensely dramatic interplay of perceptions that come finally, in memory, to be significant experience. If ever there was a man who learned to know that he almost always "had the experience but missed the meaning" and that "approach to the meaning restores the experience in a different form," it was Ford. He had become aware too that at any given moment the mind is a palimpsest of perceptions, conscious and unconscious. The task he set himself in *No Enemy* was to select incidents that had stayed alive in his memory because a large number of such perceptions had accumulated around them, to represent each incident in a way that would dramatize the process of perception rather than the occurrence of the incident, and to arrange the incidents in a way that would make clear the relations among these perceptions that constituted the meaning of the experience—in this case the experience of the war as the climactic event in the life of Edwardian England. He would make a more complete image of that experience later, in *Parade's End;* but in *No Enemy* he worked out his method of making this kind of image.[33]

The two means he uses are the careful definition of the perceptions that occur at each moment of experience and the time shift that allows him to put together moments that occurred far apart in time and space but have closely related implications. He uses both of these means cautiously. In the chapter (IX) called "The Water Mill," for example, the fact that he was reading Henry James's *What Maisie Knew* as he sat waiting for a bath in a converted water mill in Albert, behind the lines on the Somme, has important implications. But it is, on the face of it, a bizarre and improbable fact. Ford is therefore at some pains to tell us he had sent home for a batch of books in order to read them at the front and see which ones would stand up "against the facts of a life that was engrossing and perilous"—in effect to test what products of Edwardian culture would still ring true in the moment when Edwardian culture was brought to its supreme test. "It wasn't really a coincidence—that I should be reading that book." Then he links this reading up with a previous episode, his meeting in Paris with a little girl whose mother had deserted her to run off with a lover and who had said to him, "*Ils me disent que Maman est partie pour le ciel. It is very droll. But what tram do I take pour le ciel?*" Here was Maisie in the flesh. He then carefully summarizes *What Maisie Knew*, in case the reader's ignorance of the story conceal the connection from him.[34]

Then he moves back in time to describe how he and another officer had walked to the water mill, past the ruined shops of Albert "that [still] offered us, on metal placards, bicycles, chocolates, and furniture polish" and over the floor of the Cathedral's presbytery with its "great litter of books—Latin texts mostly." "Under my arm ... I had 'What Maisie Knew' in the expensive, collected edition, and we had also towels and soap. ... Whilst we were passing under the immense Madonna and Child that hung over the Cathedral steps, a Hun plane dropped a couple of bombs right into the body of the church." Thus he reached the water mill, where he sat waiting, faintly conscious of the naked men about him in the baths, of the "dirty copies of English funny periodicals" on the table before him, of the Latin texts he had just seen scattered amid the rubble, and of the expensive edition of *What Maisie Knew* in his hands; a part of him "was sitting, really, in Kensington Gardens. ... And Maisie was playing with Mrs. Wicks"; and a part of him was thinking of the little girl who wanted to find the tram *pour le ciel*; and yet another part of him was thinking of that Madonna and Child with the bombs falling around them.

> I was vaguely conscious of voices. My companion was talking to some one else—about some battalion of some regiment. ... But ...
> I was as engrossed as any schoolboy reading Ivanhoe in the twilight. It is a good tribute to pay the master. He was dying then.
> But I was vaguely unhappy too. ... I felt the queer uneasiness that, in those days, one was beginning to feel when one came in contact with civilians.

Then "a very old Tommy of the Lincolns, toothless, whitehaired, with tunic undone and tarnished buttons, told me I must still wait whilst my bath was preparing," and suddenly we are hearing the story of this simple, unselfconscious, devout Englishman who had, when the war broke out, come home from Canada to "see what we can do to 'elp the ol' gal. ... ' As if Victoria had been still on the throne." "*Et comme il était très fort, hardi, courageux et avisé*," Gringoire thinks, though this is not in any evident sense another St. Julian the Hospitalier. It is a beautiful and very quiet rendering of a moment in which an immensely complicated and subtle pattern of feelings coalesced, and it is both the experience of a single consciousness and an image of a whole culture at a moment of crisis.[35]

All the best moments in *No Enemy* are like this one, and they are connected with one another by links like those that hold each of them together internally; it is the time shift that makes it possible for Ford to limit his narrative to such moments and to put them side by side, so that their interconnected meanings are clear to us and we are able slowly to experience their total meaning and see how they lead up to the final moment of the book, when Gringoire sits after dinner under the great oak tree in the garden of the Gingerbread Cottage and Mrs. Carmody and Sélysette between them recite Ford's own "Claire de Lune" (written at "Nieppe, near Plugstreet, 17/9/16")—

> I should like to imagine
> A moonlight in which there would be no machine guns!

And Gringoire

> reached out his right hand and took Mrs. Carmody's left, and his left and took Madame Sélysette's right.
> " 'Rest,' " he said with his heavy tired voice, " 'after toil, port after stormy seas . . . ' " He paused and added after a moment: " 'Do greatly please!' "[36]

⌘ The Marsden Case

In *The Marsden Case* Ford was beginning to escape from the enslavement of the compensatory daydreams on which he had had to subsist while he was recovering from the war. He began once more to use the ironic narrative method of *The Good Soldier* and the method of representing the consciousness of his narrator that he had begun to work out in *No Enemy*. "I try, I mean, to be accurate after my own fashion," says Ernest Jessop, "which is no doubt not the fashion of the Chancellor of the Exchequer, my conscience leading me to reproduce the story only as it occurred to my attention and as it now comes back to me. . . . " This narrator's consciousness is constantly working at several levels. Jessop tells us that "I had just lately—only just two or three days before—been so badly mishandled by a woman that half the time, even then, I did not rightly know what I was doing. I would see things vividly for an hour or so, and then . . . dimness—a wavering in which I could hear myself speaking collectedly or with cynicism. This is the worst sort of 'underself' to have!" (This experience of Jessop's is of course an echo of Violet's attacks on Ford.) Or George will report that in a moment of great stress, "He desperately did not want to assault that grinning fool. . . . Yet his legs bent themselves, trembling to make the spring. . . . He said that that was the most ghastly feeling he had ever had in his life: the dread that he might act in spite of his will; or even unconsciously."[37]

The way these various selves live together in a single consciousness is frequently represented in the novel with great vividness.

I did not at first pay a great deal of attention to the conversation of Miss Jeaffreson during that walk. It began by being about Nietzsche. It was a bright July day; there were a great many people in the streets; I had to say "How do you do?" to several men whom we passed, and I was thinking really hard about Irish poetry. . . .

Miss Jeaffreson said that she supposed she could not, now, think of Mr. Podd as her publisher.

This being a personal matter, my subconscious self warned me that I must rouse my surface-self to reply with some animation. . . . My mind reverted to the misty atmosphere of the lakes of Ireland. But a portion of it was considering how I could get hold of a telephone and, if I did get hold of a telephone, how I was going, on it, to get hold of a young actress . . . of whose professional name I was not sure, though I thought it was something like Honeywill. . . .

And I was really concerned to discover whether Miss Honeywill was yet in possession of the manuscript of my shadow play that was to be produced that night. . . . My eyes explored the facias of the Salvage Station by which we were passing, absently looking for a telephone sign.[38]

But necessary as it was to tell the story as "it occurred to [the] attention" of a narrator whose "attention" was extremely complicated, it was no longer enough for Ford to describe "An Affair" and to trust the reader to feel that "the death of a mouse from cancer is the whole sack of Rome by the Goths." He had lived through the war since then; the historical dimension of experience was too immediate to him to be dealt with only by implication. He had to find some way to keep his representation of a perceiving consciousness and at the same time to represent social and political circumstances. The result is a technical compromise that is not wholly satisfactory; he inserts a long report of George's experience in Germany and the chronological summary of Chapter IV, as if he despaired of keeping so complicated a story clear if he told it exclusively as "it occurred to [the] attention" of his narrator. A little apologetically, then, he puts his narrator aside: "Perhaps it would be better," he has Jessop say, "if at this point I tried to put chronologically the story of that young pair during the year that preceded that troublesome day. I picked it up of course, only subsequently."[39]

But there are considerable triumphs of narration in *The Marsden Case,* too. The most obvious of these is the opening sequence with its succession of revelations—in Podd's office and at the lunch with George; during Jessop's walk through London with Miss Jeaffreson; amidst the only half-comprehensible confusions of Jessop's efforts, when he gets to the Ladies' Club, to make his speech about the Yeatsian poet, to endure the malice of the journalists, to cope with the unknown voice on the telephone asking if he would "vind the seggund pail," and to discover Lady Ada Pugh Gomme's purpose; and finally, in the even greater confusion of the Night Club. It is a skillful piece of sustained interior dialogue, quite coherent so far as the chronological order of Jessop's day is concerned, a nightmare of hints half understood so far as his understanding is. There are a good many lesser moments of this kind. They are as likely to belong to George Heimann as to Jessop, for this is another of Ford's novels with a doubled hero. Indeed, if Jessop's brother, Fred, were more fully developed, one might say its hero was tripled, for Fred also embodies one of Ford's ideas of the heroic life.

Fred lives on a farm with a great view, of which he is inordinately proud; "he never that I heard uttered an unkind word about a soul—except such unfortunate souls as talked in his presence about such things as the View from the Seven Hills. And even then he would say little more than that they were stupid fellows or had no sense of proportion." "So he lied, probably, about his view. But . . . in all other matters he was a saint—of the English variety. . . . He might well have been an extra-mural member of one of the great monastic orders; for perpetually, in a slow way, he reflected on the rights and wrongs of things and wished well to all the world." (Christopher Tietjens' secret ambition was to be an Anglican saint.) "He was an old-fashioned, stiff fellow, who believed that a man should make any sacrifices for a woman—any man for any woman. That was chivalry!" Here in Ernest and Fred Jessop, with the virtues distributed in a slightly different way, we have a sketch of a relation like that between Christopher and Mark Tietjens in *Parade's End.* Fred's life echoes Ford's at Bedham, and it is evidence of Ford's regained control that he takes a mildly amused view of Fred: " . . . when it came to action his mind jumped to twenty varying courses at once, ten or eleven of them being fantastic."[40]

Ford also divides himself between Ernest Jessop and George Heimann. This division is a reversal of the one he had used in *The Good Soldier* and *No Enemy;* here the unobtrusive observer of the action is the older, more worldly man, and the observed hero is the young, inexperienced one. Jessop is Ford's vision of himself as a man of the world who has known some success and acquired some skill in managing his affairs. One recognizes this Ford as soon as Jessop describes his dealings with his publishers: "[Podd] had wanted my name to give respectability to his list of books, which was not a very attractive one, and he had wanted to get it so cheaply that if the offer was not an insult it was a piece of sharp practice. I had at that date published ten or eleven rather lazy volumes. . . . I knew enough about books and the money there was in them to be aware that his offer was sheer insolence." Jessop leads, quite literally, Ford's prewar London life; he even shares Ford's idea of fighting on the "gallant-enemy" principle. He has the hard war Ford felt he had had, and is so badly disturbed by a near-miss that his nerves do not recover until 1921. "I was supposed [then] to be cured . . . having only lately come from a cold-water-cure institute. . . . There I had at last gone through what—thank God!—proved to be the last stage of a mental pilgrimage begun among beastly horrors, lasting for horrible years." This is of course the mental pilgrimage Ford took in 1904.[41]

In George Heimann, the novel's central character, Ford is describing himself as a handsome, talented, naïvely earnest young man of twenty-two who comes of very good people (but is temporarily under a shadow) and worries touchingly over his behavior—was he right to resist punching Podd in the head ("That fellow *is* practically only a tradesman")? This "courteous and visionary boy" has all the qualities Ford believed he had—the idealism, the admirable, quixotic high-mindedness, the proud devotion to "decorum of behaviour." He also has the phobias ("tics," George calls them) that Ford was inclined to feel did him credit—a numbing horror of publicity or even private discussion of his affairs, a need to live the conventionally admired life of his time. George is a "magnificent young animal, singularly in repose, with the repose of the perfectly healthy body in equilibrium, and of the quite good, generous, commonplace mind. . . . " This young man Ford exposes to precisely the emotional pressures that he had had to endure.[42]

By inventing a set of events perfectly fitted to the pressures he had experienced, he is able to dramatize his own suffering in a way he felt actuality's less well-organized events had not. The way Marie Elizabeth's obsessive selfishness, Sir Arthur's good intentions, the malice of the *Evening Paper*, and the mechanics of the law combine to crucify George just when he has reached the haven of the Irish Guards is a masterpiece of psychological Grand Guignol of a kind Ford will improve on only with the torture of Christopher Tietjens.

George is the legitimate heir of an earl, but owing to the eccentricity of his father, he cannot be sure he is not the bastard son of a nobody and he is much too proudly reticent to ask. This torturing uncertainty is complicated by his having been brought up in Germany, the enemy country, and by the passionate refinements of his own high-mindedness. This is Ford's improved version of his own situation as the descendant of German barons in wartime England. George has inherited from his father—who (like Mr. Blood and a part of Ford) "despised his kind . . . loved a row; but [was maddened by] publicity"—an agonized sensitivity to seeing his name in print. The most exquisite torture he knows is being written up in newspapers, and his sister and Miss Jeaffreson are very busy getting their friend Plowright, the American newspaperman, to write George up as much as possible, to further their scheme for getting his sister recognized as Lady Mary. It affects George in the same way the publicity about his love affair affected Mr. Blood's brother, Reginald, who became so severe a neurasthenic that he had to retire to the country, where he devoted himself to closing the shutters around the house at exactly the moment required to keep out direct sunlight.[43]

George is badly shaken by what his consideration for his sister requires him to do. Then he is forced to go to Germany just before the war breaks out. By the time he gets back he has suffered so much that his mind, like Ford's when he returned from France, "would seem to miss a stroke, as you may sometimes hear your heart do. . . . It had done that often lately. It just would not catch on to long speeches in an equable tone, though short, sharp remarks would still stir him." After his return from Germany, George spends ten happy days as a private in the Irish Guards. Then he is forced to resign and has to go back to the farm, where his sister feeds him a steady diet of Mr. Plowright's articles about him in the sensational American press.[44]

"You might put it that six of his seven minds that worked simultaneously were by then raging mad, but the seventh remained hard and practical. And he retained, of course, his passion for decorum of behaviour, so that none of them, as the phrase is, 'suspected anything.' " The wise old doctor of the novel—he has a considerable resemblance to Tebb—explains George for Ford.

> "That boy," he said, "is twice as stolid as you by nature. . . . But he has been having two years of silent worrying over a subject and at an age when worrying over that sort of thing is the most damnable influence on the brain.
>
> Of course he's jumpy. Emotional he isn't. And, mind you . . . unless the father can relieve him of those women, he's going to

have a worse time than any human being could have imagined before these days. Not physical, of course, or material, but just sheer gnawing of the mind.

This is what Ford believed he was: "jumpy" was his favorite word for describing his own condition during the war, the mental disturbance that kept him, like Ernest Jessop, neurasthenic until 1921.[45]

It is a little difficult to see how George—and Ford—could be stolid and at the same time suffer from so many esoteric "tics" that they can be driven six-sevenths mad by such things as newspaper publicity, but George is both believable and moving as a character, even if we cannot believe this diagnosis. The difficulty about *The Marsden Case* is not any inadequacy in Ford's realization of his characters. The strongest virtue of Ford's aesthetic was his concern for making things vivid; whatever impression he might be trying to convey, he always tried to "render" his subject. As he said to Stella about painting, "the Present School [of painters] is largely a reaction against the Instantaneous photograph. . . . And this leads [them] into a desire to be hyper human—to the point of producing work that is not a rendering but a comment on the inspected object. And that is a foredoomed fallacy!" The limiting difficulty about *The Marsden Case* is not any failure in the rendering of the characters and events; it is a failure to convince us that these characters and events are representative and revealing of their society. Ford has transformed the hurts, the anxieties, the desires for revenge of his private experience into convincing if somewhat specialized characters; he has not made these characters and their situations into significant images of Edwardian and wartime life. *The Marsden Case* is, as a consequence, about a group of people who are a good deal more eccentric than Ford recognizes. Even so, it is an achievement, a vivid image of a world, however odd; and it is an astonishing achievement for a man who, only a few months before he wrote *The Marsden Case*, seemed hopelessly lost in anxiety and self-pity.[46]

❦ Parade's End

The problem faced in *Parade's End* was to put the characters Ford so vividly imagined together in a fiction that would be an image not only of his own private experience but of the public life of his society, which he believed had declined disastrously. In *It Was the Nightingale* he gives an account of how he came to write *Parade's End* as he did; it may represent all he consciously grasped of the process. Sir Edward Elgar, the composer of "Land of Hope and Glory" and a neighbor of Ford's in Bedham, stops on the road past Coopers Cottage and asks Ford if they have not met at Henry James's. "Nothing in the world was further from my thoughts than writing about the late war. But I suppose the idea was somewhere in my own subconsciousness. . . . I wondered how the common friend of myself and Sir Edward would have treated that intractable subject . . . and for the rest of the day and for several days more I lost myself in working out an imaginary war-novel on the lines of 'What Maisie Knew.' "[47]

In fact, Ford seems to have started, not with a generalization about the war and a theory of narration, but with his vision of himself as an idealistic young man of great talent and unostentatious social superiority. The experiences of this young man that most deeply concerned him were his commitment to the Tory political doctrines that shall govern the world when Arthur is come again; the frustrated moral, social, and aesthetic activities they had led him into; the decision of this Tory self to serve his country and the war experience that followed it; and the emotional complications that resulted from his falling out of love with Violet Hunt and in love with Stella Bowen.

In technique he began where he had left off in *The Marsden Case* and *No Enemy*. Like *The Marsden Case, Some Do Not* . . . uses a modified chronological arrangement of events reduced to a relatively few scenes by a process of selection not unlike that of the well-made play. *Some Do Not* . . . consists of three acts. The first act takes place in and around Rye; the time is late June, 1912. This act takes us from the moment when we discover Christopher and Macmaster on the train to Rye until the moment when Christopher and Valentine's all-night ride ends with General Campion's running into them outside Mountby. The second act takes place in the dining room of Christopher and Sylvia's flat in Grays Inn; the time is late August, 1917. This act takes us through the early part of a single afternoon. The third act takes place on the street between Grays Inn and the War Office, in and about the War Office, and back at the flat. The time is continuous with that of the previous act and we are taken through the remainder of that afternoon and night.

Each of these acts is divided into scenes. For example, the first act begins with the scene in the train. It is followed by a scene at Lobscheid, where Sylvia Tietjens has just joined her mother and Father Consett. The third scene occurs at the inn where Christopher and Macmaster are staying; the fourth at the Duchemins', where they breakfast; the fifth on the path to the Wannops', and at luncheon there. The final scene begins near the finish of Christopher and Valentine's long ride to and from Plimsoll and ends with the accident. The other two acts are similarly divided into dramatically concentrated scenes.

But Ford's allusions to *What Maisie Knew* in both *No Enemy* and in his description of how he came to write *Parade's End* are important. For him, as for James, ultimate reality is not some event in time and space; it is the conception of that event in a consciousness. What distinguishes Ford's well-made play from a stageable fiction—as it distinguishes *What Maisie Knew* from a theatrical experiment like *Covering End*—is the extent to which the action is presented to us through a consciousness, much of the time at two removes—that is to say, through the consciousness of a character whose consciousness is described by the novel's narrator. Like James, Ford never frees his characters' minds entirely from the control of the narrator; both when he is writing as the omniscient narrator and when he is following the movement of a character's consciousness, he writes as a third person. This third person is not—except very occasionally in *Some Do Not...*—objective and impersonal; he is vividly present to us as a personality, as an ironic, judging mind. It is Ford's desire to let us hear his voice that makes him summarize the thoughts of his characters in the third person rather than present them to us directly. By this means he is able to show us the events as a character perceives them and at the same time to show us the narrator's judgment of the characters' thoughts and feelings.

As *Parade's End* progressed, Ford became more interested in dramatizing the perceiving consciousness, as he had in "The Water Mill" chapter in *No Enemy.* He focused more sharply on the way the conscious mind keeps several trains of thought going at once and on the extent to which the governing impulses of men come from the unconscious. Both tendencies are illustrated at the start of *Some Do Not....* Vincent Macmaster sits in the train to Rye prepared to relish the "sensuous current of his prose" in his monograph on Rossetti. He knows Christopher Tietjens, sitting opposite him, does not admire Rossetti, though he does not know why. Nor does he suspect that the prose he is about to savor and the attitude it represents illustrate all that is wrong with the society that Macmaster, with his poor-Scot ambitiousness, is so anxious to make a success in. "Gabriel Charles Dante Rossetti, the subject of this little monograph, must be accorded the name of one who has profoundly influenced the outward aspects, the human contacts, and all those things that go to make up the life of our higher civilization as we live it to-day . . . " Macmaster's monograph begins. It is all too true.[48]

Macmaster starts to read. As he does so, a second part of his mind starts to consider why he has written this monograph: it will "consolidate his position" in his department and in society, allow him to set up an elegant establishment and to furnish it with a "tall, graceful, dark, loose-gowned, passionate yet circumspect, oval-featured, deliberative, gracious" woman. The thought triggers his recurrent fear of his starved nature's occasional uncontrollable impulses to go bald-headed after "big-bosomed, scarlet-cheeked" girls of a quite different kind. So far, he thinks, Christopher has saved him from the consequences of these impulses. Yet, ironically, Tietjens himself has fallen into the trap set for him by a woman pregnant by another man and desperate for a husband.[49]

During all this time the first part of Macmaster's mind continues to be occupied—though without the relish he had anticipated (his feelings are being preempted by this second train of thought)—with his monograph. The thought of how Sylvia had trapped Christopher brings in its train a recollection of the scene that had occurred that morning when Christopher had received a letter from Sylvia announcing that she was returning to him after spending four months with a lover named Perowne. This part of his mind then forces him painfully to rehearse that scene, until he comes to the moment when Christopher said sardonically of the child he loves but is not convinced is his that Sylvia "gives me the benefit of the agreeable doubt." Wincing at the memory, Macmaster looks up from his monograph and notices that Christopher has gone gray. "Suddenly—and as if in a sort of unconscious losing of his head—Macmaster remarked: 'You can't say the man wasn't a poet!' The remark had been, as it were, torn from him. . . . "[50]

This is an illustration of how the unconscious mind seeks to shift the conscious mind from one train of thought to another when the first has become unendurable. Rossetti's spiritualized sensuality fits Macmaster's unconscious desire to make his own sensuality acceptable to his conscious self by finding for it an object not big-bosomed and red-cheeked but tall and graceful, passionate yet circumspect—to whom he can quote Rossetti's

> Since when we stand side by side
> Only hands may meet,
> Better half this weary world
> Lay between us, sweet!

His insistence that Rossetti is a fine poet gives all this away. "I can't," Tietjens says contemptuously, "say [that is not poetry] . . . I don't read poetry except Byron. But it's a filthy picture. . . . " Ironically, Macmaster's

subconscious has not even allowed him time to recognize that, in thus avoiding his own pain at the contemplation of Tietjens' suffering over Sylvia's
conduct, he is likely to have added to that suffering. It does not give him
time to consider how Christopher, brooding over his answer to Sylvia's
letter, will be affected by an insistence on the magnificence of what Christopher calls Rossetti's attempt "to justify fornication" by a pretense of spiritu-
ality.[51]

Macmaster is not a very sophisticated man, and he is scarcely aware of
how he has been victimized by his subconscious mind. Ford's intelligent
characters understand the power of their under selves. When Christopher
reviews the scene that had occurred that morning, he remembers that Macmaster, seeing his expression as he reads Sylvia's letter, had given him
brandy. "He seemed [that morning] to have no feelings about the matter";
at the same time he was aware that, subconsciously, he was feeling a great
deal and he watched himself carefully for signs of what it was; he noted that
only the brandy kept him from shivering uncontrollably.[52]

Valentine, next to Christopher the novel's most sophisticated intelligence, is equally alert for the signs of what her unconscious self is up to.

> She heard herself saying, almost with a sob, so that she was
> evidently in a state of emotion:
> "Look here! I disapprove of this whole thing. . . ."
> At Miss Wanostrocht's perturbed expression she said to herself:
> "What on earth am I saying all this for? You'd think I was trying
> to cut loose from this school! Am I?"

She is, unconsciously; for unconsciously she has already decided to seek
Christopher out at Grays Inn and to commit herself to him for life. But
consciously she does not find out about that decision till some time later.
When she finally does join Christopher at Grays Inn, her conscious mind
and her unconscious feelings fall into conflict again. "This man," her conscious mind asserts indignantly, " . . . had once proposed love to her and then
had gone away without a word and . . . had never so much as sent her a
picture-postcard! Gauche! Haughty! Was there any other word for him?
There could not be. Then she ought to feel humiliated. But she did not.
. . . Joy radiated from his homespuns when you walked beside him. It welled
out; it enveloped you. . . . Like the warmth from an electric heater, only that
did not make you want to cry and say your prayers—the haughty oaf."[53]

The determining responses of Ford's characters almost always take
place in this way, below the level of consciousness, so that their conscious
conception of themselves is always more or less at odds with the intentions

of their subconscious selves. The result is a psychic conflict that goes on continually in Christopher and Valentine and Sylvia and even, occasionally, in minor characters like Vincent Macmaster and General Campion, who, while he sits writing his letter to the Secretary of State for War "with increasing satisfaction," finds that "a mind that he was not using said: 'What the devil am I going to do with that fellow?' Or: 'How the devil is that girl's name to be kept out of this mess?' "[54]

This conflict between conscious and unconscious selves in *Parade's End* is, as was the similar but much simpler conflict in *The Good Soldier*, a genuine one. Ford does not suggest that one part of the consciousness is good, the other bad. The conscious self is the responsible, social self, and as a Tory Ford felt that this self must dominate the personality. "It is proper," as Christopher says, "that one's individual feelings should be sacrificed to the necessities of a collective entity."

> He said:
> "But it wouldn't be playing the game!"
> A long time afterwards he said:
> "Damn all principles!" And then:
> "But one has to keep on going. . . . Principles are like a skeleton
> map of a country—you know whether you are going east or north.

But when the socially determined habits of the conscious self begin to frustrate the unconscious feelings completely, as they do when society, failing to live up to its principles, ceases to provide occasions for the genuine satisfaction of these feelings (but only occasions for the meretricious satisfaction of them that Macmaster and Mrs. Duchemin will settle for), then a psychological crisis occurs in the society's best and most responsible people. The only salvation for such people—and the only way to preserve the essential principles of the society that has bred them—is for them to become "Tory radicals," to adopt a new mode of life, a new set of social conventions that will allow them to continue to live by those principles and yet satisfy the demands of their unconscious selves. After asserting that it is proper to sacrifice individual feelings to the collective entity, Christopher adds: "But not if that entity is betrayed from above."[55]

The focus of our attention in *Parade's End* is on the slow, tortured process by which Christopher becomes consciously aware that the conventional life of Edwardian society no longer embodies the principles that it professes and that he has tried with such heroic literalness to live by. Then he recognizes that if these principles are to be preserved—if, indeed, he himself is to survive as a sane man—he will have to stop living as an Edwardian Younger Son, the role for which his society had cast him. "Love, ambition, the desire for wealth. They were things he had never known of as existing—as capable of existing within him. He had been the Younger Son ...a sort of eternal Second-in-Command." He sees, to his surprise and (to Ford) comic dismay, that his unconscious self had decided to change all that long before his conscious self recognized the fact. The first hint his conscious self gets is the discovery that he wants to command the battalion, that he is ambitious. Then he discovers that he, for whom it had been a part of his duty as a member of the ruling class to lend money to anyone who asked for it, resents Colonel Partridge's request for a loan of £ 250 (it is a nice irony that Colonel Partridge—or at least Colonel Partridge's executors—are among the few who ever repay a debt to Christopher). Finally he recognizes that he intends to give up his public position in the government in London and go into the antique business in the country, to leave his luxurious social life with his wife, Sylvia, and live in chaste and frugal "sin" with Valentine Wannop. His old Edwardian self is, at first, shocked by these decisions. "Reprehensible! ... He snorted! If you don't obey the rules of your club you get hoofed out, and that's that! If you retire from the post of Second-in-Command of Groby, you don't have to ... oh, attend battalion parades! ... Reprehensible! He said." Then his newly conscious self speaks. "For God's sake *let* us be reprehensible! And have done with it!"[56]

The crisis of Christopher's consciousness that leads to this discovery illustrates the fully developed form of Ford's way of dealing with his characters. Christopher has been thinking of the Germans across no man's land, "confoundedly irritated to think of the mess they have made of his nice clean trenches." Then his mind makes an odd jump:

> The beastly Huns! They stood between him and Valentine Wannop. If they would go home he could be sitting talking to her for whole afternoons. . . .
> That in effect was love. It struck him as astonishing. The word was so little in his vocabulary. . . . He had been the Younger Son. . . .
> Now: what the Hell was he? A sort of Hamlet of the Trenches? No, by God he was not. . . . He was perfectly ready for action. Ready to command a battalion. He was presumably a lover. They did things like commanding battalions. And worse!
> He ought to write her a letter. What in the world would she think of this gentleman who had once made improper proposals to her; balked; said "So long!" or perhaps not even "So long!" And then

walked off. With never a letter! Not even a picture postcard! For two years! A sort of a Hamlet all right! Or a swine!

Well, then, he ought to write her a letter. He ought to say: "This is to tell you that I propose to live with you as soon as this show is over. You will be prepared immediately on cessation of active hostilities to put yourself at my disposal; Please. Signed, Xtopher Tietjens, Acting O.C. 9th Glams." A proper military communication.[57]

Christopher's consciousness is being dramatized as interior dialogue rather than interior monologue, and over it hovers the ironic consciousness of the author, whose amused voice we can hear in phrases like "A proper military communication." This interior dialogue shows us the way Christopher's mind struggles, against its own habitual commitments, through a series of emotionally linked perceptions rising from his subconscious, toward an understanding of his own unconscious nature. It discovers with astonishment ("It struck him as astonishing") that it is in love ("That in effect was love"), that it is ambitious ("He was perfectly ready for action"), and that it is determined to act on these feelings ("He was presumably a lover. They did things like command battalions. And worse! He ought to write her a letter").

But it was not until Ford wrote *A Man Could Stand Up—* that he worked out all the possibilities of this kind of interior dialogue and the opportunities it opened up for a new kind of narrative structure. *Some Do Not . . .* works less within the consciousness of a character than any of the other novels in *Parade's End* and, when it does, more simply. Its structure is scenic, and the scenes are usually treated dramatically. When Ford does choose to present the action through the consciousness of a character, he picks whatever character suits the immediate occasion, and he moves from the consciousness of one character to that of another without hesitation.*

No More Parades is a different matter. The rapidity with which Ford developed his new method of narration is indicated by the fact that he wrote

---

*The time shift of Macmaster's recollection in Part I, Chapter III, summarizes action Ford does not want to take the time to present scenically, as does Christopher's description of his previous evening's activity. Even Chapter VII (Valentine and Christopher's all-night ride), which is represented through the consciousnesses of Christopher and Valentine, only occasionally dramatizes their consciousnesses: for example, when Christopher is surprised by his impulse to kiss Valentine and checks himself with "Steady, the Buffs!" (I, 142). The Conradian account of the accident is also a representation of the mind of the perceiver rather than of the event: "Not ten yards ahead Tietjens saw a tea-tray, the underneath of a black-lacquered tea-tray, gliding towards them. . . . He shouted: mad: the blood in his head. His shout was drowned by the scream of the horse, etc." (I, 144). But even here there is description rather than representation ("he shouted: mad. . . . His shout was drowned. . . . ").

a concluding scene for *Some Do Not . . .* and then suppressed it so that he could use the material in the interior dialogue of *No More Parades*. *No More Parades* takes place almost entirely in the minds of Christopher and Sylvia, and we learn a great deal about the states of their minds as they live through the experiences of the novel, though these states of mind are still, much of the time, described rather than represented ("Heavy depression settled down more heavily upon him," etc.). Only at moments of great tension does Ford dramatize their consciousnesses fully. Thus when Sylvia's desire for Christopher and her hatred of him reach a climax during the air raid, and the slightly drunken, well-meaning Cowley reminds her that Christopher had not slept the night before,

> There occurred to her irreverent mind a sentence of one of the Duchess of Marlborough's letters to Queen Anne. The duchess had visited the general during one of his campaigns in Flanders. "My Lord," she wrote, "did me the honour three times in his boots!" . . . The sort of thing she would remember [being, as she sardonically recognizes, what she is and being, at the moment, mad to be possessed by Christopher] . . . She would—she *would*—have tried it on the sergeant-major, just to see Tietjens' face, for the sergeant-major would not have understood. . . . And who cared if he did! . . . He was bibulously skirting round the same idea. . . .
>
> But the tumult increased to an incredible volume. . . . She screamed blasphemies that she was hardly aware of knowing. She had to scream against the noise; she was no more responsible for the blasphemy than if she had lost her identity under an anaesthetic. . . . She was one of this crowd!

Ford dramatizes in the same way the moment Christopher's conscious mind loses control during his interview with General Campion.

> Panic came over Tietjens. He knew it would be his last panic of that interview. No brain could stand more. Fragments of scenes of fighting, voices, names, went before his eyes and ears.

For two pages they do so. Then:

> He exclaimed to himself: "By heavens! Is this epilepsy?" He prayed: "Blessed saints, get me spared that!" He exclaimed: "No, it isn't! . . . I've complete control of my mind. My uppermost mind."[58]

Ford's almost complete commitment to interior dialogue in *No More Parades* changes radically the organization of the narrative. The novel still has the tripartite structure of *Some Do Not . . .* and consists of fairly sharply defined scenes of either present or recollected action, and the present action is still chronological. Being continuously inside the mind of a character, however, allows Ford to use the time shift extensively, to rearrange the order of events by having the character "remember" scenes that occur at different times. Chapter III of Part I, for example, consists entirely of Christopher's interior dialogue at the end of the evening during which he has learned of Sylvia's presence in Rouen. This meditation, with its neat device of Christopher's putting his past relations with Sylvia in order by writing them down in the flat, impersonal style of a military report, makes it possible for us to reconstruct the history of those relations, including the episode Ford originally described in the suppressed scene of *Some Do Not...* (Sylvia also recalls this episode, in Part II). But the major purpose of Christopher's meditation is to arrange the events of this history in a nonchronological pattern that will show us the feelings they arouse in Christopher, the entanglement of those feelings with his anxieties about his job at the base, and the way these feelings together gradually change—as it were, before our eyes—his conception of himself and of the possibilities of his life. This major purpose is clear enough if we trace the pattern Ford has imposed on Christopher's meditation.

The one thing that stood out sharply in Tietjens' mind [it begins] when at last, with a stiff glass of rum punch, his officer's pocketbook complete with pencil ... he sat in his flea-bag with six army blankets over him—the one thing that stood out as sharply as Staff tabs was that that ass Levin was rather pathetic.... On the frozen hillside, he ... had grabbed at Tietjens' elbow, while he brought out breathlessly puzzled sentences....

There resulted a singular mosaic of extraordinary, bright-coloured and melodramatic statements, for Levin ... brought out monstrosities of news about Sylvia's activities, without any sequence....

And as Tietjens, seated on his hams, his knees up, pulled the soft woolliness of his flea-bag under his chin ... it seemed to him that this affair was like coming back after two months and trying to get the hang of battalion orders....

So, on that black hillside ... what stuck out for Tietjens was that ... the mysterious "rows" to which in his fear Levin had been continually referring had been successive letters from Sylvia to the harried general [Campion].... Tietjens set himself coolly to recapitulate every aspect of his separation from his wife....

The doctor's batman, from the other end of the hut, said:

"Poor ——— O Nine Morgan [whose death haunted Christopher]!..." in a sing-song mocking voice.... They might talk till half-past three.

But that was troublesome to a gentleman seeking to recapture what exactly were his relations with his wife.

Before the doctor's batman had interrupted him by speaking startlingly of O Nine Morgan, Tietjens had got as far as what follows with his recapitulation: The lady, Mrs. Tietjens....

He took a sip from the glass of rum and water.... He had determined not to touch his grog. But his throat had gone completely dry.... Why should his throat be dry?... And why was he in this extraordinary state?... It was because the idea had suddenly occurred to him that his parting from his wife set him free for his girl.... The idea had till then never entered his head.

He said to himself: We must go methodically into this!...

"Better put it into writing," he said.

Well then. He clutched at his pocket-book and wrote in large pencilled characters:

"When I married Miss Satterthwaite...."

He exclaimed:

"God, what a sweat I am in!..."...

It was no good going on writing. He was no writer, and this writing gave no sort of psychological pointers....

And his mind wanders off on half-a-dozen pages of brooding about his situation that do give him—and even more, us—psychological pointers.[59]

In part II of *No More Parades*, which takes place in Sylvia's mind, this kind of rearrangement of the events is carried much further. The present time of Part II begins exactly where the present time of Part I ends, with Christopher riding down into Rouen to reserve a room for the night at the hotel; at the beginning of Part II Sylvia, sitting in the hotel lounge with Perowne, sees Christopher come into the hotel. The presence of Perowne sends Sylvia off on a prolonged recollection of her affair with him five years before in a small French town. The scene ends in the grim comedy of her outrage at the thought that Christopher may have a girl—probably Valentine Wannop—in *this* French town, Rouen. The present time of the action—we are still in Sylvia's mind—then jumps to that evening as Sylvia sits at dinner with Christopher and Sergeant-Major Cowley. During its course Sylvia's mind drifts off into a recollection of the previous afternoon, when everyone had been at Lady Sachse's for tea, and from there into a mental debate with Father Consett in heaven.

When Christopher returns from taking a telephone call, she hands him the letters she has kept back from him all these months; one of them, which she has opened and read, is from Mark Tietjens; as Christopher reads it, she rereads it in her memory. What we have here, then, is Sylvia's recollection of Mark's sardonic description of Sylvia's efforts to persuade Mark to withhold an income Christopher has in fact refused to take from Mark. Mark had felt Christopher should take the income but had not been able to make him; Sylvia thought Christopher had taken it and wanted Mark to take it back. As Sylvia recalls Mark's letter, we hear Mark's own words about Sylvia (and Valentine) and at the same time listen to Sylvia's response to them. "Hearing" the letter repeat itself in her memory, we contemplate with her Christopher reading it to himself and—knowing well Christopher's feelings about the money, about Sylvia, and about Valentine—we imagine his response to it. Thus three minds, all intimately familiar to us, are brought before us, vivid with their own styles and voices, in response to the same matter. Part II ends with Sylvia and Tietjens dancing to a phonograph; they will go up to Sylvia's bedroom shortly to discuss their situation.

Part III begins in Christopher's mind when he awakens the next morning in his tent as General Campion and Levin enter. After a brief visit to his headquarters and a talk with Levin, Christopher is cross-examined by Campion about what had occurred the night before when he was in Sylvia's room. In this way the violent activities of the night are conveyed to us; we learn Campion's decision to send Christopher into the front lines; and we watch Christopher's mind as it comes close to breaking down. Part III ends with Campion's inspection of Christopher's cook-house.

By staying within the minds of his two major characters, Ford is able to limit both the time and the place of the novel's action. It takes place entirely at the base and in the hotel at Rouen. Part I covers part of one evening, Christopher's meditation in bed afterward, and about an hour just after noon the next day. Part II covers the succeeding hour or so and the time between dinner and bedtime that evening. Part III covers a few hours the next morning. All the rest of the events are presented in scenes—sometimes very fully developed scenes—that are remembered by Christopher or Sylvia. This concentration of presentation allows Ford to focus on the meaningful moments of the story and to bring in the rest of the events at the points in the narration where meaning rather than chronology requires them to occur; it is the meaning of a recollected scene that leads the character to remember it at the moment he does, and the way he remembers it is saturated with the meaning that made him recall it. The skeletal structure of the narrative in *No More Parades* is chronological; its three interior dialogues deal with periods that follow one another in time. But Ford arranges the events remembered in these dialogues in an order that dramatizes their meaning. A good illustration is the way Sylvia recollects, in the middle of her dinner with Christopher and Cowley, the tea that afternoon at Lady Sachse's, where Christopher handled the difficult old French duchess so perfectly that Sylvia, enraged by this successful display of tactful authority, told General Campion that Christopher was a socialist whose secret desire was to model himself on our Lord.

In *A Man Could Stand Up*— Ford completed the development of interior dialogue as a mean of representing the consciousness at war with itself. He needed to, because in this novel both Christopher and Valentine reach the climax of the long struggles by which their unconscious selves free them from Edwardian commitments and they make new ones. Ford also carried to a new extreme the rearrangement of the events in the narrative to emphasize meaning rather than chronology. *A Man Could Stand Up*— begins in the mind of Valentine Wannop at approximately eleven o'clock of November 11, 1918, Armistice Day. Valentine is at the telephone in the girls' school where she works, listening to Edith Ethel Duchemin, now Lady Macmaster, who is telling her (in the mad hope that Valentine will persuade Christopher to cancel Macmaster's debt to him) that Christopher is back in London and needs help. We stay within Valentine's mind until she has finally admitted to herself that the enlightened late-Victorian standards of her parents, which she has been trying to live by, do not work in the postwar world and have to be discarded, and has faced what she has been trying not to recognize consciously ever since she and Christopher parted in August, 1917, at the end of *Some Do Not*... —namely, that she is helplessly in love with Christopher. Having thus discarded the unworkable idea of life she has been struggling to realize and having faced the truth about herself, she determines to seek out Christopher and commit herself to him.

Part II begins "months and months before" in Christopher's mind—to be precise, six months before, at dawn of a relatively quiet morning in April, 1918, during the great battle in which Ludendorff so nearly defeated the Allies. During this morning we watch Christopher reach his decision to give up trying to be the Tory Younger Son, the role he had with such uncompromising idealism and such agony of effort been trying to live. He will cease to do what he has heretofore considered his duty, his job in the Imperial Department of Statistics (which wants him to betray the principles it stands for by faking statistics); he will give up his gentlemanly loyalty to Sylvia (who wishes he would beat her); and he will retire to George Herbert's country, join his life with Valentine Wannop's, and make a living selling antiques. Though Part II of *A Man Could Stand Up*— has no chronological relation with Part I, it parallels it very closely in meaning. In it Christopher goes through the same process of self-discovery that Valentine had gone through in Part I, and reaches the same conclusion about Edwardian society that Valentine had.

Part III begins as Valentine, following up the decision she had reached in Part I, arrives at Grays Inn and meets Christopher. Throughout the next few hours we are alternately in the minds of Valentine and Christopher as, almost wholly without words of their own, they approach complete understanding. They are much assisted in the process by another telephone call. As Edith Ethel Duchemin had, at the novel's start, put Valentine onto Christopher by her telephone call, so now Mrs. Wannop, bent on preventing Valentine and Christopher's becoming lovers if she can do so without betraying her principles, inadvertently reveals to Christopher on the telephone that Valentine had come to Grays Inn prepared to be his mistress.

Last Post carries the story on chronologically until sometime between 1926 and 1929 (Christopher is somewhere between forty and forty-three years old). Its present time covers only a few hours and it takes place entirely at Christopher and Valentine's cottage. It has almost no action; Sylvia decides to free Christopher to marry Valentine, and Christopher returns from Groby, where the Great Tree has been cut down, in time to stand with a fragment of the tree in his hand at Mark's bedside as Mark dies. Apart from brief moments when we are in the minds of Cramp, the gardener, and Christopher's son, Mark, the narrative composes into a pattern of interior dialogues: Mark, Marie Léonie, Mark, Marie Léonie; Sylvia, Valentine; Mark. Ford's emphasis is on the minds and characters of Mark and Marie Léonie, and his purpose is to conclude *Parade's End* by counterpointing the relation of Mark and Marie Léonie and the relation of Valentine and Christopher, with whom their thoughts are naturally enough much preoccupied, as his purpose in *Some Do Not . . .* at the start of *Parade's End* had been to counterpoint the relation of Macmaster and Mrs. Duchemin with that of Valentine and Christopher. Only, in *Last Post* he works mainly in the minds of Mark and Marie Léonie instead of—as he had in *Some Do Not . . .* —mainly in the minds of Christopher and Valentine.

Putting the bulk of the narration in the minds of Mark and Marie Léonie makes them the novel's most prominent characters. Both are vividly realized, and the result is striking so far as Mark is concerned, for Mark is a Christopher Tietjens without the impulse to sainthood and with a Yorkshire stubbornness so great that he would rather die with the Edwardian world than change his mode of life, as Christopher does, in order to survive into the new world. Because of this parallel, the character that is elaborated in Mark's long interior dialogues illuminates Christopher's character. The device of working within Mark's mind is, in short, successful.

But that is not true of Marie Léonie; her interior dialogue defines amusingly the French point of view which, throughout *Parade's End*, has been contrasted with the English; Marie Léonie serves the public purpose of *Parade's End* very well. In a sense, perhaps, she also serves its private purpose. Nobody could be more shrewdly practical in her conduct, more firmly bourgeois in her taste, more thoroughly and domestically marital than Marie Léonie, despite the fact that Mark picked her out of a musical-comedy chorus and has kept her as his mistress for years. Her meditation gives the maximum dramatic emphasis to the contrasting motives and attitudes of Valentine and Christopher, about whom she thinks with tolerant disapproval, in conducting their irregular union. The difficulty about Marie Léonie as a point of view is that she is not involved in the central action of *Parade's End*, not intimately linked—either logically or by the previous novels in the series—with the main characters. Ford exercised all his ingenuity to justify his abrupt introduction of her, but there is no getting around the fact that, in using her, he multiplied entities unnecessarily and shifted attention from the real center of the action; though it is easy to understand why, with his lifelong passion for the French, Ford found her irresistible.

Ford later came to dislike *Last Post* and to believe he ought to have ended *Parade's End* with *A Man Could Stand Up—*. Of this opinion the most important thing to be said is that he did not. *Last Post* cannot now be made to disappear. Ford's main objection to *Last Post* must certainly have been that it does precisely what he said in his dedication it was intended to—that is, "explain what became of Tietjens" and the people connected with him. By doing so it put the final emphasis of the series on what happened rather than on what it meant, and everything about *Parade's End* shows that what mattered most to Ford was what his story meant, not what happened in it. The arbitrary introduction of Marie Léonie may well have enforced this point for him and left him feeling that the first three novels constituted a neatly rounded-off "Affair" that begins with Valentine and Christopher as earnest Edwardians and ends with them as committed moderns about to set forth on a new life: "On an elephant. A dear, meal-sack elephant. She was setting out on...." Here is that sonata form Ford had long ago described to Wells as the ideal form for a fiction. Yet even the sonata form allows for a coda, so that *Last Post* does not really break the pattern of the series; nor does it vary in technique from the other novels of the series any more than they vary from one another.*[60]

If it is possible to argue that *A Man Could Stand Up*— completes the series by leaving Valentine and Christopher on the threshold of the new, postwar world, it is also possible to argue that in *Last Post*, as Shakespeare's shepherd says to his son, "thou met'st with things dying, I with things new-born." In *Last Post* the stubborn embodiment of the Edwardian ethos, Mark Tietjens, "chooses" to die rather than to change, while Christopher and Valentine, who have adjusted to this new world in order to preserve the essential principles they have shared with Mark, are about to see themselves newborn in the child Valentine is carrying. Perhaps the Ford who had separated from Stella thought the pastoral life of the Small Producer at Bedham with Stella and Julie was a weak manifestation of the new life of the changed soul. But the Ford who wrote *Last Post* before these changes in his circumstances would have thought exactly the opposite. Moreover, there is something to be said for this display of the hidden, honorable, frugal life ("frugal" is a key word in *Last Post*) at the end of the series, as a balance against the costly parade of Edwardian life, now drained of all meaning, with which the series had started: in *Last Post* only Sylvia can still think of living the old, luxurious, Edwardian life any longer, and even she does so with a kind of desperate weariness ("...if you rid yourself of the distinction ...of Groby Great Tree just to wound a man to the heart...you may as well take India").[61]

An odd by-product of Ford's method of narration in *Parade's End* is that what is most obvious in a conventional novel—that is, what, in the literal sense, happens—is pushed into the background, and the reader must make an effort to dig it out. In a novel arranged, as *Parade's End* is, to dramatize

*In 1930, when a one-volume reprint of the tetralogy was in prospect, Ford said, "I strongly wish to omit the *Last Post* from the edition. I do not like the book and have never liked it and always intended the series to end with *A Man Could Stand Up*." This is evidently an exaggeration. In the dedication of *Last Post* to Isabel Paterson, he said, "But... for your stern, contemptuous and almost virulent insistence on knowing 'what became of Tietjens' I never should have conducted this chronicle to the stage it has reached now"; but this is the flattering exaggeration of a dedication. In dedicating *A Man Could Stand Up*— to Gerald Duckworth, in May, 1926, Ford referred to it as "the third and penultimate" novel of the series; as early as the spring of 1926, then, he was planning *Last Post*. He began *Last Post* the minute he finished *A Man Could Stand Up*—, without being urged by anyone; when he finished it he thought very highly of it. He never explained why he turned against *Last Post*, but like most authors he often turned against books (or suddenly became very pleased with them). For example, he said in 1932: "...as far as I can remember I don't like [the *Fifth Queen* trilogy] very much and don't want to see it republished," and "[*The Portrait* is] an eighteenth century pastiche for which I have rather a tenderness."

the consciousnesses of the characters and the meaning of the events, what happens and when and where can be indicated to the reader only by references that come plausibly into the characters' or the narrator's thoughts. Ford exercises a good deal of ingenuity to provide such references, though —because he completely trusted to memory—he sometimes contradicts himself. But he tried, as Dowell says in *The Good Soldier*, to see that "You have the facts for the trouble of finding them" in *Parade's End*. That it is far from easy to do so, however, is evident from the way even careful critics of Ford have got muddled about them. One of these critics, for example, tells us that *Parade's End* begins in 1908, which is four years too early; another that Sylvia seduced Christopher in the compartment of a French train (it was "in a railway carriage, coming down from the Dukeries," the remains of Sherwood Forest, in Nottinghamshire); a third that Sylvia and Christopher are preparing for bed in Sylvia's hotel room at Rouen in *No More Parades*, when the main point of this scene is that Sylvia is trying to get Christopher to go to bed with her and he is resisting.[62]

Ford's contradictions do not disturb our "impression" of *Parade's End*'s accuracy; they emerge only when we take Dowell's advice about finding the "facts." Then we are likely to notice that sometimes Macmaster is the son of a poor shipping clerk and sometimes the son of a grocer, and that the Tietjens family is a hopeless muddle. It first consists of four boys and two girls. The boys are, in order of age, Mark, Ernest (Curly), James (Longshanks), and Christopher, fifteen years Mark's junior. Ernest and James are killed in action on the same day. Within a week one of the sisters, Caroline, a nurse, is drowned. A second sister, Effie, is married to a north-country parson. But Sylvia calls one of the dead brothers Edward and Ducket speaks of a brother John and a sister Eleanor (Effie?). In *Last Post* the Tietjens family is completely reorganized. Mr. Tietjens there has ten children, three of whom die in childhood. Only five of the remaining seven are accounted for; they are Mark, Mary (the second child, who is "killed as a Red Cross matron" and is, presumably, the former Caroline), Ted, an unnamed third boy (these two are presumably the original Ernest and James), and Christopher, who is now fourteen years younger than Mark and the son of a different mother, Mr. Tietjens' hitherto unmentioned second wife.[63]

Some Do Not... begins on June 28, 1912. Christopher Tietjens, the twenty-six-year-old youngest son of an ancient Yorkshire family is traveling down from London to Rye with Vincent Macmaster, the ambitious son of a poor Scotsman. They plan to play golf at Rye and Macmaster means to interview a wealthy clergyman who lives nearby, at Pett; this clergyman, a man named

Duchemin, has known Rossetti, about whom Macmaster is writing a monograph with a view to getting himself promoted in the Imperial Department
of Statistics for which both young men work. Tietjens' wife, Sylvia, had run
off four months earlier with a man named Perowne. Four years older than
Christopher and a great deal more experienced, she had, some years before,
trapped Christopher into marriage because she had thought herself (mistakenly, as it turns out) pregnant by an earlier lover named Drake. Just before
Christopher and Macmaster had started on this trip to Rye, Christopher had
received a letter from Sylvia announcing that she plans to return to him. She
has, with great difficulty, escaped from the violently possessive Perowne at
a remote French village, Yssingueux-les-Pervenches, and joined her mother,
who has been living at a German air resort named Lobscheid pretending, for
the benefit of London society, that Sylvia is with her. Sylvia has ordered
Christopher to come to Lobscheid and get her. It is his worry over how to
reconcile his distaste for this task with his idealistic Tory conception of the
gentlemanly attitude toward sexual relations and marriage that makes him so
furiously impatient with Macmaster's laboriously pretentious essay on Rossetti and his later Pre-Raphaelite "gurglings" over Mrs. Duchemin.

Late that afternoon of June 28, 1912, Christopher and Macmaster play a
round of golf at the Rye golf club with Christopher's godfather, General
Campion, and his brother-in-law, Paul Sandbach. During the round, Stephen
Waterhouse, a Liberal minister who is playing just ahead of them, is assailed
by a pair of suffragette demonstrators, Valentine Wannop and Gertie Wilson.
The demonstrators escape, and that evening, while Macmaster is dining at
Mountby with Campion and his sister, Claudine Sandbach, Christopher and
Waterhouse work out a way to spare these demonstrators arrest.

On Saturday morning the young men breakfast at the Duchemins' and
that night Christopher and Valentine drive Gertie Wilson to Valentine's
uncle's house twenty miles the other side of Tenterden. On the following
Tuesday, at 5:15 A.M., Christopher leaves to join Sylvia at Lobscheid. He has
worked out a plan according to which they will, before returning home,
make an appearance together at Wiesbaden to quiet gossip about Sylvia. But
when Christopher arrives at Lobscheid he learns that his mother has died,
brokenhearted at the news that Sylvia is returning to him. In these circumstances he cannot take Sylvia to Wiesbaden since they have to go into
mourning; he will not take her to England because he cannot bear to have
her at his beloved mother's funeral. He therefore takes her on an extended
trip to Kiev.

From then until 1915, Christopher and Sylvia keep up the appearance of a marriage, but they do not sleep together and Christopher refuses to let her have their son at home, keeping him at his sister Effie's in Yorkshire. Just before the outbreak of the war, in July, 1914, Sylvia and Christopher are staying together at Bamborough. Christopher leaves Sylvia there and goes to stay with Effie and his child. While he is there, Macmaster arrives, much agitated because he and Mrs. Duchemin have been spending what they hoped would be a circumspect lovers' weekend together nearby and have unexpectedly encountered friends who may at any moment realize that they are lovers. To help them, Christopher escorts Mrs. Duchemin back to London. It is August 3, 1914, the day war was declared, and everyone who is anybody is on the train from Bishop Aucklands to London. Most of them see Mrs. Duchemin weeping on Christopher's shoulder and this starts the rumor that Mrs. Duchemin is Christopher's mistress, a rumor that Sylvia sedulously encourages; this rumor is sometimes elaborated to include a bastard child because Christopher seems to have a mysterious child hidden away somewhere in the north of England.

About this time Mrs. Duchemin begins coming regularly to Macmaster's house to serve, publicly, as hostess at his weekly literary gatherings (her husband is now in an asylum); each week she brings Valentine Wannop as a sort of chaperone and, after carefully leaving in Valentine's company, slips back to Macmaster's—as Valentine knows—to spend the night with him. Christopher continues to work, along with Macmaster, in the Imperial Department of Statistics for slightly more than a year after the war begins, but by the fall of 1915 he can no longer endure the government's habit of faking statistics in order to blackmail France; and he has been growing convinced that it is his duty to be at the front. In November, 1915, at one of Macmaster's receptions, he tells Valentine Wannop he cannot reconcile it with his conscience to remain at home. He enlists, reaches the front early in 1916, and is in the fighting throughout that year. In May, 1917, he is knocked out by a near-miss at Noircourt; his mind goes blank for three weeks. When he recovers, his memory is completely gone; he also has lung trouble. He is invalided home. In August, 1917, he is declared fit again, though his memory has not returned and his lungs are still bad. The last night before he leaves for the front he asks Valentine Wannop to be his mistress; then he decides that they are both people "who do not" and leaves her at the door of her house. After a late night session with Sylvia in their flat in Grays Inn he goes out to France once more.

At the beginning of No More Parades, Sylvia has been for three months (98 days, she says) in retirement at a convent at Birkenhead, where she has been reading prewar novels. Christopher has been assigned to a base near Rouen, in charge of organizing drafts and dispatching them to the front. The commanding general at the base is Campion. Christopher has only recently got out of the hospital, to which he had been sent for congestion of the lungs. It is the beginning of December, 1917. With the help of her former lover, Perowne, who is now on General Campion's staff, Sylvia makes her way to Rouen. There she lies systematically to General Campion about Christopher, provokes Perowne by flirting with General O'Hara, and tries to seduce Christopher. She creates so much trouble, the blame for which falls on Christopher, that General Campion sends him up to the lines as second-in-command of the 9th Glamorganshires. He goes up February 14, 1918, in the company of Perowne, who is terrified of death and is killed almost as soon as he arrives at the front, and of McKechnie, a mad young officer who was formerly second-in-command of the 9th Glamorganshires. In April, 1918, during the crisis of Ludendorff's attack, Christopher is forced by the collapse of the colonel, a man named Partridge, to take over the command of the battalion. Three days later, General Campion relieves Old Puffles (General Perry) of the command of the army; almost his first act is to relieve Christopher of his command and put him in charge of a prisoner-of-war detail behind the lines.*

Some time before, as a sort of diversion, Christopher had worked out for Macmaster a set of statistics: Macmaster is still in their old department. Valentine had wondered at the time if it was not dangerous for Christopher to do that, but Christopher is confident that Macmaster is the soul of honor. Macmaster now gains a knighthood by claiming these figures as his own. Early in the fall of 1918 Christopher's weak lungs send him back to the hospital and, in October, 1918, he is invalided home, to a job at Ealing. He means to stick the war out because he wants to collect all the bonus he can. He has worked out an agreement with an American named Schatzweiler, whom he has met as a German prisoner of war, to buy up antiques for Schatzweiler to sell in America. But Christopher's brother Mark, never for a moment suspecting that Christopher will refuse to take a penny of the income from the family estate, gets Christopher demobilized just before

*The date of Sylvia's appearance at Rouen is a little indefinite. Christopher thinks of his parting from her—presumably at the end of August, 1917—as having occurred "three months ago" (I, 303); the divorce leave from which McKechnie has just returned ran "from the 14/11 to the 29/11" (I, 309). Sylvia says (I, 406) that she and Christopher parted at dawn "98 days ago." All these references place the events of *No More Parades* in the first week of December, 1917. Yet two days after Sylvia's arrival at Rouen, when General Campion asks Christopher the date, Christopher says it is "Thursday, the seventeenth, I think, of January [1918]. . . ." (I, 502), and this date seems to have been chosen with some care since January 17 was, in fact, a Thursday in 1918.

Armistice Day. Christopher had misled Mark into believing he had forgiven his family and would take money from the estate by going to see Mark when Mark fell ill with pneumonia about three weeks before Armistice Day, caring for him painstakingly and interesting himself in persuading Mark to marry his long-time mistress, Marie Léonie Rioter.

On Armistice Day, now a civilian, Christopher returns to his flat in Grays Inn. Sylvia has carried off all the priceless antique furniture Christopher had, to please her, skillfully collected for the flat; only one piece is left. Sir John Robertson, the distinguished dealer, had some years before offered Christopher £100 for this piece. Needing money desperately now, Christopher starts out with this piece under his arm to find Robertson. On his way out the front door he meets Valentine Wannop coming to look for him in order to become his mistress, having just heard from Mrs. Duchemin that he is back. He tells her to go upstairs and wait for him. Sir John—having been taught by Sylvia to believe Christopher is beneath contempt—offers him £5 for his eighteenth-century cabinet. He refuses and carries it to Mark's house and tries to borrow money from Mark on it. Mark refuses, insisting that Christopher take the money as his own, which Christopher refuses to do. "Pour le dieu d'amour," Marie Léonie lends Christopher £40.

Going up to Christopher's flat as she has been told to, Valentine finds it furnished with his camp bed; this room, cleared of all Edwardian splendors, seems to her the right place for the consummation of their relation. While she is waiting she telephones her mother to tell her what she is going to do. Christopher then arrives back at the flat in time to talk to Mrs. Wannop too. While he is doing so, Valentine admits to the flat a mixed company of Christopher's front-line friends—the one-eyed Arunjez, whose life Christopher had saved; Arunjez' Nancy from Bailleul; McKechnie; and Colonel Partridge, whose cancer has already required the amputation of his arm. They drink and dance at the flat and then go out to dinner together. McKechnie goes completely insane during the evening and Christopher and Valentine have to take him to an asylum. While they are doing so, Colonel Partridge dies in their cab and they have to take his body to Balham. They arrive back from these expeditions at Mark's flat about midnight. When they finally reach Grays Inn, Sylvia—alerted to what is going on by Lady Macmaster—is standing at the head of the stairs. She announces she is dying of cancer and then does a theatrical fall down the stairs that injures her ankle. When Christopher is tempted to help her, Valentine fiercely insists that he leave Sylvia alone and come back to Mark's flat with her. They get there about two in the morning. After they have returned to Grays Inn a second time, Lord Woolstonemark calls Marie Léonie and reveals to her that the Allies have decided not to occupy Berlin. When Marie Léonie tells Mark this news, he has a stroke. Marie Léonie calls Valentine and Christopher and they return to help her. They have not, as Marie Léonie thinks, had much of a *nuit de noces.*

Eventually, however, in *Last Post*, Christopher sorts things out. He takes a show cottage near Fittleworth and persuades Marie Léonie and Mark to join him and Valentine there. He organizes his antiques business, which he manages to finance from a supposedly worthless investment of an inheritance that suddenly becomes valuable. But he has a hard time of it. His American partner does not pay him; Valentine is highly sensitive about her status and grows increasingly so during her pregnancy; Sylvia is still harassing him: she has let Groby to a crazy American named Mrs. de Bray Pape and has persuaded her to cut down Groby Great Tree, and she has herself come down to stay with Lord Fittleworth, whom she is trying to persuade to evict Christopher and Valentine from their cottage. Most of these problems are cleared up by the end of *Last Post*. Christopher and Sylvia's son, Mark, shows every sign of growing up another Christopher; Sylvia has a vision of Father Consett and is persuaded to divorce Christopher so that he is free to marry Valentine and make their child legitimate. That frees Mark, Christopher's brother, to die.

Thus *Parade's End* ends with Valentine and Christopher and their child leading the frugal, obscure, virtuous existence that is modern life's embodiment of Christopher's Tory principles. We do not know whether Sylvia marries Campion, who has been offered the position of viceroy of India; but the suggestion is that he and she, no longer believing either in each other or what they are doing, are helpless to do anything but carry on the now meaningless Edwardian parade, perhaps in that last satrapy of empire, India.

These are the chronological facts "you have . . . for the trouble of finding them" in *Parade's End.*

A Little Less Than Gods

A Little Less Than Gods is constructed in much the same way that the Tietjens novels are, though without their consistency in point of view and with a good deal more dependence on scenes of dramatic dialogue. Ford reduces to his usual three acts the public story of Napoleon's hundred days and the private story of the love of George Feilding and Hélène de Frèjus, their discovery that they are brother and sister, and the elaborate plot by which Mr. Assheton Smith saves the life of Ney. Part I traces the involvement of young George Feilding in Napoleon's one hundred days and his passion for Hélène de Frèjus from the start at Elba to the moment at Cannes when France commits herself to Napoleon and Hélène commits herself to George. Part II begins three weeks after the battle of Waterloo, outside the Luxembourg Gardens, where Hélène and Madame Ney anxiously await their husbands, now in great danger from the royalists, and ends with Hélène's discovery that she is George Feilding's illegitimate sister. Part III rounds the whole complicated story off in four concentrated scenes. Occasionally, as in the chapters in which Gatti, the Napoleonic veteran, tells Hélène about George Feilding, whom she loves and must reject (Part III, Chapters II and III), or when George himself tells Hélène about the death of her husband (Part III, Chapter IV), Ford achieves the psychological suspense and emotional concentration of the Tietjens novels. But for the most part *A Little Less Than Gods* is an adventure story not unlike *Romance.* George Feilding is the upright, naïve Englishman that John Kemp was; he has the same sort of heroic career amidst historically spectacular events, and his story ends in a trial very like Kemp's, even to the way Hélène's testimony helps his cause, as Seraphina's did Kemp's. Ford treats the trial from George's point of view in the same way he treated Kemp's.

The nominal point of *A Little Less Than Gods* is perhaps a little more sophisticated than *Romance*'s point, that "romance" is simply the effect of the distancing of time. The title of *A Little Less Than Gods* comes from Dryden's "Song for St. Cecilia's Day":

> Less than a god they thought there could not dwell
> Within the hollow of that shell
> That spoke so sweetly and so well,

which Ford characteristically misquotes from memory part way through the novel. Napoleon's eloquence makes him seem to George Feilding scarcely less than a god. Nonetheless Napoleon fails, imperiling the lives of everyone he has convinced. George's awe-inspiring father is responsible for the horrible disaster of George's love. Mr. Assheton Smith, for all his godlike power, can save Ney only because Frèjus is willing to die for Ney. " . . . are we not all," Gatti says to Hélène, "in the end the puppets of the Gods?" "Ay," Hélène says bitterly, "but the men at whose hands we suffer are a little less than Gods!" It is a reasonable but not very striking judgment, and it is embodied in the conduct of the characters in the simplest sort of way. The most effective dramatic use Ford makes of it is the occasional suggestion that the best people are the young, who are always betrayed by the elderly mortals they mistake for gods. "Here," as Hélène thinks of Squire Feilding, "was another of these demi-Gods, another of these enormous creatures who wreck worlds—or human lives that in themselves are whole worlds. No doubt George's body was safe under that aegis; but what about his humiliation, his disillusionment, his disbelief in humanity . . . his . . . his dishonour?"[64]

The difficulty about *A Little Less Than Gods* is that there is no necessary connection between the private and the public experience it deals with; Katharine Howard's personal tragedy in *The Fifth Queen* was a result of her whole-souled commitment to a policy for England—for mankind—that Henry VIII could not finally countenance, however much he loved her. The story of Henry's career and of Katharine's love are the same story. But the innocently incestuous passion of Hélène de Frèjus and George Feilding has no necessary thematic relation with Napoleon's hundred days and the destruction of their youthful enthusiasm for Napoleon's godlike greatness is hardly a crucial aspect of the moment in history with which the novel is ostensibly concerned. Nor have their lives any special significance of their own despite the sensational character of their love.

ⅇ When the Wicked Man

The Babbitt of Ford's *When the Wicked Man*, Joseph Notterdam, is an Englishman who has immigrated to America. He has knocked about the West for years with a Dutchman named Kratch, jumping from town to town and job to job like some character in Mark Twain or Bret Harte. When the novel opens, he is—thanks to Kratch, who has become a millionaire—the head of a famous old publishing house which—like Mr. Sorrell of *Ladies Whose Bright Eyes*—he sees as a purely commercial enterprise. He means to make a fortune by selling aspiring businessmen nonbooks on how to make a fortune, and by bribing public officials to buy his textbooks.

Like Babbitt and Mr. Sorrell, Notterdam is naïvely earnest: he lives by the values of his society, and it never occurs to him that there is anything seriously wrong with them. On the other hand, he keeps thinking of the inadequacy of his life, its rootlessness, its lack of domestic happiness—his kept women, his incipient alcoholism, the confusion and fatigue of unscrupulous moneymaking. He keeps feeling ashamed of business deals that had seemed smart to him at the time. In pale imitation of "The Jolly Corner" he is haunted by a vision of himself that he cannot bear, a Doppelgänger who appears whenever he is under tension. At the end of the novel, after a complicated plot that emphasizes the contrast between Notterdam's satisfaction with his life and his sporadic awareness of its dishonesty and sterility, he makes an effort to save himself by going back to his home town in England, attempting to make restitution for the damage he has done others, giving up drinking, and settling down to permanent domesticity with the heroine. But circumstances are too much for him. He finds himself in the company of a woman who appeals strongly to his lust and decides he might as well be hung for a wolf as a lamb. He gets drunk, and just as he is about to seduce this woman, a gangster who is one of the woman's previous lovers shows up; Notterdam mistakes him for the Dopplegänger, shoots him, and becomes a hero.

> What were you to make of that? . . . Where could reform come in? . . . You could not say that whilst in a state of alcoholism you had been trying to rape a young woman [and] a phantasmagoric product of delirium tremens had appeared to you. . . . So that you tried to shoot it and hit a racketeer. . . .

On top of this, all his crooked publishing schemes succeed. This is what happens "when the wicked man turneth away from his wickedness that he hath committed, and doeth that which is lawful and right. . . . " The social system—American commercial society—is simply too strong for the sporadic efforts of a naïve man like Notterdam. He gives in and returns to America, where the heroine waits on the dock, amidst a whirl of policemen and publicity, to welcome the returning hero.[65]

The general conception of *When the Wicked Man* is perfectly reasonable, though the plot is unnecessarily fantastic and Ford's insistence on telling the story in his characteristic impressionistic manner emphasizes everything but what is important for satire, plot, and social observation. Nevertheless the book fails disastrously. Ford did not understand the world he was describing and, what is worse, was so sure he did that he exposed his ignorance freely. Describing Notterdam's scheme for using bribery to sell his school textbooks, he shows he thinks the American public-school system is operated by a "State [that is, a Federal] Education Authority" and that Notterdam can sell his textbooks only if a bill is passed by the Senate. Wanting to give Notterdam a tastelessly extravagant house on Long Island, he makes it an "imitation of a Mexican adobe patio" and gives it twelve bathrooms; at this luxurious establishment, Notterdam keeps poultry. He makes all his characters "speak American," with the result that Notterdam's children, brought up on Long Island and in private schools, assert that a fellow student at their school is "a swell fan at composition," and Lola Porter, from a superior Southern family and the wife of a proud English writer, says to a dignified publisher, "Do you see, kid, or are your brains too dusty?" All the characters resort to incomprehensible locutions, apparently intended for American colloquialisms ("Aw, Gee, Dot, can your head") and talk about dropping off a caboose (meaning a freight car) or having "the works done on" them by gangsters. These "Americanisms" are regularly accompanied by what Ford apparently does not know are exclusively British locutions—phonograms, golf house, in liquor—and some which are neither American nor British—gas-fixings (gas fixtures), roof bungalow (penthouse), distance call (long-distance call). These characters are as implausible in their conduct as in their speech; they are made up of Ford's scattered and inaccurate observations of Americans and his recollections of the life described in American books at least a generation out of date when he was writing. Ford made these unfortunate efforts to represent the manners and speech of a new age out of his deep anxiety to remain contemporary. He had been convinced—possibly by Hemingway's eloquent assertion of the point—that the dignified literary speech of his young manhood had become hopelessly dated. He liked to assert that he had learned this in the war and that it had been a fact since the nineties.

> By the nineties, in fact, not only had the literary language become unusable by the common man the world over; it had become nauseous when it was not merely grotesque.... In my battalion, after mess, when they wanted to feel good they would say to me:
> "Speak like a book, H.... Do speak like a book for a minute or two."
> And I would begin gravely:
> "After mature consideration I have arrived at the conclusion ..." There would be already titters....

Ford's all too confident ignorance of American life makes *When the Wicked Man* absurd.[66]

৶ The Rash Act *and* Henry for Hugh

When the "inverted detective story" of *The Rash Act* and *Henry for Hugh* is treated in Ford's characteristic manner, with its restriction of the point of view to the protagonist and its extensive use of the time shift, an extremely ambiguous narrative results. "The book is," as Ford said in his blurb, "the most wound-up example of the use of the time-shift that Mr. Ford has yet given us, the greater part of it passing, as is the case with our lives, in memories superimposed on the present and intimately affected by anticipations of the more or less distant future." Ford was rightly proud of his skill in managing this complicated structure; "I consider these two novels are my best books," he said, "—at any rate they fill exactly my ideas of what a novel should be. Of course the much better known *Good Soldier* is equally correct in handling, but I think it is relatively rather thin and timid in handling." This emphasis on handling is ominous; Ford was returning in these last novels to the preoccupation with technique at the expense of substance that characterized much of his early fiction; "he may sometimes," as Graham Greene gently put it, "have been over-elaborate, an accusation which after he had spent more than forty years in writing fiction can be brought against his last novels."[67]

Technically these novels are skillful and some of the episodes are entertaining. The calm assurance with which Jeanne Becquerel, in *Henry for Hugh*, ascribes her own absurdly bourgeois values to Eudoxie is quite funny, especially as we know very well what Eudoxie is really like. The treatment of the storm in *The Rash Act* is a fine illustration of how well Ford could handle a character's moment-by-moment experience of a violent event, and his representation of Henry Martin's motives as he substitutes his documents for the dead Hugh Monckton's after he has escaped from the storm is very ingenious, a careful exploitation of the conflict between Henry Martin's conscious self and his "under selves."[68]

But these technical ingenuities seem like game-playing, as if Ford were setting himself problems of no real significance to see how cleverly he can solve them, because both the world he has imagined in these novels and the creatures that inhabit it are fantastic. For example, in *Henry for Hugh* Gloria Malmström, whose refusal to become Hugh Monckton's mistress had led him to commit suicide, comes to the man she thinks is Hugh Monckton (but is really Henry Martin posing as Hugh Monckton) and asks him to let her sell the £40,000 of Monckton shares he has given her; Ford has Henry Martin grant her request because he is convinced that Hugh Monckton's honor requires him to do so.

> ... a world-famous actress had the right to at least a couple of millionaire suicides for her publicity. But consider what he [that is, Hugh Monckton] had done [when she rejected him]. Within thirty-six hours of the parting he had set himself up with a little anybody as *maîtresse en titre. And now he was living with two young women at once.*

"You could not here [in Europe]," Henry Martin tells himself, "plaster a woman with tens of thousands of banknotes of large dimensions and then refuse her . . . the natural solace her outraged honour demands." This is an ingeniously unexpected line of reasoning; it complicates the positions of both Eudoxie and Henry Martin, who both know that Henry Martin is not Hugh Monckton and are both deeply concerned to maintain the deception that he is and to protect Hugh Monckton's good name. This is clever, but it is about as humanly plausible as the motivation in a P. G. Wodehouse novel.[69]

Again and again Ford substitutes this kind of ingenuity for any possible sort of human behavior—when he maneuvers Jeanne Becquerel into the position of Henry Martin's *maîtresse en titre* just as Henry Martin and Eudoxie are falling in love; when he gives Eudoxie her fantastic moral principles to increase the difficulty of their escaping from this dilemma; when he makes it a matter of conscience for Henry Martin to protect his own reputation and that of Hugh Monckton at the same time; when he constructs the immensely complicated financial situation of Henry Martin.

Moreover, with a narrative method that limits the reader to the thoughts and feelings of the protagonist, as Ford's does, it is possible to give substance to "world circumstances" only if the protagonist is directly involved in these circumstances, as Christopher Tietjens is involved in the war. Ford tried to make Henry Martin a victim of the forces he believed had produced the Depression. He did not succeed, partly because his explanation of the Depression—Hugh Monckton's monetary theory—is ridiculous, but mainly because Henry Martin is a remote victim of it. Ford did not know enough about Americans to make him anything else. "Taylor [as Henry Martin was first called] I am afraid w^d have to be English," he wrote in his preliminary synopsis. "I could *psychologise* an American all right—but I don't know practical details—like schooling, games & such things." Even this was a self-deception; it was true that he did not know the practical details; it was also true that he had little insight into the psychology of Americans. Nevertheless he made Henry Martin an American and as a result risked the same kind of blunders he had in *When the Wicked Man*. Such blunders are disastrous with a character built up entirely from inside as Ford's hero is. Henry Martin simply collapses as a sensitive, educated American—a Dartmouth graduate and a Rhodes scholar—when he is made to express his homesickness by thinking that "he wanted to see some good up-state [Ohio] Hick who had made good in real estate . . . [who] could give a 16 h. p. grip. . . ." There are innumerable false notes of this kind in *The Rash Act* and a good many in *Henry for Hugh*.[70]

Henry for Hugh is, nevertheless, a good deal better novel than *The Rash Act*. *The Rash Act* has to support the deadweight of Ford's unsuccessful effort to create Henry Martin's American background. But Ford's knowledge of the Saint-Jean-du-Var area made it possible for him to create a convincing impression of life at the Villa Niké in *Henry for Hugh* and thus to construct a solid novel of the kind he did best. In *Henry for Hugh* a very complicated but wholly consistent—if fantastic—situation creates for Ford's protagonist a nightmare of difficulties that Henry Martin's romantic honorableness makes even more complicated. From this nightmare Henry Martin is then slowly freed by an almost equally complicated series of surprising but carefully explained events. At the conclusion of *Henry for Hugh* Henry Martin is freed to marry Eudoxie by the unexpected marriage of Jeanne Becquerel— whom his gallant rescue from suicide had given an irresistible claim on him —to Henry Martin's Communist secretary; he is released from the need to play the role of Hugh Monckton and endowed with wealth by Hugh Monckton's aunt Elizabeth Freiligrath, who on her deathbed whispers to him, "Henry Martin.... You have been a good lad.... I am happy." She knows he is not her nephew, Hugh Monckton, but thinks his deception has saved the Monckton name from the disgrace of suicide, and, thanks to Eudoxie's heroic efforts, she has learned that Henry Martin has the same great-grandfather as Hugh Monckton and is thus the best heir she can find. *Henry for Hugh* ends with Henry Martin sailing happily for America with Eudoxie because—at least according to Ford's original plan—Henry Martin "will finish in Springfield, Ohio...."[71]

⁊ Vive le Roy

The hero of *Vive le Roy*, Walter Leroy, is a young scientist who, out of vague sympathy with the Left and a love of adventure, had undertaken to deliver to the French Radicals $20,000 collected for them by the American Communists; he had just fallen in love and begun to live with a young American painter, Cassandra Mathers. They are watched over with suspicious devotion by "a great, fat, enormous, clumsy, active, obtuse, sympathetic, stupid, diabolically clever lump of flesh and intellect" called Penkethman, an old Scotland Yard hand who very much resembles Ford Madox Ford, as the young people resemble Katherine Anne Porter and Eugene Pressly—or at least Ford's conception of them.[72]

The difficulty about this *Prisoner of Zenda* in modern political dress is that it is not a very good thriller. Making a restored monarchy the salvation of a country was no doubt a romantically appealing idea in the days of Anthony Hope and the early John Buchan and the Ford of *The New Humpty-Dumpty*. But in 1936, it was not; immensely intelligent grand Chamberlains devoted to their handsome young kings were difficult to make socially sympathetic figures in the thirties, no matter how much humanitarianism and love of modern painting you ascribed to them. Ford did not diminish the old-fashioned air of his story by using a good many equally antiquated detective-story devices. He takes us unblushingly through a scene in which Penkethman dazzles everyone by making astonishing deductions about Walter, in the manner of Sherlock Holmes bowling over Dr. Watson by deducing his shaving habits at a glance. Penkethman wears a monocle that is a mirror and, without so much as turning around, breaks the arm of a villain sneaking up behind him. On top of all this, the plot of the novel is, despite Cassie's remaining in the dark up to the end, transparent from the start. Lewis Gannett said he suspected Penthièvre's plan to substitute Walter Leroy for the king on page 11 and was all but sure of it by page 22, and few readers are likely to remain mystified much beyond that point. The book's other secret—that Penkethman is Walter's father—is given away almost as promptly.[73]

Ford does not increase the excitement of his plot by presenting the climatic events—the abduction of Walter, Cassie's meeting with the bomb-throwing radical leader, her last meeting with Walter at the Caveau Rouge—through the mind of a participant. This shifts the reader's attention away from the events themselves to the interior dialogue of a mystified observer just when the interest depends most on what is happening. This defect is made more annoying by the implausibility of the observers, Ford's young Americans. Like the Americans of *When the Wicked Man* and *The Rash Act*, these characters are burdened with Ford's version of American manners and Ford complacently draws the reader's attention to the comic confusion of the French ("the American *lingua franca* is beyond most of us") over a mystery Ford is confident he has penetrated. It is not easy to believe in a heroine who, wishing to ask where a taxi driver has found some money, says, "Oh angels and ministers of grace, I don't want to spoil your home-run. ... But couldn't you ask where the jitney-guy did his gold-digging?" "Even Ford fans," as one reviewer remarked, "will not compare *Vive le Roy* with Ford's War novels."[74]

Notes

$\mathfrak{P}$

In order to avoid scattering superscript numbers over the text like confetti, I have put such numbers only at the ends of paragraphs and put together in the note references for all the material in each paragraph. After each reference I have indicated the location of the document except in the cases of Elsie Martindale's correspondence, which is in the possession of Mrs. Charles Lamb; of the letters of Ford and Stella, which are in the possession of Mrs. Roland Loewe; and of the letters of Ford and Sir Stanley Unwin, which are in the files of Allen & Unwin. Except where confusion may result, Ford's name is omitted before books written by him.

The following short titles are used in the notes:

Biala. The Janice Biala Papers, now on deposit at Cornell.

Cornell. This collection includes the Violet Hunt Papers. Many of the letters in the Violet Hunt Papers are copies; I have not attempted to distinguish these from the originals.

Harvey. David Dow Harvey, *Ford Madox Ford, 1873–1939: A Bibliography of Works and Criticism* (Princeton, 1962).

Ludwig. *Letters of Ford Madox Ford*, ed. Richard M. Ludwig (Princeton, 1965).

Naumburg. The collection of Edward Naumburg, Jr., of New York.

Soskice. The collection of Lord Stow Hill.

For convenience, all references for *The Good Soldier* are to the paperback edition published by Vintage and all references for *Parade's End* to the paperback edition published by the New American Library, but quotations themselves are from the first English editions of these five novels. All references for *The March of Literature* are to the second impression of 1947.

Introduction

1. Ezra Pound, "Ford Madox Ford," *New Directions,* Number 7 (Norfolk, Conn., 1942), p. 480. Herbert Gorman, "Ford Madox Ford: The Personal Side," *Princeton University Library Chronicle,* April, 1948, pp. 121–22. Stella Bowen, *Drawn from Life* (London [1941]), p. 63.
2. Georges Schreiber, *Portraits and Self-Portraits* (Boston, 1936), pp. 39–40.
3. Robert Lowell, "Ford Madox Ford: 1873–1939," *Life Studies* (New York, N.Y., 1959), p. 49. Campion's abrupt demotion of Christopher Tietjens (*Parade's End*, II, 146) is a less extravagant version of his story about Lloyd George's blocking his promotion.
4. *Between St. Dennis and St. George,* pp. 56–57.
5. Ford to Herbert Read, Sept. 19, 1920, in Herbert Read, *Annals of Innocence and Experience* (London, 1940), p. 169, and in Ludwig, p. 127.
6. *Portraits from Life,* pp. 1–3.
7. Violet Hunt, *The Flurried Years* (London [1926]), p. 38. For a striking example of irrelevant vanity in *Joseph Conrad,* see p. 232. Granville Hicks, "Ford Madox Ford—A Neglected Contemporary," *The Bookman,* Dec., 1930, p. 364. Jessie Conrad to Hugh Walpole, June 4, 1935 (Birmingham). When H. G. Wells said a kind word about Ford in *Experiment in Autobiography* (New York, 1934), Jessie wrote him grimly, "... perhaps I should not grudge him this, his first triumph over his fellow collaborator" (Jessie Conrad to H. G. Wells, Feb. 19, 1934 [Illinois]).
8. Robie Macauley, "The Dean in Exile: Notes on Ford Madox Ford as Teacher," *Shenandoah,* Spring, 1953, pp. 44–48.
9. *The Flurried Years,* p. 61. *D. H. Lawrence: A Composite Biography,* ed. Edward Nehls (Madison, Wis., 1957), I, 123.
10. Robert Lowell, "Foreword," *Buckshee* (Cambridge, Mass., 1966), pp. xi–xii.
11. *The March of Literature,* p. 640.
12. Ezra Pound, "Hugh Selwyn Mauberley: Mr. Nixon."
13. Ambrose Gordon, Jr., *The Invisible Tent* (Texas, 1964), p. 13.
14. Hugh Kenner, *Gnomon* (New York, 1958), p. 157.

Chapter 1

1. Extract from the Register of Baptisms, Lamerti Parish, Münster (Cornell).
2. "It was at the suggestion of Schopenhauer, or, possibly, because his own lively disposition made parts of Germany too hot to hold him, that Doctor Hueffer came to England" (*Memories and Impressions,* p. 48).
3. William Michael Rossetti, *Some Reminiscences* (London, 1906), pp. 332–33. *It Was the Nightingale,* p. 138. "Declined with Thanks," *New York Herald Tribune Books,* June 24, 1928, p. 1. Ford entertained himself in the linked novels, *The Rash Act* (1933) and *Henry for Hugh* (1934), by making the history of the hero's family, the Fabers, a variation on the history of the Hüffer family; see particularly *Henry for Hugh,* pp. 152–53. Violet Hunt's notes on Ford Madox Brown's diary (Cornell) fix the date of his emigration and show that Franz Hueffer was dining regularly at the Browns' by late 1870. Ford Madox Brown's portrait of Franz Hueffer (now in the possession of his grandson, Lord Stow Hill) shows him with eyes rather formidable than "radiant" and with sandy red hair and beard. For the Pre-Raphaelites' marriages see Rosalie Glynn Grylls, *Portrait of Rossetti* (London, 1964), p. 10.
4. *Ford Madox Brown: A Record of His Life and Works,* pp. 2–10. *Return to Yesterday,* p. 23.
5. Juliet M. Soskice, *Chapters from Childhood* (London, 1921), pp. 202–04. Juliet herself was,

according to David Garnett, "a ravishingly beautiful blonde" with "the complexion of a wild rose, masses of golden hair and enormous innocent blue eyes" (*The Golden Echo* [London, 1953], p. 38). The exhibition of Mrs. Hueffer's pictures is mentioned in *Ford Madox Brown*, pp. 219, 250. An oil sketch by her of her two sons, Ford and Oliver, made when they were about seven or eight, is in the possession of Lord Stow Hill. Her father's drawing of her is reproduced in *Ford Madox Brown* opposite p. 131.

6. Soskice, *Chapters from Childhood*, p. 201. Mrs. Charles Lamb.

7. *Thus to Revisit*, p. 53. *Memories and Impressions*, p. 78. Ford's memories of his childhood appearance are reliable. The costume he describes—except that in this instance both his stockings are bright blue—can be seen in the portrait his mother painted of him and Oliver when they were seven or eight. The "very long golden hair" can be seen in the portrait of Ford as William Tell's son painted by Ford Madox Brown when Ford was four years old. Brown is known to have painted this picture twice. The only copy I know of is in the possession of Lord Stow Hill and seems to be the copy that was at one time —during the twenties, when he was in Bedham—in Ford's possession.

8. *Memories and Impressions*, p. 46. It is typical of Francis Hueffer that he quoted this phrase from a spelling book he had used as a child in Münster. Mrs. Rossetti Angeli remembered her stays with the Hueffers as made unpleasant by "old Franz's bullying of the boys."

9. *Portraits from Life*, p. 204. *Memories and Impressions*, pp. 5–6.

10. "Not Idle," *New York Herald Tribune Books*, July 1, 1928. Mr. Blood is the leading character in *Mr. Fleight* (1913). Ford also used him frequently as a spokesman in the articles he wrote during this period. Mr. Blood evidently owes some of his characteristics to Arthur Marwood—or to Ford's idea of Arthur Marwood; but in all important respects he is an image of what Ford wanted to be himself.

11. *Memories and Impressions*, pp. 106–07, 117, 127, and 179–80. Minutes of the Society of Authors, Oct. 16, 1913, quoted in Samuel Hynes, *The Edwardian Turn of Mind* (Princeton, 1968), p. 299.

12. *Memories and Impressions*, p. 113.

13. *Return to Yesterday*, pp. 72–73. *No Enemy*, p. 64.

14. *Memories and Impressions*, pp. 115–16.

15. *Memories and Impressions*, p. 174.

16. Brown was in Manchester from April to July of 1879 and from April to September of 1880. He moved to Manchester in the fall of 1881. See *Ford Madox Brown*, pp. 327, 338–39. It is only fair to Ford to remember that he was a precocious child and that all the Pre-Raphaelite children were treated as adults. Ford was taken by his grandfather on some of his journeys to Manchester, though he was only six or seven years old, just as he was taken about by Francis Hueffer and, in crises, even used as an assistant. Once, when they were at the Three Choirs Festival at Worcester and Francis Hueffer needed the telegraph office kept open until he finished his article, he had Ford stay in the office sending anything that came into his head to keep the clerk there. What came into the fourteen-year-old's head was the church service, so that the message to the *Times* began, "When the wicked man turneth away from the sin that he has committed..." (Ezekiel, xviii, 27), a phrase that was to come into his head again over forty years later when he was looking for the title of a novel. See *Memories and Impressions*, pp. 96 and 200.

17. *Memories and Impressions*, p. 13. Charlotte Kirby seems to have had a notable touch with cab drivers. See *ibid.*, pp. 110–11. Ford retells the anecdote about Swinburne at somewhat greater length in *Portraits from Life*, pp. 185–92, where Charlotte's views of Swinburne and "Lizzie" Rossetti (Elizabeth Siddal) are also amusingly set forth.

18. Ford many times describes the Fitzroy Square house; for the details here see *Ford Madox Brown*, p. 240, and *Memories and Impressions*, pp. 2 and 13.

19. In *Provence* (p. 196) Ford recalls seeing Ellen Terry leaning over him between fits of

delirium during an illness in 1881. This is perfectly possible; Ellen Terry was a family friend. His throat was scraped by the great Sir Morell Mackenzie, who cared for Frederick III when he had cancer of the throat (*A History of Our Own Times* [Cornell], p. 354). Ford Madox Brown wrote Mrs. Alfred Hunt to cancel a dinner invitation at this time "in consequence of . . . the youngest of the Hueffer boys [Oliver] being sent here through his brother's taking scarletina" (Cornell). Ford says in *Women & Men* (p. 16) that he went to Westminster School. For Eton, see Douglas Goldring, *The Last Pre-Raphaelite* (London, 1948), p. 251.

20. Robert Skinner, "Oliver Madox Hueffer," *The Scotsman*, June 27, 1931, quoted in Harvey, p. 591.

21. *Provence*, p. 208. *The March of Literature*, p. 653.

22. *A History of Our Own Times* (Cornell). Mathilde Blind also created in him a lifelong dislike of Shelley by reading him her book on Shelley.

23. "For Poorer Travelers," *Harper's*, April, 1933, p. 620.

Chapter 2

1. For the date of Francis Hueffer's death see *Ford Madox Brown*, p. 393. Brown had moved to St. Edmund's Terrace from Manchester two years before. At Francis Hueffer's death, Watts-Dunton became Mrs. Hueffer's trustee and the boys' guardian. Ford found him very unpleasant when he went on quarter-days to collect his mother's income (*Portraits from Life*, pp. 194–97).

2. Soskice, *Chapters from Childhood*, pp. 9–19.

3. David Garnett, *The Golden Echo*, pp. 35–36. *Portraits from Life*, p. 90. Ford sometimes thought his commitment to what he called "my Tory-Papistry" was much strengthened by "the fact that my cousins, the young Rossettis . . . made my life rather a burden with their militant atheism and anarchism" (*Provence*, p. 132).

4. *Provence*, pp. 209–11 and 65. David Garnett, *The Golden Echo*, p. 109. Throughout his life Ford took pride in his command of Latin verse; it was one of the lighter accomplishments of an English gentleman. In *No More Parades* Christopher writes a sonnet to Capt. Mackenzie's (McKecknie's) set rhymes in "under two minutes and a half " and Mackenzie undertakes to turn the sonnet into Latin hexameters in under three minutes; at the end of *A Man Could Stand Up*—Mackenzie turns up at Christopher's flat on Armistice Day still worrying about that Latin translation (*Parade's End* [NAL], I, 319, and II, 163–73). This episode echoes an experience of Ford's own in 1916 with a captain named H. C. James; in an appendix to *On Heaven and Poems Written on Active Service* Ford printed two sonnets and three other poems of his together with Capt. James' Latin translations.

5. Soskice, *Chapters from Childhood*, pp. 236–38; Ford took Juliet to tea with Prince Kropotkin in 1894 or 1895. For Ford's acquaintance with anarchists and nihilists, see *Return to Yesterday*, pp. 93–94, 105–06, and 130–33; *Great Trade Route*, p. 78; and *A History of Our Own Times* (Cornell), pp. 134 and 260. H. G. Wells's *The Bulpington of Blup* (New York, 1933), pp. 53–112. Wells's description of Theodore Bulpington's exploration of the world of London's young intellectuals and radicals in this novel he wrote about Ford is probably a fair representation of this aspect of Ford's life.

6. Helen Rossetti Angeli, *Dante Gabriel Rossetti* (London, 1949), p. xii; Grylls, *Portrait of Rossetti*, p. 20.

7. Soskice, *Chapters from Childhood*, p. 30; *Memories and Impressions*, pp. 246–47.

8. *Ford Madox Brown*, pp. 354, 393, and 400–01.

9. Soskice, *Chapters from Childhood*, p. 35. *Ford Madox Brown*, p. 248.

10. *Memories and Impressions,* pp. 154–55, 249, 247–48, and 219. But when Ford first told the Harry Quilter anecdote in *Ford Madox Brown* (p. 390) all his grandfather said was, "Just as if I was living in a dog-kennel." William Rossetti recalled the specific evening Ford is remembering; see *Outlook,* April 22, 1911, p. 508. The "great picture" in Brown's studio was one his fellow artists had collected a thousand pounds to commission for the Academy, to which Brown was never elected. They had a hard time getting Brown to accept this commission: he suspected them of trying to be kind to him.

11. *Ford Madox Brown,* pp. 95–96.

12. "Mrs. Hueffer and her children are now living with me. The boys are big fellows. Ford, the eldest, has left school" (Brown to Gilchrist, Dec. 1. 1890 [Naumburg]). After Ford left the University College School he made a slight effort to enter the Royal College of Music in pursuit of his ambition to become a composer; he was, he thought, refused admission because the College so hated his father's advanced views (*Memories and Impressions,* pp. 89–90). According to Ford, he left University College School when the headmaster, learning of the publication of *The Brown Owl,* told him no boy engaged in business could remain at the school (*Memories and Impressions,* pp. 87–88). But *The Brown Owl* was not published until Sept., 1891. *Provence,* pp. 242–43. *Return to Yesterday,* p. 11.

13. *Provence,* p. 242. Soskice, *Chapters from Childhood,* pp. 235–36. *Memories and Impressions,* pp. 143–46.

14. Elsie Martindale remembered Ford's dictating poems and short stories to her at this time. *The Soul of London* has many descriptions of the London of this period; see, for example, pp. 16–18. The first passage quoted in this paragraph is from Ernest Rhys, *Everyman Remembers* (New York, 1931), p. 7; the second from *Memories and Impressions,* p. 200.

15. Ford's "In Memoriam" is in the Soskice Papers. Ford Madox Brown to Watts-Dunton, Sept. 22, 1891 (Texas). The copy of *The Brown Owl* he sent Watts-Dunton is in the Naumburg Collection. There is a similar letter from Brown to Gilchrist in the Naumburg Collection and he also sent a copy of *The Brown Owl* to Swinburne. Garnett sent Ford an advance copy of the book in August and the dates of Ford Madox Brown's letters suggest it was officially published in September rather than in October, as the reviews led David Harvey to believe.

16. *Portraits from Life,* p. 94.

17. *The Feather,* p. 8. *Portraits from Life,* p. 94.

18. *The Shifting of the Fire,* p. 295.

19. *The Shifting of the Fire,* pp. 126–27. For Ford's quotation of Berlioz in relation to his own affairs, see below, p. 30.

20. Joseph Conrad to Ford, postmarked Nov. 12, 1898 (Yale).

21. That Ford really did visit his Uncle Hermann at this time is clear from the family records of Mrs. Lamb. Ford's version of that visit is in *Return to Yesterday,* pp. 112–25. Some of the details in this paragraph come from *A History of Our Own Times,* p. 325 (Cornell). Ford wrote a short story about this visit to Germany, "The Baron (A Love Story)," *Macmillan's,* LXXXVII (Feb., 1903), 304. Violet Hunt describes his memories of this time in *The Desirable Alien* (London, 1923), pp. 127 and 256. Ford once said that before he was twenty (that is, before Dec. 17, 1894) he had "spent three winters in Paris and two summers in Germany" (*Return to Yesterday,* p. 112). That remark certainly exaggerates the length of his stays but perhaps not the number of his visits. It is almost impossible to be sure which of the incidents he later recalled belonged to which of these visits, particularly as he himself often confused them with one another. For another version of his atheist German tutor, see *When Blood Is Their Argument,* pp. 157–61. The female cousin in the almost Nihilist toque reappears in *Return to Yesterday,* pp. 125–26, where her name is given as Magdalena Schabrowsky.

22. "I Revisit the Riviera," *Harper's,* CLXVI (Dec., 1932), p. 65. *Provence,* pp. 259 and 33n.

23. There is an official copy of Ford's baptismal record at Cornell. *Between St. Dennis and St. George*, p. 75; *Return to Yesterday*, p. 104. Ford also remembered himself as having studied kitchen gardening at the Sorbonne during these many winters in Paris. The reference to Newman's circle is in *Henry James*, p. 90, where he says he has just discovered he unconsciously used Newman in one of his own novels, presumably as Don Kelleg in *An English Girl*.
24. *Provence*, pp. 132–33. Ford's history—at least as he sums it up in *Provence*—was not very accurate either. *Cromwell, Protector of the Vaudois*, is reproduced opposite p. 313 of *Ford Madox Brown*.
25. *Towards a History of English Literature*, Part II, p. 39 (Cornell). Ford to Stella Bowen, Sept. 19, 1918.
26. Soskice, *Chapters from Childhood*, pp. 235–36.

Chapter 3

1. *The Good Soldier*, pp. 111–14. *Parade's End* (NAL), II, 132. Ford to Elsie, Oct., 1893, and Jan. 6, 1894. Ford to Elsie, Jan., 1894, Martindale affidavit (when Dr. Martindale sought the court's aid in his attempt to get Elsie to return home after she had run away, he submitted an affidavit in which he included a number of letters from Ford to Elsie that he had found).
2. Ford to Elsie, March 3, 1894; Dec. 14, 1893; and March 5, 1894.
3. Ford to Elsie, May 2, 1893. There is no doubt the Martindales were trying to separate Ford and Elsie; in his affidavit, Dr. Martindale said openly that "As soon as my daughter is restored to me I intend to make arrangements for giving her a complete change of scene and surroundings for a considerable period of time."
4. For Dr. Martindale see the London *Times*, Feb. 6, 1902, p. 7.
5. When Mrs. Martindale died in 1906, there was about £ 15,000 to be divided among the children; the *Extra-Pharmacopeia* and the business, worth perhaps £ 50,000, were left to Harri Martindale.
6. *It Was the Nightingale*, pp. 273–74.
7. Oliver's early financial difficulties are documented in the family papers preserved by Darley Cumberland, their lawyers. *It Was the Nightingale*, p. 273.
8. H. G. Wells, "The Well at the World's End," *Saturday Review*, 82 (Oct. 17, 1896), 412.
9. Ford to Elsie, Feb. 26, 1894.
10. Ford to Elsie, July 19 and c. July 20, 1893.
11. Ford to Elsie, June 3, 1893; Feb., 1894; July 17, 1893.
12. Ford to Elsie (from Paderborn), Aug. 11, 1893; Oct., 1893; Oct. 26, 1893; and Jan. 7, 1894. The change may well have been a real necessity for, as always happened when Ford was under a strain, he developed all sorts of ills and his letters to Elsie during these months are filled with references to his arm being bad again or his having "gout" in his hand.
13. Martindale affidavit.
14. Elsie to Dr. Martindale, March 5, 1894 (about 11:00 p.m.); Martindale affidavit.
15. Ford to Elsie, March 5, 1894; W. M. Rossetti to Dr. Martindale, March 8, 1894; Ford to Elsie, c. March 8, 1894, and c. March 10, 1894. Ford to Edward Garnett, n.d., in Ludwig, p. 8.
16. Martindale affidavit. Mrs. Hueffer to Elsie, c/o Miss M. Hunter, 45 Victoria St., Gloucester, May 8, 1894.
17. Elsie to Dr. Martindale, May 5, 1894. This letter, like its predecessor, was sent through Shaen Roscoe in order to conceal Elsie's whereabouts. In his affidavit Dr. Martindale

indignantly denied what Elsie says about her mother and Mary, but it was quite true.
18. For the proceedings before Mr. Justice North, see the London *Times*, Aug. 10, 1894. Ford and Elsie must have learned they were in trouble with the court almost immediately after they were married; there exists a letter from Mrs. Hueffer to Robert Garnett, dated May 22, 1894, and evidently in reply to one from Ford, which says, "I enclose my letter to Ford ... as I am not certain how to address him. ... The marriage certificate is in the letter to Ford. They want it."

Chapter 4

1. The Ford Madox Brown sale realized £ 1,350, bringing Brown's net estate to £ 2,188.4.3; Lucy and Catherine therefore received what William Rossetti rightly called a "not very considerable amount" of about £ 1,000 apiece (Darley Cumberland). G. H. Perris was seven or eight years older than Ford. Five years after this episode he established, with C. Cazenove, the Literary Agency of London, which was later taken over by Curtis Brown. The issue of the *Star* of June 6 that contains the original story was an extra and is not in the British Museum's newspaper library. There were follow-up stories in the *Star* June 15, 22, and 23 and Aug., 9, and in the *Pall Mall Gazette*, June 23 and Aug. 9. For the court's action with reference to Ford and Perris' story, see the *Times*, Aug. 10, 1894.
2. Bloomfield Villa, now called Fir Trees Villa, is just off B2067 on the road that runs between the Priory Wood and the Park Wood. It is almost unchanged in appearance from the time of Ford and Elsie. Ford talks about Bonnington in *Return to Yesterday*, pp. 140ff. Elsie to Olive Garnett, Dec. 12, 1896.
3. *Return to Yesterday*, p. 175. *An English Girl*, p. 52.
4. *Return to Yesterday*, p. 170; Ford to Edward Garnett, n.d., in Ludwig, p. 9.
5. "I meant to ask about the bloody novel that Dent wouldn't have—I s'pose it is still with you?" (Ford to Edward Garnett, n.d., but 1895, in Ludwig, p. 8). There is a fragment of a novel written in Ford's earliest handwriting; it may be the novel here referred to (Cornell). The story of finding an author for *Ford Madox Brown* is in William Rossetti's *Some Reminiscences*, II, 543–44. That William Rossetti revised the book is clear from the letter to Garnett referred to just above, and the request for Garnett's assistance with the style is made in another undated letter to him from Bloomfield Villa (Texas).
6. *Ford Madox Brown*, pp. 306, 311, 386; *Return to Yesterday*, p. 46; *A History of Our Own Times*, p. 164n (Cornell).
7. Sometime early in 1896 the Hueffers bought a grandfather clock, inside the case of which they pasted sheets of paper that served as a guestbook (the first names recorded there, on April 3, 1896, are those of William Harrison Cowleshaw, the architect who had designed the cover of *Ford Madox Brown*, and his future wife, Lucy Garnett). The list of guests for August is representative. Robert Garnett and his wife, Martha, stayed with them the weekend of Aug. 1, Harri Martindale and two friends the weekend of the 7th. Two weeks later Oliver Hueffer was there ("Oliver, Baron von Hüffer-Schaumbirg, Aug 24/96") and three days later Mr. and Mrs. Martindale and Elsie's sister, Mary. This list does not include local guests like James Raynor, the "literary grocer" of Aldington, who were also there in August. James's letter to Ford, Sept. 11, 1896 (Harvard). *Return to Yesterday*, pp. 12–16; the account Ford gives there of his reasons for approaching James in the first place are apparently entirely imaginary, though they are not impossible.
8. Elsie Hueffer to Olive Garnett, Dec. 12, 1896; Ford to Walter Jerrold, n.d., but Oct. 15–21, 1896 (Cornell); *Return to Yesterday*, p. 152; E. V. Lucas, *Reading, Writing and Remembering* (London, 1932), p. 147. The Pent is shown on the Ordinance Survey's one-inch map of

East Kent; it is on the Pilgrim's Way about half a mile west of Postling.
9. Ford to Jerrold, n.d. (but fall, 1896) (Cornell). Ford to Elsie, from Manchester, Dec. 12, 1896. Ford to Jerrold, c. Jan. 5, 1897. Ford to Elsie, c. July 10, 1897. Ford tells an anecdote about Batalha-Reis, without mentioning his name, in *The Cinque Ports*, pp. 80–81. Christina's birth is recorded in the grandfather clock. Ford even tried to persuade James to use Hyde as an illustrator (James to Ford, Dec. 30, 1897 [Harvard]).
10. The descriptions of Ford and Elsie are H. G. Wells's in *Experiment in Autobiography*, p. 526, and David Garnett's in *The Golden Echo*, p. 36. The amber necklace was also worn by Ethel Duchemin; it is still in the Hueffer family's possession. Garnett, aged 5, was so charmed by Elsie that he at once proposed to marry her. Ford had grown the beard in December, 1893. *Portraits from Life*, p. 25. "The Work of William Harrison Cowleshaw," *The Artist*, xx (Sept., 1897), 432. "Sir Edward Burne-Jones," *Contemporary Review*, LXXIV (Aug., 1898), 181.
11. For the Russian novel in the 1890's see Samuel Hynes, *The Edwardian Turn of Mind*, pp. 310–11. Ford to Unwin, Jan. [*sic:* Feb.] 24, 1937.
12. Gracie's Cottage was so called because it was built for Constance Garnett's sister, Grace Black; both it and The Cearne were designed by William Harrison Cowleshaw. David Soskice was one of Constance Garnett's many Russian protégés. He had fled Russia a year or so before this time for political reasons (he had been sent to Siberia, from where he escaped to Paris and eventually arrived at The Cearne). In Sept., 1899, he married Anna Sofia Soskice at the registry office in Fulham; they had a son, Victor. In Sept., 1901, he discovered his wife living in Paris, where she had gone to study medicine, with another medical student named David Kleiman. Soskice got an uncontested divorce from her in Feb., 1902. He and Juliet were married the next October. Soskice's character is very well described by David Garnett in *The Golden Echo* (pp. 36–37), from which the description of Ford's also comes. Lawrence substituted Stepnyak for Soskice in his account of Ford and Soskice. David Garnett's firsthand version of the story is in *The Golden Echo*, pp. 37–38; Lawrence's version of it is in Kyle Chrichton's interview with Lawrence printed in *D. H. Lawrence: A Composite Biography*, ed. Nehls, II, 412. Ford to Unwin, Jan. [*sic:* Feb.] 24, 1937.
13. *Return to Yesterday*, pp. 37–38.
14. Ford describes the origin of *Seraphina* in *Return to Yesterday*, pp. 170–73, and *Joseph Conrad*, p. 13. He tells some of the local tales about smugglers in *The Cinque Ports*, pp. 175–77, and used both Thomas Wrangsley and the Old Bourne Gang in *The Portrait*, p. 112. The sample chapter of the Henry VIII book Ford wrote is typed on the backs of sheets originally used for the typing of thirty-one pages of Chap. II of *Romance* in one of its early forms (when Carlos Riego was still named Sanchez). This fragment of *Romance* cannot have been written before 1899 and was probably written a year or two later. In June Ford wrote Pinker, " . . . when [*Seraphina*] is done I hope to send you the synopsis of the Henry VIII book" (Princeton), and c. July 4, 1901, Conrad wrote Ford, "Don't let this interrupt your work on the dear old Harry. I hear you've been gathering the pollen and the sweetness of the B'sh Museum and assume you are fabricating now the specimen [honey-]combs [that is, presumably, the sample chapter]" (*Joseph Conrad, Life and Letters*, edited by G. Jean-Aubry [New York, 1927], I, 312–14, where the letter is, as David Harvey has pointed out, misdated 1903). The letter to Edward Garnett is in Ludwig, p. 8. Conrad discusses the problem of composition dates for *Romance* in a letter to Ford of Sept., 1903 (Yale).
15. Aaron Smith's trial was reported in the *Morning Chronicle* and the *Times*, Dec. 20, 1823.
16. *The March of Literature*, p. 746. Wells's comment on Ford is on p. 92 of *Boon* (London, 1915). The typescript of *Seraphina* (187 pp.) is at Cornell; its full title was written on the title page of this typescript by Edward Garnett. At several points "F. M. Hueffer/

Gracie's Cottage/ Limpsfield Chart/ Surrey" is written on the back of this ms. (see, for example, pp. 1 and 14 of Chap. XIII and the last page of L'Envoi). This fixes the approximate date of composition of *Seraphina.*

17. Pont Farm's second-story room that could be reached only by a ladder and the pane of glass with "John Kemp, 1822" scratched on it existed at the Pent (*Joseph Conrad,* p. 12). There is a summary of *Seraphina* with the fragmentary ms. of *Romance* in the Keating Collection at Yale; it corresponds reasonably well with the typescript of *Seraphina* except for its account of the book's ending, which varies considerably. Ford's later "impressions" of *Seraphina* (e.g., *Joseph Conrad,* p. 47) have almost no resemblance to the actual novel.

Chapter 5

1. *Return to Yesterday,* p. 52. In *Joseph Conrad* (p. 52) Conrad has Borys in his arms when he comes round the corner of the house. Jessie Conrad (*Joseph Conrad and His Circle* [New York, 1935], p. 63) says he cannot have: " . . . my baby was too young to trust alone with his father." In general, however, Ford's recollection of this scene appears reliable; it was also Conrad's: "The first time I saw you was in your potato-patch" (Conrad to Ford, Dec. 15, 1921 [Yale]). Wells, *Experiment in Autobiography,* p. 525. *Joseph Conrad,* p. 238. The psychological sources of Conrad's eccentric behavior—and of certain classes of characters in his fiction—have been very interestingly analyzed by Bernard Meyer, *Joseph Conrad* (Princeton, 1967). Dr. Meyer's conception of Conrad's relations with Ford suffers, however, from an unavoidable lack of information about their collaboration and, particularly, the quarrel that ended it. Conrad wrote Wells from The Cearne on Sept. 6, 1898 (Illinois), which fixes the date of his meeting with Ford.

2. *Joseph Conrad,* pp. 11–12.

3. *Return to Yesterday,* pp. 201 and 66, and *Joseph Conrad,* pp. 36–37. Conrad's letter to Henley, written Oct. 18, 1898, is in the Morgan Library (Jocelyn Baines, *Joseph Conrad* [New York, 1960], pp. 217–19). Its respectful attitude toward Henley did not prevent Conrad's saying to Cunninghame Graham "I am afraid Henley is a horrible bourgeois" (July 20, 1898 [Dartmouth]). Mr. Baines half suspects that Conrad never wrote Ford suggesting a collaboration at all: "Although all Conrad's letters to Hueffer written at this time seem to have survived there is none which contains such a proposal," he observes, p. 216n. But this statement is evidently false; Conrad's letter to Ford of Sept. 29 (Yale) clearly refers to previous correspondence that has not survived: "I've just got back from Glasgow and write without loss of time asking you to conclude the affair [of turning the Pent over to the Conrads] with the landlord. I would prefer to be a quarterly tenant. . . . This opportunity is a perfect Godsend to me. It preserves what's left of my piety and belief in a benevolent Providence and probably also my sanity." Conrad had gone to Glasgow in a last effort to find a command and return to the sea.

4. *Return to Yesterday,* pp. 170, 33, 65.

5. *Joseph Conrad,* pp. 11–12. Conrad to Ford, Oct. 2, 7, and 20, Nov. 12 and 27, 1898 (Yale); postmarked Nov. 7, 1898 (Colgate). In an undated letter of either Oct. 14 or Oct. 21 ("Friday") (Yale), Conrad says, "I am afraid we cant put off our departure from here [Stanford-le-Hope], the van arrangements being made. . . . But suppose you stay on? May I get a room in the village? . . . Jessie is coming on the 27th." They were certainly installed at the Pent by the 28th, when Conrad wrote Galsworthy that "the first letter in my new home was from you" (Birmingham). Conrad paid—or at least agreed to pay, for the money was not always forthcoming— £20 a year for the Pent. Conrad to Cunninghame Graham, Jan. 19, 1900 (Dartmouth). Immediately after the move he had written

Cunninghame Graham, "Now I am here I like it. I can write a little a very little" (Nov. 9, 1898 [Dartmouth]).

6.   E. V. Lucas, *Reading, Writing and Remembering*, pp. 146–47.

7.   Edgar Jepson, *Memories of an Edwardian* (London, 1937), p. 142.

8.   Wells, *Experiment in Autobiography*, pp. 530 and 525. *Joseph Conrad*, p. 37. In later years Ford liked to assert that he too thought in French. "Joseph Conrad—as, indeed, is the case with the present writer—habitually thought in French and translated his French into English. This helped him enormously—as it has done the present writer" (*The March of Literature*, p. 563). The sentence quoted from *Romance* is on p. 382 of the Concord Edition. Pinker's jibe at Conrad's accent is described by Jessie Conrad, *Joseph Conrad and His Circle*, p. 141; Conrad's comment on it is in a letter to Pinker, May 23, 1910. Lewis Hind, *Naphtali* (London, 1926), p. 73. Hind was staying with Wells at Voysey House. He says Conrad "had come over from his inland farmhouse [the Pent], where he was writing *The Nigger of the Narcissus*." This is impossible. Conrad did not move to the Pent until the end of October, 1898. *The Nigger of the Narcissus* was finished by February, 1897, printed as a serial in the fall, and as a book in December. Probably Hind did remember where Conrad had come from and confused his own reading of *The Nigger*—and perhaps discussing it with Conrad on this occasion—with Conrad's writing it. If so, this meeting took place sometime during the fall of 1898. E. V. Lucas, *Reading, Writing and Remembering*, pp. 145 and 147.

9.   *Return to Yesterday*, pp. 201–02.

10.   Conrad to Ford, postmarked Nov 13 99 (Yale). This letter is, somewhat inaccurately, transcribed by Mr. Baines, *Joseph Conrad*, pp. 235–36. As Conrad's addressing them both suggests, the trouble on this occasion was caused by Elsie, who felt Ford was neglecting his own work—as in fact he often did—to help Conrad. "I am sorry," Conrad says earlier in his letter, "your wife seems to think I've induced you to waste your time. I had no idea you had any profitable work to do...." What this "profitable work" was is a question. It could not have been *The Cinque Ports* because Conrad knew all about that and had, ten months before, tried to talk Meldrum of *Blackwood's* into commissioning it (Conrad to Ford, postmarked Jan. 30, 1899 [Yale]). Anyway, profitable work sounds like work for the magazines. Perhaps Elsie was exaggerating—as Ford himself sometimes did —the value of the few poems he was placing in magazines at this time; perhaps there was some vague scheme afoot for involving Ford in what always tempted him to dream of glory, editorial authority: there is a vague allusion to a weekly paper in Conrad's letter to Ford of Jan. 15, 1900 (Colgate).

11.   *Return to Yesterday*, p. 191. J. H. Retinger (*Conrad and His Contemporaries* [London, 1941], pp. 77–78) has put this same view of the relation somewhat more brutally. "It must be admitted that Conrad was a somewhat capricious friend....[Ford] soon sensed the genius of Conrad, and ... lauded him to the skies. Conrad's susceptible nature reacted easily to this homage and sincere flattery, and Hueffer became an intimate visitor at his house.... Without having any tender feelings for him, Conrad felt obliged and grateful...."

12.   Ford to Pinker, n.d. (but late Jan., 1904) (Princeton). Ford to Keating, n. d. (but Dec., 1936), in Ludwig, pp. 267–68. This letter was written to explain how Ford helped Conrad write *Some Reminiscences (A Personal Record)*, but the *Tremolino* story is in *The Mirror of the Sea* and the places Ford has Conrad reminiscing (the terrace at the Pent and Stocks Hill) fit neither book: *The Mirror of the Sea* was dictated at Airlie Gardens and *Some Reminiscences* (so far as it was dictated) at Aldington. Ford's letter describes various occasions when he persuaded Conrad to describe his life; it is an "impression." Ford could write an amateur shorthand. On a letter to Gerald Bullett, Oct. 3, 1933 (Biala), he jotted down for his secretary an answer in this shorthand. It was good enough for taking down Conrad's

dictation, though not perhaps with the ease Ford suggests. *Return to Yesterday*, p. 194. Jessie Conrad, *Joseph Conrad and His Circle*, p. 87.

13. Jessie Conrad, *Joseph Conrad and His Circle*, p. 89; Ford to Keating, n. d. (but Dec., 1936); Ludwig, pp. 267–68. The anonymous puff of Conrad is in *T. P.'s Weekly* for Jan. 4, 1904, p. 10. Ford's letters to Pinker (Princeton) show its publication involved the usual quota of complaints from Ford: the magazine outrageously failed to publish it immediately; it failed to insert a couple of late changes he sent in; it failed to pay him the day it received copy. William Rothenstein, *Men and Memories* (New York, 1932), II, 41; the portrait itself is reproduced there opposite p. 42. Conrad to Wells, Oct. 20, 1905 (Jean-Aubry, *Joseph Conrad*, II, 25).

14. *Return to Yesterday*, p. 191; Wells, *Experiment in Autobiography*, pp. 526–27.

15. *Return to Yesterday*, pp. 207 and 192. Ford did write the letter of admiration to Conrad that he describes in the first of these passages in *Return to Yesterday*, on May 31, 1924 (Yale), aboard the *Paris* (not, as he says, the *France*) as they were nearing Plymouth. There is a real pathos in this upsurge of feeling for Conrad when one considers that at this time Conrad was saying to Pinker that Ford "seems to be suffering from the idea that everybody in the world has insulted him. One would think it a mania if one did not suspect that there is a purpose in it. . . . What a luxury it would be to get rid of his nonsense. . . . You will admit that [in my letter to Ford] I have dissembled my rage successfully" (Conrad to Pinker, Feb. 7, [1924], [Yale]). *Joseph Conrad*, p. 37. Conrad's letter to Henley, Oct. 18, 1898, is in Baines, *Joseph Conrad*, pp. 217–19. See *Joseph Conrad, Letters to William Blackwood and David S. Meldrum*, ed. William Blackburn (Durham, N.C., 1958).

16. *Return to Yesterday*, p. 203.

17. *Return to Yesterday*, p. 185. *Joseph Conrad*, pp. 168–69. "On Conrad's Vocabulary," *Bookman*, June, 1928, p. 405.

18. Elsie to Mrs. Lamb, c. 1945; Jessie Conrad, *Joseph Conrad and His Circle*, p. 66. A typical instance of Jessie's self-dramatization is her story about the half-witted laborer, Hunt, besieging the Pent for two days while she heroically protected Conrad from any knowledge of the situation in order not to interrupt his work. Such, at least, was the story she told Constance Garnett (see David Garnett, *The Golden Echo*, p. 63). She gives a quite different—and no doubt equally imaginary—version of this siege in Jessie Conrad, *Joseph Conrad and His Circle*, pp. 78–84. There is a third in Borys Conrad, *My Father: Joseph Conrad* (New York, 1970), pp. 39–41.

19. *Joseph Conrad*, p. 42. Ford has improved this story; what actually happened was that Conrad pressed the bell but when he removed his finger "an invisible finger kept the button down" (Conrad to Wells, Dec. 23, 1898, in Jean-Aubry, *Joseph Conrad: Life and Letters*, I, 263). Wells's call on Ford is described in *Return to Yesterday*, p. 224, and in a canceled passage in the ms. of *Joseph Conrad* in which Ford reveals his hurt and anger (see John Hope Morey, *Joseph Conrad and Ford Madox Ford: A Study in Collaboration* [June, 1960], a Ph.D. thesis at Cornell). Henry James's disapproval is reported by David Garnett in *The Golden Echo*, p. 64. As late as 1929, Ford was still feeling injured by the opposition to the collaboration. In a canceled passage in the typescript of "Working with Conrad" (*Yale Review*, XVIII [June, 1929], 699–715), he says, "Personally I have never cared whether people liked me or not and Conrad's friends certainly did not" (Yale). The date of the visit to Sandgate is approximately fixed by Conrad's letter to Galsworthy (Birmingham), written early in November, 1898, in which Conrad says Ford is at the Pent with him.

20. "Aldington Knoll: The Old Smuggler Speaks." Conrad's letters to Ford are addressed to Limpsfield as late as January, 1899. Jessie and Joseph Conrad's names follow William Hyde's on the Fords' guest list immediately after their arrival at Stocks Hill. *Joseph Conrad*, p. 117. The novel about Cromwell is mentioned twice in Elsie's diary for October,

1899. Granger's plans for such a novel are described in *The Inheritors* (Concord Edition), p. 69. Perhaps it was Ford Madox Brown's admiration for Cromwell that led Ford to think of him as the subject for the kind of historical novel both his temperament and the market made it inevitable that he would sooner or later write.

21. *Joseph Conrad*, pp. 131 and 136–38. Conrad's inscription in Richard Curle's copy of *The Inheritors* (Yale). *Return to Yesterday*, p. 199. Jessie Conrad, *Joseph Conrad As I Knew Him* (London, 1926), p. 113. Conrad to Ford, postmarked NO 3 99 and Feb. 17, 1900; McClure to Conrad, Nov. 23, 1899 (Yale). Conrad talks of his illness to Cunninghame Graham, Feb. 13, 1900 (Dartmouth). Ford to Walter Jerrold, March 17, 1900 (Cornell).

Chapter 6

1. *Joseph Conrad*, pp. 133–34. Ford's horror of Leopold's Congo is eloquently stated in *England and the English*, pp. 333–35, and in *A History of Our Own Times*, pp. 200–01n (Cornell). He knew Roger Casement and had seen some of Casement's photographs of the Congo atrocities.

2. *Memories and Impressions*, p. 171.

3. The inhabitants of "Greenland" are Eskimo on p. 32 and blacks on p. 162 of *The Inheritors* (Concord Edition). The Conradian passage is on p. 103 (for another, see p. 120). Conrad to Garnett, July 3, 1901 (Colgate).

4. The reviews are from *The Spectator* and *The Academy* (Harvey, p. 280). *Joseph Conrad*, p. 118, and *The Nature of a Crime* (New York, 1924), p. 97.

5. The London *Times*, Sept. 3, 1901, p. 9.

6. Conrad to Meldrum, April 3, 1900, in Blackburn ed., *Letters to William Blackwood and David S. Meldrum*, p. 89. Conrad to Edward Garnett, March 26, 1900 (Colgate). When Garnett printed this letter in his edition of *Letters from Joseph Conrad* (Indianapolis, Indiana, 1928), pp. 168–69, he silently changed "fools of the Morley Roberts sort" to "fools of the N. S. sort."

7. Ford to Edward Garnett, May 5, 1928 (David Garnett). Ford's remark about Conrad "things stolen" from him refers to Elsie Hueffer's sale of various Conrad items left in her possession when she and Ford separated. In *Mr. Apollo* (pp. 113–14) the young people sing "Old Horse" when the elderly Mr. Clarges blunders his way out of the Milnes' flat. David Garnett, *The Golden Echo*, pp. 127–28.

8. *Return to Yesterday*, p. 204. *Portraits from Life*, p. 66.

9. Conrad to Ford, March 31, [1900] (Yale).

10. Jessie Conrad to Marguerite Poradowska, April 16, 1900, in *Letters of Joseph Conrad to Marguerite Poradowska* (New Haven, 1940), ed. J. A. Gee and P. J. Sturm, p. 102. In the passage about the Virgin Mary that Ford cut from the book version of "On Heaven," Mary promises Violet a son: "It is so very good to have borne a son;/ It is sad that you have no child!" (See Harvey, p. 191.) But it was Ford, not Violet, who wanted that son.

11. *The Cinque Ports*, pp. vi, 162, 168, and 208–09. *The Cinque Ports* is a beautifully made book, lavishly illustrated by William Hyde. Only 525 copies were printed, at 63s. Nesh does not appear on the Ordinance Survey map. The whole "family" pitched in on *The Cinque Ports*. Olive Garnett dug up Jeakes' *History of the Cinque Ports*, which Ford used extensively, and was told to send Ford "Any collection of Anglo-Saxon Town-charters or of Medieval English Town-charters or Customals" she could find (Ford to Olive Garnett, n.d. [Univ. of Kansas]).

12. Ford's comments on the Boer War are in *England and the English*, p. 248, and in a letter to C. F. G. Cumberland of the Oxford Press, Sept. 20, 1936 (Biala). Ford to Walter

Jerrold, March 17, 1900 (Cornell). David Harvey turned up only two reviews of *Poems for Pictures*, one of which (in the *Academy*) was inspired by Ford: it dwells on Ford's knowledge of music and its effect on Ford's metrical experiments in much the same language Ford was to use two years later in an article for the *Academy* (April 19 and 26, 1902), where he explained that "A minor poet once let me somewhat far into the secrets of his methods of work," and then analyzed the musical origins of his own "Lavender/ You make me think of lavender," the first of the six songs in "A Sequence," which he eventually published in *The Face of the Night*. Many of the poems in *Poems for Pictures* (e.g., "Aldington Knoll") were written at Bonnington during the early days of Ford's marriage.

13. *Joseph Conrad*, pp. 222–23. James B. Pinker became Conrad's agent sometime late in August, 1899 (see p. 65 below). Conrad to Galsworthy, n.d. (but July 20, 1900) (Birmingham).
14. *Joseph Conrad*, pp. 225–27. Ford was unusually skillful with his own children when they were ill, lying for hours over the foot of the bed telling them stories; he was also gifted at inventing toys for them, such as the wooden waterwheel he had made with two brightly painted figures that seemed to work very hard to turn it as the water made the wheel go round (David Garnett, *The Golden Echo*, p. 63).
15. Jessie Conrad, *Joseph Conrad and His Circle*, p. 71. Conrad to Galsworthy, Aug. 11, 1900 (Birmingham). *Joseph Conrad*, pp. 227–28.
16. *The Feather*, p. 96.
17. Conrad to Galsworthy, Sept. 19, 1900 (Birmingham). Conrad to Meldrum, Oct. 3, 1900, in Blackburn ed., *Letters to William Blackwood and David S. Meldrum*, p. 111.

Chapter 7

1. H. G. Wells, Introduction, in Catherine Wells, *The Book of Catherine Wells* (London, 1928), p. 15. Wells to Ford, Nov. 1, 1900. Wells was at Stocks Hill in September and again in October.
2. *Return to Yesterday*, pp. 9 and 225. Elsie's correspondence with Robert Garnett (e.g., for March 6, 1905) shows she owned the house. The veranda has since been removed but can be seen in family photographs. Charles Kinross, who had been a schoolmate of Ford's, later owned the Bungalow (now called "The Little House"). Kinross placed a plaque on the house recording Ford's occupancy, for the unveiling of which he held a little ceremony on June 25, 1955, that was attended by Sir Frank Soskice (now Lord Stow Hill) and several younger members of Ford's family. The description of the church is in *The Cinque Ports*, p. 81.
3. James's description of Densher is in Chap. III of *The Wings of the Dove;* Ford is responsible for the suggestion that Densher is modeled on him *(Portraits from Life*, p. 10).
4. *An English Girl*, p. 22.
5. *Return to Yesterday*, p. 372. *It Was the Nightingale*, p. 207.
6. James to Ford, May 16, 1901 (Harvard). *The March of Literature*, p. 713n. *Return to Yesterday*, p. 13. David Garnett, *The Golden Echo*, pp. 64–65. Ford to Elsie, n.d. (but "Sunday," either May 13 or May 20, 1906).
7. Robert Garnett to Conrad, July 11, 1901.
8. Robert Garnett to Conrad, July 13, 1901. Conrad was particularly given to the life-insurance-policy gambit. In March, 1902, he had borrowed from his bank, apparently against this same policy, and in order to maintain the security for this loan, Galsworthy was paying the premiums on it. Conrad then persuaded Pinker to take over the loan and assigned the policy

to him; Pinker was to pay the premiums on it. In June, 1902, he initiated a similar scheme for borrowing from Blackwood on what appears to be this same policy; poor Galsworthy was again called on to pay the premiums on the policy and also the interest on the loan (Conrad to Galsworthy, March 10 and June 19, 1902 [Birmingham]). Ford got Pinker to sell the books and autographs for him (Ford to Pinker, n.d. [Huntington]).

9. Robert Garnett to Ford, July 16, 1901. Conrad to Ford, July 19, 1901, and n.d. (but the following Thursday, which was July 25, 1901) (Yale).

10. *Return to Yesterday*, pp. 58–59. *Letters of Arnold Bennett*, ed. James Hepburn (London, 1966), I, 26.

11. James Hepburn, ed., *Letters of Arnold Bennett*, I, 27. See also Professor Hepburn's *The Author's Empty Purse and the Rise of the Literary Agent* (Oxford, 1968).

12. *Return to Yesterday*, p. 62. Hepburn ed., *Letters of Arnold Bennett*, I, 25.

13. Edward Garnett, ed., *Letters from Joseph Conrad*, p. 73. Conrad to Pinker, Aug. 23, 1899 (quoted in Hepburn ed., *Letters of Arnold Bennett*, I, 24).

14. Ford to Edgar Jepson, Feb. 12, 1922, in Ludwig, p. 138. Pinker's death is described in both *The New York Times* and the London *Times* for Feb. 10, 1922.

15. Ford to Pinker, n.d. (Princeton). The novel Ford refers to may be "Times Before Us/ A Romance of Peasant Uprising." There are three versions—all fragmentary—of this novel at Cornell in a hand that suggests they were written about this time.

16. Ford to Herbert Read, Oct. 5, 1921, in Ludwig, p. 135.

17. Conrad to John Quinn, July 15, 1916, quoted by Baines, *Joseph Conrad*, p. 427. Hepburn, *The Author's Empty Purse and the Rise of the Literary Agent*, p. 84. *Return to Yesterday*, pp. 59–60.

18. We know Ford and Conrad worked on *Romance* during the Christmas visit because when the two of them were later arguing about what dates of composition to print in the book, Conrad said, "We began [to collaborate on *Romance*] in Dec: 1900" (Conrad to Ford, [Sept., 1903] [Yale]). Conrad wrote to thank Elsie for the "holiday" at Stocks Hill "Mar 1902/Monday" (Yale), adding "I am in an hour or so going to begin my B'wood stuff—'The End of the Song' —as Ford has suggested and advised." We know Ford was at the Pent for another bout of work on *Romance* in April from a letter to Pinker saying: "I've been at the Pent until just this morning" (Ford to Pinker, n.d., but April, 1901, since it refers to the current publication of Ford's poem, "The Mother," which appeared in the *Fortnightly* for April [Huntington]). Conrad's letter about coming to Winchelsea with Jessie and Borys is postmarked "AP 28 01." The actual time of his visit is indicated by a letter to Meldrum of May 24, 1901: "I have been in Winchelsea (returned yesterday) for a fortnight; finishing a story for Heinemann, drinking bottled Carlsbad water and working with Ford Hueffer on our romance of Seraphina" (Blackburn ed., *Letters to William Blackwood and David S. Meldrum*, p. 126; the story mentioned here is "Falk": the ms. of "Falk" is inscribed: "Winchelsea, May, 1901"). See also Baines, *Joseph Conrad*, pp. 256, 261, and 265.

19. *Joseph Conrad*, p. 120. Jessie Conrad's indignant letter about *Joseph Conrad* is in the *Times Literary Supplement* for Dec. 4, 1924. Jessie Conrad, *Joseph Conrad As I Knew Him*, pp. 117–18. *The Cinque Ports*, p. 163. When Ford read Jessie's statement in *Joseph Conrad As I Knew Him*, he wrote a letter to *The New York Times* saying, "I am able to forward you the enclosed piece of writing of my own [the passage from *The Cinque Ports*], out of which I afterwards made the short story that Conrad converted into his *Amy Foster*" (Feb. 19, 1927 [Princeton]). The passage certainly proves Jessie wrong, but it does not prove Ford ever wrote the short story he mentions.

20. Conrad to Galsworthy, June 20, 1901 (Birmingham). Conrad to Ford, n.d. (but since Conrad wrote Blackwood on July 4, 1901, that the typescript of *Romance* was on its way to him, this letter must belong to late June) (Yale). Conrad's reference to the delicate state of Ford's health indicates how anxious he was to placate Ford.

Chapter 8

1. Conrad to Blackwood, July 4, 1901, in Blackburn ed., *Letters to William Blackwood and David S. Meldrum*, pp. 129–30.
2. Conrad to Kazimiriez Waliszewski, Nov. 8, 1903, in Zdzislaw Najder, *Conrad's Polish Background* (London, 1964), p. 236.
3. *Typhoon*, Chap. II.
4. Conrad to Kazimiriez Waliszewski, Nov. 8, 1903, in Najder, *Conrad's Polish Background*, p. 236. Conrad to Ford, n.d. (but immediately after reading the reviews of *Romance* and therefore early November, 1903 [Cornell]). Conrad to Meldrum, Jan. 7, 1902, and Conrad to Blackwood, May 24, 1901, in Blackburn ed., *Letters to William Blackwood and David S. Meldrum*, pp. 137 and 126.
5. Meldrum to Blackwood, Aug. 5, 1901, and Conrad to Blackwood, Nov. 7, 1901, in Blackburn ed., *Letters to William Blackwood and David S. Meldrum*, pp. 131 and 135.
6. Ford was still deeply impressed by his narrow escape from the chicken bone a year later, when he reminded his mother that "It is exactly a year since I swallowed . . . that chicken bone & since then things have gone in a most vicious string" (Ford to Mrs. Hueffer, c. Dec. 20, 1902 [Soskice]). Conrad to Meldrum, Jan. 7, 1902, Blackburn ed., *Letters to William Blackwood and David S. Meldrum*, pp. 139 and 137. *It Was the Nightingale*, p. 129. That their plan had been for Conrad to do the real writing on this version and for Ford to do the clean-up work is clear from Ford's slightly earlier announcement to Pinker that "as I am going right through the latter parts [of *Romance*] I might just as well dot the i's of the earlier," Ford to Pinker, n.d. (Huntington).
7. Ford to Elsie, n.d. (but the letter says, "Wells has seen some of it [*Romance*] & wrote to Pinker that it shall most gorgeously make all our fortunes"; Wells had seen some of it because, on Jan. 6, 1902, Conrad had tried to borrow from Pinker on the strength of the work done on *Romance*; Pinker had refused the loan, and then Wells came over to the Pent, read a bit of the book, and wrote Pinker it was good and Pinker ought to lend the money, which he did (Baines, *Joseph Conrad*, p. 268). Conrad to Galsworthy, March 10, 1902 (Birmingham).
8. The passages quoted here are from *Romance* (Concord Edition), pp. 541, 322, 337, 334, 337, and 114.
9. *The March of Literature*, p. 292.
10. The scenes referred to here are in Part Third, Chap. Five, and Part Fourth, Chap. Two, of *Romance*. The reviews quoted were in the *Academy* and *The New York Times* (Harvey, pp. 282–83). Ford to Pinker, Sept. 28, 1902, in Ludwig, p. 16.
11. Conrad to Garnett, June 10, 1902, in Edward Garnett, ed., *Letters from Joseph Conrad*, p. 180. Conrad to Ford, April 15, 1902 (Yale). Elsie wrote two novels, *Ellen Slingsby*, which was never published, and *Margaret Hever*, which was published in 1909.
12. Ford to Garnett (Texas). *Rossetti* was published in June, 1902.
13. Conrad to Ford, n.d. (Yale). Ford's poem is in Mrs. Lamb's possession.
14. Robert Garnett to Mrs. Hueffer, May 17, 1902, and Ford to Mrs. Hueffer, n.d. (Soskice). Ford added some interesting gossip about an old family friend in this letter: "Ellen Terry was in the other day; she asked to be remembered to you. She's, poor thing, getting rather groggy and old. Rheumatic, troubled with failing memory & eyesight &, I'm afraid, with failing purse too. James too has been very ill & isn't any more his charming self."
15. Ford to Mrs. Hueffer, n.d. (but June, 1902) (Soskice).
16. Ford to Mrs. Hueffer, n.d. (but June, 1902) (Soskice). Conrad to Ford, May, 1902 (Cornell).
17. Ford to Pinker, n.d. and n.d. (Princeton). Conrad had already written "a stiff letter to

Robert McClure, about Inheritor Royalties" (Conrad to Ford, April 15, 1902 [Yale]). Conrad sent McClure's check to Ford June 24, 1902 (Yale). Eventually Pinker got £ 100 for the serial rights and £ 60 for the book rights to *Romance* from McClure and £ 150 from Smith Elder for the British book rights (Ford to Pinker, Oct. 21, 1903 [Huntington], and Ford to Elsie, Feb. 21, 1903).

18. Conrad to Elsie, May, 1902 (Yale). Conrad to Ford, June 24, 1902 (Yale). Conrad had promised Blackwood the second installment on June 20; on June 23 Blackwood had written to inquire when it would arrive (Blackburn ed., *Letters to William Blackwood and David S. Meldrum*, p. 158).

19. *Joseph Conrad*, p. 243. In *Return to Yesterday*, p. 227, Ford says, "I wrote passages which [Conrad] sometimes accepted and sometimes didn't." Jessie Conrad mentions neither these passages nor the fire, but she does say "the greater part of ["The End of the Tether"] was written against time in a little cottage in Winchelsea" and that "Ford Madox Hueffer ... would appear from time to time armed with a bottle and a few sandwiches, or biscuits and cheese" (Jessie Conrad, *Joseph Conrad As I Knew Him*, p. 115). "I managed to save the 2d installment from utter collapse. . . . I finished it at 2 am today" (Conrad to Galsworthy, July 16, 1902 [Birmingham]).

20. Conrad thanked Elsie for their Winchelsea visit Aug. 5, 1902 (Yale). Only one of Ford's letters from the New Forest is dated, Aug. 12, 1902.

21. When Pinker first proposed *Romance* be cut for serialization, Conrad suggested cutting six thousand words out of 166,000 (Conrad to Ford, n.d., but probably April, 1902, since Conrad refers to taking "the last of *Romance* to London" and to an illness of Christina's of that month [Yale]). Ford to Pinker, Sept. 28, 1902, in Ludwig, p. 16. Ford to Pinker, Oct. 5, 1902 (Princeton). Ford had investments amounting to a few hundred pounds, but they hardly justified this rather grand attitude.

22. Conrad's letters to Elsie about her translations are at Yale. His comment on "Heart of Darkness" is in a letter to Elsie dated Dec. 5, 1902. Elsie's *Stories from De Maupassant* appeared in Duckworth's Green Library in 1903 as "Translated by/ E.M./ Preface by/ Ford M. Hueffer." Conrad to Elsie, Oct. 10, 1903 (Yale).

23. Ford to Mrs. Hueffer, n.d. (but Dec. 17–23, 1902 [Soskice]). Conrad to Galsworthy, Dec. 22, 1902 (Birmingham). "I've been rather seedy at W'sea," he added when he returned (Conrad to Galsworthy, Jan. 2, 1903 [Birmingham]).

24. Conrad to Ford, Jan. 2, 1903 (Yale). *Joseph Conrad*, pp. 170–71, 177–79. Ford thought all this had taken place in 1906, and it is possible they took another stab at *The Rescue* then; but Conrad's letter shows he sent the manuscript to Ford at this time. The best analysis of this tangled question is in John Morey's unpublished dissertation, *Joseph Conrad and Ford Madox Ford: A Study in Collaboration*, pp. 95–106 (Cornell).

25. *Christina's Fairy Book*, "The Three Friends," p. 46. Neither of Conrad's letters (Yale) is dated, but the one to Elsie ends by suggesting that "we—the house party shall have a quiet time on Sat: and Sun: . . . Suggest any modification you please always with the proviso that you are to stay over Sunday." This means the party was scheduled for a Friday the 16th, and if we assume that it was given on a weekend close to either Borys' birthday (Jan. 14) or Christina's (July 3), it took place on Friday, Jan. 16, 1903, the only year Jan. 16 fell on a Friday during this time; July 16 did not fall on a Friday between 1897 and 1909. Mr. Baines gives a slightly inaccurate transcription of about half Conrad's letter to Ford in *Joseph Conrad*, pp. 273–74.

26. Hyde's letters to Ford allow us to trace in detail these plans for *The Soul of London*. Ford's two letters to Elsie are dated "Gatti's 4.p.m. Wed.," and "7 Tanza Road, Hampstead. Wed. Night," and are postmarked Feb. 11 and 12, 1903. Ford's suggestion that he is breakfasting with Galsworthy in order to hurry back to Elsie is blarney: Galsworthy regularly entertained at breakfast; but that it was a sacrifice for Ford to get up for it is quite true.

27. Ford to Elsie, n.d. (*Typhoon* was published April 22, 1903, so this letter was written April 23, 1903). Conrad was still inquiring about the insomnia some time later. *Joseph Conrad*, pp. 156–57. Ford specifies the occasion of this incident in a note on the recto of the last leaf of a copy of *Romance* in the Keating Collection at Yale.

Chapter 9

1. Ford to Mrs. Hueffer, n.d., but apparently sometime near the end of 1903 (Soskice). Ford to Pinker, n.d., but the publication date of *Romance* was Oct. 16, 1903 (Princeton). McClure bought the serial rights to *Romance* but never used the novel in *McClure's*. Ford was not exaggerating Conrad's continued reliance on him for moral support. "The visit to you has started me off again with my stuff," Conrad wrote Elsie that fall. "Many thanks for all your kindness" (Conrad to Elsie, Nov. 2, 1903 [Yale]).
2. Ford to Pinker, n.d. (Huntington). The loans are shown in Robert Garnett's accounting to Elsie of March 6, 1905. Ford to Elsie, n.d. What has not been settled with Conrad must be their plans for further work now that *Romance* is off their hands. Elsie is to send the bills "down" because she was in London taking care of her mother, who had recently had a painful operation.
3. On Dec. 8, 1903, Ford told Pinker that he had already tried *The Benefactor* on Heinemann, Methuen, Murray & Isbistor "about a year ago" and that Duckworth had offered to publish it but without an advance, an offer he had refused (Texas). Ford sometimes exaggerated the extent of his revisions. Elsie's broken arm as well as the Holbein and Katharine Howard projects are discussed in William Rossetti's letters to Ford of Nov. 10 and 13, 1903.
4. Conrad to Galsworthy, n.d. (Birmingham). The Conrads stayed with the long-suffering Galsworthys until they got into their rooms in Gordon Place.
5. *It Was the Nightingale*, p. 49.
6. Ford to Pinker, n.d. (Princeton).
7. *Return to Yesterday*, p. 293. Conrad to Wells, Feb. 7, 1904, in Jean-Aubry, *Joseph Conrad*, I, 327.
8. *Return to Yesterday*, pp. 286–87. The approximate date of these events can be fixed by Henry James's letter to Elsie of "Thursday 25th 1904" (Harvard), condoling with her over Christina's accident and the family's influenza. In 1904 the 25th fell on Thursday in February.
9. *Portraits from Life*, p. 129. Galsworthy to Ford, April 14, 1904, in Goldring, *The Last Pre-Raphaelite*, pp. 117–19. The passage Galsworthy is commenting on in his letter is on pp. 123-24 of *The Soul of London*. For Lewis Hind, see *Return to Yesterday*, p. 25, and *Joseph Conrad*, p. 214.
10. Conrad to Ford, postmarked May 19, 1904 (Yale). James to Ford, April 14, 1904 (Harvard).
11. Ford to Elsie, n.d. Conrad to Ford, postmarked AP 2[?] 04 (Yale). Conrad to Ford, May 29, 1904 (Yale). Conrad to Elsie, Sept. 19, 1904 (Yale). Baines, *Joseph Conrad*, pp. 290–91. Conrad describes writing two of the papers for *The Mirror of the Sea* at the Bungalow in a letter to Galsworthy, June 30, 1905 (Birmingham). Jessie Conrad, *Joseph Conrad and His Circle*, p. 87. Ford to Elsie, n.d. (but spring, 1904). The essays in *Blackwood's* were "In Captivity" (Sept., 1905) and "Initiation" (Jan., 1906).
12. *Return to Yesterday*, p. 25. Conrad to Meldrum, April 5, 1904, in Blackburn ed., *Letters to William Blackwood and David S. Meldrum*, pp. 179–80. Ford to George Keating, July 27, 1923 [?], in Morey, *Joseph Conrad and Ford Madox Ford*, p. 120 (Cornell).

13. Conrad to Ford, July 19, 1904, quoted by Baines, *Joseph Conrad*, p. 291.
14. Baines, *Joseph Conrad*, p. 292. Mr. Baines says Mr. Keating bought this ms. fragment from Ford. This cannot possibly be true. Mr. Keating told Prof. Morey that he was "unable to trace the bookseller from whom I obtained the Ford MSS pages. Possibly from Jean Aubry himself, with whom I was in correspondence at that time" (George Keating to John Morey, Sept. 15, 1958, quoted in Morey, *Joseph Conrad and Ford Madox Ford*, p. 119). For a full discussion of this ms. fragment, see Morey, pp. 117–49 and 228–311.
15. All these errors were corrected in the first edition of *Nostromo*, but not in the installment of the story printed in *T.P.'s Weekly*, a fact that led Professor Morey to conclude that Ford also read the proofs of this installment for the serial. Professor Morey also argues that since the ms. breaks off in midsentence and since the revisions of the *T.P.'s Weekly* text of this installment made in the first edition for the pages not represented by this ms. fragment are exactly like those made for the pages that are, Ford probably wrote the whole installment. If so, about three and a half pages from the beginning of the ms. and about two and a half from the end were lost before it came into Mr. Keating's hands.
16. Morey, *Joseph Conrad and Ford Madox Ford* (Cornell), pp. 120–22.
17. Baines, *Joseph Conrad*, p. 212. The idea of going to Spain is mentioned by Hyde in a letter to Pinker of Sept. 27, 1904 (New York Public). Conrad also seems to be referring to it in the first letter he wrote after returning to the Pent from London: he mentions that he is about to write Gissing to get advice for Ford (Conrad to Ford, n.d. [Yale]). The ms. of *The Soul of London* was mailed to Pinker from the Greyhound Hotel, Fordingbridge; the covering letter to Pinker is at Texas.
18. Ford to Mrs. Hueffer, n.d. (Soskice). The two letters to Pinker here referred to are both undated, but the first was written from Settley and the second from Winterbourne Stokes (Princeton).
19. H. G. Wells, *Boon* (London, 1915), pp. 123–24. The poems quoted here are "A Sequence, III and I," and "The Great View." Ford to Mrs. Hueffer, n.d. (Soskice), and Ford to Wells, n.d. (Illinois). Both these letters were written from Winterbourne Stokes and therefore belong to May, 1904.
20. Ford to Dr. Richard Garnett, n.d. (Texas). Ford to Wells, n.d. (Illinois).
21. Conrad to Ford, May 29, 1904 (Yale).
22. *Great Trade Route*, p. 261.
23. Elsie to Mrs. Hueffer, n.d. (Soskice).
24. "Any attempt on the part of a biographer to trace the movements of Ford and his wife during the years 1904 and 1905," Douglas Goldring wrote in *The Last Pre-Raphaelite*, pp. 129–30, " . . . would now be doomed to failure." It is not quite that bad, but the story is certainly obscure in some respects. Elsie wrote to Ford at Boppard on June 6, 1904. Ford sent Elsie the poem about Romney Marsh shortly after his arrival in Germany. So intense was the feeling it describes that two or three years later, when he was writing *The Spirit of the People*, Ford recalled the poem almost word for word: " . . . in the green and sunlit valleys, by the borders of a great lake [Constance], I was obsessed always with an intense longing to see once more the sails of ships above the sea wall, the wide stretch of land, the church spire of Lydd breaking the distant horizon . . . " (*England and the English*, p. 353). *Great Trade Route*, p. 98.
25. The description of Telgte is in *When Blood Is Their Argument*, p. 100. "Tell Mummums that Pumpums has not been able to write to her for the last few days because he has had a relapse—wh. is something not at all nice.—But now he is better again & he will write her from Boppard where he is going today" (Ford to Christina and Katharine, n.d.).
26. Ford to Elsie, n.d. The details of Ford's financial situation come from an undated memorandum drawn up by Robert Garnett for Elsie, possibly—since the accumulated interest is on the money borrowed from Miss Wanostrom in December, 1903, at 5%, is £12.10—

about the middle of 1905. Robert Garnett to Elsie, Aug. 24, 1904. Conrad to Elsie, Sept. 2, 1904 (Yale); on Sept. 5, 1904, Conrad wrote Ford a number of additions of his own (Goldring, *The Last Pre-Raphaelite*, pp. 124–26). "I am quite excited about the building ..." (Ford to Elsie, n.d., but from Telgte). Robert Garnett's bill for March, 1905, which has been preserved, shows the mortgage was for £ 250.

27. Ford to Elsie, n.d., and Sept. 19, 1904.

28. W. M. Rossetti to Ford, Oct. 3, 1904. Ford repaid this £50 in April, 1906. Ford to Elsie, Sept. 23, 1904.

29. Conrad to Ford, Sept. 5, 1904 (Yale). This letter is transcribed completely but inaccurately by Goldring in *The Last Pre-Raphaelite*, pp. 124–26.

30. Ford to Elsie, n.d., and Sept. 15, 1904.

31. Ford wrote his daughter Katharine that he was going to Switzerland on Monday, Oct. 3. *Return to Yesterday*, p. 266.

32. *Return to Yesterday*, p. 266. Ford to Katharine, Oct. 15, 1904. Ford to Christina, Oct. 20, 1904. Elsie persisted in the feeling—encouraged, no doubt, by Ford's homesickness—that he would be better off back in Winchelsea under her care. In her vigorous way, she continued to assail the members of the family with this theory. "Whether it wd. be best to get Ford back to his own home is a question too delicate for me to offer an opinion on," William Rossetti wrote her, Oct. 22, 1904.

33. Ford to Elsie, Oct. 25, 1904. The unsigned letter from the relative in Boppard is dated Nov. 4, 1904. *Return to Yesterday*, pp. 267–69.

Chapter 10

1. Ford discusses his life at St. Edmund's Terrace in *Portraits from Life*, p. 52, and in "Literary Portraits—IX.: Mr. Thomas Hardy and 'A Changed Man,' " *Outlook*, XXXII (Nov. 8, 1913), pp. 641–42. *Return to Yesterday*, pp. 272–73. The description of Tebb is from Violet Hunt, *The Flurried Years*, pp. 33–34. Tebb's letters to Ford are in the Biala Papers.

2. Ford to Pinker, n.d. (but from 4 St. Edmund's Terrace) mentions the trip to Sandgate; Ford to Pinker, Feb. 1, 1905, from Winchelsea (both Huntington). Ford to Walter Jerrold, n.d. (Cornell).

3. Ford to Walter Jerrold, n.d. (but from Broadhurst Gardens) (Cornell). Ford to Pinker, n.d. (but from St. Edmund's Terrace) (Princeton). The undated letters to Pinker about the sale of *London* and the prices for his poems are at the Huntington. *The Benefactor*'s publishing history is even more confused than that of most of Ford's books. It was originally accepted, after a reading of the first two parts, by Alston Rivers, on June 26, 1905. When it was completed, however, Alston Rivers rejected it, and it was sold to Brown, Langham. After the publication of *The Soul of London*, Duckworth offered a £ 100 advance for it, and Ford was in a tearing rage when Brown, Langham refused to release it.

4. Ford to Walter Jerrold, n.d. (Cornell). *Return to Yesterday*, p. 266. As late as July Edward Garnett was telling Galsworthy that Ford "was staying with his doctor in London, as he keeps losing weight" (Garnett ed., *Letters from John Galsworthy, 1900–1932* [London, 1934], p. 59).

5. *Return to Yesterday*, pp. 236–40. For the reviews of *The Soul of London*, see Harvey, pp. 285–86.

6. The cancelled passage from "Working with Joseph Conrad" is taken from the typescript at Yale. Ford perhaps cancelled it because he remembered that the success of *The Soul of London* occurred after most of his work with Conrad was done. Edward Garnett ed., *Letters*

from John Galsworthy, 1900–1932, p. 59.

7.   *Return to Yesterday,* p. 274.
8.   Samuel Hynes, *The Edwardian Turn of Mind* (Princeton, New Jersey, 1968), pp. 62–63.
9.   *The Soul of London,* pp. 88–90, 60, 33, 133, 79, 166–67, and 176. Ford's definition of the impressionistic method is in the introduction he wrote for McClure's one-volume American edition of
the three books, *England and the English,* p. xvii, to which the sentence about the electrifica-
tion of the Underground was also added on p. 23.
10. Ford to Mrs. Hueffer, postmarked May 4, 1905 (Soskice). Ford to Pinker, n.d. (Huntington).
The information about the National Liberal Club is in Goldring, *The Last Pre-Raphaelite,* p.
131; Ford resigned in the socially disastrous year of 1908. The Mont Blanc (later called Tag-
lioni's) is mentioned in Edward Garnett ed., *Letters from John Galsworthy,* pp. 9–10, and
David Garnett, *The Golden Echo,* p. 131. In *Out and About* (New York, 1934), p. 143, Archibald
Marshall says that the Chesterton-Belloc group and the Hudson-Garnett group "never co-
alesced" at the Mont Blanc, and that Ford belonged to the latter. *Portraits from Life,* pp.
38–39. *Provence,* p. 121. R. A. Scott-James, "Ford Madox Ford When He Was Hueffer," *South
Atlantic Quarterly,* LVII (Spring, 1958), 237–53.
11. Conrad to Wells, Feb. 7, 1904, in Jean-Aubry, *Joseph Conrad,* I, 326. The first two letters from
Ford to Pinker are in the Huntington; both are undated, but the first was written from Dr.
Tebb's house and therefore belongs to early 1905. The third letter to Pinker, also undated, is
at Princeton. Conrad to Sidney Colvin, April 28, 1905, in Jean-Aubry, *Joseph Conrad,* II, 17.
Conrad to Ford, May 9, 1905, in Jean-Aubry, *Joseph Conrad,* II, 20, but I have used the copy
of this letter at Cornell. Conrad's letters to Ford about the rehearsals and the performance
are undated, but June 21–25, 1905 (Cornell). David Harvey, p. 107, was the first to notice the
significance of the ms. of *One Day More* (Cornell).
12. W. M. Rossetti to Ford, April 4 and May 15, 1905 (Cornell). Ford to Elsie, July 7, 1905.
13. *Return to Yesterday,* p. 273. For the publication dates, see Harvey, pp. 19–23. We know from
Ford's undated letter to Pinker quoted on p. 108 above that two chapters of *The Heart of the
Country* had been written by the spring of 1905 and that at least a draft of 2/3 of *The Fifth
Queen* was completed by that time. The rest of the work was done during the summer and
fall of 1905. He also found time to put together a selection of poems which he submitted to
Houghton Mifflin in August, perhaps the selection that would be published by Alston Rivers
in 1907 as *From Inland.* Houghton Mifflin turned it down. Conrad to Norman Douglas, Oct.
18, 1905 (Texas).
14. Much of this information comes from Ford's undated letters to Elsie of this summer. One
letter, dated Sept. 21, 1905, shows Elsie is back in Winchelsea. Ford had four poems in the
Academy during the next six months.
15. Ford to Pinker, n.d. (Huntington). Ford to Pinker, n.d. (but *The Benefactor* was published in
October, 1905, and this letter was clearly written very shortly after) (Princeton). Conrad had
got some of *Chance* written in Capri (see Baines, *Joseph Conrad,* p. 318). Ford was always
proud of that prediction of its success and claimed later that he collected a bet of £5 from
Conrad when *Chance* sold over 14,000 copies.
16. Ford was still submitting his work to Edward Garnett for advice and correction. Garnett read
The Benefactor in manuscript (Ford to Edward Garnett, n.d. [Texas]). Asa Briggs makes the
point about the Liberal government in his essay, "The Political Scene," in *Edwardian England* (London and New York, 1964), ed. Simon Nowell-Smith, p. 87. On p. 142 of the same
book, Marghanita Laski points out that in 1901, only 400,000 of the seven million households
in England reported incomes over £400; yet about a third of the population (the part that
called itself middle class) was trying to live in a style that only a seventeenth could afford.
17. Philip Gibbs to Ford, Nov. 2, 1905 (Princeton). Ford to Pinker, n.d. (but Dec., 1905) and n.d.
(but Jan., 1906) (Huntington).

Chapter 11

1. Hunt, *The Flurried Years*, p. 48
2. *Return to Yesterday*, pp. 235–37. Archibald Marshall, *Out and About*, pp. 111–12. Ford's account of Alston Rivers is manifestly inaccurate in some respects; for example, he calls Bathurst Henry at one point, Hervey at another: Bathurst's name was Lancelot. Marshall is also sometimes inaccurate. He thinks Alston Rivers published *The Fifth Queen* before *The Soul of London* instead of nearly a year after. *Out and About* is very severe on Ford; it was apparently even severer in ms. "As to the passages about Mr. Hueffer," Murray wrote Pinker when the ms. was submitted, " . . . we do not wish to take away from the point of the book, but obviously do not wish to run any risks" (Murray to Pinker, Jan. 5, 1933 [Northwestern]). *It Was the Nightingale*, pp. 281–82. Ford still remembered that change of name from Boileaux to Byles when he wrote *Henry for Hugh* in 1933 (p. 59). It may not have been a fact in the first place, but once established as such in Ford's mind, it stuck. This is typical of his mental processes. Ford to Pinker (about Byles), n.d. (Northwestern).
3. The Chesson affair is described in a letter to Pinker of April 26, 1906 (Huntington), and a letter to Elsie of May 17, 1906. R. H. Mottram's recollection of the dinner at Galsworthy's is in his *For Some We Loved* (London, 1956), pp. 76–77. There is an undated letter of this time to Wells in Ludwig, p. 22, that discusses Ford's visit to Sandgate and his lunching with Wells. For the quarrel with Wells over *Thus to Revisit*, see above, pp. 316–17.
4. In a letter dated Feb. 2, 1906, Ford tells Elsie he is taking the children to the doctor; on Feb. 7 he is taking them back to La Sagesse.
5. The best discussion of the whole problem of Ford's part in the invention of *The Secret Agent* is in Morey, *Joseph Conrad and Ford Madox Ford*, pp. 88–95 (Cornell). Apart from the Author's Note to *The Secret Agent*, the most important primary sources of information are *Joseph Conrad*, pp. 230–32, *Return to Yesterday*, pp. 111, 194, and 200, and *Portraits from Life*, pp. 66–67.
6. Jessie Conrad, *Joseph Conrad and His Circle*, pp. 113–16. Ford to Elsie, n.d. (but between May 9 and 20, 1906).
7. Ford to Elsie, n.d. (but Feb. 12–23), Feb. 27, and June 15, 1906. *Portraits from Life*, p. 12.
8. Ford to Elsie, n.d. (but Feb. 12–23) and March 23, 1906.
9. Ford to Elsie, Feb. 8, 12, and 23, 1906.
10. Ford to Elsie, n.d., Feb. 8 and 23, and March 23, 1906. Ford to Pinker, n.d., in Ludwig, p. 23 (the text of Ford's letter printed by Prof. Ludwig differs in some details from that of the original at Texas). Prof. Ludwig dates this letter Nov., 1905, but Ford seems not to have heard of the Soskices' plans for going to St. Petersburg until March, 1906. It seems to be true that Mrs. Hueffer had for a time concealed Father Gapon.
11. *The Nature of a Crime* (London, 1924), p. 17. Ford used a good many of his own attitudes for the narrator of *The Nature of a Crime* (see below, p. 119), and he gives the lady's husband an addiction to chloral that is very similar in its history to Gabriel Rossetti's.
12. Ford to Elsie, Feb. 27, 1906.
13. There are three undated letters to Pinker about money from this period in the Huntington Library. Ford to Elsie, March 10, 1906. Pinker jotted down on a letter of Andrew Melrose dated June 29, 1909, the sales of *The Fifth Queen* up to Dec. 31, 1908; this letter is at Northwestern. Ford mentions the American prices for *The Fifth Queen* to Elsie, March 23, 1906. Ford to Pinker, April 21, 1906 (Northwestern).
14. *Return to Yesterday*, pp. 34–35, *Great Trade Route*, p. 239, and *Portraits from Life*, p. 114. Wells had a fictional version of the Fabian episode in *The New Machiavelli*. "Hands Off

the Arts," *American Mercury*, XXXIV (April, 1935), 402–08. *Henry James*, p. 45.

15. Ford to Elsie, March 10 and April 16, 1906. The characteristic sign of Edward Burden's wealth in *The Nature of a Crime* is the purchase of a luxurious motorcar (p. 36) and in *Return to Yesterday* (pp. 6–7) Ford makes much of "a one thousand two hundred guinea motor car" in which Kipling calls on Henry James; in July, 1906, in Boppard, he was deeply impressed when the "garrison commander of Ehrenbreitstein—a splendid general with a highly decorated staff—drove . . . by in a shining car with an escort of cars as shining" ("For Poorer Travellers," *Harper's*, CLXVI [April, 1933], 620–30).

16. "The Nature of a Crime" appeared in *The English Review* in April and May, 1909. There is a letter about its publication from Ford to Pinker in Ludwig, p. 26; Prof. Ludwig is uncertain whether Ford is trying to deceive Pinker or make a joke in this letter. But Pinker knew all about the authorship of "The Nature of a Crime." Ford to Elsie, May 17, 1906. Ford to Pinker, n.d., and July 27, 1906 (Huntington), and n.d. (but Oct. 19, 1906) (Princeton); the reference to Conrad's revising is no doubt a euphemism. Jessie Conrad later recalled that in 1924 Conrad refused to believe he had ever written a word of this work until she showed him a few pages of it in his own hand; they were doubtless all the pages he had ever written.

17. *The Nature of a Crime*, pp. 21, 26, 79–80, 92, 30, 73, and 67–69. Conrad's remark is in the Preface, p. 6.

18. Ford to Elsie, April 2 and May 17, 1906. Methuen to Pinker, June 23, 1906 (Northwestern).

19. The *Times* Book Club affair is described by Derek Hudson in an essay in *Edwardian England*, ed. Simon Nowell-Smith, p. 318. Ford to Elsie, April 16 and June 27, 1906. It seems most unlikely that Ford could have cleared £ 1,500–2,000 on a £ 6,000 budget under any conditions; with his grandly generous way with contributors he certainly would not have. But the figure, though generous, is not an unreasonable one in itself. When Edmund Gosse ran the *Daily Mail* literary supplement that Harmsworth substituted for the *Academy* he was paid at the rate of £ 1,200 a year (see Archibald Marshall, *Out and About*, p. 134).

20. Marshall's account of the *Daily Mail* affair is in *Out and About*, pp. 136–52; it appears to be perfectly accurate, except that Marshall guesses wrong about some matters of which he admittedly had no firsthand knowledge. Marlowe's account of his share in the matter is in a pair of letters Marshall quotes, pp. 148–49. Ford's version of the affair is in *Return to Yesterday*, pp. 252–56. Ford may have got the idea that Harmsworth had employed him from Harmsworth's brother, with whom he also had a conference shortly after Gosse's retirement (Ford to Pinker, n.d. [Huntington]). Ford's weekly "Literary Portraits" for the *Daily Mail* Literary Supplement began April 20, 1907, with one on Swinburne; they ended fourteen issues later with one on Marie Corelli. He also contributed four poems.

21. Reginald Pound and Geoffrey Harmsworth, *Northcliffe* (London, 1959), p. 300. Ford to R. A. Scott-James, in Ludwig, p. 25. Prof. Ludwig dates this letter "[September ? 1907]," on what grounds I do not know; it must have been written shortly after Ford's first "Literary Portrait" appeared in the *Tribune*, which was, as Ford rightly says, the Saturday immediately following the appearance of the last one in the *Daily Mail* supplement, namely, July 27. Prof. Ludwig has inadvertently transcribed Harmsworth's initials as H. H. instead of A. H.

22. Ford to Elsie, May 5 and n.d., 1906. Dodd Mead, Brown, Langham, and Methuen to Pinker, May 30, June 20, June 27, and July 6 (Northwestern). Conrad to Elsie, Aug. 8, 1906 (Cornell). Conrad's dislike of America was notorious; while Ford was in America he wrote Galsworthy, "Ford I guess is being entertained in the skyscraping wigwams of the unpainted savages of the grrreat continent. I hope he'll find the war-dances agreeable and soothing to his nerves. No doubt they'll feast him on intellectual roast dog too" (Conrad to Galsworthy, Aug. 14, 1906 [Birmingham]).

23. Ford wrote Mrs. Hueffer a letter on their arrival in Rotterdam dated "Tuesday night"; we know that they reached Mannheim on Christina's birthday, so this letter must have been written Tuesday, July 3, 1906. On June 27 Ford had told Pinker that "I start for the front on Monday [July 2]" (Huntington). Ford announced their sailing plans and reviewed the financial arrangements in an undated letter to Pinker written just before they sailed (Princeton). The *Kaiserin Augusta Victoria* alone cost them £ 54.

24. Ford tells the story of working on the farm at Merion in *Return to Yesterday*, pp. 161–63, and adds to it in *Great Trade Route*, pp. 229–34. He tells of growing a garden in Charleston in the biographical sketch he wrote for Georges Schreiber's *Portraits and Self-Portraits*, where he also mentions Merion and Canaan. The dinner in Gloucester is mentioned in *A History of Our Own Times* (Cornell), p. 374, and being dined in Philadelphia in *Return to Yesterday*, pp. 163–67, and *Great Trade Route*, pp. 237–41. In *Great Trade Route*, pp. 140–41, he also hints that he spent some time on his Uncle Leopold's plantation in Virginia, though on p. 340 he says he never got to Lexington. Only the story about Philadelphia appears to have a basis in fact; he wrote Pinker from there at the time that "I've had a gayish time here—two dinners having been given in my honour & I having met a world of people & publishers who wd. be glad enough to publish me" (Ford to Pinker, n.d. [Huntington]). But even this contemporary account may be magnified in order to make Pinker believe that the money he had spent on Ford's trip had not been thrown away. Ford to Pinker, n.d. (but from Newport, where they went about Sept. 1, 1906), in Ludwig, pp. 23–24.

25. During their time in Boston they made excursions to Lexington, Marblehead, Concord, Gloucester, and Newport. The evidence for the itinerary of this American trip is largely the postcards they sent the children. Ford's comments on America are in his letter to Pinker (see previous note). He describes their trip to Philadelphia in an undated letter from there to Pinker (Huntington) and in an unpublished essay called "Weather" (Biala). The cable to Pinker is in the Naumburg Collection. The crossing on the *Minnetonka* is mentioned in *It Was the Nightingale*, p. 125.

26. McClure to Pinker, Sept. 26, 1906 (Princeton). Ford to Pinker, n.d., from Philadelphia, and n.d., from London (Huntington).

Chapter 12

1. There are a dozen undated letters to Pinker about this financial crisis and Ford's progress with his novels (Huntington). The day Ford and Elsie got back to London (Oct. 8, 1906) he told Pinker he would complete *Privy Seal* within the week; his covering letter to Pinker when he turned in the ms. is dated (apparently by Pinker) "November." *An English Girl* was in proof by May 21, 1907 (Methuen to Pinker, May 21, 1907 [Northwestern]).

2. Conrad to Ford, Jan. 8 and 27, 1907 (Cornell). In *Return to Yesterday* (pp. 242–44) Ford has a story of Byles' insulting Conrad over this cookbook. Demonstrably untrue in some respects, it yet supports the assumption that the cookbook was meant for Alston Rivers and suggests that Byles was responsible for turning it down. What apparently is this book was published by Heinemann in 1933.

3. Ferris Greenslet's misinformation is in *Under the Bridge* (Boston, 1943), p. 104.

4. Conrad to Elsie, June 15, 1907.

5. *An English Girl*, pp. 96, 38–39, 62, 116–17, and 237. *Joseph Conrad*, p. 176. The critic was the *Saturday Review*'s (Harvey, p. 292). Ford's eccentric American who distributes California oranges to lighthouse keepers turns up in *An English Girl*, p. 125; he will turn up again

as Florence's Uncle John Hurlbird in *The Good Soldier.*

6. "Literary Portraits: XXV. The Face of the Country," *Tribune*, Jan. 11, 1908, p. 2 (Harvey, p. 159). *The Cinque Ports*, pp. 74–75. Ford's description of his drawing room is in *Portraits from Life*, p. 78, Violet Hunt's in *The Flurried Years*, pp. 20–21. See also Douglas Goldring, *Life Interests* (London, 1948), p. 179, *Odd Man Out* (London, 1935), p. 98, and *South Lodge* (London, 1943), p. 16.

7. Hunt, *The Flurried Years*, p. 41. Ezra Pound to Patricia Hutchins, Dec. 21, 1956, in Patricia Hutchins, *Ezra Pound's Kensington* (London, 1965), p. 22. Edward Jepson was the recipient of Ford's confidences about his life as a country gentleman; Jepson's comment was, "I never saw his horses" (*Memories of an Edwardian*, pp. 131–33).

8. Goldring, *South Lodge*, p. 22. Goldring states as fact much that is demonstrably false (for example, that Elsie was a "fanatical Catholic" and "refused, on religious grounds," to divorce Ford). But this description of Elsie is a matter of direct observation.

9. Ford to Pinker, n.d. (Princeton). *An English Girl* was published about Sept. 6, 1907.

10. Conrad to Elsie, Jan. 1, 1908 (Yale). Goldring, *South Lodge*, p. 22.

11. Ford to Mrs. Hueffer, n.d. (Soskice); Mrs. Hueffer was in St. Petersburg, where this letter was postmarked on arrival Jan. 12, 1908. Ford to Walter Jerrold, n.d. (Cornell).

12. Ford to Mrs. Hueffer, c. Jan. 2, 1908 (Soskice).

13. Violet Hunt discusses the tea party and the quarreling in her Diary, Dec. 25, 1908. She also mentions a party on Dec. 27 with Elsie present, which Conrad also attended (Conrad to Ford, Dec. 17, 1908 [Cornell]).

14. There is a record, in Robert Garnett's hand, of the sale of the Bungalow in 1912; Elsie got £641 for it. Her additions to Hurst Cottage included the tower and much of the rest of the present structure, which is now called White Walls. Ford to Pinker, n.d. (Huntington).

15. The four letters from Ford to Pinker quoted in these paragraphs are all undated (Huntington). Bathurst to Pinker, Oct. 5, 1907 (Northwestern).

16. Edward Arnold to Pinker, May 10, 1907 (Northwestern). Pinker had asked Arnold for an advance of £250 against royalties of 20% up to five thousand copies, 25% thereafter. The sales of *The Fifth Queen* come from Pinker's note on the letter from Andrew Melrose, June 29, 1909 (Northwestern). The exact terms on which Pinker sold *The Fifth Queen* to Nash are unknown, but Nash paid royalties of £113.17.11 on March 23, 1909. This would be about what he owed if Ford had no advance, a royalty of 20%, and 3d a copy on colonial sales. These are, roughly, the terms Pinker obtained from Methuen for *Mr. Apollo* (£50 advance against a 15% royalty, of which Ford was to pay back £20 if the book did not earn the advance [Methuen to Ford, Jan. 16, 1908 (Northwestern)]). Eveleigh Nash to Pinker, Dec. 30, 1907; Ford to Pinker, n.d. (Northwestern). Ford is referring to T. Le Wyzewa, "Le Roman Anglais en 1907," *Revue des Deux Mondes*, XLII (Dec. 15, 1907), 915, which contains a flattering paragraph about the first two volumes of the *Fifth Queen* trilogy (Harvey, pp. 292–93). Ford and Eveleigh Nash were long-time fellow members of the Authors' Club (Eveleigh Nash, *I Liked the Life I Led* [London, 1941], p. 32).

17. Conrad to Galsworthy, Feb. 20, 1908 (Jean-Aubry, *Joseph Conrad*, II, 67). Conrad to Ford, March 31, 1908 (Cornell).

18. Ford to Pinker, n.d. (Huntington). Ford's *Holbein* makes a contrast between Dürer, the feudal man, and Holbein, the early modern man, that is similar to the *Fifth Queen* trilogy's contrast between Katharine and Cromwell. It also uses the same historical details —for example, the accounts of Cromwell as a collector of *objets d'art* in *Holbein*, p. 140, and *The Fifth Queen*, p. 159 (127). References in parentheses are to the contemporary one-volume reprint of the *Fifth Queen* trilogy published in England by the Bodley Head in 1962 and in the United States by Vanguard in 1963.

19. *Privy Seal*, pp. 209–10 (349).

20. *Privy Seal*, p. 74 (276).
21. The '*Half Moon*,' p. v.
22. Ford to Pinker, n.d. (Huntington).

Chapter 13

1. Ford to Pinker, n.d., but May 29, 1908 (Huntington). Goldring, *The Last Pre-Raphaelite*, p. 166.
2. Ford to Pinker, Oct. 16, 1908, in Ludwig, p. 27. Edgar Jepson, *Memories of an Edwardian*, pp. 134-39, and Goldring, *South Lodge*, pp. 50-51. *South Lodge*, p. 15; see also Goldring, *Odd Man Out*, p. 94.
3. Ford to Pinker, n.d. (but written on the back of a letter to Ford from McClure dated April 9, 1908 [Huntington]). According to Pinker's note on his letter from Andrew Melrose of June 29, 1909, *Mr. Apollo* had sold by that date 1,298 copies, plus 410 colonial sales. In America it was tried without success on half-a-dozen publishers (Paul Reynolds to Pinker, July 18, 1908 [Northwestern]). Methuen to Pinker, Dec. 8, 1908 (New York Public).
4. Ford to Pinker, n.d. (but it includes a request to Pinker to return to Ford [for *The English Review*] "the m.s. of the last collaboration with Conrad—the letters, I forget the name of it"—that is, *The Nature of a Crime;* Ford acknowledged the receipt of this ms. on Oct. 16, 1908 [Princeton]).
5. Violet Hunt's Diary, Aug. 16, 1907. H. G. Wells, *The Wonderful Visit* (New York, 1914), pp. 34-36. *Mr. Apollo*, pp. 86, 309, 40, and 78.
6. Unless otherwise indicated, material about the Hunt family comes from the Violet Hunt Papers at Cornell. Violet Hunt's Diary shows that Franz Hueffer consulted Mrs. Hunt, who had friends in Corsica, when he was writing his opera based on Merimée's *Colomba*. Douglas Goldring, *Life Interests*, p. 172. *Ford Madox Brown*, p. 249. *Parade's End* (NAL), I, 119-20 and 90.
7. The history of the Fogg Elliots' troubles runs through Violet's Diary for 1902 and 1903. Benson eventually borrowed £ 4,000 from Mrs. Hunt after Mr. Hunt's death; Fogg Elliot also borrowed from her for less productive purposes. Both of them, Violet was convinced, cheated Mrs. Hunt over their interest payments. Silvia and Venice reciprocated by suspecting Violet of taking unscrupulous advantage of the fact that Mrs. Hunt lived with her.
8. Violet Hunt's Diary, July 9, 1907 (Cornell). Wells's remark about Miss Dowie is in his review of *Gallia*, the *Saturday Review* (March 23, 1895), p. 383. Violet Hunt's Diary, Oct. 18, 1889 (Cornell).
9. Violet Hunt's Diary, Oct. 21 and Oct. 3, 1907.
10. H. Montgomery Hyde, *Henry James at Home* (New York, 1968), p. 212. Violet Hunt's Diary, Aug. 16, 1882, Jan. 4, April 25, Nov. 2 and 3, 1907. Compare with Violet Hunt, *The Flurried Years*, pp. 40-41. "To go Nap" means to bid for all five tricks in the game of Nap, thus, to go the limit.
11. Wilde's description of Violet is in a letter to Ada Leverson, in Violet Wyndham, *The Sphinx and Her Circle* (New York, 1963), p. 35. Raffalovich's attentions were marked during the summer and fall of 1884, a period during which his name appears two or three times a week in Violet's Diary. Violet Hunt's Diary, Feb. 8, 1887. Derek Patmore, *Private History* (London, 1960), p. 29.
12. Forty-five years later, Ford paid George Boughton the odd and certainly undeserved tribute of including him along with Whistler, Abbey, and Sargent among the painters who had brought new ideas from America into the world of English painting ("Tech-

niques," *Southern Review*, I [July, 1935], p. 25). Violet Hunt's Diary, Sept. 24, 1890.

13. Violet Hunt's Diary, Dec. 14 and 19 and Aug., 1890. Goldring, *South Lodge*, pp. 106–07.

14. The London *Times*, Feb. 1, 1909, and *Athenaeum*, Feb. 6, 1909. Violet Hunt's Diary, Nov. 13 and 29, 1890, and her "Notes for Autobiography" (Cornell).

15. Violet Hunt's Diary, Sept. 30, 1890.

16. Violet Hunt's Diary, Oct. 4, Sept. 8, Dec. 24, Dec. 8, Dec. 10, 1890.

17. Violet Hunt's Diary, Feb., and Dec. 20, 1900. Goldring, *Life Interests*, p. 175.

18. Under Aug. 24, 1907, Violet describes how, when she arrived at Belmont Hall, the Roscoe Brunners' place in Cheshire, for a weekend, "Ethel Brunner and her brother and Olga Lowenthal came to the gates to meet us and all I saw was [Ethel Brunner's] fair hair and very spotty face, just as mine was a year ago or so and cured by Dr. Payne." She persuaded the Brunners to consult Dr. Payne and they returned looking very depressed. "Perhaps," Violet wrote, "hers aren't caused by the same cause as mine [.] He [Dr. Payne] *said* mine was my hair . . . But Stephen Paget didn't. He was beastly to me I remember. He cut about eight and left me bleeding[,] said I must go away. And that was one of the reasons why I went . . . to Schwalbach. . . ." These notes—made much closer to the time of her discovery than the summary I have quoted in the text—show Violet was given Dr. Payne's euphemistic diagnosis of her trouble in the summer of 1906; she could have been sent to Stephen Paget by Cholmeley and been given Paget's brutally honest diagnosis no later than 1905. To some extent, however, at least during these years, she persuaded herself to believe Dr. Payne and ignore Dr. Paget, for as late as 1907 she was still expecting Dr. Propert to propose to her: "To the theatre with Angela Mond . . . and afterwards to supper at the Carlton with Dr. Propert (Angela is making a match)," she wrote on April 11, 1907. By the time she saw Paget, the disease was in its tertiary stage—"my tertiaries" she pathetically always called it—and incurable; at that time there were few means of even treating it (the usual treatment was bichloride of mercury injections; Salvarsan was not discovered until 1908). In her old age Violet exhibited many of the characteristic symptoms of tertiary syphilis—impairment of judgment, inability to concentrate, loss of memory, disorientation, incontinence; her old age is movingly described in Norah Hoult's novel, *There Were No Windows* (New York, 1946). Norah Hoult had known Violet slightly in her later years; there are several letters from her to Violet at Cornell. But *There Were No Windows* is primarily based on a very skillful reimagining of facts set forth in Violet's own *Flurried Years*. Its portrait of a lost and confused woman, "crying over herself like an ill-behaved child . . . bewailing her loneliness to all and sundry, even to strangers she picked up in the streets" (p. 69), is a vivid one.

19. There are letters of praise in the Violet Hunt Papers from most of the writers mentioned here; the others she discusses in her Diary. *D. H. Lawrence: A Composite Biography*, ed. Edward Nehls (Madison, Wisconsin, 1958), II, p. 412. Lawrence's comment about marrying Violet was made with specific reference to Ford. " '[Ford's] wife's very nice,' Frieda said. 'Why the devil he ever married Violet Hunt!' cried Lawrence, throwing up his hands. 'Why, she's too devilishly clever for a man ever to want to marry!' " Goldring, *Life Interests*, p. 171.

20. The Violet Hunt Papers show that Violet bought South Lodge for £1,200 on July 30, 1908; see also Violet Hunt, *The Flurried Years*, p. 25. South Lodge was so called for an astronomer named South who had once lived there. Grant Richards, *Memories of a Misspent Youth* (New York, 1933), pp. 211–12.

21. Violet Hunt's Diary, Aug. 6, May 13, July 30, and May 13, 1907.

22. There are frequent references to Somerset Maugham in Violet's Diary for April and May, 1907, and a good many letters from him during this period in her papers, though I have depended on other sources also for this affair. For Edward Heron Allen, see the Diary,

July 12, 1907.
23. Violet Hunt's Diary, Aug. 16, 1907. Wells to Violet Hunt, n.d. (Cornell). Hunt, *The Flurried Years*, p. 43.
24. Violet Wyndham, *The Sphinx and Her Circle*, pp. 35–36. Hunt, *The Flurried Years*, p. 18. Violet Hunt's Diary.

Chapter 14

1. *Return to Yesterday*, p. 195. *Portraits from Life*, p. 97. In *Thus to Revisit*, p. 58n, Ford says he started *The English Review* in order to publish Hardy's "A Sunday Morning Tragedy."
2. Ford to Scott-James, n.d., in Ludwig, p. 40. Wells to Ford, Sept. 26, 1908 (Cornell). There are several other letters of the same kind from Wells to Ford. M. M. Meyer, *H. G. Wells and His Family* (Edinburgh, 1956), p. 34. *Provence*, p. 60.
3. For Conrad's rushes between Someries and Aldington, see Conrad to Edward Garnett, Aug. 28, 1908 (*Letters from Joseph Conrad*, ed. Edward Garnett, p. 214), Conrad to Galsworthy, n.d., Sept. 19, 1908, and Jan. 17, 1909 (Birmingham). For the plan for Conrad's reminiscences, see Conrad to Wells, Nov. 2, 1908 (Illinois).
4. In Jan., 1914, Ford said he had stopped writing for the *Daily News* because he disliked its attitude toward women's suffrage. He probably did dislike that attitude: Violet Hunt was a passionate suffragette and had no doubt enlisted Ford's sympathies by the fall of 1909. But his work on *The English Review* made it impossible for him to go on writing for the *Daily News*. Goldring, *Odd Man Out*, p. 94. Ford to Galsworthy, Oct, 4, 1909 (Cornell). Bennett to Wells, Oct. 29, 1909, in *Arnold Bennett and H. G. Wells* (London, 1960), ed. Harris Wilson, p. 153. Hardy to Ford, Aug. 2 and Sept. 9, 1908 (Cornell).
5. *Parade's End*, I, 28.
6. Hunt, *The Flurried Years*, p. 28.
7. "Thus to Revisit: III. The Serious Books," *Piccadilly Review*, Nov. 6, 1919, p. 6. *Return to Yesterday*, pp. 371–75.
8. Hunt, *The Flurried Years*, p. 26. Conrad to Ford, [March 31, 1909] (Cornell); cp. Hunt, *The Flurried Years*, p. 37.
9. Hunt, *The Flurried Years*, pp. 26, 37, and 72. Elsie wrote Willa Cather an apology (Mrs. Lamb).
10. Bennett to Pinker, n.d., and Dec. 16, 1908 (Texas). Ford to Pinker, Jan. 4, 1908 [*sic:* 1909] (Princeton); a guinea a page was *The English Review*'s regular rate; it is what Ford offered Edward Garnett, too, Oct. 17, 1908, in Ludwig, p. 27.
11. Bennett to Pinker, postmarked Jan. 11, 1909 (Texas). Ford to Bennett, March 10, 1909 (Texas). Ford described his "sporting risk" to Edward Garnett, Oct. 17, 1908, in Ludwig, pp. 27–28.
12. Bennett to Violet Hunt, April 23, 1909 (Cornell). Bennett to Ford, March 26, 1909, and Ford to Bennett, n.d. (Texas). Ford has an improved version of this quarrel with Bennett in *Return to Yesterday*, pp. 401–02, and Violet Hunt another, no doubt learned from Ford, in *The Flurried Years*, p. 29. Both agree that Ford paid £ 40 for "A Matador of the Five Towns."
13. Thomas Seccombe, "The English Review," *Reader's Review*, Nov., 1908 (Harvey, p. 295). Seccombe was an old friend of both Violet Hunt and Ford. Ford later quarreled with him, but he had consulted Seccombe over the planning of *The English Review* and even got him to write a draft of a policy statement for it (Mrs. Lamb). *Great Trade Route*, p. 87.
14. *The New Humpty-Dumpty*, p. 297. Miss Thomas to Wells, March 31, 1909 (Illinois).

15. Ford told Violet Hunt that the *Review*'s loss per number was £ 120 (Hunt, *The Flurried Years*, p. 85); this figure apparently represents the excess of the costs of production (but not of the contributions) over income. For the National Theatre project, see Ford to Shaw, Nov. 25, 1908 (Texas).

16. For Ford's estimate that the *Review* lost £ 5,000 see p. 160. The Wells memorandum is at Cornell. Ford's description of the plan to Elsie illustrates how confusing he could become about it: "Of course the 4/5ths of the good will only belong to M[arwood] and myself. Duckworth takes 1/5th of the profits [*sic*: of the gross receipts], not of the property. The only contributors I have not paid so far are Wells and Galsworthy & the shares [of the 2/5ths of the gross receipts set aside for contributors] of those I have paid revert to us along with the [payments for] the editorial[s] etc that I write myself, so that the contributors' 2/5ths are reduced [by his paying everyone but Wells and Galsworthy in cash] to less than 1/5th of the mag. when it is reduced to paid shares [i.e., payment in shares]" (Ford to Elsie, n.d., but the first Monday in Dec., that is, Dec. 7, 1908).

17. Ford to Garnett, Oct. 17, 1908, in Ludwig, pp. 27–28. *Financial Times*, March 8, 1909. Ford to Wells, April 2, 1910, in Ludwig, p. 42.

18. Hunt, *The Flurried Years*, pp. 27–28. Ford to Elsie, c. Dec. 7, 1908.

19. Ford to Edward Garnett, Oct. 17, 1908, in Ludwig, p. 28. Ford to Wells, Oct. 6, 1908, n.d., and n.d. (but Nov.-Dec., 1908) (Illinois).

20. Ford's estimate of the *Review*'s financial prospects is at Illinois; it is undated but clearly belongs to an early stage of the magazine's planning.

21. Wells to Ford, n.d. (Cornell). Bennett to Wells, Jan. 7, 1909, in *Arnold Bennett and H. G. Wells*, ed. Wilson, p. 162.

22. Ford to Mrs. Wells, Jan. 29, 1909, in Ludwig, pp. 31–33.

23. Ford to Wells, n.d. (Illinois). H. G. Wells, Introduction, in Catherine Wells, *The Book of Catherine Wells*, pp. 6 and 7.

24. Wells to Ford, March 29 and April 2, 1909 (Cornell).

25. Miss Thomas to Wells, April 5, 1909 (Cornell).

26. Ford to Horace Shipp, March 11, 1931 (Biala). Stephen Reynolds to Ford, April 29, 1909 (Cornell). For Reynolds' career, see Archibald Marshall, *Out and About*, p. 141, and David Garnett, *The Golden Echo*, pp. 130ff. Harris to Bennett, June 17, 1909, in Harvey, p. 531. *It Was the Nightingale*, p. 316.

27. Ford to Edward Garnett, n.d., in Ludwig, pp. 30–31. Goldring once tried to discuss Ford with Edward Garnett and found him "so outrageously rude that only consideration for my hostess prevented me from . . . leaving the table" (Goldring, *South Lodge*, p. 171). Ford to Pinker, n.d. (Princeton).

28. Ford to Scott-James, n.d., in Ludwig, p. 40. What allowed Ford to think of himself as dwelling in this Manfred-like solitude is explained by his portrait of himself as Count Macdonald in *The New Humpty-Dumpty*; "A constitutional dislike to talking about his own affairs, and a strong determination to let no other person talk to him about them, rendered [Macdonald] really rather solitary"(p. 296).

29. Conrad to Ford, Oct. 10, 1908, and n.d. (Cornell). Goldring, *South Lodge*, p. 23. Jessie Conrad, *Joseph Conrad As I Knew Him*, p. 57.

30. Conrad to Ford, [March 31, 1909] (Cornell). Goldring, *South Lodge*, p. 24.

31. Hunt, *The Flurried Years*, pp. 21–22. There are several letters about lost manuscripts at Cornell, including Wells's about Sidney Olivier (Wells to Ford, March 29 and April 2, 1909).

32. Goldring, *South Lodge*, pp. 32 and 22. Hunt, *The Flurried Years*, p. 45.

33. Hunt, *The Flurried Years*, p. 21. *Return to Yesterday*, pp. 407–08. *The Letters of Wyndham Lewis* (Norfolk, Conn., 1964), ed. W. K. Rose, pp. 39–40. Goldring, *South Lodge*, p. 40. Wyndham Lewis, *Rude Assignment* (London, [1950])., p. 121. There is a third version of

Lewis's visit to Ford in *Portraits from Life*, p. 219. Later Ford was to say that Violet's work was characterized by a factor of "pure irresponsible Gothic and macabre genius, without a trace of selection, of self-consciousness, of idealism" ("Literary Portraits—V.: Miss Violet Hunt and 'The Desirable Alien,' " (*Outlook*, XXXII [Oct. 11, 1913], 497. See Harvey, p. 175).

34. *Portraits from Life*, pp. 70 and 73–74. Pound to Mencken, May 2, 1915, in *The Letters of Ezra Pound*, ed. D. D. Paige, p. 60.

Chapter 15

1. David Garnett, *The Golden Echo*, p. 129. *Return to Yesterday*, p. 396. *Portraits from Life*, p. 71.
2. Brigit Patmore, "Conversations with D. H. Lawrence," the *London Magazine*, IV (June, 1957), 31.
3. Ernest Rhys, *Everyman Remembers* (New York, 1931), pp. 243–49. Violet Hunt's Diary dates this occasion Dec. 18, 1909. "Sad about Lawrence. Do you remember bringing him to see us long ago, a poet unknown? Ah me!" (Rhys to Ford, March 15, 1930 [Biala]).
4. For the various versions of Lawrence's introduction to *The English Review*, see Jessie Chambers, *D. H. Lawrence, A Personal Record* (London, 1935), pp. 155–59; D. H. Lawrence's interview with Kyle Chrichton in *D. H. Lawrence: A Composite Biography*, ed. Nehls, I, 82, and II, 412; and Ford's *Portraits from Life*, p. 72. Lawrence's letters to Jessie, sometime in September and Nov. 1, 1909, are in *The Collected Letters of D. H. Lawrence* (New York, 1962), ed. Harry Moore, I, 56 and 57. Ford's judgment of *The White Peacock* is reported by Lawrence in the autobiographical fragment in Nehls' *Composite Biography*, I, 103. Lawrence's recollection is not quite accurate, as his own letter to Heinemann of Dec. 15, 1909, shows; he himself sent *The White Peacock* to Heinemann, along with a highly complimentary letter by Ford. In addition, it seems likely that he is remembering here what Ford said, not about *The White Peacock*, but about *The Trespasser*, since Lawrence reported to Edward Garnett at the time that Ford had said of *The Trespasser*, "The book is a rotten work of genius. It has no construction or form—it is execrably bad art, being all variations on a theme" (Lawrence to Garnett, Dec. 18, 1911, *The Collected Letters of D. H. Lawrence*, ed. Moore, I, 88).
5. Jessie Chambers, in *D. H. Lawrence: A Composite Biography*, ed. Nehls, I, 122–26. Pound disliked Lawrence, too; "Lawrence, as you know, gives me no particular pleasure . . . Hueffer, as you know, thinks highly of him" (Pound to Harriet Monroe, Sept. 23, 1913, in *The Letters of Ezra Pound*, ed. Paige, p. 22).
6. Lawrence to Ernest Collings, Nov. 14, 1912, in *The Collected Letters of D. H. Lawrence*, ed. Moore, I, 158. In 1935, when Paul Palmer asked Ford to do an essay on Lawrence for the *Mercury* series that eventually became *Portraits from Life*, Ford wrote him, "I want to reflect about Lawrence a little longer because, although he was my 'discovery,' I'm not a hell of a lot in sympathy with him and find him difficult to re-read" (Ford to Paul Palmer, Nov. 17, 1935, in Ludwig, p. 247).
7. Hunt, *The Flurried Years*, p. 44. David Garnett, *The Golden Echo*, pp. 129–30. Violet Hunt and David Garnett may be describing the same party: at least Violet mentions as present at hers "Mrs. Garnett and her boy." Violet's Diary shows the *bouts-rimés* party occurred March 4, 1909; May Sinclair was there. Ford himself describes a party at 84 Holland Park Road in *Return to Yesterday*, pp. 412–13, at which he places Hardy, Gilbert Cannan, Hugh Walpole, Galsworthy, Pound, and Wyndham Lewis. Ford had been introduced to Pound during the spring of 1909 by May Sinclair, whom he had begun to see a good deal

because she was a close friend of Violet Hunt.

8. Hunt, *The Flurried Years*, p. 49. Elsie published three essays in *The English Review* (Aug., and Oct., 1909), oddly entitled "The Art of Dining," "The Art of Manners," and "The ' Art of Contentment," that are descriptions of the life she lived in her shanty during these months.

9. Ford told Goldring that twice during the spring and summer of 1909 "he was sounded by a third party as to whether he would make it possible for his wife to divorce him" and that he "replied that he did not think a divorce would be necessary because he intended to commit suicide" (Goldring, *South Lodge*, p. 88). The only grounds for this story are that Ford wanted Elsie to divorce him and that for a moment, in the spring, he almost succeeded in persuading her to do so. Or perhaps he later rearranged in his imagination Elsie's proposal of a separation into a proposal of divorce.

10. Most of these details about Gertrud Schablowsky come from Violet Hunt's *The Flurried Years*, where Gertrud is—no doubt for safety—called Elizabeth Schultz. See pp. 50–51, 56, 65, 67–68, 80, and 85. In her correspondence with Ford Violet sometimes calls her Hedwig. There is a copy of Violet's poem in her papers at Cornell. There are also two bank drafts for money paid by Violet to Gertrud, one for £ 10 paid at Königsberg May 10, 1910, the other for £ 65, paid at Freemantle, NSW, July 18, 1910.

11. Violet Hunt's Diary, March 21, April 25, and June 14, 1907. Hunt, *The Flurried Years*, p. 18. Ford has a slightly improved version of this episode in his "Literary Portraits—V.: Miss Violet Hunt and 'The Desirable Alien,' " *Outlook*, XXXII (Oct. 11, 1913), p. 497. Ford "boomed" De Morgan in the *Daily Mail*, June 15, 1907.

12. Violet Hunt's Diary, July 20, 1907, Feb. 15, 1908; the picture of Violet and May Sinclair begging at South Kensington station appeared in *Black & White*, Feb. 22, 1908; she describes the occasion in *The Flurried Years*, pp. 41–42.

13. Hunt, *The Flurried Years*, p. 26. Ford to Violet Hunt, n.d. (but end of Dec., 1908) (Cornell). Ford to Violet Hunt, Jan. 15, 1909 (Cornell).

14. Violet Hunt's Diary, Jan.-June, 1909.

15. Ford to Elsie, c. May, 1909.

16. Hunt, *The Flurried Years*, p. 25. *The Good Soldier*, p. 114.

17. *The Good Soldier*, pp. 51, 150, and 173.

18. Hunt, *The Flurried Years*, pp. 46 and 54–55. Violet Hunt to Ford, June 11–13, 1909 (Cornell).

19. Hunt, *The Flurried Years*, pp. 55 and 57.

20. Hunt, *The Flurried Years*, p. 66. Ford to Violet Hunt, June 12, 1909 (Cornell).

21. Ford to Elsie, n.d. (but March, 1909) and March 24, 1909. Conrad to Norman Douglas, March 7, 1909 (Texas).

22. It is only fair to Elsie to notice that Violet Hunt noted in her Diary as early as Sept. 8, 1890, that "a man called arthur peason [*sic*] Marwood was [staying at Robin Hood's Bay] with a lady very queer . . . "

23. John Galsworthy, *Fraternity* (New York, 1909), pp. 166–67. *The New Humpty-Dumpty*, pp. 214, 207, and 208. But the whole scene (pp. 204–20) is important.

24. Ford to Elsie, n.d. (but dated April 10, 1909, in Elsie's hand). Ford's list is interesting. It shows him seeing a great deal of the Galsworthys: he dined with them April 3 and 8 and spent the evening of April 7 with them. It describes "an American poet" named Pound whom he has just met and "the new Polish genius" named Wyndham Lewis. It mentions Violet Hunt just once, as present at a large gathering.

25. Ford to Elsie, n.d. (but between March 24, 1909, the date of Ford's preceding letter, and March 31, the date of Conrad's letter to Ford written after Elsie had told him her story). *The New Humpty-Dumpty*, p. 332.

26. Robert Garnett to Ford, n.d. (but c. March 28–30, 1909) (Cornell).

27. *The Good Soldier*, p. 186. Conrad to Ford, March 31, 1909 (Cornell). Violet Hunt, borrowing

some phrases from this letter, hints at this whole affair in *The Flurried Years*, p. 51.
28. Conrad to Galsworthy, April 30, 1909 (Birmingham).
29. Ford to Elsie, May 8, 1909. Conrad to Ford, March 9, 1909 (Cornell). "The Learned Sock," *Outlook*, XXXVI (Aug. 14, 1915), pp. 206–07, quoted in Harvey, p. 213. *Joseph Conrad*, p. 126. *The Fifth Queen* was advertised as "By the Author and F. Norreys Connell." The *Athenaeum* (March 27, 1909) described it as "an adaptation prepared by authors who lack the sense of the theatre."
30. Conrad to Norman Douglas, n.d. (Texas). Conrad to Dr. Mackintosh, Easter Sunday (April 11), 1909 (Yale). Dr. Mackintosh came to see Conrad regularly at this time (Conrad to Galsworthy, April 30, 1909 [Birmingham]). Jessie Conrad, *Joseph Conrad and His Circle*, pp. 138–39.
31. Conrad to Galsworthy, June 5, 1909 (Birmingham); ". . . this hole here [Aldington] is growing more odious to me every day" (Conrad to Galsworthy, July 30, 1909 [Birmingham]). Conrad to Pinker, n.d., in Baines, *Joseph Conrad;* Mr. Baines dates this letter July, 1909, but it refers to Willa Cather's call on Conrad, which occurred the middle of May. Conrad to Galsworthy, Sept. 7, 1909 (Birmingham). Conrad to Douglas, Dec. 25, 1909 (Texas). Edward Davison, who did not at the time know Ford or even move in circles close to him, "gathered that Conrad had parted with him and would not meet or speak to him any more" (letter to Arthur Mizener, April 8, 1969).
32. Ford to Elsie, April 14 and May 5, 1909.
33. Conrad to Ford, July 31, 1909 (Cornell); see Jean-Aubry, *Joseph Conrad*, II, 101–102.
34. When Conrad ceased publishing his reminiscences in the *Review* he told Galsworthy that he planned to "write enough [more] to complete a vol: of Reminiscences . . . " and added in another letter "I was *prevented*, from giving an installment of my R'ces to the June [*sic:* July] N⁰ of the E. R. . . . " (Conrad to Galsworthy, April 30 and July 13, 1909 [Birmingham], my italics). When he finally made a book of these reminiscences without adding to them he told Edward Garnett that "I hesitated as to letting ["these chance-born pages"] go out in book form. . . . Still I *felt* that what was there formed a whole in itself" (Conrad to Edward Garnett, Jan. 27, 1912, in *Letters from Joseph Conrad*, ed. Edward Garnett, p. 239). But it may be Conrad found he really could not produce these reminiscences without Ford's help. His memory was bad; even as it is, parts of *A Personal Record* are borrowed from Tadeusz Bobrowski's *Memoirs* (see Najder, *Conrad's Polish Background*, p. 30). Conrad expressed his feelings about David Soskice in an undated letter to Galsworthy at Birmingham: "I hear the *ER* is sold to a friend (Englishman) of that horrible Jew Soskice [Ford's brother-in-law]." Ford to Edward Garnett, May 5, 1928 (David Garnett).
35. According to Marwood's report to Conrad, Ford was to be retained as editor at a salary of £ 300 to be paid in shares, "so," as Conrad said, "the transaction is not too brilliant" (Conrad to Galsworthy, n.d. [Birmingham]). There is a letter from Ford to David Soskice of June 8, 1909 (Cornell), in which Ford explains his view that under the interim arrangement he holds the editorial power and has been using it very fairly. A conciliatory letter from Soskice of Aug. 13, 1909, concerned with a similar quarrel is also at Cornell. Ford's view of the interim arrangement is summed up in *Return to Yesterday*, pp. 409–11. "BUT mental life of Britain was pretty DAM well strangled when the utter filth got the Eng/Rev/ away from ole Fordie" (Pound to Brigit Patmore, n.d. [Texas]).
36. Ford to Edward Garnett, Oct. 17, 1908, in Ludwig, p. 27. The kind of political article Ford had in mind is illustrated by his editorial for the July, 1909, number of *The English Review.*
37. Ford to Violet Hunt, n.d. (but from Bedburne, where Ford was staying with the Fogg Elliots the last few days of July, 1909 [Cornell]). The day was June 10, 1909.
38. Violet Hunt to Ford, Friday [June] 11, [1909]. Hunt, *The Flurried Years*, p. 25; Ford to

Violet, June 12, 1909; Violet to Ford, June 13, [1909] (Cornell); the dates were added to these letters by Violet long after and are demonstrably inaccurate in some instances (for example, the letter she dates June 12 is a reply to one she dates June 13). Throughout *The Flurried Years* Violet uses a tactful résumé of her actual correspondence with Ford. For her summary of these letters, see pp. 63 and 69.

39. Violet Hunt's Diary, July 14, 1909; Hunt, *The Flurried Years*, p. 70. Violet to Ford, n.d. (but to Bedburne, where Ford stayed with the Fogg Elliots the last few days of July, 1909); *An English Girl*, p. 31. Violet Hunt's Diary, June 28 and July 12, 1909.

40. Hunt, *The Flurried Years*, pp. 67–68 and 71.

41. Ford to Child, Aug. [16], 1909 (Cornell).

42. Silvia Fogg Elliot to Violet, n.d.; Ford to Violet, Aug. 1, 1909; Silvia to Violet, Aug. 5, 1909; Violet to Ford, [Aug.] 3 or 5, [1909]; and Ford to Violet, Aug. 5, 1909 (Cornell).

43. Violet to Ford, [Aug.] 3 or 5, [1909] (Cornell). Hunt, *The Flurried Years*, p. 66 There is a rough draft of Violet's letter to her lawyer, C. O. Humphreys, in her papers.

44. Ford to Mrs. Hueffer, n.d. (Soskice). Hunt, *The Flurried Years*, p. 202. *The New Humpty-Dumpty*, p. 304.

45. Violet to René Byles, Aug. 17, 1909 (Cornell). Mrs. Hueffer to René Byles, Aug. 18, 1909 (Cornell). Ford to Pinker, n.d. (but his letter asks for the money from the Nelson reprint of *Romance*, which appeared in July, 1909 [Princeton]).

46. Angela Mathias to Violet Hunt, Sept. 14, 1909; David Soskice to Ford, Oct, 4, 1909 (Cornell). *Return to Yesterday*, p. 409.Violet Hunt's Diary says they left for France Sept. 13, but David Soskice saw Ford, on the eve of his departure, Sept. 24.

Chapter 16

1. Hunt, *The Flurried Years*, pp. 75–76.

2. Hunt, *The Flurried Years*, pp. 78–80.

3. Ford to Sir Alfred Mond, n.d. (Cornell). Hunt, *The Flurried Years*, p. 91.

4. Ford to Pinker, n.d. (Princeton). Violet Hunt's Diary, Nov., 1909.

5. Henry James to Violet Hunt, Nov. 2 and 5, 1909; Henry James to Ford, Nov. 8, 1909 (Cornell). In *The Flurried Years*, pp. 87–90, Violet ostensibly quotes in full the first of these letters and summarizes the other. In fact, Violet almost always cut letters to suit her purpose.

6. The quotations are from the *Star*, Jan. 11, 1910; the story was also carried by the *Globe* and the *Evening News* that day and by a good many morning papers the next. Violet's comments are in *The Flurried Years*, pp. 93–95.

7. The correspondence between Violet's lawyer, C. O. Humphreys, and Ford about the payments to Elsie is at Cornell; Ford apparently made the first payment of £3.10.0 on Dec. 8, 1909. Elsie testified in *The Throne* libel suit that Ford finally discontinued these payments in June, 1912 (the *Daily Mirror*, Feb. 8, 1913). Hunt, *The Flurried Years*, p. 97.

8. Ford to Pinker, n.d. (but just after the publication of *A Call*, Feb. 12, 1910) (Texas). Ford to Jepson, Oct. 28, 1910, in Ludwig, p. 45.

9. Hunt, *The Flurried Years*, pp. 97–98.

10. Hunt, *The Flurried Years*, p. 101. The correspondence about *A Call* includes Ford to Methuen, Jan. 15, 1909 (Cornell), Ford to Pinker, March 7, 1909 (Huntington), Methuen to Pinker, May 20, 1909 (rejecting the novel), Hutchinson to Pinker, Sept. 13 and 23, 1909, Chatto & Windus to Pinker, Jan. 8, 1909 (Northwestern). Ford to Pinker, n.d., and March 30, 1910 (Princeton).

11. Pound to his father, Sept. 12, 1923, in Poli, Bernard, *Ford Madox Ford and the Transatlantic*

Review (thesis for the Doctorate of Letters, University of Paris), p. 19.

12. There is a great deal of correspondence about the Constable contract at Northwestern; see particularly, Constable to Pinker, March 17, 1909, and Ford to Pinker, June 1, 1910. On June 21, 1910 (in Ludwig, p. 43), Ford told Pinker that he was "getting along with 'The Novel for Constables' [*Ladies Whose Bright Eyes*]." For the suffragette activities see Christabel Pankhurst to Ford, June 4, 1920 (Cornell).

13. Silvia Fogg Elliot to Violet, Nov. 3 and c. July, 1909 (Cornell).

14. David Garnett, *The Golden Echo*, pp. 182–84. Cecil Beaton, in James Laver, *The Edwardian Promenade* (London, [1958]), p. 36.

15. Hunt, *The Desirable Alien*, pp. 10–16. Hunt, *The Flurried Years*, pp. 122–26. Violet to Elsie, Sept. 9, [1910]. Ford made over his profits under the Constable contract in March (Ford to Pinker, March 7, 1910 [Huntington]); there are records of payments of £ 75 and £ 34 to Elsie (Pinker to Humphreys, Dec. 20, 1910, and April 20, 1912 [Northwestern]). Elsewhere Violet acknowledged all this (Hunt, *The Flurried Years*, pp. 157–58). In Oct., 1909, Violet took out a bill of sale on Ford's furniture and pictures on which she raised £1,500 from her trustees (Goldring, *The Last Pre-Raphaelite*, pp. 158–59; most of the documents Goldring used are at Cornell, but this one is not). Violet does not name her chaperone in *The Flurried Years*, calling her "the Countess," but *The Desirable Alien* is dedicated to "Mrs. Oswald Crawfurd who led me into Germany." "Ford told me that he rarely makes an erasure or a revision in anything he writes, because he works it all out in his head beforehand, even to the actual wording, and when he sits down to write, it is all ready to come out as he intends it should. He thinks about a book about eight months and writes it in about four months. He has never kept a note of any kind, he says" (Donald Fried, *Art and Decorations* [Jan., 1927], p. 70). Ford generally asserted, too, that he thought out about a thousand words in one of those morning sessions over patience. His mss. bear out his assertion about revisions.

16. David Garnett, *The Golden Echo*, pp. 187–94. Hunt, *The Flurried Years*, p. 132; the photograph of Ford and David Garnett is reproduced opposite this page.

17. Hunt, *The Flurried Years*, pp. 132–34. Nicholas II's visits to Nauheim occurred during the first week of September.

18. Hunt, *The Flurried Years*, pp. 138–41. Hermann Hüffer to Elsie, Sept. 28, 1910. Hermann Hüffer to Harrison Martindale, Oct. 20, 1910.

19. Hunt, *The Flurried Years*, pp. 138, 141, and 167. Hunt, *The Desirable Alien*, pp. 1 and 3n. *The Desirable Alien* obscures the chronology and some of the facts of Ford and Violet's German experience, no doubt out of caution, but it also provides a good many details of their life that are otherwise unknown. In his preface to *The Desirable Alien* Ford refers to "the kindly, careless, inaccurate, and brilliantly precise mind of the author [Violet]"; that is a reasonably accurate description.

20. Hunt, *The Desirable Alien*, pp. 145–46 and 157–60. *The Good Soldier*, pp. 44–45.

21. Hunt, *The Flurried Years*, pp. 142–44. The passage in *Memories and Impressions* that Violet fell foul of is on pp. 318–19 and 328–29.

22. Hunt, *The Flurried Years*, p. 143.

23. R. Ellis Roberts, "Ford Madox Ford," in *New Directions*, Number Seven (New York, 1942), p. 485. Violet's notes on Herkomer are still in her papers at Cornell.

24. Robert Garnett to Elsie, Sept. 14 and 15, 1910. Herman Hüffer to Elsie, Sept. 15 and Oct., 1910. Hermann never forgave Ford his conduct at this time: "I passed him and Oliver in the street about a year ago," he wrote Elsie July 20, 1924, from Paris. "I was not anxious to meet [them], for . . . I do not like to seem to approve their way of acting and thinking by approaching them in a natural and unreservedly cousinly way."

25. Hunt, *The Flurried Years*, pp. 146, 147, and 155. Ford to Pinker, Jan. 27, 1911 (Huntington).

26. Hunt, *The Flurried Years*, pp. 146–50. *Memories and Impressions*, p. ix; *Memories and Impres-*

sions was not officially published until March 24, 1911. Though Arthur Waugh thought it "one of the best books we [Chapman & Hall] have published," it sold just over 600 copies (Waugh to Pinker, Aug. 9, 1920 [Northwestern]). Violet's operation was apparently a D and C. While she was in the nursing home D. H. Lawrence sent her three plays to read. When she finished them, she promptly forgot about them. Lawrence somehow got the idea that Ford had them in Germany and raised a great row when Ford denied any knowledge of them. It was not until a year and a half later, when Ford got back from Germany, that he was able to get Violet to search out these plays and return them to Lawrence.

27. William Michael Rossetti, Letter to the Editor, *Outlook*, April 22, 1911, pp. 597–98.
28. *Memories and Impressions*, p. xvii.
29. *Provence*, p. 64. Ford was fond of that comparison to interrupting the Sermon on the Mount; he began using it as early as *When Blood Is Their Argument* (pp. xiii–xiv). When he was not justifying his own habitual inaccuracy Ford could distinguish between pedantry and real scholarship. "It is of course absurd to decry scholarship. Accuracy of mind and a certain erudition are as necessary to the imaginative writer as is native genius. But I was born in the days of the full desert breath of the terrible commercial scholarship of Victorian times.... Those fellows must have done more to contribute to the barbarism of our day than all the brutalities of ten thousand big battalions thundering across a shuddering earth" *(Provence*, p. 216)—a hyperbole almost as extravagant as the one about the Sermon on the Mount.
30. *It Was the Nightingale*, p. 254.
31. Carol Ohmann, *Ford Madox Ford* (Middletown, Conn., 1964), p. 168. Paul L. Wiley, *Novelist of Three Worlds* (Syracuse, N.Y., 1962), p. 87.
32. Ernest Hemingway, *A Moveable Feast* (New York, 1964), pp. 83–88. Hemingway also says Ford was unbearable to look at—"breathing heavily through a heavy, stained mustache and holding himself as upright as an ambulatory, well clothed, up-ended hogshead"—and smelled, which is a calumny.

Chapter 17

1. Hunt, *The Flurried Years*, pp. 154–55. Ford to Mrs. Hueffer, Dec. 25, 1910 (Soskice).
2. Hunt, *The Flurried Years*, p. 159. They lunch with Arnold Bennett and his new wife while they were in Paris.
3. Hunt, *The Flurried Years*, pp. 169–70 and 172. The ms. of *Ladies Whose Bright Eyes* was sent to Pinker Nov. 13 [1910] (Huntington). Pound eventually persuaded Bird to publish the two chapters of *Women & Men* at the Three Mountains Press in May, 1923 (Pound to Kate Buss, May 12, 1923, in *The Letters of Ezra Pound*, ed. Paige, p. 186). There is a partial ms. of *The New Humpty-Dumpty*, then called *The Dark Forest*, at Cornell; it is dated Feb. 17, 1911. Ford's description of *Women & Men* is in a letter to Pinker, March 9, 1911 (Northwestern). Constable told Pinker, "We should be very interested to see the complete manuscript," but offered no contract. Shortly after the episode of the flat, Ford wrote Violet asking her for the money to give Christina and Katharine a pony-cart he said they had asked for. Violet, who was having a hard time making both ends meet as it was, burst into a rage, and Ford said she was jealous of the children and did not want him to be on good terms with them (Hunt, *The Flurried Years*, pp. 180–81).
4. Violet Hunt to Pinker, n.d. (Northwestern). Ford to Pinker, April 23, 1911 (Huntington). Harper had bought *Memories and Impressions* in February and had it in print in March, which may explain the delayed payment (Ford to Pinker, Feb. 8, 1911 [New York Public]).

5. Hunt, *The Flurried Years*, pp. 171–73. Violet Hunt, *The Desirable Alien* (London, 1913), pp. 1 and 23. Ford describes the coronation in the broadcast he did over WJZ in New York on Dec. 7, 1937, on the abdication of Edward VIII, a typescript of which is in the Biala Papers. The harem skirt and its competitor the hobble skirt of 1911 were no joke; 1,200 girls at the Brook Manufacturing Co., of Northampton struck in October because, owing to the crippling of the underskirt-making business, they had been set to the humiliating task of making pinafores; see the *Daily Mail*, Oct. 11 and 14, 1911.

6. Hunt, *The Flurried Years*, pp. 182 and 191. Ford to the editor of the *New York Herald Tribune Books*, Feb. 15, 1927, in Ludwig, p. 172.

7. Hunt, *The Flurried Years*, pp. 182 and 185–86. Ford gave his own misery at appearing toothless in public to Mr. Fleight, who felt, after his teeth were knocked out, that "he couldn't let anybody in the world see him. . . . No dishonour could have been more than that and no tragedy greater" (*Mr. Fleight*, p. 152). On the flyleaf of a copy of the *Memories of John Westlake* that is now lost, Violet later wrote: "The plan [for a real divorce] was defeated by the inertia—or malice—of the male protagonist" (Goldring, *South Lodge*, pp. 129–30).

8. Details about the trips and the correspondence with Elsie are in Violet Hunt's letters to Mrs. Hueffer, May 4, 1911, and n.d. (Soskice). Violet and Ford were indignant at the British government's bland disregard of Ford's claim to German citizenship when it attempted to collect £ 29 of income tax from him; "FMH surely hasn't got to pay income tax in two countries," Violet complained to Pinker. " . . . that money has all been earned since he took up his residence in Germany" (Violet Hunt to Pinker, n.d. [Princeton]). Not even Violet quite dared to claim that Ford was a German citizen. Conrad replied to Ford's letter on March 29, 1911 (Cornell); he was writing equally friendly letters to Elsie at the same time (Conrad to Elsie, Aug. 24, 1911 [Yale]).

9. Ford to Scott-James, May 11, 1911 (Biala), and June 30, 1911, in Ludwig, p. 52. The pseudonym may also have been adopted to prevent Elsie from claiming the profits on the book, as Ford feared she might. The *Athenaeum's* reviewer of *The Simple Life Limited* (March 11, 1911) all but identified Ford as the author.

10. *The Simple Life Limited*, p. 144. Frog's Hole, like Limpsfield, is near Westerham, Oxted, and New Hatch.

11. *The Simple Life Limited*, pp. 310 and 152.

12. *The Simple Life Limited*, pp. 42 and 43. Some of the characters such as Mr. Major (Harrison Cowleshaw) and Mr. Parmont (Edward Garnett) are straight portraits. Most of them, however, are given only one or two easily recognized characteristics of the originals. Simeon Brandetski, for example, has led a life that in many ways parallels Conrad's— including his marriage; George Everard has a physical resemblance to Frank Harris; Mr. Hangbird has many of the characteristics of Stephen Crane; and there are recognizable touches of Pinker about Mr. Gubb, of Juliet Soskice about Ophelia Bransdon, of David Soskice about Cyril Brandetski, of Constance Garnett about Miss Stobhall.

13. *Ladies Whose Bright Eyes*, pp. 4, 3, 17, and 60. Ford typically begins by calling Stapleford Castle, Stapleton and Tamworth, Tamville, just as—seeking to give an impressionistically precise sense of time—he has Mr. Sorrell think he has been "knocked . . . clean back through time—483 years" to 1327, the year after the murder of Edward II at Berkeley Castle. This makes the year of the novel's action 1810; but Ford of course meant it to be 1910.

14. Ford's comment on *The Connecticut Yankee* is in *Rossetti*, p. 93, on the boredom of winter in the Middle Ages in *The March of Literature*, p. 274. *Ladies Whose Bright Eyes*, pp. 25 and 200.

15. *Ladies Whose Bright Eyes*, p. 261.

16. The Schiffenberg excursion is described in Hunt, *The Desirable Alien*, pp. 72–74. Pound

was in Giessen at least as early as August 5, when he wrote a letter to Pinker at Ford's dictation (Naumburg). "Canzone a la Sonata/ (To E. P.)" in Ford's *High Germany* is evidently a souvenir of their argument about Pound's *Canzoni*. Pound's remark about discussing poetry with Ford is in his Editorial Comment for *Poetry*, I (Jan., 1913), and about Ford's conversation is in "Canto LXXXII." Ford's remark about the vernacular is in a letter to H. G. Wells, about 1903, in Ludwig, p. 18. *The March of Literature*, pp. 217–19 and 398.

17. Pound's letter to Ford is dated May 26, —— (Biala). See *The Letters of Ezra Pound*, ed. Paige, p. 49n, for another striking expression of Pound's debt to Ford.

18. *The March of Literature*, p. 217.

19. *Parade's End*, I, 22–23. "Mrs. W. Three Stars" is Christopher's jibe at Rossetti's "Blessed Damozel," who "had three lilies in her hand,/ And the stars in her hair were seven." One of Ford's most vivid personal memories of Rossetti's Chelsea house was of those gilt sunfish; they are carefully described in *True Love & a G.C.M.* (pp. 27–28) when the hero —who has been named Gabriel in honor of the great man—is "introduced into an immense, gloomy, coloured and dusty room, where gilded sunfishes hung from the ceiling."

20. Violet Hunt to Mrs. Hueffer, n.d. (Soskice). This letter was written from Fort-Mahon, where they were vacationing with the Farleys between bouts of work on Ford's teeth. Ford became quite an authority on false teeth, with which he provided Mr. Fleight after Mr. Fleight's heroic resistance against the disgruntled youth of Augusta Mews (*Mr. Fleight*, p. 164). Ford's teeth were a great success: "You won't know Ford again for his teeth!" Violet wrote Mrs. Hueffer. "They are really worth the money" ([Sept.] 20, 1911 [Soskice]). Violet's letter about when she became Ford's "wife" is in the Naumburg Collection. Jepson persuaded Violet not to send this letter to Ford; instead he wrote a letter for her which he sent her under a covering note dated Aug. 5, 1920, which is also in the Naumburg Collection.

21. Hunt, *The Flurried Years*, pp. 198–99. Robert Garnett to Elsie, Oct. 16, 1911; Garnett says reporters have been after him for the last three days. The *Daily Mirror*, Oct. 21, 1911, p. 3. Ford was busy advertising his marriage privately, too: "I heard from Hueffer in Germany the other day. He's married Violet Hunt over there. She writes me very sweetly" (D. H. Lawrence to Ada Lawrence Clarke, c. Oct., 1911, *The Collected Letters of D. H. Lawrence*, ed. Moore, I, 82).

22. Goldring says the house was Lady Houston's at Sandgate (*South Lodge*, p. 99); perhaps they stayed at both during this period, but Violet says the house was Lady Byron's and her address is the one Conrad used in writing Ford. The *Bystander* dinner was Jan. 19, 1912; the invitation is in the Soskice Papers. Chatto told Pinker it should be "Violet Hunt," Dec. 1, 1911 (Northwestern). Conrad to Ford, Feb. 2, 1912 (Harvard). They were certainly at Sandgate in April. Conrad's feelings were not so warm as his letter makes them sound. "The great F. M. H. . . . was here shortly after New Year with the somewhat less great V. H.," he wrote Galsworthy, March 27, 1912 (Birmingham).

23. Hunt, *The Flurried Years*, pp. 201–02. The *Daily Mirror*, Jan. 9, 1912, p. 3.

24. Lawrence to Garnett, Feb. 10, 1912, in *The Collected Letters of D. H. Lawrence*, ed. Moore, I, 98–99. Hunt, *The Flurried Years*, pp. 202–03. Violet implies that Marwood suggested some scheme for outwitting Elsie that she found too tricky: "I demurred. Everybody, he said, would not have been so scrupulous."

25. Hunt, *The Flurried Years*, pp. 206–07. Violet says *The Governess* came out in March, 1912, but there is a letter from Chatto & Windus to Pinker dated April 18, 1912, that says "We are today publishing 'The Governess' . . ." (Northwestern). "The LIBRARY: WEEK by WEEK. By Frank A. Mumby," *The Throne*, April 3, 1912, p. 28.

26. Hunt, *The Flurried Years*, p. 208. The ms. of *The Panel* was sent Pinker in two installments,

Dec. 22 and 27, 1911 (Huntington). Ford to Pinker, June 3, 1912 (Huntington). There are two other letters to Pinker on this subject in the New York Public Library; they are dated June 11 and July 3, 1912.

27. *The Panel*, p. 266.

28. Ford made some insignificant changes in *The Panel* for the American edition issued by Bobbs Merrill in Oct., 1913, as *Ring for Nancy* (see Harvey, p. 40). "I have," Ford wrote Pinker, "no objection to Mr. Bobbs Merrill doing anything he likes with 'The Panel'. He may change the title, rewrite the dedication, alter the ending into a Tragedy in which all the people stab each other. . . . " He then half seriously adds a suggestion he has made before: "Why shouldn't he call it 'The Bedroom Comedy' once for all" (Ford to Pinker, May 6, 1913 [Huntington]). There were sporadic suggestions for dramatizing *The Panel* both for the stage and the screen, and in March, 1914, a Mr. Lyell Swete completed a dramatization for the Haymarket Theatre, but it was never produced. See Bobbs Merrill to Pinker, Oct. 27, 1913 (Huntington); Haymarket Theatre to Pinker, March 31, 1914 (Northwestern); and Ford to Pinker, Dec. 27, 1914 (Princeton), and June 9, 1915, May 6 and July 8, 1920, and Jan. 7, 1921 (Huntington).

Chapter 18

1. *The New Humpty-Dumpty*, pp. 102 and 123.
2. *The New Humpty-Dumpty*, pp. 71–72. *Return to Yesterday*, p. 403.
3. *The New Humpty-Dumpty*, pp. 44, 92, and 94–95.
4. *The New Humpty-Dumpty*, p. 256. For Ford's exact words to Violet, see p. 188.
5. *The New Humpty-Dumpty*, pp. 205 and 356.
6. *The New Humpty-Dumpty*, pp. 311–12, 420, and 195. For Wells's momentary interest in Violet Hunt, see p. 150–51 above; for Ford's view of how Wells had wriggled out of his responsibilities for *The English Review* and Ford had assumed them without a murmur of complaint, see Ford's letter to Mrs. Wells, Feb. 1, 1909, in Ludwig, p. 34; for Ford's outraged conviction that Wells had mercilessly maligned him and Violet Hunt, see pp. 195–96 above.
7. *The New Humpty-Dumpty*, pp. 86, 88–89, and 93.
8. *The New Humpty-Dumpty*, pp. 92, 216, 351, and 427. Pett has connived with a sorry loyalist Galizian named Da Pinta, who seems to be Ford's version of David Soskice. The novel's rich American, Edward U. Dexter, plays the role S. S. McClure had in the affairs of *The English Review*.
9. *The New Humpty-Dumpty*, pp. 63, 303–04, and 432. "Here's my creed," wrote D. H. Lawrence, a dozen years later, " . . . this is what I believe: '*That I am I. That my soul is a dark forest.* Etc.'" (*Studies in Classic American Literature* [Anchor Books], p. 26). John Lane chose the title *The New Humpty-Dumpty* to emphasize the adventure plot.
10. Hunt, *The Flurried Years*, pp. 210–11.
11. Hunt, *The Flurried Years*, pp. 211–15. Violet to Mrs. Hueffer, May 12 [1912] (Soskice). Ralph Cope, quoted in Goldring, *The Last Pre-Raphaelite*, p. 164. Middleton Murry recalled that Ford and Masterman had called on him and Katherine Mansfield near Chichester "soon after my wife & I had first fallen in love" (Murry to Ford, Jan. 29, 1923 [Cornell]). This must have been in Aug., 1912, when Murry and Katherine Mansfield moved into a cottage at Runeton and Ford and Violet were at Selsey (see Antony Alpers, *Katherine Mansfield* [New York, 1953], pp. 175–76). Wyndham Lewis' remark is in *Rude Assignment*, pp. 121–22. Violet describes how steadily Ford worked through these months, "with aplomb dictat-

ing his daily screed of typewritten pages [which] he scorned to look over ... after his secretary had typed it." Ford's letters to Pinker for this period (Huntington) report his steady progress; he had his next novel ready for delivery by December, when he told Pinker *The Desirable Alien*, of which he wrote a part, was also ready. The heavy drinking was reported by Violet to Dr. Tebb (Goldring, *South Lodge*, p. 114).

12. Hunt, *The Flurried Years*, pp. 219 and 221. Faith Compton Mackenzie, *As Much As I Dare* (London, 1938), pp. 271–72.

13. William C. Beaumont, *A Rebel in Fleet Street* (London [1944]), pp. 72–75. Violet has quite a different story; according to her she begged Beaumont not to defend the suit but he got on his "high editorial horse" and refused to apologize (*The Flurried Years*, pp. 224–25).

14. The *Daily Mirror* and the *Daily Mail*, Feb. 8, 1913. Hunt, *The Flurried Years*, p. 230. Elsie kept *The Throne's* £ 300; this was thought by some people not very ladylike: the proper thing was to give such awards to charity; Elsie lost most of this money in bad investments. The stubbornness with which Elsie and Violet continued their battle is astonishing. Violet remained Mrs. Ford Madox Hueffer in the telephone directory until she died in 1942, and as late as 1924—sixteen years after Ford had deserted Elsie and five after he had left Violet—Violet wrote the *Weekly Westminster* a letter (Jan., 1924) about "my husband's" book, *From Inland*, and signed it Violet Hunt Hueffer and Elsie sought an injunction against her. It was during these proceedings that Elsie's counsel asserted that "Mrs. Hueffer was a Catholic, and regarded marriage as a thing which could only be dissolved by death" and thus started a false explanation of her conduct that has hardly even yet died out (the *Star*, Feb. 9, 1925). On her copy of the *Star's* report of this case Elsie wrote: "This was counsel's mistake. I was not in Court, or I would have contradicted that fact. E. H." Mrs. Lamb tried again to kill this idea with a letter to the *TLS*, June 28, 1957.

15. Goldring quotes most of Tebb's letter in *South Lodge*, pp. 104–05.

16. Hunt, *The Flurried Years*, pp. 226–28. According to Violet, Ford went back to Giessen in January, 1913, to make sure nothing went wrong with the divorce that they had both assured poor Byles had already been granted and came from there to meet her at Boulogne just before the trial. But this is impossible. On Jan. 23, 1913, Ford wrote Lucy Masterman from South Lodge that they were going "shortly" to Le Touquet (in Ludwig, p. 55) and Ford sent his daughter Katharine a postcard from Amiens on Feb. 6, the day before the trial.

17. Hunt, *The Flurried Years*, pp. 233–35.

18. Hunt, *The Flurried Years*, pp. 236–38, 241–42. Apart from what Violet paid for the girls, Elsie had £ 80 a year after Ford left her; at the end of her life she was supported by Mother Mary Matthew's order, as a dependent parent.

19. Violet to Mrs. Hueffer, *le 13* [*fevrier*] 1913, and Feb. 19, 19[13], from Carcassonne (Soskice). A few of Violet's social acquaintances did go out of their way to invite them to parties as if nothing had happened; "I'm glad I can't accept them," Violet wrote Mrs. Hueffer in reporting these invitations, "—it would embarrass kind hostesses just now—but later." But later there were very few such invitations. Conrad wrote them and, by writing to James, Violet managed to elicit a noncommittal letter from him. *Provence*, pp. 149–50.

20. Ford to Pinker, Feb. 14, 1913 (Huntington), Feb. 17 (Northwestern), Feb. 27 (Princeton), March 4 (Huntington). *Return to Yesterday*, p. 240.

21. From Carcassonne, Ford and Violet went to Arles, Avignon, and St.-Rémy, where they stayed about three weeks. They were in Corsica for about ten days in the middle of March. May Sinclair was still addressing Violet in France as late as May 10, 1913 (see Goldring, *South Lodge*, p. 111).

22. Violet Hunt's correspondence with May Sinclair and Mrs. Clifford was in the possession of Douglas Goldring and is quoted in *South Lodge*, pp. 108–12. Its whereabouts now is unknown.

23. That Howard Latimer was, on the one hand, embarrassed and, on the other, not in the hands of the sheriff is evidenced by the fact that they sold the colonial rights and five hundred sets of sheets of *Mr. Fleight* to Bell. There are too many copies of their own edition of *Mr. Fleight* in existence to allow us to believe it was not issued in some fashion, no doubt an unprofitable one. There is a letter from Ford to Pinker, of Nov. 21, 1913 (Princeton), that says, "Yes, it is not a gay report [of earnings]. . . . Of course you will reply that 'Mr. Fleight' is my own fault—and so it is. . . . "

24. *Mr. Fleight*, pp. 17, 249, 59, and 252.

25. *Mr. Fleight*, pp. 15 and 16.

26. *Mr. Fleight*, pp. 3, 249, 292, and 252. Ford quoted Mr. Blood at length on R. B. Cunninghame Graham in *The Outlook*, Dec. 20, 1913 (*Mr. Fleight* is dedicated to Cunninghame Graham), and again—here in an argument with a timid Captain Aaron Rothweil Fleight —in *The Outlook* for Jan. 23, 1915, under the title "Mr. Blood and Commonsense about the War." As late as 1921, Pound, who had always disapproved of what seemed to him Ford's idealization of the British upper-class gentleman, was referring to Ford as "my dear Col. Blood" (Pound to Ford, May 26, 1921 [Cornell]). Ford's description of the superiority of "the old feudalism" is in *Henry James*, p. 47. The passage from *Outlook* is quoted by Harvey, p. 171. All but this final one of *The Outlook* articles are reprinted in *Zeppelin Nights*.

27. Ford's cards are in the Violet Hunt Papers; examples of the stationery in the Soskice Papers. Violet describes her garden party in *The Flurried Years*, p. 243. Goldring describes later parties at South Lodge in *South Lodge*, p. 115.

28. Kathleen Cannell told me some of these things; see also her "Portrait of a Kind Eccentric," *Providence Sunday Journal*, Sept. 20, 1964, p. W-20. For other details about South Lodge see Mrs. C. A. Dawson Scott, "Violet Hunt," *The Strand Magazine*, Aug., 1923. Iris Barry to Arthur Mizener, Jan. 31, 1967. For the Gertrude Stein incident, see William Carlos Williams, *Autobiography* (New York [1951]), p. 254. Mrs. Patmore herself told me these things; see also Derek Patmore, *Private History* (London, 1960), pp. 29 and 99.

29. *Return to Yesterday*, p. 388. Pound to Brigit Patmore, n.d., Oct. 31, 1952 [postmark], and n.d. (Texas).

30. There is a note in Violet Hunt's Papers describing how she furnished Lewis' flat for him. Lewis' description of Ford is in *Rude Assignment*, p. 122. His other remarks are from *The Letters of Wyndham Lewis*, ed. W. K. Rose, pp. 440–41 and 554.

31. *Transatlantic Review*, Jan., 1924. Middleton Murry, "Thus to Revisit," *Nation and Athenaeum*, XXIX (May 28, 1921), 328–29. "The Starling," *Collected Poems*, p. 33. Goldring, *South Lodge*, p. 62.

32. The proof sheets of *Henry James* have a printer's stamp dated Sept. 2, 1913. *Henry James*, pp. 47–48 and 9. The reviews were in the *Bookman* and the Boston *Evening Transcript*; see Harvey, pp. 319 and 332.

33. *The Young Lovell*, pp. 268–69.

Chapter 19

1. For the Rhine trip see *Return to Yesterday*, pp. 420–25, and Hunt, *The Flurried Years*, pp. 245–58. Violet implies that she was anxious to get Ford to Giessen, as if the question of his German citizenship were still in doubt (see pp. 245, 257–58, especially). Mrs. Masterman says that Violet's notion the Germans had mistaken Masterman for Churchill and Ford's ascription to Masterman of great prescience about the approach of war are inven-

tions. See also Lucy Masterman, *C.F.G. Masterman* (London, 1939), pp. 259–61.

2. Pound to Amy Lowell, Nov. 26, 1913, in *The Letters of Ezra Pound*, ed. D. D. Paige, p. 26. Ford to Harriet Monroe, Nov. 12, 1913 (Chicago).

3. Ford to Pinker, Nov. 21, 1913, in Ludwig, p. 58.

4. Ford to Pinker, Nov. 21, 1913, in Ludwig, p. 58. Paul to Pinker, Jan. 29, 1914 (Northwestern). Ford to Pinker, Feb. 13, 1914, in Ludwig, p. 59.

5. The ms. of the first part of *The Good Soldier* is in a strange hand, presumably that of this "play-secretary." The idea that a novelist could not write a really good book until he was forty did not, apparently, occur to Ford until sometime in the twenties; at least he first expressed it in *Joseph Conrad*, p. 175. Hunt, *The Flurried Years*, p. 216. Violent Hunt's Diary, Feb. 3, 1914.

6. *Henry James*, p. 103. Ford to Lucy Masterman, Jan. 23, 1913; Ludwig, p. 54.

7. Hunt, *The Flurried Years*, pp. 216–19. There are only two "Agony's" and they fill only half a line. "The Hueffer good? Rather!" Pound wrote Harriet Monroe. "It is the most important poem in the modern manner. The most important single poem that is" (Pound to Harriet Monroe, May 23, 1914, in *The Letters of Ezra Pound*, ed. D. D. Paige, p. 37); but in a later, more judicious moment, Pound observed that "[Flint] and Ford and one or two others shd. by careful cataloguing have been in another group [from the Imagists]" (Pound to Glenn Hughes, Sept. 26, 1927, in *The Letters of Ezra Pound*, ed. D. D. Paige, p. 213).

8. *Return to Yesterday*, p. 429. For the shadow play, see *Return to Yesterday*, p. 430. Ford has an extended description of the evening it was performed (including a detailed account of the excellent dinner he ate) in *The Marsden Case*, pp. 87–99. The producer of the shadow play who is satirized in this description is apparently Cuthbert Hamilton (see Lewis to Cuthbert Hamilton, n.d., *The Letters of Wyndham Lewis*, ed. W. K. Rose, p. 46). The Cave of the Golden Calf, also known as the Cabaret Club, was in a cellar in Heddon Street (hence the "Cave"), just off Regent Street. Other descriptions of it are given in Edgar Jepson, *Memories of an Edwardian*, pp. 154–55; Osbert Sitwell, *Great Morning* (London, 1949), p. 207; Wyndham Lewis, *Rude Assignment*, pp. 124–25. See also Augustus John, *Chiaroscuro* (London, 1952). Lewis got £60 for his mural paintings. In the broadcast Ford did for WJZ on the abdication of Edward VIII he claimed to have seen Edward at the Cave of the Golden Calf in June of 1914. *The Marsden Case*, pp. 127–28.

9. Wyndham Lewis, *Blasting & Bombardiering* (Univ. of Calif. Press, 1967), pp. 33–36. *Return to Yesterday*, p. 419. *The Marsden Case*, p. 115.

10. *Return to Yesterday*, p. 418. Ford to Stella, May 7, 1923. *The March of Literature*, p. 533 (Ford does not actually identify the speaker of this tirade, calling him merely "a young lion then expecting to supersede [me] in the public favour"; but there can be no question this young lion is Lewis). Ford always imagined that he had announced his farewell to literature in a magazine called *The Thrush* (perhaps he recalled his own assertion that his Great Auk "was no louder than a thrush in the pages of *Blast*"). But that farewell was —as Harvey has pointed out (p. 191)—almost certainly the pair of articles on Impressionism he wrote for *Poetry and Drama* at this time, where he says, "for my part I am determined to drop creative writing for good and all" (*Poetry and Drama*, II [June, Dec., 1914], pp. 167–75, 323–34).

11. Lewis' painting was done in the fall of 1914; see Pound to Harriet Monroe, Nov. 9, 1914, *The Letters of Ezra Pound*, ed. D. D. Paige, p. 44. The South Lodge inventory made in 1926 (Cornell) lists "A large oil picture by Wyndham Lewis £40-0-0"; Violet has crossed out the "40" and written in "30," probably the price she actually sold it for, since she used this inventory for selling other things, including "A Bust Portrait of a Boy (F. M. Hueffer) by Faulkner," no doubt Charles J. Faulkner. The sale catalogue of her effects, April 14, 1942 (Cornell), does not mention Lewis' painting but does include the "tapestry

564] Notes for pages 248–50

window curtains" which the inventory calls less fancifully "three crimson spring roller blinds." The 1926 inventory includes some interesting items, a painting by Ford called *Pier and Seapiece*, 8 inches x 6 inches, and busts of Ford and his mother by Ford Madox Brown. Ford describes Mr. Croyd in the Vorticist study in *That Same Poor Man*, his unpublished novel, p. 128. Lewis' comment on Violet's clothes is quoted in Hunt, *The Flurried Years*, p. 215. Iris Barry to Arthur Mizener, Jan. 31, 1967.

12. Pound, *The Letters of Ezra Pound*, ed. D. D. Paige, pp. 33–36. *No Enemy*, p. 206. In "Henry Gaudier: The Story of a Low Tea Shop," *The English Review*, Oct., 1919, pp. 297–304, Ford described this dinner as "financed by a disagreeably obese Neutral whom I much disliked." In a letter to F. S. Flint, June 23, 1920 (Ludwig, p. 107), he apologizes for this remark, observing that, when he wrote this article, he had not the faintest recollection that Amy Lowell had given the dinner. Despite this apology, he repeated what he said in the article in *No Enemy*. These dinners are also described in John Gould Fletcher, *Life Is My Song* (New York, 1937), pp. 148–49, and S. Foster Damon, *Amy Lowell* (Boston, 1935), pp. 232–33.

13. *Return to Yesterday*, p. 436. Slightly more than three chapters of *The Good Soldier* appeared in *Blast*. Ford thought what Mary Borden read was the installments of *Ulysses* in the *Little Review;* that was chronologically impossible, and his editor decided it must have been installments of *A Portrait of the Artist*, which appeared in the *Egoist* in 1914. The argument about the Liberal government and war is described by Wyndham Lewis, *Blasting & Bombardiering*, pp. 57–59. Lewis' description of Ford's opinion about war seems to be quite precise; in a canceled passage of the unpublished *A History of Our Own Times* (Cornell) Ford says he believes the Germans would have been much more likely not to have attacked had the Tories been in power but that the Liberals were known not to fight (p. 170). In *Return to Yesterday* (pp. 434–35), in order to dramatize his reading about the murder of Archduke Ferdinand on the 28th, Ford has himself changing trains at Berwick for Duns June 29, 1914. In *Between St. Dennis and St. George*, p. 38, he gives the date as July 20, which more or less agrees with Lewis' dating of the visit ("Some weeks or so before the War appeared on the horizon, I went up to Berwickshire ... "). Lewis used this visit in his Cantleman stories, where Ford is called Leo.

14. "Literary Portraits—XLVIII.: M. Charles-Louis Philippe and 'Le Père Perdrix,'" *Outlook*, XXXIV (Aug. 8, 1914), 174–75, quoted in Harvey, p. 198.

15. *Return to Yesterday*, p. 42. Edgar Jepson, *Memories of an Edwardian*, p. 176. Lucy Masterman, *C.F.G. Masterman*, p. 267. Ford found it particularly difficult to resist exaggerating his activities during the war; "in 1915," he would write, "in common with a number of historians and economists—amongst them being Profs. Gooch, Hobhouse, Sir C. P. Scott, of the *Manchester Guardian* and others—I was approached by Mr. C.F.G. Masterman, then Chancellor of the Duchy of Lancaster—in his capacity, I think, of the Chief of the Ministry of Information—and asked for what proposals I and they thought should be made for terms of peace by the Asquith Ministry" (Ford to the Rt. Hon. Malcolm McDonald, Feb. 27, 1939 [Biala]). This is of course *only* exaggeration; peace terms were under discussion at the time and Masterman no doubt did discuss the subject with Ford. It is the implication that he was an expert of the order of Gooch and Hobhouse and that Masterman approached him as a distinguished authority that is false. The worst of this habit was that it led people to think there was no truth at all in Ford's stories, till they came to believe that his rather brave, if not very glorious, war service itself was entirely an invention.

16. Edward Heron Allen to Ford, Jan 2, 1914. Edward Heron Allen to Violet Hunt, Dec. 16, 1914. Violet's final comment, written on her copy of Brigit's letter, is: "The story (War [*sic*]) in The Bystander—Ford wrote in a morning for £10. We were hard up." Even Brigit Patmore, who seldom got involved in such affairs, wrote Violet to protest against Ford's story.

17. A. S. Williams, Chief Constable of West Sussex, to Ford, Jan. 2 and Jan. 6, 1915 (Cornell). Ford's article about the "gallant enemy" attitude is "Literary Portraits—LI.: The Face of Janus," *Outlook*, XXXIV (Aug. 29, 1914), 270–71; the phrase quoted in the text is from his summary of it in *Return to Yesterday*, p. 362. Later on he was quite properly proud of having taken this attitude; see *No Enemy*, p. 91. The remark about being insulted every two minutes is in "Literary Portraits—LIV.: The Classic Muse," *Outlook*, XXXIV (Sept. 19, 1914), 367–68. In *Return to Yesterday*, Ford says the first of these articles caused the *Outlook* to lose subscribers, but in *Portraits from Life*, p. 168, he says that it "evoked no protest from my readers." Ford wrote a poem about two soldiers who meet in hell, each of whom justifies himself with the cliché, "I at least have done my duty to Society and the Fatherland!" It ends: "For I will bet my hat that you who sent me here to Hell/ Are saying the selfsame words at this very moment/ Concerning that exploit of yours." The poem is called "That Exploit of Yours" and presumably refers to the accusations of German sympathies made against him; it first appeared in *Outlook*, Sept. 12, 1914.

18. A sample card from a copy of *Between St. Dennis and St. George* reads: "With the compliments/ of/ Professor W. Macneile Dixon/ (University of Glasgow)./ 8, Buckingham Gate,/ London, S.W.1/ England." Richard Aldington, "Ford Madox Ford," *New Directions*, Number Seven, p. 457. Aldington may be referring to the proofs of *The Good Soldier*. It is also true that Ford's weekly articles for *Outlook* used the materials of *When Blood Is Their Argument* from Oct. 3, 1914, to Dec. 12, 1914, and from Feb. 6 to 27, 1915.

19. *When Blood Is Their Argument*, pp. 76, 176, and 5.

20. *Between St. Dennis and St. George*, pp. v and 199–205.

21. The evidence for dating the completion of *The Good Soldier* is not definitive. In *Return to Yesterday* (p. 417) Ford describes it as completed on June 28, 1914; much later he told *Time* (Dec. 19, 1927) that he completed it in July. In August, 1914 (the exact day appears to be the 10th, but the second digit is not unquestionably clear), Ford wrote Lane, "I would be obliged if you could pay me the fifty pounds that became due to me on the delivery of the ms. of the Saddest Story' " (Naumburg). The last page of the printer's copy for the novel (Cornell) has a received stamp dated Oct 3 11¹⁹ AM 191[4] (the final digit of the rubber stamp did not register, but it must have been a 4). Oct. 3, 1914, would be just about the time the printer would be likely to receive the ms. if the novel had been completed when Ford said it was. Against this must be set the fact that in his letter to Lane Ford says, "I have had to give up literature and offer myself for service to George Five; so shortly you may see me popping cartridges into garrison guns directed against my uncles, cousins and aunts. . . . " Ford did not offer his services to George V until Aug., 1915; but it is hardly conceivable this letter was written then and misdated by a year, and it is reasonable to suppose he did consider enlisting before Masterman offered him the job at Wellington House. In addition, there is Richard Aldington's recollection that Ford was writing *The Good Soldier* while Aldington was his secretary. Though when Aldington was Ford's secretary is a matter of speculation, it appears to have been in the fall of 1914 (see p. 251 above). But Aldington has Ford writing the wrong propaganda book then and may also have got mixed up about *The Good Soldier*. On the whole, then, it seems likely *The Good Soldier* was completed early in July, 1914. This has the unfortunate result of making the novel's reiterated date—Aug. 4—an accidental rather than a deliberate reference to the date the Germans crossed the Belgian frontier "near," as Ford liked to say, "a place called Gemmenich" and spoils the ingenious theory worked out by Ambrose Gordon, Jr., in *The Invisible Tent*, pp. 56–57.

22. Ford spoke of the "personal reasons" influencing him in writing *The Good Soldier* in the publicity release put out by Boni & Liveright, April 6, 1928 (Biala). He spoke of what *The Good Soldier* had cost him in "Literary Portraits—LXXI.: Enemies," *Outlook*, XXXV (Jan. 16, 1915), 79–80. Violet Hunt told Goldring that "in a fit of neurasthenic depression, [Ford] consigned the MS. [of *The Good Soldier*] to the dustbin. . . . She rescued it, had it

re-typed and was responsible for getting John Lane to issue it" (Goldring, *The Last Pre-Raphaelite*, p. 170). This story may be true; Ford certainly left most of the dealings with Lane to Violet: "I did not make the agreement for the 'Good Soldier'; was told what it purported to contain and signed it in a great hurry without looking it through" (Ford to Pinker, July 28, 1920 [Princeton]). In Hunt, *The Flurried Years* (p. 244), Violet improves on this story. "I found the sheets that she [the play-secretary] had written at his dictation in the dustbin at the bottom of the orchard [at Selsey] in a hundred pieces, and it took me a week to mend each one separately and send it to a publisher." This story is not literally true: the printer's copy for *The Good Soldier* is at Cornell; it is an unmended typescript; however, pp. 113–40 are scorched.

23. Ford and Violet were at Nauheim in 1910 when the Czar and his wife were (see p. 201 above); Violet describes the occasion in *The Desirable Alien*, p. 89, but Violet's way of talking about the occasion is probably most closely represented by her description of it in *The Flurried Years*, p. 133, which is almost exactly the talk Ford ascribes to Florence in the canceled passage of *The Good Soldier*, on p. 35 of the holograph. Violet's description of their visit to the Schloss is in *The Desirable Alien*, pp. 157–60 (*The Good Soldier*, pp. 43–44), of the Grand Duke, p. 99 (*The Good Soldier*, p. 35), of the polo-playing officers, p. 97. Lelöffel is mentioned by name in *The Flurried Years*, p. 134; he turns up in *The Good Soldier*, p. 35.

24. The saturnalia at Nancy's school was something Ford had heard about in the south of France (*Provence*, pp. 42–43). Ford met the Miss Hurlbirds at his Kaltwasser-Heilanstalt in 1904 (*Return to Yesterday*, p. 270). Ford describes the drive to the station during which he played Dowell's role in *The Spirit of the People*, pp. 148–50.

25. *The Good Soldier*, p. 5.

26. Conrad's remark is reported by Wells in *Experiment in Autobiography*, p. 527. The Shaw scene is at the conclusion of *Heartbreak House*.

27. "Techniques," *The Southern Review*, July, 1935, pp. 22 and 26. *The March of Literature*, pp. 342 and 732–33.

28. *The March of Literature*, pp. 469, 519, and 730. "Dedicatory Letter," *The Good Soldier*, p. xviii.

29. "Techniques," *The Southern Review*, July, 1935, pp. 32, 35, and 33. *The March of Literature*, p. 476.

30. "But, as the lines converge, [the writer's] technique must become always tighter and more breathless, every word—but every slightest word—carrying the affair that the novelist is rendering always further and more and more swiftly to the inevitable logic of the end." So Ford defined *progression d'effet* in *The March of Literature*, pp. 529–30.

31. "On Impressionism," *Poetry and Drama*, II (June, Dec., 1914); Harvey, pp. 191–92.

32. "Some Do Not . . . ," *Nation and Athenaeum*, XXXV (May 24, 1924), 258; Harvey, p. 344.

Chapter 20

1. Mark Schorer, "Introduction," *The Good Soldier*, pp. vii and xiii; Carol Ohmann supports this view in her *Ford Madox Ford*. Robie Macauley, "The Good Ford," *Kenyon Review* (Spring, 1949), pp. 271 and 276; with some modification this view is supported by Elliott B. Gose, in his important article, "The Strange Irregular Rhythm: An Analysis of The Good Soldier," *PMLA*, June, 1957, pp. 404–509. A middle view of Dowell is taken by Paul L. Wiley in *Novelist of Three Worlds*, Richard A. Cassell in *Ford Madox Ford*, and John A. Meixner in *Ford Madox Ford's Novels*. They accept it that Dowell is, in Prof. Meixner's

words (p. 159), "a severely neurotic personality"; but, by taking the view that such personalities are peculiarly sensitive, they free themselves to take seriously the story Dowell is telling, and do not treat it merely as evidence of his neuroses. The only quite satisfactory discussion of Dowell, to my knowledge, is in Samuel Hynes' brilliant article, "The Epistomology of The Good Soldier," *Sewanee Review* (Spring, 1961), pp. 225–35.

2. Schorer, *The Good Soldier*, pp. x and xi. "Coda," *Collected Poems*, p. 318. *The March of Literature*, p. 333. *The Good Soldier*, pp. 114–15.

3. *The Good Soldier*, pp. 110–11. *Parade's End*, II, 132. Harold Loeb, "Ford Madox Ford's 'The Good Soldier,'" *London Magazine*, III (Dec., 1963), 65–73.

4. *Henry James*, pp. 153–55.

5. *The Good Soldier*, p. 79. *Parade's End*, I, 348.

6. *The Good Soldier*, pp. 147 and 93.

7. *Between St. Dennis and St. George*, p. 44.

8. *The Good Soldier*, pp. 139, 218, and 219.

9. *The Good Soldier*, pp. 83 and 87–88.

10. *The Good Soldier*, p. 253. Paul L. Wiley, *Novelist of Three Worlds*, p. 194.

11. Ford called the profit-sharing idea for *The English Review* "socialistic" (Ford to Edward Garnett, n.d.; Ludwig, p. 30), but he meant by that, of course, communistic in a feudal way.

12. *The Good Soldier*, p. 78

13. For Lawrence's description of this "nicer" Ford, see pp. 219–20 above. For David Garnett's, see p. 200 above.

14. *Return to Yesterday*, p. 191. Stella Bowen, *Drawn from Life*, pp. 79–80. Harold Loeb, "Ford Madox Ford's 'The Good Soldier,' " *London Magazine*.

15. *The Good Soldier*, pp. 71, 237, 49, 71, 120, 84, and 67.

16. *The Good Soldier*, pp. 26, 96, 8, 77, 16–17, and 13. Like Edward Ashburnham, Christopher Tietjens was too sure of his place to feel anything but contempt for status symbols; "he hadn't been able to think of going through the rest of his life with a beastly placard like Senior Wrangler hung round his neck" (*Parade's End*, I, 53).

17. *The Good Soldier*, pp. 48 and 89.

18. Robie Macauley, "The Good Ford," *Kenyon Review*, XI (Spring, 1949), 271–72. *Thus to Revisit*, pp. 53–55.

19. *The Good Soldier*, pp. 12–13 (see also p. 183), 49–50, and 104–05.

20. *The Good Soldier*, p. 20.

21. This fact does take some trouble to find. Nancy confesses her love for Edward to Leonora Nov. 12, 1913 (p. 222); the next day Edward and Leonora cable Dowell to come to Branshaw (p. 232); Dowell leaves Waterbury "quite abruptly" for Branshaw (p. 200). If we assume the trip took him about ten days, he reached Branshaw about Dec. 1, 1913, or perhaps a few days earlier. He says he started to write six months later (p. 184). Dowell's apology for "rambling" is on pp. 183–84.

22. *The Good Soldier*, pp. 184, 233, 252, and 32. There is some inadvertent confusion about the date at which Dowell wrote down Part III. He says he had his long talk with Leonora about their lives "of a windy November evening [of 1913]" "about a week after the funeral of poor Edward" (p. 104), a date Leonora reinforces during their conversation by saying "Edward has been dead only ten days" (p. 105). But if this conversation occurred ten days after Edward's death, it cannot have occurred in November, 1913. Nancy Rufford left for Brindisi a "fortnight" after Dowell's arrival at Branshaw (p. 243) and therefore about the middle of December. Edward committed suicide the day she cabled from Brindisi (p. 255); that could not have been long after her departure from Branshaw, perhaps a week. Edward then committed suicide late in December, 1913, which puts Dowell and Leonora's

conversation, ten days after his death, sometime early in January, 1914. Dowell says he is writing down this part of the story about a month after his conversation with Leonora (p. 104), that is, about Feb. 1, 1914. Ford could not have intended to suggest that; I believe he meant us to think of Dowell's writing Parts III and IV continuously, in a single stretch from October to December, 1914.

23. Samuel Hynes, "The Epistomology of the Good Soldier," *Sewanee Review*, p. 227. *The Good Soldier*, pp. 255 and 254.

24. *The Good Soldier*, pp. 103–04, 121, and 103.

25. *The Good Soldier*, pp. 111, 129, 193, and 203.

26. *The Good Soldier*, pp. 203, 85, 185, and 238.

27. *The Good Soldier*, pp. 47, 234, and 235.

28. *The Good Soldier*, pp. 146, 152, 158, and 146.

29. *The Good Soldier*, pp. 190, 159, and 161.

30. *The Good Soldier*, pp. 140, 60, 94, 144, 146, and 149.

31. *Provence*, pp. 124–25. *The Good Soldier*, pp. 44, 39, 43, and 237.

32. *The Good Soldier*, pp. 148–49, 167, and 178.

33. *The Good Soldier*, pp. 168, 169, 170, 179, 171, and 170.

34. *The Good Soldier*, pp. 175–76 and 186–87.

35. *The Good Soldier*, pp. 77, 90, 71, and 40. Mrs. Markham (Elizabeth Penrose) wrote popular school histories of England (1823) and France (1828).

36. *The Good Soldier*, pp. 71, 191, and 190. The Vintage edition follows the Boni edition of 1927 and reads (p. 71) "she annexed poor dear Edward" for "she cut out poor dear Edward"; this may well have been Ford's revision.

37. *The Good Soldier*, pp. 119, 102, 119, 121, and 120.

38. *The Good Soldier*, pp. 201–02 and 237–38.

39. *The Good Soldier*, pp. 36–37.

40. *The Good Soldier*, pp. 50 and 6. W. B. Yeats, "Meditations in Time of Civil War, I: Ancestral Houses."

Chapter 21

1. Rebecca West's review was in the *Daily News;* the other reviews quoted were in the *Outlook* and the *New York Times;* Harvey, pp. 321 and 323. For the details of the *New Witness* affair see Harvey, pp. 329 and 598–99. J. K. Prothero was Ada Elizabeth Jones, who later became the wife of G. K. Chesterton's brother, Cecil. Wells's letter is in Maisie Ward, *Gilbert Keith Chesterton* (Penguin Books, 1944), p. 244.

2. Goldring, *South Lodge*, p. 115. Ford to Masterman, June 28, 1919, in Ludwig, p. 95. Ford learned of Violet's syphilis, and perhaps a good deal more about her previous affairs than he had hitherto known, when a doctor who was caring for her insisted on talking to her "husband." Exactly when this occurred is not clear, but it may be that Florence Dowell's affairs with Jimmy and Edward Ashburnham and her deception of Dowell embody Ford's feelings about this aspect of his relation with Violet. If so, they indicate how strong his response to it was. Ford's unhappiness at this time was, as Wells said to Chesterton, "notorious."

3. Wyndham Lewis, *Blasting & Bombardiering*, p. 185. Ford to Mrs. Hueffer, Sept. 18, 1915 (Soskice). Wells makes particularly effective satiric use of this mixture of feelings in *The Bulpington of Blup*, p. 205: "One might be all for the War to end War but nevertheless one had to keep cool. . . . Be English; be phlegmatic. . . . That wasn't altogether satisfactory to the Bulpington of Blup. It didn't stage well. It jarred with the spirit of leadership in him. But for a time it kept him from positive action." But by the time Wells was writing that, Ford too could be

ironic about it, in a Hemingway vein: "The Big Words ... Loyalty, Heroism, Chivalry, Conscience, Self-Sacrifice, Probity, Patriotism, Soldierly Piety, Democracy even ... those big words and the golden naïvetés that they stood for were probably in that year [1915] going stronger than they ever before had gone. . . . We were going—all volunteers at that date—to damn well *make* the world fit for Heroes and Democrats and Patriots!" (*Portraits from Life*, p. 169). *The Marsden Case*, p. 242.

4. Ford to Mrs. Hueffer, Sept. 18, 1915 (Soskice). Ford used almost the same words in his letter to Lucy Masterman announcing his commission: "I can assure you, for what it is worth, that it is as if the peace of God had descended on me" ("A Jubilee," *Outlook*, XXXVI [July 10, 1915], 46–48).

5. Ford to Lucy Masterman, July 31, 1915, in Ludwig, pp. 60–61.

6. Hunt, *The Flurried Years*, pp. 260–61. Ford to Mrs. Hueffer, n.d. (Soskice).

7. Violet apparently never sent Ford the letter quoted here; Goldring found it in a copy of *The Good Soldier* at South Lodge (Goldring, *South Lodge*, p. 118), where he also found the inscription in Lawrence's *Love Poems* (*South Lodge*, p. 63).

8. "Merciful Aphasia" appeared in *Outlook*, XXXVI (Aug. 28, 1915), 271; see also "Is It Worth While?" in *Poetry*, XII (April, 1918), 21, and her review of Pinero's *The Big Drum, Outlook*, XXXVI (Sept. 11, 1915), 332–33.

9. "The appointment of Mr. Ford Madox Hueffer to be a second lieutenant (on probation) in the 3rd Battalion Welch Regiment was gazetted last night" (the London *Times*, Aug. 14, 1915). Ford's "Officer's Record of Services, Army Book 439," gives the official date of his commissioning as Aug. 10, 1915 (Biala). The War Office, apparently echoing the *Times*, told Goldring the date was Aug. 14 (*The Last Pre-Raphaelite*, p. 185). Ford mentions training at Chelsea at least three times: in the dedication of *The Good Soldier* (1927), p. xxi, in a letter to Stella, Nov. 1, 1918, and in *No Enemy*, p. 33. In *The Marsden Case* (pp. 201 and 265) George Heimann spends eleven days training with the Irish Guards at Chelsea Barracks; perhpas Ford did too. Ford was eager to get into uniform at the very first opportunity (Ford to Oliver Hueffer, Oct. 5, 1915 [Soskice]). The description of him in uniform is from a letter of Iris Barry to Arthur Mizener, Dec. 21, 1966.

10. The erroneous notion that Ford could not have been in uniform until after Aug. 14 has confused attempts to clarify this episode. Prof. Harry T. Moore (*The Intelligent Heart* [London, 1955], p. 194) is convinced Ford's description of the occasion is "romancing" because he mistakenly believes Ford could not have been in uniform before the Lawrences left Greatham at the end of July and that Frieda's version of the story is therefore correct. But Frieda is not very reliable either. During Kyle Chrichton's interview with Lawrence (*D. H. Lawrence: A Composite Biography*, II, 412) she has Ford instead of Violet denying his German ancestry by implying he is Dutch instead of Russian. The later variations on her story that are quoted in the text are in a letter to Prof. Moore about *The Intelligent Heart*, written Jan. 14, 1955 (*Frieda Lawrence: The Memoirs and Correspondence*, ed. E. W. Tedlock, Jr. [New York, 1964], p. 389). It is difficult to reconcile the assertions that Violet was calling Ford Russian and Ford suggesting he was Dutch at the same time. T. S. Eliot once called *Antwerp* "the only good poem I have met with on the subject of the war" (quoted in Harvey, p. 333). *Portraits from Life*, p. 89. Hunt, *The Flurried Years*. Ford's answer to Frieda's letter to the *American Mercury* is in Ludwig, p. 269.

11. Goldring, *South Lodge*, p. 118; *The Last Pre-Raphaelite*, p. 184. Official Copy of Public Records Office Enrollment (Supreme Court of Judicature), 1915. Vol. 14, p. 221 (Cornell).

12. *The Marsden Case*, pp. 156–57 and 225. Pound to Harriet Monroe, Sept. 25, 1915, in *The Letters of Ezra Pound*, ed. D. D. Paige, p. 63. Pound found the war's interference with his literary projects very annoying. He was as busy as ever promoting good poets and seeking recommendations for them: "You can take Hueffer's commendation of Eliot to back up mine, if it is any use to you," he wrote Harriet Monroe (Oct. 2, 1915, *The Letters of Ezra Pound*, ed. D.

D. Paige, p. 64). But it was getting harder to pin Hueffer down. "F.M.H. is taken up with his soldiering and one only sees him when he's on leave," he complained (Pound to Harriet Monroe, Jan. 21, 1916, in *The Letters of Ezra Pound,* ed. D. D. Paige, p. 68). Ford to Masterman, Aug. 28, 1915; Ludwig, p. 61. Ford to Mrs. Hueffer, n.d. (Soskice). Ford to Lucy Masterman, Feb. 15, 1916; Ludwig, p. 63.

13. Frank MacShane, *The Life and Work of Ford Madox Ford* (London, 1965), p. 129; the young officer was Thomas A. Lloyd. Ford to Lucy Masterman, May 13, 1916; Ludwig, pp. 64–65. *Portraits from Life,* p. 211; *No Enemy,* pp. 31–32. With his habitual confusion about dates, Ford tells a story in *Portraits from Life* (pp. 167–68) about reviewing Dreiser's *The Titan* in "late 1914" when he was Battalion Orderly Officer in Cardiff. He was not, of course, at Cardiff until late 1915 and his review of *The Titan* appeared in *Outlook* as one of his then regular weekly articles March 6, 1915.

14. The companion poems are "The Silver Music" and "The Iron Music"; both are dated in *On Heaven,* the one quoted July 22, 1916, so that if we take that "nine weeks" literally, the trip to Chepstow was made on Sunday, May 14. "What the Orderly Dog Saw" appeared in *Poetry* in March, 1917. Ford to F. S. Flint, Feb. 19, 1917; Ludwig, p. 83. "I have been writing silly little lyrics wh. no one will print," he wrote Lucy Masterman on July 11, 1916 (Ludwig, p. 66), possibly in the hope that, if someone did publish them, she might believe their subject was imaginary.

15. Ford to Wells, March 22, 1916; Ludwig, pp. 63–64.

16. "I have been warned to hold myself in readiness for the front—& shd. go about 14.6.16" (Ford to Pinker, June 1, 1916 [Princeton]). Conrad refused to be the guest of honor at Violet's garden party in a letter of June 2, 1913. He accepted the literary executorship in a letter to Ford, Aug. 12, 1915. The letter about binoculars is undated; Conrad's letter to Violet about Borys is dated Sept. 28, 1915, and his assertion that he almost called at South Lodge is in a letter of Oct. 26, 1915. Ford liked to tell a story about receiving a £5 note from Conrad when he was on the Somme in July, 1916, because he had bet Conrad *Chance* would sell over 14,000 copies (*Return to Yesterday,* p. 234; in 1927, in an interview with Fanny Butcher, he placed this incident in February, 1917; see Harvey, p. 371). Ford apparently did combat Conrad's pessimism about the book, but he was proved right long before he reached France. "Tell Ford he was right and I was wrong about [*Chance's*] success," Conrad wrote Violet on Feb. 23, 1914. "Thank him too for the *James* & say I'm sorry I didn't write." These letters are at Cornell. For the farewell meeting with Conrad see *Return to Yesterday,* p. 198.

17. The general impression was that Christina had been a very naughty small child and then suddenly became very good and almost desperately self-abnegating. This abrupt change frightened both Elsie and Ford, who, rightly or wrongly, were haunted by the possibility that Christina had inherited something of Mary Martindale's instability; they did not dare to oppose her beyond a certain point.

18. "Footsloggers," *Collected Poems,* p. 79. "[Ford] . . . took no active part in the fighting. . . . He was most anxious to obtain front line experience . . . but Colonel Cooke would not allow him, on account of his age" (letter from Thomas Sugrue to Arthur Mizener, April 19, 1966. Thomas Sugrue was a fellow officer and Ford's closest friend during his days in France). To the best of Captain Sugrue's knowledge, Ford was never gassed, though when he was hospitalized later on he was convinced his lungs had been affected by "the touch of gas I got at Nieppe" (Ford to Mrs. Hueffer, Dec. 15, 1916 [Soskice]), and he later told Jepson a story of gas getting into his portmanteau as he was packing for a leave so that, when he opened it in England, he got a lung full of gas (Edgar Jepson, *Memories of an Edwardian,* pp. 212–13). Ford to Lucy Masterman, July 11, 1916; Ludwig, p. 66. Goldring, *The Last Pre-Raphaelite,* p. 188.

19. The best account of the battle of Mametz wood is that of L. W. Griffith, who was at Brigade Hdqtrs., at the time (*Up to Mametz* [London, 1931]). The history of the 58th Brigade, of which the 9th Welch was a part, can be traced in detail in Everard Wyrall's *The History of the 19th*

Division, 1914–1918 (London, n.d.). See also *The History of the Welch Regiment* (Cardiff, 1932). In later years Ford told a great many stories about this brief and terrible period on the Somme. Some of these are vivid vignettes, as of the old French butler at Albert (*It Was the Nightingale*, p. 117). Some are descriptions of himself carrying out what appear to be the duties of a staff officer ("A Day of Battle" [ms. at Cornell], pp. 3 and 5; *It Was the Nightingale*, p. 113; the broadcast for WJZ, Dec. 7, 1936 [Biala]). One describes how he began to translate *The Good Soldier* into French "in Bécourt-Bécordel wood in July 1916" (*Return to Yesterday*, p. 429; the ms. of this translation is in the Biala Collection); another describes how he reread *Youth* and *Heart of Darkness* "in a regimental ammunition dump that had been dug out in the side of a hill in Bécourt wood" ("Literary Causeries: IV. Escape . . . " *Chicago Tribune* [Paris], March, 1924). A few of the very late ones are clearly imaginary, for example the story of how he marched "my battalion" into the lines during the battle of the Somme (*Great Trade Route*, pp. 339–40). *The Marsden Case*, p. 305. Ford to Lucy Masterman, July 28 and Sept. 6, 1916; Ludwig, pp. 67 and 74.

20. Ford to Masterman, Jan. 5, 1917; Ludwig, p. 82. "Met Hueffer's brother-in-law [David Soskice] on the plaisaunce. He said a shell had burst near our friend and that he had had a nervous breakdown and was for the present safe in a field hospital" (Pound to Lewis, July, 1916, *The Letters of Ezra Pound*, ed. D. D. Paige, p. 86). Ford to F. S. Flint (June 23, 1920; Ludwig, p. 108). Ford's remark about the nerve tangle is in a letter to H. G. Wells, Oct. 14, 1923; Ludwig, p. 154.

21. The description of the Casualty Clearing Station at Corbie is in *Portraits from Life*, p. 205. Ford frequently referred to this loss of memory, for example, in *Portraits from Life*, p. 165, *It Was the Nightingale*, pp. 80 and 194–96.

22. Ford to Lucy Masterman, n.d.; Ludwig, p. 68. I have substituted "nurses" in this quotation for the "muses" of Prof. Ludwig's text. Ford wrote his mother (n.d. [Soskice]) that he was in the hospital about a week. The exact location of the 9th Welch is given in *It Was the Nightingale*, p. 116. Ford to Mrs. Hueffer, Sept. 6, 1916 (Soskice). "Copy it ["A Solis Ortus Cardine"] out, will you & send it to V. for publication but keep the autograph." He gave a carbon copy of this ms. to Thomas Sugrue; it is now at Cornell. Letter from Thomas Sugrue to Arthur Mizener, April 19, 1966.

23. Ford to Mrs. Hueffer, Sept. 6, 1916 (Soskice). Ford to Lucy Masterman, Sept. 6, 1916; Ludwig, pp. 74–75. Ford to Lucy Masterman, Aug. 23, 1916; Ludwig, p. 69. Ford hated being Mess Officer, which did, as the "Ration Book" in which he kept his accounts shows, involve a great deal of work (Cornell). Ford to Conrad, Sept. 7, 1918; Ludwig, p. 75. Ford to Lucy Masterman, n.d.; Ludwig, pp. 67–68. Ford to Lucy Masterman, Aug. 25, 1916; Ludwig, p. 70. Simultaneously he was telling the battalion M. O. that "I can hardly move" because of rheumatism and agoraphobia; see below, p. 290.

24. Ford to Conrad, n.d. (but if we take literally Ford's statement that he has been at the front six weeks, c. Aug. 29, 1916), Sept. 6, and Sept. 7, 1916; Ludwig, pp. 71–76. The reference to reading *The Red Badge of Courage* is taken from the unrevised typescript of Ford's essay on H. G. Wells (Cornell); in the somewhat different version he printed (*Portraits from Life*, p. 122) he specifically mentions that he was "obsessed by insomnia." The description of reading the proofs of *Their Lives* is in the Preface. He later told his daughter Katharine that most of the poems in *On Heaven* were written in Albert and at Kemmel Hill, just in front of Bailleul (Ford to Katharine Hueffer, April 13, 1918, in Goldring, *The Last Pre-Raphaelite*, p. 199). *That Same Poor Man*, Chapter I (Cornell). Ford also reproduces the facts—and presumably the impressions—of his own experience of the war in the unfinished novel he wrote immediately after it called *True Love & a G.C.M.* (Cornell).

25. There is a carbon of Ford's letter to Masterman in his "Ration Book" at Cornell. Col. Cooke's letter was addressed to the headquarters of the 58th Brigade, Aug. 6, 1916; a copy was sent to Ford at South Lodge by the Battalion Adjutant, Capt. R. R. Whitty, because no one at

Battalion Headquarters knew where Ford was until he turned up there from the hospital. Col. Cooke's exact words were, "I consider that he is quite unsuitable to perform the duties required of an officer in this campaign. He would not inspire his men with confidence and his power as a leader is nil. . . . I recommend that he be sent home as early as possible as there is no use to which I can put him. I could not place him in command of men in the field. I cannot recommend him for employment at home" (Cornell). In *True Love & a G.C.M.* (pp. 76–78), Gabriel Morton's colonel accuses him of both inefficiency and cowardice "at 11.45 ach emma this 17 9 16." Ford also wrote a short story, "The Colonel's Shoes," about this episode, about a Capt. Gotch who "came from a Reserve Battalion that wasn't popular in that Regiment. So things were said about him—they were probably untrue. They ranged from nasty —very nasty things about him and women and the Colonel of his Reserve Battalion, to the allegation that a firm, in which he had been junior partner before the war, had been fined heavily for trading with the enemy" (Cornell).

26. There are carbons of Ford's letters to the adjutant and the M.O. in his "Ration Book" at Cornell; they are dated Sept. 7 and 8, 1916. The descriptions of Paris in *No Enemy* are in Chapters VIII and X; see also *Provence,* p. 292. Ford to Masterman, Sept. 13, 1916; Ludwig, p. 76. Some of the French reviewers of *Entre Saint Denis* were less kind than the Minister of Instruction; David Harvey (p. 331) quotes one who said it was "un livre déroutant et bizarre . . . horriblement touffu, diffus, gesticulant, désordonné. . . . "

27. Ford to Masterman, Oct. 12 and 25, 1916; Ludwig, pp. 76–77. "I cd. get along personally on my pay," he wrote Lucy Masterman (Oct. 27, 1916; Ludwig, p. 78), "—but I have outside liabilities too, you see. And V's campaign of vilification makes people very shy of publishing my work." "I rather suspect V (though I may be unjust) of suppressing them [his poems] for ends of her own" (Ford to Lucy Masterman, Aug. 25, 1916; Ludwig, p. 70).

28. Ford to Masterman, Nov. 29, 1916, and Jan. 5, 1917; Ludwig, pp. 78 and 81–83. The description of the Red Cross hospital is in "I Revisit the Riviera," *Harper's,* CLXVI (Dec., 1932), p. 66. Ford told Stella ten years later that he was hospitalized Dec. 5, 1916. He tells a story about one of the prisoners he guarded at Rouen in *Return to Yesterday,* p. 119. In some of his letters from the hospital (for example, to his daughter Katharine, December, 1916) Ford says he was "blown up by a 4.2 & shaken into a nervous breakdown," as if he knew the breakdown had begun when he was knocked down by that shell concussion on the Somme. There is a vivid description of what he suffered at Rouen in *True Love & a G.C.M.,* pp. 33–36.

29. Ford to Mrs. Hueffer, Dec. 15, 1916 (Soskice). "One Day's List," *Collected Poems,* p. 66.

30. Wells, *Experiment in Autobiography,* pp. 530–31. Wells to Douglas Goldring, May 30, 1945, in *The Last Pre-Raphaelite,* pp. 89–90.

31. H. G. Wells, *The Bulpington of Blup,* pp. 326 and 322–23. "I have a weakness for . . . Theodore Bulpington," Wells said. " . . . [He] is as good as Kipps. Please" (*Experiment in Autobiography,* pp. 414 and 420).

32. Like Ford, Theodore Bulpington claimed (in Theodore's case falsely) to have been stunned by a near miss. Like Ford, he blames his weak lungs on poison gas. He hangs around Parville, out of fright, as Ford hung around Rouen because neither he nor Col. Cooke could endure his returning to the 9th Welch. Theodore appealed to Sir Lucien Brood for help in getting out of his military job as Ford appealed to Masterman (*The Bulpington of Blup,* pp. 326, 250, and 241).

Chapter 22

1. Ford left Rouen for Menton on Jan. 8, 1917. The description of the Cap Martin Hotel is in "I Revisit the Riviera," *Harper's,* CLXVI (Dec., 1932), 67; it reappears in *Provence,* pp.

265–66. See also Humphrey Waterfield to Arthur Mizener, July 31, 1966. Château Pavie was Ford's favorite wine.

2. *It Was the Nightingale*, p. 192. Ford's Service Record shows him to have been at Rouen from Feb. 3 to Feb. 24 and at Abbeville from Feb. 25 to March 15, 1917. He describes the Canadian company at Rouen in his unpublished *Toward a History of Literature*, pp. 93–94, and the prisoner-of-war camp in a letter (Biala). The description of the cold north is in a letter to F. S. Flint, Feb. 19, 1917; Ludwig, p. 83.

3. Ford to Mrs. Hueffer, April 19, 1917 (Soskice). Ford to Lucy Masterman, Sept. 8, 1917; Ludwig, p. 84. Ford has an improved version of Col. Powell's letter of commendation in *It Was the Nightingale*, p. 21. He gave Col. Powell a copy of *On Heaven* as a wedding present (Ford to the Poetry Bookshop, Sept. 9, 1920 [Texas]). Ford occasionally confused the issue about this period of his life by suggesting he had returned to France; for example, "Before the great attack on Wytschaete in the Salient I . . ." (*Provence*, p. 298). This refers to the so-called third battle of Ypres, which began with an attack on Wytschaete-Messines on June 7, 1917. Ford also placed himself at Vimy Ridge for Ferris Greenslet, *Under the Bridge*, p. 162.

4. Ferris Greenslet, *Under the Bridge*, p. 161. Ford to Mrs. Hueffer, March 23, 1917 (Soskice). Ford to Lucy Masterman, Jan. 13, 1918; Ludwig, p. 86.

5. Ford to Harold Monro, May 30 and June 9, 1920, and Violet Hunt to Harold Monro, n.d. (but approximately the same time) (Texas). There is a note in the Violet Hunt Papers at Cornell describing their establishment at Redcar. Pound to Mencken, Aug. 12, 1917, in *The Letters of Ezra Pound*, ed. D. D. Paige, p. 114. Ford first mentions *Women & Men* in a letter to Pinker, Jan. 31, 1911; a year later he is still trying to find a publisher for it (Ford to Pinker, Jan. 31, 1911, and Feb. 12, 1912 [Huntington]). *Provence*, p. 61. Ford has an improved account of his meeting with Greenslet in *Return to Yesterday*, p. 329.

6. Ford to Pinker, Jan. 6, 1918 (Princeton). When *No Enemy* was finally published, a decade later, Ford wrote his agent, Ruth Kerr, that "The sort of line they [Macaulay, the publisher] ought to take is this: This is the only book about the war and the state of things after the Armistice by a novelist and thinker of Mr. F's position and experience actually to go through the war as an infantry officer in the line . . ." (Ford to Ruth Kerr, Nov., 1929 [Biala]). Collins turned down Pinker's proposal that they commission a novel by Ford (Jan. 11, 1918 [Northwestern]). Ford to Katharine Hueffer, March 15, 1918; there is some confusion about the date of Ford's staff appointment. Ford told Katharine it was màde "about a month ago" (that is, about March 15); but his Service Record gives the date as April 15. *Great Trade Route*, p. 46, and *No Enemy*, p. 30. Ford to Pinker, n.d. (New York Public).

7. Ford to Katharine Hueffer, April 13, 1918. For Harriet Monroe's review, see Harvey, p. 335.

8. Stella Bowen, *Drawn from Life* (London, 1941), pp. 36 and 48–49.

9. Bowen, *Drawn from Life*, p. 62.

10. Ford to Stella, June 26, 1918. Bowen, *Drawn from Life*, p. 63 (this passage summarizes Ford's letter to Stella of Aug. 28, 1918).

11. *No Enemy*, pp. 64 and 70. *Collected Poems*, p. 78.

12. *No Enemy*, p. 10. Bowen, *Drawn from Life*, pp. 64 and 165.

13. Interview with Fanny Butcher, *Chicago Tribune*, Jan. 22, 1927. The novel he speaks here of having suppressed is presumably *True Love & a G.C.M.* In later years Ford sometimes claimed (mistakenly) that he had suppressed *No Enemy* in 1919. Ford to Martin Secker, Aug. 18, 1918; Ludwig, pp. 88–89. In May, 1919, Ford asked Stella to look into the firm of Cobden Sanderson, which had approached him (Stella to Ford, n.d., but c. May 9, 1919). At the same time he was trying his idea of a collected edition on John Lane, who—he later came to believe—promised to publish such an edition (Ford to Pinker, n.d., but c. July 15, 1920 [Huntington]). He therefore submitted *The Wheels of the Plough* to Lane on the understanding that Lane was going to publish a collected edition. In rejecting *The Wheels of the Plough*, Lane said, "Though Mr. Hueffer mentioned the Collected Edition,

the terms were not even touched on. . . . At any rate, I could not consider the publication of his Collected Works on such terms [as Ford has proposed]. . . . The impression Mr. Hueffer has regarding the terms makes it quite useless for us to enter into further controversy on the subject." Ford had not improved his relations with Lane by asserting that Lane had got *The Good Soldier* at cut rates. "On *The Good Soldier*," Lane observed in his letter to Pinker, "Mr. Hueffer has earned £ 67.11.11 and I have lost £ 54.10.0, which does not tend to prove that Mr. Hueffer gave me his book at a 'cheap' price" (Lane to Pinker, July 26, 1920 [Northwestern]). This was Ford's old problem. By Ford's standards of what society should pay for so good a book as *The Good Soldier*, Lane's price was highway robbery; by the standard set in the marketplace, Lane had overpaid him. Ford took his revenge on Lane by presenting him in *The Marsden Case* as the crooked publisher, Podd, who cheats George Heimann over his translation of Prof. Curtius' epic poem and gets humiliatingly exposed in court.

14. *Great Trade Route*, p. 204. Ford to Stella, Aug. 22, Sept. 19, Oct. 2, and Nov. 1, 1918.

15. Ford to Stella, Nov. 1 and Dec. 10, 1918. It is difficult to imagine precisely what relations between Stella and Violet were during this period. When Stella went to Redcar to look after Ford she wired Violet at Knap Cottage, "Shall stay here till you come or he leaves as doctor says he must have nursing" (Stella to Violet, Oct. 12, 1918 [Cornell]). Perhaps Ford got well quickly enough to escape Violet's coming.

16. *The Letters of Arnold Bennett*, ed. Hepburn, I, 237, 262, and 265-66. *Return to Yesterday*, pp. 404-05. *It Was the Nightingale*, pp. 18-20 and 24. Ford to Stella, Nov. 7 and 13, 1918. *Parade's End*, II, 279.

17. Bowen, *Drawn from Life*, p. 60. Ford to Stella, Nov. 11 and Dec. 13, 1918. *It Was the Nightingale*, pp. 18-20 and 22. In literal fact Ford had, since 1912, written two novels, two books for Wellington House, *On Heaven*, parts of two unpublished novels (*True Love & a G.C.M.* and *No Enemy*), and over a hundred articles, mostly for the *Outlook*. His statement that he had written nothing for seven years means "nothing significant since *The Good Soldier*," which was completed in 1913. His object is, of course, to dramatize the extent to which he had been forgotten, not to record trivial facts.

18. Alec Waugh dined with Ford and Violet at South Lodge in January and during these months attended a number of evening parties there with them both present (Goldring, *The Last Pre-Raphaelite*, pp. 206-07). Ford received his first promotion, to lieutenant, July 1, 1917, when he was serving under Col. Powell; he was made captain Jan. 7, 1918. He held the temporary rank of brevet major from March 14, 1918, to Aug. 1, 1918.

19. Violet mentions Ford's lack of a bed in a letter to him, n.d. (Cornell). The description of his dress is from *That Same Poor Man*, p. 238. *It Was the Nightingale*, pp. 151 and 111-12. Ford always remembered that he was in category nineteen of the discharge lists, which included "authors, gypsies, travelling showmen and unemployables. We were all non-productive and so to be discharged last!" ("Literary Causeries: III.—And the French," *Chicago Tribune* [Paris], March 2, 1924). *Parade's End*, I, 202-03.

20. Ford warned Stella about Child's opening his letters March 31, 1929. Violet Hunt had tea with Mary Martindale and Mrs. Hueffer at their flat in Blythe Road Nov. 24, 1909 (Diary). In *The Flurried Years* (p. 73), published in 1926, she says that Mary "had gone to live in Germany."

21. Ford to Stella, n.d., and Stella to Ford, n.d.

22. Bowen, *Drawn from Life*, pp. 65-66.

23. Ford to Stella, April 6, 1919. In *It Was the Nightingale* (pp. 111-19) the meal is a stew of mutton and shallots and a half bottle of port bought in Pulborough on the way down. Ford says he made a pact with himself that, if the skins came off the shallots, he would go on with his life; otherwise he would not. There is a third version of his arrival at Red Ford in *No Enemy*, p. 148. Pound's description of Red Ford is in *Mauberley*, X. Ford kept

his studio at 20A Campden Hill Gardens until quarter-day for visits to London.

24. Gardening bulks very large in Ford's letters to Stella through these months. For the potatoes and pigs, see *It Was the Nightingale*, pp. 123–24 and 126–27. The remark about Ford's gardens was made by Edward Crankshaw, about the garden at the Villa Paul. When Ford sent Pinker the ms. of *Mr. Croyd* in October, 1920, he said, "I have been hammering at it now for about eighteen months" (Ford to Pinker, Oct. 21, 1910 [Princeton]); if so, he started it just about the time he arrived at Red Ford.

25. Stella reported Tom's departure late in May. The precise date of her arrival at Red Ford is uncertain, but as late as June 9 Ford was writing his mother that he was very much alone there (Soskice). The deed poll, dated June 4, 1919, is in the Biala Collection.

26. Ford to Pinker, June 5, 1919; Ludwig, p. 93. Violet to Mrs. Hueffer, n.d. (Soskice). This letter is dated simply "Thursday," probably June 19 or 26. Violet was told nothing until the middle of June, when Stella joined Ford; Ford wrote Mrs. Hueffer the news July 3.

27. Ford to Mrs. Hueffer, July 3, 1919 (Soskice). Ford did, for some time, make social appearances with Violet: there are letters to Ethel Mayne and Violet herself about his doing so (Cornell). "I shan't appear again in London," he wrote Masterman on June 28, 1919 (Ludwig, p. 96), "except that, in order to spare Violet the mortification of the appearance of an official abandonment, I shall figure at her larger parties from time to time—as, for instance, Monday next [June 30]. I don't like doing it, but I take it to be a duty."

28. Ford to Masterman, June 28, 1919; Ludwig, p. 95. Ford to Mrs. Hueffer, July 3 and c. 24, 1919 (Soskice). Bowen, *Drawn from Life*, pp. 66–68. Ford also suffered intermittently from certain aftereffects of the war; one leg bothered him, and in May, 1919, he had an operation for a tumor on his neck (Ford to Violet, July 1, 1919 [Cornell]).

29. Bowen, *Drawn from Life*, p. 68.

30. Ford to Mrs. Hueffer, n.d., but c. Aug. 15, 1919 (Soskice). "English Country" appeared in the *New Statesman*, Aug. 23 and 30 and Sept. 6, 1919. Ford described the book to Pinker July 24, 1919; Ludwig, p. 96. In an undated letter to his mother, c. July 24, 1919 (Soskice), he says, "I took up my novel again three days ago & shall try to finish it if no more earthquakes intervene—or even if they do." This is the novel that started as *Mr. Croyd*, became *The Wheels of the Plough* and, later, *That Same Poor Man.*

31. *No Enemy*, p. 9. The passage about Gaudier Brzeska in Chapter X (pp. 204–06) was part of a review in *The English Review*, Oct., 1919. Ford used it once again in *Thus to Revisit*, pp. 173–84. The account of the trip to Paris in "Maisie" (Chapter VIII) and "From the Balcony" (Chapter X) is based on "Trois Jours de Permission," *Nation* (London), Sept. 30, 1916. Ford sent Pinker "the complete m.s." Oct. 9, 1919, though whether of *No Enemy* or the earlier version, it is impossible to say. Pinker reported that Cobden Sanderson turned the book down Oct. 17, 1919 (Northwestern). It was also turned down by John Bale Sons and Danielson (John Bale to Pinker, July 24, 1920 [Northwestern]).Ford then said, "I don't know that 'English Country' is much good, really, I was rather ill when I wrote it. I fancy it might anyhow be best to put it into a drawer for a year or two" (Ford to Pinker, July 28, 1920 [Princeton]). Perhaps that last sentence is the source of Ford's later conviction that he had refused to publish *No Enemy* at the time it was written because it was too frank.

Chapter 23

1. Bowen, *Drawn from Life*, pp. 77–78. Ford signed the agreement for the sale of the movie rights to *Romance* June 16 (Texas). His acknowledgment of Pinker's check, with a com-

plaint about Pinker's deductions, is dated June 28, 1919 (Huntington). The movie was eventually produced under the title *The Road to Romance;* Ramon Navarro played the lead. It was reviewed in *The New York Times* Oct. 10, 1927; Harvey, p. 17. Ford was horrified when he came on a poster for it that fall in New York. Ford to Masterman, June 28, 1919; Ludwig, p. 95; "various cinema rights" refers to an inquiry about *The Panel* (Bobbs Merrill to Pinker, Feb. 22, 1919 [Northwestern]). *The Panel* was never sold, though Ford was asking Pinker for the $500 he thought it had brought in June (Ford to Pinker, June 25, 1919, and Jan. 7, 1921 [Princeton]). Ford to Mrs. Hueffer, June 9, 1929 (Soskice).

2. Ford to Pinker, June 29, 1919; Ludwig, pp. 93–94. Bowen, *Drawn from Life,* p. 69. Ford to Herbert Read, Sept. 2, 1919, and June 11, 1920; Ludwig, pp. 98 and 103. Ford to Harold Monro, June 9, 1920; Ludwig, p. 101. Bedham is in Sussex, three miles north of Fittleworth on B2188.

3. Ford to Pinker, May 6, 1920 (Huntington). Ford to Harold Monro, June 9, 1920; Ludwig, p. 101. The typescript of "A House" (Cornell) is inscribed "For my dear Stella. First draft finished 5/6/20. Final copy . . . 10/6/20."

4. Penny is mentioned to Herbert Read, June 11, 1920 (Ludwig, p. 104), and his name is explained to Isador Schneider, Sept. 14, 1929; Ludwig, p. 190.

5. Ford to F. S. Flint, June 23, 1920; Ludwig, pp. 106–08. Ford to Herbert Read, June 11, 1920; Ludwig, p. 104. *The Marsden Case,* p. 304.

6. "Immortality" was printed in *The Chapbook* in July, 1920. Ford never reprinted it but it is reproduced in Harvey, pp. 219–22. The poem is a very specific summary of Ford's view of himself as one who "wrote all your life for Immortality/ Of a Parnassian, most impersonal shape"; it also calls him "watchful, aviséd," in an echo of the phrase he had used in *No Enemy:* "très fort, hardi, courageux et avisé."

7. Ford to Pound, July 27, 1920; Ludwig, p. 117. For the history of *Mr. Croyd* and *Thus to Revisit,* see Ford to Herbert Read, June 30 and July 24, 1920; Ludwig, pp. 109 and 114; Ford to Ezra Pound, June 29, 1920, in Ludwig, p. 118; Ford to Pinker, Sept. 7, 1920 (Princeton), and Oct. 21, 1920 (New York Public); Alec Waugh to Pinker, July 26, 1920 (Princeton); Arthur Waugh to Pinker, Aug. 9, 1920 (Northwestern); Ford to Pinker, Aug. 8, 1920 (Huntington). Waugh chose *Thus to Revisit,* But Ford hopefully tried *Mr. Croyd (The Wheels of the Plough)* on him as soon as it was finished.

8. Ford to Pound, Aug. 30, 1920; Ludwig, p. 122. Sylvia Tietjens put detectives on Christopher and Valentine in much the same way (*Parade's End,* II, 283). Pound to Ford, July, 30, 1920 (Cornell). Ford to Pound, Sept. 19, 1920; Ludwig, p. 124. Goldring, *The Last Pre-Raphaelite,* p. 206. Bowen, *Drawn from Life,* p. 72.

9. There are five letters, written between July and December, 1920, from Mrs. Hunt to Violet, at Cornell. Ford evidently knew about Mrs. Hunt's correspondence with Violet, for Sylvia Tietjens, whose treatment of Christopher in *Last Post* is closely modeled on Violet's treatment of Ford, was—according to her son—"In correspondence with Father's servants," as well as in the habit of "Dressing up as a housemaid and looking over the hedge." Indeed, as we know from Mark Tietjens' blunter Yorkshire comment, she had "gone caterwauling about it to [the wife of] of the carpenter" Christopher employed, exactly as Violet had (*Last Post,* pp. 215 and 228). Wells to Violet, postmarked March 9, 1923 (Cornell).

10. Violet Hunt to Elsie, Aug. 10, [1920]. Violet was trying to persuade Mary Martindale to take on the care of the aging Mrs. Hueffer, but Mary refused and the task fell to Juliet Soskice. Nothing ever came of that legacy to Katharine. Violet published as a short story a somewhat different account of her meeting with Elsie called "Read, Mark . . . ," *Saturday Review,* LXXXIV (Aug. 5, 1922). This story outraged Ford (Ford to Jepson, Aug. 15, 1922; Ludwig, p. 144). It determined him never to see Violet again and he wrote F. S. Flint of something Violet had said, "I feel inclined to say 'Don't be idiotic!'—& I don't know that I don't say it. For, really, you ought to be a better judge of humanity than to

be agitated by the pronouncements of Camden Hill. Put it out of your mind" (Ford to F. S. Flint, Sept. 9, 1920 [Texas]).

11. Bowen, *Drawn from Life*, pp. 69 and 74.

12. Bowen, *Drawn from Life*, pp. 84, 75, 78, and 83.

13. Northern Newspaper Syndicate to Pinker, Aug. 20, 1920 (Northwestern). The short story was "The Colonel's Shoes." Ford to Eric Pinker, Jan. 10, 1921, n.d., and May 17, 1921 (Princeton). Ford to Herbert Read, June 25, 1921; Ludwig, p. 133. Ford to Eric Pinker, April 21, 1922 (Northwestern). Ford to Alec Waugh, July 27, 1920; Ludwig, p. 117. Ford to Herbert Read, Oct. 5, 1921; Ludwig, p. 135. One of the novels he proposed to Macmillan was *True Love & a G.C.M.* This was the novel they preferred, but Ford now wanted to write *The Marsden Case*, which he eventually persuaded them to take (Ford to Macmillan, Aug. 14, 1921 [Huntington]).

14. Ford to Pinker, July 25, 1921 (Huntington). Chapter IX of *Thus to Revisit* appeared in the *New York Evening Post*, March 19 and 25, 1921, "A House" in *Poetry*, XVII (March, 1921). Professor Price had written an article about Ford for *Poet Lore*, XXXI (Autumn, 1920). Bowen, *Drawn from Life*, p. 80.

15. *Thus to Revisit*, pp. 18, 19, 8, and 25.

16. *Toward a History of Literature*, pp. 87–89 (Cornell). *Thus to Revisit*, pp. 62 and 14.

17. The *New Statesman*'s critic is quoted in Harvey, p. 337. *Thus to Revisit*, p. 35. *Toward a History of Literature* is undated, but in a note on p. 80 of Part I Ford refers to the *Saturday Review* of Aug. 12, 1922, as current, and other references support this date (see, for example, Part I, p. 98, and Part II, Chapter III, p. 41); in the Introduction to Part II he refers to himself as at Bedham.

18. *Thus to Revisit*, pp. 29 and 45–46. H. G. Wells, Letter to the Editor, *The English Review*, Aug., 1920, p. 178. It is characteristic of Ford that when he himself was lecturing on the writing of novels, he too stuck to homely, practical matters such as the importance of a character's first speech in fixing his type for the reader, the effect of broken speech, unfinished sentences, and the failure of characters to listen to one another. See the notes taken on a Ford lecture at Olivet in June, 1938, in Robie Macauley's "Observations on Technique," *Shenandoah*, IV (Spring, 1953), 49–50.

19. Ford to Wells, Aug. 1. 1920; Ludwig, pp. 119–22.

20. *Return to Yesterday*, pp. 248–51. A canceled passage in the typescript of the Wells chapter of *Portraits from Life* (Cornell) identifies Wells as the "eminent politician" of this occasion. Ford was still using his version of this episode as late as *Provence* (1935), p. 67.

21. *Return to Yesterday*, p. 251.

22. Pound to Ford, Dec. 27, 1933, and Sept. 11, 1936 (Biala), and May 22, 1921 (Cornell). Pound was always ready to help Ford, however difficult his own circumstances. "Here iz the hors d'oeuvres. I will try to make up the rest of the hundred bucks within a fortnight" (Pound to Ford, Aug. 20, 1931 [Biala]; Pound sent the rest of the $100 the next day); "Am relieved to know I neednt try to invent something to cover the rest of the 100 bucks you mentioned in anterior epistle.... We all OUGHT to have plenty of money. I have thought so for twenty years" (Pound to Ford, March 10, 1932 [Biala]). "That bloody minded nurse" is nurse Atterbury, for whom see *Return to Yesterday* pp. 72–73.

23. Pound to Ford, July 30, 1920 (Cornell). Pound's enthusiasm for the "advance" in *Mauberley* later waned. When, a decade later, Ford asked him to write about the proper form for a modern poem he said, "Mauberley has got some structure ... but I ain't ready to theorize about major form YET" (Pound to Ford, Sept. 5, [1933] [Biala]).

24. Pound to Ford, Jan. 13, [probably 1922] (Cornell); this canto was first published in *The Dial*, May, 1922. Pound to Ford, n.d. (but obviously shortly after the preceding letter) (Cornell).

25. Ford to F. S. Flint, May 12, 1921; Ludwig, p. 131. *The Marsden Case*, pp. 138–39. Mrs. Hueffer to Frank Soskice, n.d. (Soskice).

26. Ford to Mrs. Hueffer, Feb. 28, 1921 (Soskice). Bowen, *Drawn from Life*, pp. 82–83. Composi-

578] Notes for pages 320–25

tion dates for *The Marsden Case* are given with the dedication to Edgar Jepson.

27. "I am forwarding to-day to . . . Macmillan . . . the complete manuscript of . . . *The Marsden Case*" (Ford to Eric Pinker, Feb. 29, 1922 [Princeton]). Ford mentions his editorship to Anthony Bertram, June 16, 1922; Ludwig, p. 139 (see also p. 141). In a letter of March 26, 1923 (Texas), he tells A. E. Coppard that he hears "rather lugubrious rumors as to their solvency . . . " It was with Roth's *Two Worlds Monthly* that Joyce had the terrible struggle over the pirating of *Ulysses*. Ford told Eric Pinker on July 6, 1922, that Macmillan had turned down *The Marsden Case* (Huntington). Ford to Edgar Jepson, Nov. 25, 1922; Ludwig, p. 146. Bowen, *Drawn from Life*, pp. 84–86.

28. Ford to Clifford Bax, March 26, 1922 (Texas). Bowen, *Drawn from Life*, pp. 84–85. Ford even tried to extract from Conrad some money for that fire at the Pent during which "The End of the Tether" had been destroyed. "It was very long ago," Conrad said, "and all I remember is that the claim was satisfied by the repolishing of the table and replacing the carpet by another one of the same size and character. Jessie's recollection agrees with mine"—which no doubt puts it mildly (Conrad to Ford, Oct. 16, 1922 [Yale]).

29. Bowen, *Drawn from Life*, pp. 85–86. *The Marsden Case* was never published in the U.S.; it was rejected by Macmillan, Liveright, Knopf, Brentano's, Holt, Scribner's, and Dodd Mead (Brandt and Kirkpatrick to Pinker, May 12, 1923 [Northwestern]). There was even some uncertainty about Monro's villa; "I am happy to hear," A. E. Coppard wrote them Nov. 15, 1922 (Cornell), "that the scoundrel Monro has apparently behaved well after all & that the villa will be available . . . "

30. *Mister Bosphorus*, pp. 103 and 125–26. On Oct. 8, 1922, Stella wrote Jepson from Bedham that Ford was struggling with a great poem; on Nov. 25, 1922, Ford himself wrote Jepson, from Paris, that he had finished it (Naumburg). Harvey found only two reviews of *Mister Bosphorus* and when, about 1933, Duckworth remaindered 800 copies of it, Duckworth himself remarked that " . . . it was a failure right from the announcement"; simultaneously Duckworth remaindered 900 copies of *Joseph Conrad*, "as there is no longer any interest in Conrad" (Duckworth to Bradley, n.d. [Biala]). Elsie was convinced that Ford and Stella had an additional reason for going to Paris, to escape Mary Martindale, who certainly pursued them at Bedham. But Elsie was inclined to believe Ford's life was affected to a greater degree than it was by circumstances connected with her part in it.

31. *The Marsden Case*, p. 335.

32. *The Marsden Case*, p. 1.

33. *The Marsden Case*, pp. 97–134, 11, 49, 333, 4, 271, 194, and 176. For Madame Strindberg's Cabaret Club, p. 246.

Chapter 24

1. Ford to Jepson, Nov. 25, 1922; Ludwig, pp. 146–47. Bowen, *Drawn from Life*, pp. 87–90. *It Was the Nightingale*, pp. 199–201.

2. Bowen, *Drawn from Life*, pp. 92 and 93. *It Was the Nightingale*, p. 205.

3. *It Was the Nightingale*, pp. 223 and 227.

4. Bowen, *Drawn from Life*, pp. 190, 96–98, and 100. Ford to Jepson, May 8, 1923; Ludwig, p. 150. Stella must have painted many pictures during her life, even if one does not count what she called her "quickies," the sketch portraits that her knack for catching a likeness made easy for her. The only living she ever made after she and Ford separated was from her painting; she spent a year in the U.S. doing portraits, including a pair of Sinclair Lewis and Dorothy Thompson; and for two years she was an official painter for the Australian government (1942–44). But apart from her war paintings in Canberra and a

dozen or so pictures in the hands of friends and her daughter, there is little trace of her work.

5. Bowen, *Drawn from Life*, pp. 102–08. *It Was the Nightingale*, pp. 250–51.
6. Bowen, *Drawn from Life*, pp. 110–11. Lucy was quickly replaced by Madame Annie, "one of my mistakes," Stella said. "For three years she ruled me with a rod of iron..." (*Drawn from Life*, p. 122). Without someone to care for Julie in the evenings, Stella could not accompany Ford to the cafés. Stella says that this was her first meeting with Oliver, but her memory has betrayed her: she certainly saw him the previous May, when she was in Paris studying (Ford to Stella, May 7, 1923) and probably met him the previous November, when Ford saw him (Ford to Jepson, Nov. 25, 1922; Ludwig, p. 147). Alice Halicka, *Hier (Souvenirs)*, p. 157. Harvey, p. 530. Harold Loeb, *The Way It Was* (New York, 1959), pp. 207–08. In *Drawn from Life* (p. 121), Stella describes what appears to be this same fight and suicide attempt as occurring at the studio in the Boulevard Arago rather than the cottage, and, in *Postures* (p. 63), Jean Rhys places it in the studio at 84 rue Notre Dame des Champs.
7. *It Was the Nightingale*, p. 253. Pound called *Some Do Not...* "the best he has done since *Good Soldier* or *A Call*" (Pound to Homer Pound, Sept. 12, 1923, in Bernard Poli, *Ford Madox Ford and the Transatlantic Review* [Syracuse, 1967], p. 19. Professor Poli's work comes in two forms, the mimeographed thesis he submitted to the University of Paris and this book; they vary slightly. I have quoted the thesis where it is more useful, but all page references are to the book, since the thesis is difficult to get hold of). Bowen, *Drawn from Life*, pp. 109 and 111. Ford to Wells, Oct. 14, 1923; Ludwig, p. 154. Charles Norman, *Ezra Pound*, p. 50. Harold Loeb, *The Way It Was*, p. 189.
8. Bowen, *Drawn from Life*, pp. 112–14 and 119; Ford has a different version of how this decision was made, in *It Was the Nightingale*, pp. 259–60. Ford to Wells, Oct. 14, 1923; Ludwig, p. 154. The Nègre de Toulouse was so called for a carved figure that stood before it. In 1926–27 Stella did an amusing triptych for it (reproduced opposite p. 96 of *Drawn from Life*). The central panel has portraits of the proprietor, M. Lavigne, and his wife before a table on which rests an overflowing basket of fruit; each of the two side panels has an arrangement of portraits of four waitresses. Stella says they moved from Oliver's cottage in December, 1923 (*Drawn from Life*, p. 119); William Carlos Williams says he attended a party there in January, 1924 (William Carlos Williams, *Autobiography* [New York, 1951], p. 135).
9. *It Was the Nightingale*, pp. 283–84 and 277. Stella Bowen, in *Drawn from Life*, p. 114, frankly confesses her memory of this episode is vague and repeats what Ford says.
10. The meeting at Pound's flat was the occasion for *The New York Times*'s famous photograph of Quinn, Joyce, Pound, and Ford. Professor Poli (*Ford Madox Ford and the Transatlantic Review*, pp. 20 and 22) has worked it out that this meeting must have taken place Oct. 12, 1923. Bowen, *Drawn from Life*, pp. 115 and 110. Stella adds, with similar generosity, that "Ford, in recognition of [her financial contributions], subsequently made over his English royalties to me"; it was not quite that simple (see pp. 364–65 below). But it is true that with *The Transatlantic Review* Ford began to accumulate a debt to Stella that amounted, by the time they parted, to £ 2,500 "advanced...at various dates between November, 1923 and the above [Dec. 22, 1932]...." (Biala). Ford's own estimates of the investment in the *Transatlantic* vary with the occasion from the $2,000 (35,000 francs) mentioned in the *Transatlantic*'s letterhead to $18,000. Ford told Gertrude Stein he himself has lost "over frs 100,000 in all" on the *Review* (Ford to Gertrude Stein, Sept. 18, 1924; Ludwig, p. 163); this figure is not impossible. As late as 1927 the financial problems of the *Transatlantic* pursued him; when Ford sent Coppard $23 as his share of the advance on the volume of *Transatlantic Stories* Ford had edited for Dial (Oct. 25, 1926), Coppard ungraciously rejoined that he had never been paid for his story in the first place. Ford wrote

him, "I do not think the publication can have done you any harm . . . —at least in this country where I am a tremendously boomed person inclusion in a volume under my editorship ought to have a certain value as what is called 'publicity' " (Ford to A. E. Coppard, Feb. 17 [1927] [Texas]).

11. Poli, *Ford Madox Ford and the Transatlantic Review*, pp. 26 and 28–29. Bowen, *Drawn from Life*, p. 116. "The Gossip Shop," *Bookman* (N.Y.), LXIV (Jan., 1927), 648. Ford to Gertrude Stein, Sept. 18, 1924, in *Flowers of Friendship* (New York, 1953), ed. Donald Gallup, p. 165.

12. Conrad to Ford, Nov. 18, 1923 [*sic*: Oct. 23, 1923] (Naumburg); this letter is transcribed in Morey, *Joseph Conrad and Ford Madox Ford* (Cornell), p. 222.

13. *It Was the Nightingale*, p. 259. Lloyd Morris, *A Threshold in the Sun* (New York and London, 1943), p. 244. Joyce's debate with himself about publishing in the *Transatlantic* runs through his correspondence for several months (see *Letters of James Joyce*, [New York and London, 1957], ed. Stuart Gilbert, I, 209). Joyce to Harriet Weaver, April 8, 1928 in Richard Ellmann, *James Joyce* (New York, 1959), pp. 574–75.

14. The prospectus of the *Transatlantic* is reproduced in Poli, *Ford Madox Ford and the Transatlantic Review*, pp. 37–40. "Editorial," *Transatlantic Review*, Dec., 1924. William Bird to Poli, Nov. 10, 1961, in Poli, *Ford Madox Ford and the Transatlantic Review*, p. 43.

15. Lloyd Morris, *A Threshold in the Sun*, pp. 216 and 217. Robert McAlmon, *Being Geniuses Together* (New York, 1968), p. 127. Ford almost never criticized young writers, but he had said, "The two worst writers I have met in Paris . . . are Waldo Frank and Robert McAlmon" ("From a Paris Quay [II]," *New York Evening Post Literary Review*, Jan. 3, 1925). McAlmon describes his comment on Ford as a counterattack.

16. Bowen, *Drawn from Life*, p. 101. Herbert Gorman, "Ford Madox Ford: The Personal Side," *Princeton University Library Chronicle*, IX (April, 1948), 121. Harold Loeb, *The Way It Was*, p. 189. Samuel Putnam, *Paris Was Our Mistress*, p. 122.

17. Poli, *Ford Madox Ford and the Transatlantic Review*, pp. 55–57.

18. "I had forgotten about [The Nature of a Crime]," Ford wrote Conrad, "till the other day when Dents asked me if I could not print a page or two of ROMANCE with indications of which passages were yours and which were my writing. They say they have received thousands of requests for this. . . . [And] I think that to reprint the *Story of a Crime* . . . would have a certain literary and sentimental interest and I should very much like to do it" (Ford to Conrad, Nov. 8, 1923 [Princeton]). The date of this letter shows how early in his thinking about the *Transatlantic* Ford conceived this scheme. Jessie Conrad, *Joseph Conrad as I knew Him*, p. 152.

19. Ford to Jepson, Oct. 14, 1923; Ludwig, p. 153. Goldring, who was then Thomas Seltzer's agent, had put Ford in touch with Seltzer and Ford, as he so often did, assumed the contract with Seltzer was completed when he presented his terms. Seltzer went bankrupt before anything came of this proposal (Goldring, *South Lodge*, pp. 141–42). Bowen, *Drawn from Life*, pp. 117 and 124. The most detailed account of the McAlmon dinner is in Williams's *Autobiography*, pp. 194–95; see also Harold Loeb, *The Way It Was*, p. 202.

20. Bowen, *Drawn from Life*, p. 119. *The Sun Also Rises*, Chap. III. The restaurant Hemingway is describing is the Nègre de Toulouse; its proprietor, Lavigne, is mentioned by name. Markham Harris noticed "Stella Bowen's big teeth and loud laugh" ("A Memory of Ford Madox Ford," *Prairie Schooner*, XXIX [Winter, 1955], p. 254).

21. Juliet Soskice to Frank Soskice, postmarked Jan. 28, 1924, and April 15, 1924; Mrs. Hueffer to Frank Soskice, Feb. 4, 1924 (Soskice). Mrs. Hueffer died June 3, 1927, aged 76.

22. Bowen, *Drawn from Life*, pp. 123–25. There is considerable confusion over just when Hemingway joined the *Transatlantic*. Ford says in *It Was the Nightingale* (p. 295) that Hemingway was present at the famous meeting with Joyce and Quinn at Pound's studio in October; but that is impossible since Hemingway was then in Canada. Harold Loeb (*The Way It Was*, p. 194) describes discussing Ford with Hemingway in October, too. Heming-

way told Carlos Baker that he met Ford at Pound's studio after he got back from Canada in January, 1924 (Poli, *Ford Madox Ford and the Transatlantic Review*, pp. 58–59; Hemingway's letter to Prof. Baker, April 1, 1951, is quoted in Poli's thesis. See also Carlos Baker, *Ernest Hemingway* [New York, 1969], pp. 122–23). Ford's remark about Hemingway is quoted in Gertrude Stein, *The Autobiography of Alice B. Toklas* (New York, 1933), p. 271.

23. Stein, *The Autobiography of Alice B. Toklas*, p. 264. Hemingway to Gertrude Stein, Feb. 17, 1924, and Ford to Gertrude Stein, Sept. 18, 1924, in *The Flowers of Friendship*, pp. 159 and 165.

24. Sisley Huddleston, *Paris Salons, Cafés, Studios* (New York, 1928), p. 219. Joyce to Harriet Weaver, Feb. 8, 1924, in *Letters of James Joyce*, ed. Stuart Gilbert, I, p. 210. Poli, *Ford Madox Ford and the Transatlantic Review*, pp. 69 and 75.

25. For the reviews quoted see Harvey, pp. 342–45.

26. Stein, *The Autobiography of Alice B. Toklas*, p. 309. *It Was the Nightingale*, pp. 361–63. *Transatlantic Review*, Dec., 1924, p. 685. Prof. Poli has a detailed discussion of this financial crisis, pp. 92–98.

27. Gertrude Stein's copy of the letter offering shares is signed E. G. Bowen (Yale); Poli, *Ford Madox Ford and the Transatlantic Review*, pp. 95–96.

28. Conrad to Eric Pinker, Feb. 4, 1924, in Baines, *Joseph Conrad*, p. 432. Ford to Conrad, Feb. 14, 1924 (Yale). Conrad to Eric Pinker, Feb. 17, 1924 (Yale).

29. Ford to Edgar Jepson, Sept. 15, 1921 (Naumburg).

30. Conrad to Eric Pinker, Feb. 17, 1924 (Yale). Conrad to Ford, May 3, 1924 (Yale). Conrad to Pinker, May 1, 1924, in Baines, *Joseph Conrad*, p. 433. Ford to Pinker, March 30, 1924 (Yale). "I saw Mr. Eric Pinker, the son . . . and also Conrad himself on the 9th and 10th of May 1924 . . . " (Ford to W. H. Thompson, Feb. 5, 1926; Ludwig, p. 167). Ford benefited considerably from the constant reissuing in editions of Conrad of their collaborations; in 1925, for example, he collected £ 237.5.5 as his share of the royalties on them. But he continued to be indignant over Dent's failure to put his name on the covers and dust jackets of the edition they had printed before this agreement was reached. On Jan. 7, 1926 (Biala), he wrote his agent, Bradley, "I have seldom read a cooler letter than Hugh Dent's . . . I do not propose to put up with less than the letter of apology for which I stipulated and an undertaking not to issue any more copies with only one name on the back, dust-sheet etc." This was not very reasonable; there was nothing to be gained by forcing Dent to apologize for the original blunder, and Ford knew enough about publishing to understand that the so-called Gresham Edition of Conrad that he was here complaining about was merely a reprinting, from the same plates, of the edition he had agreed to let Dent get by with if they would make the correction in later editions. When he carried his objections to the point of writing a solicitor, W. H. Thompson replied, " . . . it does not seem to me that Pinkers are to blame, or that Dents can do more that [*sic*] they have offered to do. Also I would point out that you have had royalties on this account [and accepted them] and can hardly now complain of it . . . " (Thompson to Ford, May 4, 1926 [Biala]).

31. Ford to Conrad, May 21, 1924 (Yale).

32. *Return to Yesterday*, p. 207. Ford to Conrad, May 31, 1924 (Yale). Perhaps because Elsie's anger was freshly aroused, perhaps because the *Transatlantic* publicity for *Romance* made them seem more salable, Elsie sold at this time the corrected proofs of *Romance*. She told Robert Garnett these proofs showed "the *final* corrections" (Elsie to Robert Garnett, Feb. 19, 1924, at Darley, Cumberland). She offered these proofs to T. J. Wise for £ 400; he thought the price outrageous. She then put them up for auction, but the bidding failed to reach the reserve price of £ 60 (Elsie's diary, June 27, 1924). They were finally sold for £ 70 (Katharine Lamb to Arthur Mizener, Nov. 12, 1966). This sale distressed Ford; it was a matter of great pride with him that he had never sold anything connected with Conrad.

He wrote a letter to the *New York Herald Tribune* (Feb. 20, 1927) to say that "It has come to my knowledge that a Mr. Wise who I understand is a collector of autographs is advertising in his catalogue the fact that he is in possession of private letters addressed to myself by the late Joseph Conrad. I desire to state that I never either sold or authorized the sale of any letter, presentation copy from, or anything in the nature of an autograph or personal memento of, the late Mr. Conrad." The Violet Hunt Papers at Cornell show that about this time Violet sold to Wise some of the letters she had used in writing *The Flurried Years* and on Nov. 21 and 23 the American Art Association held a sale of *First Editions, Inscribed Copies & Autograph Letters of Joseph Conrad, the Property of Mrs. Ford Madox Hueffer*—that is, Elsie. The catalogue of this sale is in the Naumburg Collection. There is a single, partial exception to Ford's statement (see Harvey, p. 63), but it is otherwise absolutely true.

Chapter 25

1. Burton Rascoe, *A Bookman's Daybook* (New York, 1929), pp. 257–59. Mr. Naumburg possesses a copy of *Some Do Not...* inscribed by Ford for John Cornos aboard the *Paris* on June 1, 1924.
2. *Transatlantic Review*, Aug., 1924, p. 213.
3. *Transatlantic Review*, Sept., 1924, pp. 300–02. There is a badly mangled reprint of Ford's article for the *Journal Littéraire* in *Joseph Conrad*, pp. 251–56.
4. *Transatlantic Review*, Sept., 1924, pp. 341–42.
5. Bowen, *Drawn from Life*, p. 131. Markham Harris, "A Memory of Ford Madox Ford," *Prairie Schooner*, XXIX (Winter, 1955), p. 257. It is a guess that the phrase on the card was "C'est toi qui dors dans l'ombre"; Mr. Markham says Ford wrote in French: " 'And thou also hast descended into the shadow.' " "C'est toi qui dors dans l'ombre..." is the title of Ford's elegy for Conrad in the *Transatlantic* (Sept., 1924, p. 327). Ford's description of *Joseph Conrad* is on p. 39, the remark about biographers in a letter to the *American Mercury* (Nov., 1936); Ludwig, p. 266. *Joseph Conrad* started to run in the *Transatlantic* in Sept., 1924. Perhaps in memory of their struggles there with *Romance* in 1900, Ford dates the completion of *Joseph Conrad* "Bruges, *October 5th*, 1924."
6. For the reviews of and comments on *Joseph Conrad*, see Harvey, pp. 352–57. In *Return to Yesterday* (p. 198) Ford says that at their interview in July, 1916, Conrad "ask[ed] me to write a memoir of him." This does not sound like Conrad at any time, even less so at that time; perhaps Ford suggested he might do so and Conrad, as was his way, did not argue. Ford himself once said of this occasion that "we fell to discussing the question of literary biographies in general and our own in particular. We hit, as we generally did, very quickly upon a formula.... We agreed that... this life might well be the subject of a monograph... and a biography... should be a novel..." (*Transatlantic Review*, Sept., 1924, p. 337). This would be Ford's view, and one can easily imagine his stating it to Conrad and Conrad's nodding as he talked.
7. Robert McAlmon to Gertrude Stein, n.d.; Hemingway to Gertrude Stein, Aug. 9, 1924, in *The Flowers of Friendship*, pp. 167 and 162–64.
8. Hemingway to Gertrude Stein, Aug. 15, [1924], in *The Flowers of Friendship*, p. 164. Nathan Asch describes the Friends in the broadcast about Ford taped by KPFA in Berkeley, Nov. 21, 1961, of which there is a copy in the Naumburg Collection. Hemingway to Gertrude Stein, Oct. 10, [1924], in *The Flowers of Friendship*, p. 167.
9. Herbert Gorman, "Ford Madox Ford: A Portrait in Impressions," *Bookman*, LXVII (March, 1928), 56–57. Rascoe has an account of an evening at the *bal musette* that includes

an inaccurate account of Hemingway's quarrel with Ford in *We Were Interrupted*, pp. 184-86. Harold Loeb, *The Way It Was* (p. 252), describes an evening there when Max Eastman and Hemingway nearly came to blows. Goldring describes an evening there in *South Lodge*, p. 156. In *The Sun Also Rises*, Jake meets Brett at the Bal du Printemps; "Pat Gutherie, a well-known Montparnasse play-boy whose services to the arts have not been recorded, was there with Duff Twysden" the night Goldring describes.

10. Jean Rhys, *Postures* (London, 1928), pp. 91-92. Nina Hamnett, *Laughing Torso* (London, 1932), p. 297. Bowen, *Drawn from Life*, p. 130.

11. *Sunday Times* (London), Nov. 6, 1966. Rhys, *Postures*, pp. 13, 39-40, and 195. Bowen, *Drawn from Life*, pp. 166-68.

12. Rhys, *Postures*, pp. 97-98 and 246. Bowen, *Drawn from Life*, p. 166.

13. Rhys, *Postures*, pp. 86-87, 102, and 68. How literal Jean Rhys's representation of Stella is is indicated by the fact that in *Postures*, written in 1928, Lois says of Marya, "It's appalling . . . to think of the difference money makes to a woman's life" (p. 69), and in *Drawn from Life*, written in 1941, Stella says of Jean, "[knowing her] taught me that the only really unbridgeable gulf in human society is between the financially solvent and the destitute. You can't have self-respect without money" (p. 167). Ford wrote a preface for Jean Rhys's first book, a volume of short stories called *The Left Bank & Other Stories*, published by Cape in 1927. He also wrote a preface for her translation of Francis Carco's *Perversité* which, through a series of publisher's blunders, was published as by him. What happened was that he originally agreed to translate the book; then he proposed to find a competent translator for it and to write an introduction (this was apparently an effort to find work for Jean Rhys, since he refers in this letter to the translator as "she"). When he sent the translation and preface to Covici, Covici lost them and Ford had to send the carbons, which did not indicate the separate authorships, which Covici managed not to remember; thus the translation as well as the preface were published as Ford's. The correspondence covering this affair is in the Biala Collection. Alice Halicka, *Hier (Souvenirs)*, p. 157.

14. Bowen, *Drawn from Life*, p. 167. Rhys, *Postures*, pp. 93-94, 100, 158, 140, 143, 96, and 124. The epigraph of *Postures* is by "R[ichard] C[heever] Dunning," "a typical romantic figure, long, lanky, and always sad looking, who soon died of malnutrition, tuberculosis, and drug addiction." Pound thought highly of his work for a time and Ford published twelve of his poems in the November number of the *Transatlantic* (see Poli, *Ford Madox Ford and the Transatlantic Review*, p. 122).

15. Rhys, *After Leaving Mr. Mackenzie* (London, 1931), pp. 30 and 66. Bowen, *Drawn from Life*, pp. 166 and 168. "A man," Stella observed, "seldom shows to advantage when trying to get rid of a woman who has become an incubus" (*Drawn from Life*, p. 168), and there was plenty of gossip to make him look worse: people said Miss Rhys had had a child by him and that, coming across him six months after their affair ended, she walked straight up to him and slapped him hard in the face. In fact Ford and Stella provided an allowance for Miss Rhys at least until the end of 1926 (see Stella to Ford, Oct. 29, 1926).

16. Bowen, *Drawn from Life*, pp. 162 and 168-69.

17. Bowen, *Drawn from Life*, p. 171. Stein, *The Autobiography of Alice B. Toklas*, p. 270.

18. *A Mirror to France*, pp. 202, 82, and 14. Pages 31-58 of *A Mirror to France* are, with the omission of three or four too revealing paragraphs, taken word-for-word from pp. 194-222 of *Between St. Dennis and St. George*, despite the fact that Ford says in *A Mirror to France* (p. 9) he thinks "the time for [the] republication [of *Between St. Dennis and St. George*] is hardly now."

19. Bowen, *Drawn from Life*, pp. 125 and 131. George Slocombe, *The Tumult and the Shouting* (New York, 1936), p. 226. Rhys, *Postures*, pp. 80-81. By an unfortunate slip, Stella places their move to the rue Notre Dame des Champs in the fall of 1924 (*Drawn from Life*, p. 130). As a result she dates everything one year too early thereafter. All Ford's correspond-

ence shows they remained in the rue Denfert Rochereau until they moved for the summer of 1925 to Guermantes and that it was in the fall of 1925 that Nina Hamnett found them their new flat in the rue Notre Dame des Champs.

20. Juan Gris to Pedro Penzol, Jan. 10, 1926, in *Letters of Juan Gris, 1913–1927* (London, 1956), ed. Douglas Cooper, p. 177. Bowen, *Drawn from Life,* pp. 132 and 181–82. Hamnett, *Laughing Torso,* pp. 188–89.

21. Juan Gris to Kahnweiler, Dec. 29, 1925, and Jan. 4, 1926, in *Letters of Juan Gris,* ed. Douglas Cooper, pp. 175 and 176. Bowen, *Drawn from Life,* p. 137. *Saturday Review,* Dec. 11, 1926.

22. Stella herself blued the remainder of her capital—and more—after she separated from Ford, trying to maintain a studio of her own in the rue Boissonnade. Bowen, *Drawn from Life,* p. 142.

23. Bowen, *Drawn from Life,* pp. 148–49.

24. Ford to Gerald Duckworth, March 3, 1926 (Biala). Bowen, *Drawn from life,* p. 154.

25. Bowen, *Drawn from Life,* p. 152.

26. Mary Bromfield, "A la Recherche du Temps Perdu," *Town and Country,* Jan., 1943, p. 28. For some reason Mrs. Bromfield remembers Ford's studio as in the rue des Acacias and the only work of his she had ever heard of was "some very good novels about a misunderstood hero . . . with a dreadful wife."

27. The Seltzer-Boni business can be traced through Ford's correspondence for a long time: see particularly Brandt & Brandt to Ford, Jan. 27, 1926; Bradley to Ford, March 29 and May 13, 1926; Ford to Arthur Spingarn (his lawyer), June 2, 1927; Boni to Spingarn, July 25, 1927; Bradley to Ford, Nov. 6, 1927; Ford to Boni, July 25, 1927 (Biala). The composition dates given at the end of *A Man Could Stand Up*—are:

TOULON, 9th January, 1926
PARIS, 21st, July, 1926

But the dedication to Gerald Duckworth is dated May 18, 1926.

28. The date of their stay at Avignon is fixed by Juan Gris' letter of July 24, 1926, to Gertrude Stein (in *Letters of Juan Gris,* ed. Cooper, p. 193) saying the Fords are dining with them "next Wednesday [July 28] before they go to Avignon." Ford crossed to America on the *Savoie* and reached New York on Saturday, Oct. 30, the day his letter to Stella (dated only "Saturday") was written. Stella to Ford, Oct. 29 [1926].

29. Ford to Harriet Monroe, Nov. 3, 1926 (Chicago). Ford to Stella, [Oct. 30] and "Tuesday 2d." [Nov., 1926]. But the second of these letters was actually written on election day.

30. The Boni negotiations can be traced through Ford's letters to Stella. When Ford's dedication of *The Good Soldier* to Stella, written for Boni's reprint of 1927, appeared in England in 1928, Ford added a note: "This letter was written as a special introduction to *The Good Soldier* in the collection of the author's work published in America." Harvey (p. 46) suggests this statement is misleading, but in fact Boni's reprint of *The Good Soldier* is uniform with their edition of *New York Is Not America* and *Last Post,* and these volumes are described, on the dust jackets (and, in the cases of the last two, on the spines), as the Avignon Edition. Boni clearly intended, if all went well (which it did not), to continue to publish Ford in this way and gradually to add further reprints of old books, including *Ladies Whose Bright Eyes, Joseph Conrad,* the *Collected Poems,* and "possibly some of my historical novels" (see Ford to Duckworth, Jan. 12, 1927 [Biala]). Harvey quotes Albert Boni's description of their contract with Ford, p. 59.

31. Ford to Stella, Sunday 9th [of Jan., 1927].

32. Ford to Stella, Saturday 22 Jan [1927]. References to the lecture engagements mentioned here are scattered through several letters to Stella.

33. Burton Rascoe, "Contemporary Reminiscences," *Arts and Decoration,* XXVI (Dec., 1926),

55. "The Gossip Shop," *Bookman*, LXIV (Jan., 1927), 648. Ford wrote Stella the next day that his Plaza talk was "a triumphant success." New York *World*, Nov. 4 and Nov. 8, 1926. For Masefield's authorship of the first review of *Romance*, see Harvey, p. 245.

34. Ford to Stella, Nov. 11, 1926, and Jan. 22, 1927. Markham Harris, "A Memory of Ford Madox Ford," *Prairie Schooner*, XXIX (Winter, 1955), 260. A fragment of an itinerary of Ford's fall lecture tour (Cornell) shows he was at Dartmouth Dec. 10 and at Williams Dec. 12, 1927. Samuel Putnam (*Paris Was Our Mistress*, p. 120) reports Ford's giving what sounds like his standard lecture in Chicago too.

35. Ford mentions a great many social engagements during these months in his letters to Stella. The P.E.N. dinner was reported in the *Herald Tribune*, Dec. 21, 1926, and Ford's own dinner in Isabel Paterson's "Turns with a Bookworm," *Herald Tribune*, Dec. 19, 1926. In dedicating *Last Post* to her, Ford called Isabel Paterson his "fairy godmother." Ford expressed his anxiety about *I Have This to Say* in two undated letters written in November to Stella.

36. On Dec. 17, 1926, Ford wrote Stella, "What really has harmed me here—oddly enough—is Jessie's letter to the *Times*." For the details of his debate with Jessie over "Amy Foster," see pp. 69–70 above. McFee told Ford at this time that, when he published his defense of *Joseph Conrad* (see above, p. 342), he received from Jessie a letter of Billingsgate (Ford to Stella, Dec. 25, 1926).

37. Ford to Harriet Monroe, Jan. 13, 1927 (Chicago). George Dillon, "Homage to Ford Madox Ford," *New Directions*, Number Seven, 1942, p. 469. Ford to Stella, Jan. 22, 1927. Samuel Putnam, *Paris Was Our Mistress*, p. 121. Clarence Hemingway to Ernest Hemingway, Jan. 27, 1927. I owe my knowledge of this letter to Prof. Carlos Baker.

38. Stella to Ford, Nov. 9 and Dec. 27, 1926. Bowen, *Drawn from Life*, p. 169. Ford to Stella, Jan. 9 and 22, 1927.

Chapter 26

1. Ford had hoped to cross the Atlantic with "a jovial crew" on the *Ansonia* but finally sailed on *The American Banker* on Feb. 24 (Ford to Ferris Greenslet, Feb. 20, 1927 [Harvard]; Ford to Stella, Feb. 13, 1927). Bowen, *Drawn from Life*, p. 146. The composition dates at the end of *Last Post* say it was begun in "Paris, *7th* June [1927]," but that is impossible: Ford was at the Hotel Belgravia in London on June 7. He had begun dictating *Last Post* to Caroline Tate before he left New York. In June, Courtney of the *Fortnightly Review* turned down two stories (Courtney to Pinker, June 15, 1927 [New York Public]); in July the *Saturday Review* turned down Ford's suggestion of a weekly article (*Saturday Review* to Pinker, July 29, 1927 [Northwestern]). Ford to Pinker, July 18, 1927 (Huntington); the *Sunday Express* to Pinker, Aug. 3, 1927 (Northwestern).

2. *New York Times*, July 23, 1927; London *Times*, July 23, 1927. Ford to Pinker, July 18, 1927 (Princeton).

3. Jane Dransfield, "Ford Madox Ford," *New Directions*, Number Seven, 1942, pp. 470–71. *Parade's End*, I, 110.

4. The composition dates of *Last Post* describe it as completed in the "ST. LAWRENCE RIVER, *24th September*—NEW YORK, *12th November*." But Ford wrote Stella on Thursday night (Sept. 22), "I finished *Last Post* ten minutes ago." They reached Montreal Sept. 24. C. F. Crandall, "When Sinclair Lewis Wrote a Sonnet in Three Minutes, Fifty Seconds," *New York Herald Tribune Book Review*, Sept. 2, 1951. Ford to Stella, Oct. 1 and 22, 1927.

5. Ford to Stella, Oct. 1 and Dec. 21, 1927. Stella to Ford, Oct. 14, 1927.

6. Goldring, *South Lodge*, p. 181. Ford to Stella, Oct. 30, 1927.

7. Ford to Stella, n.d. (but Nov., 1927). Allen Tate to Arthur Mizener, Aug. 7 and 17, 1968.

8. Boni' s royalty reports (Biala) show that, when the Tietjens novels went out of print in Dec., 1931, Boni had sold 1,003 copies of *Some Do Not . . .* (there is no record of Seltzer's sales), 12,601 copies of *No More Parades*, 4,613 copies of *A Man Could Stand Up—*, and 3,238 copies of *Last Post*. For the reviews quoted, see Harvey, pp. 362 and 367. *The Literary Digest*, March 20, 1926, p. 29. The issue of *Wings* (the house organ of the Literary Guild) that is devoted to *Last Post* estimates the Guild's membership at 30,000–40,000 (p. 6) and Ford told Stella he expected the Guild to sell 25,000–40,000 copies, worth $3,500–$5,500 (Dec. 10, 1927). Ford gave Percival Hinton that figure of 50,000 copies (in Goldring, *The Last Pre-Raphaelite*, pp. 244–45). Ford also told Hinton that the Tietjens novels sold about 1,000 copies apiece in England, and the fragmentary royalty reports from Duckworth that have been preserved suggest that estimate is about right. There were Grosset and Dunlap reprints of the first three Tietjens novels; there is no evidence of how well they sold.

9. Goldring, *South Lodge*, pp., 181–83; Goldring, *Odd Man Out*, p. 305. Ford to Stella, Oct. 30, 1927.

10. George Hartman's portrait of Ford has often been reproduced. Burton Rascoe, *We Were Interrupted*, pp. 228–30. Ford to Rascoe, Nov, 9, 1927 (about *The Sisters*) (Biala). In 1927 Ford prepared synopses of four novels (apparently for Viking) that are at Cornell; one is a synopsis of *A Little Less Than Gods* and its incest plot; another of a Lesbian story which was never written, though there are Lesbians in *The Rash Act*.

11. *A Little Less Than Gods*, p. v. This is the way the name is given in the American edition; in the English, "David" is omitted. Ford's walk with Rene in Central Park must have taken place early in September, 1906; Ford and Elsie left New York for Philadelphia in the middle of September. Ford later told Harold Loeb that he and Mrs. Wright had met at his Uncle Leopold's tobacco farm in Lexington, Virginia, and had been childhood sweethearts. There is some doubt whether Ford ever visited his Uncle Leopold's farm (Harold Loeb, *The Way It Was*, p. 189, and "Ford Madox Ford's 'The Good Soldier': A Critical Reminiscence," *London Magazine*, III [Dec., 1963], 65–67).

12. Ford's "Winter-Night Song" appeared almost simultaneously in the *Herald Tribune Books* and in *New Poems* in January, 1927. The description of Mrs. Wright as she appeared to Ford's young friends is Harold Loeb's. The story of the Wrights' marriage can be traced in the columns of the *St. Louis Post-Dispatch* and I am indebted to Mrs. Sally Defty of that paper for my information about it. Guy Wright, who had inherited about a half million dollars from his father, never worked. Rene was his second (and also his third) wife.

13. Harrison Smith to Ford, Sept. 27, 1927 (Biala). Ford to James Babb, Oct. 8, 1927 (Yale). The account of this weekend comes from the Babbs themselves. Ford to Wilbur Cross, Oct. 22, 1927 (Yale).

14. Ford to Stella, Nov. 13, Dec. 21, and Oct. 30, 1927. Stella to Ford, Oct. 14 and Nov. 1, 1927.

15. Ford to Stella, Dec. 21 and 30, 1927. Stella to Ford, Jan. 3, 1928. Bowen, *Drawn from Life*, p. 169.

16. Stella to Ford, April 18, 1928.

17. Stella to Janice Biala, n.d. (Biala).

18. The official agreement between Ford and Stella is in the Biala Papers. There is also a letter from Ford to Bradley (May 11, 1928) in which Ford repeats the substance of this agreement. There were difficulties about it from the start; when Ford went to America that spring, he left debts of about 2,000 francs that Stella had to pay (Bradley to Ford, July 5, 1928 [Biala]).

19. Ford sent Stella a copy of *Last Post* from New York, Dec. 21, 1927. All references to *Parade's End* are to the two-volume Signet Classic edition published by The New Ameri-

can Library in 1964 (Volume I: *Some Do Not . . .* and *No More Parades;* Volume II: *A Man Could Stand Up—* and *Last Post*). All quoted passages have, however, been checked against the original Duckworth texts. The text of *Parade's End* is in very bad shape. For this Ford is partly to blame; he was careless about spelling, punctuation, and other things that tempt copyreaders to tamper with texts; he was a bad proofreader; and he wrote a nearly illegible hand. Of the original editions Duckworth's is far superior to Boni's. For example, where Duckworth reads, obviously correctly, "[Duckett] continually rubbed his ankles with his shoe, . . . " Boni reads, "[Duckett] continually moved his ankles with his soles. . . . " A copyreader might fairly be tempted to correct Ford's mixture of singular and plural in "ankles" and "shoe," but Boni's "moved" and "soles" are pretty certainly simply misreadings of Ford's longhand. Boni's texts of all four novels contain a great many careless errors of this kind. The Penguin text of 1948 was carefully made from the Duckworth texts and is so far superior to the Knopf text of 1951, which reproduces the Boni text, complete with errors, and supplies a remarkable number of additional errors of its own. The Knopf text is by far the worst text in existence, both unforgivably careless and very free with ignorant emendation. For example, both the Duckworth and Boni texts read (I, 380) "It meant he was aware a frightful row with the provost-marshal. . . . " The Knopf copyreader, unable to make sense of this sentence because of the omission (probably by Ford himself) of the commas around "he was aware," blithely rewrote it into nonsense as "It meant he was aware of a frightful row with the provost-marshal." On the other hand, the Knopf copyreader seldom corrects the Boni text's obvious errors; when the Boni text makes Marie Léonie speak of "that obscene street" (II, 275), the Knopf text happily accepts this misprint for "obscure." When Ford has Tietjens' sergeant in *A Man Could Stand Up—* say, "They do say the first consignment of bombs was it n smashed. Hin a gully; well beind the line," Boni gets it, "They do say the first consignment of bombs was it not smashed. Hin a gully; well behind the line." The Knopf copyreader thought this reading quite satisfactory. Unfortunately the editor of the NAL text was not able to prevent NAL's copyreader from providing assistance for kindergarten readers at this point, so that the NAL text reads (II, 57), "They do say the first consignment of bombs was 'it 'n smashed. Hin a gully; well be'ind the line." The NAL text has a good many "improvements" of this kind; it is nonetheless the best text we have. The Viking text of *A Little Less Than Gods* is similarly—though not so extremely—inferior to the Duckworth.

20. In *No More Parades* (I, 497–98) Christopher recalls a scene Ford had originally described in *No Enemy,* pp. 79–87; it was undoubtedly a real experience, though not literally in this form. Colonel Partridge, whom Christopher replaces as commander of the 9th Glamorganshire, and Slocombe, the soldier who writes music-hall sketches in his spare moments in the trenches, in *A Man Could Stand Up—* (II, 11of., and 101), both appear in *Mr. Croyd,* the unpublished autobiographical novel Ford wrote immediately after the war. The skylarks of *A Man Could Stand Up—* with the "won'erful hinstinck set in the fethered brest by the Halmighty!" (II, 49) were a part of Ford's repertoire of personal anecdotes (see Samuel Putnam, *Paris Was Our Mistress,* p. 125). "Old Puffles" (General Perry) suffers the fate of Gough's Fifth Army of March, 1918, in *No More Parades* and *A Man Could Stand Up—.* Ford even enjoyed a few private jokes with personal details of this kind: Sylvia (I, 405) quotes to Christopher the line from Pound's translation of Arnaut Daniel—"*Ah me, the dawn, the dawn it comes too soon!*"—that it had so amused Ford to hear Pound reading (see p. 239 above), and a Canadian soldier refers to the "flagitious mineral-water company . . . at the Ten Sen spring near Kobe" that René Byles had worked for (I, 332). Ford to Stella, Oct. 1, 1927.

21. *Parade's End,* I, 84. For the attack on Asquith, see Wilfred Blunt, *My Diaries* (New York, 1932), p. 689.

588] NOTES for pages 366–75

22. Ford to Stella, Oct. 22, 1927. The Boni edition of *Last Post* is called *The Last Post*.
23. *Parade's End*, I, 42, 47, 168, and 205–06.
24. *Parade's End*, I, 47.
25. *Parade's End*, I, 419, 430, and 480.
26. *Parade's End*, II, 303, 307, and 327. Ford revised this part of *Last Post* for the Duckworth edition on which the NAL text is based; Boni and Knopf read differently here. We know that the business of Groby Great Tree has its source far back in Ford's life because he used it in *The Portrait* (1910), where "the immense cedar that shaded the banqueting hall" at Winterbourne Manor-house is cut down (p. 233; on p. 14 it is a yew tree).
27. *It Was the Nightingale*, pp. 178 and 211. Violet Hunt to Ethel [Colburn Mayne], n.d., but immediately after the publication of *Some Do Not...* in April, 1924 (Naumburg). This may be the draft of a letter never sent. *Parade's End*, II, 283.
28. *Parade's End*, I, 369, 389, and 420. Violet Hunt to Ethel [Colburn Mayne], n.d. (Naumburg).
29. *Return to Yesterday*, p. 247. Stella to Ford, Oct. 14, 1927; speaking of Valentine, Stella says, "I am glad you did not have a scene between Helen Luther [Lowther] and Valentine"; this indicates that Helen Lowther is also based on a real person, but I do not know who she is. *Parade's End*, I, 58–60 and 274. Given the way Ford's imagination worked, it is likely Mark Jr.'s never writing Christopher ("But the son's letters would have been stopped by the mother" [*Parade's End*, II, 138]) derives from Ford's belief that Elsie prevented Ford's getting letters from his daughter Katharine.
30. *It Was the Nightingale*, p. 222. For the Marwood family's opinion of the Tietjens, see p. 370. *Parade's End*, II, 318–19.
31. *Parade's End*, I, 22–23. *Memories and Impressions*, pp. 69–70 and 149.
32. James Joyce, *A Portrait of the Artist As a Young Man* (New American Library), p. 168. *Parade's End*, II, 132–33; this passage is quoted in full on pp. 501–02. *True Love & a G. C. M.*, pp. 97–98.

Chapter 27

1. *Parade's End*, I, 310–11. In *It Was the Nightingale* (pp. 161–62) Ford describes himself feeding his pig, Anna, at Coopers "in old khakis, shorts and an old khaki army shirt," when Sir Edward stopped to speak to him. "I knew him for the local great man—and of course as the composer of ... *Land of Hope and Glory*. ... There came into my mind suddenly the words: 'The band will play: "*Land of Hope and Glory*"' ... The adjutant will say: "There will be no more parades. ... " ' " But this was of course written after *No More Parades*.
2. *Parade's End*, I, 111; II, 146 and 67; I, 28.
3. *Parade's End*, I, 242–43, 494, and 279–80.
4. *The March of Literature*, pp. 441–42. Ford has just quoted Crashaw's

> He left His father's court, and came
> Lightly as a lambent flame
> Leaping upon the hills to be
> The humble King of you and me.

5. *Parade's End*, I, 179, and 370–71. For Ford's argument that the Germans should be treated as gallant enemies, see p. 251.
6. *Parade's End*, I, 248.

7. *Parade's End,* I, 55, 80, and 79.
8. *Parade's End,* I, 69, 62–63, 64, and 97.
9. *Parade's End,* I, 23, 22, 86, 104, 87, 90, 63, and 72.
10. *Parade's End,* I, 409 and 420.
11. *Parade's End,* I, 82.
12. *Parade's End,* I, 369. Ford's batman in the Welch Regiment was O Nine Evans.
13. *Parade's End,* I, 448.
14. *Parade's End,* I, 404 and 465–66.
15. *Parade's End,* I, 504 and 310–11.
16. *Parade's End,* II, 23.
17. *Parade's End,* II, 335–36.

Chapter 28

1. *The Rash Act,* pp. 182–83. How literally Ford was describing his own life in *The Rash Act* is evident from Samuel Putnam's description of it. "Ford was very lonely, that was plain to be seen. Especially at night. He . . . would stroll down to the Deux-Magots and sit at a table waiting for an audience of one or two. . . . Most often it was Arabella Yorke . . . and her mother, Mrs. Selina Yorke, now in her seventies. . . . With them Ford would sit for hours and reminisce. Others might come and be invited to drop down, it made little difference; all that was needed was a pair of listening ears, and Ford the fictionist was at his best" *(Paris Was Our Mistress,* p. 125).
2. Putnam, *Paris Was Our Mistress,* pp. 122–24. Ford to Gerald Duckworth, Feb. 13, 1928; Ludwig, p. 176.
3. Ford to Gerald Duckworth, Feb. 13, 1928; Ludwig, p. 175. Ford followed this complaint with a request that Duckworth end their contract with the publication of *Last Post* (Ford to Gerald Duckworth, Feb. 26, 1928 [Biala]). Ford to Hugh Walpole, Dec. 2, 1929; Ludwig, pp. 190–91. Ford published *A Little Less Than Gods* with Duckworth in October, 1928, after trying it on W. & R. Chambers of Edinburgh. Pinker also got Jonathan Cape to consider a one-volume edition of the Tietjens novels for his Travellers Library at this time, but nothing came of the proposal (W. & R. Chambers to Pinker, March 15, 1928, and Cape to Pinker, March 25, 1928 [Northwestern]).
4. Ford to Stella, May 12, 1928.
5. Mrs. Wright divorced Guy Wright on May 11, 1928; she must have come almost immediately to New York to meet Ford.
6. Harold Loeb, *The Way It Was,* pp. 189–90, and "Ford Madox Ford's 'The Good Soldier': A Critical Reminiscence," *London Magazine,* III (Dec., 1963), 65–67. Mr. Loeb dates his meetings with Ford and Mrs. Wright 1930, but this is a slip; Ford's affair with Mrs. Wright was at an end by 1930. By then she was back in St. Louis and perhaps seeing Guy, for in March, 1933, Guy divorced Mrs. Nellie Moore, whom he married a month after his divorce from Rene, and, in August, 1933, remarried Rene. Guy died in 1946 and Rene— of cancer—in 1957.
7. *The Good Soldier,* p. 115. *When the Wicked Man,* pp. 232 and 243. *No Enemy,* p. 292.
8. The dedication of *A Little Less Than Gods* is dated "Off Nantucket, 28*th July,* 1928." The covering letter Ford wrote Brandt when he sent in the typescript is dated July 12, 1928 (Biala). He had begun the novel "last night—or rather this morning after I came in from the Horse Show where I had been with Keating and Mcfee" (Ford to Stella, Nov. 13, 1927). Ford to Bradley, Aug. 13, 1928; Ludwig, p. 179.
9. Ford to Mrs. Loewe, Sept. 20, 1928. Ford to Gertrude Stein, Sept. 8 [1928]; Ludwig, p. 180.

Ford to George Oppenheimer of Viking, Nov. 9, 1928; Ludwig, p. 181. "On Conrad's Vocabulary," *Bookman*, June, 1928, pp. 405–08.

10. L. P. Hartley, "A Little Less Than Gods," *Saturday Review*, CXLVI (Nov. 24, 1928), 692. For other reviews see Harvey, pp. 380–83. Viking to Ford, Oct. 31, 1928 (Biala). Viking did a first printing of 5,000 and a second of 1,000 (Harvey, p. 72).

11. Putnam, *Paris Was Our Mistress*, p. 125. Allen Tate to Arthur Mizener, Sept. 23, 1968.

12. Ford to Ruth Kerr, Feb. 4, 1929 (Biala).

13. Ford to Janet Adam Smith, June 3, 1934; Ludwig, p. 232.

14. Ford to Bernice Baumgarten, Dec. 31, 1928 (Biala).

15. Ford to Brandt & Brandt (cable), n.d. (Biala).

16. Ford to Darley Cumberland, Jan. 3, 1929. Ford knew all about Elsie's suit against Violet Hunt before it even came to trial (see Ford to Conrad, May 21, 1924 [Yale]).

17. Robert Garnett to Ford, Jan. 22, 1929 (Mrs. Loewe).

18. Ford began *When the Wicked Man* in Paris, Dec. 17, 1928, and finished it in New York May 15, 1929 (see *When the Wicked Man*, p. 352). Ford to Bernice Baumgarten, July 10, 1929 (Biala). Ford to Cape, March 14, 1931 (Biala).

19. Ford to Bernice Baumgarten, July 10 and 7, 1929 (Biala).

20. Ford's review of *Dodsworth* appeared in the *Bookman*, April, 1929; see Harvey, p. 255.

Chapter 29

1. Ford's ill-advised displays of the American language begin as early as *The Benefactor* (1905); " 'The American novel is played out,' Mr. Beale suddenly announced. Philadelphia, in the shape of his firm, was waiting for it at the last base or he wasn't any judge of base-ball" (p. 166)—as evidently neither he nor Ford is. For the reviews of *When the Wicked Man*, see Harvey, pp. 390–91. Ford's move to Pinker meant a break with William Bradley, who had been his European representative for a long time. Ford to Walpole, May 28, 1930; Ludwig, p. 196.

2. Ford to Ralph Pinker, Aug. 17, 1929, from the Authors' Club in London (Princeton). Ford included in this letter a list of the books he wished to put in a collected edition. They are: *The Good Soldier*, the four Tietjens novels, *Joseph Conrad* and *Henry James* (in a single volume), *Ladies Whose Bright Eyes*, *Romance*, *A Mirror to France*, a volume of poems, *Ancient Lights*, *The Inheritors* and *The Nature of a Crime* (in a single volume).

3. Cape published *When the Wicked Man* in June, 1932. It was shortly after this time (*Bookman*, December, 1930) that Granville Hicks, also impressed that, though "Ford's individual books have, as they appeared, been greeted as unusual achievements," his "work as a whole has made little impression on the contemporary mind," tried to put the matter right with one of the most intelligent articles on Ford written during Ford's lifetime. Cape also rejected *The English Novel* and said he could not consider a collected edition of Ford. Chapman & Hall, too, rejected *The English Novel*; it was finally published by Constable, for a royalty of 10% on the first five thousand (Chapman & Hall, to Pinker, Jan. 31, 1929, and Constable to Pinker, Aug. 29, 1929 [Northwestern]; Pinker to Ford, Aug. 17 and 28, 1929 [Biala]). At this same time Farrar, in New York, rejected Ford proposals for a cookbook (Ford had had some success in America with articles on cooking and wines) and a volume of crossword puzzles. Ford kept on trying to place *No Enemy* in England, meeting publishers' objections ("I confess I found much the greater part of it extremely dull . . . ") with more and more extravagant claims for it (". . . the best piece of prose I ever wrote but I suppose that in England that does not count") (Gollancz to Pinker, Nov. 13, 1929 [Princeton]). In October, Benn had turned down *No Enemy* for the

same reason (Benn to Pinker, Oct. 7, 1929 [Northwestern]). Walpole's comment on the neglect of Ford appeared in an article in the *New York Herald Tribune Books*, Nov. 24, 1929, and Ford's expression of gratitude in a prefatory letter to the English edition of *The English Novel* (see Harvey, pp. 73 and 384).

4. "When I got the cables of acceptance [from publishers] I confess I was a little perturbed at what I had done," Aldington later said. " . . . However, I got to work, Ford and H. D. laboured nobly, and the *Imagist Anthology, 1930,* contained poems from everyone who had ever contributed . . . except poor Amy [Lowell] who was dead, Skipwith Cannell whom we couldn't trace, and Ezra who was sulky. Ford wrote one of his genially discursive introductions, and we sold several thousand copies . . . " (Richard Aldington, *Life for Life's Sake* [New York, 1941], p. 143). For the anonymous reviewer of the *Imagist Anthology,* see Harvey, p. 535.

5. Janice to Liveright, Jan. 26, 1932 (Biala). Ford had a "troublesome form of blood-poisoning" in November, 1929, and some sort of operation then (Ford to Hugh Walpole, Dec. 2, 1921; Ludwig, pp. 191–92). The Davisons met Janice and Ford at the Writer's Conference at Boulder, Colorado, in 1937 (Edward Davison to Arthur Mizener, April 8, 1969).

6. "Buckshee," *Collected Poems*, pp. 293–94. The first line of this passage is an ironic echo of "On Heaven," written twenty-odd years before, which says, "For God is a good man; God is a kind man."

7. Bowen, *Drawn from Life*, p. 190.

8. Susan Jenkins to Ford, Feb. 10, 1930 (Biala).

9. Ford to Ruth Kerr, Nov. 19, 1929, and Liveright's royalty reports for *When the Wicked Man* (Biala). In the course of these maneuvers, Ford ran up a bill of $500 with Spingarn, his lawyer; it was still unpaid in 1933 (Bradley to Ford, May 12, 1933 [Biala]).

10. Bowen, *Drawn from Life*, pp. 191–92.

11. Ford to Walpole, March 30, 1930; Ludwig, p. 193. This letter is misdated; it was written March 30, 1931. *Return to Yesterday* was not begun until Nov. 4, 1930 (*Return to Yesterday,* p. 436).

12. Ford to Ruth Kerr, March 11, 1930, Sept. 20, 1929, and Dec. 8, 1931 (Biala).

13. Ford to T. R. Smith, March 14, 1921; Ludwig, p. 200. Bowen, *Drawn from Life*, pp. 183–85. *Provence*, p. 148. Ford told Wells on July 28, 1930 (Biala), that, "having last autumn got together a sum sufficient to keep myself for a year I invested it, not at all speculatively, in stocks that stood at 115 but which are now at 50. . . . " But it seems unlikely he had invested much, for in June, 1929, well before the Crash, George Keating wrote him not to worry about the $300 Ford had recently borrowed: it would not have been like Ford to borrow when he had shares that could have been sold without loss in June, 1929 (Keating to Ford, June 25, 1929 [Biala]). He did realize some of these investments. "I cannot," he told Brandt when he was trying to get Brandt to finance his trip to Europe in the summer of 1929, "go on disturbing my investments in order to live here very expensively and unsatisfactorily" (Ford to Carl Brandt, n.d., but at the same time that he was writing Miss Baumgarten similar letters that are dated July, 1929 [Biala]). Ford's investment was probably in Anaconda Copper, which he may have been persuaded to invest in by some well-meaning relative of Harold Loeb's. At least, it is Anaconda that Henry Martin Smith is persuaded to buy by an imposing relative of Mr. Kuhn in *The Rash Act;* Henry Martin buys at 115 and the shares fall to 13.

14. Ford to Keating, May 26, 1930, and Ford to Wells, July 28, 1930 (Illinois). Shortly after this Ford asked Ralph Pinker for a loan of £50 on the security of the manuscript of the first volume of *A History of Our Own Times* (Ford to Pinker, Aug. 21, 1930 [Biala]). Dent rejected *A History* at this time (" . . . in our opinion, Mr. Ford has carried out the work . . . indifferently . . . "), as Benn and Gollancz had earlier (Dent to Pinker, Sept. 16, 1930, Benn to Pinker, Oct. 7, 1930, and Gollancz to Pinker, Oct. 25, 1929 [Northwestern]). In

September Ford borrowed another £25 or £50 from Wells (Ford to Wells, Sept. 3, 1930 [Illinois]).

15. *Great Trade Route*, p. 227. Bowen, *Drawn from Life*, p. 191. *Henry for Hugh*, pp. 101–102. Ford's love of the Villa Paul is very clear from his description of the Villa Niké in *Henry for Hugh*.

16. "L'Oubli—, Temps de Sécheresse," *Collected Poems*, pp. 308–09.

17. Louise Bogan to Janice, Feb. 25, 1934 (Biala).

18. Ford to Pinker, Aug. 17, 1930 (Princeton).

19. Review of Paul Morand's *New York, New York Herald Tribune Books*, Nov. 9, 1930; Harvey, pp. 256–57. Harold Loeb, "Ford Madox Ford's 'The Good Soldier,'" *London Magazine*, III (Dec., 1963), 65–73. Mr. Loeb says Mr. Tate had arranged a lecture for Ford in Tennessee. This is not true, though Mr. Tate did arrange a lecture for Ford when Ford came to see the Tates in Memphis in 1935. *Great Trade Route*, p. 32.

20. *When the Wicked Man* was completed "off the Scillias, 1st December, 1930." Joyce to Harriet Weaver, Feb. 16, 1931, in Richard Ellmann, *James Joyce*, p. 649n. Joyce also observed that Ford had one less wife than Earwicker's seven. "I don't understand," said Mary Butts in her blunt way, "why all those women want to leap into bed with old Ford." Ford refers to Father O'Flynn in *The March of Literature*, p. 620.

21. Ford to Joyce, March 9, 1931; Ludwig, p. 199. Richard Ellmann, *James Joyce*, p. 627. Lucia Joyce to Signora Svevo, Jan. 25, 1931, in *Letters of James Joyce*, ed. Gilbert, I, 299. Svevo's publishers rejected the idea of a Ford introduction.

22. "On Heaven," *Collected Poems* (1936), p. 11. Ford to T. R. Smith of Liveright, March 14, 1931; Ludwig, p. 200. Ford to Dreiser, April 18, 1931; Ludwig, p. 201. "Inconsiderately" is a guess; Prof. Ludwig found the word here illegible. Ford to Gollancz, Feb. 23 and March 7, 1931. Ford went through an elaborate pantomime with Gollancz about "my agent, Mme. E. G. Bowen, 18 rue Boissonade, Paris," so that when the confusion arose over the serial rights, he was able to blame it on "his agent's" assumption that it was customary trade practice for the author to sell the serial rights, regardless of any contract stipulation.

23. Keating to Ford, May 21, 1931 (Biala). Ford was also pressing *When the Wicked Man* on Gollancz, whom he now thought of as his English publisher (Ford to Gollancz, June 6, 1931). Gollancz was much embarrassed. He had obtained a copy of *When the Wicked Man* from Curtis Brown and found it unpublishable but urged Curtis Brown to silence on the grounds that Ford "is a very difficult man and he may be irritated if he knows I have actually read it and rejected it" (Gollancz to Curtis Brown, n.d.). Ford to Henry Kohn, Oct. 17, 1931 (Biala) (this is a draft of Ford's letter to Kohn and may not represent what he finally sent). Henry Kohn to Ford, April 8, 1932 (Biala). Kohn also reports in this letter that Liveright "is not inclined to publish" *That Same Poor Man.*

24. Bowen, *Drawn from Life*, p. 190. The completion date given in *Return to Yesterday* is "Cap Brun, *8th August, MCMXXXI.*" *Buckshee* consisted of eight poems at this point; "Coda" was added later, in 1936. *Buckshee* first appeared in Lascelles Abercrombie's collection called *New English Poems*, published by Gollancz on Nov. 9, 1931. *Poetry* printed them in two installments, in Feb., and March, 1932. Ford to Harriet Monroe, April 28, 1932 (Chicago).

25. *Buckshee* was put back into print in 1966 by the Pym-Randall Press with forewords by Robert Lowell and Kenneth Rexroth and a jacket design by Janice Biala.

26. *The March of Literature*, p. 405.

27. They had rented the flat at 32 rue Vaugirard to Mary and Padraic Colum and could not return to Paris until the Colums found another place (Ford to Padraic Colum, Sept. 21, 1931 [Biala]). Bowen, *Drawn from Life*, p. 191. *Return to Yesterday*, pp. 434–35.

28. Even as Prince of Wales, George V was politically active; he seems to have worked closely with the Liberals in their planning to limit the power of the Lords (see Kenneth Young,

Arthur James Balfour [London, 1963], p. 294; this story, however, comes from Mrs. Masterman). Ford to Victor Gollancz, Nov. 9, 1931 (Biala). There was no second edition of *Return to Yesterday,* the English edition of which sold 1,121 copies at list price; 87 were remaindered (see Harvey, p. 74).

29. The remarks of Arthur Waugh and Morton Zabel were made in reviews that are quoted in Harvey, pp. 394 and 396. Much of *Return to Yesterday* covers ground Ford had already been over in the first half of *Thus to Revisit.*

30. Ford to Ruth Kerr, Dec. 8, 1931 (Biala). Ford to Ray Long, July 2, 1932, Ludwig, pp. 208–11.

31. For Stella's trip to America see *Drawn from Life,* pp. 200–19; during this trip she did portraits of Carl Van Doren, Dorothy Thompson, and Sinclair Lewis, among others. Mrs. Lamb has a copy of her letter to Ford written at this time. Possibly Ford never received it; it was sent to Paris and he was at Cap Brun.

Chapter 30

1. Bradley, who was again serving as Ford's agent, welcomed Ford back to Paris Jan. 3, 1932; there is a memo from Long to Bradley outlining the terms of the contract with Ford dated Feb. 12, 1932 (Biala). Ford granted Long all English rights to his books and the royalty terms were nothing special (10% for the first 5,000, 12½% for the second, 15% thereafter). For the history of Long and Smith, see *The New York Times,* April 27, 1933, p. 15.

2. Ford to Bradley, March 12, 1932, Bradley to Ford, March 14, 1932 (Biala). The description of Henry Martin Smith's state of mind after he has committed the rash act, when, despite his physical vigor, he finds that his "brain . . . had been too much tried," reflects Ford's conception of his own condition at this time (*The Rash Act,* pp. 305 and 319).

3. *The Rash Act,* pp. 179–80, 184–85, and 190.

4. For the Alston Rivers episode, see pp. 130–131. Janice to Bradley, May 14, 1932, Bradley to Ford, May 14, 1932 (Biala).

5. Bradley to Ford, June 5, 1932 (Biala). Ford to Bradley, June 8, 1932; Ludwig, pp. 205–08. Ford became more and more concerned with the Jewish question as the horror of German anti-Semitism became plainer. He felt he had an insider's understanding of the Balfour Declaration of 1917 and he was eager to write about Zionism. In March, 1933, he tried to persuade the *Daily Mail* to let him do so and in June he tried to get *Scribner's* to take an article on the subject (Ford to the *Daily Mail,* March 13, 1933, and to Maxwell Perkins, June 18, 1933 [Biala]).

6. We do not have the alternate endings for *The Rash Act.* Ford was forced to reveal he was writing a trilogy when Smith wrote Bradley that he had solved the puzzle by "more or less of a combination use of both endings" (Smith to Bradley, Dec. 22, 1931, quoted by Bradley in a letter to Ford, Jan. 3, 1932 [Biala]). Ford to Ray Long, July 2, 1932; Ludwig, pp. 208–11; this is the letter in which Ford says the character of Henry Martin is partly based on Hart Crane, possibly on what Allen Tate and Katherine Anne Porter had told Ford about Crane. Smith reported to Ford on Jan. 13, 1933, that they had, as Ford suggested, sent *The Rash Act* to the printer without the last chapter (Biala).

7. Ford to Hugh Walpole, Oct. 25, 1932 (Texas). Bradley to Janice, Aug. 31 and Sept. 11, 1932; Richard Smith to Ford, Oct. 28, 1932, and Jan. 20, 1933 (Biala). The publication date of *The Rash Act* is given in Ford's letter to Pound, March 8, 1933; Ludwig, p. 217–18.

8. In Biala there is an unidentified newspaper clipping, rubber-stamped Aug. 3, 1933, describing how Smith staved off bankruptcy. This clipping is attached to Bradley's letter of Sept. 2, 1933, containing that unfortunate remark about how much money they had got for *The Rash Act.* Bradley is of course referring to Long and Smith's monthly payments of $200,

nine of which had been paid by this time (there would be two more before Smith ceased to pay). Ford had specifically asked Bradley to return the newspaper clipping; it proved that Smith was not only not bankrupt but rich.

9. Ford to Bradley, Sept. 10, 1933 (Biala).

10. Smith to Bradley, Jan. 20, 1933 (Biala).

11. Ford told Bradley they left for Rapallo June 21 and were back by July 4 (Ford to Bradley, July 19 and Aug. 11, 1932 [Biala]). Charles Norman (*Ezra Pound*, p. 312) credits Pound with "the words in parenthesis" in the interview with Ford, but it seems likely he composed more than that. Ford and Janice were in Paris for a few days on their way back from Germany (Ford to Ruth Kerr, Sept. 7, 1932 [Biala]). Ford dates the start of *It Was the Nightingale* "PARIS, JAN. 12TH."

12. *Provence*, pp. 356–58. Ford was exhausted by his work on *The Rash Act*, which he had written faster than he wanted to to please Long (Ford to Bradley, May 23, 1932 [Biala]). Ford to Alfred Goldsmith, Jan. 31, 1933; the "mixed type-holograph ms" of *A History of Our Own Times* is still in the Janice Biala Papers. Ford to Pound, March 8 and 27, 1933; Ludwig, pp. 217–19.

13. *Provence*, pp. 285–88. Caroline Gordon returned the compliment of Ford's dedication by dedicating to him her finest novel, *Aleck Maury, Sportsman*. Ford often exploited the Greco-Roman background of Provence too, as in *The Rash Act* with its references to the Roman remains of Provence and in *Henry for Hugh* with its references to Ulysses.

14. *Collected Poems*, p. 306.

15. Ford to Caroline Gordon, Sept. 11, 1933; Ludwig, pp. 227–28. Ford to Horace Shipp, Aug. 25, 1933 (Biala). Shipp, the editor of *The Second English Review Book of Short Stories*, proposed to dedicate the book to Ford; Ford urged him not to, on the grounds that his name would be less than helpful to it in England. His consolation, he told Shipp, was that "At any rate, thank Goodness, the Middle West and some French army messes and the district round the Pantheon, consume a sufficiency [of his books] to let me continue working on this Mediterranean hillside...." He even began to believe he no longer admired James; "... as the years have gone on," he said, "I have grown more and more antipathetic to the Master of Rye" (Ford to Janet Adam Smith, June 3, 1934; Ludwig, p. 232). For the sales of *The Rash Act*, see Harvey, p. 77.

16. For the reviews of *It Was the Nightingale*, see Harvey, pp. 399–402. The critical remarks quoted in this paragraph were made about *Some Do Not.... It Was the Nightingale* sold 2,930 copies in America and approximately 2,000 in England (Harvey, pp. 78–79).

17. *It Was the Nightingale*, pp. 17–23 and 24.

18. *It Was the Nightingale*, pp. 114 and 119.

19. Lippincott's reply to Ford's proposal of a collected edition was reported to Ford by Jenny Bradley, Dec. 6, 1933 (Biala). *The March of Literature*, p. 769.

20. Katherine Anne Porter to Rosemary Mizener, April 7, 1967.

21. *It Was the Nightingale*, p. 9.

22. Pound to Ford, Nov. 3, [1933] (Biala). Pound is replying to Ford's request that he boom René Béhaine, in support of whose work Ford conducted a long campaign that included persuading Edward Crankshaw to translate Béhaine's *The Survivors* (1938), for which Ford wrote a preface. Ford to Ferris Greenslet, Aug. 24, 1938 (Biala).

23. Ford to Herbert Gorman, Feb. 18, 1934 (Naumburg). Ford sent *Henry for Hugh* to Lippincott Jan. 1, 1934 (Biala). Goldring, *South Lodge*, pp. 192–94. *Provence*, p. 77.

24. *Provence*, pp. 23–24.

25. Allen & Unwin necessarily published Ford's books in a somewhat different order from that of their American publication: *Great Trade Route*, Jan., 1937; *Vive le Roy*, July, 1937; *Portraits from Life* (under the title *Mightier than the Sword*), Feb., 1938; *Provence*, Nov.,

1938; *The March of Literature*, Sept., 1939.

26. *Provence*, Part III, Chap. I. Ford to Bertram, Sept. 27, 1935; Ludwig, p. 243.
27. Goldring, *South Lodge*, pp. 194–95 and 200. The London *Times*, Jan. 19, 1942. Violet did not steal Ford's possessions; she bought them when she moved him from Holland Park Avenue to South Lodge.
28. Ford to Stella, June 19, 1933; Heinemann to Ford, May 1, 1934; Janice to Stella, Aug. 4, 1934 (Biala).

Chapter 31

1. Ford sent his blurb for *As Thy Day* to Jefferson Jones of Lippincott Jan. 1, 1933, with a covering letter in which he says, "I am forwarding to you on an attached sheet some notes about the book that may possibly be useful for your announcements" (Biala). Elizabeth Freiligrath quotes Ford's title at the end of *Henry for Hugh*, p. 299. Henry Martin mentions the Pilgrimage of Children and Hugh Monckton describes him as trustworthy in *The Rash Act*, pp. 233 and 251. The references to the inscription to the boy dancer are in *The Rash Act*, p. 33 and *Provence*, p. 49.
2. *The March of Literature*, p. 759.
3. Bonamy Dobrée, "*The Rash Act*," *Spectator*, Sept. 8, 1933, p. 311. Herbert Agar, "*The Rash Act*," *The English Review*, Oct., 1933, p. 435 (Harvey, pp. 398 and 399).
4. Ford describes their crossing and this winter in New York in *Great Trade Route*, pp. 48–90. For the gout, see J. Jefferson Jones to Ford, Dec. 5, 1934 (Biala).
5. *Great Trade Route*, pp. 87, 192, and 251.
6. *Provence*, p. 21. *Great Trade Route*, pp. 25 and 39. The first thing Ford wrote for the *American Mercury* after he had made his arrangement with Paul Palmer in the summer of 1935 was an article on The Small Producer; it begins, "Very soon now the Small Producer shall again inherit the earth and the fulness thereof . . . whatever we may say or do. So it has always been and so it will be again" (*American Mercury*, XXXV [Aug., 1935], 445).
7. *Great Trade Route*, p. 25.
8. Ford to Stanton Campbell, Aug. 24, 1928, quoted in Harvey, p. 80. *Great Trade Route*, p. 224. "If you will read very carefully Provence, Great Trade Route and the last two poems L'oublie and Coda, you will get a pretty good idea of our life and what Ford thought about the world in general" (Janice Biala to Goldring, April 14, 1945 [Biala]).
9. *Great Trade Route*, p. 142.
10. *Provence*, pp. 138, 64, and 67.
11. *Great Trade Route*, pp. 145–46 and 330. Ford's scorn of science and its supposedly crass, rationalistic dependence on "fact" was of course commonplace among literary men of his time. Yeats was offended by science; Pound used "scientists" like Frobenius to suit his own mythic purposes; D. H. Lawrence said, "Our science is a science of the dead world" (Foreword to *Fantasia of the Unconscious*).
12. Caroline Gordon to Stella, n.d. (Mrs. Loewe). *Provence*, p. 19. Graham Greene, "Provence," *London Mercury*, Dec., 1938, pp. 217–18 (Harvey, p. 422).
13. Katherine Woods, "*Provence*," *New York Herald Tribune Books*, March 24, 1935, p. 1; Noel Sauvage, "*Provence*," *New York Times Book Review*, March 24, 1935, p. 9 (Harvey, pp. 403–04). Mr. Sauvage not only describes *Provence* as Ford wanted it described but refers to its joie de vivre, the parallel to Sterne, and the wit of Biala's illustrations, all favorite points with Ford. For the sales of *Provence* see Harvey, p. 80. Ford had now completed the first volume of his projected three-volume *History of Our Own Times*. On March 11,

1935, Curtis Brown wrote him that there was no market for volume I (1870–1895) or for a three-volume history either (Biala).

14. Ford was paid $100 apiece for the two articles he wrote for the North American Newspaper Alliance about the Hauptmann trial (for the first of which see the *New York World-Telegram*, Jan. 24, 1935, p. 1; for the second, *The New York Times*, Feb. 14, 1935, p. 11). Curtis Brown to Ford, Feb. 15, 1935; Jefferson Jones to Ford, Feb. 20, 1935; Ford to Lippincott, Dec. 11, 1935 (Biala).

15. *Great Trade Route*, pp. 26–27 and 380–84. Ford's article on "Techniques" appeared immediately after this occasion, in the first number of the *Southern Review*, July, 1935.

16. *Great Trade Route*, pp. 362–63 and 405. Curtis Brown reported to Stella (April 10, 1935 [Biala]) that they had tried *Provence* and *Henry for Hugh* on Cape, Heinemann, Nicolson & Watson, Faber & Faber, Putnam, Cassell, Dent, Methuen, Lovat Dickson, Peter Davies, Chatto & Windus, and Wishart. Juliet Soskice helped Stella out with Julie's school bills at this time (Stella to Janice, April 16, [1935] [Biala]).

17. Janice to Stella, June 6, 1935 (Biala).

18. Ford to Palmer, June 6, 1936; Ludwig, pp. 250–51.

19. *Great Trade Route*, pp. 406–07, 421, 391–92, and 439.

20. Stella to Janice, Dec. 8, [1935] (Biala).

21. Ford to Julie, Sept. 11, 1935; Ludwig, pp. 238–41.

Chapter 32

1. Ford to Anthony Bertram, Oct. 15, 1935; Ludwig, pp. 245–46. *The March of Literature*, p. 210. Ford to Julie, Dec. 25, 1935 (Mrs. Loewe).

2. Edward Crankshaw to Ford, April 8 and 23, 1936 (Biala).

3. Janice to Stella, Aug. 31, 1935, and Easter Saturday [April 11], 1936 (Biala).

4. *Vive le Roy*, pp. 258, 68–73, and 139. Lenin was an "admirable tyrant" because he acknowledged that the Small Producer "would be too much for the digestion of his Machine" (p. 70). This was a favorite point with Ford; he quotes the relevant passage from Lenin in *Great Trade Route*, p. 79.

5. Ford to Henry Goddard Leech, Feb. 18, 1938; Ludwig, pp. 288–89.

6. *Collected Poems*, p. 319. An unrevised version of "Coda" appeared in the *London Mercury*, Sept., 1936. *Vive le Roy* sold 2,498 copies in America and 1,160 in England (see Harvey, p. 80). Janice to Stella, June 24, 1936 (Biala). Ford to Paul Palmer, July 24, 1936; to Allen Tate and to Ezra Pound, both Sept. 6, 1936; Ludwig, pp. 253, 258, and 261–62.

7. Ford to Ruth Aley, Sept. 7, 1936 (Biala). As soon as Ford got to New York he transferred his affairs to George Bye (Bye to Ford, Dec. 6, 1938 [Biala]). Ford to Eugene Pressly, Aug. 20, 1936; Ludwig, p. 255.

8. The Oxford Press of New York printed 750 copies of the *Collected Poems* and bound 550. When it was declared out of print in January, 1944, they destroyed 195 sets of unbound sheets (Harvey, p. 81). Edward Crankshaw was reading the galleys of the English edition when the war broke out. When it was over, he wrote the Oxford Press about the book; the Press told him they had no knowledge of it. He then sent them his set of the galleys; they neither wrote nor returned the galleys. There is a long series of letters between Howard Lowry and Ford about their problems (Biala).

9. Ford to Paul Palmer, Nov. 17 and July 24, 1936 (Biala). Ford reread Swinburne that summer at the Crankshaws'. Ford to Allen Tate, Sept. 6, 1936; Ludwig, pp. 257–58.

10. Edward Dahlberg, "Ford Madox Ford," *New Directions*, Number Seven, 1942, p. 468. Ford to Paul Palmer, Dec. 9, 1936 (Yale). Ford's talk was broadcast Dec. 7, 1936, 5:00–5:30; some

of those who did hear it reported they could not understand what Ford was saying, but it must have been true the radio people admired it, because WABC, only a fortnight later, got Ford to do a half-hour talk on the W.P.A. and the arts. There are scripts of both radio talks (Biala).

11. Williams' description of Ford inspecting the Jersey truck garden is in the typescript fragment of an article entitled "Les Amis de For Maddox Forde [*sic*]!" (Yale). Ford describes the same occasion with considerable grace in *Great Trade Route*, pp. 184–85. Williams' other comment is in his *Autobiography*, p. 300. Ford's remark about his wounded foot is in a letter to Mrs. Force, Jan. 11, 1937 (Biala); at the same time he was telling another correspondent that "we all have got colds and gout" (Ford to Jefferson Jones, Feb. 17, 1936 [*sic*: 1937]) (Biala).

12. Horace Reynolds, "Portraits from Life," *Christian Science Monitor Weekly Magazine*, April 28, 1937, p. 28. Ford to Unwin, Jan. 24, 1937. Ford to Greenslet, Jan. 30, 1937 (Biala). For Ford's earlier opinion of *Mr. Croyd*, see p. 295 above. Greenslet to Ford, Feb. 15, 1937. Ford to George Bye, March 8, 1937 (Biala). *Great Trade Route* sold about 1,000 copies in America, about 1,400 in England; *Portraits from Life* something less than 2,500 in America, 1,290 in England; see Harvey, pp. 84–85.

13. Ford to Unwin, March 15, 1938. The terms Ford proposed for Doubleday were, sadly enough, a comedown for him. In 1936 he had told Unwin he must have $2,000 on the American rights and £100 on the English (Ford to Unwin, Nov. 3, 1936). Ford invented a marvelously subtle variation on the lonely old buffalo figure in Commandatore Raymondo Poggio of *Professor's Progress* (see p. 459).

14. Ford's talk at the Town Hall Club was reported in the *New York Herald Tribune*, March 10, 1937, p. 10. Apparently in an effort to help Stella and Julie, Juliet Soskice offered in March to sell at Sotheby's a series of Ford manuscripts and typescripts then in Stella's possession—*The Rash Act, Henry for Hugh, Toward Tomorrow (It Was the Nightingale), A History of Our Own Times*, "Conrad and the Sea." But the bidding did not reach the reserve prices, modest though these were at £5 to £10, and the material remained in Stella's hands (see Sotheby's *Catalogue of Valuable Printed Books*, March 16, 1937).

15. Ford to Stanley Unwin, May 29, 1937. Dale Warren. Edward Crankshaw's report on *Portraits from Life* is in Allen and Unwin's files. *Portraits from Life*, pp. 205, 221, and 206. Harvey lists an unusually large number of reviews in both America and England (see pp. 412–19). A characteristic comment is that of James Stephens in the *Sunday Times* (Harvey, p. 416): "Each of these essays is readable from the first word to the last.... Critically, however, the matter is deplorably otherwise."

16. Robie Macauley, "The Dean in Exile: Notes on Ford Madox Ford as Teacher," *Shenandoah*, IV (Spring, 1953), 47. Caroline Tate to Ford, n.d., but fall, 1936 (Biala). Ford to Paul Palmer, July 29, 1937; Ludwig, p. 280. Robert Lowell, "Visiting the Tates," *Sewanee Review*, LXVII (Autumn, 1959), 557.

17. Janice to George Davis, June 21, 1937 (Biala).

18. Ford wrote his new agent, George Bye, on Dec. 28, 1936, that Dial would soon communicate with Bye "about the HISTORY OF WORLD LITERATURE that he [Vernon, the editor] wants me to write" (Biala). Robert Lowell, "Foreword," *Buckshee*, p. xi, and "Visiting the Tates," pp. 598–99. As early as June 3, 1921, Ford had written Pinker (Huntington) suggesting he write a two-volume history of English literature (100,000–150,000 words). "You might say," he wrote, "that it will contain as much of the history of literature as a gentleman ought to know; or in the alternative that it will be an account of English literature by a man of the world for men of the world—not a handbook with condensed annotations by a half dead don." A considerable portion of this history of literature was written despite Ralph Pinker's inability to find a publisher for it (Biala). Ford's progress with *The March of Literature* can be traced almost chapter by chapter

through Ford's letters to Bye and Vernon (Biala). By the beginning of June he was "through Greece"; by the middle of August through Book I, Part II. He told Vernon (June 9, 1937 [Biala]) that he was producing a thousand words a day. Ford was uncomfortable with Robert Lowell; he predicted Lowell would later describe him *en pantoufles*, a constant subject of anxiety with him. When one of their friends at Boulder heard from Jean Stafford that Lowell was secretly planning to be on the boat the next time Ford and Janice went to Europe, she warned them. "... if I were in your boots," she said, "and he succeeded in his little plan, I am sure I would push him off the rail before we reached Cherbourg" (Natalie Davison to Janice, Oct. 27, 1937 [Biala]).

19. Robert Lowell, "Visiting the Tates," p. 558. Allen Tate. Ford to George Bye, June 11, 1937 (Biala).

20. Ford to Stanley Unwin, May 29, 1937. Ford spoke at *Poetry*'s fund-raising dinner at the Arts Club the evening of May 26 and on the evening of May 27 at Chicago. He described *A Little Tour at Home* in a synopsis he wrote for publishers. He proposes to deal with Detroit, a village in south Michigan, Chicago, Kansas City, Pittsburgh, Richmond, Washington, Charleston, and Baltimore. Janice said the book would include New Orleans, New York, Boston, Washington, Nashville, Chicago, Detroit, Denver, San Francisco, Havana, Paris, Dijon, Marseilles, etc. (Janice to George Davis, June 21, 1937 [Biala]). Both lists were probably influenced to some extent by where the writers were longing to go. There is a preliminary description of this book, then called *Portraits of Cities* and described as largely Janice's idea, in a letter to Greenslet, June 12, 1937; Ludwig, p. 279.

21. Allen Tate to Arthur Mizener, Jan. 29, 1969. Ford to Dale Warren, June 11, 1937; Ludwig, p. 278.

22. Ford to Dale Warren, June 11, 1937; Ludwig, p. 278. Robert Lowell, "Visiting the Tates," p. 557. Allen Tate, "Ode to the Confederate Dead."

23. The Tates returned to Benfolly, taking Katherine Anne Porter with them; there she met Albert Erskine, whom she shortly after married. Lowell followed Ford to Boulder; there he met Jean Stafford, whom he shortly after married.

24. Edward Davison to Arthur Mizener, April 8, 1969. Ford reported casually to Vernon of the Dial Press (Aug. 18, 1937 [Biala]) that Boulder had been "enervating on account of the altitude and the want of oxygen in the air."

25. Robert Lowell, "Foreword," *Buckshee*, p. xi.

26. Ford to George Keating, June 1, 1938; Ludwig, p. 295. The lecture tour was the idea of Burton Hoffman, president of Dial; Lee Keedick handled it. The only firm engagements Keedick got Ford were The Friends of American Writers in Chicago, Northwestern University, and Western State Teachers College in Kalamazoo (Hoffman to Ford, June 14, 1938, and Keedick to Hoffman, July 13, 1938 [Biala]).

27. Ford to Unwin, Sept. 5, 1937; Ludwig, p. 282.

28. Robie Macauley, "The Dean in Exile," *Shenandoah*, pp. 46–47.

29. Robie Macauley, "The Dean in Exile," pp. 44–45.

Chapter 33

1. They spent three days in New York with Prof. Richard Cox (for whom see *Great Trade Route*, pp. 52–53) and sailed on the *Lafayette* Dec. 4, reaching Paris Dec. 14. Ford to Christopher Morley, Nov. 27, 1937; Ford to Stanley Unwin, Dec. 4, 1937; Ford to Joseph Brewer, Feb. 19, 1938 (Biala). Ford to Unwin, Feb. 24, 1938. Ford to Julie [March 20, 1938]; Ludwig, p. 292.

2. Ford to Burton C. Hoffman of the Dial Press, June 16, 1938 (Biala). Ford to Stanley Unwin, March 15, 1938.
3. Ford to Pound, Feb. 17, [1938], in Ludwig, pp. 270-72; Ford inadvertently dated this letter 1937 instead of 1938, and Prof. Ludwig has followed him. Ford neither saw Olivet nor held a position there until the summer and fall of 1937, nor was he in Paris (where this letter was written) in February, 1937, but in New York. Brewer to Ford, Jan. 20, 1938 (Biala).
4. Pound to Ford, postmarked Feb. 21, March 18, and March 22, 1938 (Biala).
5. Ford to Pound, March 16, 1938; Ludwig, p. 290. Ford to Brewer, Feb. 19, 1938 (Biala). Ford to Stanley Unwin, March 15, 1938.
6. Ford to Paul Palmer, April 19, 1938 (Biala); Ford told Unwin that "the American doctors ... seem to think that my heart is less weak than the French doctors thought" (April 16, 1938). Ford had told Unwin at the time of his illness that "I had written about half ... the HISTORY OF LITERATURE by the beginning of December ... and I have only managed to crawl through about half a chapter since then" (Feb. 24, 1938). "Half" *The March of Literature* is Book I, the first 408 pages of the Allen & Unwin edition; Ford always thought of it as the first volume of a two-volume work and perhaps he sent it to his publishers separately because he still hoped to get the book published in two volumes; he wanted the money for the first volume.
7. Ford to George Keating, June 1, 1938; Ludwig, p. 295.
8. There is a copy of Prof. Akley's citation in the Janice Biala Papers. "Professor Emeritus" was what Ford had proposed to President Brewer; Brewer made him a professor on leave (Ford to Unwin, June 8, 1938). The degree was a Litt. D., not an LL. D. Ford to Julie, Aug. 30, 1938 (Biala).
9. Ford to Unwin, July 15, 1938; Ford to Hoffman, July 13, 1938 (Biala).
10. Ford to Hoffman, July 28, 1938, and Ford to Vernon, Aug. 1, 1938 (Biala).
11. Hoffman to Ford, Aug. 1, 1938; Ford to Hoffman, Aug. 3, 1938 (Biala). Ford made a strenuous effort to have the quotations put back when Unwin published *The March of Literature* in England a year later, and Unwin too pointed out that the cost would be prohibitive. Ford to Hoffman, July 31, 1938 (Biala). Ford had a subsidiary quarrel with Vernon over Vernon's refusal to pay the exorbitant prices Pound demanded for his translations of Chinese poetry, which Ford had used at every possible opportunity.
12. Ford to Hoffman, Aug. 3, 1938, and Hoffman to Ford, Aug. 1, 1938 (Biala).
13. Ford to Paul Palmer, July 21, 1938 (Yale). Ford to Unwin, Aug. 4, 1938.
14. Ford to Hoffman, Sept. 7, 1938 (Biala). Ford's pocket engagement book for these months shows him doing radio broadcasts for WHN Oct. 7 and NBC Oct. 14.
15. Robie Macauley, "The Dean in Exile," *Shenandoah*, IV (Spring, 1953), p. 45. *The March of Literature*, pp. 724n, 674-75, 698, and 486. We are also urged to note that "it had been [the Athenians' and the Sicilians'] pleasure ... to house sumptuously, and richly reward ... itinerant poets" (p. 132).
16. *The March of Literature*, pp. 331, 382, 457, 482, and 729.
17. *The March of Literature*, pp. 619-20, 681, 469, 547, 649, and 653-54.
18. *The March of Literature*, pp. 194, 229-30, 212-13, 418, and 703.
19. The pocket diary is in the Biala Papers. In it Janice recorded Ford's weight (Nov. 22 and 29) and the diet laid out for him (Dec. 11, 1938). George Keating got him the tickets for the Cornell-Columbia game (Ford to Keating, Nov. 3, 1938 [Biala]). He went to Boston for the Book Fair in November and lectured there at the Women's City Club. Ford to Unwin, Oct. 12, 1938.
20. Ford to Brewer, Oct. 24, 1938; Brewer to Ford, Nov. 1, 1938 (Biala).
21. Ford to Unwin, Oct. 12, 1938, and Feb. 16, 1939. Hoffman to Ford, Oct. 13 and 17, 1938 (Biala). We do not know just what writers Ford and Dial disagreed about, but shortly

after this he urged Unwin to publish a volume of Eudora Welty's short stories and a novel by Wanda Tower (Mrs. William Picard) called *Salute to the Ladies* (Ford to Unwin, Feb. 3, 1939).

22. The P.E.N. dinner was on Nov. 22, 1938. After it Ford wrote Lewis, "I was so struck all of a heap by your reference to me the other night that...I omitted any thanks to yourself or expression of admiration for your work—for which the merest decency would have called" (Ford to Lewis, Nov. 25, 1938 [Yale]). Ford to Unwin, Feb. 16, 1939. Ford to Hoffman, Oct. 19, 1938 (Biala).

23. Ford to Unwin, Feb. 16 and March 23, 1939. Ford outlined what he had proposed to Howe in a letter to George Bye, Nov. 29, 1938 (Biala). Ford to Unwin, Nov. 3, 1936. Howe to Bye, Nov. 30, 1938 (Biala).

24. Ford to Unwin, Jan. 4, 10, and Feb. 3, 1939. Ford to Brewer, Feb. 17, 1939, and Brewer to Ford, March 17, 1939 (Biala). There are three different versions of the opening chapters of *Professor's Progress*, as if, in his illness, Ford had had an unusually difficult time getting started.

25. Williams to McAlmon, May 25, 1939, in Harvey, p. 604. William Carlos Williams, *Autobiography*, p. 300. "To Ford Madox Ford in Heaven," *Furioso*, I (Spring, 1940) 4-5.

26. Ford to Brewer, Feb. 17, 1939, and Pound to Ford, Jan. 31, 1939 (Biala).

27. "We have given further study to the Transatlantic Review Project, but with the best will in the world toward you yourself...we are still forced to the conclusion that it would be a mistake for us to lend our imprint to it or undertake its direct distribution" (George Shively of Frederick A. Stokes to Ford, March 22, 1939 [Biala]). Ford to Edward Crankshaw, March 14, 1939, and Ford to George Keating, March 13, 1939; Ludwig, p. 315. Ford to William Bird, May 23, 1929, and Ford to Allen Tate, March 24, 1939 (Biala).

28. Office memo from George Bye announcing Ford's signing with Stokes, March 14, 1939 (Biala). The details of the contract are in Stokes' letter to Allen & Unwin, July 18, 1939. Ford to Unwin, Sept. 23, and Unwin to Ford, Oct. 6, 1938; Ford to George Bye, Nov. 29, 1938 (Biala). Ford to Henry Goddard Leach, Feb. 18, 1938; Ludwig, p. 288. When Ford signed with Stokes, he assigned his American royalties to Janice (Stokes to Bye, March 13, 1939 [Biala]). The typescript and ms. of *Professor's Progress* are in the Biala Collection. On the last page of the ms. Janice has noted that these were the last words Ford wrote. Ford to George Shively, April 21, 1939 (Biala).

29. Ford to Unwin, May 25, 1939. *Professor's Progress*, pp. 8, 15, and 18. It is just possible that the idea of Bullen's inheriting a fortune from his brother reflects Ford's awareness that Allen Tate's brother Ben was a wealthy businessman; Ford was thinking a good deal about this at the time he was writing *Professor's Progress* because he hoped Mrs. Tate might be persuaded to finance the revival of the *Transatlantic Review.*

30. *Professor's Progress*, pp. 6-7, 9, 68. Ford to Hoffman, June 16, 1938 (Biala).

31. *Professor's Progress*, pp. 65, 54, and 55-59.

32. *Professor's Progress*, p. 62.

33. Ford to T. Rokotov, Editor, *International Literature*, Oct. 29, 1938 (Biala). *Professor's Progress*, second typescript, pp. 111 and 75.

34. As early as March 13, 1933 (Biala), Ford had written the editor of the *Daily Mail* to ask if they would use an article on the Jews in Europe. "I think," he said, "I was the first to suggest to the Asquith Cabinet when asked by C. F. G. Masterman, then Chancellor of the Duchy of Lancaster, that an independent Jewish state in Palestine should be part of British peace terms—in 1915." When this suggestion was refused he asked the London *Times* to let him write them "an article for your editiorial page" on the subject (March 20, 1933 [Biala]). In July, 1937, he told Paul Palmer of the *American Mercury* that if Palmer would let him "write something about Zionism...I'd put off everything else to let you have it—I mean on approval" (Ludwig, p. 280); these were almost unprecedented conces-

sions for Ford. *Professor's Progress*, pp. 111, 75, 99, and 108. Commandatore Poggio is based on Ford's recollection of Borschitzky, with whom he had studied the violin as a boy (*Return to Yesterday*, pp. 80–81).

Chapter 34

1. Caroline Gordon, "The Story of Ford Madox Ford," *Highlights of Modern Literature* (Mentor, 1954), p. 114. Mrs. Tate dates this occasion April, 1938, but the letter she wrote Mrs. Loewe after Ford's death, in which she also describes Ford's visit, shows it was April, 1939.
2. Ford to Tetley, April 26 and May 23, 1939 (Princeton). Ford to Allen Tate, May, 19, 1939 (Biala). Ford to Brewer, May 8, 1939 (Biala).
3. Charles Norman, *Ezra Pound* (New York, 1960), pp. 363–64. Williams to McAlmon, May 25, 1939, in *Selected Letters of William Carlos Williams*, ed. John C. Thirlwall (New York, 1957), p. 177.
4. Ford to Bye, May 30, 1939, and Bye to Ford, May 31 and June 6, 1939 (Biala). Ford to Unwin, May 25, 1939; in this letter Ford made a last attempt to persuade Unwin to publish *Mr. Croyd*.
5. Janice to Stella, June 11, 1939 (Biala). Bowen, *Drawn from Life*, p. 244.
6. Edward Crankshaw to Stanley Unwin, July 2, 1939. Janice to Julie, Tuesday [June 30], 1939 (Mrs. Loewe).
7. Janice to Julie, Tuesday [June 30], 1939 (Mrs. Loewe). For the Le Sons see the dedicatory letter to *Great Trade Route*.
8. When, after the war, Janice married the painter Daniel Brustlein, they put up the headstone that now marks Ford's grave in the Deauville cemetery.

Appendix

1. H. G. Wells made sly fun of Ford's fourth-dimensionist inheritors in *The Bulpington of Blup*, his novel about Ford (see, for example, p. 337).
2. *The Inheritors* (Concord Edition), pp. 9, 184, and 152.
3. *The Inheritors*, pp. 185, 7–8, and 6.
4. *The Inheritors*, pp. 156–57 and 5. Conrad discusses their idea for a novel about "an old and famous painter" in a letter to Kazimier Waliszewski, November 8, 1903, quoted by Zdzislaw Najder, *Conrad's Polish Background*, pp. 236–37. Jenkins, like Brown, owns the death mask of Oliver Cromwell and looks like the king of hearts.
5. *The Inheritors*, p. 33.
6. *The Inheritors*, pp. 55, 110, and 189.
7. *The Benefactor*, pp. 347–49.
8. Richard A. Cassell, *Ford Madox Ford* (Baltimore, 1962), p. 118. *The Benefactor*, pp. 232 and 251.
9. *The Benefactor*, pp. 214 and 50. That George Moffat is a self-portrait is shown by many small particulars of the novel. George's father, a famous painter, has impressed on him "that you must never lose a chance of helping any lame dog over a stile" (p. 15); these are almost the exact words Ford Madox Brown addressed to Ford (see p. 13 above). The novel's American, Mr. Beale, says George's house "has a bully Gothic window" (p. 176); this is the voice of Stephen Crane speaking of Gracie's Cottage (see p. 38 above). George's

naive delight in admiration, in disciples, and in being called "Cher Maître," his talk about the techniques of fiction, his—to him—inexplicable enbroilments with everyone he helps, his family background; all these things are evidently Ford's. The remark that Ford did not know what to think is quoted by him in *Provence*, p. 120. The reviewer was *The English Review's* (see Harvey, p. 286).

10. *The Fifth Queen*, pp. 20, 102ff., and 169ff. (24, 85ff., and 134ff.). References in parentheses are to the new, one-volume American edition of the *Fifth Queen* trilogy published in New York in 1963.

11. Synopsis of a projected life of Henry VIII (Cornell). *Joseph Conrad*, p. 176.

12. *The Fifth Queen Crowned*, p. 307 (588).

13. *The Fifth Queen*, pp. 214–15, 195, 219 (168, 154, 172).

14. *The Fifth Queen*, p. 28 (30–31); *Privy Seal*, pp. 259, 119, and 115 (376, 300, and 298). The remark about Cromwell is in *When Blood Is Their Argument*, p. 11.

15. *The Fifth Queen Crowned*, pp. 181–82 (520); *Privy Seal*, p. 91 (285).

16. *The Fifth Queen Crowned*, pp. 306–12 (587–91).

17. *The 'Half Moon'*, p. 333.

18. Hunt, *The Flurried Years*, pp. 60–61. The "Epistolary Epilogue" of *A Call* is addressed to "my dear———" but Ford filled in the blank with the name "Violet" in the copy he inscribed to her: " 'Every way and altogether,' she answered./ To Violet Hunt/ Ford Madox Hueffer/ Feb 8th MCMX" (Naumburg). The inscription is the last sentence of the novel.

19. *A Call*, pp. 30 and 281. Ford's emphasis on the shaping effect of Robert Grimshaw's "English public-school training" shows Violet Hunt was right to think Robert is modeled on Ford's conception of himself. Christopher Tietjens is also a product of such training. "It is not good to have taken one's public school's ethical system seriously," he tells General Campion. "I am really, sir, the English public-school boy. That's an eighteenth-century product" (*Parade's End* [NAL], I, 494). Ford believed the best kind of Englishman—he himself—was characterized by a feudal, chivalric sense of public duty, and he was so sure this sense of duty was inculcated only by English public schools that he convinced himself he had attended one of them.

20. *A Call*, pp. 275 and 291.

21. *A Call*, pp. 121–22.

22. Bennett's review was in *The New Age*, March 17, 1910, p. 471; his other comment in *The Journal of Arnold Bennett* (New York, 1932), p. 370 (see Harvey, p. 303). D. H. Lawrence said *A Call* had "more art than life" (Lawrence to Blanche Jennings, Nov. 1, 1909, *Letters*, I, 57). Hunt, *The Flurried Years*, p. 155.

23. *A Call*, pp. 9–12 and 110–11. Ohmann, *Ford Madox Ford*, p. 56, says Kitty is implausible, and she certainly is; but Ford uses her cleverly.

24. *A Call*, pp. 163 and 18.

25. *A Call*, pp. 272–74. Violet Hunt told Ford he was like Robert Grimshaw in a letter dated Aug. 7, 1909 (Cornell). Ohmann, *Ford Madox Ford*, pp. 57–58.

26. "Prospectus," *Transatlantic Review*. The *March of Literature*, p. 398. "Stocktaking: Towards a Revaluation of English Literature," *Transatlantic Review*, May, 1924. "You see, *after I left Eton*, I came to study at the Sorbonne and I was greatly attached to an old professor ..." (Goldring, *The Last Pre-Raphaelite*, p. 251).

27. *The Good Soldier* (Vintage), pp. 60–61. For Ford's letter to Robert Garnett, see pp. 54–55. In *Ladies Whose Bright Eyes* Ford makes characteristically ingenious use of Elsie's acceptance of the Hüffer policy of pretending that Ford's interest in Violet Hunt was a mere passing fancy. He has the Lady Blanche, who is very hot after Mr. Sorrell, think that Mr. Sorrell's attachment to the Lady Dionissia is "a mere passing whim ... a temporary clouding of [the] intellect." "That," says the Dean, "is so exactly like the overwhelming

pride of the Lady Blanche . . . " (*Ladies Whose Bright Eyes*, pp. 244–45). The Lady Blanche is, in physical appearance, very like Elsie and, in character, like the conception of Elsie which Ford was slowly working up and which he would develop fully in the Countess Macdonald of *The New Humpty-Dumpty.*

28. *Ladies Whose Bright Eyes*, pp. 231–32. *The Young Lovell*, p. 189. *The Fifth Queen*, p. 195 (154).

29. *The March of Literature*, pp. 274–75. *Ladies Whose Bright Eyes*, pp. 237–38.

30. *Ladies Whose Bright Eyes*, pp. 344 and 358.

31. There are detailed descriptions of the changes between the 1911 and the 1935 versions of *Ladies Whose Bright Eyes* in John A. Meixner, *Ford Madox Ford's Novels*, pp. 74–77, and Richard A. Cassell, *Ford Madox Ford*, pp. 90–106.

32. *The Young Lovell*, pp. 12, 292, 302, 133, 224, 306, and 127. Ford wrote Pinker from St. Rémy on March 26, 1913 (Princeton), to say the book was well along and announced its completion from South Lodge on July 7 (Huntington). His comment on the quality of *The Young Lovell* is in a letter to Pinker of March 17, in Ludwig, p. 56. For Pound's remark, see p. xiv.

33. The quoted phrases are from T. S. Eliot, "The Dry Salvages."

34. *No Enemy*, pp. 176, 177, and 164.

35. *No Enemy*, pp. 179, 180, 182, 183, and 184–86.

36. *No Enemy*, pp. 290–92.

37. *The Marsden Case*, pp. 84 (see also p. 17) and 217. For the origin of the last detail in Ford's life, see p. 289.

38. *The Marsden Case*, pp. 18 and 19–21.

39. *The Good Soldier*, p. 5. *The Marsden Case*, p. 45.

40. *The Marsden Case*, pp. 135–36, 185, and 149.

41. *The Marsden Case*, pp. 2, 165, and 324. Compare Jessop's attitude toward Podd and Ford's toward Stanley Paul, p. 244.

42. *The Marsden Case*, pp. 22, 334, 281, and 206–07.

43. *The Marsden Case*, p. 240.

44. *The Marsden Case*, pp. 236–37.

45. *The Marsden Case*, pp. 281 and 164.

46. Ford to Stella, May 7, 1923.

47. *It Was the Nightingale*, p. 162. Though Ford's anecdote appears to exaggerate the direct influence of *What Maisie Knew* on the conception of *Parade's End*, the general influence of James's novel on Ford's imagination may have been considerable. One of the haunting images of *The Good Soldier* is the mad Nancy Rufford's habit of saying "Shuttlecocks!" Sane, she had "felt like a shuttlecock being tossed backwards and forwards between the violent personalities of Edward and his wife" (*The Good Soldier*, p. 253). "The wretched infant" of *What Maisie Knew*, James says in his Preface, "was thus to find itself practically disowned [by both parents], rebounding from racquet to racquet like a tennis-ball or shuttlecock."

48. *Parade's End*, I, 20.

49. *Parade's End*, I, 18–19.

50. *Parade's End*, I, 22.

51. *Parade's End*, I, 22.

52. *Parade's End*, I, 14.

53. *Parade's End*, II, 38, 153, 149.

54. *Parade's End*, I, 469.

55. *Parade's End*, I, 362 and 149.

56. *Parade's End*, II, 132 and 301, and II, 137–39.

57. *Parade's End*, II, 132–33 (the first edition mistakenly prints quotation marks before Xtopher).

58. The ms. of the suppressed ending of *Some Do Not . . .* is in the Naumburg Collection. It

has been printed by Frank MacShane in "A Conscious Craftsman: Ford Madox Ford's Manuscript Revisions," *Boston University Studies in English*, Autumn, 1961, pp. 182–98. There are a couple of pages at the beginning of Part I of *No More Parades* before Ford moves unquestionably into Christopher's mind; there are several passages of third-person summary about Perowne in the middle of Sylvia's interior dialogue in Part II (I, 392–93). In the middle of Part III we are for a moment in Campion's mind (I, 469–74), and the transition back to Christopher's mind is made by another three or four pages of dramatic dialogue (I, 474–79). The quoted passages are from *Parade's End*, I, 445 and 497–98.

59. *Parade's End*, I, 345–53.

60. *Parade's End*, II, 177. *Thus to Revisit*, p. 45. Ford to Eric Pinker, Aug. 17, 1930, in Ludwig, p. 197. Ford to Stella, Oct. 6, 1927. Ford to Ruth Kerr, Sept. 2 and 7, 1932 (Biala). John A. Meixner (*Ford Madox Ford's Novels*, p. 219) argues against the inclusion of *Last Post*; he is mildly supported by Paul L. Wiley (*Novelist of Three Worlds*, p. 239). But his arguments are not very persuasive, or at least have not persuaded such critics as Mrs. Ohmann, Mr. Cassell, and Mr. Gordon, Jr.

61. *Parade's End*, II, 295.

62. There is a casual reference in *Some Do Not . . .* (I, 286) that implies the story begins in 1907. But later Christopher places his ride with Valentine about July 1, 1912, and General Campion twice places his talk with Christopher at the Rye golf club in 1912. Sylvia also recalls that Christopher came for her at Lobscheid "two or three years . . . before . . . 1914" (II, 26; I, 499 and 160). For the circumstances in which Sylvia seduced Christopher, see I, 127.

63. The contradiction about Macmaster's parentage is at I, 11 and 18; the facts about the first version of the Tietjens family are given at I, 132, 174–76, 182 and II, 136, the facts about the second version at II, 238.

64. *A Little Less Than Gods*, pp. 108, 255, and 201. References here are to the Duckworth edition, which is superior to the Viking edition. Ford quotes the whole stanza from "A Song for St. Cecilia's Day" in *The March of Literature*, p. 553. The real Assheton Smith owned the Quorn hounds in 1806.

65. *When the Wicked Man*, p. 350.

66. *When the Wicked Man*, pp. 105, 345, 110, 126, 187, 114, 289, 166, 225, 65, 91, 21, 176, and 251. *Portraits from Life*, p. 210.

67. Ford to George Keating, June 1, 1938; Ludwig, p. 295. Graham Greene, Introduction, *The Bodley Head Ford Madox Ford*, I, 8.

68. *Henry for Hugh*, pp. 251–60. *The Rash Act*, pp. 211 and 322–32. Ford makes an unconvincing effort to trace these three Henry Martins to Henry Martin's Luxembourg and Massachusetts ancestors (*The Rash Act*, p. 376).

69. *Henry for Hugh*, pp. 129–30.

70. Ford's synopsis is in the Biala Papers. *Henry for Hugh*, p. 134. In *The Rash Act*, Henry Martin calls a show room a "show-store" and an electric fan a "wind fan" (p. 9), a grade crossing a "level-crossing" (p. 12), bindle-stiffs "bundle-stiffs" (p. 76), the University of Chicago "Chicago University" (p. 108), electric fixtures "electric fixings" (p. 123), a beer baron a "Beer Lord" (p. 175); he talks about wanting "to kick his legs about like a nigger at a barn dance" (p. 37), about "playing craps" (p. 50), about being "very flush of money" (p. 54), about his wife's going "back to Paris so that she might without censure can herself" (p. 127), and about "interstate railway commissions" (p. 317). There are similar blunders in *Henry for Hugh*, where Ford makes matters worse by having Henry Martin correct the mistakes of the English about America ("Fall River is not in Rhode Island," p. 112) and then makes geographical mistakes of his own ("When Wanda had lived with him at Reading Ridge, Conn.," p. 125). In spite of everything that was said to him about the damaging effect of these blunders, he continued in his later books to go out of his

way to use "Americanisms." "M. de la Penthièvre had a gun in his hand ... A blue nickelled gat!" (*Vive le Roy* [Lippincott], p. 75); "police ... are practicing their gats ..."; "large fellows and fine dames who have jumped blind baggages ... in all the dangerous places of the globe will exclaim: 'Swell! ... Fine! ... Great guy, you ... Put it there! ... What have you?" (*Great Trade Route*, pp. 280 and 190). Even Isabel Paterson, one of Ford's staunchest supporters, felt obliged to comment on the "manifest defects ... in [*The Rash Act*'s] occasional views of American life (*New York Herald Tribune Book Review*, Feb. 26, 1933, p. 4; see Harvey, p. 397). The brilliant impression of New York during the winter of 1934–35 in *Great Trade Route* is also marred by inaccuracies, though Ford's knowledge of New York was far greater than his knowledge of America as a whole. He calls the Pulaski Skyway "the Pulaski Speedway" (p. 56), and "the Pulaski Highway" (p. 183 and 405), and Columbus Circle "Columbia Circle" (p. 75).

71.   The Villa Niké of *Henry for Hugh* is of course based on the Villa Paul; Ford even uses the queer trick the frogs in the cistern at the Villa Paul had of going suddenly silent when an owl flew over (*Henry for Hugh*, p. 72; compare *Provence*, p. 222). *Henry for Hugh*, p. 299. Ford to Ray Long, July 2, 1932, in Ludwig, p. 209. Ford's original outline cannot be taken as a reliable account of his final plan for Henry Martin; for one thing he says Henry Martin "will find Mlle. Becquerel dully insupportable and suspect her and the dark girl [Eudoxie] of being Lesbians," but as he actually wrote the books, Eudoxie becomes the heroine and it is Henry Martin's first wife, Alice, and Mrs. Percival who are lesbians.

72.   *Vive le Roy* (Lippincott), p. 159. Lippincott's edition of *Vive le Roy* is inferior to Allen & Unwin's of the next year. Some of the mistakes are clearly Ford's: for example, the confusion over whether Penthièvre and Walter are riding in a car or carriage when they are attacked (p. 75) and over whether Walter's putative father is a shoe-seller (p. 14), a trunk-seller (p. 57), or a seller of leather goods in general (pp. 107 and 213). Some, however, are careless misreadings, possibly of Ford's difficult handwriting; for example, the substitution of "Penkethman" for "Penthièvre" (p. 173) and of "rue d'Annam" for "rue d'Assas" (p. 60), and such gross errors as "with thirty medal-ribbons on his cheek" (p. 55). Cassandra Mathers is descended from both Brigham Young and Cotton Mather—Ford's little joke about Katherine Anne Porter's obsession with Cotton Mather: she and Walter Leroy live in Ford's flat in Paris, as did the Presslys. The political young, Cassie says, are "a pack of schoolboys playing games," and Penkethman is "all their Godfather" (pp. 100–101), as Ford felt himself the sympathetic but mature godfather of the young intellectuals.

73.   The Sherlock Holmes scene is on pp. 24–28; the monocle flourishes all through the book; it is explained on p. 341. Lewis Gannett, "*Vive le Roy*," *New York Herald Tribune*, April 9, 1936, p. 21 (Harvey, p. 407); Mr. Gannett is being quite literal about where the plot is given away. The first time Penkethman had to mention his acquaintance with Walter's mother, "he broke off and remained silent for quite a time, looking unseeingly in front of him. Finally he said: 'It was a long time ago ... I was almost as slim in those days ...'" (p. 108; compare Ford's remark to Rene Wright about their first meeting, in the dedication of *A Little Less Than Gods*, "When you were in ... stiff little frilly things and I, oh dear, as slender as a gazelle...."). Willy Cuppy thought *Vive le Roy* "a perfectly swell mystery story" (*New York Herald Tribune Books*, April 19, 1936, p. 16 [Harvey, p. 407]).

74.   For the scenes referred to see *Vive le Roy*, pp. 71ff., 181ff., and 290ff. For Cassie's speech see p. 145. Cassie is also made to talk of someone's wanting to "do a rape on me" (p. 91) and of going "clean cuckoo" (p. 304); she describes her father as "a floor headman in a department store" (p. 56). These "Americanisms" alternate in the characters' speeches with exclusively British idioms such as "$20,000 in notes" (p. 9) and "phoned through to" (p. 262). *Time*, April 13, 1936, p. 91 (Harvey, p. 407).

Index